D0952194

COMPARATIVE
ECONOMIC SYSTEMS

H. STEPHEN GARDNER
Baylor University

COMPARATIVE ECONOMIC SYSTEMS

THE DRYDEN PRESS CHICAGO NEW YORK SAN FRANCISCO PHILADELPHIA
MONTREAL TORONTO LONDON SYDNEY TOKYO

Acquisitions Editor: Elizabeth Widdicombe
Developmental Editor: Deborah Acker
Project Editor: Teresa Chartos
Design Director: Jeanne Calabrese
Production Manager: Barb Bahnsen
Permissions Editor: Cindy Lombardo
Director of Editing, Design, and Production: Jane Perkins
Text and Cover Designer: Frances Hasegawa
Copy Editor: Siobhan Granner
Indexer: Joyce Goldenstern
Compositor: Weimer Typesetting Company, Inc.
Text Type: 10/12 Garamond

Library of Congress Cataloging-in-Publication
    Data
Gardner, H. Stephen.
    Comparative economic systems.
    Includes bibliographies and index.

    1. Comparative economics.   I. Title.
HB90.G37   1988   330   87-24563
ISBN 0-03-000064-5

Printed in the United States of America
890-038-987654321
Copyright © 1988 by The Dryden Press,
a division of Holt, Rinehart and Winston, Inc.

Address orders:
111 Fifth Avenue
New York, NY 10003

Address editorial correspondence:
One Salt Creek Lane
Hinsdale, IL 60521

The Dryden Press
Holt, Rinehart and Winston
Saunders College Publishing

To my parents, Evelyn Gardner and the late C. E. Gardner, and my "other" parents, Lynn and Joy Stokes—my bridges to the past; and to my children, Danny and Jessica—with hope for the future.

The Dryden Press Series in Economics

PREFACE

These are unusually exciting times in the international economy. China, the Soviet Union, and the nations of Eastern Europe are engaged in revolutionary programs of economic and social reform. Industrial capitalist countries are experimenting with privatization programs, industrial policies, financial deregulation, and new forms of international cooperation. A few of the Third World nations are successfully emerging from poverty; many more are struggling with rapid population growth, hunger, indebtedness, and civil strife. In *Comparative Economic Systems,* I have attempted to provide the conceptual tools, historical background, and current information that are needed to make sense of these developments.

This book is designed to serve as a basic text for undergraduates or as a supplementary survey text for graduate students. My approach to the subject is nontechnical, and most of the book can be understood by readers who have a limited background in economics. This is important because all of us— businesspeople, journalists, public servants, educators and students, as well as professional economists—need to recognize the important changes that are happening in the world around us.

Distinctive Features

This text has several unique features that distinguish it from other books in the field.

Broad Country Coverage.   Many countries and country groups are given full-chapter coverage. These include the United States, Great Britain, Germany, Sweden, France, Japan, the Soviet Union, China, Yugoslavia, Hungary and Eastern Europe, and the developing countries. Three chapters are devoted to the Soviet Union alone because of its importance in the socialist world. Thus, this book gives instructors the flexibility to accommodate their individual interests and time constraints.

Pedagogical Approach.   Conceptual material is integrated into chapters that discuss actual economies. The theory of the labor-managed firm, for example, is discussed in the chapter about Yugoslavia, and technical features of the theory are discussed in an appendix at the end of the chapter. Similarly, input-output economics is introduced in the context of the Soviet economy. Most of the chapters also include boxed items that provide real-world applications of broader concepts.

A uniform style of organization is used in the chapters about capitalist countries to facilitate comparisons between countries. In each case, the environment, industrial organization, labor market and relations, financial sector, and governmental institutions and policies are discussed. In all chapters, key terms appear in bold type within the text. Each chapter ends with a summary, discussion and review questions, and a list of suggested readings.

Statistical Emphasis.   A unique chapter on comparative economic statistics is included early in the book to introduce students to the methods and definitions used by professionals in the field. Tables in individual chapters are supplemented by an extensive end-of-book appendix of comparative statistics.

Historical Perspective.   The longer I teach this subject, the more I am convinced that historical and cultural factors play a leading role in economic structure and performance. It is impossible to understand the roots of American individualism, Soviet authoritarianism, British economic decline, or Chinese population growth without looking into the distant past. Thus, I have included more historical material than is common in this field. Full chapters are included on the institutional and theoretical histories of capitalism and socialism. The largest part of the book, however, is devoted to current conditions, trends, and issues. Every effort has been made to keep these discussions relevant and up-to-date.

Ancillary Materials.   A comprehensive *Instructor's Manual and Test Bank* is available for professors. It includes outlines, lecture suggestions, multiple choice questions, and essay questions for each chapter.

Acknowledgments

Many people contributed to this book and I cannot possibly thank them all. Ed Hewett (now at the Brookings Institution), Gregory Grossman, and Benjamin Ward (both at the University of California, Berkeley) introduced me to the field of comparative economics in the early 1970s. In subsequent years, my students at Baylor University have influenced my opinions on the scope and teaching of this subject. Among them, Chris Barnes worked as my research assistant, and Charles Patterson assisted in preparation of the maps. Several drafts of the manuscript were tested in my classes, and my students provided many helpful suggestions.

Useful comments on the manuscript were provided by Katherine Huger (Baptist College at Charleston), Lubomyr Kowal (University of Michigan, Flint), Mark Lutz (University of Maine), Dennis O'Connor (Loras College), and Bruce Reynolds (Union College). Valuable suggestions on individual chapters and on the initial plan for the project were provided by Elizabeth Clayton (University of Missouri, St. Louis), Edwin Dolan (George Mason University), Ken Gray (now at the U.S. Department of Agriculture), Bill Rushing (Georgia State University), Roger Skurski (University of Notre Dame), several anonymous reviewers, and by my colleagues at Baylor including Gerald Fielder, Art King, Joe McKinney, Mark Vaughan, and Keith Rowley. Although all of these people contributed greatly to the project, I alone am responsible for any errors or omissions, and I welcome suggestions for subsequent editions.

I owe special thanks to the administration of Baylor University, the Hankamer School of Business, and the Ben Williams Endowment for supporting this project. The staff at The Dryden Press provided unrelenting encouragement, creativity, and attention to detail. I was particularly aware of the efforts of Liz Widdicombe, Debby Acker, Barb Bahnsen, Jeanne Calabrese, Teresa Chartos, Siobhan Granner, Stephanie Hill, Carol Mikenas, Jane Perkins, and Terry White.

Finally, I want to thank my wife, Kathy, my son, Danny, and my daughter, Jessica, for their patience, pressure, and perseverance. Danny suggested that I close with these lines from *The Adventures of Huckleberry Finn:*

. . . *and so there ain't nothing more to write about, and I am rotten glad of it, because if I'd 'a' knowed what a trouble it was to make a book I wouldn't 'a' tackled it, and ain't a-going to no more.*

Without the help of so many good people, I don't know how I'd 'a' tackled it either.

H. Stephen Gardner
February 1988

About The Author

Stephen Gardner is the Ben Williams Professor of Economics at Baylor University. He holds a B.A. degree in economics and Russian studies from the University of Texas, Austin, and a Ph.D. in economics from the University of California, Berkeley. Professor Gardner's primary research interests are Soviet and Eastern European economics, international trade, and the history of economic thought. As a guest of the Soviet Academy of Sciences, he has conducted research at the Central Mathematical Economics Institute and the Institute for World Economy and International Relations, both in Moscow. He has also acted as a consultant for the U.S. Department of Commerce and for several corporations and public agencies. Professor Gardner's published works include *Soviet Foreign Trade: The Decision Process* (Boston: Kluwer-Nijhoff, 1983) and many articles in academic, business, and governmental publications.

CONTENTS

COMPARATIVE
ECONOMIC SYSTEMS

I

BASES OF COMPARISON

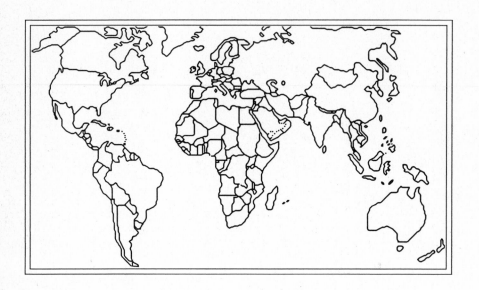

1

Economic Systems: Classification and Performance

If the U.S. is to enter seriously the competition to sway men's minds in every country of the world, including the Soviet Union, . . . we [must] understand not only what we are against but also what we are for.
—David Satter
   The Wall Street
   Journal, May 23, 1983

"Would you tell me, please, which way I ought to go from here?" [said Alice.] "That depends a good deal on where you want to get to," said the [Cheshire] Cat.
—Lewis Carroll
   Alice's Adventures in
   Wonderland, 1865

If you live in an industrially developed market economy, you enjoy a fate accorded to only 16 percent of the world's population. Nearly 9 percent of the earth's inhabitants live in the Soviet Union and in the other centrally planned industrial economies of Eastern Europe. A quarter of mankind lives in China, Cuba, Vietnam, and several other socialist developing countries. The remaining half of humanity lives in a host of traditional and market-oriented developing countries, ranging from Ethiopia and India to Brazil and Singapore.

As socially, politically, and developmentally diverse as the countries of the world may be, they all face the basic economic problem of allocating limited productive resources to the satisfaction of seemingly unlimited human wants. The means that have been devised to achieve that end, and the effectiveness of those means, are what this book is all about.

In this introductory chapter we will first explore the concept of an "economic system" and consider its role in economic performance. Second, we will survey the various criteria that are used to classify economic systems and briefly discuss the countries that are covered in later chapters in light of these criteria. Finally, we will discuss a few of the problems encountered when attempting to compare the performance of different economic systems.

The Economic System, the Environment, and Policies

According to the useful framework suggested by Tjalling Koopmans and John Michael Montias, the **economic performance** of a country is determined by its economic system and environment, and by the policies of its leaders.[1] Let us briefly consider what is meant by each of these terms.

An **economic system** is a set of institutions involved in making and implementing economic decisions.[2] An **institution,** in turn, is an organization, practice, convention, or custom that is material and persistent in the life or culture of a society. The most familiar institutions are formal organizations, such as business corporations, labor unions, and government agencies. Equally important, however, are those institutions that exist in the form of practices, conventions, and customs, such as the profit motive, property rights, racial discrimination, market exchange, planning, and taxation. We may think of the American economic system, therefore, as a particular collection of institutions, and we may think of the Soviet system as a very different collection.

Following Koopmans and Montias, the **environment** includes the nation's resources (land, initial labor, and the initial capital stock), initial technology, and a range of external factors, such as the economic performance of trading partners and the existence of military rivals and allies. In other words,

[1]Tjalling Koopmans and John Michael Montias, "On the Description and Comparison of Economic Systems," in *Comparison of Economic Systems: Theoretical and Methodological Approaches,* ed. Alexander Eckstein (Berkeley: University of California Press, 1971), 27–38. Koopmans and Montias usually use the term *outcomes* where we use *performance.*

[2]Our definition is closest to that of Gregory Grossman in *Economic Systems,* 2d ed. (Englewood Cliffs, N.J.: Prentice-Hall, 1974), 3.

the environment roughly consists of those factors that are beyond the control of participants in the economic system under consideration.

Factors that can be manipulated and controlled to influence economic performance are the substance of economic **policies.** Koopmans and Montias admit that the "boundary between system and policies is not a sharp one and may depend on the period for which a comparison is made."[3] Persistent practices, such as the collection of an income tax in the United States since World War I, are considered part of the economic system. Less persistent practices, such as a temporary change in tax rates, are considered policies which affect the operation of the system.

The distinctions between an economic system, environment, policies, and performance can be clarified using a simple, but imperfect, analogy. An automobile is a system composed of several persistent mechanisms (institutions), each of which is designed to perform a particular task. The performance of the car will depend on how well it is driven (policies) and on the external environment (road conditions, the climate, and the actions of other drivers).

Notice that if an automobile performs badly, this may be the result of a deficiency in the car itself, or it may be caused by the manner and environment in which the car is driven. Likewise, poor performance of an economy may or may not be due to shortcomings in the economic system. Also consider the fact that an individual's decision to purchase a particular car depends on the kind of performance desired (such as rapid speed, fuel economy, or safety) and on the environment in which the car will be driven (a large radiator may be preferable in a hot climate). Similarly, it is not likely that a single economic system could be optimal for all purposes, populations, times, and places.

Modes of Classification

There are far too many countries in the world for us to study all of their economic systems in this book. Instead, we shall follow the convention of establishing classifications for economic systems. We will then study one or two representative countries in each class.

We should acknowledge at the outset that classification of economic systems is a rather difficult enterprise. Just as we can classify people according to their height, weight, sex, age, nationality, political philosophy, and temperament, we can classify economic systems according to a wide range of overlapping criteria. Furthermore, the economic systems of actual countries are never purely capitalist or socialist, market or planned, free or controlled. Most accurately, we say that they are all "mixed economies," and that their mixtures of institutions change from year to year through processes of evolution and revolution.

Nevertheless, over a certain period of time, the actual economic system in a particular country may serve as a useful approximation to one of the pure,

[3]Koopmans and Montias, "Description and Comparison," 33.

idealized, theoretical economic systems, and may provide some indication of the relative merit of that theoretical system. Conversely, an economic theory based on the operation of an idealized economic system (such as the theory of perfect competition) may contribute to our understanding of the operation of actual economic systems. We should always be careful, however, to separate theory from reality.

Classification According to Ownership

The most venerable classification of economic systems, dating back at least to Karl Marx, distinguishes between economies according to the predominant form of ownership of the factories, farms, and other productive assets. Although capitalism and socialism may differ from one another in many different ways, the *definitional* distinction between the two systems is usually expressed in terms of ownership.

Unfortunately, ownership is itself an imprecise concept and is variously taken to include any or all of the following: (1) the right to control how the asset will be used and to delegate that responsibility to others; (2) the right to retain all or part of the income generated by the asset; and (3) the right to transfer ownership of the asset to others by sale, as a gift, or by bequest. These rights usually are limited by zoning laws and other legal restrictions even in the most libertarian of economic systems, and they seldom are totally denied in the most repressive countries (see "When Is an Owner an Owner?" page 7).

Medieval **feudalism** was an economic and social system wherein all ownership rights over land were ultimately held by the king. Those rights were conditionally delegated down through the hierarchy of princes, dukes, marquis, earls, viscounts, and barons, subject to their loyalty, payment of tribute, and military and civil service. At the bottom of the hierarchy were the serfs, who were "tied to the land" they were given to cultivate, and who were required to pay tribute to their lords. Vestiges of the feudal system persist in many countries, as in Latin America where the owners of a small number of *latifundios* control a large proportion of the agricultural land.

Capitalism is an economic and social system in which the greater part of the means of production are owned outright (not subject to feudal obligations) by private individuals. Laborers are no longer tied to the land, and are free to move between employers (except in slave states). Marxist critics of capitalism say that the freedom of the laborers is limited and illusory because their survival requires that they work for the capitalist class—the owners of the means of production. Proponents of the capitalist system say that laborers who are willing to work, save, and invest may be able to join the capitalist class themselves.

Socialism is an economic and social system in which the greater part of the means of production are owned "socially." According to various definitions, social ownership may include possession by the government, by cooperatives, by syndicated bodies of workers, and/or by communes. Under Soviet

WHEN IS AN OWNER AN OWNER?

The fine line between ownership and what might be called "perpetual rentership" is illustrated by the situation in much of Soviet, Chinese, and Eastern European agriculture. In the Soviet Union, the big collective and state farms are owned and managed socially, but each family is also allowed to till a small private plot near their house. The private plot is managed by the family and the family can consume or sell the food and livestock grown on the plot with considerable freedom. Although they use only 3 percent of the sown land, the plots account for about 26 percent of the gross value of agricultural output (discussed further in Chapter 13).

The comments of Viktor Kulinich, a collective farm worker in southern Russia, paint an interesting picture of the ambiguous legal and perceptual nature of private plot ownership: "The house is my personal property, and the land belongs to me. Well, it's not really mine; we rent the land—nominal rent, about $30 per year. The state owns all of the land," he says with a smile, "but if the land is attached to my house, it sort of belongs to me."

Source: The quotation is taken from "October Harvest," an installment of the *Comrades* series aired on the PBS television program, *Front Line,* in 1986.

socialism, for example, the government maintains effective ownership rights over most of the means of production, whereas Yugoslav socialism delegates most of these rights to the workers' councils of individual factories. As we shall see, this is a distinction of considerable operational importance.

We distinguish between economic systems in terms of the "predominant" form of ownership because very few countries are purely capitalist or socialist. In the so-called "industrial capitalist" world, publicly owned enterprises account for a share of gross investment that ranges from 4.9 percent in the United States to about 10 percent in France and Japan, and up to 20 percent in Austria, Australia, and the United Kingdom (Table A.15).* Largely because of its persistence in agriculture, the private sector accounts for 14, 20, and 48 percent, respectively, of national income in "socialist" Yugoslavia, Poland, and Vietnam (Table A.16). In the developing world, we find countries that are spread all along the continuum between private and social ownership.

*Statistical tables A.1 to A.28 appear in the Appendix at the end of this book.

Classification According to Coordinating Mechanism

In any economic system a large number of decisions must be made each year concerning the production, sale, and purchase of commodities and resources. Since millions of people are usually involved in making these decisions and in carrying them out, every economic system must employ one or more **coordinating mechanisms** to insure that the decisions taken are mutually consistent—intended purchases are roughly equal to intended sales for each commodity, the number of people who enter a given occupation is roughly equal to the number of jobs available in that occupation, and so on. Economic systems are often classified, therefore, according to their predominant coordinating mechanism. Once again, however, we should note that all existing economic systems employ not one, but several, forms of coordination.

A **traditional economy** is one in which coordination is perpetuated through simple maintenance of the status quo.[4] What products will be produced? Those that were produced last year. How will they be produced? The way they were produced in the past. The sons follow their fathers in their choice of occupation, and the daughters follow their mothers. In most countries, the traditions take on a social, political, and religious momentum that is difficult to break.

Tradition can predominate as a coordinating mechanism only in rather small, simple, and stationary economies. In fact, it would be a contradiction in terms to speak of a dynamic and growing economy that is coordinated primarily by tradition. Nevertheless, elements of tradition can be found in any functioning economy. In the form of racial and sexual discrimination, for example, tradition has a significant effect on occupational choice in the United States and many other countries. Many Japanese sons, to this day, are honor-bound to work for their family's business if that is their father's wish. Soviet planners never "start from scratch" when they compile a new plan, but always build on the results achieved in the previous year.

A **market economy** is one in which coordination is predominantly achieved through the free and spontaneous movement of market prices and through their effect on quantities supplied and demanded. Thus, under competitive conditions, a shortage (or surplus) of any commodity will cause its relative price to rise (fall). The resulting increase (decrease) in the quantity supplied and decrease (increase) in the quantity demanded will reduce or eliminate the shortage (or surplus).

In addition to its spontaneous coordination of decisions, a market economy tends to provide for **consumer sovereignty** automatically. Consumer demand, which is usually (in peacetime) the largest component of final demand, will ultimately determine what is produced in the economy. John Kenneth Galbraith and others have noted that the sovereignty of the consumer is manipulated by the marketing programs of producers. Nonetheless, if the con-

---

[4] Notice that tradition cannot, in itself, coordinate decisions, but can only perpetuate a set of decisions that has been coordinated by some other means.

sumers cannot be convinced to buy a particular product, production will not continue. This is not always true in centrally planned economies, where shortages and surpluses of products arise from the mismatch between planners' priorities and consumer demand.

Again, we should note that the market mechanism often is employed even in countries where it is not allowed to predominate. In the Soviet Union, for example, about 25 percent of agricultural output is sold on free and legal markets, and a significant (but difficult to quantify) volume of consumer goods is traded illegally in the black market (or second economy).

A **planned economy** is, quite simply, one in which coordination of long-run and/or short-run decisions is attempted by means of a central plan, which is designed to guide the economy toward certain goals or objectives.[5] Given the generality of this definition, a planned economy can take one of at least two forms.

Directive planning (or **command planning**), such as that employed in the Soviet Union, China, much of Eastern Europe, and in the U.S. military, is a system whereby the most important long-run *and* short-run decisions are made or approved by a central planning authority and are then passed down to subordinates in the form of instructions, directives, or commands. From the central planners' point of view, the effectiveness of this system will depend upon the quantity and quality of economic and technical information at their disposal, the effectiveness with which they can use that information to construct a consistent and meaningful plan, and the degree to which they can induce fulfillment of the plan from their subordinates.

Indicative planning, employed in France, Japan, Yugoslavia, and a number of other countries, is a hybrid mechanism that uses the market system for coordination of short-run decisions (how many apples to pick this week) in combination with a plan for coordination of long-run decisions (how many trees to plant this year). Fulfillment of plan targets usually is not compulsory for anyone other than government employees. In fact, an indicative plan typically specifies only very general (that is industry-wide) targets over a long (usually five-year) time horizon. In contrast, a directive plan typically includes an annual target for each factory and each important product. Ideally, since an indicative plan is meant to specify a set of consistent goals that are mutually beneficial to all segments of society, it should evoke voluntary compliance, and it should serve as a self-fulfilling prophecy. Realistically, fulfillment of the plan frequently requires governmental support through monetary, fiscal, and regulatory policies.

Quite often, countries that engage in indicative planning also conduct an active **industrial policy (IP).** An IP may include several different kinds of programs. First, a list of "winning" and "losing" industries may be formulated,

---

[5]We reject John Kenneth Galbraith's assertion that corporate planning *within* each major industry has transformed the United States into a planned economy. By our more restrictive definition, the plan must, in some sense, be formulated to achieve coordination *between* industries. See John Kenneth Galbraith, *The New Industrial State* (Boston: Houghton Mifflin, 1956).

with measures designed to support the former and phase out the latter. For example, the Japanese government supported development of the steel and auto industries in the 1950s, consumer electronics in the 1960s, computer chips in the 1970s, and "knowledge-intensive" industries in the 1980s. Second, an IP often includes measures to strengthen industrial stability and/or competition. Where monopoly power is pervasive, existing companies may be regulated, nationalized, or split into smaller units. Conversely, small companies may be merged into larger units to enhance their financial strength, production efficiency, and competitive position on the world market.

Classification According to Incentive Systems

Any coordinating mechanism must include a system of incentives to reward socially desirable behavior and to discourage inappropriate actions. These are usually divided into three broad classes: coercive, material, and moral incentives.

When **coercive incentives** are used, behavior is modified by actual or threatened force and punishment. In a number of societies—including the Old South, Egypt under the Pharaohs, and the Soviet Union under Stalin—coercion played a very important role. More recently, the Soviets have allegedly used political and religious prisoners on Siberian construction projects.[6] Even the most libertarian societies make occasional use of coercion to raise tax revenues, to staff the military, and to prevent theft, fraud, violence, and other illegal actions.

Material incentives are those which reward desirable behavior with a claim over material goods, usually through some form of monetary payment. In a competitive market economy, material incentives arise more or less automatically from the operation of the system. If there is a shortage of any product, the resulting increase in its relative price will give producers a material incentive to increase the quantity they supply, and it will give consumers a material incentive to reduce the quantity they demand.

In an economy coordinated by a directive plan, a material incentive system must be consciously designed and administered if it is to elicit compliance with the plan. Very often, this is accomplished using bonus pay arrangements that are tied to fulfillment of production targets. We shall find, however, that countries like the Soviet Union have found it very difficult to design an incentive system that simultaneously encourages accurate reporting of economic information to central planners and compliance with both the letter and the intent of the plan.

Moral incentives are those which elicit desirable behaviors by appealing to a wide range of emotions, including nationalism, company or personal pride, compassion for the sick and the poor, and the desire for acceptance by one's peers. Moral incentives are involved in "socialist competitions" between

---

[6]Steve Mufson, "Allegations Soviets Using 'Slave Labor' Heat Up Debate Over Pipeline to Europe," *Wall Street Journal,* August 17, 1982, 28.

factories in the Soviet Union, in the singing of company songs in Japan, and in the use of slogans, such as "Just Say No" and "Buy American."

Again, economic systems are often classified according to their dominant incentive systems. According to Karl Marx, in the early stages of socialism, goods should be distributed according to the principle, "to each according to his labor," whereas the ultimate communist system will be characterized by distribution "to each according to his needs." In other words, immature socialism will be based on material incentives, but full communism will be based on moral incentives and the creation of a "new socialist man." Similarly, distinctions often are drawn between **command socialism,** which makes extensive use of coercion; **utopian socialism,** which leans heavily on moral incentives; and **market socialism,** with its stronger reliance on material incentives.

Classification According to Objectives

Earlier we noted that automobiles are often classified according to the purposes they are meant to serve: race cars, economy cars, military vehicles, etc. Similarly, different economic systems are established to pursue different objectives, and they may be classified accordingly. Among the objectives that nations may choose to pursue are the following:[7]

- Individual freedom.
- High levels of per-capita consumption.
- High rates of growth in output or in per-capita consumption.
- Economic and military power.
- Equity in income distribution.
- Full employment.
- Allocative and/or dynamic efficiency.
- Protection of the natural environment.
- Price stability.

As its name implies, a **free-enterprise economy** is one in which protection of individual freedom is a dominant objective. Defenders of free enterprise—from Adam Smith to Ludwig von Mises, Friedrich Hayek, and Milton Friedman—have always drawn a close connection between economic and political freedoms:

Economic freedom is an essential requisite for political freedom. By enabling people to cooperate with one another without coercion or central direction, it reduces the area over which political power is exercised. In addition, by dispersing power, the free market provides an offset to whatever concentration of political power may arise. The concentration of economic and political power in the same hands is a sure recipe for tyranny.[8]

---

[7]For a longer list of objectives, see Koopmans and Montias, "Description and Comparison," 41–48.

[8]Milton Friedman and Rose Friedman, *Free To Choose: A Personal Statement* (New York: Harcourt Brace Jovanovich, 1979), 2–3.

Furthermore, advocates of free enterprise would argue that other, less important, objectives, such as economic growth and an equitable distribution of income, are also best achieved by the free market system:

Wherever we find any large element of individual freedom, some measure of progress in the material comforts at the disposal of ordinary citizens, and widespread hope of further progress in the future, there we also find that economic activity is organized mainly through the free market.[9]

A society that puts freedom first will, as a happy byproduct, end up with both greater freedom and greater equality.[10]

In a **welfare state,** an equitable distribution of income and full employment are among the leading objectives, and positive governmental action is employed to pursue those objectives. Advocates of the welfare state find it hard to believe that free and unregulated capitalism will best promote the welfare of society. In the words of John Maynard Keynes, "The outstanding faults of the economic society in which we live are its failure to provide for full employment and its arbitrary and inequitable distribution of wealth and incomes."[11] Governmental programs, including countercyclical monetary and fiscal policy, redistribution of income, health and employment insurance, and many other services are supported in the welfare state.

Of course, equity, like beauty, is in the eye of the beholder. Is an equitable income distribution one that divides the national income equally across the population? Is it one that divides income according to work performed? If so, should inherited wealth be confiscated by the government? How can the work of carpenters, lawyers, artists, and legislators be reduced to a common denominator to divide the national income equitably? These are among the questions that must be considered in the welfare state.

A number of different labels have been attached to economic systems that set the attainment of economic and military power as a preeminent objective. **Mercantilism,** which held sway in England and much of Europe during the sixteenth, seventeenth, and eighteenth centuries, was a system of economic thought and policy that held that national economic power could be augmented by governmental support of domestic monopolies, subsidization of exports, and restriction of imports, all aimed toward the accumulation of wealth embodied in gold and silver.

With wealth one could finance and equip armies and navies, hire foreign mercenaries, bribe potential enemies, and subsidize allies. Power could be exercised to acquire colonies, to win access to new markets, and to monopolize trade routes, high-seas fisheries, and the slave trade with Africa.[12]

When capitalist ownership is combined with a totalitarian government bent on national economic and military power, the result is an exaggerated

[9]*Ibid.,* 54–55.

[10]*Ibid.,* 148.

[11]John Maynard Keynes, *The General Theory of Employment, Interest, and Money* (New York: Harcourt, Brace, and World, 1964), 372.

[12]Jacob Viner, "Mercantilist Thought," *International Encyclopedia of the Social Sciences* (New York: Macmillan, 1968), 4:438.

form of mercantilism, known as **fascism** or **Nazism.** The relationship between individual rights and the national interest under such a system was described by the Fascist Labor Charter of 1927:

> *The Italian Nation is an organism having ends, a life and means superior in power and duration to the single individuals or groups of individuals composing it. . . . In view of the fact that private organization of production is a function of national concern, the organizer of the enterprise is responsible to the state for the direction given to production.* [13]

An Operational Classification System

Again, classification of economic systems is an imprecise enterprise that invites disagreement. We have considered four dimensions along which economic systems may be classified: ownership, coordinating mechanisms, incentive systems, and objectives. Many other dimensions can be considered, including centralization of decision making, modes of distributing information, the role of money in the economy, and the state of excess supply or excess demand in product markets.[14] Furthermore, when we attempt to classify economic systems, we should remember the following:

1.   Economic systems may be either real or theoretical.

2.   Theoretical systems may be "pure," but real systems generally include a mixture of different forms of ownership, coordination, incentives, and objectives.

3.   Theoretical systems may stand still, but real systems change through time.

4.   Reasonable persons will disagree on the assignment of actual countries to conceptual categories.

5.   Ideally, assignment of actual countries to categories should be based on objective criteria, not on the rhetoric of politicians.

Pushing aside all of the ambiguities, in Table 1.1 we identify seven very broad categories of economic systems that encompass all of the real and theoretical cases that we will consider in this book. Countless numbers of other subcategories could be created by filling in more detail. For example, we could say that democratic socialism is a form of market socialism with a democratic set of objectives. Command socialism could be divided into its Stalinist, Maoist, and reformed variants, and so forth.

We shall examine countries that represent each of these systemic varieties in the following chapters. Our brief study of the developing world will

---

[13]This translation is given in Earl Sikes, *Contemporary Economic Systems* (New York: Henry Holt, 1940), 670–75.

[14]For a discussion of this last criterion, see Janos Kornai, "Resource-constrained versus Demand-constrained Systems," *Econometrica* 48 (1979): 801–819.

Table 1.1   An Operational Classification of Economic Systems

	Dominant System of Ownership	Dominant System of Coordination	Dominant System of Incentives	Dominant System of Objectives
Traditional	Tribal	Tradition	Various	Various
Feudalism	Shared with superiors	Tradition, Market	Material, Coercion	Various
Free-Enterprise Capitalism	Private	Market	Material	Individual freedom
Regulated Capitalism	Private	Market, Indicative plan	Material	Various
Fascism, Nazism	Private	Market	Coercion, Material	National power
Command Socialism	Social	Directive plan	Mixed	Various
Market Socialism	Social	Market, Indicative plan	Material	Various

explain the difficulties involved in breaking out of traditional and feudal modes of organization. A pure system of free-enterprise capitalism has never existed outside of textbooks and our closest approximation to that archetype is probably the U.S. economy. Among our examples of regulated capitalism, the United Kingdom, West Germany, and Sweden will represent the capitalist welfare states (with an aside on the Nazi regime in Germany during World War II), and France and Japan will demonstrate the operation of indicative planning.

When we turn to the socialist world, we find that command socialism has played a dominant role, but all of the major countries have engaged in interesting experiments with other systems. After the 1917 revolution, the first Soviet economic system was a utopian form of command socialism known as War Communism. The Soviets tried market socialism during the 1920s, under Lenin's New Economic Policy (NEP), and they are taking careful steps back in that direction today. The Chinese adopted Stalinist command socialism after World War II, created their own Maoist version during the Great Leap Forward (1958–1960) and the Cultural Revolution (1966–1976), and are now moving in the direction of market socialism. Yugoslavia and Hungary have accumulated the longest and most extensive experience with market socialism, and the other countries of Eastern Europe have fashioned a variety of other reforms of the Stalinist command model.

Comparisons of System Performance

Given our competitive, nationalistic, and ideological leanings, we inevitably wish to know which economic system is best—capitalism or socialism, American or Soviet, German or Japanese? Let us briefly consider some of the problems involved in making such comparisons.

Isolation of the Economic System

Earlier we noted that economic performance is influenced jointly by the economic system, the environment, and policies. If we find, for example, that Soviet agriculture has not performed as well as American agriculture, we should not immediately conclude that the Soviet economic *system* is inferior. We should first ask whether the shortcomings in Soviet agriculture can be fully explained by environmental factors and Soviet policies. If not, then the economic system would fall under suspicion.

Actual and Ideal Economic Systems

Polemical defenders of capitalism and socialism are often guilty of comparing a theoretical version of one system with a description of the actual problems of the other. Western commentators often discuss the shortages of goods that exist under Soviet socialism, and then describe how those problems are solved in a perfectly competitive free-enterprise economy. Soviet writers tend to emphasize the unemployment, inflation, and social injustice of capitalist economies, followed by a description of perfect coordination of economic activity under a central plan. If we remember their limitations, abstract models of idealized economic systems can be quite useful in our understanding of actual economic systems. However, they should be handled with care when performance comparisons are made.

Measurement Problems

The statistical problems involved in making international comparisons of income, unemployment, income distribution, and the like are so complex that we cover them in the next chapter. Differences in monetary systems, accounting standards, and data collection systems, as well as international secrecy, all contribute to the problems. Furthermore, many important performance criteria, such as individual freedom, are not readily quantifiable.

Assigning Priorities

Finally, even if we could isolate the influences of economic systems and quantify them fully, any broad performance comparison must be based on value judgments. Is the "better" economic system the one that provides more individual freedom, more economic growth, less inflation or unemployment, more technological progress, or more equitable distribution of income? If a single economic system does not excel according to all of these and other criteria, then people or groups of people with different values may disagree on the question of performance. Indeed, even if one system out-performs the other according to all objective criteria, the "loser" may still maintain support on ideological grounds. In other words, as you read the remainder of this book, you are invited to draw your own conclusions.

Summary

The economic performance of a country is determined by its economic system and environment, and by the policies of its leaders. An economic system is a set of institutions involved in making and implementing economic decisions.

Economic systems can be classified according to ownership of productive assets (feudalism, capitalism, or socialism), according to the mode of coordination (tradition, market, plan, or industrial policy), according to incentive systems (coercive, material, or moral), or according to objectives (free enterprise, welfare state, fascism, utopianism). Economic systems can be either real or theoretical, and real systems generally employ complex mixtures of ownership relations, coordination mechanisms, incentive systems, and objectives.

When we compare the performance of two economic systems, we should remember that: (1) poor economic performance of a country may be caused by environmental factors or poor policies, rather than a faulty economic system; (2) it is unfair to compare the real system in one country to a theoretical model of the system in the other country; (3) international statistical comparisons should be handled with care; and (4) performance comparisons ultimately are based on a system of values and priorities, about which opinions may differ.

Discussion and Review Questions

1.   In addition to those we have discussed in this chapter, what other criteria could be used to classify economic systems?

2.   Who owns your college, university, or business? Does that system of ownership have a significant influence on the way the institution is governed?

3.   Countries that rely on the market system during times of peace have been known to use rationing and central control during times of war. How might this be explained?

4.   What is the difference between a directive plan and an indicative plan? What are the different purposes they serve?

5.   What are a few examples of coercive, material, and moral incentives that influence the behavior of college students?

6.   According to your own system of values and priorities, what are the most important performance criteria for an economic system?

Suggested Readings

Comparative Economic Studies (CES) and *Journal of Comparative Economics* (JCE). *These are two professional journals that are devoted to the field of comparative economic systems. The articles in JCE tend to be more mathematically technical than those in CES.*

Dahl, Robert A., and Charles E. Lindblom. *Politics, Economics, and Welfare*. New York: Harper & Row, 1953. *Written by a political scientist and an economist, this book examines eco-*

nomic and political systems under four broad categories: the price system, hierarchy, polyarchy, and bargaining.

Kornai, Janos. *Contradictions and Dilemmas.* Cambridge, Mass.: MIT Press, 1986. *This book provides a unique Eastern European perspective on a range of definitional and conceptual issues.*

Neuberger, Egon, and William Duffy. *Comparative Economic Systems: A Decision-Making Approach.* Boston: Allyn and Bacon, 1976. *This book devotes ten chapters to fully developing a decision-making framework for classifying and analyzing economic systems.*

Wiles, Peter J.D. *Economic Institutions Compared.* New York: John Wiley, 1977. *Written with insight and biting wit by an iconoclastic professor (one of several in this field) at the London School of Economics. Long and sometimes difficult, but rewarding, this book is organized by institutions rather than national case studies.*

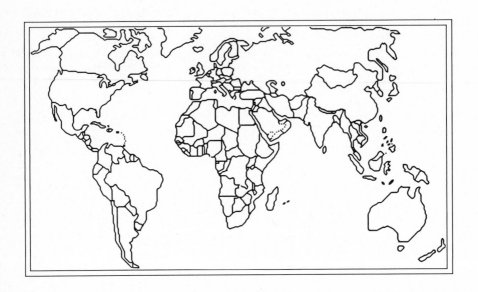

2

COMPARATIVE ECONOMIC STATISTICS

Thou shalt not have in thine house divers measures, a great and a small. But thou shalt have a perfect and just weight, a perfect and just measure shalt thou have.
—Deuteronomy 25: 14–15

As we compare the operation and performance of economic systems, we will base many of our judgments on statistical data. Comparisons of this kind are important for many reasons. First, statistical measurements lend greater objectivity to a field of study that provokes strong opinions. They allow us to formulate and test complex hypotheses and to check our simpler preconceived notions. In which country, for example, would you expect that exports represent a larger proportion of national income—Japan or France? You may be surprised to learn that the answer is France (see Table A.27). In which of these countries is governmental indebtedness larger in relation to national income? The answer this time is Japan (Table A.23).

International statistical comparisons are particularly important when they are used to guide governmental policy. The World Bank, for example, provides aid to low-income countries that can pass a needs test that is based on GNP per capita.[1] Comparisons of American and Soviet defense expenditures prepared by the U.S. intelligence community, which reflect a higher level of spending in the Soviet Union, have been used to support military programs in the United States.

Because of their importance and complexity, international statistical comparisons should be handled with caution. They are complicated, first of all, by differences in the definitions and accounting methods that are used by different countries. Second, there are major national differences in statistical reporting and collection systems. Third, there are difficult theoretical and methodological issues involved in the interpretation of international data. Finally, because of state secrecy and a number of other considerations, many important statistics simply are not available. The Soviet Union, for example, does not publish data on the level or growth of its money supply or on its international balance of payments, international indebtedness, domestic crime, unemployment, or gold production.

In this chapter we will examine the methods and problems involved in making international comparisons for several broad classes of data, including national income, unemployment, inflation, and income distribution statistics. Our examination of the actual data will raise several questions to be discussed in later chapters.

National Income Comparisons

Since 1665, when Sir William Petty compiled the first estimate of the "income of the people" of England, measures of national income have played a prominent role in international comparisons, and international comparisons have played an important role in national income measurement. John W. Kendrick

---

[1]Under these circumstances, national income estimation can become entwined in international politics. For example, Hungary once applied for $239 million of World Bank loans, and claimed that its income per capita was $2,100. Although the World Bank estimate was $4,180, the loan was eventually approved. See Lawrence Rout, "Study Questions World Bank Policies," *Wall Street Journal,* May 19, 1983, 33.

notes that "the most frequent motivation of the individual scholars" who developed national income accounting before 1920 "was nationalism—the desire to compare the economic performance of rival nations."[2]

Today, national income comparisons are used for a number of purposes. Total national income or product is the most common measure of the economic size or power of a country. Ratios of imports or exports to national income are commonly used to measure the "openness" of countries to foreign trade, ratios of military spending to national income are used to measure the "burden" of defense, and so on. When we speak of the economic growth of a country, we usually mean growth of real national income and product. Finally, national income per capita is the yardstick most commonly used to compare levels of economic development or standards of living.

National Income Definitions

If we are to carry out an international comparison of national incomes, we must first recognize the fact that different countries and international agencies employ different national income concepts and definitions. For our purposes, the three most important measures of national income are gross national product, gross domestic product, and net material product. It is not meaningful to compare, for example, the gross national product of one country with the net material product of another. Furthermore, if we compare the gross national products of two countries, we are likely to obtain results quite different from those that would be obtained by a comparison of net material products.

Gross national product (GNP), the income concept employed by the U.S. Commerce Department and several international agencies, is defined as the market value of all final goods and services produced by the nation in a year. *Nation* does not refer to the geographical confines of a country, or to its citizens, but rather to its residents—those who resided in the country for more than 6 months of the year. The income of a U.S. citizen, whether it is earned in the United States or abroad, would not be included in U.S. GNP if that citizen is not also a resident. On the other hand, the income of a U.S. resident is included in the U.S. GNP even if it is earned abroad. The U.S. resident may, for example, spend part of the year working abroad, or he may obtain an income on investments abroad. In either case, his income would be included in the U.S. GNP.

Gross domestic product (GDP), the national income measure included in the United Nations system of national accounts, is defined to be the annual market value of final goods and services produced within the geographic boundaries of a nation, whether it is produced by citizens, residents, or migrant workers.[3] The income generated by international investments is included in the GDP of the country where actual production of goods or

[2]John W. Kendrick, *Economic Accounts and Their Uses* (New York: McGraw-Hill, 1972), 10.
[3]Kendrick, *Economic Accounts,* 33–34.

Table 2.1   GNP as a Percentage of GDP in Selected Countries (Averages for 1970–1981)

Argentina	97.9	Kuwait	111.4
Bahrain	73.5	Liberia	84.4
Brazil	97.1	Mexico	97.6
Canada	97.8	Oman	84.8
Cape Verde	138.8	Sweden	99.8
France	100.5	United Kingdom	100.4
Japan	100.0	United States	101.4
Jordan	122.4	West Germany	100.2

Source: World Bank, *World Tables,* 3d ed., 1 (Baltimore: Johns Hopkins University Press, 1984).

services is conducted, which may not be the country where the recipient of that income resides.

For most countries, the difference between GNP and GDP is relatively small—less than 3 percent of GDP (see Table 2.1). However, for a few countries, such as Bahrain, Cape Verde, Jordan, Kuwait, and Oman, that pay or receive large incomes through international investments or remittances, the difference can be quite substantial.

Net material product (NMP), the national income concept employed by the Soviet Union and most other socialist nations, is equal to the total value, measured in final selling prices, of final material production, net of amortization (depreciation) of fixed assets.[4] Unlike GNP and GDP, NMP does not include the value of nonmaterial services. These are excluded in keeping with the classical notion, propounded by Adam Smith and amplified by Karl Marx, that productive workers are those who participate in the production of "vendable" commodities, whereas service workers do not create anything of lasting substance—they are "unproductive."

Ideally, services are included in NMP only if they contribute to the value of a material product, such as the services of furniture and shoe repairmen. Governmental, medical, educational, legal, and recreational services are excluded from NMP by all of the socialist countries. Public transportation and communication are excluded by the USSR and Czechoslovakia, but they are included in material production by the other socialist countries.[5]

The differences between international comparisons based on GNP (or GDP) and NMP measurements can be quite substantial. In 1985, for example, when the Soviet NMP was equal to about 66 percent of the U.S. level, their

[4]For a full discussion, see Abraham S. Becker, "National Income Accounting in the USSR," in *Soviet Economic Statistics,* ed. Vladimir Treml and John Hardt (Durham, N.C.: Duke University Press, 1972).

[5]For a full list of activities included in national income by various capitalist and socialist nations, see United Nations Economic Commission for Europe, *Economic Survey of Europe in 1984–1985* (ECE(XXXX)/1 Add. 1), 4.157.

GNP was only about 51 percent of the American total.[6] The reason for the difference is quite clear. Since the U.S. economy has a highly developed service sector, NMP calculations exclude a much larger portion of economic activity for the United States than they do for the Soviet Union.

Uncounted Production and Income

Certain forms of production and income are not fully included even in the broader measures of national income, such as GNP and GDP. Generally speaking, GNP measurements include only the value of goods and services that are produced legally and sold on open markets. Let us briefly consider how this restriction affects international comparisons of income.

First, GNP measurements do not include many of the goods and services that are produced by a family for consumption in their own household because such goods and services are never sold on an open market. Thus, the value of housework and childcare performed at home and the value of food produced in back yards and on family farms for home consumption are seldom included in GNP calculations. As significant as those omissions may be for industrialized countries, they are proportionally more significant for underdeveloped subsistence economies with rudimentary market systems. This helps explain how the World Bank can report, while keeping a straight face, that GNP per person was $110 per year (30 cents per day!) in Ethiopia in 1984. Clearly, a great deal of Ethiopian production in 1984 was never sold on a market and was not included in GNP. It is generally agreed that GNP measurements seriously understate the production and income levels of underdeveloped countries.

In addition to the problem of unmarketed output, national income estimates also exclude the value of goods and services produced in the **underground** (or **second** or **shadow**) **economy**—production that is hidden from governmental authorities to escape taxation or criminal charges. According to various estimation techniques, inclusion of the underground economy would raise American GNP by somewhere between 3 and 20 percent.[7] The estimates in Table 2.2 indicate that underground activities grew in relation to GDP in all of the major Western countries between 1960 and 1978; they ranged in importance from 4 percent of GDP in Japan to 13 percent in Sweden in 1978. With the notable exception of Italy, where the shadow economy seems to have a unique cultural basis, the countries with the largest underground sectors are generally those with the highest rates of taxation.

In the socialist world, the underground or second economy fills some of the gaps left by the system of central planning. In several socialist countries,

---

[6]The NMP estimate is from Central Statistical Board of the USSR, *The USSR in Figures for 1985* (Moscow: Finansi i Statistika, 1986), 50. The GNP estimate is the geometric mean of dollar and ruble comparisons in U.S. Central Intelligence Agency, *Handbook of Economic Statistics, 1986* (CPAS 86-10002, September 1986), 38.

[7]Carol Carson, "The Underground Economy: An Introduction," *Survey of Current Business* 64 (May 1984): 21–37.

Table 2.2   Taxation and Estimated Underground Production in OECD Countries

| | Underground Income as a Percentage of GDP | | Current Receipts of Government as Percentage of GDP |
	1960	1978	1978
Sweden	5.4	13.2	57.5
Belgium	4.7	12.1	42.4
Denmark	3.7	11.8	49.6
Italy	4.4	11.4	36.0
Netherlands	5.6	9.6	50.9
France	5.0	9.4	42.3
Norway	4.4	9.2	52.0
Austria	4.6	8.9	46.2
Canada	5.1	8.7	36.2
West Germany	3.7	8.6	44.7
United Kingdom	4.6	8.0	37.5
Finland	3.1	7.6	38.0
Ireland	1.7	7.2	35.2
Spain	2.6	6.5	27.1
Switzerland	1.1	4.3	33.8
Japan	2.0	4.1	24.5

Sources: First two columns are estimates of Weck, Pommerehne, and Frey, reported in Dieter Cassel and E. Ulrich Cichy, "Explaining the Growing Shadow Economy in East and West," *Comparative Economic Studies* 28 (Spring 1986): 21. Third column is from *OECD Economic Outlook* 40 (December 1986), Table R9.

enterprises have been uncovered that produce goods during the day for the planned economy and then operate all night to supply the second economy. These enterprises obtain inputs from other factories that operate illegally at night and all this clandestine production requires the payment of hush money to local police and governmental officials. How large is the socialist second economy? One Western scholar estimates that its inclusion would have increased Soviet GNP by 5 percent in 1965 and 10 percent in 1980.[8] Others estimate that it is much larger.

Conversion of National Incomes to a Single Currency

Before the national incomes of various countries can meaningfully be compared, they must, of course, be converted to a single currency, usually the U.S.

[8]Estimates by Peter Wiles as cited in Dieter Cassel and E. Ulrich Cichy, "Explaining the Growing Shadow Economy in East and West," *Comparative Economic Studies* 28 (Spring 1986): 21. They broadly agree with the results of a survey of Soviet immigrants in Israel that found incomes received away from the main place of employment to account for about 10 percent of total earnings. See Gur Ofer and A. Vinokur, *Private Sources of Income of the Soviet Urban Household* (Rand Corporation, R-2359-NA, August 1980).

dollar. The simplest method for such conversions, commonly used by the World Bank and other organizations, is the application of official or market exchange rates to the data in marks, pounds, francs, yen, and so on. The justification for this procedure is that a market exchange rate should roughly translate the prices of one market economy into the prices of another. Suppose, for example, that a ton of steel sells in Japan for a price in yen that, when converted to dollars at the market exchange rate, is much lower than the current dollar price of steel on the U.S. market. What will happen? Americans will want to buy the relatively cheap Japanese steel. The American import demand may be expected to cause the Japanese to raise the price of their steel, or it may cause the exchange rate of the dollar to fall relative to the yen until the dollar price of a ton of steel is roughly the same in Japan and in the United States. Either way, the market exchange rate would reflect the relative purchasing power of the two currencies.

Unfortunately, the world does not operate quite as simply as described above. In socialist countries exchange rates and prices generally are set by central planners rather than markets. In market economies they are often influenced by governmental intervention in foreign exchange markets, price controls, taxes, and foreign trade restrictions. Many products are not traded internationally because of high transportation and marketing costs, so their prices are not equalized by international market forces. Moreover, exchange rates can be rendered meaningless by wild speculative activities. Official and market exchange rates provide only crude approximations of the relative purchasing powers of national currencies.

Because of the unreliable character of national income comparisons based on official or market exchange rate conversions, the U.N. International Comparison Project (ICP) has adopted an alternative approach.[9] The output of each country is divided into 151 product groups and the value of each group is calculated according to a set of average **international prices** (expressed in terms of U.S. dollars). When the product groups are added together, the resulting comparisons of GDP are roughly equal to those that would be obtained by application of purchasing-power–parity exchange rates. A similar approach is employed by the U.S. Central Intelligence Agency to estimate the dollar value of the Soviet GNP and military spending.

The data in the first two columns of Table A.2 demonstrate that international comparisons based on purchasing-power–parity exchange rates differ substantially from those based on market and official exchange rates. Comparisons for 1984 indicate that most nations, and particularly the poor nations, compare more favorably with the United States in terms of GDP per capita when the purchasing-power–parity method is used.

---

[9]See Irving Kravis et al., *World Product and Income: International Comparisons of Real Gross Product* (Baltimore: Johns Hopkins University Press, 1982); and Robert Summers and Allan Heston, "Improved International Comparisons of Real Product and Its Composition: 1950–1980," *Review of Income and Wealth* 30 (June 1984): 207–262.

The Index Number Problem

Although international comparisons of national income based on purchasing-power–parity calculations are, in principle, superior to those based on official exchange rates, they still do not solve one nagging problem. As we have seen, national products can be converted to a single currency by applying a single set of prices to the outputs of the various countries. The question remains: Whose prices do we use? The so-called **index number problem** refers to the fact that comparisons of macroeconomic aggregates (such as national income, industrial production, and the consumer price level) can be greatly influenced by the prices (or quantity weights, in the case of price indexes) that are used to add the values of products together.

Suppose, for example, that we wish to compare the national products of the United States and the Soviet Union, and, for the sake of simplicity, suppose that both countries produce only two products—wheat and steel. According to the hypothetical data in Table 2.3, U.S. agriculture is highly productive; thus, U.S. wheat production is greater than Soviet wheat production and the price of wheat is relatively low in dollars. The Soviet Union, on the other hand, is assumed to have a relatively efficient steel industry, with a high level of production at a relatively low price.

If we calculate the U.S. GNP using rubles, we apply the relatively high ruble price for wheat to the high level of U.S. wheat production and thus derive a U.S. GNP that is nearly twice the Soviet level. The Soviet Union, however, looks better if the comparison is done in dollars: the Soviet GNP includes its large volume of steel production valued at the high U.S. steel price.

Our hypothetical example illustrates the **Gershchenkron effect**—when the production levels of two countries are compared, the GNP of country X will appear to be relatively larger if the prices of country Y are used to sum the products of each of the countries. This regularity is supported by the actual, rather than hypothetical, estimates of U.S. and Soviet GNP in Table 2.4. According to the Central Intelligence Agency, Soviet GNP was less than half the U.S. level in 1985 when measured in rubles and almost two-thirds of the

---

Table 2.3   Hypothetical GNP Calculations

	Final Output (billion tons)		Prices per Ton	
	USSR	U.S.	Rubles	Dollars
Wheat	10	50	16	15
Steel	50	30	8	20

	Gross National Product		
	USSR	U.S.	USSR/U.S.
Rubles (billion)	$(10)(16)+(50)(8)=560$	$(50)(16)+(30)(8)=1040$	.54
Dollars (billion)	$(10)(15)+(50)(20)=1150$	$(50)(15)+(30)(20)=1350$	.85

Table 2.4   United States and Soviet GNP, 1985

	Soviet Union	United States	USSR/U.S.
Rubles (billion)	572	1356	.42
Dollars (billion)	1406	2252	.62

Source: U.S. Central Intelligence Agency, *Handbook of Economic Statistics, 1986* (CPAS 86-10002, September 1986), 38.

U.S. level when measured in dollars. Which estimate is more meaningful or valid? The one in dollars? The one in rubles? Some average of the two? Unfortunately, this question has no straightforward answer.[10]

As we mentioned earlier, the U.N. International Comparisons Project (ICP) handles the index number problem by employing a set of average international prices. In principle, this is undoubtedly better than using the prices of any single country. In practice, though, the prices used in the ICP studies are closer to those of the industrial countries than they are to those of the developing countries. The Gershchenkron effect would suggest that the use of industrial world prices is likely to impart an upward bias to the estimates of national income for the developing countries. Indeed, the estimates of developing-country incomes that are obtained by the ICP studies are two to three times larger than those obtained by simple market exchange rate conversions (Table A.2). Thus, the ICP estimates have been criticized by Third World economists, who fear that the larger income estimates may reduce their nations' access to foreign aid.[11]

Alternative Measures of the Standard of Living

As was mentioned earlier, national income per capita is the measure most commonly used for international comparisons of economic development and living standards. However, because of the deficiencies discussed above—disagreements over how national income should be defined, exclusion of unmarketed and hidden output, and the problems involved in converting national incomes to a common currency—the search is under way for alternative measures of the standard of living.

One revealing statistical series, for example, is food consumption per capita, measured in calories. The Food and Agriculture Organization of the

---

[10]For an interesting discussion of the index number problem as it applies to comparisons of U.S. and Soviet military spending, see Franklyn Holzman, "Is There a Soviet-U.S. Military Spending Gap?" *Challenge* (September–October 1980): 3–9.

[11]For further explanation of this and other problems, and a defense of the ICP position, see Irving Kravis, "Comparative Studies of National Income and Prices," *Journal of Economic Literature* 22 (March 1984): 1–39.

MILITARY SPENDING:
THE INDEX NUMBER GAME

In its comparisons of U.S. and Soviet defense spending, the CIA encounters the same problems that occur in GNP comparisons. To prepare its annual estimates of Soviet military spending, the CIA first compiles an inventory of military purchases in physical terms—numbers of personnel, aircraft, ships, missiles, etc.—based on satellite reconnaissance and other intelligence sources. It then attaches approximate dollar prices to each of those items (wage rates paid to U.S. military personnel and prices of American weapons that are more or less similar to Soviet weapons) and adds them together. Thus, the CIA calculates the approximate number of dollars that the Soviet Union would have to spend at American prices to purchase its military. That hypothetical dollar amount is compared to the actual level of U.S. military spending.

From time to time, the CIA analysts also prepare comparisons in rubles, but they have less confidence in these estimates because of uncertainty about ruble prices. Thus, the ruble estimates are given little publicity.

According to the Gershchenkron effect, we would expect the Soviet military to appear somewhat larger in the dollar estimates than in the ruble estimates. Indeed, according to the CIA estimates for 1981, the Soviet military cost 45 percent more than the American military in dollar prices and 25 percent more in ruble prices. By 1985, after several years of the Reagan defense buildup, the CIA estimates that U.S. and Soviet spending were roughly equal in dollars. A ruble comparison was not published for 1985, but presumably it would indicate that the United States outspent the Soviet Union. Some critics of the CIA estimates (Franklyn Holzman, for one) believe that they overestimate the relative size of the Soviet military, and others (for example, Steven Rosefielde and William T. Lee) believe that they seriously underestimate the Soviet threat.

Sources: The CIA estimates are reported in annual hearings of the Joint Economic Committee of the U.S. Congress, titled *Allocation of Resources in the Soviet Union and China*. See also Franklyn D. Holzman, "Soviet Military Spending: Assessing the Numbers Game," *International Security* 6 (Spring 1982): 78–101; and Steven Rosefielde, *False Science: Underestimating the Soviet Arms Buildup* (New Brunswick: Transaction Books, 1982).

United Nations regularly prepares estimates of food consumption, based on data provided by national governments, for 164 countries covering over 500 primary and processed food products.[12] Food consumption is not, of course, as broad a gauge of the standard of living as is national income, and consumption above some caloric level is not even healthy, as many of us know from personal experience.

Nevertheless, it is interesting to note that in terms of the basic provision of nutrition, the developing and socialist countries compare much more favorably with the industrial capitalist countries than they do in terms of national income per capita (Table A.2). Bangladesh, for example, with a GDP per capita equal to only 5 percent of the U.S. level, achieved over half the U.S. level of calorie consumption per capita in 1984.

The **Physical Quality of Life Index (PQLI),** adopted by the Overseas Development Council, is meant to measure economic and social development in terms of human results (health and education) rather than in terms of inputs (consumption of food and other goods and services). The PQLI is a simple unweighted average of index numbers for three development indicators: infant mortality rate, life expectancy, and adult literacy.[13] It is attractive in its simplicity, in its apparent lack of bias toward any economic system, and in its emphasis on results. Furthermore, because public health and literacy are positively correlated with income equality, the PQLI tells us something about the distribution, as well as the average level, of real income in each country. On the other hand, the PQLI neglects certain aspects of the quality of life (freedom, leisure, etc.); it is based on health and education statistics that are notoriously deficient; and the assignment of equal weights to the three indicators seems arbitrary.[14]

The data in Table A.2 indicate, again, that the developing and socialist nations compare much more favorably with the industrial capitalist economies in terms of the PQLI than they do in terms of per capita national income. Indeed, given the high priority that socialist countries supposedly place on income equality and public health, we can hypothesize that a socialist country with a particular level of per capita income should have a higher PQLI than a capitalist country at that same level of income. Statistical tests have yielded mixed results, but they provide some support for this hypothesis.[15]

---

[12]*FAO Production Yearbook, 1981* (Rome: Food and Agriculture Organization of the United Nations, 1982), 9.

[13]The PQLI is fully explained in Morris D. Morris, *Measuring the Condition of the World's Poor* (New York: Pergamon Press, 1979).

[14]On the poor quality of infant mortality statistics, see William McGreevey, "Measuring Development Performance," in *Third World Poverty,* ed. William McGreevey (Lexington, Mass.: Lexington Books, 1980), 24–27.

[15]Edward F. Stuart, "The PQLI as a Measure of Comparative Economic Performance," *The ACES Bulletin* 26 (Winter 1984): 43–53; and John P. Burkett, "PQLI as a Measure of Comparative Performance: Comment," *Comparative Economic Studies* 28 (Summer 1986): 59–68.

Income Distribution Comparisons

We noted in the previous chapter that the performance of an economic system may be assessed not only by the size and growth of the national income it generates, but also by the equity with which that income is distributed across the population. We also noted, however, that one man's equity is another man's injustice. An equitable income distribution may be one that divides income evenly, or according to work, inheritance, market forces, or any number of other standards. We should establish at the outset, therefore, that measures of income *equality* may not be the same as measures of income *equity.*

Measures of Income Inequality

Data relating to the distributions of income in the United States, Sweden, and Brazil are presented in Table 2.5. Based on these data, the Swedish distribution of income is more even than that of the United States, and the Brazilian distribution, like that of many Third World countries, is less even. These observations can be illustrated in several ways. First, and most simply, the poorest decile (tenth) of households received only 0.6 percent of total income in Brazil, compared to 1.6 percent in the United States and 2.6 percent in Sweden.

Another simple measure of income inequality is the **decile ratio**—the share of income received by the richest decile of the population of households divided by the share of the poorest decile. A larger decile ratio would, of course, denote a less equal distribution of income. According to the data in Table 2.5, the decile ratios are 18.1 for the United States, 8.2 for Sweden, and 84.3 for Brazil. While the decile ratio is a simple and useful measure of inequal-

Table 2.5 Distribution of Household Income in the United States, Sweden, and Brazil

	Percentage of Total Household Income Received by Each Decile		
	United States	Sweden	Brazil
Poorest Decile	1.6	2.6	0.6
Second Decile	3.4	4.6	1.4
Third Decile	4.7	6.1	2.1
Fourth Decile	6.1	6.7	2.9
Fifth Decile	7.5	7.5	4.0
Sixth Decile	8.9	9.9	5.4
Seventh Decile	10.6	11.8	7.1
Eighth Decile	12.6	13.6	9.9
Ninth Decile	15.6	16.0	16.0
Richest Decile	29.0	21.2	50.6

Source: Wouter van Ginneken and Jong-goo Park, *Generating Internationally Comparable Income Distribution Estimates* (Geneva: International Labour Office, 1984), Tables 1 and A.1. Reference years are 1971 for the United States, 1972 for Brazil, and 1979 for Sweden.

Figure 2.1 Lorenz Curves

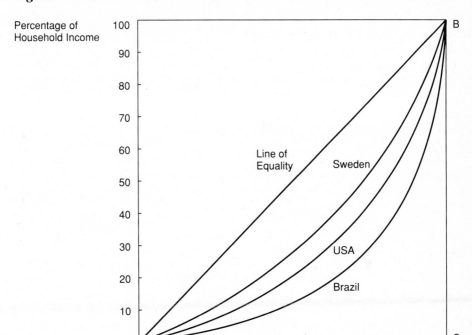

Percentage of Household Income

100
90
80
70
60
50
40
30
20
10

Line of Equality

Sweden

USA

Brazil

B

C

A

10 20 30 40 50 60 70 80 90 100

Percentages of Households

ity, it utilizes data concerning only the richest and poorest members of the population, ignoring those in the middle.

A second tool for analysis and comparison of income distributions is the **Lorenz curve,** which illustrates the percentage of total income received by each cumulative percentage of the population. Lorenz curves based on the data in Table 2.5 are presented in Figure 2.1. Clearly, all Lorenz curves must pass through points A and B on the graph, because zero percent of households must logically receive zero percent of total income, and 100 percent of households must logically receive 100 percent of income. It is the *shape* of the Lorenz curve between these points that reflects the degree of income inequality.

If there were a country in the world with a perfectly even distribution of income (there is not), its Lorenz curve would be the straight diagonal line, AB. Along that line, the poorest 20 percent of households receive 20 percent of total income, the poorest 40 percent of households receive 40 percent of total income, and so forth. The greater the income inequality in a country, the more the Lorenz curve for that country will bend away from the line of equality. Thus, it is clear by inspection that Brazilian income is distributed less equally than American income, and Swedish income is distributed more equally. In the extreme and unsustainable case of perfect income inequality (one person receives all the income) the Lorenz curve would be the right-angled line, ACB.

A third tool for comparison of income distributions is the **Gini ratio,** named for the Italian statistician who introduced it in 1912. The Gini ratio is equal to the measured area between the diagonal line of equality, AB, and the Lorenz curve, divided by the total area of the triangle, ABC. In the case of perfect equality there would be no area between the Lorenz curve and the diagonal line (they would be the same line) and the Gini ratio would equal zero. In the case of perfect inequality the Gini ratio would equal the area of triangle ABC divided by itself, or 1. For any real country, the Gini ratio falls somewhere between 0 and 1, with a larger coefficient denoting more income inequality.

Because the curved area between a Lorenz curve and the line of equality can be difficult to measure, exact calculation of the Gini ratio is somewhat complex, and several different estimation techniques are available. The simplest formula is:

$$\text{Gini ratio} = 1 - 2 \sum_{i=1}^{n} \left(\frac{1}{2n} + \frac{(n-i)}{n} \right) P_i$$

Where:

n = number of income groups (n = 10 in Table 2.5)
i = a particular income group (i = 1 for poorest group)
P_i = fraction of total income received by
income group i, expressed as a decimal fraction
rather than a percentage (P_1 = .016 for the United States).

If the population is divided into ten income groups (as in Table 2.5), then:

Gini ratio = $1 - (1.9P_1 + 1.7P_2 + 1.5P_3 + 1.3P_4 + 1.1P_5 + .9P_6 + .7P_7 + .5P_8 + .3P_9 + .1P_{10})$

Applying this formula, the Gini ratios calculated from the data in Table 2.5 are 0.30 for Sweden, 0.39 for the United States, and 0.61 for Brazil (in ascending order of inequality). Data for several other countries are presented in Table A.24. These data have been selected and adjusted to ensure a reasonable level of comparability, but they should be treated with caution. In general, the developing countries (with notable exceptions, such as Bangladesh) have the greatest levels of income inequality, the socialist countries (with the possible exception of Yugoslavia) and the capitalist welfare states (Denmark and Sweden) have the most egalitarian distributions of income, and the other industrial capitalist countries seem to fall somewhere in the middle.[16]

---

[16]The range of Gini ratios among industrial capitalist countries is actually quite similar to the range among socialist countries, but the socialist countries seem to have a higher level of

Problems in Making Income Distribution Comparisons

If international comparisons of income inequality are to be made—whether we employ decile ratios, Lorenz curves, or Gini ratios—we must carefully consider the comparability of the underlying income distribution data, such as those presented in Tables 2.5 and A.24. First, the data should be comparable in their coverage and segmentation of the population. For example, data that cover only employed persons or workers (as is often true of data released by socialist countries) will indicate a greater degree of income equality than data that include retired persons, the unemployed, and others with zero incomes. With regard to segmentation, the measured distribution of income among households comes closer to being equal than the distribution of income among individuals because relatively high and low incomes tend to be pooled within each household.[17]

Second, the data should be comparable in terms of the forms of income that are included, that is, wages, profits, rents, capital gains, transfer payments, income in kind, etc. Inclusion of capital gains, for example, usually increases measured income inequality. Comparisons are preferably based on income after taxes, because many countries design their systems of taxation expressly to redistribute income.

With regard to industrial capitalist countries, the significance of these considerations can be illustrated with data relating to the Swedish income distribution. In 1976–1977, the Swedish Gini ratio for the distribution of individual pretax incomes was equal to 0.52. The ratio for household incomes before taxes was lower, 0.37, indicating greater equality. The ratio for household incomes after taxes was still lower at 0.30. When another adjustment is made for differences in the size of households, the Swedish coefficient falls to 0.25—about half the level for individual pretax incomes.[18]

Estimates of income inequality in developing countries are hampered by poor statistical reporting systems and by the important role of nonmarket income. For reasons that we shall consider below, unemployment is often underestimated in Third World countries, possibly causing an underestimation of income inequality. On the other hand, the governments of these countries have poor information on nonmarket incomes, possibly causing an overestimation of inequality. According to estimates for Malaysia, if monetary incomes are adjusted to include in-kind income, transfer payments, and the value of housing services, the Gini ratio falls from 0.62 to 0.57 (denoting greater equal-

---

income equality if their lower levels of economic development are taken into account. See Christian Morrisson, "Income Distribution in East European and Western Countries," *Journal of Comparative Economics* 8 (June 1984): 121–138; and Gustav Papanek and Oldrich Kyn, "The Effect on Income Distribution of Development, the Rate of Growth, and Economic Strategy," *Journal of Development Economics* 23 (September 1986): 55–65.

[17]See Harold F. Lydall, "Some Problems in Making International Comparisons of Inequality," in *Income Inequality,* ed. John R. Moroney (Lexington, Mass.: Lexington Books, 1979), 21–37.

[18]*Ibid.,* 31.

ity) and the inclusion of several other forms of nonmarket income reduces the ratio to 0.48.[19]

For the socialist countries, Table A.24 presents two sets of estimates—one based on monetary income and another that includes estimates of the nonmonetary income received by the elite in the form of access to special shops, the use of official cars, and other perquisites. Clearly, international comparisons based on inconsistent coverage and definition of incomes can produce misleading results.

Unemployment Comparisons

International comparisons of unemployment are facilitated by the fact that international agreements were reached in 1954 and 1982 under the auspices of the International Labour Organization on a standard definition for unemployment.[20] Nevertheless, national practices vary with respect to age limits, reference periods, criteria used to determine whether a person is actively seeking work, treatment of persons who are temporarily laid off, handling of military personnel, and other details that are not included in the standard definition. Moreover, some nations have ignored the international agreement.

Aside from definitional problems, the international comparability of unemployment rates is also damaged by differences in the methods of data collection. Some 36 countries, including most of North and South America and several Western European nations, base their unemployment estimates on periodic labor force sample surveys. Sample surveys are generally believed to yield the best estimates of unemployment because they include groups of persons who are often missed by other methods.

However, a much larger number of countries, including most of the developing nations, as well as West Germany, Great Britain, Switzerland, and Denmark, base their estimates on registrations at governmental employment and social security offices. These may, of course, overlook unemployed persons who choose not to register, particularly in Third World countries where the government has little to offer to the unemployed. By way of illustration, the unemployment rate in Spain was 21.7 percent in 1984 according to a labor market survey and 18.8 percent according to employment office registrations.[21]

In Table 2.6, three different sets of unemployment estimates for ten countries are assembled. The first column lists the rates that are published by each of the countries, according to their various definitions and methods of data collection. The second column lists estimates prepared by the U.S. De-

---

[19]Michael Kusnic and Julie Davanzo, "Accounting for Non-Market Activities in the Distribution of Income," *Journal of Development Economics* 21 (May 1986): 211–227.

[20]The standard definition and a description of the various systems of data collection are given in *Yearbook of Labour Statistics* (Geneva: International Labour Office, 1985), 477–78.

[21]*Ibid.,* 491.

Table 2.6   Unemployment Rates According to Three Definitions, 1985

	National Definitions	U.S. Definition	OECD Definition
Australia	8.3	8.3	8.2
Canada	10.5	10.5	10.4
France	10.8	10.4	10.1
Great Britain	11.5	13.1	13.0
Italy	10.6	6.0	10.5
Japan	2.6	2.6	2.6
Netherlands	15.9	14.1	13.0
Sweden	2.5	2.8	2.8
United States	7.2	7.2	7.1
West Germany	9.3	7.9	8.6

Sources: Column 1: United Nations, *Monthly Bulletin of Statistics* 41 (January, 1987), Table 8. Column 2: U.S. Department of Labor, *Monthly Labor Review* 110 (February, 1987), p. 88. Column 3: *OECD Economic Outlook* 40 (December, 1986), Table R12.

partment of Labor that include rough adjustments of the data to conform with the U.S. definition. In the third column (and in Table A.12 for a larger number of countries and years) are Organization for Economic Cooperation and Development (OECD) estimates of unemployment rates that are supposed to roughly "conform with the definitions drawn up by the International Labour Organization."[22] The OECD estimates are adjusted to improve the comparability of data gathered by sample surveys and governmental employment offices. Whereas the U.S. estimates (second column) are based on unemployment in the *civilian* labor force, the OECD estimates are calculated for the total labor force.

By far, the most significant adjustment is the one for Italy, where the unemployment rate according to the U.S. definition is little more than half the rate obtained by the Italian and OECD definitions. According to Italian practice, a person who has made no effort to find work in the last month may be counted as unemployed . According to the American definition, such inactive persons are dropped from the unemployment rolls and placed in another category known as "discouraged workers."[23]

International comparisons of unemployment are also complicated by the existence of underground, unreported employment. Those who hide their incomes in order to obtain welfare benefits, to hide illegal activities, or to avoid taxation are often counted as unemployed. We might hypothesize, there-

[22]*OECD Economic Outlook* 40 (December 1986): 167.

[23]For a full discussion of the adjustment methods used by the U.S. Department of Labor, see *U.S. Bureau of Labor Statistics, International Comparisons of Unemployment,* Bulletin 1979 (August 1978); and Joyanna Moy and Constance Sorrentino, "Unemployment, Labor Force Trends, and Layoff Practices in 10 Countries," *Monthly Labor Review* (December 1981): 4–5.

fore, that reported unemployment rates are inflated in countries with high tax rates, large welfare systems, and high crime rates, because of the prevalence of underground employment.

On the other hand, published unemployment rates fail to capture the significant amount of underemployment that exists in countries where large numbers of workers are forced to accept part-time jobs or jobs below their skill levels, or where employers are unwilling or unable to fire unproductive workers. In the Netherlands, for example, where the unemployment rate increased from 5 percent in 1979 to 14 percent in 1983, the share of part-time employment in total employment increased during those same years from 8 percent to 21 percent.[24] In Japan, the permanent commitment system of employment causes a substantial amount of "unemployment within the company." According to one estimate, the total unemployment and underutilization of Japanese labor during the late 1970s was about 10 percent of the labor force, while the official unemployment rate was only 2 percent.[25] Likewise, the American unemployment rate would increase substantially if it included disgruntled part-time workers and the so-called discouraged workers who have stopped looking for jobs.

Most of the socialist countries do not report unemployment rates, but the perpetual state of excess demand that is maintained in most of these countries has generally kept the rates very low. Indeed, the system of central planning gives enterprise managers a strong incentive to hoard labor, which reduces unemployment at the expense of underemployment. In market-socialist Yugoslavia, the reported unemployment rate was 13.8 percent in 1985— one of the highest rates in Europe. That rate would have been even higher if large numbers of Yugoslav workers had not left the country to find jobs.

Comparisons of Inflation

Few international comparisons are more dramatic than those for price inflation. During the 1970s, the reported average annual rates of consumer price inflation ranged from 0.2 percent in the Soviet Union (and similarly low rates in most of Eastern Europe) to 5 percent in West Germany and Switzerland, 7 percent in the United States and Japan, 15 percent in Britain, Ireland, Spain, and Italy, and in excess of 100 percent in Argentina and Chile.

Although it is clear that inflationary experiences differ widely between countries, there are several considerations to bear in mind when international comparisons are made. First, there is significant variation across countries in the quantity and quality of price data collected. In underdeveloped countries,

[24]Chris de Neubourg, "Part-Time Work: An International Quantitative Comparison," *International Labour Review* 124 (September–October 1985): 563.

[25]For example, see Koji Taira, "Japan's Low Unemployment: Economic Miracle or Statistical Artifact?" *Monthly Labor Review* 106 (July 1983): 9.

consumer price data are generally collected only in the capital cities and may cover as few as 30 items. In developed countries, the price surveys ordinarily include several cities and 200–400 items.

Second, recall that even in countries where nearly complete data are collected, the "true" rate of inflation is a matter of disagreement. In the United States, for example, it is commonly alleged that the consumer price index (CPI) overstates the rate of inflation because of its use of fixed commodity weights from a year in the past and its insufficient adjustment for improvements in product quality. From 1970 to 1986, the CPI (using 1967 weights) increased at an annual rate of 6.7 percent, while the implicit price index for personal consumption expenditures (using 1982 weights) increased at a rate of 6.0 percent.[26]

Special care must be taken when international comparisons include countries that exercise price controls. In the Soviet Union and most of Eastern Europe, the vast majority of prices are set and controlled by governmental agencies. In these countries, inflation is likely to take three forms: (1) open, reported inflation; (2) hidden inflation; and (3) repressed inflation.

Open, reported inflation occurs in planned economies because some prices are not controlled and because the authorities themselves occasionally increase the controlled prices. In the Soviet Union, Eastern Europe, and China, for example, part of agricultural output is sold to consumers on collective farm markets where it is legal to charge any price the market will bear. The Soviet authorities have increased the controlled prices of gasoline, vodka, and a number of other products in recent years.

Hidden inflation occurs when there are violations of "price discipline." If a new product is introduced at a higher price than the product it replaced, for example, without a corresponding improvement in quality, the price increase is not likely to be reflected in the official measured rate of inflation. Likewise, if products are secretly sold (perhaps on black markets) at prices that exceed their controlled levels, the resulting inflation is hidden.

Repressed inflation is a condition in which price controls are effective, so that inflationary pressures (such as rapid growth in the money supply) cannot be relieved by open or hidden price increases. Instead, the inflationary pressures manifest themselves in the form of shortages, which require the distribution of products through queues and/or rationing. It should be emphasized that widespread shortages do not necessarily indicate the presence of repressed inflation. The shortages could be caused by a faulty set of *relative* prices, rather than a low *general* price level.

Four different measures of Soviet and Eastern European inflation are presented in Table 2.7. First, we have the official estimates, which are generally

---

[26]Calculated from index numbers in *Economic Report of the President* (Washington: USGPO, 1987), 250, 307. For further discussion of this point, see Richard Wahl, "Is the Consumer Price Index a Fair Measure of Inflation?" *Journal of Policy Analysis and Management* 1 (Winter 1982): 496–507.

Table 2.7 Alternate Measures of Inflation in the Soviet Union and Eastern Europe (Average Annual Percentage Rates)

| | Consumer Price Indexes: | | Indexes of Inflationary Pressure Based on: | |
	Official Estimates	CIA Estimates	Black-Market Exchange Rates	Money Income Growth
Soviet Union				
1961–1970	−0.1	0.9	7.2	3.8
1971–1980	0.3	2.1	2.9*	2.7
1981–1984	1.0	2.0	n.a.	1.2
Bulgaria				
1961–1970	0.9	3.2	3.2	n.a.
1971–1980	2.1	4.9	1.7*	4.2
1981–1984	0.7	2.8	n.a.	1.9
Czechoslovakia				
1961–1970	1.2	3.2	4.4	n.a.
1971–1980	1.0	2.3	1.1*	2.2
1981–1984	2.2	1.6	n.a.	1.9
East Germany				
1961–1970	−0.1	1.2	3.3	n.a.
1971–1980	−0.1	1.1	1.8*	0.7
1981–1984	0.1	1.5	n.a.	2.1
Hungary				
1961–1970	0.7	2.1	4.3	n.a.
1971–1980	4.7	5.2	1.8*	5.8
1981–1984	6.8	7.4	n.a.	7.4
Poland				
1961–1970	1.9	2.5	5.7	n.a.
1971–1980	4.3	7.3	4.8*	8.1
1981–1984	35.6	34.4	n.a.	34.1

*1971–1979

Sources: Column 1—*Statisticheskii ezhegodnik stran-chlenov Soveta Ekonomicheskoi Vzaimopomoshchi* (Moscow: Finansi i Statistika, various years). Column 2— Central Intelligence Agency, *Handbook of Economic Statistics, 1986* (CPAS 86-10002, September 1986), 53. Column 3—William Patton Culbertson, Jr. and Ryan C. Amacher, "Inflation in the Planned Economies: Some Estimates for Eastern Europe," *Southern Economic Journal* 45 (October 1978): 387, 391. Updated to 1979 using the Culbertson-Amacher procedure. Column 4—Annual growth of personal disposable money income minus growth of real consumption. For Eastern Europe, calculated from data in Thad Alton and Assoc., *Research Project on National Income in East Central Europe* (New York: L. W. International Financial Research, 1985), OP-88, 9 and OP-87, 8–12. For the Soviet Union, state wages and salaries were used as a surrogate index of money income, and were calculated from *Narodnoe khoziaistvo SSSR* (Moscow: Finansy i Statistika, various years). The CIA index of real consumption was taken from the CIA *Handbook of Economic Statistics, 1986,* 66.

based on the prices on state lists, rather than on prices actually paid. They indicate very low rates for all of the countries in the 1960s, moderate rates for Hungary and Poland in the 1970s, and a very high rate for Poland during the crisis of the early 1980s.

The second set of estimates, compiled by the Central Intelligence Agency, is based on comparisons of official indexes of personal consumption (or retail sales in the case of the Soviet Union) in current prices with estimated indexes of consumption (or retail sales) in constant prices. This procedure is meant to capture at least some hidden inflation, but its authors emphasize that "if anything, it understates the increase in prices."[27] In most cases, the CIA estimates are a little higher than the official estimates, but they still indicate rather low inflation rates for most of the countries and time periods.

The third set of estimates, devised by Culbertson and Amacher, is formulated on the assumption that black-market exchange rates for the currencies of the Eastern countries should roughly reflect the relationships between the price levels of those countries and price levels in the rest of the world.[28] Since foreign currency is used by Eastern European residents to purchase goods that are in short domestic supply, the demand for foreign exchange may provide some indication of all of the forms of inflation: open, hidden, and repressed. Still, these estimates are extremely speculative, because a number of other factors influence black market exchange rates (including the risk of prosecution), and because a narrow assortment of goods is bought with foreign exchange.

Nevertheless, it is interesting to note that the Culbertson-Amacher estimates produce an unweighted average inflation rate for the six socialist countries from 1960 to 1970 of 4.7 percent, which is very close to the 4.4 percent average recorded during the same years by 19 industrial market economies. However, the same method provides much lower estimates of Eastern European inflation from 1970 to 1979—lower, in fact, than the CIA estimates for four of the countries, and lower than the official estimates in the cases of Hungary and Poland.

Finally, the last column of Table 2.7 presents an index of purchasing power imbalance—the amount by which the annual growth of the population's money income exceeds the growth of real production of consumer goods. In other words, it is a rough estimate of the extent to which "too many rubles are chasing too few goods." For the Eastern European countries, the inflationary pressure indicated by the index is very close to the CIA estimates. For the Soviet Union, the index indicates a higher level of inflationary pressure in the 1960s and 1970s than we find in the official or CIA statistics—possibly pointing to repressed inflation.[29] Alternatively, the extra income may flow into voluntary saving.[30] With the exception of the Polish crisis, all of these estimates

---

[27]Gertrude Schroeder and Barbara Severin, "Soviet Consumption and Income Policies in Perspective," in U.S. Congress, Joint Economic Committee, *Soviet Economy in a New Perspective* (Washington, D.C.: USGPO, 1976), 631.

[28]William Patton Culbertson and Ryan C. Amacher, "Inflation in the Planned Economies: Some Estimates for Eastern Europe," *Southern Economic Journal* 45 (October 1978): 380–393.

[29]For further discussion of purchasing power imbalances in the Soviet Union and China, see Gavin Peebles, "Aggregate Retail Price Changes in Socialist Economies: Identification, Theory, and Evidence for China and the Soviet Union," *Soviet Studies* 38 (October 1986): 477–507. For evidence of repressed inflation based on supply shocks and bank lending, see Gregory Grossman, "Inflationary, Political, and Social Implications of the Current Economic Slowdown," in *Economics and Politics in the USSR: Problems of Interdependence,* ed. Hans-Hermann Hohmann, Alec Nove, and Heinrich Vogel (Boulder: Westview, 1986): 173–197.

[30]For estimates of repressed inflationary pressure (or the lack of it) that take account of saving and other factors, see Richard Portes and David Winter, "Disequilibrium Estimates for Consumption Goods Markets in Centrally Planned Economies," *Review of Economic Studies* 47 (1980): 137–159.

of inflation and inflationary pressure are rather low for the centrally planned economies.

Summary

Statistical information is invaluable in assessing economic systems, but it should always be handled cautiously. First, there are problems of definition. National income can be defined as gross national product, gross domestic product, net material product, or in a number of other ways. Income distribution statistics may cover the income of households or individuals, before or after taxes. Unemployment statistics may or may not include those who have failed to look for a job in the past month. Inflation may be measured at the consumer, wholesale, or GNP level.

Second, there are inconsistencies between countries in the methods and quality of data collection. In the case of national income measurement, a significant amount of output may not be reported if it is produced for home consumption or the underground economy. Unemployment statistics may be collected through market surveys or from employment office statistics. Price indexes may be based on large or small numbers of geographic areas and commodity groups and price increases may be hidden in countries that exercise price controls.

Finally, there are problems of interpretation. The very meaning of national income comparisons is clouded by the index number problem. The significance of income distribution statistics depends on one's concept of social equity. The dividing lines between the unemployed, the underemployed, and the "discouraged workers" may be difficult to draw. The rate of repressed inflation may be impossible to measure. These are analytical problems that, even while unsolved, must not be ignored.

Discussion and Review Questions

1.   What is the difference between GNP and GDP? Between GNP and NMP?

2.   How should the value of services performed by lawyers, accountants, and college professors be measured for inclusion in GNP?

3.   In national income comparisons, what is the advantage of using a common set of average international prices to evaluate each nation's output, rather than converting total national incomes with exchange rates? What problems are not solved by this procedure?

4.   If you were asked to prepare a comparison of national standards of living, and you were given an unlimited budget, how would you proceed?

5.   Suppose that you are appointed Minister of Propaganda for your country and you wish to say that your country has an even distribution of income. Without actually falsifying the data, how will you collect and arrange them to make your point? What forms of income and taxation will you

include? What population unit will you use? With what country will you compare your country's income distribution?

6. What are the differences between open, hidden, and repressed inflation? For the general population (or for various segments of the population) what would be the advantages and disadvantages of living in a country with repressed inflation rather than open inflation?

7. If you have a background in statistics or econometrics, how would you test the hypothesis that a socialist country at a particular level of per capita income tends to have a higher PQLI than a capitalist country at the same level of income?

Suggested Readings

Kravis, Irving, et al. *World Product and Income: International Comparisons of Real Gross Product.* Baltimore: Johns Hopkins University Press, 1982. *Gives a full description of the objectives, methods, and results of the U.N. International Comparisons Project.*

Pryor, Frederic L. *A Guidebook to the Comparative Study of Economic Systems.* Englewood Cliffs, N.J.: Prentice-Hall, 1985. *Pryor has collected an enormous amount of comparative data for capitalist and socialist countries and is a pioneer in the kind of hypothesis testing that is mentioned in discussion question 6, above.*

Treml, Vladimir and John Hardt, eds. *Soviet Economic Statistics.* Durham, N.C.: Duke University Press, 1972. *This is a classic work on the socialist statistical system, with chapters on national income, industry, agriculture, wages, prices, and money.*

Below are a few of the many sources of current comparative statistical data. You can learn much about comparative statistics by reading the explanatory notes and appendices.

Alton, Thad P., et al. *Research Project on National Income in East Central Europe.* New York: L.W. International Financial Research, Inc. Occasional papers, published annually.

Handbook of Economic Statistics. U.S. Central Intelligence Agency, annual.

Handbook of Labor Statistics. Washington, D.C.: U.S. Department of Labor, Bureau of Labor Statistics, annual.

International Financial Statistics. Washington, D.C.: International Monetary Fund, monthly, with annual compilations and supplements.

Monthly Bulletin of Statistics. New York: United Nations Statistical Office, monthly.

OECD Economic Outlook. Paris: Organization for Economic Cooperation and Development, biannual.

Sivard, Ruth Leger, ed. *World Military and Social Expenditures.* Washington, D.C.: World Priorities, annual.

Statistical Yearbook. New York: United Nations Statistical Office, annual.

World Bank. *World Development Report.* New York: Oxford University Press, annual.

World Bank. *World Tables.* Baltimore: Johns Hopkins University Press, occasional.

World Economic Outlook. Washington, D.C.: International Monetary Fund, annual.

Yearbook of Labour Statistics. Geneva: International Labour Office, annual.

II

PART

CAPITALISM

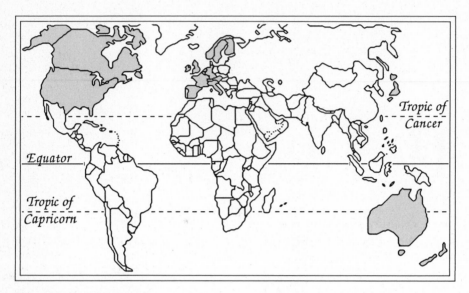

Industrial Capitalist Countries

3
CHAPTER

History and Theories of Capitalism

The starting-point of the development that gave rise to the wage-laborer as well as to the capitalist, was the servitude of the laborer. The advance consisted in a change of form of this servitude, in the transformation of feudal exploitation into capitalist exploitation.
—Karl Marx
  Capital, 1867

The exigency, complexity, and multiplicity of life on earth become yearly more unfathomable to any tyrant or planner. No nation can grow and adapt to change except to the extent that it is capitalistic, except to the extent, in other words, that its productive wealth is diversely controlled and can be freely risked in new causes, flexibly applied to new purposes, steadily transformed into new shapes and systems.
—George Gilder
  Wealth and Poverty, 1981

In the first chapter we defined capitalism to be an economic and social system in which the nation's farms, factories, and mines are predominantly owned by private individuals, partners, and stockholders. The industrial capitalist economies account for only 16 percent of the world's population and 24 percent of its bounded land area, but they contribute about half of the world's production and two-thirds of its exports (Tables A.1 and A.26).

Because the market system and the institution of private property are so intimately involved in our present way of life, we must be reminded that these are relatively recent developments in the history of civilization. Let us consider, for a moment, our precapitalist roots and the development of modern capitalist institutions. Afterwards, we will briefly survey the history of economic analysis of capitalism from the eighteenth century to the present.

Precapitalist Economic Systems

At the dawn of civilization, in the fifth millennium B.C., the social systems that developed on the plains of Egypt and Mesopotamia bore a closer resemblance to the modern Soviet system than to anything that can now be found in the Industrial West. Nearly all the land and other productive assets were owned by the state and individual freedom was severely restricted. As Stephan Viljoen reports:

Already when the riverine economies emerged in history, all economic activity was controlled, coordinated, canalized, and directed by the managerial bureaucracy, and all large enterprises undertaken by the state. After the irrigation works had been completed, the most important functions of management and control were those involved in the maintenance of the works, the distribution of irrigation water, and flood control.[1]

The pyramids and the walls of Babylon demonstrated the ability of a strong central authority to mobilize society toward the fulfillment of a few high-priority projects.

The outstanding feature of these works was that the builders invariably tried to achieve the requisite effect with the maximum use of material—a reflection of the inherent love of bureaucracy for the spectacular rather than for the aesthetic or the practically useful. Kings often boasted of the amount of material used and the number of workers employed.[2]

Again the similarities with modern Soviet society are striking, but they should not be overstated. The Soviet Union is ruled by a Communist Party hierarchy rather than by a king with divine pretensions, it has reached a much higher level of economic development, and its institutional structure is much more complex. Still, the ancient civilizations held even less in common with modern capitalist societies.

---

[1]Stephan Viljoen, *Economic Systems in World History* (London: Longman, 1974), 16.
[2]Ibid.

Greece and Rome

Beginning in the twelfth century B.C., the rise of the Greek and Roman city-states ushered in a new era of individual freedom, including economic freedom, for a significant segment of the population. Although perhaps 50 percent of the Greek and 80 percent of the Roman population lived in slavery, a significant number of people were free to choose their occupations and the craftsman, merchant, and banking professions began to thrive in the cities. Indeed, their prosperity gained the attention of the classical philosophers. Aristotle, for one, was quite disturbed by the fortunes amassed by merchants and bankers:

[Gaining wealth through retail trade] is justly censured; for it is unnatural, and a mode by which men gain from one another. The most hated sort, and with the greatest reason, is usury, which makes a gain out of money itself, and not from the natural object of it. For money was meant to be used in exchange, but not to increase at interest. Wherefore of all modes of getting wealth this is the most unnatural.[3]

Interestingly, although Aristotle argued that the unlimited capitalist pursuit of wealth was "unnatural," he argued in favor of the right of individuals to own private property—obviously a necessary precondition for the capitalist system. Property should be held privately, he said, because "when every one has a distinct interest, men will not complain of one another, and they will make more progress, because every one will be attending to his own business."[4] In other words, Aristotle noted in the fourth century B.C. that an economic system based on private property rights would provide stronger incentives for production than a communal society. On the other hand, he believed that the inequities caused by private property should be balanced with charity: "It is clearly better that property should be private, but the use of it common; and the special business of the legislator is to create in men this benevolent disposition."[5]

Although one author contends that "the Graeco-Roman economy was a free economy in the sense that a number of markets were more or less free to regulate themselves," the system was still quite unlike modern market capitalism.[6] Again, the use of slave labor was a dominant characteristic of the system and retail trade existed for little more than the provision of luxury goods to the upper class. Most of the important economic achievements of the Greek and Roman societies were prompted by governmental commands rather than by market forces, and surplus productive power was used to build impressive public buildings, city walls, and standing armies, rather than factories, machinery, and equipment.

[3]Aristotle *Politics* 1.10.1258a38–1258b7.

[4]Aristotle *Politics* 2.5.12663a25–29.

[5]Ibid., 1263a38.

[6]Viljoen, *Economic Systems in World History,* 55.

The Middle Ages

Progress toward the establishment of a market capitalist system was interrupted when the western part of the Roman Empire fell in the fifth century
A.D. The relative peace and unity that had been imposed by Rome disintegrated
into chaos. Long-distance trade became extremely hazardous and it was further restricted by the lack of a common language, legal code, or currency. The
countryside was carved into a large number of small, self-sufficient, feudal
estates. Each estate was held in trust by a feudal lord, who was responsible for
the physical and economic welfare of his vassals. In turn, the serfs were required to work in the lord's fields and shops and to provide him with a portion
of their product. Little money changed hands and little trade was conducted
with neighboring estates.

The system of mutual obligations between lords and servants in the
countryside was paralleled by the craft guilds in the cities. Master craftsmen
and their apprentices were bound by a system of indentures, which required
faithful service by the apprentices in exchange for instruction by the masters,
together with suitable provision of food, clothing, and shelter. The guild organizations enforced a rigid set of regulations concerning everything from hours
of work, methods of production, tools, prices, and raw materials that could be
used, to the number of apprentices and journeymen that could fall under a
single master's control. Thus, labor mobility, entrepreneurship, market flexibility, and technological progress were seriously restricted.

The medieval social structure was legitimized and maintained in the
West by the dominant institution of the era, the Roman Catholic Church.
Thomas Aquinas and other church theologians maintained that the master-
servant authority structure, including the institution of slavery, was ordained
by God. Indeed, the theologians of the day believed that charitable contributions should be limited in order to allow the upper class to live "in keeping
with their social station," because "no man ought to live unbecomingly."[7] On
the other hand, Aquinas declared that the inordinate accumulation of wealth
was sinful, particularly if it was acquired by selling goods above their "just
price" or by charging interest on loans.

A number of forces caused the slow demise of the feudal system. The
gradual rebuilding of strong centralized governments in Europe and England
restored the unity of languages, monetary systems, and laws, and reopened
trade routes. In the countryside, the slow substitution of money rents for labor
services transformed the relationship between lord and serf.

In the thirteenth century, the **enclosure movement** began, whereby
the landed aristocracy "enclosed" lands for their exclusive use that had previously been accessible to peasant farmers. As a result, a new class of landless
peasants was formed—a class dependent on the wages they could earn by
working for others. Thus, the enclosure movement began the stage of devel-

---

[7]Thomas Aquinas, *Summa Theologica,* quoted in Jacob Viner, *Religious Thought and Economic Society* (Durham, N.C.: Duke University Press, 1978), 74.

opment that Karl Marx called "primitive capitalist accumulation," which, in his opinion, "plays in Political Economy about the same part as original sin in theology."[8]

According to Werner Sombart, the "spirit of capitalism" first manifested itself in the thirteenth century in Italy, and by the fourteenth century the Florentines "were filled with a feverish (I had almost said an American) desire for gain, and a devotion to business that almost amounted to passionate love."[9] Italian commerce was facilitated, according to Sombart, by the substitution of Arabic for Roman numerals in the early thirteenth century, without which "quick and exact calculation would be well-nigh impossible," and by the development of a well-ordered system of bookkeeping by the end of the century.[10]

Renaissance and Reformation

The end of the Middle Ages and the beginning of the Renaissance are usually associated with the fall of Constantinople, the capital of the Byzantine Empire, in 1453. Refugees from Byzantium, where the study of Greek and Roman literature and art had continued, reintroduced those ideas in the West and a new era of creativity began. The inventiveness and vision of Leonardo da Vinci and his peers laid the necessary groundwork for the Industrial Revolution that would follow three centuries later.

As the Renaissance continued, Martin Luther unwittingly initiated the Protestant Reformation in 1517 when he attacked the papal practice of indulgences. The rise of Protestantism may have contributed to the rise of capitalism in a number of ways. First, it weakened the legitimizing force behind the feudal order—the Roman Catholic Church. Second, the new Protestant theology was more individualistic than Catholic doctrine—confession and interpretation of scripture did not require the intervention of the clergy. The new spirit of individualism may have encouraged the replacement of hierarchical social systems with decentralized markets. Third, according to the German sociologist Max Weber, the Calvinist belief that worldly success was a sign of divine favor inspired a work ethic and an attitude toward thrift that supported economic development more effectively than Catholic doctrine and practice.

The Development of Capitalism

The forces of Renaissance, Reformation, enclosure, urban growth, international trade, mathematics, and monetary exchange converged in the late sixteenth and early seventeenth centuries as capitalism spread from the merchant

---

[8]Karl Marx, *Capital,* vol. 1 (New York: International Publishers, 1967), 713.

[9]Werner Sombart, *The Quintessence of Capitalism* (New York: Howard Fertig, 1967), 132. Interestingly, Marx agreed that capitalistic production developed earliest in Italy. See Marx, *Capital,* 716.

[10]Sombart, *Quintessence,* 126–127.

sphere to the productive sphere of the Western economies. In its early stages, a large part of capitalist production was organized around the so-called **putting-out system,** whereby the capitalists bought raw materials, "put them out" to artisans working in their own homes for a piece-wage, and then sold the final product. The scale of such operations could be quite large, as was the case of a British clothier who employed 3,000 home laborers.[11]

In the late 1700s, Britain was shaken by the Industrial Revolution and the American Revolution. The former was initiated by an amazing succession of technical innovations. After 1760, for example, British iron production expanded rapidly as methods were developed that made it possible to use relatively abundant coke, rather than scarce charcoal, in the smelting process. In 1770, James Hargreaves patented the first machine capable of spinning more than one cotton thread at a time and in 1776 James Watt constructed his first successful steam engine. In all, 976 patents were granted in Great Britain for new inventions between 1760 and 1789, compared to only 230 patents between 1730 and 1759.[12]

The new technologies necessitated and supported a number of other developments. First, their effective use required that laborers move their places of work from their homes to mechanized factories. The capitalist or entrepreneur, who previously provided his workers only with raw materials under the putting-out system, became an owner of factories and machinery. Thus, the share of capital formation in British national income rose from approximately 3 percent during the first half of the eighteenth century, to 5 percent in 1780, and to 10 percent in the mid-nineteenth century.[13] The result? Between 1770 and 1800, British iron production increased five-fold and cotton textile production increased twelve-fold. Overall industrial production, which had risen by only 1.0 percent per year between 1700 and 1783, grew by 3.4 percent per year between 1783 and 1802.[14]

The Industrial Revolution had begun in England. At Manchester cartloads and boatloads of people of both sexes and all ages poured into the city to work in the new factories. Of the 12,000 houses in Birmingham in 1790, two-thirds were built after 1760.[15] The share of the British labor force working in agriculture dropped from 60 percent in 1700 to 40 percent in 1820 and to 16 percent in 1980.[16]

Similar movements toward industrialization, mechanization, and urbanization occurred in France, Germany, and the United States after 1830, and in

[11]E. A. J. Johnson and Herman E. Krooss, *The American Economy: Its Origins, Development, and Transformation* (Englewood Cliffs, N. J.: Prentice-Hall, 1960), 58.

[12]Viljoen, *Economic Systems in World History,* 176n.

[13]Ibid, 178.

[14]Walter G. Hoffmann, *British Industry, 1700-1950* (Oxford: Basil Blackwell, 1955), 331.

[15]Witt Bowden, et al., *An Economic History of Europe Since 1750* (New York: Howard Fertig, 1970), 190.

[16]Angus Maddison, *Phases of Capitalist Development* (Oxford: Oxford University Press, 1982), 35.

Sweden, Japan, and Russia after 1860. As the volume of world trade grew by approximately ten-fold between 1830 and 1900, the resulting diffusion of new technology, creation of new markets, and growth of specialization and competition caused industrial development to spread from one country to another. Just as important, in stark contrast to the slow, unsteady pace of economic development before the 1780s, economic growth in the newly emerging capitalist countries was *self-sustaining*. The surplus capacity that had been used to build pyramids by the Egyptians, coliseums by the Romans, and castles by the feudal lords was used by the new capitalist class to build machines and factories, which could be used to build even more machines and factories. Real GDP per capita roughly tripled in England, France, Germany, and Sweden between 1820 and 1913 and it grew more than four-fold in the United States (Table A.4).

Early Views of Capitalism

Mercantilism

We noted previously that the late feudal era was marked by the consolidation of national governments and by the rise of a merchant class with considerable economic and political power. Beginning in the fifteenth century, legislation was passed throughout Europe and England that served the purposes of the ascending civil servants and merchants. The new governments raised needed revenues, for example, by selling "patents of monopoly," which granted the exclusive right to trade with certain foreign countries to a few favored merchants. As a result, by about 1600, the ordinary Englishman could trade only with France, Spain, and Portugal without the intervention of the East India Company or one of the other monopolistic trading companies.

An equally important source of governmental revenue was the collection of tariffs on imported goods. Once again, import tariffs served the purposes of domestic manufacturing and merchant interests by protecting them from foreign competition. Their interests were served so well that the merchants put forth an influential—if self-serving—argument for further import protection.

The **mercantilist** foreign trade doctrine was based on the proposition, stated most clearly by the French Finance Minister Colbert, that "the quantity of gold in a state alone determines the degree of its greatness and power."[17] A large stock of monetary gold was believed to stimulate trade within the nation and it could be used to hire mercenaries and purchase munitions in wartime. Since gold was earned through the sale of exports and was sacrificed through the purchase of imports, the mercantilists argued that active measures should be taken by the government to encourage the former and limit the latter. In short, the mercantilists maintained that the wealth of a nation was advanced most effectively by active governmental intervention in the economy, promotion of monopolies, and restriction of trade.

---

[17]Quoted in Sombart, *Quintessence,* 84.

Adam Smith and Classical Theory

Just as many modern-day proponents of governmental regulation of the capitalist economy can trace their roots back to the mercantilists, advocates of laissez-faire capitalism continue to draw inspiration from the Scottish philosopher and economist, Adam Smith (b.1723, d.1790). In *The Wealth of Nations* (1776), Smith declared that provision of consumer goods, not accumulation of gold, "is the sole end and purpose of production."[18] What kind of economic system would serve the needs of consumers most efficiently? Certainly not the mercantile system, which placed limits on imports and encouraged the formation of monopolies. Instead, Smith proposed a system of "natural liberty"— a system that would mobilize the self-interested acts of individuals to pursue social goals:

It is not from the benevolence of the butcher, the brewer, or the baker, that we expect our dinner, but from their regard to their own self-interest.[19]

Every individual necessarily labours to render the annual revenue of the society as great as he can. . . . He intends only his own gain, and he is in this, as in many other cases, led by an invisible hand to promote an end which was no part of his intention. . . . By pursuing his own interest he frequently promotes that of the society more effectually than when he really intends to promote it.[20]

In reply to Aristotle, Aquinas, and other philosophers and theologians who feared the free exercise of self-interest, Smith was confident that competitive forces would protect the consumers. If one butcher, brewer, or baker charged exorbitant prices, the consumers would buy their meat, ale, or bread from another. Indeed, Smith believed that a competitive system would establish itself—with little need for antitrust legislation—if the government-sponsored monopolistic practices of the mercantilists were abandoned:

All systems either of preference or of restraint, therefore, being thus completely taken away, the obvious and simple system of natural liberty establishes itself of its own accord. Every man, as long as he does not violate the laws of justice, is left perfectly free to promote his own interest in his own way, and to bring both his industry and capital into competition with those of any other man, or order of men.[21]

Adam Smith contributed far more, of course, than assertions in favor of his system of natural liberty. He also provided a rather sophisticated—for his day—explanation of the laws of supply and demand that lay behind the "invisible hand" of the market. As Smith put it, if the quantity of a product brought to market on any given day is insufficient to meet the effectual demand, the price of that product will rise, and the self-interest of producers will be elicited

---

[18]Adam Smith, *An Inquiry into the Nature and Causes of the Wealth of Nations,* vol. 2 (Oxford: Clarendon Press, 1976), 660.

[19]Ibid., 26–27.

[20]Ibid., 456.

[21]Ibid.

to supply more of the product in the future. In the long run, the effectual demand for the product will be met, and the price will settle at a level sufficient to provide for the ordinary payment of wages, profit, and rent.

According to Smith, the government would have only three duties in his system of natural liberty, although they are duties of great importance—to provide for national defense, to administer justice, and to provide public goods ("certain public works . . . which it can never be for the interest of any individual or small number of individuals to erect and maintain").[22] Efficient management of the production system, he believed, was far beyond the capacity of any system of central planning:

The sovereign is completely discharged from a duty, in the attempting to perform which he must always be exposed to innumerable delusions, and for the proper performance of which no human wisdom or knowledge could ever be sufficient, the duty of superintending the industry of private people, and of directing it towards the employments most suitable to the interest of the society.[23]

Adam Smith's arguments were refined and extended by successive members of the classical school. Jean-Baptiste Say (b.1767, d.1832), Smith's French disciple, continued the campaign against those latter-day mercantilists who argued that a large stock of monetary gold was needed to support the demand for products. With an insufficient supply of money, they contended, the economy would suffer recession or depression. Say's reply was quite simple: the quantity of money in a nation is not terribly important because commodities are ultimately purchased with other commodities. Money is not the source of demand, but only a medium of exchange. As Say put it:

Sales cannot be said to be dull because money is scarce, but because other products are so. . . . A product is no sooner created, than it, from that instant, affords a market for other products to the full extent of its own value. When the producer has put the finishing hand to his product, he is most anxious to sell it immediately, lest its value should diminish in his hands. Nor is he less anxious to dispose of the money he may get for it; for the value of money is also perishable. . . . Thus, the mere circumstance of the creation of one product immediately opens a vent for other products.[24]

Thus, **Say's Law,** as Keynes stated it over a century later, holds that supply creates its own demand. The government need only create a healthy environment for production and trade and the free play of the market will insure that the nation's output is sold. "It is the aim of good government to stimulate production," Say concluded, "and of bad government to encourage consumption."[25] This, in a nutshell, is the idea behind what is now called **supply-side economics.**

[22]Ibid., 687–88.

[23]Ibid.

[24]Jean-Baptiste Say, "Of the Demand or Market for Products," in *Classics of Economics,* ed. Charles W. Needy (Oak Park, Ill.: Moore Publishing, 1980), 58.

[25]Ibid., 61.

Say's Law was a controversial proposition from the very beginning, even among members of the classical school. Thomas Malthus (b.1766, d.1834), for one, was skeptical: "I by no means think that the power to purchase necessarily involves a proportionate will to purchase, and I cannot agree . . . that in reference to a nation, supply can never exceed demand."[26]

Of course, Malthus was pessimistic about far more than the ability of the market system to generate a demand for goods. He was more concerned about the ability of the system to generate a sufficient supply of food. It was Malthus who suggested that mankind was destined to endure wars, famine, and plagues because "the power of population is indefinitely greater than the power in the earth to produce subsistence for man."[27] Foreshadowing the arguments of modern-day conservatives, Malthus argued that governmental programs to help the poor would only exacerbate the population problem. Little wonder that Thomas Carlyle, after he read Malthus, called economics "the dismal science."

Say's Law was accepted uncritically by Malthus's contemporary and close friend, David Ricardo (b.1772, d.1823). According to Ricardo, the prospective problems of capitalist society would not stem from an insufficient demand for products or from an insufficient supply of food, but from an undesirable trend in the distribution of national income between laborers, capitalists, and landlords.

The real wages earned by laborers would tend to remain at the physical subsistence level, Ricardo reasoned, because higher wages would encourage population growth, which would eventually drive wages back down. At the same time, the owners of scarce land would earn progressively larger rents as the population, the demand for food, and food prices all rose. Rising food prices would mean that the capitalist must pay his employees higher *money* wages in order to maintain their *real* wages at the bare subsistence level. Caught between rising money wage costs and land rental costs, the profits retained by capitalists would tend to diminish. As profits continued their decline, Ricardo believed that capitalists would eventually refuse to invest in additional production, and economic growth would come to a halt.

Fortunately, however, Ricardo believed that England could postpone or avoid this chain of events by adopting a policy of free international trade. If mercantilist restrictions on the importation of grain—the Corn Laws—were lifted, Ricardo predicted that food prices, money wages, and land rents would fall and profits would rise.

England should import grain at whatever rate because its "comparative advantage" (another concept contributed by Ricardo) lay in industrial production, not agriculture. Put differently, the opportunity cost of agricultural pro-

---

[26]In a letter to David Ricardo. See David Ricardo, *The Works and Correspondence of David Ricardo,* ed. Piero Sraffa, vol. 6 (London: Cambridge University Press, 1951–1955), 132.

[27]Thomas Robert Malthus, *An Essay on the Principle of Population* (New York: W. W. Norton, 1976), 20.

duction, measured in terms of foregone industrial production, was higher in England than in Europe and America.

Twenty-three years after his death, Ricardo's arguments finally carried the day (with support from the Anti-Corn Law League and food shortages caused by the Irish potato blight of 1845) and the Corn Law was repealed in 1846. England adopted a policy of free trade that persisted until the outbreak of World War I. Between the decades of the 1820s and the 1860s, British imports of wheat multiplied sixteen times over and British exports of coal increased by a multiple of twenty-nine.

John Stuart Mill (b.1806, d.1873), who is usually considered the last of the great classical economists, perceived still another set of problems in capitalist society. Mill accepted Say's Law, and was not terribly worried about the macroeconomic stability of capitalism. He accepted Ricardo's argument that a falling rate of profit would eventually lead to a cessation of economic growth, but he did not consider this to be a problem:

I cannot . . . regard the stationary state of capital and wealth with the unaffected aversion so generally manifested towards it by political economists of the old school. I am inclined to believe it would be, on the whole, a very considerable improvement of our condition. I confess I am not charmed with the ideal of life held out by those who think that the normal state of human beings is that of struggling to get on; that the trampling, crushing, elbowing, and treading on each other's heels, which form the existing type of social life, are the most desirable lot of human kind, or anything but the disagreeable symptoms of one of the phases of industrial progress.[28]

Whereas Smith and Say took it as a foregone conclusion that the benefits of economic growth and industrialization would filter down to the working class, nearly a century after the advent of the Industrial Revolution, Mill concluded that "it is questionable if all of the mechanical inventions yet made have lightened the day's toil of any human being."[29] To Mill, therefore, what was lacking in nineteenth-century capitalism was not an ample supply of gold, food, or profits, but an adequate code of social justice. Charles Dickens, Mill's contemporary, wrote in *Hard Times* and *Oliver Twist* of the overcrowded, disease-ridden cities created by the Industrial Revolution and of the Poor Law that required the children of paupers to labor in mines and factories for 14-hour workdays, often under horrendous conditions.

The situation was so desperate, Mill lamented, that "if this, or Communism, were the alternative, all the difficulties, great or small, of Communism, would be but as dust in the balance."[30] Nevertheless, Mill believed that other alternatives were available. He advocated the reform, rather than the immediate elimination, of capitalism, through governmental taxation of large inheri-

---

[28]John Stuart Mill, *Principles of Political Economy,* in *Masterworks of Economics,* vol. 2, ed. Leonard D. Abbott (New York: McGraw-Hill, 1973), 163–64.

[29]Ibid., 166.

[30]Ibid., 138.

tances, redistribution of income to the poor, and provision of public education, health, and sanitation services. Thus, Mill may be considered an early advocate of welfare capitalism, but an advocate who was concerned with maintenance of work incentives:

> *Relief must be given; no one must be allowed to starve; the necessaries of life and health must be tendered to all who apply for them; but to all who are capable of work they must be tendered on such terms, as shall make the necessity of accepting them be regarded as a misfortune. . . . To this end, relief must be given only in exchange for labour, and labour at least as irksome and severe as that of the least fortunate among independent labourers.*[31]

Karl Marx: The Socialist Critique

Adam Smith and his followers were not blind to the economic problems of their day. Smith was concerned about the spread of monopolistic privileges, Ricardo was worried about the prospects for continued economic growth, Malthus was fearful of population growth, and Mill was disturbed by the living conditions of the lower classes. Nevertheless, none of the classical economists suggested that conditions would deteriorate so severely that the entire capitalist system would be overthrown. Indeed, most of them believed that more extensive application of laissez-faire and free-trade principles would alleviate the remaining problems. Even Mill called only for the legislative reform of capitalism, not for its overthrow.

A very different picture of the history, nature, and future of capitalist society was painted by Karl Marx (b.1818, d.1883) and his collaborator, Friedrich Engels (b.1820, d.1895). In keeping with their materialist conception of history, Marx and Engels argued that each society spontaneously adopts an economic system that is appropriate for its current stage of economic development. As Engels put it:

> *The materialist conception of history starts from the proposition that the production of the means to support human life and, next to production, the exchange of things produced, is the basis of all social structure; that in every society that has appeared in history, the manner in which wealth is distributed and society divided into classes or orders is dependent upon what is produced, how it is produced, and how the products are exchanged.*[32]

Accordingly, primitive societies naturally adopt a simple tribal or communal form of organization. At a higher level of economic development, slavery and feudal institutions are developed as a means of extracting surplus production for the use of the upper class. As society grows still more techni-

---

[31]John Stuart Mill, "The Proposed Reform of the Poor Laws," cited in Robert Ekelund and Robert Hebert, *A History of Economic Theory and Method* (New York: McGraw-Hill, 1983), 182.

[32]Friedrich Engels, *Socialism: Utopian and Scientific* in *The Marx-Engels Reader,* ed. Robert Tucker (New York: W. W. Norton, 1978), 700–701.

cally advanced, the need for greater labor mobility requires that laborers be free to move between employers and capitalism emerges. Nevertheless, Marx maintained that the freedom of the working class in capitalist society is only illusory: "The worker, whose sole source of livelihood is the sale of his labor power . . . belongs not to this or that capitalist, but to the capitalist class."[33] In other words, the laborer is enslaved to the capitalist class by the fact that he cannot work for himself. He cannot work for himself because all of the means of production are owned by the capitalists. Thus, the laborer is exploited in capitalist society in very nearly the same sense that he is exploited in feudal or slave societies, but his position is obscured by the apparent freedom of the labor market.

Interestingly, although Marx believed that capitalist society is evil, he believed it to be a necessary evil—necessary for the eventual attainment of socialism:

Fanatically bent on making value expand itself, [the capitalist] ruthlessly forces the human race to produce for production's sake; he thus forces the development of the productive powers of society, and creates those material conditions, which alone can form the real basis of a higher form of society, a society in which the full and free development of every individual forms the ruling principle.[34]

In other words, Marx and Engels believed that the socialist system was appropriate only for countries that had achieved high levels of economic development and that market capitalism, with its high rate of investment and its heavy-handed treatment of the labor force, was the *only* system capable of driving society to the level of economic development necessary for the transition to socialism.

A large part of Marx's writing was devoted to the forces that would, in his view, *inevitably* lead to the downfall of capitalism. The root problem is the capitalist himself and his continual accumulation of wealth. The capitalist lives to accumulate, according to Marx, for he derives his enjoyment from amassing wealth rather than from consumption: "He shares with the miser the passion for wealth as wealth."[35] Furthermore, the capitalist must accumulate in order to live—he must invest in machinery and equipment that reduces his costs of production in order to remain competitive.

Driven by desire and necessity, the capitalists' exploitation of labor and accumulation of wealth eventually would cause several other economic and social problems, according to Marx. First, they would combine to cause a chronic underconsumption of goods—a state of excess aggregate supply. The rapid growth of the capital stock and harsh treatment of the labor force would create a fertile environment for the production of goods, but not for their sale. The ability of the working class to purchase the flood of new goods is limited by low income levels, while the capitalist class has a strong preference for

---

[33]Karl Marx, *Wage Labour and Capital,* in *The Marx-Engels Reader,* 205.
[34]Karl Marx, *Capital,* vol. 1 (New York: International Publishers, 1967), 592.
[35]Ibid.

saving over consumption. In a word, Marx did not accept Say's law. Insufficient demand for final products would inevitably lead to a series of business depressions.

Second, Marx believed that the process of capital accumulation would cause the general rate of profit to trend downward. In the long run, he argued, the source of all profits is exploitation of live labor. Investment in machinery and equipment may provide the capitalist with a short-term windfall profit if it reduces his costs of production below those of his competitors, but in the long run his rivals will also invest in the new technology and the price of the final product will fall to a level consistent with the lower industry-wide costs of production. In the end, all of the capitalists will invest in the new technology, but none will gain a lasting profit from it. As the capitalists are forced by competition to devote more of their investment to machinery and equipment which does not provide an enduring profit, the rate of profit will fall.

The falling rate of profit, Marx predicted, would encourage the capitalists to further exploit their laborers by lengthening the working day and reducing wage rates. Furthermore, the profit squeeze would drive the smaller and weaker capitalists out of business as their companies are "gobbled up" by the larger capitalists and the small capitalists themselves would be cast into the growing "reserve army of the unemployed." In the end, the capitalist system would self-destruct:

Along with the constantly diminishing number of the magnates of capital . . . grows the mass of misery, oppression, slavery, degradation, exploitation; but with this too grows the revolt of the working class . . . The knell of capitalist private property sounds. The expropriators are expropriated.[36]

In retrospect, many of the predictions made by Marx and Engels were no more, and no less, accurate than the predictions made by Adam Smith, David Ricardo, Thomas Malthus, and John Stuart Mill. For example, the notion that the rate of profit would tend to drift downward in capitalist countries was not originated by Marx, but by Adam Smith. Smith believed that profits would fall as markets grew more competitive, and as economic growth increased the demand for labor and increased real wages. He believed, in other words, that a falling rate of profit would be a sign of economic health. Ricardo believed that profits would decline as money wages were driven up by rising food prices. He predicted that the falling rate of profit would eventually cause investment to cease and would lead to a dismal, no-growth, "stationary state." On the other hand, Marx viewed the falling rate of profit as one of the factors that would cause the breakdown of capitalist society. The actual historical trend in the rate of profit is still a subject of considerable controversy.

Critics of Marx can point to several failed predictions. The long-term trend in the living conditions of the working class in industrial countries has been toward improvement, rather than toward greater "misery, oppression,

[36]Ibid., 763.

slavery, and degradation."[37] The first socialist revolution did not occur in one of the most developed capitalist countries, as Marx's analysis suggested, but in relatively backward Russia.

On the other hand, Marx was one of the first economists to formally challenge Say's Law and to present an analysis of business cycles. Furthermore, in a day when small businesses were still the norm, Marx foresaw the emergence of the giant business enterprises. Finally, with respect to his prediction of the eventual breakdown of capitalism, orthodox Marxists would suggest that the final chapter is yet to be written.

The Great Depression and J. M. Keynes

If there was ever a time when the Marxian "death knell of capitalism" seemed to toll loudly, it was in 1933. Between 1929 and 1933, some 85,000 American businesses were forced to close their doors, causing a 30 percent drop in national income and an increase in the unemployment rate from about 3 percent to nearly 25 percent. Literally millions of Americans who had never known poverty were faced with the threat of starvation. The nightmare of the Depression quickly spread to all of the other major industrial capitalist countries and many Americans and Europeans turned to the Communist Party for leadership and inspiration.

Among those who were not convinced by the Marxian interpretation of the Depression, we find the eminent British economist, John Maynard Keynes (b.1883, d.1946). In 1931, Keynes made his opinion of Marxian economics quite clear:

How can I accept a doctrine which sets up as its bible, above and beyond criticism, an obsolete economic textbook which I know to be not only scientifically erroneous but without interest or application for the modern world? How can I adopt a creed which, preferring the mud to the fish, exalts the boorish proletariat above the bourgeois and intelligentsia who, with all their faults, are the quality of life and surely carry the seeds of human advancement.[38]

Whereas many Marxists believed that the capitalist system was doomed to extinction, Keynes suggested that the system could and should be preserved by appropriate governmental action. In late 1933, Keynes prescribed a program of expansionary fiscal and monetary policies to the new American president, Franklin D. Roosevelt, in an open letter published in the *New York Times*. The influence that this letter, and a meeting between Keynes and Roosevelt in the summer of 1934, may have had on the formulation of the New Deal policies of the 1930s is uncertain. The Roosevelt program, though revolution-

---

[37]For a recent opposing view, see Xenophon Zolotas, *Economic Growth and Declining Social Welfare* (New York: New York University Press, 1981).

[38]J. M. Keynes, *Essays in Persuasion* (New York: Harcourt, Brace, and Company, 1932), 300.

ary in its own right, apparently was not designed to draw the nation out of the Depression through fiscal and monetary stimulus, but only to provide a minimum level of relief for those in the greatest need.[39] It would require the fiscal stimulus of World War II to prove Keynes's point once and for all.

Nevertheless, although his proposals may not have been fully implemented during the Depression, Keynes was certainly correct (if immodest) when, in 1935, he wrote to his socialist friend, George Bernard Shaw, that he was writing a book which would eventually "revolutionize . . . the way the world thinks about economic problems." His *General Theory of Employment, Interest, and Money,* first published in 1936, has done exactly that. In effect, Keynes rejected elements of both the classical and Marxian views of capitalism and formed his own middle ground.

Keynes broke with his classical heritage most fundamentally on the subject of Say's Law. As we noted earlier, the classical economists (with the notable exception of Malthus) believed that a market economy would spontaneously generate enough demand to purchase all of the goods produced by a fully-employed work force. Production creates income, they reasoned, and income creates demand. If some individuals choose to save their income rather than spend it, their savings will ordinarily be transferred to borrowers who will, in turn, purchase investment goods. On this last point, Keynes was not convinced:

Those who think in this way are deceived . . . by an optical illusion, which makes two essentially different activities appear to be the same. They are fallaciously supposing that there is a nexus which unites decisions to abstain from current consumption with decisions to provide for future consumption, whereas the motives which determine the latter are not linked in any simple way with the motives which determine the former.[40]

If the market could not be trusted to automatically generate investment demand sufficient to absorb the savings of a fully employed labor force, the government must take action to fill the void: "I conceive, therefore, that a somewhat comprehensive socialization of investment will prove the only means of securing an approximation to full employment; though this need not exclude all manner of compromises and of devices by which public authority will cooperate with private initiative."[41]

Although Keynes agreed with Marx on the invalidity of Say's Law, he disagreed on a number of equally important issues. As we have seen, Marx believed that regardless of any governmental action, the internal contradictions of capitalism would inevitably lead to: (1) a violent overthrow of the system, (2) establishment of social ownership of the means of production, and (3) social control of the allocation of resources and the distribution of income.

---

[39]For a full discussion of this point, see Herbert Stein, *The Fiscal Revolution in America* (Chicago: University of Chicago Press, 1969), Chapter 4.

[40]John Maynard Keynes, *The General Theory of Employment, Interest, and Money* (New York: Harcourt, Brace, and World, 1964), 21.

[41]Ibid., 378.

In contrast, Keynes believed: (1) that "it is not the ownership of the instruments of production which it is important for the State to assume," but control of the aggregate level of demand for goods; (2) that the measures necessary to achieve that control "can be introduced gradually and without a break in the general traditions of society"; and (3) that the allocation and distribution of goods and resources should be left to private, rather than social, initiative:

If our central controls succeed in establishing . . . full employment as nearly as is practicable, the classical theory comes into its own again from this point onwards. If we assume the volume of output to be given, . . . then there is no objection to be raised against the classical analysis of the manner in which private self-interest will determine what in particular is produced, in what proportions the factors of production will be combined to produce it, and how the final product will be distributed between them.[42]

Put briefly, Keynes hoped that his analysis and proposals would make it possible to "cure the disease [of unemployment] whilst preserving efficiency and freedom."[43] The first explicit exercise of Keynesian policy on American soil would not be undertaken, however, until the Kennedy administration took office in 1961. Faced by a rising rate of unemployment in that year, Walter Heller, the president's unabashedly Keynesian economic advisor, called for a major program of tax cuts, despite the fact that the federal budget was already in deficit.

The tax cut was finally enacted in 1964, during the first year of the Johnson administration. Soon thereafter, Johnson laid on two additional programs of fiscal stimulus. First, under the Great Society program, federal expenditures on social welfare were more than doubled between 1965 and 1970. Second, as U.S. participation in the Vietnam War escalated, defense spending increased by about 56 percent between 1965 and 1968. The result? The federal budget deficit, which stood at $1.6 billion in 1965, ballooned to over $25 billion in 1968. The unemployment rate, which stood at 6.5 percent when the Kennedy administration took office in 1961, steadily fell to 3.4 percent in 1969.

The Keynesian policies had worked, but at a heavy cost (in addition to the human cost of the Vietnam War). Fueled by the rising fiscal deficits, which were financed by the creation of new money, the annual rate of inflation (measured by the GNP deflator) escalated from 0.9 percent in 1961 to 5.4 percent in 1970. Efforts by the Nixon and Ford administrations to control the inflation and unemployment rates simultaneously through a combination of monetary and fiscal policies and price controls seemed only to make the situation worse. In 1975 the unthinkable happened—the inflation rate, at 9.3 percent, and the unemployment rate, at 8.5 percent, both hit new postwar record levels *in the same year.* Keynesian demand management policies came under attack from several quarters.

[42]Ibid., 378–79.
[43]Ibid., 381.

New Twists on Old Ideas

Monetarism

The first well-organized attack against activist Keynesianism came from the monetarist school, led by Professor Milton Friedman. Reaffirming Say's Law, the monetarists believe that the market system will spontaneously achieve full employment (or, as Friedman puts it, the unemployment rate will fall to its "natural" level) if two basic requirements are met. First, the government must allow the market system to operate as freely as is possible. Governmental regulation of production and price controls cripple the market system, Friedman believes, in its effort to achieve a full-employment equilibrium. Thus, monetarists are generally opposed to minimum wage laws, agricultural price supports, regulation of exchange rates, and direct wage and price controls.

Second, the monetary authorities must maintain a slow but steady growth of the nation's money supply. The Great Depression, Friedman believes, did not prove the inability of capitalist economies to regulate themselves. Instead, the Depression proved the importance of a stable monetary policy. Between 1929 and 1933, as unemployment ravaged the country, the nominal supply of money (M1) fell by 25 percent. In 1937, when the United States began to climb out of the Depression, the Federal Reserve doubled the reserve requirements on bank deposits and the economy fell into a new downturn. Friedman claims that the Federal Reserve "continues to promote the myth that the private economy is unstable, while its behavior continues to document the reality that government is today the major source of economic instability."[44]

In the late 1970s and early 1980s, a number of countries—including the United States, France, the United Kingdom, and Chile—experimented with monetarist policies to cure inflationary problems. Speaking very generally, monetarist policies have been effective against inflation (witness the drop in U.S. consumer price inflation from 13.5 percent in 1980 to 1.9 percent in 1986), but at the expense of very high rates of unemployment (in the United States, 9.5 percent in 1983, compared to 7.0 percent in 1981). Monetarists insist that a *temporary* escalation of unemployment is the price that must be paid for adjustment to a lower rate of inflation. According to many observers, however, including the editors of *Business Week,* "the monetarist experiment failed because it beat inflation to the ground only at the expense of record-high interest rates and the worst recession in postwar history."[45]

Supply-Side Economics

Disillusionment with monetarism set the stage for new strands of economic thought at the conservative end of the political spectrum. Perhaps the most influential of these is the supply-side movement, which declares that Keyne-

---

[44]Milton Friedman and Rose Friedman, *Free to Choose* (New York: Harcourt Brace Jovanovich, 1980), 90.

[45]*Business Week,* April 4, 1983, 64.

sians and monetarists have overemphasized the importance of the demand for goods and have paid too little attention to the factors that influence productivity. Productivity is considered the appropriate focus of governmental concern because supply-siders firmly believe that supply creates its own demand. As Gilder observes: "Say's Law in all its variations is the essential enactment of supply-side theory."[46]

Actually, the supply-siders can be divided into two camps. The traditional wing is headed, in the United States, by Martin Feldstein, a Harvard professor, president of the National Bureau of Economic Research, and former chairman of the President's Council of Economic Advisors. He and his colleagues have long favored reductions in marginal tax rates, deregulation of industry, and a flexible antiinflationary monetary policy. In their view, these policies would contribute to economic growth, in the *long run,* principally by encouraging growth in the stock of productive capital.

The "new" supply-siders, led by Arthur Laffer and Paul Craig Roberts, make more extravagant claims. Reductions in marginal tax *rates,* they say, will stimulate work incentives to such an extent that national income will increase significantly in the *short run* and *total* tax revenues will increase. According to Feldstein, the claims of these supply-side "extremists" have been disproved by the record of economic growth and budget deficits that followed the Tax Reform Act of 1981, which provided a 25 percent across-the-board reduction in personal tax rates.[47]

Post-Keynesian Economics

On the liberal reformist wing of the political spectrum, we find the so-called post-Keynesians (PKs)—a diverse group of dissident economists who joined forces in the mid-1970s to oppose monetarism and to adapt Keynesian theory to the conditions of the latter years of the twentieth century. Among the PKs, we find American institutionalists (such as John Kenneth Galbraith), Keynes's colleagues and students at Cambridge (for example, Joan Robinson and Lord Kaldor), and a broad array of other critics of neoclassical economics.

According to Alfred Eichner, five essential elements distinguish PK theory from the neoclassical orthodoxy. First, PK theory is usually concerned with economic growth, where neoclassical theory (including the textbook version of Keynesian theory) emphasizes static equilibrium. Second, the key determinant of growth is taken to be the rate of investment and the rate of growth is directly related to the distribution of income. Third, the money supply is believed to play an important role in long-term economic growth, where the neoclassical model would say that it only determines the general price level. Fourth, the competitive assumptions of neoclassical theory are replaced with an explicit treatment of the influence of multinational corpora-

[46]George Gilder, *Wealth and Poverty* (New York: Bantam Books, 1981), 56.

[47]Martin Feldstein, "Supply Side Economics: Old Truths and New Claims," *American Economic Review* 76 (May 1986): 26–30.

WHO SAID IT FIRST?

"If a bank lends you $1,000, the bank controls you. If a bank lends you $1 million, you control the bank." A few years ago, when the international banking crisis became the lead story in the daily news, a *Wall Street Journal* reporter attempted to find the origin of this saying and learned an important lesson about the history of ideas.

After several false starts, the reporter was directed to Donald Moggridge, a professor at the University of Toronto, who is a joint managing editor of the collected works of J. M. Keynes. In volume 24 (of 30 volumes), Moggridge located the following passage from a paper that Keynes sent to the British Cabinet in 1945: "The old saying holds: Owe your banker 1,000 pounds and you are at his mercy. Owe him one million pounds and the position is reversed."

Now, all that remains is to find out whom Keynes was quoting.

Source: Lawrence Rout, "Keynes (or Maybe Publius) Speaks on the International Banking Crisis," *Wall Street Journal,* February 24, 1983, 29.

tions and labor unions. And fifth, PK analysis aspires to include treatment of nonmarket forms of resource allocation—including the operation of the government.[48]

A more concise definition is offered by Joan Robinson: "To me, the expression *post-Keynesian* has a definite meaning; it applies to an economic theory or method of analysis which takes account of the difference between the future and the past."[49] Like their namesake, the post-Keynesians recognize that the future is uncertain and they believe that speculative behavior lends instability to the capitalist system. Unlike Keynes, who believed that the government should primarily involve itself in macroeconomic stabilization, many of the PKs support an active public role in the distribution and allocation of income and resources.

Radical Economics

Finally, somewhere to the left of the average PK, we find a group of neo-Marxists and other radicals who believe that the capitalist system is beyond reform—it must be replaced. The radicals have their own professional jour-

[48]Alfred Eichner, "Post-Keynesian Theory: An Introduction," *Challenge* 21 (May–June 1978): 4–17.

[49]Joan Robinson, "Keynes and Ricardo," *Journal of Post Keynesian Economics* 1 (Fall 1978): 12.

nal—*The Review of Radical Political Economics*—and their own cast of prominent authors, including Paul Sweezy, Samuel Bowles, Richard Edwards, Herbert Gintis, Michael Reich, and Thomas Weisskopf.

With some updating and revisions, the radicals generally accept the Marxian analysis of exploitation and class struggle in capitalist society. Indeed, most of them believe that imperialist practices and unequal exchange between nations have carried capitalist exploitation to the international realm. On the other hand, few of the radicals believe that capitalism will inevitably be replaced by socialism. The transition, they believe, will require positive democratic or revolutionary action.

In response to Friedman and others who say that freedom and democracy are inexorably linked with the capitalist system, the radicals suggest that capitalism and democracy may have "reached a parting of the ways."[50] The risk, they say, is that business interests may find the democratic system of government hostile to their purposes in an economic crisis (for an extreme example, consider the formation of the Nazi regime in wartime Germany). Thus, the Radicals believe that democratic socialism—which they are careful to distinguish from Soviet socialism—may be the only sustainable form of democracy.

Summary

Several historical preconditions had to be fulfilled before the capitalist economic system could develop. Growth of market exchange required the development of monetary institutions and a relatively safe area of travel. In the political and legal sphere, capitalism requires the development of a system of property rights and a reasonable measure of political freedom for a large segment of society. In the areas of religion and philosophy, capitalism requires the relaxation of taboos against individualism and accumulation of wealth. Finally, it requires the formation of a class of people (capitalists) who direct savings into productive investment rather than into the erection of monuments.

The mercantilists were among the first to call for an active governmental role in the market economy, particularly in the regulation of foreign trade. Adam Smith argued that the mercantilist controls were counterproductive and he proposed a system of "natural liberty" regulated by the competitive market mechanism. Smith's followers in the classical school supported his recommendations, but they foresaw problems in the operation of capitalism. Malthus feared overproduction of goods and population crises. Ricardo predicted a trend toward a no-growth, "stationary state." Mill decried the social injustice of capitalism.

---

[50]See Samuel Bowles and Richard Edwards, *Understanding Capitalism* (New York: Harper & Row, 1985), 388–391.

According to Karl Marx, capitalism is an exploitive system and its eventual replacement by socialism is an inevitable law of history. During the Great Depression, when it seemed that the Marxian prediction was becoming reality, J. M. Keynes argued that the capitalist system could be saved through macroeconomic stabilization. The popularity of Keynesian ideas peaked in the 1960s and then declined during the stagflation of the 1970s.

At the current time, the capitalist system is interpreted in many different ways by different groups of economists. Monetarists and supply-siders draw their inspiration from Adam Smith and his classical school. They generally believe in the stability of the capitalist system and advocate a limited role for the government. Post-Keynesians question the competitiveness, equity, and stability of modern capitalism and many of them favor broad programs of macroeconomic stabilization and social reform. Radical economists expand on Marx in their analysis of domestic and international capitalist exploitation and argue that growing frictions between democracy and capitalism require the adoption of democratic socialism.

Discussion and Review Questions

1. What basic preconditions had to be fulfilled for the development of capitalism? What role was played by the enclosure movement? The Renaissance? The Protestant Reformation?

2. What was the mercantilist argument in favor of governmental control in a market economy? How did Adam Smith respond?

3. What was Say's Law? Which economists rejected it? On what grounds?

4. What, according to Ricardo, would cause economic growth to cease in a capitalist country? What was Mill's attitude toward the "stationary state?"

5. According to Marx, what are the causes of the "inevitable" downfall of capitalism?

6. How does Keynesianism differ from Marxism? How does supply-side economics differ from monetarism?

Suggested Readings

Bowles, Samuel and Richard Edwards. *Understanding Capitalism: Competition, Command, and Change in the American Economy.* New York: Harper & Row, 1985. *This introductory textbook presents a cogent analysis of American capitalism from a radical perspective.*

Heilbroner, Robert L. *The Making of Economic Society.* 6th ed. Englewood Cliffs, N.J.: Prentice-Hall, 1980. *By the author of* The Worldly Philosophers, *this is probably the most accessible introduction to the history of capitalism.*

Maddison, Angus. *Phases of Capitalist Development.* Oxford: Oxford University Press, 1982. *Provides a statistical analysis of productivity growth during the development of capitalism.*

Smith, Adam. *An Inquiry into the Nature and Causes of the Wealth of Nations.* Oxford: Clarendon Press, 1976. *If you intend to study the history and theories of capitalism from original texts, this is a good place to begin.*

Spiegel, Henry William. *The Growth of Economic Thought.* Durham, N.C.: Duke University Press, 1983. *A comprehensive survey of the history of economic thought.*

Sweezy, Paul. *The Theory of Capitalist Development.* New York: Monthly Review Press, 1968. *A classic, and readable, introduction to Marxism.*

Viljoen, Stephan. *Economic Systems in World History.* London: Longman, 1974. *Provides a particularly strong discussion of pre-capitalist economic systems.*

United States: Share of Services in Employment
- ☐ 51%–57%
- ▨ 58%–62%
- ☐ 63%–77%

Source: U.S. Bureau of Labor Statistics

4

THE UNITED STATES: THE SERVICE ECONOMY

In the United States a man builds a house in which to spend his old age, and he sells it before the roof is on; . . . he brings a field into tillage and leaves other men to gather the crops; he embraces a profession and gives it up; he settles in a place, which he soon afterward leaves to carry his changeable longings elsewhere.
—Alexis de Tocqueville
  Democracy in America,
  1840

Here individuals of all nations are melted into a new race of men, whose labors will one day cause great changes in the world.
—J. H. St. John de
  Crévecoeur
  *Letters from an
  American Farmer,* 1782

Most of the readers of this book—including those who are not Americans—will already know something about the economic system of the United States. However, a quick review of the U.S. economy is warranted for at least two reasons. First, the comparative perspective of this book should allow us to gain new insights into the nature of the American system. We will ask, what is it about the U.S. economy that is truly unique?

Second, the United States produces more goods and services—valued at over four *trillion* dollars in 1986—than any other country in the world. Despite the spectacular growth that has been experienced in a number of other countries since World War II, the American GNP is still larger than the *combined* products of the United Kingdom and the other members of the European community. It is nearly twice as large as the Soviet GNP and nearly three times as large as the Japanese GNP. Clearly, our analysis of world economic systems would be incomplete without an analysis of this superpower.

The Environment

Natural Resources

A significant part of American economic growth and prosperity can be attributed to the richness of its natural resources. The United States claims only 5 percent of the world's population, but approximately 7 percent of its land area, over 15 percent of its copper and cadmium reserves, and over 20 percent of its reserves of coal, lead, silver, and zinc.[1] American croplands are among the most fertile in the world and benefit from an exceptionally mild climate. Nonetheless, the prosperity of America is only partially explained by its rich endowment of natural resources. The Soviet Union, for example, has a land area more than twice as large as the United States and has much larger reserves of fossil fuels, gold, diamonds, manganese, and platinum-group metals. Some of the world's poorest countries, including many in Africa, are more favorably endowed than America (on a per capita basis) with land and minerals.[2]

Cultural Heritage and Human Resources

Above all else, it must be recognized that the American labor force is descended from a multinational assortment of religious and political dissidents, opportunists, and slaves. Each group, for its own reasons, developed a disdain for higher authorities. Thus, America is a "melting pot" nation and the home of "rugged individualism." These two aspects of American society have left a lasting imprint on the economy.

---

[1]U.S. Bureau of Mines estimates found in D. Hargreaves and S. Fromson, *World Index of Strategic Minerals* (New York: Facts on File, 1983), 31ff.

[2]For a ranking of nations in terms of their potential organic and mineral production, see S. R. Eyre, *The Real Wealth of Nations* (New York: St. Martin's Press, 1978), 116–129.

The philosophy of individualism, for example, is the basis of the so-called American Dream—the idea that anyone can "pull himself up by his bootstraps" to a higher standard of living through frugality and hard work. The dream was personified by men such as Andrew Carnegie, the son of poor Scottish immigrants. Carnegie started work at the age of thirteen as a bobbin boy in a Pennsylvania cloth mill and eventually built a steel empire that he sold in 1900 for over $400 million. He argued that individual freedom and competition are "best for the race" because they insure "the survival of the fittest in every department."[3]

Americans generally believe that individual wealth is the reward for hard work and frugality, where Europeans are more likely to attribute large accumulations of wealth to inheritance. As a result, Americans are relatively uncomfortable with governmental schemes to redistribute income. A number of public-opinion surveys have found little support for major redistribution schemes, even among the poorest Americans.[4] Governmental outlays on social security and welfare constitute a much smaller fraction of national income in the United States than in most European countries (Table A.17).

The philosophy of individualism also entails the belief that the individual citizen can have a significant impact on society. In a classic five-nation survey, 75 percent of the American respondents believed they could do something about an unjust national regulation, compared to 62 percent of the British, 38 percent of the Germans and Mexicans, and only 28 percent of the Italians.[5] The idea that the individual makes a difference may help to explain the American preoccupation with higher education. In 1983, 56 percent of Americans age 20–24 attended colleges and universities, compared to about 30 percent of the Japanese, French, East Germans, and West Germans, and about 20 percent of the British and Soviets.[6]

The "melting pot" also has its economic ramifications. On the positive side of the ledger, the United States benefits from the diversity of skills and talents that its ethnic groups have mastered.[7] On the other hand, some economic problems are obviously caused by racial discrimination and by the fact that millions of Americans have serious difficulty with spoken English.

Furthermore, the "melting pot" may provide another explanation for the relatively low level of U.S. welfare spending. In France, Italy, West Germany, and Sweden, each population is relatively homogeneous in terms of race and

[3]The *North American Review* of 1889, quoted in Daniel Fusfeld's *The Age of the Economist* (Glenview, Ill.: Scott, Foresman and Co., 1972), 82.

[4]For a review of these surveys, see Jennifer L. Hochschild, *What's Fair? American Beliefs about Distributive Justice* (Cambridge: Harvard University Press, 1981), 15–19.

[5]Gabriel A. Almond and Sidney Verba, *The Civic Culture: Political Attitudes and Democracy in Five Nations* (Princeton, N.J.: Princeton University Press, 1963), 185.

[6]The World Bank, *World Development Report 1986* (New York: Oxford University Press, 1986), 237.

[7]For a provocative assessment of the role of ethnicity in U.S. economic development, see Thomas Sowell, *The Economics and Politics of Race* (New York: William Morrow, 1983), Chapter 6.

religion. As a result, there is little perception in these countries that welfare payments represent a transfer of income from one identifiable segment of society to another. In the United States, despite the fact that two-thirds of the people living below the poverty line are white, the perception persists that welfare payments only serve to redistribute income from whites to other races. Not too surprisingly, this perception provokes an unusual amount of political opposition.

The Changing Structure of the Economy

Compared with the nations of Western Europe, America is a relative latecomer to industrialization. In 1840, when only 23 percent of the British labor force was working in agriculture, about 69 percent of American laborers continued to farm. As late as 1900, more Americans were employed in agriculture than in the industrial or service sectors (Table 4.1). Even today, although agriculture accounts for only 4 percent of U.S. employment, it accounts for 19 percent of commodity exports.

According to Adam Smith, writing in the 1770s, America's commitment to agriculture was extremely beneficial:

It has been the principal cause of the rapid progress of our American colonies towards wealth and greatness, that almost their whole capitals have hitherto been employed in agriculture. They have no manufactures, those household and coarser manufactures excepted which necessarily accompany the progress of agriculture, and which are the work of women and children in every private family.[8]

In this, Smith undoubtedly was influenced by his French acquaintances, the Physiocrats. The Physiocrats argued that agricultural workers are always more productive than industrial workers because they cooperate more directly with nature. According to Smith, "As a marriage which affords three children is certainly more productive than one which affords only two; so the labor of farmers and country laborers is certainly more productive than that of merchants, artificers, and manufacturers."[9] In addition, Smith undoubtedly realized that American soil and climate were perfect for agriculture.

The French Revolution and the Napoleonic Wars (1785–1815) further enhanced the benefits of American agriculture. As a neutral power, America was able to export agricultural goods to all sides and foreign demand was so great that U.S. export prices more than doubled between 1794 and 1799.[10] The resulting agricultural boom frustrated Alexander Hamilton's desire to launch America into an early industrialization.

[8]Adam Smith, *An Inquiry into the Nature and Causes of the Wealth of Nations* (New York: P. F. Collier, 1909 [1776]), 308.

[9]Ibid., 460.

[10]D. C. North, *The Economic Growth of the United States* (Englewood Cliffs, N.J.: Prentice-Hall, 1961), 25–26.

Table 4.1   Distribution of American Employment, 1870–1986

	Agriculture	Industry	Services
1870	47%	27%	26%
1900	35	34	31
1920	24	41	35
1940	19	35	46
1960	8	41	51
1980	3	33	64
1986	3	29	68

Sources: 1870–1940—Victor Fuchs, *The Service Economy* (New York: National Bureau of Economic Research, 1968), 24, 30; 1960–1986—*Economic Report of the President 1987* (Washington, D.C.: USGPO, 1987), Tables B-31 and B-40.

Industrial Growth

Led by the creation of national transportation and communication networks, America finally embarked on a stage of industrial growth during the first half of the nineteenth century. The successful completion of the Erie Canal in 1825, linking New York City with the agricultural regions in western New York, reduced transportation costs in that region by 90 percent. A boom in canal-building resulted and by 1859 some 1.6 billion ton-miles of cargo were being transported on canals. In 1828, the first steam railway in America, the Baltimore and Ohio, commenced operations. By 1840, America had a rail network of over 3,000 miles of track; by 1860 it exceeded 30,000 miles. Samuel Morse invented a practical telegraph in 1837 and the telegraph lines of Western Union reached the Pacific by 1861.

These rapid advances in transportation and communication formed a national market. Coal could now be moved from the rich fields in Pennsylvania to the industrial centers of the East. Large factories could be built with the assurance that their output could be sold throughout the country and overseas. Industrialization had begun and it was sustained by two distinctively American production technologies—the system of interchangeable parts (introduced by Eli Whitney in 1801) and the moving assembly line (introduced at Ford Motors in 1913). By the 1880s, many of the classic American industrial giants were well established—Standard Oil, Westinghouse, Edison General Electric, Western Electric, Singer, John Deere, and National Cash Register, to name a few. By the mid-1880s, America had bypassed Great Britain to become the world's leading producer of industrial goods. It still holds that position today.[11]

[11]W. W. Rostow, *The World Economy: History and Prospect* (Austin: University of Texas Press, 1978), 52–53.

The Rise of the Service Sector

Although the United States is still the largest industrial power in the world, the dominance of the industrial sector *within* the American economy was relatively short-lived. Industry employed more laborers than agriculture and the service sector for less than 30 years—from the early 1900s to the mid-1920s (Table 4.1). In contrast, the plurality of British workers was involved in industrial production for over 100 years—from the 1840s until the late 1960s.[12]

By 1960, over half of the U.S. labor force was employed in the service sector, and that proportion has continued to rise. In other words, the majority of American workers are what Adam Smith called "unproductive laborers"—people who do not produce a physical, tangible commodity.[13] Although the labor force has shifted from industry to services in all of the advanced countries, the shift has been more rapid and complete in the United States than in any other country.

The first phase of service growth, between the end of the Civil War and the beginning of the Great Depression, was based on expansion of wholesale and retail trade. Growth in the trade network was a natural concomitant of the industrial growth that occurred during that era and was made possible by the improvements in transportation and communication noted earlier. Thus, the second half of the 1800s ushered in the large chain stores—A&P, Kroger, J. C. Penney, Woolworth, and Walgreen—and the giant mail-order houses—Montgomery Ward and Sears Roebuck.

The second stage of growth in service employment was launched by the expansion of public services during the Great Depression. Government employment, which absorbed only 9 percent of the nation's labor force in 1929, encompassed 17 percent of the labor force in 1939. Since that time, the governmental share of employment has remained relatively stable.[14]

Since the end of the 1930s, growth in service employment has been concentrated in the nonprofit sectors (education and health) and in business services (accounting, finance, insurance, real estate, and computer programming). The increased commitment to education and health undoubtedly reflects the rising affluence of the American people. Many of the business-service enterprises (for example, accounting firms) were established to provide a highly specialized service at the lowest possible cost. Furthermore, as women began to enter the labor force in increasing numbers after World War II, many of them chose the service industries. In 1984, when women accounted for

---

[12]Simon Kuznets, *Modern Economic Growth* (New Haven: Yale University Press, 1966), 106; and Organization for Economic Cooperation and Development, *National Accounts: 1964– 1981,* vol. 2 (Paris, 1983), 275. Here, as elsewhere, I have adopted the method of aggregating detailed sectors into agriculture, industry, and services as described in Victor Fuchs, *The Service Economy* (New York: National Bureau of Economic Research, 1968), 16–17. In particular, transportation, communications, and utilities are included in industry rather than services.

[13]Smith, *The Wealth of Nations,* 270–71.

[14]Thomas M. Stanback, Jr., et al., *Services: The New Economy* (Totowa, N.J.: Allanheld, Osmun, & Co., 1981), 12–13.

only 20 percent of employment in agriculture and 26 percent in industry, they held 54 percent of the service positions.

Finally, part of the growth in service employment can possibly be attributed to the deindustrialization of America, whereby industrial jobs are lost to foreign competition and the released workers are forced to find service jobs. Although this scenario has been repeated in the lives of millions of individual Americans, the macroeconomic validity of the deindustrialization thesis is open to question. After reaching a peak of 26 million in 1979, employment in the goods-producing industries declined to 23 million in 1983, but recovered to 25 million in 1986.[15] Most of the growth in service employment represents an addition to total employment, not necessarily a replacement of existing jobs.

Significance of the Shift to Services

The shift to services has profoundly influenced the structure and performance of the American economy. First, and most obvious, it has changed the nature of work and employment. More Americans are now engaged in sales (wholesale and retail) than in manufacturing. College students who may have prepared for professions in engineering in the 1950s and 1960s are more likely to specialize in business and legal services, computer programming, recreation, or gerontology in the 1990s. Many service workers are self-employed (for example, doctors, lawyers, auto mechanics) and relatively few are unionized.

One important question that we cannot presently answer is: What effect will the service revolution have on the distribution of income? Many people fear that the replacement of middle-class industrial jobs with low-paying (fast-food workers, housecleaners, etc.) and high-paying (doctors, lawyers, accountants, etc.) service jobs will cause the gap between the rich and the poor to widen. On the other hand, we should remember that many industrial pursuits provide both high- and low-paying jobs (executives and janitors) and many service jobs employ the middle class (for example, teachers, nurses, and insurance agents). As we will see later in this chapter, the American distribution of income has been remarkably stable since World War II, despite the growth of the service sector.

It is often alleged, on a macroeconomic level, that the service revolution has slowed the rate of growth of the U.S. economy. According to most measurements, labor productivity has grown more slowly in the service sector than in the goods-producing sectors and thus growth in service employment has supposedly reduced the average growth of productivity. Many economists fear that continued emphasis on services will lead to further deceleration in U.S. productivity growth.

Of course, this may be nothing more than a statistical illusion because the output of service workers is very difficult to measure. How can the govern-

---

[15]*Economic Report of the President 1987* (Washington, D.C.: USGPO, 1987), 290.

mental statisticians know, for example, whether a college professor has performed her duties as a teacher and researcher more effectively this year than she did last year? A lawyer? A social worker?

Even if service productivity has grown slowly, the shift toward service employment may have actually contributed to the growth of overall productivity. This is possible because the absolute level of productivity (total output per worker) is higher in the service sector than in agriculture. Movement of workers from agriculture to services may encourage economic growth, even if productivity is growing more rapidly (in percentage terms) in agriculture.[16]

Possibly because of the slow growth of service productivity, and possibly because the service sector faces little foreign competition, the rate of price inflation in the service sector is relatively high. Between 1970 and 1986, while the average annual rate of inflation for commodities was about 6 percent, the inflation rate for services was about 8 percent.[17] According to the minutes of a 1986 meeting of the Federal Reserve Open Market Committee, "basic cost pressures appeared to be well contained . . . in manufacturing industries, although price and wage pressures in the service industries remained disturbing."[18]

Regardless of the effect of service production on productivity growth and inflation, it has clearly increased the stability of employment and output. Service employment has grown in every single year since 1958, while industrial employment has moved up and down with the business cycle.

Several factors may account for the apparent immunity of the service sector to recessions. First, about 13 percent of service workers are self-employed, compared to only 5 percent in industry.[19] Many other service employees, including salespeople, waiters and waitresses, barbers and beauticians, realtors, and insurance agents, are paid on a commission or piecework basis. In all of these cases, a drop in the market demand for services is likely to reduce the incomes of service workers, but it is not likely to cause them to lose their jobs. In industry, where wages are less flexible, a reduction in demand is likely to result in unemployment.

Second, unlike manufactured goods, the output of the service sector usually cannot be stored in inventories. It is unlikely, therefore, that a surplus of services (which must be sold before production can resume) will be produced. The standard Keynesian theory of unemployment, based on an assumption of inflexible wages and an inventory adjustment mechanism, may have lost some of its relevance in an economy dominated by services.

---

[16]For further explanation and statistical evidence on this point, see Angus Maddison, *Phases of Capitalist Development* (Oxford: Oxford University Press, 1982), 115–121.

[17]*Economic Report of the President 1987,* 310. Again, this may be little more than a statistical illusion. Can we be sure, for example, how much the increased cost of health care was caused by higher prices per unit of care, and how much it was caused by an improvement in the quantity and quality of care?

[18]Rose Gutfeld, "The Prices of Services, Unlike Those of Goods, Keep Rising Strongly," *Wall Street Journal,* September 9, 1986, 30.

[19]Fuchs, *The Service Economy,* 185. These figures are for 1960.

A third reason for the stability of service employment is that governmental services usually are not reduced during recessions. Actually, new government workers may be needed to process the expanded load of claims for unemployment and welfare benefits.

The service sector also has a positive impact on the nation's balance of international payments. In 1986, when American exports of merchandise fell short of imports by $149 billion, the deficit was partially offset by a $44 billion surplus on service transactions.[20] As a net exporter of services, one of the major U.S. objectives in recent negotiations has been to reduce international barriers to service trade.

Even if service productivity has grown slowly in the past, and even if this has retarded economic growth and fueled inflation, these trends may not continue in the future. If the technological achievements of the past were oriented toward goods production (for example, the assembly line), the recent technological advances in computer hardware and software, xerography, and telecommunications are particularly useful for accounting firms, banks, educational institutions, and other services. In 1982, service and information firms invested $140 billion in new technologies and this figure has certainly grown.[21] The service revolution, it would seem, has only just begun.

Industrial Organization

Before the Civil War, the U.S. economy approximated the textbook model of perfect competition. Over half of the labor force worked on small, owner-managed farms. In manufacturing, no single plant was known to control as much as 10 percent of the output of any product in the early 1800s. As late as 1870, the average firm in the iron and steel industry employed fewer than 100 people. Each firm produced a relatively homogeneous product, and the government played a very limited role in the economy.

The nationwide network of transportation and communication, in place by the end of the Civil War, enabled the age of Big Business to begin, led by the so-called captains of industry. By 1879, the Standard Oil trust (controlled by John D. Rockefeller) controlled about 90 percent of American oil refining, and by 1900 the Carnegie empire produced nearly half of the nation's steel.

The trend toward bigness accelerated after 1889 when the New Jersey legislature legalized the formation of holding companies. The resulting merger movement, which lasted until 1904, created the largest private corporations the world had known. In 1901, for example, J. P. Morgan formed America's first billion-dollar company, U.S. Steel, by merging the old Carnegie company

[20]*Economic Report of the President 1987,* 266. For a detailed statistical description of U.S. service trade, see Anthony DiLullo, "Service Transactions in the U.S. International Accounts, 1970–1980," *Survey of Current Business* 61 (November 1981): 29–46.

[21]Ronald Shelp and Gary Hart, "Understanding a New Economy," *Wall Street Journal,* December 23, 1986, 18.

with its eight largest competitors. By 1904, one or two giant firms controlled at least half of the output of 78 different industries. Just as significant, the age of the owner-managers—the captains of industry—began to give way to an age in which large corporations were run by professional managers who often had little stake in ownership.

The Antitrust Movement

A backlash against monopoly began in 1887 when the Interstate Commerce Commission was established to regulate railroad rates. The Sherman Antitrust Act, passed in 1890, prohibited any contract, combination, or conspiracy "in restraint of trade" or any attempt to monopolize "any part of the trade or commerce among the several States." Filling in more detail, the Clayton Antitrust Act of 1914 declared the following four specific practices to be illegal if their "effect was to substantially lessen competition or tend to create a monopoly":

- Merger of competing companies.
- Price discrimination—charging different prices to different customers for the same product.
- Tying contracts—requiring a buyer to purchase goods from one seller.
- Interlocking directorates—directors of one company sitting on the boards of directors of competing companies.

At a time when the European and Japanese governments were encouraging the formation of monopolies, conglomerates, and cartels, the Sherman and Clayton Acts established an American tradition of relatively strict (by international standards) antitrust policy. The enormity of the American domestic market may help to explain this distinction. On the American market, it is usually feasible for several competing companies to exploit economies of large-scale production, making it possible for them to compete on the international market. In fact, because of the United States' relative independence of the foreign market, more governmental attention has been given to the protection of consumers from the abuses of big business. In Europe, where large corporations are viewed as artillery on the battlefield of international trade, governmental support for industrial concentration and mergers is often designed to create a few internationally competitive corporations. It is assumed that domestic consumers will be protected by foreign competition.

In recent years, the most significant American antitrust action was the breakup of the world's largest corporation—the American Telephone & Telegraph Company. After a 7-year court battle with the Justice Department, AT&T agreed in 1984 to divest itself of 22 subsidiary companies, reducing its assets from $155 billion to about $43 billion. In return, the company was given permission to enter areas of the telecommunications business—including computers—from which it had been barred by a 1956 agreement with the Justice Department.

Trends in Business Size and Concentration

Although it is fairly clear that big businesses became more influential in America between 1860 and 1900, the more recent trends are difficult to assess. On the one hand, the United States still has more than its share of corporate giants. In 1985, 86 of the 200 largest industrial corporations in the world were based in the United States (Table A.10). On the other hand, 56 percent of the U.S. labor force worked in establishments with less than 100 workers in 1983—up from 54 percent in 1975. It is debatable whether large corporations play a more dominant role in the United States than they do in other countries, and whether their influence has grown in recent years.

Trends and levels of industrial concentration are measured in several ways. The yardstick used most often is the **four-firm concentration ratio**— the percentage of total sales of the four largest firms in an industry. Concentration ratios for several American industries are presented in Table 4.2. According to these data, the levels of concentration range from very high (aluminum in 1947 and automobiles in 1982) to very low (sporting goods and jewelry). The share of the four largest firms has risen dramatically in some industries (synthetic rubber) and fallen in others (aluminum and sporting goods).

In international perspective, comparisons conducted by F. M. Scherer and Frederic Pryor indicate that the average level of industrial concentration in America is less than or roughly equal to levels in France, West Germany, Italy, Japan, and the United Kingdom (Table A.9). Concentration seems to be highest in countries such as Belgium, Canada, Sweden, and Switzerland where the domestic markets (measured by population or GNP) are too small to accommodate a large number of competitors.[22]

In his classic study of trends in American industrial organization, Warren Nutter defined an industry to be effectively monopolistic if its four-firm concentration ratio exceeded 50 percent. Applying that criterion to the period between 1899 and 1937, he detected only a very slight increase—from 19 to 20 percent—in the fraction of private production originating in monopolistic industries.[23] Likewise, for the 1947–1972 period, estimates by Scherer indicate a very small rise (about 2 percentage points) in the average concentration ratio for manufacturing industries.[24]

A more comprehensive assessment of recent trends (including those in agriculture and services) has been assembled by William Shepherd.[25] In Shep-

[22]Frederic L. Pryor, *Property and Industrial Organization in Communist and Capitalist Nations* (Bloomington, Ind.: Indiana University Press, 1973), 199–205. Pryor's conclusions are generally consistent with those reached by Joe Bain, in his *International Differences in Industrial Structure* (Westport, Conn.: Greenwood Press, 1966).

[23]G. Warren Nutter and Henry A. Einhorn, *Enterprise Monopoly in the United States: 1899– 1958* (New York: Columbia University Press, 1969), 50.

[24]F. M. Scherer, *Industrial Market Structure and Economic Performance,* 2d ed. (Chicago: Rand-McNally, 1980), Table 3.7.

[25]William G. Shepherd, "Causes of Increased Competition in the U.S. Economy, 1939–1980," *Review of Economics and Statistics* 64 (November 1982): 613–626.

**Table 4.2   Four-Firm Concentration Ratios
in Selected American Industries, 1947–1982**

	1947	1958	1967	1977	1982
Motor Vehicles	n.a.	n.a.	92%	93%	92%
Aircraft	n.a.	83%	69	59	64
Aluminum	100%	n.a.	n.a.	76	64
Synthetic Rubber	5	13	33	56	63
Steel Mills	50	53	48	45	42
Men's Suits	9	11	17	21	25
Radio, TV Equipment	n.a.	n.a.	22	20	22
Sporting Goods	24	41	27	21	17
Jewelry	13	18	23	18	16

Source: U.S. Department of Commerce, Bureau of the Census, *1982 Census of Manufactures: Concentration Ratios in Manufacturing,* MC82-S-7 (Washington, D.C.: USGPO, 1986), Table 5.

herd's study, each industry or sector of the economy is assigned to one of four categories:

- *Pure Monopoly*—Market share near 100 percent, effective barriers to entry, control of prices.
- *Dominant Firm*—A market share of 50 to 90 percent, no close rival, high entry barriers, control of prices.
- *Tight Oligopoly*—Four-firm concentration ratio above 60 percent, stable market shares, medium or high entry barriers, rigid prices.
- *Effective Competition*—Four-firm ratio below 40 percent, unstable market shares, flexible pricing.

Obviously, Shepherd was forced to make many judgment calls in his assignment of industries. In the end, he found that the market structure of the U.S. economy was rather stable between 1939 and 1958, but he detected a "remarkable" growth in competitiveness after 1958. According to his estimates, the share of national income originating in industries that are effectively competitive rose from 56 percent in 1958 to 77 percent in 1980 (Table 4.3).

Table 4.3   Competitive Structure of the American Economy, 1939–1980

Year	Percentage Share of National Income Originating in:			
	Pure monopoly	Dominant firm	Tight oligopoly	Effective competition
1939	6.2	5.0	36.4	52.4
1958	3.1	5.0	35.6	56.3
1980	2.5	2.8	18.0	76.7

Source: William G. Shepherd, "Causes of Increased Competition in the U.S. Economy, 1939–1980," *Review of Economics and Statistics* 64 (November 1982): 618.

In Shepherd's opinion, over half of the increase in American competition was caused directly or indirectly by stricter enforcement of antitrust laws. In addition, he notes the importance of rising import competition and deregulation of the transport, communication, and banking industries. To these causes, we might add the rise of the service economy. Some 67 percent of service workers are employed by establishments with less than 100 employees, compared to only 28 percent in manufacturing.[26] According to Victor Fuchs:

> *As these and other facts become better known, we may see an end to the myth of the dominance of the large corporation in our society. Most people do not work and never have worked for large corporations. . . . In the future, the large corporation is likely to be overshadowed by the hospitals, universities, research institutes, government agencies, and professional associations that are the hallmarks of a service economy.*[27]

The Social Costs of Industrial Concentration

Although large corporations may not dominate the entire U.S. economy, they certainly dominate a number of important markets. For this reason, economists and other social scientists have long studied and debated their influence. The neoclassical theory of monopoly, which may be found in any text on the principles of economics, predicts that firms with market power will tend to restrict output below the competitive level, charge higher prices, and collect larger profits. Statistical investigations by Joe Bain, Michael Mann, and a number of others have found that profit rates tend to be significantly above the norm in industries where the four-firm concentration ratio exceeds a threshold between 45 and 59 percent.[28] These "excessive" monopoly profits are disturbing to many people because of their influence on the distribution of income and wealth. About 57 percent of all personal holdings of corporate stocks are owned by the wealthiest 1 percent of the population.[29] Nonetheless, according to one recent study, if the four-firm concentration ratios for all American manufacturing industries were reduced to a maximum of 40 percent, the incomes of the most affluent households would fall by only 1.4 percent and the remaining income groups would experience gains of only 0.3 to 0.7 percent.[30]

Apart from their distributional effects, large corporations are criticized on a number of other grounds. Many of these criticisms relate to the alleged inefficiency of large corporations. First, by restricting their output below the

[26]U.S. Bureau of the Census, *Statistical Abstract of the United States: 1986* (Washington, D.C.: USGPO, 1985), Table 880.

[27]Fuchs, *The Service Economy,* 10.

[28]This literature is briefly reviewed in Scherer, *Industrial Market Structure and Economic Performance,* 276–282.

[29]U.S. Bureau of the Census, *Statistical Abstract: 1982–83,* 449.

[30]Irene Powell, "The Effect of Reductions in Concentration on Income Distribution," *Review of Economics and Statistics* 69 (February 1987): 75–82.

competitive level, large corporations are said to reduce the allocative efficiency of the economy—goods are produced in the wrong proportions to maximize national income. Estimates of the magnitude of this loss in the American context range from paltry (0.1 percent of GNP) to significant (4 to 7 percent of GNP).[31]

Second, as Adam Smith noted two centuries ago, "monopoly . . . is a great enemy to good management." Picking up on this theme, Harvey Leibenstein argues that when competition is absent, corporations are likely to be guilty of what he calls "X-inefficiency"—failure to minimize their costs of production. Although the evidence of monopoly-induced cost inefficiency is primarily anecdotal, the problem is undoubtedly a real one. In several cases, when former monopolists have been confronted by the pressure of competition, they have been able to cut their unit costs by 10 to 20 percent and more.[32] Furthermore, large corporations allegedly waste national resources and distort the operation of the political system through their political lobbying and advertising.

A number of observers believe that large corporations pose a threat to the macroeconomic stability of the American economy. In recent years, the federal government concluded that the pending failures of Chrysler Corporation (with $13 billion in sales in 1983) or the Continental Illinois National Bank (with $44 billion in assets) would have such a detrimental effect on the entire economy that it stepped in to bail them out. If large corporations are reasonably sure that the government will not allow them to fail, they may be even more prone to X-inefficiency.

Moreover, it is often alleged that the corporate giants contribute to macroeconomic instability through their handling of capital investment. About half of all capital expenditures in manufacturing are controlled by the 200 largest firms. If a relatively small number of corporate executives become pessimistic about the business outlook, a significant downturn in investment spending may occur, possibly resulting in a business recession. According to John Kenneth Galbraith, recessionary trends in competitive industries are "self-limiting and, eventually, self-correcting," but concentrated industries are "inherently unstable."[33]

Big Business Defended

In defense of the large corporations, many economists believe that the standard measures of market power (for example, the four-firm concentration ratio) significantly overstate the extent of monopoly. They point to several sources of competition that are commonly ignored. For example, the ratios seldom take account of competition from imports or from substitutes that are

---

[31]Scherer, *Industrial Market Structure and Economic Performance,* 459–464.

[32]Ibid., 464–466.

[33]On the macroeconomic stability of competitive and concentrated industries, see John Kenneth Galbraith, *Economics and the Public Purpose* (Boston: Houghton Mifflin, 1973), 179.

produced by other industries (for example, competition between aluminum foil and waxed paper producers).

William Baumol argues that monopoly profits are constrained by the threat of potential competition. Concentrated markets operate very much like competitive markets, he says, as long as they are "contestable"—that is, as long as other companies are free to enter.[34]

John Kenneth Galbraith contends that the power of monopolistic sellers is often withstood by the countervailing power of monopolistic buyers. Large steel producers, for example, are faced by large, powerful purchasers of steel in the automobile industry, and large producers of consumer goods are faced by Sears and the other large retail chains.

Even if it can be shown that the exercise of monopoly power results in various forms of inefficiency, these costs must be balanced against the savings that accrue from large-scale research, production, and marketing. According to Yale Brozen of the University of Chicago:

Concentration occurs and persists where it is the efficient structure for producing and distributing a product and for adapting to changing technical possibilities, shifting demand, and increasing regulatory requirements. . . . Where centralization is not efficient, industries do not become concentrated.[35]

The Labor Market

Neoclassical theory suggests that employment and wages are determined by the supply and demand of labor if labor markets are sufficiently competitive. In comparison with many other industrial capitalist countries, the U.S. labor market seems to be relatively competitive, and it may be growing more competitive through time.

On the employers' side of the market, there is little evidence of widespread monopsonistic power of the kind that would depress wages below their competitive levels. Studies of local labor markets have found that a very small percentage of American workers live in towns where the ten largest firms employ over half of the labor force.[36] Furthermore, the average American manufacturing establishment had a smaller number of employees in 1982 than in 1947.[37]

---

[34]William J. Baumol, "Contestable Markets, Antitrust, and Regulation," *The Wharton Magazine* 7 (Fall 1982): 24.

[35]Yale Brozen, *Concentration, Mergers, and Public Policy* (New York: Macmillan, 1982), 56–57.

[36]Thomas J. Kniesner, *Labor Economics,* 2d ed. (Englewood Cliffs, N.J.: Prentice Hall, 1980), 202–204.

[37]U.S. Department of Commerce, Bureau of the Census, *1982 Census of Manufacturers,* MC82-S-1 (Washington, D.C.: USGPO, 1986), 1–2.

On the employees' side of the market, labor unions are the most important expressions of market power. In the United States, however, union members now represent less than 20 percent of the labor force. That proportion
has been falling since the mid-1950s, when it peaked at about 27 percent.
Union membership is much less pervasive in the United States than in any of
the major Western European countries, with the exceptions of France and
Switzerland (Table A.11).

Thus, the American labor market would seem to be relatively competitive, but this raises another question. Neoclassical theory suggests that unregulated competitive markets should adjust to a supply-demand equilibrium,
leaving no surplus or shortage of the commodity in question. However, the
United States and other capitalist countries have experienced a persistent
labor surplus, or unemployment. How can this be explained?

A full discussion of the causes of unemployment would take us far afield,
but a few words are in order. Neoclassical theory suggests that unemployment
is caused by downward inflexibility of nominal wages, stemming from long-
term labor contracts, minimum wage laws, unemployment compensation, and
the like. Keynesians would say that a reduction in nominal wage rates may not
reduce unemployment, because it may reduce the total income of the labor
force and the aggregate demand for goods.

Structural unemployment arises because labor is highly differentiated by
skill and location and job information is costly to obtain. Equalization of the
total supply and the total demand for labor cannot eradicate unemployment if
the jobs and workers do not match or if they cannot find one another.

According to comparative data, while unemployment rates increased in
all major capitalist countries between 1970 and 1985, the rate increased by a
smaller amount in the United States than in most other countries (Table A.12).
Thus, the United States had a relatively high unemployment rate (compared
to other industrial countries) in 1970, but a relatively low rate in 1985. According to a study by the International Monetary Fund, the smaller increase in
U.S. unemployment may be explained by greater flexibility of American wages,
which again may reflect the competitiveness of the American labor market.[38]

Reasons for Declining Unionization

Earlier, we noted that American union membership declined from about 27
percent of the labor force in the mid-1950s to less than 20 percent today.
Approximately half of this decline can be attributed to the growth of the
service economy. As we have seen, firms in the service sector tend to be
smaller than industrial firms, and many service workers are self-employed. For
these and other reasons, the service sector is less susceptible than industry to

[38]Charles Adams, Paul Fenton, and Flemming Larsen, "Differences in Employment Behavior
among Industrial Countries," in *Staff Studies for the World Economic Outlook* (Washington,
D.C.: International Monetary Fund, July 1986), 24–36.

union activity. In 1986, union members accounted for only 16 percent of service employment, compared to 26 percent in industry.[39]

The other half of the decline in unionism is more difficult to explain. According to one hypothesis, the unions have suffered because many of their functions have been taken over by the government. Guarantees that were once embedded in union contracts—unemployment insurance, retirement benefits, health and safety requirements—are now subjects of legislation. Accordingly, a recent study found that unionism has declined most rapidly in those states that have done the most to uphold workers' rights.[40] On the other hand, the governmental substitution hypothesis is not consistent with the fact that union membership is generally highest in countries where governmental spending on social security and welfare represents a large percentage of national income (compare Tables A.11 and A.17).

Labor Legislation

One reason for the low level of union membership in the United States (by international standards) is that pro-labor legislation came late to America. In Sweden, for example, the major employers agreed in 1906 that they would not attempt to disrupt unionizing activities. In America, these guarantees were not extended until the passage of the Norris-LaGuardia Act of 1932 and the National Labor Relations Act of 1935. In 1938, the Fair Labor Standards Act enacted a minimum wage rate (25 cents per hour!) and a maximum work week (44 hours) for labor engaged in interstate commerce.

Public opinion turned against the labor unions toward the end of World War II, when a long series of strikes disrupted the coal, steel, telephone, automobile, and meat-packing industries. In 1946, approximately 116 million man-hours were lost due to labor disputes. In the aftermath, the Labor-Management (Taft-Hartley) Act of 1947 was enacted to exercise control over the unions. Under the act, the **closed shop,** which requires job applicants to join the union before they may be hired, was outlawed. The **union shop,** which requires employees to join the union within a specified period after they are hired, was not prohibited by the act, but the individual states are free to pass right-to-work laws which prohibit union shops. Twenty states, most of them in the South and West, presently have right-to-work laws.

The Taft-Hartley Act also placed restrictions on the right of unions to call strikes. If the government feels that a strike is likely to create a national emergency, it can require an 80-day cooling-off period and intervention by the Federal Mediation and Conciliation Service.

[39]U.S. Department of Labor, Bureau of Labor Statistics, *Employment and Earnings* 34 (January 1987): 220.

[40]George R. Neumann and Ellen R. Rissman, "Where Have All the Union Members Gone?" *Journal of Labor Economics* 2 (April 1984): 175–192.

The Economic Impact of Labor Unions

The most important goal of labor unions traditionally has been to raise and maintain the wages of their members. They pursue this goal by bargaining collectively with management (with the threat of a strike if bargaining fails), by restricting the supply of union labor, by increasing the demand for their labor through featherbedding (creation of new, and sometimes useless, jobs), and through efforts to increase the demand for their final product (for example, "Look for the union label" and "Buy American" slogans).

The actual impact of unions on wage levels can be estimated in a number of different ways, and economists disagree on the methods that should be used. Nevertheless, few economists would question the proposition that union members receive higher wages, on average, than nonmembers. According to one set of estimates, for example, the wages of union laborers exceeded those of nonunion laborers by the following percentages between 1920 and 1980:[41]

1920–1924	25–31%	1950–1954	16–26%
1925–1929	41–45	1955–1959	23–31
1930–1934	48–64	1960–1964	23–32
1935–1939	23–25	1965–1969	22–29
1940–1944	5–16	1970–1974	8–17
1945–1949	1–15	1975–1980	1–7

The estimated union effect on wages reached an all-time high during the early years of the Depression, declined until the late 1940s, climbed to a new plateau during the 1950s and 1960s, and declined during the 1970s. These trends may suggest that the money wages of union members are less responsive to changes in the general price level than the wages of nonmembers. In the early 1930s, for example, when the price level fell, the reduction in union wages was relatively small. Hence, the ratio of union to nonunion wages increased. Conversely, union wage increases were apparently smaller than nonunion increases during the inflation of the 1970s, reducing the advantage of union membership.[42]

Although labor unions apparently have succeeded in raising the wages of their members, this does not necessarily imply that they have raised the average level of wages for all workers. A number of economists believe that the gains of union laborers have been won at the expense of nonunion laborers rather than at the expense of corporate stockholders. If high wages cause

---

[41]Derived from the estimates of John Pencavel and Catherine E. Hartsog, "A Reconsideration of the Effects of Unionism on Relative Wages and Employment in the United States, 1920–1980," *Journal of Labor Economics* 2 (April 1984): 206. For a survey of the voluminous literature on this subject, see C. J. Paisley, "Labor Union Effects on Wage Gains," *Journal of Economic Literature* 18 (March 1980): 1–31.

[42]Again, it should be emphasized that these observations are based on a fragile set of estimates. According to Pencavel and Hartsog, "these relative wage effects are not measured with precision, and a large number of different possible values for the effect of unions on relative wages are consistent with the evidence." Pencavel and Hartsog, "A Reconsideration," 216.

unemployment in the unionized sector and the unemployed spill over into the nonunion sector, then competition for jobs may reduce the wages of nonmembers.

In fact, the share of U.S. national income received by all laborers (union and nonunion) has been remarkably stable for over 50 years. In 1933, when only 7 percent of the labor force was unionized, laborers received about 73 percent of national income. In 1954, when the unionized share of the labor force peaked at 27 percent, labor's share of national income was 69 percent. In 1986, unions claimed less than 20 percent of the labor force and labor received about 74 percent of national income.[43]

The Financial Sector

Financial institutions—including banks, securities firms, insurance companies, and others—perform a number of important functions in capitalist-market economies. They provide efficient and safe methods for payment between buyers and sellers (checking accounts, letters of credit, bankers' acceptances, etc.); they provide for safe storage of financial wealth (savings accounts, etc.); they extend credit (bank loans, bond sales, etc.); they allow individuals to share their risks with larger numbers of people (insurance policies); and they facilitate efficient transfers of ownership of businesses, housing, and other capital goods (stock market and real estate transactions).

Although banks and other financial institutions perform many of these same functions in socialist countries, particularly in market-socialist countries, their responsibilities are far more limited. Most obvious, there is no need for a stock market in socialist countries (although bond markets have been established in some countries) or for a commercial real estate industry (because individuals are not allowed to own the means of production). For the most part, the allocation of land and capital goods is tightly controlled by central planners.

For reasons that we shall discuss more fully in Part III, banks and other financial institutions play a limited role in socialist countries. Only about 0.4 percent of Soviet GNP is produced in the finance and insurance industries, compared to about 4.4 percent in the United States.[44] Stated simplistically, this means that the importance of the financial sector is about ten times greater in the American economy than in the Soviet economy. Furthermore, the contri-

---

[43]Here, I take compensation of employees, as defined by the Commerce Department, to represent labor's share of national income. Labor's share is even more stable if we include proprietor's income. These data are taken from *Economic Report of the President 1986*, 270.

[44]These figures are for 1980. The Soviet estimate, prepared by the U.S. Central Intelligence Agency, is taken from U.S. Congress, Joint Economic Committee, *USSR: Measures of Economic Growth and Development, 1958–1980* (Washington, D.C., 1982), 61. The U.S. estimate is from *Survey of Current Business* 63 (April 1983): 23.

bution of the (more broadly defined) financial sector is greater in the United States than in the other industrially developed capitalist countries (Table A.8).

Trends in American Bank Regulation

Before 1863, the U.S. banking system was almost wholly unregulated by the national government. With the exception of the First and Second Banks of the United States, which were chartered by the U.S. Congress, the 2,500 banks established between 1781 and 1861 were all chartered by authorities at the state level. Many of these banks were unsound and nearly two-fifths of them were forced to close within 10 years after they opened. To make matters worse, each bank was able to issue its own banknotes, which were used as currency. In the mid-1800s, literally thousands of different kinds of currency were in circulation in the United States, making it very difficult to detect counterfeit notes.

The National Banking Acts of 1863 and 1864 put the state banks out of the business of issuing currency and established a uniform and safe currency system. Furthermore, the acts established the office of the Comptroller of the Currency in the Treasury Department and empowered it to charter and supervise a system of national banks. Hence, a unique (by international standards) system of **dual banking** was created, with national banks chartered by the comptroller and state banks chartered by state banking authorities.

Although the national banking system established a uniform currency, it did not provide an efficient national system for clearing checks, that is, for moving funds from one bank to another. Likewise, the system did not provide an efficient means for banks that were short of funds to borrow from banks with excess reserves. Most important, the National Banking Acts did not establish a central bank that could adjust the supply of money to meet the needs of the economy. The establishment of a central bank was resisted strongly by conservative Democrats who feared encroachment on states' rights.

The Federal Reserve Act of 1913 struck a compromise between the demands for state autonomy and the need for a central bank. The act established 12 Federal Reserve district banks, each of which is owned by the member banks in its district. To this day, the district banks are the only central banks in the world that are wholly owned by commercial banks. Furthermore, each district bank is controlled by a board of nine directors, six of whom are elected by the member banks in the district.

A seven-member board of governors, appointed by the president, was placed at the head of the Federal Reserve system. All national banks were required to become members of the system and state banks were invited to join. Member banks were allowed to borrow money at the discount window of the Federal Reserve and could use its check-clearing facilities, but they were regulated more tightly (for example, larger reserve and capital requirements) than many of the state banks that did not choose to join the system.

The authority of the Federal Reserve expanded during the Great Depression, but it began to decline after World War II. In order to escape the stringent reserve requirements placed on member banks, a number of banks dropped out of the Federal Reserve system. The proportion of all commercial banks that retained their membership in the system dropped from a peak of 49 percent in 1947 to 42 percent in 1980. This exodus allegedly threatened the safety of the banking system and crippled the Federal Reserve's efforts to control the growth of the money supply.

In order to deal with these and other problems, Congress passed the most significant and wide-ranging piece of banking legislation since the 1930s—the Depository Institutions Deregulation and Monetary Control Act of 1980. Among the important provisions of the act were the following:

- The Federal Reserve was given the authority to set reserve requirements on checking accounts at *all* federally insured depository institutions— member banks, nonmember banks, savings and loan associations, credit unions, etc.
- Federal Reserve loans and other Federal Reserve services (for example, check collection) were made available (at a fee) to *all* depository institutions.
- All depository institutions were given the authority to offer interest-earning checking accounts.
- A phaseout of interest rate ceilings on deposits and other accounts was initiated.

The 1980 legislation was meant to reassert the authority of the Federal Reserve and to place all depository institutions—member and nonmember banks, savings and loan associations, and others—on an equal footing. The new power that was given to the Federal Reserve would have delighted Alexander Hamilton (who fought to establish the First Bank of the United States), but would have horrified Thomas Jefferson and other advocates of states' rights.

The deregulation of deposit interest rates under the 1980 act contributed to the efficiency of the financial system, but it also caused problems for many banks and thrift institutions. In order to compete, many of them were forced to pay higher interest rates on deposits than the average yield on their investment portfolios. For this reason and several others (including nonpayment of debt by oil companies and Third World borrowers), hundreds of banks and thrift institutions have been forced to close their doors. The average number of bank failures jumped from about 5 per year in 1945–1980 (with a maximum of 16 in 1976) to about 73 per year in 1981–1986.[45]

The United States, with its tradition of individualism and states' rights, still has a banking system that is unique from an international perspective. The Federal Reserve remains a *federal* system, with its network of locally-owned district banks. Moreover, the banking authorities in the individual states still have the authority to establish regulations on branch banking and a wide range of other issues.

---

[45]See the annual reports of the Federal Deposit Insurance Corporation.

The Governmental Sector

By international standards, the activities of the U.S. government are rather limited. Taken as a percentage of GNP, for example, government expenditures are smaller in the United States than in any other major industrial nation, with the notable exceptions of Japan and Switzerland (Table A.17).

From a historical and international perspective, the United States was slow to adopt a strong central government. In keeping with the philosophy of federalism, the focus of governmental power was kept close to the electorate—at the state and local levels. After independence was won from the British, the Articles of Confederation denied the central government the power to collect taxes. When the Constitution was adopted in 1789, it gave a broad range of economic powers to the Congress, but these were used sparingly. For 140 years, over half of all U.S. governmental spending was carried out at the local level (Table 4.4). It took nothing less than the Great Depression and World War II to elevate the central government to a position of dominance.

Along with the shift toward centralization of government, the post-war generations also witnessed a dramatic shift in the functional distribution of governmental spending. Before World War II, the government spent more money on the postal and transportation systems than it spent on national defense, social security, and welfare, combined (Table 4.5). During the war, the military absorbed over three-fourths of all governmental expenditures. The military share dropped again after the war, but not to the pre-war level. American participation in the Korean War, the Vietnam War, and the arms race have kept military spending at a relatively high level. At the same time, the governmental commitment to social security and welfare, which began during the Depression, grew rapidly after the war. Taken together, the share of national defense, social security, and welfare in U.S. governmental spending increased from 8 percent in 1927 to 45 percent in 1983.

Table 4.4   The Distribution of Federal, State, and Local Governmental Expenditures in the United States, 1902–1984

Year	Federal	State	Local	Total
1902	35%	11%	55%	100%
1913	30	12	58	100
1922	41	14	46	100
1927	32	17	52	100
1936	55	19	27	100
1944	91	4	5	100
1950	64	18	18	100
1960	64	17	19	100
1970	63	19	18	100
1980	64	20	16	100
1984	64	20	16	100

Source: *Facts and Figures on Government Finance 1986* (Washington, D.C.: The Tax Foundation, Inc., 1986), a12.

Table 4.5   The Functional Distribution of Federal, State, and Local Governmental Expenditures in the United States, 1902–1983

	1902	1936	1944	1950	1970	1983
Defense, Foreign Relations	9.9% *	5.6%	77.8%	26.1%	25.3%	16.9%
Education	15.5	14.1	2.6	13.7	16.7	13.1
Postal, Transport	19.5	17.7	6.4	9.6	8.5	5.2
Social Security, Welfare	2.5	7.3	1.8	14.0	19.8	28.2
Health	6.9	4.7	1.0	5.0	5.1	5.3
Police, Fire	5.4	3.2	0.7	1.9	2.1	2.1
Interest on Debt	5.8	8.7	2.4	6.9	5.5	9.8
Other	34.5	38.7	7.3	22.8	17.0	20.2
Total	100.0	100.0	100.0	100.0	100.0	100.0

*Percentages of total expenditure.

Sources: U.S. Department of Commerce, Bureau of the Census, *Historical Statistics of the United States, Colonial Times to 1970,* Part 1 (Washington, D.C.: USGPO, 1975), Series Y 533–566; and *Facts and Figures on Government Finance, 1986* (Washington, D.C.: Tax Foundation, 1986), Table A7.

Regulation of the Economy

We have already taken note of the important role that the government plays in regulating the American product, labor, and financial markets. Regulation of banking began in earnest in the 1860s, antitrust action began in the 1890s, and guidance of labor relations began in the 1930s.

Governmental concern for public health and safety began with the passage of the Pure Food and Drug Act of 1906, prompted by the publication of Upton Sinclair's novel, *The Jungle,* that same year. In more recent years, the regulatory umbrella has been expanded to cover consumer and occupational safety, environmental protection, energy production, transportation, communication, and a number of other concerns.

Most of the regulatory agencies were established to deal with important national problems and very few economists or politicians would advocate abolishing the entire governmental rulebook. Nevertheless, the regulatory process has fallen under broad criticism in recent years. First, many would say that governmental regulations are too expensive. In addition to the billions of dollars that are spent to operate the regulatory agencies, private businesses must spend billions to comply with the regulations, and these costs are passed down to consumers in higher taxes and prices. According to Murray Weidenbaum, a former chairman of the President's Council of Economic Advisors, the cost of governmental regulation exceeds $100 billion annually.[46]

Another dysfunctional aspect of governmental control is suggested by the **regulatory capture** theory, which states that in time, and sometimes quite innocently, regulators become tools of the industries they are supposed to regulate. For example, governmental agencies barred the entry of new com-

[46]Leslie Goldwater, "Regulation in America," *Iron Age* 226 (June 6, 1983), 20.

petitors into the trucking and airline industries for many years, granting monopoly power to the existing companies. The Civil Aeronautics Board did not grant a single long-distance route to a new airline between 1938 and 1978. Officials of the Federal Reserve often lobby in Congress for legislation that favors the banking industry. Early on, Adam Smith attacked the feudal system of apprenticeships, which regulated the employment and training of craftsmen, because it "restrain[s] the competition in some employments to a smaller number than might otherwise be disposed to enter into them."[47]

Partially reversing the earlier trend, a wave of deregulation has recently swept the United States. The Airline Deregulation Act of 1978 and the Motor Carrier Act of 1980 reduced the restrictions on entry and pricing in those industries. The Depository Institutions Deregulation Act of 1980 and the Garn-St. Germain Act of 1982 initiated a phaseout of interest rate ceilings and provided for interstate acquisition of failing banks.

Deregulation has undoubtedly injected new competitiveness and flexibility into the economy, but it also carries risks. We have already noted the epidemic of bank failures experienced in recent years in the United States. In 1984, when the government was forced to bail out the Continental Illinois Corporation—the ninth-largest bank holding company in the nation—Federal Reserve Chairman Volcker admitted to Congress that "in hindsight, it's an unassailable argument that the central bank should have been tougher with Continental."[48]

Fiscal and Monetary Policy

Superficially, the institutional machinery that sets fiscal and monetary policy in the United States is quite simple. On the fiscal side, the national budget is prepared by the executive branch under the coordination of the Office of Management and Budget. It is sent to Congress for amendment, debate, and approval, and then it is returned to the president to be signed into law. At each step, the formation of fiscal policy is influenced by the actions of lobbyists and by the demands of the electorate.

Monetary policy is set by the governors of the Federal Reserve System, each of whom is appointed by the president of the United States for a 14-year term. Because of these long terms of office, and because the Federal Reserve is able to cover its operating expenses without appropriations from Congress, the board of governors is well insulated from political pressure.

As we noted in the previous chapter, the U.S. government did not adopt an active program of fiscal and monetary measures to stimulate employment during the Great Depression. Indeed, in 1937 the government reduced its expenditures, and the Federal Reserve acted to reduce the size of the money supply. In the end, however, the World War II experience confirmed the

[47]Adam Smith, *The Wealth of Nations* (New York: Collier, 1909), 126.

[48]G. Christian Hill and Edwin Finn, "Big Depositors' Runs on Beleaguered Banks Speed the Failure Rate," *Wall Street Journal,* August 23, 1984, 12.

Keynesian proposition that unemployment could be reduced by a program of governmental spending. Indeed, wartime spending successfully reduced the rate of unemployment in America from 17 percent in 1939 to 2 percent in 1945.

After the war, a new attitude toward fiscal policy was reflected in the Employment Act of 1946, which declared that the federal government had an obligation to promote maximum employment, production, and purchasing power. For several years, these goals were attained rather effectively: one major study found that between 1955 and 1965 the American government used fiscal policy more successfully than any of the major European governments to stabilize the growth of national income.[49]

In more recent years, American fiscal policy seems to have gotten out of control. The federal government has run budget deficits in every year since 1969, and no end to the deficits seems to be in sight. In 1970, about 62 percent of government expenditures consisted of social security payments, interest on the national debt, and other payments that were uncontrollable under present law, according to the Office of Management and Budget. By 1985, the portion of federal spending that was uncontrollable had risen to 73 percent of the total.[50]

Aside from the use of fiscal and monetary policy to stabilize employment and the price level, the U.S. government has made little use of indicative planning or industrial policy to influence the structure of the economy. There is no American counterpart to the Japanese Ministry of International Trade and Industry, which uses subsidies and other means to encourage the development of favored industries. On the other hand, many Americans seem to be ready to experiment with the Japanese system. In a 1984 survey of leaders in American business, labor, government, and other segments of society, 51 percent said that they favored the establishment of a long-range industrial policy, and 54 percent said that tax breaks and subsidies should be given to certain industries.[51]

Redistribution of Income

We noted above that Americans traditionally have been uncomfortable with governmental schemes to redistribute income. "We Still Believe That God Helps Those Who Help Themselves," is the title of a *Psychology Today* study of American attitudes toward wealth and poverty.[52] This attitude may help to

---

[49]Bent Hansen, *Fiscal Policy in Seven Countries: 1955–1965* (Paris: Organization for Economic Cooperation and Development, 1969), 69–73.

[50]U.S. Bureau of the Census, *Statistical Abstract of the United States: 1986,* Table 497.

[51]Results of the survey, conducted by Opinion Research Corporation, are reported in the *Wall Street Journal,* October 2, 1984, 11. In his book, *The Zero-Sum Solution: Building A World-Class Economy* (New York: Simon and Schuster, 1985), Lester Thurow argues for the establishment of an American industrial policy, and he claims that the nation's success in agriculture can be attributed to governmental aid to that sector—for example, agricultural colleges, federal crop insurance, export credit, electrification, etc.

[52]*Psychology Today,* November 1972, 107–108.

Table 4.6   The Influence of Federal, State, and Local Transfer Payments and Taxes on the U.S. Distribution of Income, 1980

| | Percentage of Total Income Received by: | | | | | |
	Poorest 20%	Second 20%	Third 20%	Fourth 20%	Richest 20%	Gini Ratio
Income before Taxes and Transfers	1.7	8.0	15.0	22.8	52.5	.49
Income after Transfers	4.1	9.7	15.4	21.9	48.9	.43
Income after Taxes and Transfers*	4.6	10.4	15.9	22.0	47.2	.41

*According to the most progressive assumptions in Pechman's study of tax incidence.

Sources: Distribution of income including transfers before taxes (second line of data in the table) is from Joseph Pechman, *Who Paid the Taxes, 1966–1985?* (Washington, D.C.: The Brookings Institution, 1985), Table 4–6. Transfer payments were subtracted to obtain the first line of the table, using data in Edgar Browning, "Pechman's Tax Incidence Study: A Note on the Data," *American Economic Review* 76 (December 1986): 1217. The third line was calculated using effective tax rates for 1980 found in Joseph Pechman, "Pechman's Tax Incidence Study: A Response (Erratum)," *American Economic Review* 77 (March 1987): 233.

explain why the United States has a relatively unequal distribution of income in comparison with other industrial capitalist countries (Table A.25).

An assessment of the impact of taxes and governmental transfer payments on the U.S. distribution of income is presented in Table 4.6. According to these estimates, the system of transfer payments (that is, social security, aid to families with dependent children, and unemployment compensation) redistributes a significant amount of American income from the rich to the poor and reduces the Gini inequality ratio by 6 percentage points. However, the system of taxation apparently has a rather minor impact on income distribution. This may seem surprising, since the United States has a progressive national income tax, but the progressivity of the income tax is reduced considerably by treatment of deductions and capital gains and is offset further by regressive state and local sales and property taxes.

Thus, the system of transfer payments has a progressive impact on the distribution of income and the share of transfer payments in personal income has increased as follows:[53]

1950   6.7%
1960   7.2
1970 10.3
1980 14.4
1986 14.7

Taken together, these observations would seem to suggest a rising level of income equality. Nevertheless, the data in Table 4.7 (which include monetary

[53]*Economic Report of the President 1987,* 272–73.

Table 4.7   The Distribution of Family Income in the United States, 1950–1984

	Percentage of Total Family Income Received by:				
	Poorest 20%	Second 20%	Third 20%	Fourth 20%	Richest 20%
1950	4.5	12.0	17.4	23.4	42.7
1960	4.8	12.2	17.8	24.0	41.3
1970	5.4	12.2	17.6	23.8	40.9
1980	5.1	11.6	17.5	24.3	41.6
1984	4.7	11.0	17.0	24.4	42.9

Source: U.S Department of Commerce, Bureau of the Census, *Current Population Reports,* Series P-60, No. 151 (Washington, D.C.: USGPO, 1986), Table 12.

transfer payments but not taxes) indicate that the American income distribution has been remarkably stable during 1950–1984. That stability is particularly surprising when we consider the other changes that have occurred in the American economy: the rising participation of women in the paid labor force, the improvement in educational levels, and the establishment of affirmative action programs to counteract the lingering effects of racial and sexual discrimination. If the data were adjusted for the effects of taxation, the distribution of income apparently became somewhat less equal from 1966 to 1985 because the progressivity of the overall tax system was reduced during those years.[54]

How do we reconcile the rising significance of transfer payments with the stable distribution of income? Apparently, while the distribution of market income has become less equal over time in America, this trend has been offset by the growth of governmental transfer payments so that the distribution of total income has changed very little.[55]

What has caused the rising inequality of market incomes? According to supply-side economists, the growing system of transfer payments has reduced work incentives among the poor and created an underclass of permanent welfare recipients.[56] Alternatively, many economists believe that rising inequality is another symptom of the service economy. After comparing the distributions of earnings in the service and industrial sectors of the economy, a team of researchers reached the following conclusion:

For services as a whole, the most important observation is that there tends to be a concentration of employment in better-than-average and

[54]Joseph A. Pechman, *Who Paid the Taxes, 1966–1985?* (Washington, D.C.: The Brookings Institution, 1985), Chapter 5; and Joseph A. Pechman, "Pechman's Tax Incidence Study: A Response (Erratum)," *The American Economic Review* 77 (March 1987): 232–234.

[55]This was the conclusion reached for the 1950–1970 period by Morgan Reynolds and Eugene Smolensky in their *Public Expenditures, Taxes, and the Distribution of Income* (New York: Academic Press, 1977). Their conclusion seems to hold true into the 1980s.

[56]See, for example, Charles Murray, *Losing Ground: America's Social Policy, 1950–1980* (New York: Basic Books, 1984).

poorer-than-average jobs. In contrast, in manufacturing and construction the distributions are more heavily weighted toward medium and above-average income jobs.[57]

Paradoxically, the process of economic development has given rise to the service economy, and the service economy has made new and difficult demands on the American economic system.

Summary

The United States has built the largest system of production in the world on the basis of an excellent endowment of natural resources and a labor force dedicated to the philosophy of individualism. The plurality of the workers remained in agriculture until the twentieth century and then, after a brief period of industrial dominance, moved rapidly into services. The growth of the service sector contributed to a growth in self-employment and weakened the role of the labor unions. It may have retarded the overall rate of economic growth (although this is debatable) and exacerbated the problem of price inflation, but it apparently stabilized the growth of employment and output.

A relatively competitive system gave way to rising industrial concentration after the Civil War, leading to the adoption of antitrust legislation around the turn of the century at a time when merger and concentration were encouraged in other countries. Partly for this reason, the United States has an average or relatively low level of industrial concentration (by international standards), and the level of concentration has been fairly stable during the twentieth century.

In the labor market, trade unions play a relatively limited role (in comparison to their role in other industrial countries) and their share of the labor force has declined. Relative competitiveness of the U.S. labor market is also suggested by the record of employment and wage flexibility.

In the financial sector, American federalism led to the creation of a dual system of state and national banks and a unique central banking system with elements of local ownership and control. Likewise, the focus of governmental authority was maintained at the state and local levels until the Great Depression and World War II. Governmental regulation of the economy expanded through most of the twentieth century, but a trend toward deregulation has received bipartisan support in recent years.

Active use of monetary and fiscal management methods have been employed, but a formal system of indicative planning and industrial policy has never been established. Despite the influence of the progressive national income tax and the growing program of transfer payments, the distribution of income has been remarkably stable.

[57]Thomas M. Stanback, Jr., et al., *Services: The New Economy,* 71.

Discussion and Review Questions

1.   How can we explain the fact that employment is more stable in the service sector than in the industrial sector?

2.   How does American policy toward industrial concentration differ from European policy? What are the costs and benefits of concentration?

3.   How can we explain the trends in the wage differential between union and nonunion labor? How can we explain the fact that the wage share of national income has been relatively stable while the power of the unions has increased and decreased?

4.   How has American federalism influenced the system of financial regulation?

5.   How can we explain the fact that the American distribution of income has remained relatively stable, despite the progressive income tax system and the growth of governmental transfer payments?

Suggested Readings

Brozen, Yale. *Concentration, Mergers, and Public Policy.* New York: Macmillan, 1982. *A review of American industrial organization by a defender of concentration. Compare to Shepherd, below.*

Economic Report of the President. Washington, D.C.: USGPO, annual. *Includes an annual review of macroeconomic policy and a wealth of statistical material.*

Feldstein, Martin, ed. *The American Economy in Transition.* Chicago: University of Chicago Press, 1980. *Published to mark the 60th anniversary of the National Bureau of Economic Research, this volume includes excellent surveys on everything from demography and technology to macroeconomic policy and industrial structure.*

Hession, Charles H. and Hyman Sardy. *Ascent to Affluence.* Boston: Allyn and Bacon, 1969. *An excellent introduction to American economic history.*

Murray, Charles. *Losing Ground: America's Social Policy, 1950–1980.* New York: Basic Books, 1984. *Proposes to scrap the entire federal welfare and income support structure for working-age persons—purportedly to "save the poor." Compare to Schorr, below.*

Papers and Proceedings of the meetings of the American Economic Association, *The American Economic Review,* May issues, annual. *The record of the annual convocation of the nation's largest economics association, these volumes include accessible essays (quite unlike the technical reports that are found in the other issues of this journal) on a broad range of issues concerning the American economy.*

Pechman, Joseph A. *Who Paid the Taxes, 1966–85?* Washington, D.C.: The Brookings Institution, 1985. *A brief statistical review of trends in the American income distribution.*

Schorr, Alvin L. *Common Decency: Domestic Policies After Reagan.* New Haven: Yale University Press, 1986. *Calls for a renewed emphasis on income redistribution, full employment, racial integration, national health insurance, and a range of other social issues. Compare to Murray, above.*

Shepherd, William G. *The Economics of Industrial Organization.* 2d ed. Englewood Cliffs, N.J.: Prentice-Hall, Inc., 1985. *Generally opposes industrial concentration and supports antitrust action. Compare to Brozen, above.*

Stanback, Thomas M., Jr., et al. *Services: The New Economy.* Totowa, N.J.: Allanheld, Osmun, & Co., 1981. *Reports on several studies relating to the operation and productivity of the service sector.*

Thurow, Lester C. *The Zero-Sum Solution: Building A World-Class Economy.* New York: Simon and Schuster, 1985. *In this, a sequel to his* Zero-Sum Society, *Thurow argues that "the huge technological edge enjoyed by Americans in the 1950s and 1960s has disappeared" (p. 47), and a positive industrial policy is needed to reverse the trend.*

Tocqueville, Alexis. *Democracy in America.* New York: Harper, 1966. *A penetrating analysis of the roots of American individualism, based on his visit in the 1830s. See the opening quotation for this chapter.*

Shetland Islands

Lewis

*North
Sea*

*Atlantic
Ocean*

Skye

Scotland

Glasgow

Edinburgh

Londonderry

Belfast

**N.
Ireland**

Isle of Man

Ireland

Leeds

Liverpool

Sheffield

England

Wales

•Birmingham

• Cardiff

London •

Channel
Islands

France

Great Britain

5

THE BRITISH ECONOMY: DECLINING CAPITALISM

Men of England, Heirs of Glory, Heroes of unwritten story, Nurslings of one mighty mother, Hope of her, and one another,
Rise, like lions after slumber, In unvanquished number, Shake your chains to earth like dew, Which in sleep had fall'n on you.
—Percy Bysshe Shelley
   The Masque of Anarchy, 1819

Great Britain was the undisputed superpower of the nineteenth century.[1] Wellington's victory over Napoleon in 1815 silenced any doubts concerning British military superiority that may have been raised during the American Revolution. In the years that followed, Brittania ruled the waves and established an empire on which the sun never set. By the end of the century, Britain controlled over one-fifth of the world's land surface and ruled one-quarter of the world's population.

More importantly for our purposes, British military power during the nineteenth century was only a reflection of her economic power. England was the birthplace of the Industrial Revolution, the so-called workshop of the world. In 1870, the British had the highest per capita income on earth (Table A.4). With only 2 percent of the world's population, they accounted for 32 percent of the world's industrial production and 25 percent of world trade.[2] London was the dominant commercial and financial center of the world economy, and the pound sterling was the key currency in the international monetary system.

Today, however, all that has changed. Seventeen countries, including three that were formerly part of the British Empire—the United States, Canada, and Australia—have per capita incomes that are higher than the British.[3] The British share of world industrial production has fallen from 32 percent in 1870 to about 3 percent in 1986. In recent years, the United Kingdom has experienced simultaneously a higher rate of inflation, a higher rate of unemployment, and a slower rate of economic growth than the average for other industrial market economies (Table 5.1). The relative position of Britain in the world economy declined more dramatically in the last century than that of any other country.

Table 5.1   Relative Performance of the British Economy, 1971–1985

	United Kingdom	All Industrial Capitalist Countries*
Average Annual Growth of GNP Per Capita	1.9%	2.9%
Average Annual Rate of Inflation	11.4	8.3
Average Annual Unemployment	7.1	5.6

*Members of the Organization for Economic Cooperation and Development (OECD).

Sources: *OECD Economic Outlook* 40 (December 1986), Tables R1, R10, and R12.

[1]Great Britain was formed in 1707 by a union of England, Wales, and Scotland. The United Kingdom was formed in 1801 by the union of Great Britain and Ireland. The Irish Free State withdrew from the United Kingdom in 1922, but Northern Ireland was retained.

[2]W. W. Rostow, *The World Economy: History and Prospect* (Austin: University of Texas Press, 1978), 52, 70.

[3]World Bank, *World Development Report 1986* (New York: Oxford University Press, 1986), 181.

Reasons for Decline: An Overview

What went wrong? Why did British dominance come to an end? That question has been debated for years by scores of social scientists in and out of England. Most of their explanations revolve around the British failure to maintain a technological lead after initiating industrialization.

Although the British quickly adopted the first generation of technologies in the textile, iron, and steel industries, they were slow to install the second generation of technologies. In 1870, the average open-hearth furnace in the British steel industry was roughly the same size as a furnace in Germany. Twenty years later, the German furnaces were 50 percent larger and total production was 65 percent greater. The method of continuous rolling of steel was invented in England in the 1860s, but it was first employed on a large scale in the United States in the 1890s.

The British were not only slow to adopt new techniques in the old staple industries (iron, coal, steel, and textiles), but they were slow to develop capacities to produce electricity, chemicals, and automobiles—the new industries of the early twentieth century. Thus, understanding the British decline requires understanding why the British failed to maintain technological leadership. This is a question that has been widely debated in recent years; it is particularly interesting now when many claim that the United States is losing its technological and competitive edge.

Disadvantages of a Head Start

It may seem that Britain, the first country to pass through the Industrial Revolution, should have been able to establish and maintain a technological advantage over her competitors. On the other hand, since England was the first country to build a network of large, capital-intensive industries, it was also the first country to be saddled with a large, outdated capital stock. According to one interpretation, the small, owner-managed companies that launched British industrialization created a vested interest against a modern system of corporate capitalism.[4]

The latecomers to industrialization were able to learn from the British experience. They had the advantage of starting afresh with the newest technologies in the most progressive industries. They could sell their products on a growing British market that was free from import barriers. They also benefited from huge infusions of British capital investment. In 1913, over 80 percent of the issues in the London capital market were directed toward investment overseas: "No country, before or since, has invested as high a proportion of its resources abroad over such a sustained period."[5]

[4]Bernard Elbaum and William Lazonick, "An Institutional Perspective on British Decline," in *The Decline of the British Economy,* ed. Bernard Elbaum and William Lazonick (Oxford: Clarendon Press, 1986), 1–17.

[5]M. W. Kirby, *The Decline of British Economic Power Since 1870* (London: George Allen and Unwin, 1981), 14.

Governmental Policy and Relative Decline

Analysts of all persuasions tend to lay a considerable amount of blame on the British government, but they disagree on the policies that should have been pursued. One view suggests that the government should have conducted a much more active industrial policy to promote the adoption of advanced technologies and the production of advanced industrial goods. Proponents of this view claim that an active governmental role was played in all of England's major competitors—in France, Germany, Russia, Japan, and the United States— while England held to a policy of laissez faire. Hence, Britain was the only industrial country in which the government neither built nor financed any part of the railway system. The average German tariff on British industrial products was 25 percent in 1904 and the average American tariff was 73 percent, but no tariff was charged on manufactured goods entering Britain.

Cut off from the fast-growing markets enjoyed by their competitors, British manufacturers didn't stand a chance. . . . The [Great Depression] was the culmination of a bitter competitive struggle [of] British laissez faire *against the continental weapon of state-protected, bank-financed industrialization.* Laissez faire *lost.*[6]

According to another viewpoint, the British government has routinely sacrificed its domestic policy goals to its foreign policy.[7] Unwilling to accept the declining role of the pound sterling in the world economy, the British government made a fetish of defending its international value. This prompted a destabilizing "stop-go" pattern of fiscal and monetary policy. Furthermore, the British have devoted a larger proportion of their GNP to military production than any other Western country, aside from the United States (Table A.20).

Finally, supply-side economists blame the British government for creating a poor system of investment and work incentives. Until the Thatcher administration adjusted the tax system in 1979–1980, the United Kingdom had the highest marginal tax rates in the capitalist world, except for the welfare states of northern Europe (Table A.22). To a strict supply-side economist, this alone is sufficient to explain the slow growth of labor productivity that has stunted the British economy.

Sociological Reasons for Decline

Another group of observers would hold responsible British society at large, rather than the government alone, for the relative decline of the economy. The Industrial Revolution, they argue, was created by the entrepreneurial spirit of the lower-middle classes. By the final quarter of the nineteenth century, however, the symptoms of third-generation decline began to appear: "a growing antipathy towards the conduct of their businesses which manifested itself in an increasing proclivity to squander the hard-won wealth of their

[6]John Eatwell, *Whatever Happened To Britain?* (New York: Oxford University Press, 1982), 66–67.

[7]Andrew Shonfield, *British Economic Policy since the War* (Middlesex: Penguin, 1958).

IF THINGS ARE SO BAD, WHY DO THEY FEEL SO GOOD?

In 1981, in its World Values Survey, the Gallup organization asked residents of several countries to rate their level of happiness on a scale of 1 ("not at all happy") to 4 ("very happy"). If we list these countries in descending order of their reported happiness (according to their average score on the 4-point scale) and include each of their income levels (GNP per capita in U.S. dollars) and "misery indexes" for 1981 (the sum of the unemployment and inflation rates), we obtain the following:

	Happiness	Income	Misery
Britain	3.33	$ 9,000	21.7%
Netherlands	3.30	10,103	14.2
United States	3.26	12,759	17.9
Belgium	3.25	10,441	18.4
Sweden	3.24	10,831	14.6
Norway	3.21	12,397	15.7
France	3.09	10,688	20.8
Finland	3.03	9,842	17.1
Spain	2.98	6,929	28.5
Germany	2.96	11,037	10.7
Japan	2.96	9,163	7.1
Italy	2.84	8,615	26.1
Average	3.12	10,150	17.7

The relative happiness of the Netherlands, with its low level of misery, and the United States, with its high level of income, are easy enough to explain. Likewise, Italy and Spain seem to be justified in their unhappiness. But why do the British, with their low incomes and their high misery index, claim to be among the happiest people in the world? Does this simply say that money cannot buy mirth? Perhaps, but Gallup researchers suggest another interpretation. The "stiff upper lip" aspect of the British culture may not allow them to admit their problems.

Sources: Ronald Inglehart and Jaques-Rene Rabier, "If You're Unhappy, This Must Be Belgium," *Public Opinion* 8 (April–May 1985), 10–15; OECD, *Purchasing Power Parities and Real Expenditures in the OECD* (Paris, 1985), 94; and *OECD Economic Outlook* 40 (December 1986), Tables R10 and R12.

forebears in ostentatious and extravagant living."[8] In the lower ranks of society, labor productivity was stifled by an antiquated and militant trade-union establishment. Simply put, according to one Labour party official, "For generations this country has not earned an honest living."[9]

An elitist educational system was established to serve the upper classes and the humanities were stressed in the curriculum to the exclusion of the natural sciences, engineering, and business. According to a 1977 study by the British Department of Industry, "Attitudes toward industry . . . are less favorable in Britain than in other major industrialized countries, and are reflected in our educational system."[10]

To this day, very few British universities offer a business degree. Only 20 percent of the college-aged population is engaged in any form of higher education (compared to 26 percent in France, 30 percent in West Germany and Japan, and 56 percent in the United States).[11] Lured away by higher pay, better research facilities, and more progressive attitudes, many of Britain's best and brightest have left the country for greener pastures. According to the National Science Foundation, British scientists and engineers are moving to America at a rate of about 1,000 per year—a greater "brain drain" than the total for other European countries.[12]

According to another sociological perspective, the entire notion of British decline is a statistical artifact. Walter Neale, for one, believes that the British have willingly sacrificed economic growth to form a decent society—"a society which puts more emphasis on kindliness than on efficiency, more emphasis on considerateness than on productivity—a society that puts more emphasis on the pleasant enjoyment of the even tenor of one's way than rapidly increasing material wealth."[13] In other words, the British may have experienced an improvement in social welfare that is not reflected in the standard growth statistics. Nonetheless, it should be noted that an international survey taken in the early 1960s found that only 10 percent of the British people were proud of their economic system, compared to 23 percent of the Americans and 33 percent of the West Germans.[14]

Industrial Organization

The British traditionally have displayed a rather permissive attitude toward industrial concentration and monopoly. Restrictive arrangements among firms

---

[8]Kirby, *The Decline,* 9.

[9]Ray Gunter, Minister of Labor, 1964–1968, quoted in Andrew Gamble, *Britain in Decline* (Boston: Beacon Press, 1981), 23.

[10]Quoted in *The Managed Economy,* ed. Charles Feinstein (Oxford: Oxford University Press, 1983), 224.

[11]World Bank, *World Development Report 1986,* 237.

[12]"Britain's Brains Go Down the Drain," *The Economist* 302 (March 28, 1987): 59.

[13]Walter C. Neale, *The British Economy: Toward a Decent Society* (Columbus: Grid Publishing, 1980), 209.

[14]Gabriel Almond and Sidney Verba, *The Civic Culture: Political Attitudes and Democracy in Five Nations* (Princeton: Princeton University Press, 1963), 102.

to set prices and divide markets have been illegal in the United States since the passage of the Sherman Act of 1890. Legislation of this kind did not appear in Britain until 1948, when the Monopolies Commission was established, and no specific list of monopolistic practices was prohibited by law until 1956. Even then, a price-fixing agreement could be approved by a special Restrictive Practices Court if it reduced unemployment, promoted exports, or had some other beneficial effect.

Although the government has placed some controls on monopolistic practices and mergers in recent years, it has also played an active role in the rationalization of certain industries—that is, the government has sometimes *encouraged* the merger of small enterprises into larger ones in order to increase their strength, efficiency, and international competitiveness. In 1966 the Labour government established an Industrial Reconstruction Corporation (IRC) to support and finance these merger schemes. The IRC was dissolved by the Conservative government in 1971, not because the Conservatives opposed rationalization, but because they did not feel that it should be directed by the government. The dissolution of the IRC was followed by a record number of mergers in 1972 and 1973.

How have these governmental policies influenced the British industrial structure? In a study of the largest firms in 41 European industries, it was found that the average British firm was 2.2 times as large as its German counterpart and 3.5 times as large as the leading French firms. The authors of the study attribute the difference to laws that permit mergers in Britain, where the Continental countries are more tolerant of cartel agreements and other forms of collusion among firms.[15] Likewise, another study found that the average British manufacturing establishment was larger (in terms of employment) than in any other Western nation.[16]

The Labor Market and Labor Relations

By almost any measure, the performance of the British labor market has deteriorated seriously in recent years. After hovering in the 2–3 percent range during 1950–1970, the unemployment rate climbed to 13 percent in 1985 (Table A.12). According to a recent econometric study, about 3 percentage points of that increase can be attributed to the growth of social security and employment protection, which reduces the willingness of employers to fill vacancies with permanent employees.[17] Hence, the employment manager for Tetley Tea reports that he never keeps temporary workers on the payroll for more than 12 weeks: "After that," he says, "they start to get certain rights."[18]

---

[15]Kenneth G. George and T. S. Ward, *The Structure of Industry in the EEC* (Cambridge: Cambridge University Press, 1975), 23–26.

[16]Frederic L. Pryor, *Property and Industrial Organization in Communist and Capitalist Nations* (Bloomington, Ind.: Indiana University Press, 1973), 157.

[17]Richard Layard and Stephen Nickell, "Unemployment in Britain," *Economica* (Supplement) 53 (1986): 121–169.

[18]Barry Newman, "High Unemployment Wreaks Vast Changes on Life in Britain," *Wall Street Journal,* November 10, 1986, 10.

Labor Unions

According to the same econometric study, another 3 percentage points of the increase in unemployment can be attributed to the rising level of conflict between labor and management. From 1955 to 1970 and 1971 to 1982, the annual average number of workdays lost to labor unrest more than doubled, giving Britain one of the worst strike rates in the industrial world (Table A.11). Although there is plenty of blame to divide between labor and management, one cause of the British malaise seems to be its antiquated trade-union structure.

British labor unions differ from their American counterparts in a number of important ways. First, they involve a much larger proportion of the labor force. With about half of the workers organized, the British fall in the mid-range of industrialized countries in terms of numerical union strength (Table A.11).

Second, British unions play an unusually important role in the national political system through their strong affiliation with the Labor Party. The unions provide 90 percent of the party's funds and control four-fifths of the votes at the party's annual conferences. James Callaghan (prime minister from 1976 to 1979) and two-thirds of his cabinet were former union officials.

Third, in comparison to the relatively conservative stance of American labor leaders, British labor has a strong socialist tradition. The unions are strong supporters of nationalization of industry and economic planning. Arthur Scargill, the Marxist leader of the National Union of Mineworkers, still speaks of "class war" and "toppling the ruling class."

Fourth, all of the major unions in England are members of a single confederation, the Trades Union Congress (TUC). The closest thing to this confederation in the United States, the AFL-CIO, does not include the United Automobile Workers, the United Mine Workers, or the Teamsters. Given its size, the TUC is able to play an important political role and an important role in mediating labor disputes. However, unlike the labor confederations in some countries (notably Sweden), the TUC does not participate directly in collective bargaining.

Fifth, with the exception of the National Union of Mineworkers, British unions are not organized according to industry. Instead, the unions that represent unskilled and semiskilled workers attempt to recruit workers from all industries. As a result, workers in a given company who have very similar jobs may be represented by several different unions. One automobile plant, for example, employs members from 22 different unions, and a 1968 study of several companies found an average of 7.4 unions represented per plant.[19]

Finally, the union organizations at the company level are allowed to act quite independently of their national leadership. Ordinarily, each of the national unions in each company has one or more shop stewards who conduct plant-level negotiations with management. Although they serve as agents of the national unions, the shop stewards have primarily represented the interests

---

[19]Thomas Kennedy, *European Labor Relations* (Lexington, Mass.: Lexington Books, 1980), 3.

of their own work groups. They are allowed, even encouraged, by the leaders of their national unions to call unofficial wildcat strikes to support their demands.

Thus, it is very difficult to organize industrywide, or even companywide, collective bargaining in the United Kingdom. A single employer must deal with the shop stewards of several different unions. In some cases, committees of shop stewards have been established to represent all of the workers in a firm or an industry, but any agreement that they reach with management must still be approved by the individual unions. Hence, wage negotiations are often long and complex and are interrupted too often by demonstrations and strikes.

Labor Legislation and Union Growth

Until the nineteenth century, the formation of labor unions was tightly restricted by British law. As Adam Smith said in 1776, "We have no acts of parliament against combining to lower the price of work; but many against combining to raise it."[20] In 1799, the home secretary warned that if labor unions were allowed to exist, they could become "a most dangerous instrument to disturb the public tranquility."[21]

In 1825, a more liberal parliament gave labor the freedom to organize and unions began to form in the cotton factories around Manchester. The new unions were given the right to picket in 1871 and a 1906 law gave them legal immunity for acts performed by their members while picketing. Encouraged by these and other new freedoms, the unions expanded their membership from 13 percent of the labor force in 1906 to 45 percent in 1920.

Between 1920 and 1970, the forces that influenced British union growth seem to have been very similar to those that influenced American growth (Figure 5.1). Statistical analysis by Bain and Elsheikh suggests that union growth in both countries is affected by the inflation rate, the unemployment rate, and the rate of change of money wages.[22] Inflation encourages union growth because it strengthens the need for an institution that can bargain for wage increases. Unemployment discourages union growth because the unemployed are likely to drop their union membership and those who manage to keep their jobs are not as likely to demand wage increases. Wage increases seem to encourage union growth, perhaps because they demonstrate the benefits of union membership.

After 1970, the close correlation between American and British union growth breaks down. As we have seen, the shift to a service economy in the United States caused union membership to continue its downward slide throughout the 1970s. On the other hand, union membership grew rapidly in

[20]Adam Smith, *An Inquiry into the Nature and Causes of the Wealth of Nations* (Oxford: Clarendon Press, 1976), 84.

[21]Albert Tucker, *A History of English Civilization* (New York: Harper and Row, 1972), 563.

[22]George S. Bain and Farouk Elsheikh, *Union Growth and the Business Cycle: An Econometric Analysis* (Oxford: Basil Blackwell, 1976); and Farouk Elsheikh and George S. Bain, "American Trade Union Growth: An Alternative Model," *Industrial Relations* 17 (February 1978): 75–79.

Figure 5.1   U.S. and U.K.: Trade Union Membership As a Percentage of Civilian Labor Force, 1900–1986

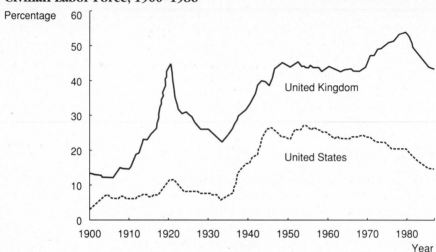

Sources: George Sayers Bain and Robert Price, *Profiles of Union Growth* (Oxford: Basil Blackwell, 1980), Tables 2.1 and 3.1. U.S. Department of Labor, Bureau of Labor Statistics, *Directory of National Unions and Employer Associations, 1979* (Washington, D.C., 1980), Table 6.
U.S Department of Labor, Bureau of Labor Statistics, *Employment and Earnings* (January issues).
Department of Employment, *British Labour Statistics Year Book, 1975* (London: HMSO, 1977), p. 304.
Department of Employment, *Employment Gazette* (January issues).

the United Kingdom during that decade, despite the fact that the British, too, were shifting toward the production of services. One explanation for the rise in British unionism may be the high British inflation rate (about 14 percent annually during the 1970s, compared to 7 percent in the United States), which may have increased the demand for union services.[23]

The policies of Margaret Thatcher's administration have caused a rapid reduction in union membership in more recent years. Her tight monetary policy resulted in the highest unemployment rate since the 1930s and a low inflation rate, both of which discourage union growth. In addition, she has taken a hard line in her dealings with labor unions. A legislative initiative during 1980–1984 introduced the following major changes in labor relations law:

- Secret-ballot elections, requiring an 80 percent majority vote, were introduced to approve or confirm closed shops.
- Industrial action (such as strikes) must now be approved in advance by a secret ballot of members.
- Legal immunities were removed from the unions for damages caused during unlawful industrial actions.
- Executive committees of unions must be elected (or reelected) by secret ballot at least every 5 years.

[23]David C. Smith, "Trade Union Growth and Industrial Disputes," in *Britain's Economic Performance,* ed. Richard E. Caves and Lawrence B. Krause (Washington, D.C.: The Brookings Institution, 1980), 83–107.

The new regulations, coupled with the high rate of unemployment, have noticeably influenced the balance of power between labor and management. In 1984 and 1985, when union executives in the automotive and railway industries attempted to call strikes, the workers rejected that advice by secret ballot. Despite the long and violent coal miners' strike of 1984–1985, Thatcher persisted in her plan to close unprofitable mines. The unions must be pacified, she said, in order to "banish from our land the dark, divisive clouds of Marxist socialism."[24]

The Financial Sector

Although it no longer occupies the dominant position it enjoyed in the nineteenth century, London is still among the most important financial centers in the world. In an area of one square mile, the City of London contains over 400 foreign banks, 200 stockbroking firms, and a range of other financial services. It is the world's most important center for international lending, insurance, shipping contracts, and trading of gold bullion, Eurocurrencies, and Eurobonds. Its stock exchange is the world's third largest (behind the United States and Japan) and is nearly as large as the rest of Europe's combined.[25]

As is true in the United States, all British commercial banks are privately owned. Banking is dominated by the "big four": Barclays, National Westminster, Midland, and Lloyds. All together, they account for about 75 percent of all domestic deposits. Thus, the banking industry is far more concentrated in the United Kingdom than in the United States (where the ten largest banks account for only 16 percent of deposits).

The Bank of England and Financial Regulation

Founded in 1694 to finance a war with France, the Bank of England is the world's second oldest central bank (Sweden's Riksbank was established in 1668). The bank was nationalized in 1946 and is still the only state-owned bank in the United Kingdom. Its governors and directors are all nominated by the Prime Minister and appointed by the Queen.

The Chancellor of the Exchequer has the power to issue directions to the bank, after consultation with the governor. Thus, the bank is not allowed to operate quite as independently as the U.S. Federal Reserve. This fact may help explain the chronically high inflation rate in Britain since World War II.

The responsibilities of the bank are essentially the same as those of the Federal Reserve system in the United States. It exercises control of the money supply, performs banking services for the government, regulates the banking system, and acts as a lender of last resort. Monetary control is implemented through open-market operations and through changes in the bank's minimum

---

[24]*Wall Street Journal,* June 2, 1983, 22.

[25]*The Economist,* July 14, 1984, supplement, 4; *Wall Street Journal,* December 6, 1983, 20; and L. J. Kemp, *A Guide to World Money and Capital Markets* (London: McGraw-Hill Book Company (UK) Limited, 1981), 333–335, 379.

lending rate, the minimum rate of interest at which the bank will lend to discount houses, which in turn lend money to the banking system.

Regulation of the British banking system traditionally has been very permissive. The first banking act, introduced in 1979, established the qualifications necessary for an institution to be designated as a recognized bank or a less auspicious licensed deposit taker. The Bank of England was initially given the authority to inspect the licensed deposit takers, and in 1985, after the failure of Johnson Matthey Bankers with more than $260 million in bad loans, the central bank was also given the power to inspect the fully recognized banks.

For centuries, British stockbrokers, insurers, and other financial groups have been allowed to police themselves through their own trade groups. Until very recently, for example, the United Kingdom had no counterpart to the U.S. Securities and Exchange Commission (established in 1934). In 1985, however, after a number of securities scandals, the Secretary of Trade and Industry called for a radical reform of existing law to protect the public against fraud, negligence, and monopolistic practices.

The first and most radical reform was introduced in October 1986, when the so-called "Big Bang" shook the London Stock Exchange. Trading in stocks and government bonds, previously the exclusive domain of 19 British firms, was opened to foreign competition. Barriers that protected brokers from other kinds of financial firms were removed. Fixed commissions, which had been established by collusive arrangements for 85 years, were abolished. In the new competitive environment, commissions fell by 53 percent in the first 4 months.[26]

A new Securities and Investments Board (SIB) was established to regulate stock and commodity traders, and the Marketing of Investments Board (MIB) was established to oversee life insurance companies and mutual funds. Unlike the powerful Securities and Exchange Commission in the United States, the SIB has very limited judicial powers, a small enforcement division, little direct access to corporate information, and is financed by the industry it is supposed to regulate. In effect, the SIB is expected to do little more than oversee the work of self-regulatory organizations within the financial community.[27]

The Governmental Sector

By all accounts, the role of the government in the British economy was relatively small before World War II. Great Britain embraced the writings of Adam Smith in the eighteenth century and a policy of free trade in the nineteenth. Some observers believe that England's present problems are a legacy of past governmental inactivity. The British were slow to impose regulations on mon-

---

[26]Gary Putka and Matthew Winkler, "Gloom Prevails 110 Days After Big Bang," *Wall Street Journal,* February 18, 1987, 28.
[27]Gary Putka, "London's Exchange Braces for Big Bang Set to Occur Monday," *Wall Street Journal,* October 24, 1986, 18.

opolies, banks, and other financial institutions. Very few industries were nationalized before the war, and according to the data presented in Table A.18,
the British government purchased a smaller percentage of the nation's GNP in
1870 and 1938 than the average for other nations.

During World War II, the governments of many countries were given
emergency powers and England was no exception. The airlines were nationalized in 1939 by a Conservative government, food and clothing were rationed, prices were controlled, and men were conscripted into the service—
all contributing to the notion that individual freedom could be subordinated
to the national welfare.

In 1941, as the war raged on, the Beveridge Committee was formed by
Parliament to formulate recommendations for a system of social services to
heal British society at the end of the war. Their report called for a national
system of health and unemployment insurance, family allowances, old-age
pensions, and funeral benefits—that is, it called for the establishment of a
comprehensive welfare state. This sounded quite promising to a generation of
Britons who feared that the end of the war could mean a return to the Depression. When the war ended in 1945, Winston Churchill shrugged the Beveridge
Report aside as little more than "a cloud of pledges and promises," and his
Conservatives were soundly defeated by the Labour Party under Clement
Attlee.

The Attlee government (1945-1951) moved quickly to implement the
most important provisions of the Beveridge Report, establish the National
Health Service, and nationalize the "commanding heights" of the economy—
the Bank of England; the steel, coal, electricity, and gas industries; the railroads,
trucking, and civil aviation.[28] Nondefense governmental expenditures jumped
from 6 percent of GNP in 1946 to 15 percent in 1951.[29] Furthermore, the
wartime systems of wage and price controls and rationing were phased out
very slowly. Altogether, the government began to play an unprecedented role
in the British economy.

More significantly, a succession of Conservative governments between
1951 and 1964 did not dismantle the essential elements of the welfare state.
The National Health Service was preserved and nondefense governmental
expenditures declined only slightly as a percentage of GNP—to 14 percent in
1965.[30] Of the industries that were nationalized by Labour, only steel and
trucking were returned to private ownership by the Conservatives. Further-

[28]The notion that a socialist government can exercise sufficient control over the economy by
nationalizing only the commanding heights of industry was introduced by V. I. Lenin during
the 1920s to explain his decision to return several industries to private ownership during his
New Economic Policy. The commanding heights doctrine is also an important part of the
current Chinese reforms.

[29]B. R. Mitchell and H. G. Jones, *Second Abstract of British Historical Statistics* (Cambridge:
Cambridge University Press, 1971), 151, 161.

[30]Governmental outlays on social services actually increased during this period, from 13 per-
cent of GNP in 1950 to 17 percent in 1965. See William G. Shepherd, "Alternatives for Public
Expenditure," in *Britain's Economic Prospects,* ed. Richard E. Caves (Washington, D.C.: The
Brookings Institution, 1968), 383.

more, it was the Conservative government that set up a limited program of national economic planning in 1961.

Much of this has changed, of course, since Margaret Thatcher's Conservative administration entered office in 1979. Many of the nationalized industries have been privatized, and a plan to replace state pensions with private programs has been proposed. On the other hand, there are no plans to dismantle the National Health Service and many welfare-state programs have escaped the budget ax. Unemployment benefits can be collected for an unlimited period of time and families are still paid allowances for their children, regardless of family income.

Taken together, governmental transfer payments and subsidies have risen from 15 percent of GNP in 1979 to 17 percent in 1985. Clearly, the Thatcher administration has found it difficult to reverse the momentum of governmental growth. Although the Labour Party contends that Britain has abandoned the fundamental principles of a welfare state, social historian David Piachaud of the London School of Economics feels there has been "no major change in the basic principles that have underlain social policy since World War II."[31]

The Nationalized Industries

A list of the principal British nationalized industries is presented in Table 5.2. As the data show, the companies were nationalized over a long span of years and in a fairly wide range of industries. Why were these particular companies nationalized? We can isolate several different motivations that help to explain the pattern of nationalization.

First, there is the ideological motive. Many of the industries were nationalized at the end of World War II by a socialist Labour government that wished to exercise greater control over the economy and reduce the level of capitalist exploitation. Thus, they chose the Bank of England and the commanding heights of industry as takeover targets and established the National Health Service as the centerpiece of their social welfare program.

Second, a number of industries have been nationalized for purposes of national security. This was the case when the post office, the petroleum industry (at the beginning of World War I), and the airlines (at the beginning of World War II) were acquired. Interestingly, in a number of ancient despotic societies the postmaster general was simultaneously the director of internal security.[32]

Third, many failing companies have been nationalized to maintain employment. In the 1970s, for example, when Rolls Royce and British Leyland were facing bankruptcy, they were taken over by the government to keep them alive with subsidies. In contrast, when the American government was faced with the imminent collapse of Chrysler Corporation in 1980, nationalization never was seriously considered. Instead, the company was left in private

[31]*Wall Street Journal,* June 4, 1985, 39.

[32]Pryor, *Property and Industrial Organization,* 40.

Table 5.2   Principal Nationalization and Privatization of British Enterprises

	Year Initially Nationalized	Privatized during 1979–1986	Proceeds of Privatization ($ million)
Communications			
Post Office	Before 1850	No	
British Telecom	Before 1900	Yes	5,600
Cable and Wireless	Before 1900	Yes	1,466
British Broadcasting	1927	No	
Transportation			
British Railways	1948	No	
British Waterways	1948	No	
British Airways	1939, 1946	Pending	1,500*
National Freight	1969	Yes	n.a.
Associated British Ports	1963	Yes	139
British Airports Authority	1966	Pending	715*
Energy			
Electricity Council	1948	No	
British Gas	1949	Pending	7,865*
National Coal Board	1947	No	
British Petroleum	1913	Yes	1,040
Britoil	1976	Yes	1,513
Enterprise Oil	n.a.	Yes	543
Other Industrial			
Royal Ordnance	Before 1800	Yes	305
British Steel	1951, 1967	Pending	
Rolls Royce	1971	Pending	715*
Jaguar Cars	1975	Yes	425
British Leyland	1975	Pending	
British Aerospace	1977	Yes	556
Amersham International	n.a.	Yes	92
Water Authorities	1983	Pending	7,150*
Financial			
Bank of England	1946	No	
Social			
National Health Service	1948	No	

*estimated

n.a.—not available

Sources: William G. Shepherd, *Public Enterprise: Economic Analysis of Theory and Practice* (Lexington, Mass.: Lexington Books, 1976), 106–107; Peter J. Curwen, *Public Enterprise: A Modern Approach* (Brighton: Wheatsheaf Books, 1986), 2–8; and *Wall Street Journal*, November 11, 1986, 36.

hands and bailed out with a package of governmental loan guarantees and union wage concessions.

Fourth, natural monopolies are often nationalized to prevent their abuse of market power. These primarily include the network industries—postal services, electricity, gas, and telephone—that are difficult to divide between several competitors. By contrast, the usual American practice has been to leave natural monopolies in private hands, but to regulate them heavily.

Fifth, economic theory suggests that a market economy will tend to allocate too few resources to industries that provide external benefits—benefits that are received by someone other than the buyer and seller of the product. A product such as health care provides direct benefits to those who receive treatment and indirect benefits to those who are spared from contracting infectious diseases. Therefore, an economic argument can be made in favor of subsidizing the health-care industry. In the British case, that subsidy is provided through the National Health Service. In the United States, the governmental subsidy is more limited and much of it is provided to doctors in the private sector through programs such as Medicare and Medicaid.

A final motive for nationalization in many countries—eliminating foreign ownership and control—has not played a prominent role in the United Kingdom. In countries such as the Soviet Union and Cuba, overthrow of foreign imperialism was one of the primary objectives of their socialist revolutions. More recently, reduction of foreign control was mentioned by President Mitterrand as one of his reasons for nationalizing several industrial groups in France.

Problems and Privatization

The performance of the nationalized industries has been a subject of debate in Britain throughout the postwar era. When a company is taken over by the government, it is inevitably transformed into a political creature. Interest groups of all kinds attempt to determine how the enterprise is run. There is an old saying in England: The private sector is the part of the economy that the government controls; and the public sector is the part that nobody controls.

Compounding the problem, there is no consensus on how one should judge the performance of the nationalized industries. The industries are often criticized, for example, because many of them fail to operate at a profit, requiring that they be subsidized by the government. This criterion may be less than fair, however; most of the industries were nationalized precisely in order to pursue some objective other than profit maximization. Until recently, the National Coal Board continued to operate a number of unprofitable mines in order to maintain employment. Likewise, British Airways flew several unprofitable routes to provide service to outlying communities. On a number of occasions, the industries have been required to play a leadership role in the government's fight against inflation by holding their prices steady in the face of rising labor costs.

All things considered, it is not surprising that many of the nationalized industries require governmental subsidies to fulfill their many objectives. Despite some evidence to the contrary, their accounting losses are nonetheless often ascribed to excessive union pressure and poor, bureaucratic management.[33]

[33]Richard Pryke, *Public Enterprise in Practice: The British Experience of Nationalization over Two Decades* (New York: St. Martin's Press, 1972); and J. A. Kay and D. J. Thompson, "Privatization: A Policy in Search of a Rationale," *The Economic Journal* 96 (March 1986): 18–32.

Accordingly, when Thatcher took office in 1979 she quickly set about the task of privatizing as many of the nationalized industries as possible. By the end of 1986, more than 25 companies were sold to private stockholders, raising about 7 billion pounds (roughly $10 billion) for the Treasury; another 12 billion pounds ($18 billion) were raised by local authorities through the sale of public housing.[34] Another $18 billion of assets are scheduled for sale over the next few years (Table 5.2). In addition, the government has signed contracts with private companies to provide a host of services, such as garbage collection, that were formerly handled by the government.

Those industries that have not been privatized are now being operated more commercially. In several cases, business executives have been appointed to their governing boards. The miners' strike of 1984–1985 was precipitated by a governmental decision to close 18 unprofitable coal mines employing some 20,000 workers.

Predictably, Thatcher's privatization program has drawn both praise and protest. Supporters of the program emphasize the gains to the Treasury from sale of company stock and elimination of subsidies. They point to several companies that have become profitable since they were placed in private hands. Finally, they claim that privatization has turned workers into capitalists. The National Freight Consortium, for example, was sold to its 12,000 workers; and over 90 percent of the employees of British Telecom bought stock in their company when it was sold. Another 750,000 families have purchased the houses that they previously rented from the government. All this, they say, has improved efficiency and given the public a greater pride of ownership.

Critics of privatization claim the government has "sold the family silver"—sometimes at cut-rate prices—to handle its budgetary problems. After holding their stock for one week, the traders who purchased companies such as Amersham International, British Telecom, and Associated British Ports were able to sell their shares on the open market for 35 to 98 percent more than they paid the government.[35]

Critics also point back to the original purposes of nationalization. Monopolies, such as British Telecom and British Airways, should not be allowed to exercise their market power. Firms that play a vital national security role, such as British Aerospace and Royal Ordnance factories, should be controlled by the government. Employment of coal miners and other workers should be maintained without strict adherence to profitability criteria. Nevertheless, as this is written, the privatization drive continues and has spread to Canada, Germany, Italy, Spain, and several other countries.

Macroeconomic Policy and Planning

Little needs to be said about economic planning in Great Britain because it has never played an important role. In 1961, impressed by the French record of

---

[34]*OECD Economic Outlook* 40 (December 1986): 16.

[35]Kay and Thompson, "Privatization: A Policy in Search of a Rationale," 28.

Table 5.3   The Stop-Go Cycle in the United Kingdom, 1955–1984

Balance of Payments Problems in:	Followed by Fiscal Tightening in:	Followed by Rising Unemployment in:	Followed by Fiscal Stimulus in:
1955	1955	1956–1959	1959–1960
1960	1961–1962	1962–1963	1963
1964–1965	1966	1966–1972	1972
1973–1976	1977	1977	1978
1979	1979	1980–1983	1983
1984	1984–1985	1984–1985	1986

Notes: Balance of payments is measured by current account in U.S. dollars. Fiscal stimulus or tightening is indicated by changes in the central government budget balance as a percentage of GDP. Based on the author's calculations from OECD data.

rapid economic growth, the Conservative government in England attempted to invigorate the economy by adopting a system of indicative planning. The task of formulating plans was turned over to the newly formed National Economic Development Council (NEDC), consisting of representatives from industry, labor, and the government. Unfortunately, the NEDC was given no effective levers of control over the economy to encourage the fulfillment of its plans. The Treasury, which has enough difficulty controlling the government's budget and the balance of payments, has paid little attention to the plans. Several other attempts have been made to use economic planning in England, but none have been successful.

Ironically, the home of John Maynard Keynes also has a poor reputation for its handling of fiscal and monetary policy. According to a classic study of seven industrialized countries in the years 1955 to 1965, the United Kingdom was the only country whose government actually destabilized the economy through its use of fiscal policy.[36] Since that time, England has been plagued continually by macroeconomic instability.

The problem seems to lie in the British penchant for a **stop-go** style of policy implementation. This, in turn, is caused by the conflict between labor's demand for full employment and the financial community's demand for a strong balance of payments. When the unemployment rate rises, the government usually switches to an overly expansionary macroeconomic policy. This reduces the unemployment rate, but it also increases the inflation rate, stimulates the demand for imported goods, and often leads to a balance-of-payments crisis. To deal with this problem, the government switches to the stop phase of contractionary fiscal and monetary policies. The unemployment rate rises and the cycle repeats itself. This process can be found in many countries, but

[36]Bent Hansen, *Fiscal Policy in Seven Countries 1955–1965* (Paris: Organization for Economic Cooperation and Development, 1969), 69–71. For a critique of the Hansen study, and a slightly less negative appraisal of British fiscal policy, see John Bispham and Andrea Boltho, "Demand Management," in *The European Economy,* ed. Andrea Boltho (Oxford: Oxford University Press, 1982), 306–308.

it is reinforced in the United Kingdom by the unique balance of power between the labor and financial communities.

The British "stop-go" cycle is illustrated by Table 5.3. On average, there has been a 5-year cycle from the end of one balance-of-payments crisis to the beginning of the next one. In each case, the crisis has led to fiscal contraction, followed by rising unemployment, fiscal stimulus, and another balance of payments crisis.

Thatcher's Monetarism

When Margaret Thatcher entered office in 1979, the unemployment rate stood at 5.7 percent, the lowest level in 3 years, but the inflation rate was running at 13.4 percent, five points higher than in the previous year. Control of inflation, therefore, was chosen as the first priority of macroeconomic policy. According to the monetarist philosophy of the Thatcher administration, control of inflation is *the* legitimate objective of macroeconomic policy: economic growth and employment will revive if the government allows the spontaneous forces of the market to operate.

Accordingly, the administration implemented a range of monetarist policies in 1979, and in 1980 they were formalized in a 4-year program entitled the Medium-Term Financial Strategy. First and foremost, the growth rate of the broad money supply (sterling M3) was reduced from 13.3 percent in 1979 to 9.7 percent in 1984. The purpose here, of course, was to reduce the inflation rate.

Second, in an effort to keep monetary restraint from leading to higher interest rates, the so-called public-sector borrowing requirement (roughly equal to the budget deficit) was reduced from 4.8 percent of GDP in 1979–1980 to 1.6 percent in 1985–1986.[37] This was accomplished through a combination of tax increases, selective spending cuts (although the overall level of government spending increased), and sale of nationalized industries.

Third, the system of taxation was adjusted along supply-side lines in an effort to improve the climate for economic growth. Marginal income tax rates were reduced and the loss in revenue was replaced by an increase in the value-added tax (VAT, a national sales tax). Theoretically, this should have given the public a stronger incentive to produce and earn income, and a stronger incentive to save and invest that income, rather than spend it on goods that are taxed. Still, some supply-side economists have disavowed the Thatcher program because it has led to an increase in the overall level of taxation.[38]

The primary objective of the Thatcher program was certainly accomplished. Consumer price inflation fell from an annual rate of over 13 percent in 1979 to 4 percent in 1986. On the other hand, the unemployment rate jumped from 6 percent to 13 percent over the same period—the highest

[37]*OECD Economic Surveys 1985/1986: United Kingdom* (Paris, 1986), 9; and *OECD Economic Outlook* 40 (December 1986): 92.

[38]Arthur Laffer, "Margaret Thatcher's Tax Increase," *Wall Street Journal,* August 20, 1979, 20.

unemployment rate the United Kingdom has experienced since 1933. A similar reduction in inflation was experienced in the United States, but it was accomplished with half the increase in unemployment.

Critics of Thatcher contend that the large increase in unemployment proves that her policies were overly contractionary. A more modest program, they say, would have yielded the same benefits. Her supporters maintain that the rise in joblessness was not caused by fiscal or monetary policy, but by an increase in the natural rate of unemployment, resulting from demographic and structural changes in the British economy.[39] According to one set of estimates, the natural rate of unemployment rose more rapidly in the United Kingdom than in any other major industrial country during the early 1980s.[40]

Redistribution of Income and Wealth

The British government has concerned itself with the distribution of income in one way or another since 1723, when the Poor Law made it possible for rural parishes to build workhouses for the able poor. Even this limited form of help was controversial at the time: Thomas Malthus argued that the Poor Laws would exacerbate the problem of population growth. In the years before World War II, the British government fell far behind the other governments of Western Europe in social welfare spending.

The postwar government, prodded by the memory of the Great Depression and guided by the report of the Beveridge Commission, made the establishment of a welfare state one of its top priorities. This objective has been pursued to a greater or lesser extent, respectively, by subsequent Labour and Conservative administrations. Even the Thatcher government claims that the "charge that we want to dismantle the welfare state" is "totally unfounded."[41] In 1983, British governmental expenditures on health, education, and welfare represented a larger percentage of national income than those of the United States, Canada, Japan, Australia, or several of the socialist countries, but a smaller percentage than those of Sweden, the Netherlands, France, or Germany.

Aside from governmental expenditure, income is also redistributed through progressive or regressive taxation. The available evidence suggests that in the early 1970s the British tax system was more progressive than the tax systems of the United States, Western Europe, and Japan, but less progressive than those of the northern European welfare states (Table A.25). Progressive taxation has not been a priority of the Thatcher administration: the largest income tax cuts have gone to the rich and the value-added (sales) tax has been increased.

[39]Both of these positions are discussed in Willem H. Buiter and Marcus H. Miller, "Changing the Rules: Economic Consequences of the Thatcher Regime," *Brookings Papers on Economic Activity* 2 (1983): 338–352, 366–379.

[40]United Nations Economic Commission for Europe, *Economic Survey of Europe in 1984–85,* Part 1 (New York: United Nations, 1985), 2.106–113.

[41]*Wall Street Journal,* May 19, 1983, 32.

**Table 5.4   Percentage of Total Income Received
by the Richest 5 Percent of Families**

Year	United Kingdom	United States
1949	24%	17%
1953	22	16
1961	19	17
1967	19	15
1975	17	16
1983	17	16

Sources: *National Income Blue Book* (London: Central Statistical Office, 1984), 20; and U.S. Department of Commerce, Bureau of the Census, *Current Population Reports,* Series P-60, No. 151 (Washington, D.C.: USGPO, 1986), Table 12.

How have British social welfare programs affected the distributions of income and wealth? According to the data in Table 5.4, British income inequality has gradually declined since World War II, while the American distribution has been relatively stable. In 1949, the share of total income received by wealthy British families was significantly larger than the share received by rich Americans, but the income distributions of the two countries were rather similar by the mid-1970s.

Table 5.5, concerning the distribution of wealth, supports this observation. Nearly half of British wealth was concentrated in the hands of the richest one percent of the population at the end of World War II, but that proportion was cut to 21 percent by 1982. The American distribution of wealth, which did not change appreciably between 1950 and 1982, was roughly comparable to the British distribution at the end of the period.

**Table 5.5   Percentage of Personal Wealth Held by the Richest
1 Percent of the Adult Population, 1922–1982**

Year	Great Britain	United States
1922–1923	61%	32%
1938–1939	55	31
1949–1950	47	21
1962	32	22
1972	32	21
1976	25	21
1982	21	20

Sources: A. B. Atkinson and A. J. Harrison, "Trends in the Distribution of Personal Wealth in Britain," in *Wealth, Income, and Inequality,* ed. A. B. Atkinson 2d ed. (Oxford: Oxford University Press, 1980), 218; *Income and Wealth* (London: Central Statistical Office, 1985), Table 22; U.S. Department of Commerce, Bureau of the Census, *Statistical Abstract of the United States 1985* (Washington, D.C.: USGPO, 1984), 463; and Marvin Schwartz, "Preliminary Estimates of Personal Wealth, 1982," in U.S. Internal Revenue Service, *Statistics of Income Bulletin* 4 (Winter 1984–1985): 1–7.

The United Kingdom in the European Community

In 1951, when formation of the European Communities (EC) commenced under the Treaty of Paris, the British chose not to participate.[42] In the view of the ruling Labour Party, membership in a free-trade organization would weaken their control of the domestic economy. Indeed, the British felt they had little need to trade with war-ravaged Europe. At the time, they still had strong links to their Commonwealth and enjoyed a special relationship with the United States.

The events of the 1950s and 1960s prompted a heated debate over EC membership—a debate that continues to the present. Comparisons are often drawn between the rapid economic growth of the member countries and the relative stagnation of the British economy. Membership in the EC, it was argued, would provide a larger trading area. This would allow efficient producers to exploit economies of scale and would place inefficient producers under competitive pressure. Representatives of the Conservative party spoke of an additional benefit: competitive pressure in the labor market would keep the country's powerful trade unions in line.

In 1961, the Conservative government of Prime Minister Harold Macmillan offered Britain's first application for admission to the EC. It was vetoed 2 years later by the French president, General de Gaulle, who feared that Britain would serve as a vehicle for U.S. influence in the Communities. A second application was filed in 1967 by the moderate Labour government of Harold Wilson and was negotiated and debated for 5 years. This time, the most serious opposition came not from abroad (de Gaulle resigned the French presidency in 1969), but from the left wing of the Labour party at home. Eventually, the European Communities bill was passed in the House of Commons by a majority of only 8 votes and the United Kingdom became a member in 1973.

The impact of EC membership on British foreign trade was clear and immediate. Between 1973 and 1981, British exports to EC countries increased by 27 percent per year, compared with a 19 percent average for their exports to the rest of the world. It is impossible to say how much additional trade was created by British membership in the Common Market and how much trade was simply diverted from the United States and other nonmembers. To the extent that Britain was encouraged to expand its overall levels of trade and specialization, the impact of membership presumably was beneficial. On the other hand, to the extent that tariffs on imports from nonmember countries caused Britain to replace low-cost agricultural imports from the Commonwealth and America with more expensive food from Europe, EC membership was costly.

Because Britain was a latecomer to EC membership, it was not able to influence the structure of the organization in its formative stages. Thus, a

---

[42]The 1951 treaty established the Steel and Coal Community, and the Treaty of Rome established the European Atomic Energy Community (Euratom) and the better-known European Economic Community (EEC) in 1958. The three bodies were merged to form the European Communities (EC) in 1967.

budgetary system was established in the EC that is ill-suited to British interests. The largest expenditure item, absorbing about 70 percent of the EC budget, is support for the Common Agricultural Policy (CAP). The CAP is a scheme to equalize agricultural prices in all of the member countries, and to stabilize them at target levels. In order to keep prices from falling below the targets, agricultural surpluses must be purchased and stored.

On the revenue side of the budget, the EC receives all of the levies that are charged on imports of food from outside the Communities. Thus, the largest contributors to the EC budget are the large agricultural importers (the United Kingdom and West Germany), and the largest recipients of subsidies from the CAP are the major food exporters (France and Holland). Balancing expenditures against receipts, the United Kingdom is consistently a large net contributor to the EC budget while some of the more affluent members, such as the Netherlands, are usually net recipients. This, the British are quick to say, is patently unfair and Thatcher has pressed for budgetary reform at EC summit conferences.

At any rate, membership in the EC did not cause the rapid improvement in British productivity that was originally hoped for and expected. The relative decline of the British economy continued for a decade and the budgetary inequities grew ever larger. By 1981, the number of Britons who believed that EC membership was detrimental outnumbered those who considered it beneficial by a 2-to-1 margin.[43] Since its 1980 conference, the Labour Party has supported withdrawal from the Communities. For this and other reasons, several of the leading moderates in the Labour Party broke away to form the Social Democratic Party, which supports continued membership. Continuation of membership is also supported by the Conservative government, but efforts are under way to reform the Common Agricultural Policy and the budget mechanism.

A British Revival?

Despite the preceding discussion, a number of signs seem to indicate that the British economy may be on the mend—its relative decline may have finally come to an end. British national income grew more rapidly in 1983 than in any other major Western country (including Japan) and kept pace with the European average from 1984 to 1986. Furthermore, the British balance of payments remained in the black during each of the years between 1980 and 1986, and their rate of consumer price inflation was slightly below the European average for 1983 to 1986. If unemployment can be arrested, the British performance may become one of the best in the West.

Is this merely another turn on the "stop-go" cycle? Perhaps. But recent Gallup polls indicate for the first time in a decade that more Britons expect

[43]N. Webb and R. Wybrow, *The Gallup Report: Your Views in 1981* (London: Shere Books, 1982), 99.

the immediate future to be better than the past. A British author who is usually critical of Thatcher remarks:

The Thatcher government, for all its faults, has created a new element of national confidence. . . . I think there is a very different feeling than there was ten years ago. The man on the street feels Britain can hold its head high again.[44]

Summary

Great Britain, the economic and political superpower of the nineteenth century, has suffered a long and deep decline in its relative world standing. According to one explanation, the countries that experienced later industrial revolutions were able to adopt newer technologies and benefit from British financing. Another says that the laissez faire policies of the nineteenth-century British government allowed foreign producers to invade the British market, and that the economic and political costs of superpower status outweighed the benefits. Other explanations lay blame on the peculiarities of British fiscal policy, the decline of entrepreneurial spirit, the elitist educational system, and the inordinate power of trade unions.

Governmental policies toward industrial concentration usually have been permissive and have encouraged the merger of small enterprises into larger ones. British financial markets are also relatively unregulated and are among the most important in the world. In the labor market, British trade unions differ from their American counterparts in their broader membership, stronger political role, strong socialist tradition, organization by craft rather than industry, and local autonomy.

The role of the government expanded during the Labour government after World War II, with broad programs of nationalization, national health insurance, and social welfare reform. Arguments for nationalization included ideology, national security, maintenance of employment, control of natural monopolies, and provision of other public goods. The evidence seems to indicate that the social welfare system contributed to a significant reduction in inequality of income and wealth. Since 1979, the Thatcher administration has returned many of the nationalized companies to private ownership, employed tight money policies to reduce the inflation rate at the expense of higher unemployment, and exerted stronger legal and economic authority over the trade unions.

Great Britain was a latecomer (in 1973) to membership in the European Communities and has been required to finance a heavy share of the EC budget. Membership in the EC did not provide a quick fix for the relative decline of the British economy. Nevertheless, aside from the persistence of high rates of unemployment, the most recent data seem to suggest a significant improvement in British economic performance.

[44]Anthony Sampson, quoted in *Wall Street Journal,* August 27, 1984, 8. For an even more positive assessment, see Alan Walters, *Britain's Economic Renaissance* (New York: Oxford University Press, 1986).

Discussion and Review Questions

1.   Of the suggested reasons for British economic decline, which ones seem to be applicable in the United States today? Which ones are likely to trouble Japan in the future?

2.   Why is it difficult to organize industrywide and factorywide collective bargaining in Great Britain?

3.   How can we explain the correlation between fluctuations in American and British labor union membership?

4.   What were the motivations for nationalizing British industries? What are the arguments for and against privatization?

5.   What are the arguments for and against British participation in the European Communities? Would you favor the formation of a common market including the United States, Canada, and Mexico?

Suggested Readings

Batstone, Eric and Stephen Gourlay. *Unions, Unemployment, and Innovation.* Oxford: Basil Blackwell, 1986. *Based on case studies and a survey of over 1,000 shop stewards, this study provides a micro view of the organization and operation of British trade unions and their impact on technological innovation.*

Caves, Richard E. and Lawrence B. Krause, eds. *Britain's Economic Performance.* Washington, D.C.: The Brookings Institution, 1980. *An extremely useful compendium of studies by American authors on subjects ranging from trade union growth and industrial productivity to fiscal and monetary policy and the impact of North Sea oil.*

Curwen, Peter J. *Public Enterprise: A Modern Approach.* Brighton: Wheatsheaf Books, 1986. *Provides comprehensive coverage and useful case studies of the history and performance of nationalized companies and the impact of the program of privatization.*

Eatwell, John. *Whatever Happened To Britain?* New York: Oxford University Press, 1982. *One of the more accessible books in the "decline" literature, this one blames the laissez faire policies of the government.*

Elbaum, Bernard and William Lazonick, eds. *The Decline of the British Economy.* Oxford: Clarendon Press, 1986. *A collection of industry studies, organized around the thesis of decline caused by institutional rigidities.*

Mack, Joanna and Stewart Lansley. *Poor Britain.* London: George Allen & Unwin, 1985. *Based on interviews in the so-called Breadline Britain survey, this is a survey of changing public attitudes concerning poverty and an assessment of the living conditions of the poor.*

Norton, Philip. *The British Polity.* New York: Longman, 1984. *A survey of the British political environment, including an analysis of relations with the European Communities.*

Walters, Alan. *Britain's Economic Renaissance.* New York: Oxford University Press, 1986. *An unusually positive assessment of the policies of the Thatcher administration and of prospects for the British economy.*

West Germany

6

WEST GERMANY: THE SOCIAL MARKET ECONOMY IN TRANSITION

*We in West Germany
have resorted to anything
but a secret science. . . .
I have merely attempted
. . . to overcome the age-
old antithesis of an
unbridled liberalism and
a soulless State control,
to find a sound middle
way between out-and-out
freedom and
totalitarianism.*
—Ludwig Erhard
*Prosperity Through
Competition,* 1958

The Federal Republic of Germany and Japan are the two great success stories of the post–World War II era. Both countries came back from the ashes of defeat to take their place among the industrial powers of the world. West Germany has the world's fourth largest GNP (after the United States, the Soviet Union, and Japan) and is the world's second largest exporter (after the United States).

A few common elements may help to explain the successes of Germany and Japan. Both cultures are renowned for the value they place on hard work and efficiency. After the war, the occupying forces restricted military spending in both countries, which enabled them to set aside a large part of national income for investment. Thus, both countries were able to begin anew with a modern capital stock. Furthermore, the Japanese quality circles and the German system of codetermination allow workers in both countries to play an active role in management.

On the other hand, the German and Japanese successes were accomplished within very different institutional settings. Germany established a social market economy (SME) after the war, with one of the most extensive social welfare systems in the world, while the Japanese welfare system is very limited. The Japanese set up a system of indicative planning; the German SME expressly rejected the notion of planning. Most Japanese labor unions operate only at the company level; German unions are organized by industry and cooperate in a nationwide confederation of unions.

Clearly, the German SME has a unique orientation, structure, and method of operation. It serves as a model to other countries that wish to combine the allocative efficiency of the market system with the decency of the welfare state. Because the modern German system was created in reaction to events before and during World War II, we begin with a brief historical sketch.

The Historical Legacy

Late in the Middle Ages, when strong, centralized national governments were being formed in England and France, Germany remained a disunited, feuding collection of states. It was not until 1871 that the Prussian statesman Otto von Bismarck was able to consolidate the German states into a great empire.

Bismarck

Bismarck, who served as chancellor between 1871 and 1890, was a pragmatic politician who boasted that experience, not theory, was his guide. He maintained popular support by giving concessions to a number of interest groups. For the agriculturalists and upper-class businessmen, he enacted a protective tariff on imports in 1879. Behind this wall of protection, and encouraged by governmental policy and new technologies, German industry began to form itself into a concentrated system of monopolies, cartels, and syndicates.

For the working class, Bismarck created the world's first comprehensive social security system in a series of laws passed between 1881 and 1889. The system included coverage for work accidents, sickness, retirement, and death. In all of this, Bismarck admitted that his motive was to draw the workers away from the siren song of the socialists.

After Bismarck, Germany continued its program of colonial expansion until it suffered defeat in World War I. In that war, Germany lost about 3 million of its people and all of its overseas colonies. Wartime spending was financed by money creation and this caused the worst round of postwar inflation in world history—prices increased by a multiple of 15 thousand billion times between 1914 and 1923. The harsh terms of the Treaty of Versailles caused a continuation of national decline and national decline was both the cause and the effect of political instability. When these troubles were compounded by the unemployment of the Great Depression, Germany turned to the promises of another empire builder—Adolf Hitler and his National Socialist (Nazi) party.

German Fascism[1]

The economic system established by the Nazis beginning in 1933 was based on totalitarian state control within the framework of private property—capitalism without free enterprise. The private sector was controlled by a comprehensive system of governmental regulatory agencies, headed by the Department of Economics, and by private trade groups that were subservient to the government. Production was controlled directly through quotas and rationing of raw materials and indirectly through price controls, taxes, and tariffs.

Formation of monopolies and cartels was not only condoned by the Nazis, it was encouraged. Large monopolies, they believed, could project German power overseas more effectively than thousands of small businesses and could be regulated more easily by the government. A 1933 statute gave the Department of Economics authority to force small businesses to join cartels if it was found to be "desirable from the point of view of the entire economy."[2]

In the labor sector, the Nazis dissolved all of the independent labor unions (under the pretext that they were dominated by Jews) and replaced them with a puppet organization, the German Labor Front. Final authority over the setting of wages, salaries, and work conditions was left in the hands of 20 regional government officials—the Trustees of Labor—whose decisions could not be appealed. The purpose was to insure labor peace and reduce the share of national income going to labor so that more could be set aside for investment and the military.

---

[1]For a full discussion, see Otto Nathan, *The Nazi Economic System: Germany's Mobilization for War* (Durham, N.C.: Duke University Press, 1944).

[2]Ibid., 71.

The Social Market Economy[3]

After the Third Reich was defeated and Germany was divided into East and West, the occupying authorities and the new economics minister, Ludwig Erhard, set several requirements for the new West German economic system. First, given the excesses of the Nazi era, it was clear that the power of the central government and the business cartels must be limited. Second, it was important to reignite economic growth in order to speed recovery from the war. Third, economic growth and the release of price controls could not be allowed to rekindle the inflation that destroyed the German currency after World War I. And fourth, the efforts to control inflation must not be hampered by public fears of unemployment and income insecurity.

In order to meet these requirements, Erhard borrowed a number of ideas from the Freiburg School of neoliberalism, headed by Walter Eucken, and designed an economic system for Germany that he called the **social market economy** (SME). As the opening quotation of this chapter indicates, the SME was based on a compromise between classical liberal (laissez faire) and interventionist philosophies. From the classical liberals, the SME adopted the ideas that the market system is the best means for coordinating economic activity and that the proper role of government is to provide a healthy environment for the operation of the market. Economic planning and Keynesian efforts to fine-tune the economy through short-run fiscal and monetary measures were ruled out. Instead, a monetarist program for price stability was mixed with a supply-side program of tax cuts and investment incentives to encourage economic growth.

From the interventionists, the architects of the SME inherited the doubt that market economies are inherently competitive and equitable. Recall that Adam Smith and his classical school believed that monopolies were usually the result of governmental action and restriction of government would automatically give rise to competition. Eucken and Erhard believed, however, that cartel arrangements were so firmly entrenched in the German economy that positive governmental action would be necessary to break them. In the words of Eucken:

> *More or less state activity—this kind of question misses the point. . . . Far more essential is a positive policy which aims at bringing the market form of complete competition into being. . . . It is here that the policy of the competitive order differs completely from the policy of* laissez faire *which, according to its own basic principles, did not recognize the need for a positive economic policy.*[4]

The 1957 Law Against Limitations of Competition was designed to per-

---

[3]For a discussion of the historical forces that gave rise to the social market economy, see Willi Semmler, "Economic Aspects of Model Germany," in *The Political Economy of West Germany: Modell Deutschland,* ed. Andrei S. Markovits (New York: Praeger, 1982), 22–52. For a discussion of the philosophy and formation of the social market, written by its architect, see Ludwig Erhard, *Prosperity Through Competition* (London: Thames and Hudson, 1958).

[4]Walter Eucken, quoted in Sima Lieberman, *The Growth of European Mixed Economies, 1945–1970* (New York: John Wiley and Sons, 1977), 198.

form this positive function, but it did not go as far as the proponents of the SME would have liked. To provide for social security and welfare, an extensive welfare state was established, building on the tradition of Bismarck.

To limit the power of the central authorities, a federal form of government was established by the Basic Law of 1949. The 11 state (Lander) governments were given control of the police, education, and all other matters that were not delegated expressly to the central government, and the wartime systems of planning, rationing, and price control were phased out. A staunchly independent central bank (the Bundesbank) was created to carry out the monetarist program of slow and stable monetary growth without governmental interference. The power of both government and business were counterbalanced by the revival of the independent labor unions and by the system of codetermination.

The SME seemed to operate beautifully through the 1950s and 1960s; it was given much of the credit for West Germany's success in achieving political stability, rapid growth, low inflation, and labor peace, even as it absorbed over 13 million refugees from East Germany and other Eastern European countries. In the 1970s and 1980s, however, as new challenges have arisen and memories of the war that gave rise to the SME have begun to fade, the West German economic system has strayed from the blueprint laid by Ludwig Erhard.

Industrial Organization

West Germany is the most industrial of the major Western industrial countries. The share of industry in employment and production is larger than in other countries and the share of the service sector is smaller.

In contrast to traditions in the United States and Britain, where industrial market power is exercised most commonly through the formation of oligopolies and monopolies, German enterprises have a long history of open collusion through cartels and other price-fixing agreements. A **cartel** is an association of legally independent enterprises that are contractually bound to control prices and other market conditions. In many cases, the cartel sets up a unified sales organization to market the goods of all of its members, but the participants maintain their identity as independent producers.

The German cartel movement began early in the nineteenth century and accelerated during the Bismarck era. An 1897 law affirmed the legality of cartel agreements and in 1923, when price-fixing agreements were already prohibited in the United States, German law merely restricted their abuse of monopoly power. The number of cartel agreements grew from 385 in 1905 to over 3,000 in 1930.[5] They accounted for 93 percent of sales in the mining sector, 96 percent in chemicals, 95 percent in steel, and 87 percent in electrical

---

[5]Nathan, *The Nazi Economic System,* 65; and Eric Owen-Smith, "Government Intervention in the Economy of the Federal Republic of Germany," in *Government Intervention in the Developed Economy,* ed. Peter Maunder (New York: Praeger, 1979), 163.

engineering.[6] More cartels were established by the Nazis to control prices and mobilize for war.

After World War II, the architects of the SME called for a general prohibition of cartels and dissolved existing agreements in the steel, coal, and chemicals industries. They introduced a draft law on cartels in 1951, but strong opposition forced the addition of a number of amendments and exceptions. By the time the Law Against Limitations of Competition was finally passed in 1957, it allowed the existence of cartels to promote exports, to ease the adjustment problems of dying industries, to reduce research and development costs, or to deal with other exceptional circumstances. Amendments to the law in 1965 and 1973 added even more loopholes. The law is weak by American or British standards and falls far short of the social market ideal.

On the other hand, German enforcement of its antitrust laws is said to be second only to that in the United States.[7] Unlike their counterparts in many countries, German antitrust authorities are armed with subpoena powers and are able to assess fines commensurate with the excess profits gained through violation of the law. According to several comparative studies, West Germany has one of the lowest levels of industrial concentration in the industrial world (Table A.9).

Further improvement of German competitiveness has been restricted by a preference among workers and investors for the stability of large, well-established corporations. Entrepreneurs have the reputation of gamblers in most societies and it is a particularly negative reputation in conservative West Germany. Apple Computer, which was born in a California garage, "would still be in the garage here," according to the head of a Munich underwriting company.[8] Indeed, the German computer industry is one of the weakest in the Western industrial countries.

Attitudes toward small business have begun to change in recent years as hard times have befallen the previously stable smokestack industries. About 170,000 new companies were founded in 1984, one-third more than in the previous year. To finance the new firms, the number of venture capital firms grew from 2 in 1983 to 30 in 1985.[9] This growth is still modest by U.S. or British standards, but it reflects an important change in the West German environment.

The Labor Market and Labor Relations

The operation of the German labor market since World War II has been nothing short of phenomenal. The country has maintained one of the world's

[6]Helmut Bohme, *An Introduction to the Social and Economic History of Germany* (New York: St. Martin's, 1978), 109.

[7]F. M. Scherer, *Industrial Market Structure and Performance,* 2d ed. (Chicago: Rand McNally, 1980), 508.

[8]Roger Thurow, "New Vigor Is Infusing Small-Business Sector of West Germany," *Wall Street Journal,* August 28, 1984, 1.

[9]Louis Richman, "Testing Time for Germany's Miracle," *Fortune,* May 13, 1985, 120.

lowest unemployment rates and lowest rates of labor unrest (Tables A.11 and A.12), while it has simultaneously held to one of the lowest rates of wage and price inflation. Credit for this performance is variously given to the German system of collective bargaining, to codetermination, to the apprenticeship program for youth, and to the flexible use of guest workers from other countries. Let us consider each of these briefly.

Collective Bargaining

Approximately 35 percent of the German labor force is unionized, a proportion that has been remarkably stable since World War II.[10] This percentage is higher than in the United States and France, but much lower than in the United Kingdom and most of northern Europe (Table A.11). The closed shop, which requires employees to join a union, is illegal.

German unions, as reorganized after the war, represent workers in relatively broad groups of industries. For example, IG Metall, the nation's largest union with 2.5 million members, represents almost all of the workers in the iron, steel, and automobile industries, and in several other industries that involve metalworking. About 90 percent of all union members belong to one of the 16 unions that form the German Confederation of Labour. As a result, there is little of the British-style trouble with interunion rivalry and collective bargaining is easy to organize along industry lines.

Chastened by the memory of hyperinflation in the 1920s and repressed inflation in the 1940s, the German unions have a reputation for moderation. The oil price shocks of the 1970s that set off inflationary wage-price spirals in most Western countries were simply absorbed by lower real incomes in West Germany. According to the London *Economist,* the moderation of the unions in the face of falling real wages between 1981 and 1983 was "a feat their British colleagues would have found inconceivable."[11]

German labor peace is strengthened by the bargain that was struck after World War II, whereby labor accepted limitations on its right to strike in exchange for a voice in management (codetermination). Under German law and union rules, a strike may not be called until the current contract has expired, peaceful means of settlement have been exhausted, the strike has been authorized by the national union, and 75 percent of the workers approve it in a secret ballot. Employees who take part in an illegal strike may be fired by their employer, expelled by the national union, and fined by a labor court.[12]

In a major departure from its usual conciliatory stance, IG Metall staged a bitter 8-week strike in the summer of 1984 to demand a 35-hour workweek with no decrease in pay. In the end, the workweek was reduced to 38.5 hours,

[10]George S. Bain and Robert Price, *Profiles of Union Growth* (Oxford: Basil Blackwell, 1980), 134; and *Business Week,* November 26, 1984, 88.

[11]*The Economist,* February 4, 1984, 24.

[12]Thomas Kennedy, *European Labor Relations* (Lexington, Mass.: Lexington Books, 1980), 180.

but the strike had a devastating effect on the economy and on the public opinion of labor unions. More than 300,000 people were involved in the strike and it reduced the national income by about $75 million per day.

Codetermination

One of the most interesting aspects of the German economic system is the system of **codetermination,** wherein workers are given a voice in the management of their companies. German employees are able to participate in management through works councils and through representation on corporate supervisory boards.

German **works councils** date back to the safety legislation of 1891, when employers were required to consult with their employees before drafting shop rules. Under current law, councils of labor representatives are required in all factories having five or more employees. They have an equal voice with management on matters relating to (1) job evaluation; (2) overtime, breaks, and holiday schedules; (3) recruitment, selection, and dismissal; and (4) training and safety. Strikes over these matters are prohibited by law and disputes are usually resolved through binding arbitration.

Thus, the councils represent labor on most issues other than the wage contract, which is reserved for the unions. Union wage negotiations are generally held at the industrial level, while the works councils negotiate with management at the factory level. In a survey of the automobile and metal industries in the Munich area, workers said that their works councils had done more than their unions to represent and advance their interests.[13]

The second form of codetermination involves labor representation on corporate supervisory boards. Each German company has two boards of directors—a supervisory board, which meets about four times per year to handle broad policy issues, and a management board, which is appointed by the supervisory board to handle the day-to-day operation of the firm. In 1951, in order to prevent a disastrous strike in the iron, coal, and steel industries, one-half of the positions on supervisory boards in those industries were turned over to representatives of labor. The stockholders' representatives reserved the right to nominate the chairperson of the board, but the labor representatives were allowed to designate a neutral member to cast tie-breaking votes. In other industries, the Works Constitution of 1952 gave labor one-third representation on the supervisory boards.

In 1976, a new law gave equal representation to labor on the supervisory boards of *all* companies with over 2,000 employees (or 1,000 employees in the iron, coal, and steel industries). Companies outside of iron, coal, and steel with 500 to 2,000 employees must provide one-third representation to labor.

[13]Charles J. Hobson and James B. Dworkin, "West German Labor Unrest: Are Unions Losing Ground to Worker Councils?" *Monthly Labor Review* 109 (February 1986), 47.

About one-quarter of the German labor force is affected by one of these forms of codetermination.[14]

In the industries outside of iron, coal, and steel, the chairperson of the supervisory board, rather than a labor designee, is allowed to vote twice in the event of a tie. If the board is deadlocked on the choice of a chairperson, a simple majority of the stockholders' representatives can overrule the labor representatives. Thus, the stockholders' representatives still have effective control of companies outside of the iron, coal, and steel industries, even in those cases where the workers have equal representation on the board.[15]

How has labor participation on supervisory boards influenced corporate policy in West Germany? This was the question posed to a bipartisan investigating committee appointed by Chancellor Kiesinger in 1967. According to their report, published 3 years later, codetermination has exerted very little influence on the overall direction of corporate policy. To those who claimed that employees with no ownership stake in the company were likely to take a short-run view of things, the committee responded that the "interest of the employees in the continued prosperity of the enterprise was never less than that of the shareholders or owners."[16] Indeed, service on a supervisory board sometimes causes labor representatives to forget their identity as workers. They often are unwilling to share privileged information with their fellow employees and sometimes side with management against union demands.

In many cases, codetermination has strengthened cooperation between labor and management. When it has been necessary to close excess iron and coal mines with the danger of causing unemployment, the labor representatives have been able to bargain for long adjustment periods. After an agreement is reached with management, the representatives have helped to sell unpopular policies to the workers—without causing the strikes one might expect in many countries.

Critics of codetermination say that it threatens the institution of private property and gives too much power to the unions. They admit that worker participation may have contributed to labor peace in the booming 1950s and 1960s when unemployment was not a serious problem, but in the more difficult environment of the 1970s and 1980s they say that it has exacerbated tensions between labor and management and slowed corporate decision making. Nonetheless, Germany has continued to have one of the lowest strike rates in the world (Table A.11).

[14]Egon Overbeck, "Codetermination at Company Level," in *German Yearbook on Business History, 1983* (Berlin: Springer-Verlag, 1984), 11.

[15]Hobson and Dworkin, "West German Labor Unrest," 47; and Robert J. Flanagan, David Soskice, and Lloyd Ulman, *Unionism, Economic Stabilization, and Incomes Policies: European Experience* (Washington, D.C.: Brookings Institution, 1983), 290.

[16]The committee report, quoted in Z. Almanasreh, "Institutional Forms of Worker Participation in the Federal German Republic," in *The Economics of Codetermination,* ed. David F. Heathfield (London: Macmillan, 1977), 98.

Apprenticeships

Germany has one of the lowest rates of teenage unemployment in the Western world, although its performance has deteriorated in recent years (Table A.13). Much of the credit goes to the unusual German system of vocational education and training that has operated for the past 150 years.

Full-time compulsory education ends at age 16 in West Germany and almost three-quarters of the young people quit their formal education at that age. Of those, about 90 percent enter a 2- to 3-year apprenticeship—a dual program of vocational education (usually 2 or 3 days per week) and on-the-job training (usually 3 days per week). An apprenticeship is required for 451 different jobs, including auto mechanic, electrician, glassblower, jeweler, cashier, and furniture salesman.

The state and local chambers of commerce oversee the apprenticeship programs. They establish curriculum, health, safety, and compensation standards, approve companies that wish to participate, and provide guidance to young people entering the programs. The federal and state governments provide a small amount of financing (about $400 million annually), but the bulk of the annual training costs (about $4.1 billion) are borne by the companies. Apprentices are not required to stay with the employer who trained them and employers are not required to keep them, but about 80 percent of apprentices stay with the same employer when their training is over.[17]

Guest Workers

Guest workers (*Gastarbeiter*) from other countries have performed an important shock-absorbing role in the German economy. In the early 1960s, a serious labor shortage developed as economic growth continued and immigration from East Germany was halted by the building of the Berlin Wall. To alleviate the problem, German firms actively began to recruit workers from other countries. The number of foreigners working in Germany rose from less than 100,000 in 1956 to a peak of 2.6 million in 1973. Almost half of these came from Turkey and Yugoslavia and primarily worked in unskilled and semi-skilled jobs.[18]

In 1973, when unemployment started to rise during the first oil crisis, Germany imposed a ban on further recruiting of labor from outside the Common Market. By 1983, the number of guest workers had fallen to about 1.8 million, two-thirds of whom had been living in Germany for over 6 years. Germany still had the largest migrant population in Europe in the early 1980s (Table 6.1). About 80 percent of the native Germans felt the number of foreigners was too high. Late in 1983, Parliament passed a new law offering

[17]*Wall Street Journal,* September 15, 1981, 27; and *The Economist,* February 4, 1984, 20.

[18]Hermann Korte, "Labor Migration and the Employment of Foreigners in the Federal Republic of Germany Since 1950," in *Guests Come to Stay: The Effects of European Labor Migration on Sending and Receiving Countries,* ed. Rosemarie Rogers (Boulder, Colo.: Westview Press, 1985), 29–49.

Table 6.1   Migrant Workers in Selected European Countries, 1981 (Thousands)

Sending Countries	Host Countries							
	Austria	Belgium	France	Germany	Netherlands	Sweden	Switzerland	Total
Greece	—	11	—	132	2	7	5	157
Italy	2	91	157	316	11	—	235	812
Portugal	—	6	434	57	6	—	9	513
Spain	—	32	129	86	13	—	63	323
Turkey	30	23	—	637	60	—	23	773
Yugoslavia	114	3	—	358	8	23	34	114
Algeria	—	3	382	—	—	—	—	386
Morocco	—	37	172	—	40	—	—	249
Tunisia	—	5	73	—	2	—	—	79
Other	30	122	244	496	98	203	146	1,337
Total	176	332	1,592	2,082	239	234	515	5,169
Percentage of Labor Force	5.3	8.0	6.9	7.6	4.4	5.4	16.8	

Source: OECD estimates, cited in Rosemarie Rogers, "Post–World War II European Labor Migration," in *Guests Come to Stay* (Boulder: Westview, 1985), Table 1-1. Reprinted with permission.

foreign workers prepaid social security benefits—as much as $14,000—to go home.

What would happen to Germany if all the *Gastarbeiter* were to return home? Presumably there would be some reduction in native unemployment. On the other hand, a study commissioned by the city of Dusseldorf concluded that garbage collection, construction, hospital, and public transport services would collapse; a sizeable number of German teachers would lose their jobs; and whole residential quarters of the city would become derelict.[19]

Financial Markets

The deregulation of financial markets is now under way in the United States, the United Kingdom, and many other countries was largely complete in West Germany by the late 1960s, when interest rate controls were removed. The financial system is headed by the nation's fiercely independent central bank, the Bundesbank. Founded in 1957, the Bundesbank is required by law to safeguard the currency as its first priority. The bank is directed by a Central Bank Council, which consists of the president, the vice-president, the other eight members of the bank directorate, and the presidents of the 11 state (Land) central banks. Members of the directorate are appointed by the federal president for 8-year terms; the presidents of the Land central banks are chosen by the Bundesrat, the house of Parliament representing all the Lander.

The German government plays an important role in financial markets through programs designed to encourage saving and investment. Workers can

[19]*The Economist,* February 4, 1984, 24.

avoid taxation on part of their income by setting it aside in a special account that cannot be touched for 7 years. Interest on the account, which is normally managed by the employer, is subsidized by the government. A similar program supports the formation of accounts at savings banks for down payments on homes.[20] Saving is also encouraged by the absence of a tax on long-term capital gains and by the relatively low rate of inflation. The result? West Germans saved 22 percent of their GDP in 1985, compared to 20 percent for all OECD countries.[21] Among the major capitalist countries, only Japan has been able to finance a more rapid growth in its capital stock (Table A.6).

The Banking Sector

Banks play a predominant role in the German financial system, accounting for about 70 percent of the funds raised by enterprises and households from 1970 to 1985.[22] The system includes commercial banks, savings banks, cooperatives, and other specialized financial institutions.

Among the commercial banks, over 40 percent of all business is handled by the Big Three—Deutsche Bank, Dresdner, and Commerzbank—and by their networks of over 3,000 branches located all over the country. In contrast to the situation in the United States, where commercial banks are just now winning the right to engage in some investment banking activities, the Big Three have been allowed to broker securities, underwrite stock and bond issues, and provide investment counseling for many years. Working beside these three nationwide all-purpose banks, the system of state and regional commercial banks generally restricts itself to conventional deposit and commercial loan activities.

The savings banks are mostly owned by local authorities and operate according to local regulations. They obtain most of their funds from household deposits and lend to households and small businesses. The cooperatives were originally established to meet financial needs in agriculture, but they now pursue a full range of banking activities.

Securities Markets

In comparison to the role played by direct bank lending, the securities markets play a relatively small role in the German financial system. There are eight securities exchanges in West Germany. The largest one, in Frankfurt, accounts for some 46 percent of all transactions and handles nearly all of the open-market operations of the Bundesbank.

Trading in the bond market is about six times greater than trading in the stock market. The banks are the largest issuers of bonds; they own over one-

---

[20]Interestingly, schemes very similar to these were used by the Nazis during World War II. See Nathan, *The Nazi Economic System,* 297–298.

[21]*OECD Economic Outlook* 40 (December 1986), 159.

[22]Organization for Economic Cooperation and Development, *OECD Economic Surveys: Germany 1985/1986* (Paris, 1986), 45.

third of all the bonds outstanding. In recent years, large budget deficits have forced the government to become a more important issuer of bonds.

Because of the small scale of the securities market, German companies obtain a relatively large part of their financing through bank lending and a relatively small part through equity ownership (Table A.8). In 1983, only 440 companies were listed on a German stock exchange (compared with 5,300 on the London exchange), and only 30 of these were actively traded. Thus, the average debt-to-equity ratio of German companies is dangerously high and has increased steadily since 1970. The number of insolvencies increased from 7,700 in 1974 to 18,900 in 1985.[23]

The government, beginning in 1977, has taken several actions to strengthen the equity market. In 1977, double taxation of dividends was abolished. More recently, legislation was introduced to give small companies access to the stock market through investment companies, to establish a new market for unlisted stocks, and to allow institutional investors to purchase a broader range of stocks. Still, it may be difficult to convince cautious German investors to gamble in the stock market.

The Governmental Sector

As we have seen, the German government has a long tradition of active involvement in the economy. Under Bismarck, a progressive system of social welfare was established and tariff policy was used to promote industrialization. Under the Nazis, the power of government was pervasive. A significant proportion of authority was returned to the private sector after the war, but the government continued to play an important role in promoting economic growth, providing a system of social welfare, controlling monopolies and cartels, and establishing a legal framework for codetermination.

Fiscal Policy and Planning

We noted earlier that the postwar architects of the social market economy explicitly rejected the use of economic planning or Keynesian demand management. Instead, they coupled an antiinflationary monetary policy with a supply-side package of tax cuts and investment incentives. As Chancellor Konrad Adenauer told Parliament in 1949, "The primary function of the state is to encourage capital formation."[24] Supply-side economists continue to point to Germany's success during the 1950s to support their policy proposals.[25]

---

[23]Ibid., 53–54.

[24]Quoted in Willi Semmler, "Economic Aspects of Model Germany," 28.

[25]See, for example, Bruce Bartlett, *Reaganomics: Supply-Side Economics in Action* (New York: Quill, 1982), 192.

During the 1960s German economic growth decelerated and became more unstable. In 1963, an independent Council of Economic Experts (loosely patterned after the Council of Economic Advisors in the United States) was established to study the problem and to submit annual reports to the government. The recommendations of the "Five Wise Men," as they are known, are not always followed by the government, but they have enhanced the visibility and sophistication of public policy discussions.

In 1967, when Germany experienced its first serious postwar recession, a new coalition government was formed that included the Social Democrats, and economic policy began to shift in the Keynesian direction. The Stability and Growth Law was passed in 1967, setting four overall goals for economic policy: stable prices, full employment, balance of payments equilibrium, and stable economic growth. To give the government greater short-run flexibility in fine-tuning the economy, the law allowed the use of some new policy instruments, such as temporary tax surcharges, without prior legislative approval.

The Stability and Growth Law also established a framework for medium-term fiscal policy. It requires the government to formulate its annual budget within a 5-year financial plan that rolls forward each year. The financial plan is accompanied by 5-year target projections, prepared by the Ministry of Economic Affairs, for aggregates such as GDP growth, unemployment, inflation, the balance of payments, and the shares of profits and wages in national income.

Finally, the 1967 law created a discussion group known as Concerted Action, with representatives from the government, private business, the labor unions, the Bundesbank, and the Council of Economic Experts. The group meets two or three times a year to consider the state of the economy, to exchange information, and to formulate coordinated strategies, particularly those involving wage increases.[26] Although Concerted Action has no real authority of its own, it has served as an important forum for debate and compromise.

Does this mean that Germany has adopted a system of indicative planning? Opinions differ. According to Gregory and Stuart, "A striking characteristic of the West German economic apparatus is the virtual absence of planning machinery at the federal level."[27] Certainly, there is no close German counterpart to the French General Planning Commissariat or the Japanese Economic Planning Agency. Still, the late Andrew Shonfield argued that "Germany, for all its anti-planning rhetoric, became adept at it," and "the great differences in the approach to policy-making at the turn of the 1970s decade were between Britain, on the one hand, and France and Germany on the other, rather than between France and Germany."[28]

---

[26]Concerted Action did not meet between 1977 and 1979 because its labor representatives withdrew during a Supreme Court test of the 1976 codetermination law.

[27]Paul Gregory and Robert Stuart, *Comparative Economic Systems,* 2d ed. (Boston: Houghton Mifflin, 1985), 336.

[28]Andrew Shonfield, *In Defense of the Mixed Economy* (Oxford: Oxford University Press, 1984), 39.

The more active macroeconomic policy after 1967, along with the shift to floating exchange rates in 1971 and the oil price shocks of 1974 and 1979, sent Germany through a succession of "stop-go" cycles. Then, in 1982 the major conservative parties, the Christian Democratic Union and the Christian Social Union, regained power under the leadership of Helmut Kohl, and fiscal policy returned to a supply-side orientation.

The share of governmental expenditures in GNP, which grew from 39 percent in 1967 to 50 percent in 1982, was cut by the Kohl government to less than 48 percent in 1985 and is budgeted to fall below 43 percent in 1995. A $6 billion package of tax cuts was introduced in 1986, and a $24 billion package was prepared for introduction in 1990—the biggest tax reduction in West German history. If successful, marginal tax rates will be reduced by up to 5.5 percentage points, with the largest cuts going to the middle class.

Monetary Policy

Although German fiscal philosophies may have zigzagged since World War II, the policy of the Bundesbank has remained staunchly monetarist. As we noted earlier, the central bank is legislatively required to "safeguard the currency" as its first priority. It is also obliged to "support the general policy of the federal government," but it is legally "independent of instructions" from the government.[29]

If safeguarding the currency means total price stability, the German record has not been perfect. However, it has been much better than that of other industrial countries. Between 1957 and 1984, German consumer prices rose by a total of 162 percent (3.6 percent annually), compared with an average of 336 percent (5.6 percent annually) for all OECD countries. If the bank was supposed to safeguard the international value of the currency, its performance has been even better. Despite the strength of the U.S. dollar in recent years, a deutsche mark that was worth only 24 cents in 1957 could be exchanged for about 52 cents in 1986. During that same period of time, the values of the British, French, and Italian currencies fell precipitously against the dollar.

The antiinflationary stance of the Bundesbank was graphically demonstrated during the oil price explosion of 1974. While the central banks of many Western countries accelerated monetary growth in an effort to forestall a world recession, the German authorities attempted to decelerate monetary growth in order to prevent more inflation.[30] The result? The inflation rate remained stable in West Germany between 1973 and 1974, while nearly doubling in other OECD countries. On the other hand, the German unemployment rate more than doubled between 1973 and 1974, while it was relatively stable in other OECD countries.

---

[29]*Encyclopedia of Banking and Finance,* ed. F. L. Garcia (Boston: Bankers Publishing Co., 1973), 106.

[30]John Bispham and Andrea Boltho, "Demand Management," in *The European Economy,* ed. Andrea Boltho (Oxford: Oxford University Press, 1982), 311–312.

Table 6.2   West German Monetary Growth Targets

	Percentage Growth of Central Bank Money	
Year	Target Range	Actual Growth
1975	8	9.9
1976	8	9.3
1977	8	9.0
1978	8	11.4
1979	6–9	6.4
1980	5–8	4.8
1981	4–7	3.5
1982	4–7	6.1
1983	4–7	7.0
1984	4–6	4.6
1985	3–5	4.4
1986	3.5–5.5	8.3

Sources: Peter Isard and Liliana Rojas-Suarez, "Velocity of Money and the Practice of Monetary Targeting," *Staff Studies for the World Economic Outlook* (Washington, D.C.: International Monetary Fund, July 1986), 84; Organization for Economic Cooperation and Development, *OECD Economic Surveys 1985/86: Germany* (Paris, 1986), 18; and Organization for Economic Cooperation and Development, *Main Economic Indicators* (March 1987), 122.

The Bundesbank was also one of the first central banks in the world to set annual targets for monetary growth—a practice that has now been adopted by almost all of the OECD countries. The projections are meant to communicate central bank intentions, to impose discipline on the central bankers themselves, and to subdue inflationary expectations. Since 1975, the bank has announced growth targets each year for central bank money, a narrow measure of the monetary base that includes currency and required bank reserves, but excludes excess reserves. As the data in Table 6.2 indicate, the Bundesbank consistently overshot its targets in 1975–1978, but faithfully stayed within the target ranges in 1979–1985. The monetary targets were exceeded again in 1986–1987, but not in response to domestic political pressure. The impetus at that time came from the U.S. government, which called on Germany to stimulate its demand for American goods and support the international value of the dollar.

Industrial and Regional Policy

As is true in all of Europe, the German government plays an active role in attracting new industries and keeping old ones alive. In contrast to the rest of Europe, however, much of this activity goes on at the state (Lander) level in Germany. The Lander are able to offer free land, tax holidays, housing grants for workers, and credit guarantees to businesses that locate within their borders.

Unprofitable businesses are kept afloat by the government in the coal, steel, railroad, and shipbuilding industries and in agriculture. In most of these cases, the subsidies are paid to prevent unemployment and, in the case of coal, to exploit the country's only indigenous source of energy. As the president of the miners' union bluntly said, "This sector will need subsidies not just temporarily, but forever."[31]

Among the new industries that have been supported by the government, the most important is nuclear power. The nuclear industry has been encouraged by the government since the early 1960s and not without results. Other new companies that have received government assistance may be found in the aircraft, computer, and shipping industries. Special efforts are made to encourage the formation of small and medium-sized companies to offset the power of big business.

Of the 4.6 billion deutsch marks (about $1.6 billion) of federal subsidies that were paid to support troubled regions of the country in 1984, 3.6 billion deutsch marks were directed to West Berlin. A capitalist island in the middle of East Germany, Berlin requires a huge amount of aid to attract investment and to maintain its transportation and communication links with the outside world. Federal financial aid is also given to the unemployment-plagued industrial regions in the northern part of the country.

Redistribution of Income

Bismarck's Germany led the world in the enactment of social insurance legislation in the nineteenth century. Untouched by the laissez faire philosophy that inhibited the British and the French, and alarmed by the inroads of the socialists (Marx and Engels were Germans, not Russians), Bismarck and his successors established national insurance programs against sickness in 1883, against accidents in 1884, for the old and disabled in 1891, and for widows and orphans in 1911. National unemployment insurance was not established until after World War I, but local programs were adopted in some cities as early as 1894.

Given this tradition and the German fear of unemployment and inflation after World War II, the conservative architects of the social market economy were forced to rebuild an extensive system of social welfare programs—even though they believed that "economic freedom and compulsory insurance are not compatible."[32] In the early 1950s, the German and French governments redistributed a larger percentage of GDP through transfer payments than any other major capitalist country (Table A.19). Since that time, German social welfare expenditures have not grown as rapidly, expressed as a percentage of GDP, as those of other major countries. By the early 1980s, the Germans had been overtaken by the Swedes, Norwegians, Italians, and British, and advanced upon by the Americans and Japanese.

Nevertheless, Germany has one of the most extensive social welfare systems in the world. As is true in most of Europe, the German social security

[31]*The Economist,* February 4, 1984, 11.

[32]Erhard, *Prosperity through Competition,* 186.

system includes a number of programs that are not found in the United States and Japan. New mothers are paid maternity grants and a 1985 law allows them to take a paid child-care vacation for 12 months after the birth of their child, with protection against dismissal. Family allowances are paid to all households with school-age children. A monthly allowance of 50 deutsch marks (about $25) is paid for the first child, another DM 120 ($60) for the second child, and DM 240 ($120) for each additional child. For those who qualify, the state provides a free university education. The German unemployment insurance system covers a number of occupational groups, such as agricultural employees and at-home workers, that are excluded by the American system. The pensions paid under the social security system are larger than those in the United States and the government contributes about $2,000 to funeral costs.[33]

What the German government gives with one hand, however, it takes away with the other. Like other European countries and unlike the United States and Japan, Germany raises a large part of its governmental revenue with regressive consumption taxes (Table A.21). Hence, the available evidence indicates that the American tax system redistributes more income from the rich to the poor than the German system. Although German distribution of income is significantly more even than the American distribution before taxes are paid, it is very similar to the U.S. distribution after taxes (Table A.25).

Finally, we should note that the German distribution of income, like the American, has changed very little since World War II. Despite Germany's large and growing social welfare programs, the Gini coefficient for after-tax household income showed only slight change between 1950 and 1975—from 39.6 to 38.8, respectively.[34] As in America, it seems that the German welfare state has done little more than offset a trend toward greater inequality of privately-earned income. Critics of the welfare state claim that it is actually the cause, rather than the cure, of income inequality, because it weakens work incentives. How would German incomes be distributed today if there were no social welfare system? Nobody really knows.

What's Left of the Social Market Economy?

The social market economy (SME) was created in West Germany after World War II in response to a unique set of circumstances. The end of the Nazi era, the inflow of refugees, the fresh memory of hyperinflation and repressed inflation, the presence of Allied occupation authorities, the leadership of Erhard and Adenauer—all influenced the structure of the SME. Since that time, the

[33]U.S. Department of Health and Human Services, *Social Security Programs throughout the World, 1981* (Research Report No. 58), 90–91; Organization for Economic Cooperation and Development, *OECD Economic Surveys: Germany 1985/1986,* 67; and Thomas O'Botle and Peter Gumbel, "Bonn Now Faces Task of Finding a Solution for Its Welfare Crisis," *Wall Street Journal,* January 28, 1987, 1.

[34]Royal Commission on the Distribution of Income and Wealth, "The International Comparison of Income Distributions," in *Wealth, Income, and Inequality,* 2d ed., ed. A. B. Atkinson (Oxford: Oxford University Press, 1980), 95.

German environment has changed dramatically and a new generation has replaced the old. The SME imprint may still be found on the German economic system, but it has faded with age.

With respect to fiscal policy, the SME called for a package of supply-side tax incentives rather than a Keynesian system of demand management. This plank of the SME was broken by the Stability and Growth Law of 1967, which introduced a system of economic planning and Keynesian policy. However, the German planning machinery is very limited and the Kohl government has moved back toward a supply-side program of tax cuts.

With respect to monetary policy, the SME called for a monetarist effort to safeguard the currency. In the 1960s and 1970s, the Bundesbank did allow some acceleration in the rate of inflation, but much less than was experienced in other countries. Again, allegiance to the SME weakened, but it did not disappear.

The architects of the SME were forced to compromise their ideals concerning the control of monopolies and cartels from the beginning. The 1957 Law Against Limitations of Competition was riddled with loopholes by the time it was passed and was weakened further by amendment. By international standards, Germany has an unusually good record of antitrust enforcement and a relatively low level of industrial concentration.

Finally, an important aspect of German economic success of the 1950s and 1960s was the strong national work ethic and the low level of labor unrest. Since that time, the level of labor unrest has risen and the work ethic has been weakened, it is alleged, by the system of social welfare. However, the German strike rate is still one of the lowest in the Western world; the average German manufacturing worker puts in more hours per week than his counterparts in most other industrial nations.

The legacy of the social market economy is still quite evident and continues to provide the West German people—and the families of two million guest workers—with one of the highest standards of living that the world has known.

Summary

West Germany and Japan, the two "miracle" countries of the postwar era, both benefited from a strong work ethic and a high saving rate, a light military burden, and an active program of worker participation in management. On the other hand, Germany developed an extensive social welfare system, while Japan did not, and Japan engaged in indicative planning, while Germany did not.

German national unity, industrial policy, and social welfare policy have their roots in the nineteenth century leadership of Bismarck. Drawing on this heritage, and determined to put away the hyperinflation, cartel power, and political repression of the war years, Ludwig Erhard and his associates fashioned the social market economy (SME). The SME model is based on a rejection of central planning and an affirmation of the market system, an active effort to abolish cartels and to establish competition, a supply-side fiscal policy, a monetary policy dedicated to price stability, and an extensive social welfare system.

As a result of political opposition, the framers of the SME were unable to enact the very strict anticartel law that they favored. The law that was finally passed in 1957 included a number of loopholes, which were expanded in subsequent legislation, but the law is firmly enforced.

Although not a part of the original SME model, labor participation in management (codetermination) is another important component of the German economic system. Codetermination is handled through works councils, which consult with management on working conditions, and labor representation on corporate supervisory boards. Together with well-organized systems of collective bargaining and youth apprenticeships, and flexible use of migrant guest workers, the system of codetermination has contributed to labor peace, price stability, and relatively low unemployment in most years.

The financial sector is characterized by a strong and independent central bank that has remained dedicated to price stability and by a pervasive banking system and limited stock market. Although a Keynesian approach to fiscal policy was adopted in the mid-1960s and the governmental share of the economy increased steadily until the early 1980s, the government has returned to a supply-side program of tax and spending cuts in recent years. The original SME has been altered in many ways, but its legacy is still apparent in the structure and performance of the German economy.

Discussion and Review Questions

1.   What were the essential elements of the Nazi economic system? How did the Nazi legacy influence the postwar years?

2.   How does the philosophy of the social market economy differ from the classical liberalism of Adam Smith?

3.   What are the specialized roles of the labor unions, works councils, and labor members on supervisory boards in representing the interests of German workers?

4.   How do the relative roles of banking and securities markets differ in the American and German financial systems?

5.   In an effort to avoid the centralized concentration of power that characterized the Nazi era, postwar Germany was organized as a *federal* republic. What are some of the economic functions of the state (Land) governments?

6.   What are the essential elements of the social market economy? How faithfully does the German economy fit that model today?

Suggested Readings

Erhard, Ludwig. *Prosperity through Competition.* London: Thames and Hudson, 1958. *A fascinating, if somewhat self-serving, first-hand account of the German miracle in the making.*

Flanagan, Robert J., David Soskice, and Lloyd Ulman. *Unionism, Economic Stabilization, and Incomes Policies: European Experience.* Washington, D.C.: Brookings Institution, 1983. *A survey of labor-market operations in nine countries; its 100-page chapter on Germany discusses that country's success from institutional, cultural, and econometric perspectives.*

Heathfield, David F., ed. *The Economics of Codetermination.* London: Macmillan, 1977. *A compendium of papers comparing German codetermination with similar systems in other countries.*

Markovits, Andrei S. *The Political Economy of West Germany: Modell Deutschland.* New York: Praeger, 1982. *Written by a team of economists, historians, and political scientists; several of the papers in this book emphasize the active role of the government in the German economic system and the applicability of the German model to other countries.*

Nathan, Otto. *The Nazi Economic System: Germany's Mobilization for War.* Durham, N.C.: Duke University Press, 1944. *Provides a clear description of the institutional structure of the Nazi system and its influence on the mobilization effort.*

Organization for Economic Cooperation and Development, *OECD Economic Surveys: Germany.* Paris, annual. *An annual survey of macroeconomic policy. The 1986 issue includes an extended discussion of financial markets; the 1985 issue provides an extended analysis of labor markets.*

Rogers, Rosemarie, ed. *Guests Come to Stay: The Effects of European Labor Migration on Sending and Receiving Countries.* Boulder: Westview Press, 1985. *Includes three chapters on the role of guest workers in Germany, other chapters on France, Sweden, and Switzerland, and four chapters on the sending countries.*

Thimm, Alfred L. *The False Promise of Codetermination.* Lexington, Mass.: Lexington Books, 1980. *Argues that the system of codetermination has contributed little to the German success and that the system has generated more discord than harmony.*

Sweden

7

SWEDEN: WHITHER THE WELFARE STATE?

"Journalists used to come because we were a successful welfare state; now they come because we are an unsuccessful one," chuckles Professor Erik Lundberg. . . . "Disaster is more interesting."
—The Wall Street Journal, February 21, 1979

Sweden has combined perhaps the highest standard of living in the world with a highly developed social welfare system to create what is perhaps the closest thing to a utopian society in existence.
—Martin Schnitzer
The Economy of Sweden, 1970

Although Sweden is a very small country in terms of population—smaller than eight of the American states—it deserves a prominent place in this book as an example of the capitalist welfare state pushed to its limits. Beginning in the Depression years of the 1930s, Sweden sought to find a middle way between the instability and perceived inequity of free-enterprise capitalism and the inefficiency and repression of Soviet-style socialism. In more recent years, with its comprehensive assortment of lifelong benefits and a system of taxation that absorbs about 60 percent of national income, the Swedish economic system has been considered utopian by some and disastrous by others. Swedish per capita income is second only to that of the United States (measured at purchasing power parity) and the Swedish physical quality of life is second to none (Table A.2).

What are the historical and sociological roots of the Swedish welfare state? How has the social welfare system affected the overall performance of the economy? With perhaps the most heavily unionized labor force in the world, how has Sweden maintained one of the lowest levels of labor-management conflict? These are a few of the issues that will concern us in this chapter.

The Environment

Geography has been kind to Sweden. Relatively isolated on the Scandinavian peninsula, the Swedes have not been forced to participate in a major war since they joined the fight against Napoleon in 1813. They were spared the human and economic devastation of the World Wars; neutrality has allowed them to devote a relatively small share of national income to the military (Table A.20). Furthermore, because of its rich endowment of natural resources, Sweden is the top Western European producer of timber, wood pulp, and iron ore and is second only to Germany in production of gold.

Unlike the United States or the Soviet Union (but similar to Japan), the Swedish population has a high degree of ethnic and religious homogeneity. No foreign nation, except for neighboring Denmark, has ever invaded or occupied the country. Hence, over 90 percent of the population are Germanic Scandinavians of the Lutheran faith.

What is the economic significance of this racial, cultural, and religious homogeneity? Most important, it seems to contribute to a strong sense of equalitarianism and solidarity among the Swedish people. Even during the Middle Ages, feudalism and serfdom never took hold, and the peasants maintained their freedom. With the establishment of the modern welfare state, the perception that income is redistributed from one racial or cultural group to another has never taken hold. The "haves" are difficult to distinguish from the "have nots."

The solidarity among Swedish workers and the consequent popular support for welfare state policies are reflected in a number of international polls and surveys. For example, a 1980 Gallup Poll found that 18 percent of the Swedes believed that unemployment was their country's most important problem, compared to only 11 percent of Americans—and the poll was taken at a time when the Swedish unemployment rate (2 percent) was less than one-third the U.S. level (Table A.5). Thus, the politics of the welfare state are less divisive in Sweden than they are in the United States and other melting pot societies.

The Swedes, like the Japanese, have a penchant for cooperation and consensus, rather than conflict and litigation. Preceding each of the major reforms in Sweden, a governmental commission has been established to conduct a 2- to 5-year study. When the findings and recommendations of the commission are published, all interested parties are invited to submit their responses to the government. The governmental position is forged (ideally) out of the ensuing discussion and debate. Although it may take a very long time to complete this process, it has led to the eventual acceptance of a number of reforms that initially seemed too radical or innovative. This, too, may be more difficult to accomplish in a heterogeneous society.

Another aspect of the political environment that has left its mark on the Swedish economic system is the traditional dominance of the Social Democratic Party (SDP). Aside from a brief period in 1936 and a longer period between 1976 and 1982, the SDP has held power since 1932, either alone or in a coalition. From its inception in 1889, the SDP has been a socialist party, but one that believed socialism was best pursued through gradual reform of the capitalist system, rather than through violent revolution. After half a century in power, the SDP has had an extensive opportunity to nudge that evolutionary process along.

Industrial Organization

Unlike the British Labor Party, the SDP has never championed a program for the widespread nationalization of industry. The advocates of nationalization split away from the SDP in 1921 to form the Communist Party, which has played a limited role in Swedish politics. Hence, until recent years, over 90 percent of industry remained in private hands. When companies have been nationalized, socialist ideology has seldom been the motive. For example, some of the major iron ore mines were purchased by the government in 1907, long before SDP rule, in order to oust foreign control of the nation's industry.

During the recession of the late 1970s, the government nationalized a number of financially troubled companies in order to save them from bankruptcy. These included the entire shipbuilding and commercial steel industries and several smaller firms. In 1982, the revenues of state-owned companies and utilities amounted to $16.7 billion, or 21 percent of GNP.[1] Ironically, this latest wave of nationalization was undertaken when the relatively conservative Center Party controlled the prime minister's office. When the SDP socialists returned to power, they announced their intention to sell nationalized firms back to private owners and some have already been sold. According to an

---

[1]*Wall Street Journal,* March 20, 1984, 31.

official in the Industry Ministry, "We have no hesitation about selling if a company can have a better future with private owners."[2]

Because it is a small country, with little room for competition in each market, Sweden has one of the highest levels of industrial concentration in the developed world. On average, the three largest firms in each industry produce about 83 percent of that industry's output. This is roughly double the American level of concentration (Table A.9). On the other hand, Swedish companies face a high level of foreign competition. Imports amounted to about 28 percent of GNP in 1984, compared to a 9 percent share in the United States.

The power of domestic monopolies is also counterbalanced by the fact that Sweden has one of the most extensive systems of consumer cooperatives in the world. Nearly half of the Swedes are members of Kooperativa Forbundet (KF), the national confederation of cooperatives. Organized in 1889, KF subsidiaries operate thousands of department stores, food stores, automobile dealerships, specialty shops, insurance companies, and other outlets for consumer goods and services. As the nation's largest purchaser of many consumer products, KF is in a good position to bargain with manufacturers for cut-rate prices passing the savings on to the consumers who own the organization.

The Labor Market and Labor Relations

One of the hallmarks of the Swedish welfare state is the smooth operation of its labor market. Although its reputation has tarnished in recent years, Sweden traditionally has maintained one of the lowest unemployment rates and one of the lowest levels of labor unrest (as measured by days lost to strikes) of any Western nation (Tables A.11 and A.12). In this respect, the Swedish and German economies have both been very successful. However, the Swedish and German formulas for harmonious labor relations are quite dissimilar.

Collective Bargaining

Industrialization did not come to Sweden until the 1870s. When it arrived it set off an unusually rapid growth in the number and size of labor unions. Several nationwide union organizations were established by the 1880s; in 1898 they combined to form the Swedish Confederation of Trade Unions (the LO), which has played a major role ever since. By 1929, when union members made up about 10 percent of the labor force in the United States and 25 percent in the United Kingdom, they already accounted for 33 percent of the labor force in Sweden. This proportion has grown to over 80 percent today. Swedish unions now include industrial and service workers, policemen and soldiers, and even members of the clergy.

Although Swedish labor relations have been remarkably calm since World War II, they were not always so. At the beginning of this century Sweden

---

[2]Ibid.

and Norway had the highest levels of industrial conflict in the West.[3] In 1902, during one of the worst conflicts—a general strike in support of demands for universal suffrage—the Swedish Employers Association (SAF) was created to countervail the power of the LO.

After years of conflict and violence, faced with a governmental threat to pass laws limiting strikes and lockouts, the representatives of the LO and the SAF met in 1938 in the suburban town of Saltsjobaden to settle their differences. Under the terms of the Basic Agreement of Saltsjobaden, as amended in 1947 and 1948, the representatives of management agreed to recognize the unions as legitimate bargaining partners and to establish a system of general rules concerning layoffs and dismissals. Both sides pledged that they would no longer resort to strikes or lockouts without first holding direct negotiations and would not attempt to force the renegotiation of existing contracts. The Saltsjobaden Agreement, reached and enforced with little governmental involvement, led to an immediate reduction in industrial unrest.

The rules of Swedish labor relations were refined further after World War II, when the employers pressed successfully for a system of **centralized collective bargaining.** Under this unique system, wage negotiations were first carried out at the national level between the labor union confederation (the LO) and the employers' confederation (the SAF), resulting in a binding framework agreement concerning average wage increases, working hours, and fringe benefits.[4]

Within the economywide guidelines established by the LO-SAF frame agreement, industrywide and local negotiations were held between employers' groups and union affiliates. If the industrial and local negotiators did not abide by the provisions of the national framework agreement, they risked the loss of financial and administrative support from the LO and the SAF. Local union members, for example, could be deprived of financial aid from the LO during a strike or a lockout.

The employers initially pressed for centralized bargaining for two reasons. First, they believed that greater coordination and control of negotiations would reduce the level of industrial conflict. Second, they believed that centralization would strengthen their bargaining power. Under the decentralized system, the unions would use the wage gains in early settlements as a basis for additional demands in later settlements. This leapfrogging process allegedly added fuel to inflation and caused the unions to delay their negotiations.[5]

The unions agreed to the system of centralized bargaining in order to prevent governmental control of wages and to support their own policy of

[3]Walter Korpi, "Industrial Relations and Industrial Conflict: The Case of Sweden," in *Labor Relations in Advanced Industrial Societies,* ed. Benjamin Martin and Everett Kassalow (Washington, D.C.: Carnegie Endowment for International Peace, 1980), 93.

[4]Two other labor groups are also involved. Whereas the LO (with 2.1 million members in 1981) primarily represents blue-collar workers, the Central Organization of Salaried Employees (TCO, with 1.1 million members) and the Swedish Confederation of Professional Associations and Federation of Government Employees (SACO-SR, with 234,000 members) were formed in the 1940s to represent the growing white-collar community.

[5]R. Bean, *Comparative Industrial Relations* (New York: St. Martin's Press, 1985), 83–84.

wage solidarity. Originally introduced in 1936, wage solidarity is the practice of granting the largest wage increases to the lowest-paid workers. In the beginning, its aim was simply to promote equity—equal pay for equal work.

In the 1950s, the equity motive for wage solidarity was buttressed by a productivity motive. Gosta Rehn, a prominent SDP economist, argued that equality of wage costs would force inefficient firms to either make improvements or close. Thus, the policy of wage solidarity would encourage a rapid adjustment to the long-run equilibrium structure of wages and employment.[6] To deal with the transitory unemployment that would be caused by this structural adjustment, Rehn designed an active labor market policy (discussed in the next section).

Between 1945 and 1970, the system of centralized collective bargaining worked beautifully. Wage agreements were reached peacefully, without recourse to strikes or lockouts, and the demands of the LO and its union affiliates were modest, resulting in a moderate amount of inflation. The low rate of inflation contributed, in turn, to favorable balances of international payments.

The performance of the Swedish system of collective bargaining began to deteriorate after 1970. Departures from the LO–SAF framework agreements became quite common, resulting in an inflationary wage drift. Between 1971 and 1984, wage drift accounted for about one-third of the overall increase in industrial wages.[7] The Swedish inflation rate, somewhat lower than the average for other industrial countries from 1966 to 1975, accelerated to a relatively high average in 1976 to 1985 (Table 7.1). This, in turn, damaged the international competitiveness of Swedish industry.

Also during the years since 1970, the traditional tranquility of labor-management relations has been interrupted by several instances of open conflict. During the so-called Luxury Strike of 1971, over 50,000 civil servants walked out, closing the railroads, courts, and schools. This was little more than a prelude to the massive conflict of 1980, when the nonsocialist Center government attempted to cut public spending. Nearly half of the industrial labor force was idle during that year, as public-sector strikes led to supportive strikes and lockouts in the private sector.

The system of centralized collective bargaining began to unravel in 1983, when the metalworkers union and the engineering industry's employers group broke away from the national talks to hold their own negotiations. The well-paid metalworkers received more generous pay increases than those allowed under the system of wage solidarity. In response, the LO announced that it would replace the system of central negotiations with a series of separate talks with each industry group. The LO said that it would attempt to "reach the same results with individual talks as we have with central negotiations," but

---

[6]Erik Lundberg, "The Rise and Fall of the Swedish Model," *Journal of Economic Literature* 23 (March 1985): 18–19.

[7]Robert J. Flanagan, "Efficiency and Equality in Swedish Labor Markets," in *The Swedish Economy,* ed. Barry Bosworth and Alice Rivlin (Washington, D.C.: The Brookings Institution, 1987), 166–169.

Table 7.1   Consumer Price Inflation in Sweden and in All OECD Countries

	Average Annual Percentages	
	1966–1975	1976–1985
Sweden	6.2	9.8
All OECD	7.8	8.1

Source: *OECD Economic Outlook* 40 (December 1986); Table R10.

the late Prime Minister Palme predicted that collective bargaining would become an inflationary "free for all."[8]

In 1986, the country was shaken by another round of public-sector strikes, but this time the unions were confronted by an SDP government. In another effort to control budget deficits at the national and local levels, the government decided to discontinue the 20-year-old practice of guaranteeing public-sector workers the same pay increases as those won in the private sector. The strike began with 14,000 health and welfare workers, and several thousand blue-collar workers quickly joined. Another 600,000 workers supported the strike by refusing to work overtime. Eventually the conflict included transport workers, teachers, postal employees, and thousands of other civil servants in a strike lasting for one month. The government was successful in its bid to decouple public and private wages in the settlement that followed.

Active Labor Market Policy

During the postwar era, the Swedish unemployment rate remained at an extremely low level despite the nation's rapid adjustment from a semi-industrial state to a modern technological economy and the structural changes caused by the system of wage solidarity. A major share of credit for this accomplishment is due to the **active labor market policy** pursued by the Swedish government.

According to Gosta Rehn, the architect of the Swedish system, an active labor market policy includes three components: programs to increase the demand for labor (relief work and industrial subsidies), programs to tailor the labor supply to new job openings (retraining and relocation of laborers), and efforts to match supply and demand through job information and placement services.[9] About 50 percent of Swedish expenditures on these programs are devoted to demand expansion, 40 percent to retraining and relocation, and 10 percent to information and placement. Together, these expenditures are about three times as large as those devoted to unemployment compensation.[10]

[8]*Wall Street Journal,* September 6, 1983, 34; and *Wall Street Journal,* April 13, 1984, 30.

[9]Gosta Rehn, "Swedish Active Labor Market Policy: Retrospect and Prospect," *Industrial Relations* 24 (Winter 1985): 62.

[10]Ibid., 71.

The management of Swedish labor market policy is the responsibility of the National Labor Market Board and the 24 County Labor Market Boards, each of which includes representatives from government, business, and labor. Because a wide range of governmental programs are administered by the boards, they can respond to a problem (for example, a plant closing) in a variety of ways. They can increase public-service employment, attract new firms or help existing ones through subsidies, increase the issue of building permits, expand occupational training courses, and pay for job searches and moving expenses for those workers who must leave the target area.

Although the Swedish success in controlling unemployment is a matter of record, the impact of extensive public-sector employment and private sector subsidies on productivity is more difficult to assess. Defenders of the Swedish system usually admit that relief employment may not be as desirable as regular employment, but they contend that it is preferable to the psychological and economic impact of unemployment. Nonetheless, the system seems to accord well with the spirit of equalitarianism in Swedish society.

Codetermination and Employee Ownership

As is true in West Germany, Swedish workers are able to participate in management through their involvement in works councils (which play a consulting role on hiring and firing policy, employee safety, and other manpower issues) and through their representation on company boards of directors. Under legislation passed in the mid-1970s, each company with 25 or more employees must allow the local union to appoint two board members. The employee representatives are not allowed to participate on the board when it considers industrial relations and collective bargaining issues.

Although the system of codetermination has been controversial, it has been eclipsed in importance by the movement to transfer a large share of corporate ownership to laborers through the formation of **employee investment funds.**[11] Debate over the funds has been raging since they were first proposed by Rudolph Meidner, the chief LO economist, in a report presented in 1975. The issue dominated the 1982 parliamentary elections and played a prominent role in the 1985 elections.

The investment funds were established by an act of parliament in 1982 and became operational in 1984. They are financed through a tax on excess corporate profits and through a 0.2 percent increase in the payroll tax. Whereas the original Meidner plan would have created one large fund under the control of the LO, the actual legislation avoided any new concentration of economic power by establishing five regionally-based funds. Each is controlled by a government-appointed board of worker representatives, and political

[11]The following discussion draws on Kristina Ahlen, "Sweden Introduces Employee Ownership," *The Political Quarterly* 56 (April–June 1985): 186–193; Flanagan, "Efficiency and Equality in Swedish Labor Markets," 169–172; and Lundberg, "The Rise and Fall of the Swedish Model," 30–31.

manipulation of the funds is suppressed by the fact that each is required to earn a 3 percent real rate of return. Together, the five funds cannot own more than 40 percent of the voting shares in any one corporation; they will control about 5 to 6 percent of the value of all listed shares by 1990.

Why were the employee investment funds established? Several reasons were given by the LO for championing this cause. First, they are obviously meant to redistribute the ownership and control of Swedish industry—not for the socialization but for the democratization of industry. By European standards, a small share of Swedish industry is nationalized; half of all corporate stock is owned by fewer than 0.3 percent of households.

Second, the funds are meant to capture the "excess profits" created by the Swedish wage system. According to the usual argument, the solidarity system holds wages below their market levels in industries where labor productivity is the highest, causing profits in those industries to be unusually large and capital formation to be unusually rapid. Hence, a share of ownership in those industries should be transferred to the workers whose low wages made these developments possible.

Third, the LO claims that the funds will make the public more tolerant of large corporate profits and cause laborers to be more moderate in their wage demands. (The funds actually were established in exchange for a pledge from the LO to accept very small wage increases for its members in 1984—a 1 percent *cut* in real wages.) Moderation of wage increases should, in turn, contribute to simultaneous reductions of inflation and unemployment. While we should not overstate the impact of the investment funds, the Swedish inflation and unemployment rates did simultaneously decline in 1984, 1985, and 1986, while unemployment was rising in most of Europe.

On the other hand, public opinion polls have found that a majority of Swedes are opposed to the investment funds. Critics say that the funds will increase the power of the already-powerful union bureaucrats. The funds will be used, it is feared, to protect employment by bailing out inefficient enterprises, rather than to promote economic growth. Furthermore, employee ownership may distort the operation of the collective bargaining system. For example, the accountants at Volvo and several other highly profitable firms were able to avoid any payment of profit-sharing taxes into the funds in 1985. Several small corporations have threatened to circumvent the system by moving their operations to other countries.

The Financial System

The Swedish financial system is similar, in most respects, to the financial systems of other Western nations that we have considered. It is directed by the Sveriges Riksbank, the oldest central bank in the world, which has been governmentally owned and operated since its establishment in 1668. The nation's largest commercial bank, PK-Banken, is state-owned, but all of the other commercial banks are owned privately. The system also includes a small stock exchange and networks of savings banks, cooperative agricultural credit societies, mortgage institutions, and finance companies.

Accounting for over half of all long-term funds, the largest lender in the Swedish credit market is the National Pension Insurance Fund. Unlike the employee investment funds, the pension funds cannot buy corporate stock—they can buy only bonds. Financed by employer contributions, the funds are managed by three boards of directors, each consisting of nine members appointed by the national government. Thus, the government is able to implement its investment priorities through the credit market. In particular, a large part of the money has been used to support the housing industry.

The Governmental Sector

As we have emphasized, the influence of the government is seen everywhere in Sweden, the preeminent welfare state. First-time visitors to Stockholm are usually impressed by the clean streets, the artwork in the subway stations, and the staccato sound that coincides with green lights at crosswalks to help the blind. Generally speaking, the Swedes have led the rest of the world in stabilization policy, redistribution of income, health insurance, and environmental and consumer protection. On the other hand, until the bailouts of recent years, direct control of production through nationalized industries has been very limited.

Fiscal and Monetary Policy

In 1930, even before the Great Depression reached Sweden, a group of Social Democrats made a proposal to the Parliament to use expansionary fiscal and monetary policies to reduce the rate of unemployment. When the Social Democrats entered office in 1932, these recommendations became governmental policy. The result? The annual unemployment rate, which hit a Depression peak of 15 percent in Great Britain and 22 percent in the United States, never exceeded 7 percent in Sweden.

Fiscal activism has remained an important element of the Swedish model in the postwar era. Beginning in 1955, the traditional instruments of monetary and fiscal policy were supplemented with the use of the **investment reserve funds system.**[12] The investment reserve is designed to stabilize investment expenditure by awarding tax advantages to companies that save during boom periods and invest during downturns. The system is flexible and responsive because it can be used without the approval of Parliament.

The reserve system works roughly as follows. A Swedish company can escape taxation on up to 40 percent of its profits in any year by setting them aside in an investment reserve. Two basic conditions are attached to the tax concession. First, a portion of the reserve (46 percent since 1961) must be placed in a noninterest-bearing account with the central Riksbank. Second, the

---

[12]The investment reserve funds were actually established in 1938, but they were not used for countercyclical purposes until 1955.

money in the fund must be used for capital investment, and the timing, nature, and location of the investment must be approved by the Labor Market Board.

It is this last provision that allows the funds to be used as a stabilization device. Through its control over the funds, the Labor Market Board is able to influence the timing of about one-eighth of all private investment. According to a careful econometric investigation by John B. Taylor, the system was quite successful in stabilizing Swedish investment during the 1950s and 1960s. Taylor concludes that a system like this one may be especially useful to a number of countries under current conditions, when monetary policy is being used less for countercyclical purposes and more as a means for achieving long-run price stability.[13]

In its handling of monetary policy, the Swedish central bank utilizes a broader arsenal of controls than its counterparts in the United States, Great Britain, and West Germany. In addition to its use of traditional tools such as open-market operations, reserve requirements, and discounting, the Riksbank also exercises direct control over bank lending. In 1985, for example, the banks were instructed to increase their lending in Swedish kroner by no more than 4 percent for purposes other than housing.[14]

The most serious macroeconomic problem that has plagued Sweden in recent years has been its relatively high rate of inflation, which discourages saving and capital formation and threatens the competitiveness of Swedish goods on world markets. Swedish prices climbed more rapidly than the OECD average in every year between 1980 and 1985, causing a 50 percent depreciation of the kroner against the U.S. dollar. The Swedish government has attempted with some success to remedy the inflation problem without sacrificing its goal of full employment. The governmental budget deficit, which amounted to more than 6 percent of GNP in 1982, was gradually reduced to less than 1 percent in 1986. This made it possible to slow the growth of the money supply without slowing the growth of production. In addition, the government enacted several rounds of compulsory price controls and the employee investment funds were established in exchange for moderate wage demands from the unions. Consumer price inflation slowed from nearly 14 percent in 1980 to less than 6 percent in 1986; this contributed to a rise in gross saving from 14 percent of GNP in 1982 to 18 percent in 1985.

Social Welfare and Income Redistribution

The welfare states of northern Europe—Sweden, Germany, Belgium, Denmark, and the Netherlands—spend over 30 percent of their national incomes on social programs (Table 7.2). The Swedish welfare system includes cash maternity benefits; family allowances of $400 per year for each child under sixteen

---

[13]John B. Taylor, "The Swedish Investment Reserve Funds System as a Stabilization Policy Rule," *Brookings Papers on Economic Activity,* No. 1 (1982): 97.

[14]Organization for Economic Cooperation and Development, *OECD Economic Surveys: Sweden 1984/1985* (Paris: May, 1985), 71.

Table 7.2   Social Expenditures* in OECD Countries

| | Percentage of GDP | |
	1960	1981
Australia	10.2	18.8
Belgium	17.4	37.6
Canada	12.1	21.5
Denmark	—	33.3
France	13.4	29.5
Italy	16.8	29.1
Japan	8.1	17.5
Netherlands	16.2	36.1
Norway	11.7	27.1
Sweden	15.4	33.4
Switzerland	7.7	14.9
United Kingdom	13.9	23.7
United States	10.9	20.8
West Germany	20.5	31.5

*Social expenditure includes general government spending on education, health, pensions, unemployment compensation, and other factors.

Source: Organization for Economic Cooperation and Development. *Social Expenditure 1960–1990: Problems of Growth and Control* (Paris, 1985), Table 1.

years of age, regardless of family income; free childcare; and free public education through graduate school.

The nation's system of comprehensive health insurance, which is administered by the 23 county governments, covers medical and dental treatment, hospitalization and surgery, and pharmaceutical costs. The government also provides vacation grants for housewives, free marital counseling, generous retirement and disability pensions, and a network of paid Samaritans to dispense home help to the elderly.[15] The redistributive effect of all of this welfare spending is enhanced by a progressive tax system. Thus, Sweden has the most even distribution of after-tax income in the Western world (Table A.25).

Moreover, Swedish social welfare spending has had a demonstrable impact on the health and education of the population. No other nation has a longer life expectancy or a lower level of infant mortality than Sweden. No country, other than the United States, enrolls a larger percentage of its young people in college. On the other hand, the Swedes have one of the highest suicide rates in the world.

A Swedish Tax Revolt?

Of course, such a large amount of social welfare and other governmental spending has its cost. Governmental receipts absorb about 60 percent of Swed-

---

[15]Reacting to this last provision, a Swedish critic of the system has observed that the welfare state is "fundamentally based on the dogma that in child care, education, sick care, and old-age care, commercially 'hired love' is as good as love given and taken without payment. . . ." See Sven Rydenfelt, "The Swedish and Japanese Welfare Systems," *Wall Street Journal,* September 30, 1981, 23.

ish national income—roughly double the American or Japanese proportions. Marginal tax rates can amount to 85 percent on the incomes of middle-level managers. In the words of a Swedish executive, "The government takes the salary and leaves you the tip—15 percent."

The impact of heavy taxation on the Swedish economic and social system is a subject that has received a lot of attention. First, it is widely believed that income taxation has damaged work incentives. The average Swedish work-week is one of the shortest in the world (Table A.14). Of course, this may only reflect the value placed on leisure by an increasingly affluent society. In a 1981 survey, 1,000 salaried workers were asked, "If you had to choose between a salary raise and a longer vacation, which would you choose?" Fifty-eight percent answered that they would prefer a longer vacation—on top of the 5 weeks they already receive.[16]

Second, high taxes have undoubtedly driven a significant part of income and production underground. One reason why Swedes desire long vacations is to engage in untaxed do-it-yourself home improvement projects and barter activities. According to survey research, about one-fifth of respondents admit that they have engaged in illegal black market activities, designed to hide taxable income. Econometric estimates place the size of the underground economy at about 15 to 25 percent of GNP.[17] According to Gunnar Myrdal, a Nobel laureate and one of the architects of the welfare state, Sweden has become a nation of hustlers. He advocates reform of the tax system—less progressive income taxation and more taxation of consumption and wealth— rather than dismantling the social welfare system.[18]

Finally, the tax system has caused a number of the most affluent Swedes to leave the country. In 1984, the outflow of Swedish wealth due to emigration tripled over the previous year, to the equivalent of $330 million.[19] In 1983– 1984, Sweden's two most successful family-owned businesses of the postwar era transferred their majority stockholdings out of the country in an effort to escape the high wealth and inheritance taxes.

Nevertheless, while resistance to the tax system may be growing, support for the social welfare system remains very strong. Even Gunnar Heckscher, the leader of the Swedish Conservative Party, believes that "On the whole, the welfare state has been more of a success than a failure in Denmark, Finland, Norway, and Sweden."[20] Most significantly, the Social Democrats were

---

[16]Hans Zetterberg and Greta Frankel, "Working Less and Enjoying It More in Sweden," *Public Opinion,* August-September, 1981, 43.

[17]Ibid., 42, for the survey results. For econometric results, see Table 2.2 and the estimates of Edgar Feige reported in Edward Gramlich, "Rethinking the Role of the Public Sector," in *The Swedish Economy,* ed. Barry Bosworth and Alice Rivlin (Washington, D.C.: The Brookings Institution, 1987), 271.

[18]Robert L. Bartley, "A Conversation with Gunnar Myrdal," *Wall Street Journal,* February 14, 1979, 20.

[19]*Wall Street Journal,* January 25, 1985, 20.

[20]Gunnar Heckscher, "Equality versus Democracy," *Sweden Now* 3 (1984): 42.

reelected yet again in 1985. Ingvar Carlson assumed leadership of the SDP after the mysterious assassination of Olaf Palme in 1986; within a year he achieved a public confidence rating of 62 percent—the highest ever for a Swedish prime minister.[21] The Swedish model is alive and well; it demonstrates the feasibility of pursuing egalitarianism without sacrificing a high standard of living.

Summary

Sweden is a small, geographically isolated country. Its isolation has lightened its military burden and promoted a cultural homogeneity that is conducive to cooperation and egalitarianism. The reform-socialist Social Democratic Party has ruled with few interruptions since 1932, but it has never pressed for nationalization of industry. Because Sweden is a small country, many of its industries are highly concentrated; they face foreign competition and a strong system of consumer cooperatives.

Sweden has a tradition of peaceful labor-management relations, despite the fact that over 80 percent of the labor force is unionized. This is explained in part by the orderly system of conflict resolution established in the Basic Agreement of 1938 and in part by the centralized system of collective bargaining created in the 1950s. However, centralized collective bargaining has begun to unravel in recent years as the labor unions have split on the issue of wage solidarity. The labor movement gained some additional control over corporate policy through the new employee investment funds, which became operational in 1984.

Unemployment has been kept at very low levels through an active labor market policy of governmental support for job creation, information, training, and relocation, and through an expansionary fiscal policy. The latter includes a special investment reserve program that allows the government to stimulate and stabilize the level of investment expenditure. The high priority given to unemployment reduction has caused serious inflationary problems, requiring tighter control of budget deficits and monetary growth in recent years.

The lifelong social welfare system is one of the most comprehensive in the world, and the tax system is highly progressive. Thus, Sweden has the most even distribution of after-tax income in the Western world and one of the healthiest and best-educated populations. High taxes seem to weaken work incentives and encourage a large and inefficient underground economy, but popular support for the SDP and its welfare-state policies is very strong.

Discussion and Review Questions

1.   Describe the Swedish industrial structure. What is the government's policy concerning nationalization? Is industry relatively concentrated? Why? How is monopoly power contained?

---

[21]Steve Lohr, "Palme Successor Alters Style of Swedish Politics," *New York Times,* March 2, 1987, A3.

2.   Explain the operation of centralized collective bargaining. What caused labor and management to adopt the system? How has it been weakened in recent years?

3.   What is the purpose of an active labor market policy? What does it include? Does it have any drawbacks?

4.   What are employee investment funds? What are the arguments for and against the program?

5.   How is the investment reserve fund used to stabilize the economy? How does it differ from the conventional tools of fiscal policy?

6.   How has the high level of welfare-state taxation affected the operation of the Swedish labor market?

Suggested Readings

Arestis, Philip. "Post-Keynesian Economic Policies: The Case of Sweden." *Journal of Economic Issues* 20 (September 1986): 709–723. *Discusses the Swedish employee investment funds and argues that they represent the socialization of investment that is the hallmark of post-Keynesian economic policy.*

Bosworth, Barry P. and Alice M. Rivlin, eds. *The Swedish Economy.* Washington, D.C.: The Brookings Institution, 1987. *Based on a conference held in 1986, this book includes eight chapters by American authors with comments by Swedes. The emphasis is on macroeconomic policy, but attention is also given to the operation of the labor market, the systems of public expenditure and finance, and the political foundations of economic policy.*

Lundberg, Erik. "The Rise and Fall of the Swedish Model." *Journal of Economic Literature* 23 (March 1985): 1–36. *A good general survey; this article asserts that the Social Democrats were radicalized under Olaf Palme while they were out of office in 1976–1982 and that their subsequent policies (such as the employee investment funds) have departed from those in the "golden decades" of the 1950s and 1960s. However, since this article was written, the SDP has apparently returned to moderation under Ingvar Carlson.*

Rehn, Gosta. "Swedish Active Labor Market Policy: Retrospect and Prospect." *Industrial Relations* 24 (Winter 1985): 62–89. *Written by an architect of the Swedish system, this article gives a full and accessible account of its operation and performance.*

Schnitzer, Martin. *The Economy of Sweden.* New York: Praeger Publishers, 1970. *This book is somewhat dated, but it is one of the few general surveys of Swedish economic institutions in the English language.*

France

FRANCE: PLANNING IN THE MARKET ECONOMY

Our government is entirely arranged on a new system, which is the absolute will of the ministers in each department; everything that shared that authority has been abrogated. Thus, the court resembles all that the heart is in the human body; everything passes and re-passes through it several times before circulating to the body's extremities.
—Marquis d'Argenson
  Considerations sur le Gouvernement de la France, 1672

France was always very different from other capitalist countries, so different indeed that it should perhaps never have been included in any list of them.
—Peter Wiles
  Economic Institutions Compared, 1977

France always has been a great exporter of ideas. French philosophers, from Descartes and Rousseau to Sartre and Camus, have inspired the creation of democratic institutions and have lamented their limitations. The French contribution to economic theory and policy has been equally important. In the eighteenth century, the French physiocrats inspired Adam Smith with their belief in a natural economic order, with their conception of a circular flow of national income, and with their call for a policy of laissez faire. In the nineteenth century, Jean-Baptiste Say laid the groundwork for classical macroeconomic theory, Cournot and Walras contributed to the establishment of mathematical economics, and Saint-Simon proposed a system of national economic planning under an industrial parliament.

In the twentieth century, after World War II, the French actually established a unique system of indicative planning, although it bore little resemblance to the scheme suggested by Saint-Simon. Subsequently, the French record of economic growth was transformed from one of the worst in the industrialized world to one of the best. Real GDP, which grew at a rate of only 1 percent per year between 1913 and 1950, advanced by more than 5 percent per year between 1950 and 1973.[1] Correctly or not, many observers attributed that achievement to the system of indicative planning, and several other countries engaged in the sincerest flattery by establishing their own planning systems (recall the formation of the National Economic Development Council in Great Britain).

How has indicative planning influenced the operation of the French economy? What is its purpose? How is an indicative plan formulated and implemented? Is the French style of planning likely to work in other countries? How has the system fared through the competition and cohabitation of the French socialist and conservative parties? These are only a few of the questions that will concern us in this chapter.

The Environment

Of the many environmental factors that have influenced the operation of the French economic system, perhaps the most important is the domestic political culture, formed by a long search for national unity. For centuries, the French have been bitterly divided into social and ideological factions. Recurrent clashes between the aristocracy and the industrialists, the industrialists and the workers, the farmers and the landowners, and various other social groupings have resulted in chronic political instability. Between the French Revolution, beginning in 1789, and the establishment of the Fifth Republic in 1958, no less than 16 constitutions were enacted, establishing nearly every conceivable type of regime. The Fourth Republic (1946–1958) had 20 cabinets in 12 years—a new government every eight months!

[1]Angus Maddison, *Phases of Capitalist Development* (Oxford: Oxford University Press, 1982), 45.

Throughout its history, the divisiveness of French politics has invited the creation of autocratic regimes, which have established a tradition of strong central control over the economy. The prestige of the French monarchy reached its highest point during the reign of Louis XIV, the so-called Sun King, between 1661 and 1715. Louis tranquilized the feuding nobility, built the great palace at Versailles, and carved out colonies in Canada, Louisiana, and India. His finance minister, Jean Baptiste Colbert, established a comprehensive mercantilist system of import tariffs, quality standards for manufactured goods, and subsidies for manufacturers, trading companies, and the merchant marine.

A more exaggerated form of mercantilism was exercised during the despotic rule of Napoleon Bonaparte, between 1799 and 1814. Louis's quest for colonies became Napoleon's grab for world domination, and Colbert's import restrictions were enlarged to an outright ban on trade with Britain. In order to replace the textiles that previously were imported from England, Napoleon subsidized the domestic cotton industry to the tune of some 62 million francs.[2]

Created in 1958 under the authoritarian direction of General Charles De Gaulle, the French governmental system under the Fifth Republic is highly centralized. In contrast to the American, German, and Canadian federations, where power is geographically dispersed, the French central government exercises strong control over local authorities.[3] Unlike the Fourth Republic, which delegated a larger measure of authority to the legislature, the Fifth Republic provides for an unusually strong presidency. The president is able to appoint the prime minister and his cabinet and can dissolve the National Assembly—the lower house of Parliament—at any time and call for new elections. Furthermore, the president is able to submit legislative proposals directly to the public by referendum and, in cases of national emergency, is able to rule by decree.

In contrast to the political instability experienced under the Fourth Republic, a measure of normalcy has characterized the Fifth Republic. Between 1958 and 1981, the country was governed continuously by a coalition of Gaullists and other relatively conservative parties, and the cabinet was reshuffled only 11 times. The Socialist Party, which often participated in the governing coalition in the 1950s, was forced into an opposition role. In 1981, with unemployment and inflation soaring, a socialist-communist coalition led by Francois Mitterrand gained control of the presidency and the parliament. When a balance of payments crisis forced Mitterrand to adopt an austerity program in 1983, the communists left his government in protest, and unemployment continued to rise. A coalition of the centrist Union for French Democracy (UDF) and the neo-Gaullist Rally for the Republic Party (RPR) regained control of the parliament in 1986, and socialist President Mitterrand

---

[2]Shepard Bancroft Clough, *France: A History of National Economics* (New York: Octagon Books, 1970), 81.

[3]Since 1982, a series of reforms have initiated a transfer of power from the central government to the local authorities that some observers believe will be massive, and others describe as a legal fiction. For the former view, see Michael Harrison, "France's Uncertain Transition," *Current History* 85 (November 1986): 361. For the latter, see Jack Hayward, *The State and the Market Economy* (New York: New York University Press, 1986), 162–169.

was forced to share power in "cohabitation" with Prime Minister Jacques Chirac of the RPR.

The precarious French political environment has required the creation of a strong central government. The government, in turn, has established a tradition of intervention in the economy. Perhaps the most unique form of governmental intervention is the system of indicative planning.

Indicative Planning

Due to prewar stagnation and wartime destruction, France emerged from World War II in a state of economic and technological backwardness. National income per capita, which was over 80 percent of the American level in 1933, slipped to about half of the U.S. level by the end of the war (Table A.4). The average age of the stock of machine tools was 6 years in the United States, 9 years in England, and 25 years in France. There was one tractor for every 43 farmers in the United States, but only one for every 200 farmers in France. Jean Monnet, director of the Commissariat for Armaments, Supplies, and Reconstruction during the final days of the war, concluded that a national plan was needed for modernization and that all segments of French society would have to make additional sacrifices to rebuild the capital stock. Thus, Monnet proposed the creation of a Planning Commissariat and insisted that planning must be a cooperative enterprise. As he told General De Gaulle in 1945:

The French economy can't be transformed unless the French people take part in its transformation. And when I say "the French people," I don't mean an abstract entity: I mean trade unionists, industrialists, and civil servants. Everyone must be associated in an investment and modernization plan.[4]

The Planning Commissariat was established in 1946 and Monnet was appointed as its first director. Under the leadership of Monnet and his successors, Etienne Hirsch and Pierre Masse, the basic principles of French planning were established. First, and most important, indicative planning was never meant to replace the market system, but to improve its operation. Planning was intended to improve the flow of information between participants in the market and to encourage risk-averse businesspeople to base their investment decisions on more optimistic assumptions. In order to emphasize the limited role of planning, the Planning Commissariat was never allowed to become a large organization. Until it was merged into a new ministry by the socialist government in 1981, the Commissariat had a staff of approximately 100, in contrast to the thousands of workers at the Soviet State Planning Commission.

Second, it was decided that compliance with the plan should not be compulsory, even for nationalized industries. Unlike Soviet directive plans, the French plans have never included detailed production targets for individual companies. At most, they include quantitative projections for broad product and industrial groups.

---

[4]Jean Monnet, *Memoirs* (Garden City, N.Y.: Doubleday, 1978), 234–235.

Although it is not compulsory, compliance with French plans is encouraged in three ways. First, the plan is supposed to be a self-fulfilling prophesy. That is, the plan ideally represents a consensus view, based on input from all segments of society, of the most probable and desirable path for the economy over the plan period (usually 5 years). Hence, it is ideally in everyone's self-interest to act in accordance with the plan. Second, the French government is able to encourage plan compliance through its influence over nationalized industries and nationalized banks and through its monetary, fiscal, and regulatory powers. Finally, under the 1982 planning reform, a new system of plan contracts was established, whereby the government agrees to provide financial aid to a region or enterprise in exchange for the performance of tasks that are included in the plan.

Planning Institutions and Procedure

We have already noted that the Planning Commissariat, which was attached to the prime minister's office, was responsible for coordinating the planning process until 1981. Monnet preferred this arrangement because "no Ministerial post would have offered as much scope as the indefinable position of Planning Commissioner," and he kept his staff small so that "no one will be jealous, and we shall be left in peace . . . we'll get others to do the work."[5] The Commissariat was upgraded into a new Ministry for Economic Planning and Regional Policy in 1981, but it is not clear whether the new arrangement has strengthened the position of planners in the government.[6]

As Monnet proposed, much of the planning work is done outside of the Commissariat by the 30-odd **modernization commissions,** each including representatives from business, labor, and the government. Most of these are vertical commissions, which prepare plans for individual sectors such as agriculture, industry, energy, and transport. The horizontal commissions study problems that cut across all sectors, such as the balance of payments, manpower, research and development, and the input-output balance of the economy. Beginning with the Sixth Plan (1971–1975) there have also been several social commissions, dealing with issues such as health, education, housing, and rural affairs.

Several agencies perform support and advisory roles in the formulation of the plan. Statistical research and support is provided by the National Institute of Statistics and Economic Research (INSEE) and the forecasting directorate of the Ministry of Finance. These two agencies have developed several large econometric models that have been used extensively in plan preparation since the 1960s. The Economic and Social Council, a constitutionally established advisory body with representatives from business, labor, government, and academia, reviews plan documents as they are formulated. In addition, to

[5]Ibid., 241.

[6]Martin Cave, "French Planning Reforms 1981–1984," *The ACES Bulletin* 26 (Summer–Fall 1984): 29–38.

study and propound the needs of the provinces, a set of Regional Development Commissions was set up in the Fifth Plan (1966–1970), and the regions were given representatives on the National Planning Commission, an advisory body established in 1982. Taken together, approximately 5,000 people are involved in the planning commissions, councils, and study groups.

The procedure used to formulate and approve the plans has changed continuously through the years, but it works roughly as follows. First, the Planning Commissariat (or Ministry) and its statistical support agencies prepare an options report, which outlines the various macroeconomic strategies that are available to the government, and their probable influences on economic growth, inflation, unemployment, and the balance of payments. The report is discussed and debated in the governmental ministries, the Economic and Social Council, and the National Planning Commission, and the options are adjusted and revised, until one of the options is chosen and approved by Parliament.

Based on the macroeconomic assumptions in the final options statement, the vertical modernization commissions prepare output and investment programs for their individual industries. These are checked and adjusted for consistency (input-output, balance of payments, etc.) by the horizontal commissions. The final draft of the plan is compiled by the Planning Commissariat (or Ministry) and it is given final approval by Parliament. Since 1982, the Parliament has passed one law approving the strategic choices and objectives embodied in the plan and a second law indicating how the objectives are to be achieved.

The Planning Record

Throughout the postwar era the objectives stated in the French national plans and the role of the planning process in the economic system have gradually changed. The Monnet Plan (1947–1951, extended to 1952–1953) was a rather simple program for economic reconstruction, modernization, and growth, with a large share of investment directed to six high-priority sectors: electricity, coal, steel, agricultural machinery, transport, and cement. In the spirit of postwar cooperation, everyone from the business community to the Communist-dominated labor unions worked together on the formulation and execution of the plan, and the government used almost every power it possessed to enforce compliance with the plan. For these reasons, and with the help of Marshall Plan aid from the United States, the Monnet Plan was quite successful.

Beginning with the Second Plan (1954–1957), a number of new trends began to emerge. First, the scope of the plans gradually expanded. Whereas the Monnet Plan covered only six priority sectors, the Second Plan initiated coverage of the entire economy, the Third Plan included international trade, and the Fourth Plan covered social and regional issues. Monetary targets and incomes policies were incorporated for the first time in the Fifth Plan, and industrial policies were outlined in the Seventh and Eighth Plans.

Second, the statistical information and methods that are used in the planning process have continually improved. The Monnet Plan was based on scattered data and little statistical analysis. Far better information was available for the Second Plan, and input-output tables were used extensively in the Third Plan. Beginning with the Sixth Plan, a number of large econometric models have been constructed to prepare forecasts and analyses for the planners.

On the other hand, the planning process grew less consensual as labor leaders and small businessmen complained that they were not given an equal voice on the modernization commissions. They claimed that the meetings were dominated by civil servants and the managers of big business, many of whom were schoolmates in the elite *Grandes Ecoles.* According to one observer, "when a trade union representative arrives in a modernization commission he feels like an uninvited guest at a family reunion."[7] Furthermore, the largest labor confederation in France (the CGT), with ties to the Communist Party, withdrew from participation in planning during the Cold War and lost much of its interest when it became clear that planning would not transform France into a socialist society.

After 1950, when Monnet left the Planning Commissariat to direct the European Coal and Steel Community, even the government demonstrated little fidelity to the plans. In 1952, the new prime minister, Antoine Pinay, replaced the Monnet Plan in its final year with his personal plan to slow inflation. In 1953–1954, the Second Plan was overshadowed by the Eighteen Month Plan for Economic Expansion, formulated by Finance Minister Edgar Faure. The Third Plan, originally programmed for 1958 to 1965, was quickly rendered obsolete by the Algerian War, the resulting balance of payments crisis, and the ascent of General De Gaulle's Fifth Republic in 1958. After a study by a "Committee of Experts," Pinay (who was now De Gaulle's finance minister) replaced the Third Plan with a contractionary Interim Plan for 1960–1961. Similarly, the Fourth Plan (1962–1965) was compromised by the 1963 Stabilization Plan of Finance Minister Giscard d'Estaing, and the Sixth Plan (1971–1975) was interrupted by the OPEC oil price explosion, which prompted President Pompidou to introduce a mini-plan in 1974.

When the Mitterrand government took power in 1981, a draft of the Eighth Plan for 1981 to 1985 had just been completed by the previous administration. A decision immediately was taken to abandon that plan and to replace it with an Interim Plan for 1982–1983. Once again, though, when faced by a worsening balance of payments situation in 1983, even the socialist government abandoned its growth targets and introduced a strict austerity program.

The Ninth Plan (1984–1988), prepared by the Mitterrand government during the balance of payments crisis of 1983, ventured few macroeconomic forecasts or targets. It did, however, establish a closer connection with the

[7]Stephen S. Cohen, *Modern Capitalist Planning: The French Model* (Cambridge: Harvard University Press, 1969), 66.

Table 8.1   Priority Programs of the Ninth French Plan, 1984–1988

	Expenditures (millions of francs)	
Priority Implementation Program	First Year 1984	Total 1984–1988
1. Modernize industry by introducing new technologies and mobilizing savings.	3,176	19,880
2. Modernize educational system and youth industrial training.	16,554	91,237
3. Encourage innovation, develop services to firms, and provide training in the new technologies.	10,683	64,305
4. Develop the communications industries.	3,594	21,191
5. Reduce energy dependence.	2,767	15,462
6. Active employment policy, especially in the organization of the workweek.	5,356	36,278
7. Better marketing at home and abroad.	4,776	28,190
8. Provide an environment favorable to the family and the birth rate.	226	1,309
9. Decentralization, deconcentration, and regional balance.	3,296	21,042
10. Improve urban life.	2,576	15,086
11. Modernize the health system and control health expenditure.	4,837	28,698
12. Improve justice and personal security.	1,275	7,861

Source: The Ninth Plan, reported in Jack Hayward, *The State and the Market Economy* (New York: New York University Press, 1986), 188. Reprinted with permission.

governmental budget through the inclusion of 12 detailed Priority Implementation Programs (PIPs). The PIPs, which were formulated on the basis of close consultation between the Planning Commissariat and the Finance Ministry, devote specific budgetary allocations over a 5-year period to several high-priority projects (Table 8.1). The three largest PIPs involved youth training, training in new technologies, and the funding of a Swedish-style active employment policy, all designed to alleviate the unemployment caused by austerity measures. As we shall see, these training programs were preserved and expanded in 1986, despite the center-right victory in the parliamentary elections.

Has Planning Helped?

Considering the unwillingness of the French government to stick to its plans and the unwillingness of some labor unions to participate in their formulation, one begins to wonder if this is a useful exercise. An indicative plan is supposed to be a self-fulfilling prophesy, but why would a private corporation voluntarily comply with a plan that has lost its credibility? Although the plans provided fairly accurate forecasts of economic growth in the 1950s and 1960s, they have provided little more than wishful thinking in the 1970s and 1980s (Table 8.2). Indeed, the Ninth Plan does not even include a specific target for growth of GDP. According to Jack Hayward, "Planning may seem to be too pretentious

Table 8.2　French Plans and Performance

Plan	Years	Annual Percentage Growth of GDP: Planned	Actual
Monnet	1947–1953	**	7.1
Second	1954–1957	4.4	5.4
Third	1958–1961	4.7	3.8
Fourth	1962–1965	5.5	5.8
Fifth	1966–1970	5.7	5.9
Sixth	1971–1975	5.9	3.7
Seventh	1976–1980	5.7	3.3
Eighth	1982–1983	3.0	1.3
Ninth	1984–1988	**	

**No specific growth target for GDP stated in the plan. The Ninth Plan calls for a rate of growth 0.7–1.0 percent higher than that of major trade partners in 1988.

a label when all that is possible is improvising interim remedies to intractable problems. . . ."[8]

Defenders of French planning admit that the forecasts have not been accurate, but claim that they are better than the guesses of individual economists. A 1967 governmental study found that managers in enterprises accounting for about 80 percent of industrial production were aware of the Fifth Plan's growth projection, and over half of the large firms (those with more than 5,000 employees) reported that the plan forecasts had a significant impact on their investment decisions.[9] Undoubtedly, those proportions would be smaller today.

Regardless of their accuracy, many proponents would agree with Pierre Masse (a former director of the Planning Commissariat) that "the planning process is more meaningful than the plan itself."[10] Until recent years, the planning process contributed to a national fixation on economic growth and modernization, which may have encouraged a higher level of investment expenditure. At the very least, the planning process stimulates communication between business, labor, and government, and within each of these groups. The impact of that communication on the economy cannot be measured, but the French success in postwar economic growth may be vindication enough.

Industrial Organization
Nationalized Industries

France has long and extensive experience with nationalized industries. The state-run tobacco monopoly dates all the way back to Napoleon; other com-

[8]Hayward, The State and the Market Economy, 225.

[9]The findings of J. J. Carre and associates, whose work is discussed in Martin Cave and Paul Hare, Alternative Approaches to Economic Planning (New York: St. Martin's Press, 1981), 81–82.

[10]Quoted in J. R. Hough, The French Economy (New York: Holmes and Meier, 1982), 123.

panies were taken over during the 1930s and more—including half of the banks—were nationalized in the aftermath of World War II. The largest post-war nationalization program in the Western world was carried out in 1982, when the socialist government took over 39 banks, two financial holding companies, and nine major industrial groups, at a cost of some $8 billion. This gave the government control over 29 percent of sales, 22 percent of the labor force, 52 percent of investment in industry, and about 90 percent of bank deposits.[11]

Mitterrand offered several reasons for his program of nationalization.[12] First, several companies were taken over because they "exercise a monopoly or because they are evolving toward a monopoly position." The nationalized companies employ nearly half of all French industrial workers who are em-ployed by very large enterprises—those with over 2,000 employees.[13] Some were acquired to protect them from foreign control and others were targeted for subsidies to give them new life. According to private estimates, between 1981 and 1985 the government invested more than $5 billion in the newly nationalized companies, 20 times more than their private stockholders spent in two decades.[14]

The nationalized companies fall under the general oversight and direc-tion of the Ministry of Industry; their top executives are appointed by the government, but they are usually allowed to handle their own affairs. In the first 2 years of the Socialist administration the executives of the companies complained of excessive governmental meddling and one of them resigned in protest. After that time, the executives claimed that contact with the govern-ment "isn't much greater for a nationalized company than for a private one," and, according to a government official:

At first, we had several priorities for nationalized companies, but now the priority is profits. It's the only way to get really efficient management.[15]

When Jacques Chirac gained control of the prime minister's office in 1986, he announced his intention to return 65 nationalized companies to private ownership over a 5-year period. Socialist President Mitterrand refused to enact the privatization by decree, saying that he was afraid the firms would fall into foreign hands. The parliamentary majority subsequently turned the tables by passing an amended bill that loosened the restrictions on foreign ownership.

The 5-year privatization program is expected to reduce the number of public-sector employees from 1.9 million to about 1 million and to raise about $50 billion for the treasury.[16] Taking a cue from Margaret Thatcher in England,

[11]Estimates of the Ministry of Industry, reported in Organization for Economic Cooperation and Development, *OECD Economic Survey 1982–1983: France* (Paris: 1983), 50.

[12]*Wall Street Journal,* October 7, 1981, 23.

[13]Organization for Economic Cooperation and Development, *OECD Economic Survey 1982–1983: France,* 50.

[14]*Wall Street Journal,* November 12, 1985, 33.

[15]*Wall Street Journal,* April 18, 1985, 1, 22.

[16]Organization for Economic Cooperation and Development, *OECD Economic Survey 1986/87: France* (Paris: 1987), 35.

Chirac mounted an enormous advertising campaign to sell stock to the general public. In the first 6 months, the campaign roughly doubled the number of individual shareholders in France, and the demand for stock exceeded the supply by a factor of 65.[17] About 70 percent of the stock in each enterprise has been sold to the French public, 20 percent has been sold to foreigners, and 10 percent has been reserved for the company's employees.

Industrial Concentration and Plant Size

France has a higher level of industrial concentration than the United States, West Germany, or the United Kingdom, as measured by three-firm concentration ratios (Table A.9). This merely reflects the fact that the French domestic market is too small to accommodate a large number of firms.[18] French enterprises are generally smaller than those in the other major industrial countries. In 1963, each of the 20 largest plants in the typical French industry employed about 2,000 workers, compared to more than 3,000 in the United Kingdom and Germany.[19]

Accordingly, the French government is more interested in creating monopolies and oligopolies than it is in controlling them. No antitrust agency has ever been created along the lines of those existing in the United States, Great Britain, Germany, and Japan. Instead, domestic control of monopolies is often handled through nationalization.

Afraid that its small firms cannot take full advantage of economies of scale and compete effectively on the world market, the government initiated a program of loans and bonuses in 1955 and created tax incentives in 1965 and 1967 to facilitate merger. Support for industrial concentration was given a high priority in the government's Fifth (1966–1970) and Sixth (1971–1975) Plans. The result? The number of business mergers jumped from an annual average of 61 in 1950 to 1958 to 166 in 1959 to 1965, then peaked at 213 in 1966 to 1972.[20] The proportion of the industrial labor force working in establishments with over 500 employees (a remarkably stable figure between 1931 and 1966) grew rapidly between 1966 and 1975, and then stabilized (Table 8.3).

Industrial Policy

Intimately connected with its programs of planning, nationalization, and merger, the French government has attempted (with limited success) to develop a comprehensive program to modernize and rationalize the structure of

[17]*Wall Street Journal,* May 11, 1987, 18.

[18]French GNP, which is used to measure the size of the domestic market, is smaller than the British, American, or German GNP.

[19]Kenneth D. George and T. S. Ward, *The Structure of Industry in the EEC* (Cambridge: Cambridge University Press, 1975), 30.

[20]Francois Caron, *An Economic History of Modern France* (New York: Columbia University Press, 1979), 301–303.

Table 8.3 Distribution of French Industrial Employees by Size of Establishment

| | Percentage of Industrial Labor Force Employed in Establishments with: | | | |
Year	1–10 Workers	11–500 Workers	Over 500 Workers	Total
1906	32	49	19	100
1931	20	53	27	100
1954	16	57	27	100
1966	13	61	26	100
1975	6	58	36	100
1983	8	60	32	100

Sources: 1906–1966—Francois Caron, *An Economic History of Modern France* (New York: Columbia University Press, 1979), 280; and 1975–1983—*Annuaire Statistique de la France 1985* (Paris: INSEE, 1985), 107.

industry. Since its reorganization in 1969, the Ministry for Industry and Research has assumed general responsibility for coordination of industrial policy and for supporting scientific research that is useful to industry.

An important role in industrial policy is also played by the Industrial Development Institute (IDI), established in 1970 along the lines of the British Industrial Reorganization Corporation. Financed and operated cooperatively by private corporations and public agencies, the IDI primarily provides financial aid and advice to rapidly growing medium-sized firms. Likewise, the government established an Industrial Modernization Fund in 1983 and gave it an appropriation of 9.5 billion francs in 1985 to encourage capital investment in small- and medium-sized enterprises, which generate the bulk of new jobs.

The government has aided larger companies in troubled industries through its program of restructuring, whereby unprofitable enterprises are merged with successful ones, and early retirement and retraining are provided to surplus workers. Major restructuring has already been accomplished in the French chemicals industry and a program was initiated in 1984 for the steel, shipbuilding, and coal industries. The program provides tax concessions to companies that take over unprofitable businesses and calls for a reduction of employment in these industries of 40,000 to 60,000 by the year 1990.[21]

The Labor Market and Labor Relations

At first glance, the French system of labor relations seems to have much in common with the American system. About 20 percent of the workers in both countries are members of labor unions, a very small proportion by European

[21]*Wall Street Journal,* February 9, 1984, 28.

standards (Table A.11). Furthermore, the labor movements in both countries are fragmented. In neither country does one find a unified confederation of labor unions, similar to the British Trades Union Congress or the German Confederation of Labor. This, though, is where the resemblance ends.

Although roughly the same proportions of the French and American labor forces are unionized, they are distributed very differently. French unions include many more white-collar workers and less manual workers than in the United States. They include a large number of public employees, where most American unions are dominated by the private sector.[22]

French union members are divided between five major confederations, each of which exercises strong control over its affiliate unions. The oldest and largest confederation, the CGT, was established in 1895 and has close ties to the French Communist Party.[23] The subordination of the CGT to the needs of the Communist Party may help to explain the low level of union membership in France.[24] The other four confederations were formed by various anti-Communist groups, including the Roman Catholic Church, as alternatives to the CGT. In general, each confederation has an affiliate union for each major industry. Hence, an employer is often required to deal with five different unions in collective bargaining situations.[25]

Because they are small and fragmented, the French labor unions are relatively weak. Because they have very limited financial resources to aid striking workers, French strikes are usually of short duration. Even the Socialist Mitterrand administration has operated more or less independently of union influence and enacted an austerity program that was bitterly opposed by the unions. However, the unions can be pushed only so far. A general strike in 1968 almost caused the government to collapse, and a far less serious round of strikes at the beginning of 1987 inflicted serious damage on Prime Minister Chirac in the public opinion polls.[26]

Worker Participation in Management

In order to quell the general strike of 1968, General De Gaulle promised to establish an ill-defined system of worker participation in management. In fact, a very limited participation law was passed in 1969, but it fell far short of the demands of the Left. When the Socialist and Communist Parties forged their so-called Common Program in 1972, they included a proposal for *autogestion*

---

[22]Frederic Meyers, "France," in *International Handbook of Industrial Relations,* ed. Albert A. Blum (Westport, Conn.: Greenwood Press, 1981), 182. It should be noted, however, that U.S. union participation has been growing in the public sector and falling in the private sector.

[23]In 1981, when all of the other French confederations organized demonstrations condemning the suppression of the Solidarity trade union in Poland, the CGT decided not to participate.

[24]For development of this thesis, see Robert Flanagan, David Soskice, and Lloyd Ulman, *Unionism, Economic Stabilization, and Incomes Policies: European Experience* (Washington, D.C.: The Brookings Institution, 1983), 580–593.

[25]Thomas Kennedy, *European Labor Relations* (Lexington, Mass.: Lexington Books, 1980), 47.

[26]*Wall Street Journal,* January 12, 1987, 26.

THE EVENTS OF MAY 1968

The French labor unions are relatively weak, but for a brief period in 1968 they joined with rebelling college students and the combination almost toppled the Gaullist government. The students were dissatisfied by the elitism of the French educational system, by their fear of unemployment after graduation from classical programs, and by the overcrowded and decrepit facilities at their universities.

Repeated riots led to brutal repression by the police and the Latin Quarter in Paris became a battleground. On May 10th and 11th, the students built barricades with paving stones and overturned automobiles, and the police attacked with tear gas and shock-producing hand grenades. The barricades were broken down and hundreds of students were arrested. Two days later, hundreds of thousands of demonstrators took to the streets to protest the repression. Prompted by governmental austerity measures, wildcat strikes began the next day, on May 14th, and by the end of the next week they were joined by eight to ten million workers.

Interestingly, the Communist Party and the CGT, afraid that the anarchist element in the rebellion would weaken their control of the working class, took a moderate stance. They criticized the students for their irresponsibility, and attempted to mediate the differences between labor and management. When their efforts were rejected by the striking workers, General De Gaulle agreed on May 30th to hold new parliamentary elections and offered a program of labor and educational reforms. A massive demonstration was held the next day in support of De Gaulle and the voters registered a massive backlash against the revolution in the June election. The Gaullist party won the first single-party majority in French republican history.

Source: Richard Johnson, *The French Communist Party versus the Students: Revolutionary Politics in May-June 1968* (New Haven: Yale University Press, 1972).

(workers' consultation in management). According to the proposal, the workers' representatives would not participate directly in management, but they would be consulted on major decisions and would have the right to veto layoffs and dismissals of workers.

Legislation to that effect—known as the Auroux laws after the labor minister at that time—was adopted in 1982 when the Socialist-Communist coalition controlled the parliament. When the RPR–UDF coalition gained the parliamentary advantage in 1986, they repealed the provisions that required employers to obtain authorization before they could lay off workers, and worker participation has stopped far short of the German or Swedish models.[27]

The Financial Sector

As stated previously, the French financial system traditionally has been characterized by a significant level of state ownership and regulation. The Bank of France (the central bank) and the three largest commercial banks were nationalized in 1945; 39 other commercial and savings banks were nationalized in 1982, placing more than 90 percent of all bank deposits under state control. The government also owns many of the major insurance firms and financial holding companies and operates a number of specialized lending institutions, which raise money from bond offerings, the social security system, and the savings banks, and make loans to sectors of the economy that are favored by the government. A few of the banks and insurance companies have been privatized by the Chirac government and several others are scheduled for sale, but public ownership will continue to play an important role in the financial sector.

In comparison to other Western nations, strict control is exercised over private financial institutions through regulation of lending, foreign exchange operations, and the issue of stocks and bonds. Because of these controls and the dominant role of governmental agencies in the absorption and lending of funds, the activity of the stock exchanges in Paris and six other French cities is relatively limited. At the beginning of the 1980s, less than 4 percent of domestic saving was invested in the stock exchange.[28]

In an effort to help Paris compete with New York, London, and Tokyo as a financial center, the Socialist government initiated a program in 1985 to strengthen and liberalize the securities market. Trading hours at the Paris exchange were extended, bond issues were liberalized, foreign-exchange controls were loosened, trading in commercial paper, negotiable CDs, and negotiable stock options and franc futures contracts was approved, and a system of stock jobbers (specialists who maintain orderly markets) was established.[29]

The importance of financial institutions in the French economic system is quite clear. Through its control over bank lending, the French government is able to operate a **selective monetary policy.** That is, the government is able to control both the growth of the money supply and its distribution to priority sectors. This is one of the most powerful tools the government has at its disposal to provide for the fulfillment of its indicative plans.

[27]For a description of the autogestion proposals, see Volkmar Lauber, *The Political Economy of France* (New York: Praeger, 1983), 33–37, 196–199.

[28]L. J. Kemp, *A Guide to World Money and Capital Markets* (London: McGraw-Hill, 1981), 184.

[29]*Wall Street Journal,* July 31, 1985, 21. For a more complete discussion, see Organization for Economic Cooperation and Development, *OECD Economic Survey 1986/87: France,* 39–58.

The Governmental Sector

We have already taken note of the active role that the French government traditionally has played in economic planning, nationalization of industries and financial institutions, industrial policy, and regulation of the financial market. The government has also been aggressive in its fiscal and monetary policy, but has a mixed record in its efforts to redistribute income.

Fiscal and Monetary Policy

While Germany ended World War II with a legacy of hyperinflation, the new French leaders inherited a legacy of stagnation. At 1 percent per year, the French economy grew more slowly from 1913 to 1950 than any other country in the industrial West, with the sole exception of Austria.[30] Thus, while the Germans placed a higher priority on fighting inflation, the French directed their efforts to stimulate economic growth and modernization.

Given these objectives, both countries were quite successful. Throughout the postwar period, the French economy grew more rapidly than the average for other Western countries. How much of that success is attributable to governmental policy? We cannot say with certainty, but one set of estimates for 1955 to 1971 suggests that fiscal policy eliminated 50 percent of the fluctuation of French GNP around its potential—the highest degree of stabilization achieved anywhere in Western Europe.[31]

On the other hand, the excellent French growth performance was achieved at the cost of a relatively high rate of inflation and was punctuated by recurrent balance of payments crises. Between 1959 and 1973, France posted an annual average balance of payments deficit of $193 million, while all of the other major Western European nations posted average surpluses.[32] The situation turned from bad to disastrous when rising oil prices drove the balance of payments deficit to $6 billion in 1974 and 1976.

Raymond Barre, the former economics professor who became prime minister in late 1976, decided to attack the balance of payments with a dose of monetarism. He established strict monetary growth targets, lifted price controls, and cut industrial subsidies. As one might expect, these policies caused an improvement in the balance of payments—including a large surplus in 1978—but they also caused a steep rise in unemployment.

The socialist government of Francois Mitterrand entered office in 1981 with reduction of unemployment as its top macroeconomic goal. Governmen-

---

[30]Angus Maddison, *Phases of Capitalist Development,* 45.

[31]John Bispham and Andrea Boltho, "Demand Management," in *The European Economy,* ed. Andrea Boltho (Oxford: Oxford University Press, 1982), 305–307. J. R. Hough, in *The French Economy,* argues that the government did not use Keynesian demand-management policies until after 1965 (p. 134), but Francois Caron, *An Economic History of Modern France,* reports that "modulation of public expenditure in order to regulate the economic situation dates from the early fifties" (p. 314).

[32]John Llewellyn and Stephen Potter, "Competitiveness and the Current Account," in *The European Economy,* 141.

tal fiscal policy, which had been contractionary in 1979 and 1980, became expansionary in 1981 and 1982.[33] Likewise, the target for growth of the money supply, which had been reduced steadily by Barre, was increased in 1982.

As before, these measures resulted in good news and bad news. On the positive side, employment and output grew in 1982, although only modestly. On the other hand, the balance of payments deficit ballooned to $12 billion in 1982, almost wiping out the nation's foreign exchange reserves. In a rapid reversal of its previous policies, the socialist government launched an austerity program in mid-1982 and expanded it in March 1983. The program included new taxes, forced loans to the state by individuals and corporations, a slowdown in social security increases, several devaluations of the franc, and limitations on tourist spending abroad. Wage increases for government employees were held down by tying them to the government's targets for future price inflation, rather than to the higher rates of past inflation. Money supply growth targets were reduced sharply in 1983 to 1985 and fiscal policy returned to a contractionary stance.

The good news? After years of escalation, the inflation rate and the balance of payments deficit both followed a downward trend during 1982 to 1986. In the words of *The Economist:*

Against expectations, a Socialist government, having seen its own mistakes, is correcting chronic weaknesses which its conservative predecessors failed to deal with. Even opposition politicians are forced to acknowledge, through extremely pursed lips, that macroeconomic policy is going in the right direction.[34]

Of course, austerity programs are given their name for good reason. During 1983 to 1985 national income grew by only one-third of the rate experienced in other OECD countries, and the unemployment rate climbed from 8.3 percent to 10.1 percent. All around the world the question was asked, Is this socialism? Thus, the center-right RPR–UDF coalition won the parliamentary elections of March 1986, and Jacques Chirac entered the prime minister's office.

The Chirac government hopes to stimulate the economy with a package of supply-side tax and spending cuts. The top tax rate on personal income was cut from 65 percent to 58 percent in 1986, and a further reduction to 50 percent is scheduled for 1989. The wealth tax has been abolished, and two million low-income taxpayers are being dropped from the tax roles. Unfortunately, all of these reductions will be roughly counterbalanced by higher social security contributions, which are necessary to keep the system solvent. Corporate tax rates were cut from 50 percent to 45 percent in 1986, with a reduction to 42 percent planned for 1988.[35]

---

[33]As measured by the fiscal impulse index. See International Monetary Fund, *World Economic Outlook* (Washington, D.C.: April 1986), 121–123, 196.

[34]"France: A Survey," *The Economist,* February 9, 1985, 9.

[35]Organization for Economic Cooperation and Development, *OECD Economic Survey 1986/ 87: France,* 28–29.

The government has also taken several direct measures to alleviate the unemployment problem. By the middle of 1986, about 193,000 young people were employed under a community work scheme that was introduced in 1985. Another 600,000 young people found jobs during May to October 1986 under a program that allowed employers to escape payment of social security contributions. The practice of requiring employers to obtain official authorization before they can lay off workers was discontinued at the beginning of 1987, with the hope of encouraging new employment.[36]

Redistribution of Income

Dating back to the excesses of Louis XIV, France has a tradition of social stratification, and, by most accounts, it still has the highest level of income inequality in the industrial West (Table A.25). In 1975, the richest 10 percent of households received over 30 percent of national income (compared to 23 percent in the United States and Britain).[37]

The causes of French income inequality are not at all clear. One cause may be the low level of unionization of the labor force. Another may be the relatively large number of low-income farm workers in the country. About 8 percent of the French labor force is still working in agriculture, compared to 4 percent in West Germany, and 2 percent in the United States and the United Kingdom.

What do the French do to redistribute income from the rich to the poor? Very little redistribution of income is effected through the French system of taxation. Judging by the differences between before-tax and after-tax distributions of income, France had one of the most neutral tax systems in the industrial West in the 1970s (Table A.25). France derives an unusually small proportion of its revenues from a mildly progressive income tax and relies heavily on regressive social security contributions, property taxes, and consumption taxes (Table A.21).[38]

President Mitterrand made several changes in the tax system to increase its progressivity. Exemptions were increased for low-income groups, a surtax was levied on high income, and a new wealth tax was established, which fell on the richest 2 percent of the population. These measures, however, were repealed by the Chirac government.

On the expenditure side, France devotes a relatively large percentage of its national income to social welfare programs and this percentage has grown rapidly since the 1960s (Tables A.17 and A.19). Prenatal and maternity benefits cover 90 percent of a mother's earnings before and after a birth or adoption.

---

[36]Ibid., 37.

[37]The World Bank, *World Development Report 1985* (New York: Oxford University Press, 1985), 229.

[38]On the progressivity or regressivity of these taxes in France and other European countries, see Malcolm Sawyer, "Income Distribution and the Welfare State," in *The European Economy,* 194–203.

Birth grants and monthly family allowances help defray the cost of raising children. Sickness benefits cover half of the earnings that are lost, and national health insurance covers up to 100 percent for hospital bills, 75 percent for doctor bills, and 70 percent for drugs. The system also includes generous unemployment and disability benefits, pensions, and survivor benefits.[39]

Soon after his election in 1981, Mitterrand increased family allowances by 25 percent, old-age pensions by 20 percent, and housing subsidies by 50 percent. Expansion of the welfare system was slowed by the austerity program that began in 1982 and some planned increases in social spending were scaled back. The trend toward austerity continued under the Chirac government; the share of social benefits in national income declined slightly in 1986.[40]

New Life for Indicative Planning?

By most accounts, French indicative planning passed through a period of decline in the 1970s. The unstable international environment of the late 1960s and 1970s—including the Vietnam war, the breakdown of the Bretton Woods monetary system, and the rise of OPEC—required French leaders to give short-run stabilization precedence over long-range planning. Skepticism grew as discrepancies persisted between planned outcomes and actual results. The French leaders of the 1970s became quite indifferent, or even hostile, toward indicative planning.

Although the enthusiasm of the early 1960s has yet to be regained, the role of planning in the French economic system has been reaffirmed in the 1980s. A more stable international environment has made planning more plausible, and the challenge of a new wave of technology has dramatized the need for long-range decision making. Under the Mitterrand administration, the Planning Commissariat was upgraded to a ministry and a new National Planning Commission was formed to encourage participation of the regions and localities in plan formulation and execution. The system of plan contracts was established to enforce the fulfillment of agreements between state agencies, regions, and public enterprises that are included in the plan.[41]

Most important, the business community has not given up on planning. In a 1985 poll of French corporate executives, only 26 percent believed that companies should make large investment decisions without governmental consultation. About 24 percent believed that either the state or the governmental economic plan should make the big decisions, and 26 percent said that the state and the company should decide together.[42]

[39]U.S. Department of Health and Human Services, Social Security Administration, *Social Security around the World 1981,* Research Report No. 58, 82–83.

[40]Organization for Economic Cooperation and Development, *OECD Economic Survey 1986/87: France,* 31.

[41]Cave, "French Planning Reforms, 1981–1984," 29–37.

[42]*Wall Street Journal,* July 22, 1986, 32.

The shift of the Mitterrand and Chirac administrations from a plan for growth to a policy of austerity reminds us how difficult it is for any French administration to plan the activity of a market economy. Yet, they keep trying. We are reminded again, in our study of economic systems, of Samuel Johnson's observation about a dog walking on its hind legs: It may not be done well, but you are surprised to find it done at all.

Summary

France has a tradition of social discord, which encouraged the development of strong governmental institutions under Colbert, Napoleon, and De Gaulle to maintain order. This led to a tradition of governmental intervention in the economy. One important form of that intervention has been the system of indicative planning, established after World War II. Indicative planning is meant to improve the operation of the market mechanism through cooperation and exchange of information. Compliance with the plan is voluntary, but it is encouraged by governmental financial and regulatory actions and by the relatively new system of plan contracts. The record of plan fulfillment in recent years has not been good.

France also has long experience with nationalized industries; a wide range of operations were nationalized by Mitterrand in 1982. The Chirac government, however, initiated a privatization program in 1986. French industry is concentrated, but firm sizes are relatively small. Mergers are encouraged. The labor union movement is relatively weak.

The financial system also has a tradition of governmental participation in ownership and regulation. A program of financial deregulation was initiated in 1985.

During the postwar years, the general stance of fiscal and monetary policy has been pro-growth, with occasional austerity programs to handle balance of payments problems. The Mitterrand government was forced to adopt an austerity program in 1982–1983, followed by a series of tax and spending cuts and a broad-based program to alleviate unemployment.

Discussion and Review Questions

1. Describe the organizational structure and procedure used to formulate an indicative plan in France.

2. What would be the arguments for and against the adoption of indicative planning in the United States?

3. How are the French and American labor markets similar? How are they different?

4. Describe the measures that have been taken in recent years to alleviate the unemployment problem. Do you believe that they will help or hurt in the short-run and the long-run?

Suggested Readings

Caron, Francois. *An Economic History of Modern France.* New York: Columbia University Press, 1979. *Provides a wealth of statistical data and analysis on developments between 1815 and 1975.*

Cave, Martin. "French Planning Reforms 1981–1984." *ACES Bulletin* 26 (Summer–Fall 1984): 29–38. *Describes the efforts of the Mitterrand administration to breathe new life into indicative planning.*

Cohen, Stephen S. *Modern Capitalist Planning: The French Model.* Cambridge: Harvard University Press, 1969. *Provides an interesting description of the interplay between planning institutions and a good account of the formulation of the first four plans.*

Estrin, Saul and Peter Holmes. *French Planning in Theory and Practice.* Boston: Allyn and Unwin, 1983. *One of the few surveys of the theoretical literature on indicative planning, including its capacity to reduce uncertainty.*

Hayward, Jack. *The State and the Market Economy.* New York: New York University Press, 1986. *Particularly strong on the policies of the Mitterrand administration and the relationship between national and local economic authorities.*

Hough, J. R. *The French Economy.* New York: Holmes and Meier, 1982. *A brief overview of the system, with a particularly strong chapter on regional policy.*

Lauber, Volkmar. *The Political Economy of France.* New York: Praeger, 1983. *Primarily covers the period from Pompidou to Mitterrand, concentrating on political aspects.*

Monnet, Jean. *Memoirs.* Garden City, N.Y.: Doubleday, 1978. *A fascinating first-hand account of the establishment of indicative planning, the founding of the European Community, and a broad range of other experiences.*

Organization for Economic Cooperation and Development. *OECD Economic Survey 1986/87: France.* Paris: 1987. *Along with the usual review of macroeconomic events, this issue includes an extended discussion of financial deregulation and reform.*

China

U.S.S.R

North
Korea

South
Korea

Sea of
Japan

Sapporo

Hokkaido

Aomori

Sendai

Honshu

Nagano

Kyoto Nagoya Tokyo
Kobe Yokohama

Hiroshima Osaka

Kitakyushu
Fukuoka Matsuyama Pacific
Nagasaki Shikoku Ocean

Kyushu

Japan

9

JAPAN: MIRACLE OR MYTH?

*When I inquire about
Ohira on my latest
Japanese trip, there is
embarrassed silence.
"We had to let him go,"
the chairman says. "He is
an oldest son and his
father, who owns a small
wholesale business . . .
demanded that he take
over the family
company." "Did he want
to leave?" I ask. "Of
course not, but he had no
choice . . . Executives,
after all, have to set an
example—and in Japan
an oldest son is still
expected to follow his
father in his business."
—Peter Drucker
  The Wall Street
  Journal, August 21,
  1980*

By most accounts, Japan is the economic success story of the postwar era. Between 1950 and 1985, Japanese national income multiplied 10 times and income per person multiplied about 7 times. This record is unmatched by any other industrial country, capitalist or socialist. Economists of all stripes have attempted to claim Japan as proof of their model. Conservatives are quick to say that the Japanese miracle was performed with a low level of government spending and taxation. Liberals are equally eager to emphasize the active role of the Japanese government in industrial policy and indicative planning.

Ironically, praise of the Japanese economic system in other countries has coincided with rising criticism of the system within Japan. The miracle lost some of its magic when the oil shocks of the 1970s caused a rapid deceleration of economic growth. In surveys that have been taken every year since 1974 by the prime minister's office, only 2 to 5 percent of the respondents say that their standard of living has improved over the previous year. The proportion who say that their living level has declined during the year was never lower than 25 percent and in 1986 the figure was 35 percent.[1] Somehow, the growth in real national income that transpired during these years seems to have bought little happiness.

How did Japan rise from the ashes of World War II to become the world's third largest industrial power? What role did Japanese culture play, and what role was played by the government? Can the Japanese system be exported to other countries? Should it be? Why do the citizens of this successful, paternalistic country have a relatively high suicide rate? Japan, as we will see, is a most fascinating and enigmatic country.

The Environment

Japan is a country with little land and many people. A population more than half the size of America is squeezed onto a group of islands that are collectively smaller than California. To make matters worse, most of the country's terrain is mountainous; only about 18 percent is arable. In 1984 Japan depended on imports for 82 percent of its energy and for practically all of its iron ore, copper, tin, aluminum, nickel, and uranium.

Sociologists tell us that the Japanese are driven by a survivor mentality, a result of the lack of natural resources and the trauma and nuclear devastation of World War II. The refrain, "We must work very hard because we are a poor island nation," has become a cliché. The American belief, "All things are possible in a land of opportunity," stands in stark contrast.

Having lived in isolation from the rest of the world for more than two centuries (1603 to 1867), the Japanese population is among the most homogeneous in the world. The people share a common race, culture, language, and

---

[1] *Survey on People's Living,* cited in Jon Woronoff, *The Japan Syndrome* (New Brunswick, N.J.: Transaction Books, 1986), 26; and Masayoshi Kanabayashi, "The Japanese, Despite Great Affluence, Perceive Themselves as Poor, Insecure," *Wall Street Journal,* June 4, 1987, 22.

value system. Japanese homogeneity again contrasts sharply to American individualism. One positive aspect is that the unity of Japanese society encourages the settlement of disputes through conciliation, compromise, and other honorable means, rather than through conflict and litigation. Labor-management relations are generally peaceful, and there are fewer lawyers in Japan than in the city of Philadelphia.

On the negative side, Japanese homogeneity is said to stifle the initiative and creativity that one finds in an individualistic society. The Japanese educational system, which emphasizes rote memorization rather than critical thinking, offers little reward to those who have a capacity for original thought. Technologically, this renders Japan a nation of copiers, not inventors. During 1946 to 1984, Japan won only 4 Nobel prizes in chemistry, physics, and medicine, compared with 6 in France, 8 in the Soviet Union, 13 in Germany, 45 in the United Kingdom, and 115 in the United States.[2]

As technological imitators, however, the Japanese have done extremely well. Their success in this area can be explained in many ways, but part of the explanation is cultural. In contrast to the superstitions and taboos that have inhibited the advance of technology in many underdeveloped countries, Japanese Confucianism is an intellectual and rationalistic system. Thus Morishima believes it was entirely owing to the intellectualism of Confucianism that Western science was transplanted quickly and painlessly in Japan.[3]

Also on the negative side, Japanese homogeneity apparently has contributed to racist and xenophobic tendencies. The Japanese public was not alarmed by, and most probably agreed with, Prime Minister Nakasone's assertion in 1986 that American intellectual development is held back by the black and Hispanic populations. The 700,000 Korean residents in Japan, many of whom are children of laborers who were brought to the country forcibly during the 1910 to 1945 occupation of Korea, cannot obtain automatic citizenship even if they were born and raised in Japan. And despite their proximity, less than 5,000 Indochinese refugees settled in Japan from 1971 to 1984, compared with over 600,000 in the United States.[4]

Finally, the homogeneity of the Japanese population reinforces a tight system of familial and social obligations. As the introductory quotation for this chapter indicates, the father-dominated family is still a very important institution in Japan. Beyond that, the Japanese worker experiences a familial relationship with his employer, particularly if the worker has a commitment for lifetime employment. Furthermore, the Japanese company engages in a familial relationship with other companies in its *zaibatsu* or *keiretsu* conglomerate and with the paternalistic government. While these family ties contribute to a

---

[2]U.S. Department of Commerce, Bureau of the Census, *Statistical Abstract of the United States 1986* (Washington, D.C.: USGPO, 1985), 581.

[3]Michio Morishima, *Why Has Japan 'Succeeded'?* (Cambridge: Cambridge University Press, 1982), 61.

[4]George Fields, "Racism Is Accepted Practice in Japan," *Wall Street Journal,* November 10, 1986, 19; and U.S. Department of Commerce, Bureau of the Census, *Statistical Abstract of the United States 1986,* 86.

sense of security, cooperation, and communication, they discourage social and occupational mobility. A Japanese elder son may be compelled to continue in his father's business; a worker under the permanent commitment system is tied to his employer by a set of neo-feudal mutual obligations.

A Brief History

From the seventh century A.D., when the monarchy was established, until 1603, when a unified military dictatorship was founded by the Tokugawa family, Japan experienced a chronic state of civil war. The Tokugawa regime gave Japan 250 years of peace, law, and order, but it imposed a feudal economic order and a policy of total isolation from the outside world. Thus, the country developed culturally, but fell far behind the West in the fields of science and technology.

The Japanese became aware of their backward state in 1853, when Commodore Perry arrived with his fearsome fleet of steam-powered ships and delivered a letter from the president of the United States (Franklin Pierce) demanding the opening of trade relations. The ensuing domestic debate led to a civil war in 1867; the military dictatorship was overthrown and the monarchy restored under the young emperor Meiji.

The new Meiji regime opened the door to foreign trade, abolished many of the feudal institutions, and attempted to close the technology gap. It established the legal equality of all social classes and gave everyone the legal (if not social) freedom to choose their trade or occupation. Feudal guilds were eliminated, the agricultural estates were divided between the peasants, and monetary taxes replaced payments in kind. Primary education (with a Western curriculum) was made compulsory, and foreigners were employed as educators, advisors, and corporate officers. The government established a number of large state-run businesses and supported private industry through extension of loans and subsidies. Government enterprises accounted for about 40 percent of total investment during the Meiji period.[5]

The Meiji reforms drew Japan into the modern world and ushered in a period of rapid economic growth between 1913 and 1938. This ended with the devastation of World War II. The war destroyed about one-fourth of the nation's buildings and structures, one-third of its industrial machinery, and more than 80 percent of its ships. Japan was stripped of its colonies and investments in Manchuria, Korea, and Formosa; reparations payments required the dismantling of some industrial capacity. Unlike Germany, Japan was not surrounded by other countries with rapid recoveries and expanding markets. Japanese recovery was slow and the prewar level of GNP was not reached until 1954.[6]

[5]Angus Maddison, *Economic Growth in Japan and the USSR* (New York: W. W. Norton, 1969), 23.

[6]Ibid., 46.

Table 9.1   Size Distribution of Japanese and American Manufacturing Establishments

	Percentage of Manufacturing Output Produced by Establishments with:		
	0–99 Workers	100–499 Workers	Over 499 Workers
Japan (1983)	39	26	35
United States (1982)	23	31	46

Sources: Statistics Bureau, Management Coordination Agency, *Japan Statistical Yearbook 1986* (Tokyo: 1986), 214; and U.S. Department of Commerce, Bureau of the Census, *1982 Census of Manufactures*, General Summary, Part 2 (Washington, D.C.: USGPO, 1985), 1–3.

The outbreak of the Korean War in 1950 caused a rapid growth in the demand for Japanese exports. It also induced the United States to recognize the importance of Japan as an outpost against communism in the Far East. Hence, American policy toward Japan shifted from punishment to encouragement. For these and other reasons, a period of miraculous growth began around 1953 and continued until the oil shock of 1974.

Industrial Organization

Japanese business is characterized by a dual market structure—very large businesses and very small businesses with very few in the middle. As shown in Table 9.1, medium-sized companies (those with 100–499 employees) account for only a quarter of manufactured output in Japan, compared to almost a third of output in the United States. On the other hand, small firms account for a much larger percentage of output and employment in Japan than they do in the United States. Thus, according to conventional measurements, the average level of industrial concentration in Japan is relatively low.[7] Conventional measurements, however, do not reflect the hierarchical nature of Japanese business, wherein many small firms are members of industrial families that are dominated by the large firms. The control of Japanese industry is probably far more concentrated than the figures suggest.

Big Business

In 1985, Japan was the home of 28 of the world's 200 largest industrial corporations (Table A.10). Only the United States had a larger share. The 20 largest Japanese industrial corporations, most of which are automotive, electrical, electronic, and steel manufacturers, are listed in Table 9.2. Japan is also

[7]Richard Caves and Masu Uekusa, "Industrial Organization," in *Asia's New Giant*, ed. Hugh Patrick and Henry Rosovsky (Washington, D.C.: The Brookings Institution, 1976), 472. See also, Takatoshi Nakamura, "Japan's Giant Enterprises—Their Power and Influence," *Japanese Economic Studies* 12 (Summer 1984): 62.

Table 9.2   Japan's Largest Industrial Corporations, 1985

Company	Sales (U.S. $ million)	Employees
Toyota Motor	26,040	79,901
Matsushita Electric	20,749	133,963
Hitachi	20,525	164,951
Nissan Motor	18,226	108,500
Mitsubishi Heavy Ind.	14,111	90,300
Toshiba	13,502	114,000
Nippon Oil	13,478	10,300
Nippon Steel	12,535	72,081
Honda Motor	10,753	50,609
Idemitsu Kosan	9,439	5,921
NEC	9,246	90,102
Mitsubishi Electric	8,201	68,745
Showa Shell Sekiyu	6,819	3,157
Mazda Motor	6,680	29,148
Fujitsu	6,396	74,187
Nippon Kokan	6,286	36,851
Sanyo Electric	6,228	25,429
Maruzen Oil	6,015	1,992
Sony	5,776	44,908
Kobe Steel	5,314	32,524

Source: "The International 500," *Fortune,* August 4, 1986, 181–182.

the home of the world's largest trading companies and some of the world's largest banks.

A few of the large companies, including the Mitsui and Sumitomo groups, date back to the feudal Tokugawa years. The big jump in industrial concentration began, however, in the 1880s, when a fiscal crisis forced the government to sell some of its nationalized companies to the public. Since few people could afford to buy them, the privatized companies fell into the hands of a few wealthy families and eventually grew into conglomerates that were known as the *zaibatsu* (the financial clique).[8]

By the turn of the century, the four major *zaibatsu* groups—Mitsui, Mitsubishi, Sumitomo, and Yasuda—developed their own characteristic form of organization. Each was organized around a family-owned holding company that controlled shares in a diversified and interdependent group of industrial corporations, banks, trading companies, and other businesses. The larger firms controlled shares in smaller subsidiaries and suppliers, creating a pyramid arrangement under the holding company. The *zaibatsu* bank provided financing for all of the firms in the group, the trading company handled the intelligence and marketing function for the entire group, and other firms performed other specialized functions for the *zaibatsu* family.

[8]Edwin O. Reischauer, *Japan: The Story of a Nation,* 3d ed. (New York: Alfred A. Knopf, 1981), 130–131.

Aided by their close connections with the government, by the total lack of antitrust legislation, and by their participation in world trade, colonialism, and mobilization for war, the *zaibatsu* organizations grew in economic and political influence. By the end of World War II, the four largest *zaibatsu* owned about one-fourth of the paid-in capital of Japanese incorporated business.[9]

After the war, the American occupation forces attempted to create a more competitive and decentralized industrial structure in Japan. Through a series of laws, some of which were drafted by the Antitrust Division of the U.S. Justice Department, the *zaibatsu* were broken up, their holding companies were dissolved, and thousands of their officers and stockholders were purged for their wartime activities. Banks were forbidden to hold more than 5 (later 10) percent of the stock of a given company, mergers were placed under strict limits, and a number of unfair business practices were prohibited.

After the Allied occupation ended in 1952, the Japanese government relaxed its enforcement of the antitrust laws. A restoration of big business was considered to be necessary if Japan was to exert its economic power on world markets. Because the *zaibatsu* holding companies were not allowed to reorganize, the banks and trading companies took on a more important role. A new kind of industrial conglomeration developed, the *keiretsu* (group)—a loose confederation of companies that borrow from the same bank and sell through the same trading company. The limited development of the Japanese securities market, making businesses dependent on bank lending for their capital needs, strengthens the *keiretsu* arrangement. Coordination of each group is also accomplished through interlocking directorates and presidents' clubs.

Several of the *keiretsu,* including Mitsui, Mitsubishi, and Sumitomo, were formed by the regrouping of former *zaibatsu* firms. Others were created anew around the large banks. Today, except for a few companies such as Honda and Sony, most of the large companies have some relationship with one of the *keiretsu* organizations. In 1985, the nine major trading companies had combined sales of $380 billion (about one-third of Japan's GNP) and handled about half of all exports and imports.[10]

According to the available evidence, the profitability of *keiretsu* members is no greater than the profitability of large unaffiliated firms.[11] Companies apparently join the groups principally for the familial security that they provide. The members provide steady markets for the products of other members, while the *keiretsu* bank provides financial support for all of the members. When one company has excess labor, it is possible to transfer workers to another member without violating the permanent commitment. The *keiretsu* are a natural expression of the Japanese culture (see "Why Can't We Sell on the Japanese Market?").

Although little competition exists between companies that are members of a single *keiretsu,* competition between the groups is fierce. When one group

[9]Caves and Uekusa, "Industrial Organization," 462.

[10]*Wall Street Journal,* March 31, 1986, 22.

[11]Caves and Uekusa, "Industrial Organization," 502–504.

WHY CAN'T WE SELL ON THE JAPANESE MARKET?

In the wake of enormous Japanese trade surpluses (for example, $86 billion in 1986), the United States and other countries have called on Japan to open its markets. This will not be accomplished easily, however, because protectionism is deeply ingrained in Japanese trade, both international and domestic. Often, it is difficult for a member of one *keiretsu* corporate family to sell its goods to a member of a different *keiretsu.* This point is illustrated by the observations of a banker in Tokyo:

> *My office used to be located in a building owned by Mitsubishi Real Estate. The elevators in it were built by Mitsubishi Elevator. Last year when my firm moved to a new building owned by a real estate company associated with Toshiba, it wasn't necessary to ride in the elevators to learn who manufactured them. It was nearly preordained—they were Toshiba elevators. Were the price and quality the factors governing the owners' decisions to purchase those elevators? Could Westinghouse or Otis have sold their elevators to either owner if they had offered them at competitive prices? It's unlikely.*

Source: Laurence Bresler, "You Won't Find a Bargain in Tokyo," *The Wall Street Journal,* October 20, 1986, 23. Reprinted by permission of *The Wall Street Journal,* © Dow Jones & Company, Inc. 1986. All Rights Reserved.

develops a new product, the other groups usually are eager to offer their own model, battling for market share. This has been the pattern for everything from bicycles and radios to ships, robots, and genetic engineering products.

In a few industries, including textiles and shipbuilding, the government has sponsored the formation of rationalization cartels to forestall excessive competition. The government also allows the formation of temporary recession cartels during economic downturns. The latter may actually contribute to the level of competition in the long run preventing the bankruptcy of large numbers of competitors.

Finally, the large corporations wield an unusual measure of influence over the government through their participation in four big business federations, whose leaders are collectively known as the **zaikai.** The most important of these is the Keidanren (Federation of Economic Organizations), which includes 118 smaller business federations and 845 prominent corporations. Keidanren has 60 departments and committees that formulate policy on everything from taxation and transportation to space research and cooperation with Venezuela.[12]

[12]Kenjiro Horikawa, "Federation of Economic Organizations: Keidanren," *Journal of Japanese Trade and Industry* (May–June 1985): 14–16.

Prominent members of the *zaikai* hold regular breakfast meetings with government leaders and serve as chairmen of scores of governmental advisory boards and panels. These include, for example, the Economic Council (attached to the Economic Planning Agency), the Industrial Structure Council (which advises the Ministry of International Trade and Industry), and the Commission on Administrative Reform (established to reduce the size of the governmental bureaucracy).

Recommendations from the business community are backed by tens of billions of yen donated to election campaigns. They are also supported by the practice of *amakudari* (descent from heaven), whereby senior bureaucrats are allowed to retire into well-paid jobs in the private sector in exchange for political favors. According to some, "No legislation strongly opposed by the *zaikai* is introduced by the government or passed by the Diet."[13] A more extreme position is taken by Woronoff, who claims that "the country's economic policy is not really determined by the Prime Minister or the bureaucrats," but by "three old men in their seventies and eighties who are in charge of the leading businessmen's associations."[14]

Small Businesses

The dominance of the large companies and conglomerates should not obscure the fact that 99 percent of all Japanese companies, accounting for more than 75 percent of the labor force, have fewer than 100 employees. These small companies take several forms. Japan has a relatively large number of very small retail and wholesale establishments. The average Japanese retail establishment has only three employees, compared with more than seven in the average American establishment.[15] Because economies of scale are substantial in retailing, the Japanese system is inefficient. This pattern is gradually changing, however, as Japanese youth become less interested in taking over the family business. The number of stores run by individuals declined by 8 percent during 1982 to 1985, while the number of corporate-run stores increased by 35 percent.[16]

In manufacturing, almost two-thirds of the small firms are primarily subcontractors for larger firms. In some specific sectors—including machinery, motor vehicles, clothing, and construction—subcontracted work can amount to 70–90 percent of the value of the finished products. Subcontractors provide everything from manufactured components to marketing and janitorial services.

---

[13]S. Prakash Sethi, Nobuaki Namiki, and Carl Swanson, *The False Promise of the Japanese Miracle* (Boston: Pitman, 1984), 21.

[14]Woronoff, *The Japanese Syndrome,* 125.

[15]The American figure is taken from U.S. Department of Commerce, Bureau of the Census, *Statistical Abstract of the United States 1986* (Washington, D.C.: USGPO, 1985), 779. The Japanese figure is from Keizai Koho Center, *Japan 1985: An International Comparison* (Tokyo: 1985), 29.

[16]Christopher Chipello, "Mom-and-Pop Stores Lose Favor in Japan," *Wall Street Journal,* March 18, 1987, 20.

The large firms derive several advantages by contracting much of their work out to smaller companies. Some say that the large companies unfairly exploit the dependent position of the smaller companies. First, because the wages of workers in small firms are generally lower than those in large firms (about 21 percent lower in 1984), large firms can reduce their labor costs by subcontracting.[17]

A second advantage to prime contractors is their ability to shift the cost of holding inventories of parts and assemblies to subcontractors. This is known in Japan as the "just in time" inventory method. Third, during recessions the large firms are able to maintain the employment of their own permanent commitment laborers by reducing the amount of subcontracted work. For this reason, and because they find it difficult to obtain the bank financing needed during lean years, small firms are far more vulnerable to business cycles than large firms. Finally, according to Woronoff, the subcontractors are given "the most painful, tedious, and unproductive jobs while the more pleasant, mechanized, and profitable ones are kept in-house."[18]

The Labor Market and Labor Relations

Japan has few significant natural resources other than its people. Management and motivation of the labor force, therefore, are most important aspects of the economic system. Japan has been successful in this regard. Labor productivity has grown rapidly, unemployment has been kept at very low levels (between 1.5 and 3 percent), strike activity has been moderate (Table A.11), and new manufacturing technologies have been introduced with a minimum of resistance from the labor unions. These are the achievements of a unique system of labor-market institutions.

Collective Bargaining

Organized labor does not have a long history in Japan. Before World War II, a few experiments with unionism were attempted with little success. After the war, in line with its effort to break up the power of the *zaibatsu* organizations, the Allied occupation authorities instituted reforms that encouraged the formation of labor unions and guaranteed basic rights to organized labor. In response, union membership soared to almost 7 million by 1948, reaching more than 50 percent of the industrial labor force.[19] The unions, which had socialist ties, lost some legislative ground during the Cold War and were dealt another blow by the ascent in 1955 of the conservative Liberal Democratic

---

[17]Organization for Economic Cooperation and Development, *OECD Economic Surveys 1986/ 1987: Japan* (Paris: 1986), Table 25B.

[18]Woronoff, *The Japan Syndrome,* 79.

[19]Solomon Levine, "Japan," in *International Handbook of Industrial Relations,* ed. Albert Blum (Westport, Conn.: Greenwood Press, 1981), 323–330.

Party (which has controlled Japanese politics since that time). Together with the rise of the nonunionized service economy, these forces have reduced union membership to about 22 percent of the labor force—roughly the U.S. level (Table A.11).

The majority (about 85 percent) of Japanese union members are organized in comprehensive enterprise-based unions. The unions are comprehensive in that their membership includes all of the permanent employees of the enterprise, including white-collar personnel with ranks lower than section chief. Most of the enterprise-based unions are affiliated with industrial, regional, and national federations, but little authority is given to the latter to conduct collective bargaining, strikes, and grievance procedures. Relations within the Japanese company families are not always harmonious, but every effort is made to keep all disagreements within the family. Thus, Japan experiences very few "sympathy" strikes.

The three large national federations serve as political lobbying units for the labor movement, as forums for information and discussion, and as organizers of the so-called Spring Labor Offensive. Sohyo, the largest federation (accounting for about one-third of all union members) supports the Socialist Party, and Domei (which represents almost one-fifth of union members) supports the Democratic Socialist Party. Thus, they stand in perpetual opposition to the ruling, business-backed Liberal Democratic Party. The third federation, Churitsu-Roren (including about 11 percent of union members) attempts to remain politically neutral.

The **Spring Labor Offensive** (*Shunto*) is the most coordinated activity of the Japanese labor unions. Formally initiated in 1955 under the leadership of Sohyo, it usually begins in December or January when the national federations announce targets for basic wage increases. These are usually countered by a recommendation from Nikkeiren, the Federation of Employers' Associations. On several occasions, corporate executives have voluntarily reduced their own salaries when asking labor to reduce wage demands. In early April, while the corporations are hiring new graduates for permanent employment, the unions stage a number of brief 1- or 2-day strikes and demonstrations to assert their solidarity. Following this, negotiations are conducted at the industry level and settlements are reached at the company level. In 1986, for example, the iron and steel workers demanded a raise of 5.8 percent and settled for 2.7 percent. In 1987, faced by rising unemployment, they did not ask for any wage increase.[20]

Like the Swedish system of centralized collective bargaining, Shunto provides a forum for coordinated negotiations between national labor and employer confederations, thus setting guidelines for subsequent local negotiations. Unlike their Swedish counterparts, however, the Japanese labor confederations have neither the need nor the ability to discipline the docile company unions. The Spring Labor Offensive has worked so smoothly, gener-

[20]Masayoshi Kanabayashi, "Japanese Unions Lower Wage Demands Amid Concerns About Rising Joblessness," *Wall Street Journal,* January 23, 1987, 18.

ating reasonable wage increases and limited strike activity, that an adaptation of the system has been proposed for the United States.[21] It is difficult to say, however, whether it would work as well in the adversarial American environment.

Lifetime Employment

Perhaps the most distinctive feature of the Japanese labor market is the permanent commitment system of employment. Under this arrangement, the large corporations and selected employees are honor-bound to maintain their employment relationship until retirement. The corporations promise that they will not dismiss their permanent employees, except under the most extreme circumstances (for example, embezzlement). The employees pledge that they will not abandon their employer for a more attractive job. The system is another reflection of the family aspect of Japanese business.

The permanent commitment system does not apply to everyone. It generally excludes women, who traditionally join the labor force after graduation, drop out after marriage, and then take up work again in their late thirties and forties when their children are grown. Only 48 percent of Japanese women between the ages of 25 and 34 are economically active, compared to 69 percent in the United States and France, and 74 percent in Sweden.[22] In the large Japanese corporations, the average female employee has less than half as many years of service as the average male, and her income is about 40 percent smaller.[23]

The permanent commitment system is not practiced in smaller enterprises, which employ the majority of Japanese workers, and it does not apply to all of the male workers in large corporations. According to most estimates the system covers about 25 to 30 percent of the labor force. Thus, while the system does not give a universal guarantee of employment to the labor force, it is large enough to influence the operation of the economic system.

A positive aspect of the permanent commitment system is that it provides security to those workers who are covered and reinforces their sense of loyalty to the company family. Thus, it contributes to the relatively low level of labor unrest and encourages the workers to identify their own destiny with that of the company. This, in turn, may help explain the willingness of employees to participate after working hours without pay in quality control circles and other programs to improve the efficiency and quality of production. According to Toyota, the suggestions of the quality control circles have generated annual savings of $230 million for the company.[24]

[21]Robert Evans, "Lessons from Japan's Incomes Policy," *Challenge* 27 (January–February 1985): 33–39.

[22]*Yearbook of Labour Statistics 1984* (Geneva: International Labour Office, 1984), 26–42.

[23]Organization for Economic Cooperation and Development, *OECD Economic Surveys 1986/ 1987: Japan* (Paris: 1986), Table 25B.

[24]Kenichi Ohmae, "Quality Control Circles: They Work and Don't Work," *Wall Street Journal,* March 29, 1982, 22.

The permanent commitment system may also help to explain the excellent performance of the Japanese in adopting modern production technologies. Employees under the system, who have little fear of technological unemployment, are not likely to resist the introduction of robots and other innovations that make their jobs easier. Employers are willing to spend time and money to train their employees for new technologies, knowing that their company—not a competitor—will reap the benefits.

The system also presents a number of problems. From the employer's perspective, many workers who are redundant, incompetent, or unmotivated must be retained. Japanese manufacturers kept about two million extra workers on their payrolls during the oil crisis of the late 1970s; and estimates of the number of expendable workers ranged from 500,000 to 1,200,000 in 1987.[25] Some of these are assigned such tasks as messengers and doorkeepers; sidelined middle managers are sometimes assigned to the *madogiwa-zoku,* "the window-seat tribe." As the name implies, they are expected to do little more than look out the windows, while the valued employees work in the inner offices (which often have no windows).[26]

From the workers' perspective, the lifetime employment system, together with the seniority wage system, makes it very difficult to leave a job for a better one with another employer. According to a survey by the Japanese prime minister's office, only 59 percent of young Japanese workers say that they are satisfied or more-or-less satisfied with their place of work, compared to 83 percent in the United States.[27] The proportion of male workers between the ages of 20 and 45 who change jobs in any given year is about four times larger in the United States than it is in Japan.[28] The fate of the lifetime employee is in the hands of his employer.

The lifetime employees are considered an elite class of workers. According to Woronoff, "this means that the others are much worse off," because they serve as a buffer. "Since they are the buffer and regular employees are not fired, the ordinary worker is exposed to even greater chances of losing a job than otherwise."[29]

Despite Japanese reverence for the elderly, older employees are another buffer group. The mandatory retirement age in most companies is 55, although Japanese life expectancy (77 years) is among the longest in the world. When employment cuts are needed, companies often resort to the "golden handshake"—payment of bonuses to employees, aged 45 or older, who agree to early voluntary retirement. After losing their prestigious permanent position, these older workers are often forced to find a new job at lower pay. While

[25]Karl Schoenberger, "The Trauma of Job Uncertainty Is Confronting Workers in Japan," *Wall Street Journal,* June 1, 1987, 15.

[26]Sethi, Namiki, and Swanson, *The False Promise,* 232, 235.

[27]Toyohiro Kono, "An Excerpt from Strategy and Structure of Japanese Enterprises," *Japanese Economic Studies* 13 (Fall–Winter 1984–85): 194.

[28]Isao Ohashi, "A Comparison of the Labor Market in Japan and the United States," *Japanese Economic Studies* 11 (Summer 1983): 63.

[29]Woronoff, *The Japan Syndrome,* 66.

cause and effect is impossible to establish, it should be noted that the elderly Japanese have one of the highest suicide rates in the industrial world.[30]

In recent years, with Japanese economic growth decelerating and unemployment rising, the buffer of retiring workers and subcontractors has not been large enough to protect even the younger permanent employees. For example, Nippon Steel, the world's largest steelmaker, suffered a 19 percent decline in sales for the 1986–1987 fiscal year. In response, the company developed a plan to rationalize 19,000 jobs, accounting for one-third of its work force, over 4 years. Approximately half of the job cuts are to be handled through early retirement and some surplus workers will be added to the *madogiwa-zoku.* In many cases, however, the permanent employees will be forced to find jobs elsewhere (with help from Nippon); more than 2,000 have already faced temporary layoffs.[31]

Seniority Pay and Bonuses

The Japanese wage system is characterized by two interesting practices. First, in many private and public organizations, wage levels are determined largely by the length of service of the employee, rather than by skill, performance, or position. Although the seniority system does not completely exclude other considerations (and many Japanese corporations say that they base wages on merit alone), the statistical evidence indicates that seniority has a greater impact on wages in Japan than in the United States.[32] The seniority system reinforces the permanent commitment system because it is costly for an employee to lose seniority with a job change. It also encourages companies to force their older, higher-paid, workers into early retirement.

The other unique aspect of the compensation system is the extensive use of bonuses. In contrast to the practice in other Western countries, where salary bonuses usually are paid only to top management, Japanese companies pay semiannual bonuses to all regular employees—from janitors to presidents. For managerial employees, the size of the bonus varies according to individual performance; all other employees usually receive the same percentage of their regular salary. On average, production workers in manufacturing receive about 20 percent of their compensation in bonuses, compared with less than 1 percent in the United States and the United Kingdom.[33]

The system of bonuses is important in many ways. First, like profit-sharing schemes in other countries, it may contribute to the employees' interest in the performance of their company and to their motivation to work. Second,

---

[30]U.S. Commerce Department, Bureau of the Census, *Statistical Abstract of the United States 1986,* 841.

[31]Schoenberger, "The Trauma of Job Uncertainty," 15; and *Wall Street Journal,* October 30, 1986, 34.

[32]Ohashi, "A Comparison," 60.

[33]U.S. Department of Labor, Bureau of Labor Statistics, *Handbook of Labor Statistics* (Washington, D.C.: USGPO, 1985), 439–440.

if the bonuses are regarded as transitory income by the workers, Friedman's permanent income hypothesis suggests that a relatively large portion of bonus income will be saved. Thus, the bonuses may help explain the Japanese population's high savings rate, which finances the high rate of investment and economic growth.

Is Japan a Share Economy?

One interesting result of the bonus system is suggested by Martin Weitzman of MIT. According to Weitzman, Japan is a living laboratory for an economic system that he calls a **share economy,** in which workers are paid a fixed share of the revenue of their company instead of a fixed wage.[34] In a pure share economy, Weitzman claims that profit-maximizing employers would expand employment and output until "every qualified person in the economy seeking work has a job."[35] Briefly put, this is based on the fact that revenue-sharing employers would maximize their profits by maximizing revenues, which would usually call for a larger level of production than profit maximization with a fixed wage. Thus, Weitzman argues that the bonus system may help explain the very low level of unemployment in Japan and advocates the adoption of a similar system in other countries.

Weitzman's assertion that the wage system is *the* cause of unemployment in capitalist economies, and his argument that unemployment can be eradicated by the adoption of a share economy, have both met stiff disagreement.[36] Critics say that a theory of unemployment based on wage rigidity cannot explain, for example, how the world economy slipped into the Great Depression and takes little account of the influence of expectations and uncertainty.

There was a time when a share economy—better known as sharecropping—dominated the world agricultural system. It gradually disappeared as the need to economize on labor and to introduce new agricultural technologies increased. If we were to return to a pure share economy today, Paul Davidson argues, unemployment may decrease, but "we would see an auto industry where workers hand-carried car frames down the assembly line . . . ."[37]

Even if a pure share economy can theoretically deliver what Weitzman claims it can, the bonus system may not explain the low rate of unemployment

[34]Martin L. Weitzman, *The Share Economy: Conquering Stagflation* (Cambridge: Harvard University Press, 1984), 73.

[35]Ibid., 6. For a technical proof of this proposition, see Martin L. Weitzman, "The Simple Macroeconomics of Profit Sharing," *The American Economic Review* 75 (December 1985): 937–953.

[36]See Kurt Rothschild, "Is There a Weitzman Miracle?" and Paul Davidson, "The Simple Macroeconomics of a Nonergodic Monetary Economy versus a Share Economy: Is Weitzman's Macroeconomics Too Simple?" both in *Journal of Post Keynesian Economics* 9 (Winter 1986–1987): 198–225; and papers by William Nordhaus and James Tobin in *The Share Economy: A Symposium,* ed. William Nordhaus and Andrew John, *Journal of Comparative Economics* 10 (December 1986): 414–473.

[37]Davidson, "The Simple Macroeconomics," 220.

Table 9.3 Gross Saving As a Percentage of GDP

	1966	1975	1985
United States	20.2	18.1	16.5
Japan	32.1	32.3	31.4
Germany	26.8	20.9	22.2
France	25.8	23.0	18.0
United Kingdom	19.6	15.5	19.2
Italy	22.8	20.1	17.7
Canada	23.9	21.1	18.6
Average of Countries Above	22.5	21.1	20.0
Austria	28.6	25.9	24.4
Belgium	23.6	21.8	15.9
Denmark	22.9	19.4	15.4
Greece	20.3	23.3	12.2
Ireland	19.0	21.8	18.1
Netherlands	26.3	23.1	24.1
Norway	27.9	26.7	30.0
Spain	22.8	23.5	21.0
Sweden	25.2	23.8	17.8
Switzerland	30.2	27.8	30.0
Total OECD	22.7	21.5	20.2

Source: *OECD Economic Outlook* 40 (December 1986): Table R4.

in Japan. The bulk of Japanese income is still paid in wages rather than bonuses, and the bonus rate is usually settled in the annual Shunto wage negotiations. In Japan, bonuses may be little more than another form of wage payment. According to econometric estimates, the fluctuation of bonus payments is correlated more closely with wages than with profits.[38] Weitzman's critics propose that the low rate of Japanese unemployment is explained by several factors that are not included in his theory:

1. The rapid rate of output growth caused by the high savings rate, assimilation of foreign technology, and other factors;

2. The stabilizing influence of the permanent commitment system of employment on aggregate demand; and

[38]Merton J. Peck, "Is Japan Really a Share Economy?" in *The Share Economy: A Symposium*, 428–431.

3.   The observed tendency of unemployed Japanese workers (particularly women) to leave the labor force during times of recession, so that they are counted only as discouraged workers.[39]

The Financial Sector

The high rate of economic growth in Japan is explained, in large part, by the nation's high rate of saving and investment (Table 9.3). The high saving rate, in turn, may be explained by a number of factors. First, young workers are motivated to save for the enormous down payments that are required to purchase a home and to provide for their old age. Retirement comes early in Japan and social security benefits are modest. Second, as discussed above, the system of semiannual bonuses may encourage saving.

Third, the government provides tax incentives to savers, including tax-free interest income on small saving accounts (up to $15,000). In the past, the government often generated its own savings in the form of budget surpluses. Finally, the high savings rate may be not only a cause but also an effect of the high rate of economic growth. Growth contributes to personal saving because consumer spending tends to lag behind the growth of national income.

Whatever the case may be, the Japanese have maintained a high level of saving and various financial institutions have successfully channeled those funds from savers to investors. Under the leadership of the Ministry of Finance and the Bank of Japan (the central bank), the financial system is dominated by the large urban commercial banks. Four Japanese banks—Dai-ichi Kangyo, Sumitomo, Fuji, and Mitsubishi—are among the five largest banks in the world.[40] In 1985, Japanese banks surpassed their American competitors to become the world's largest lenders on the international market.[41]

The primacy of banks in the Japanese financial system is derived from their central role in the *zaibatsu* and *keiretsu* groups and from governmental regulation of the markets for stocks and bonds. Japanese manufacturers finance much more of their investment through debt than through equity and a large part of their debt is owed to banks rather than to bond holders. In this respect, the Japanese financial system differs markedly from the American system (Table 9.4).

Heavy reliance on short-term debt exposes Japanese companies to the risk of insolvency. Traditionally, this risk has been dispelled through the mutual support of *zaibatsu* and *keiretsu* members and through the cushion of rapid economic growth, but it has been an increasing cause of concern since the slowdown of the 1970s. Some corporations have managed to replace their

[39]Koichi Hamada and Yoshio Kurosaka, "Trends in Unemployment, Wages, and Productivity: The Case of Japan," *Economica* 53 (Supplement 1986): S285–S286; and Stuart Weiner, "Why is Japan's Unemployment Rate So Low and So Stable?" *Federal Reserve Bank of Kansas City Economic Review* (April 1987), 3–18.

[40]Keizai Koho Center, *Japan 1985: An International Comparison,* 30; and *Wall Street Journal,* April 20, 1987, 16.

[41]*Wall Street Journal,* January 31, 1986, 18.

Table 9.4   The Composition of Liabilities of American and Japanese Nonfinancial Corporations, 1984

	Percentages of Total Liabilities	
	United States	Japan
Equity	61.8	17.3
Short-term Debt	18.3	59.6
Bank Loans	5.2	23.5
Trade Credits	9.0	23.2
Long-term Debt	19.9	23.0
Bonds	11.0	2.4
Bank Loans	3.2	15.8
Total Liabilities	100.0	100.0

Source: Organization for Economic Cooperation and Development, *Non-Financial Enterprises Financial Statements 1986* (Paris: 1986), 30–31, 80–81.

short-term indebtedness with long-term bonds and common stock. By 1981, for example, Toyota Motor had repaid all of its bank debts and earned $334 million more in interest and dividends than it paid out.[42]

In order to meet the financial needs of their corporate clients, the banks often engage in overlending. In 1982, the loans of private financial institutions exceeded deposits by about 10 percent in Japan, whereas loans were about 30 percent less than deposits in the United States.[43] Accordingly, Japanese banks are highly dependent on the Bank of Japan as a source of loanable funds and discount policy is the most important instrument of monetary control.

The Bank of Japan uses its discounting authority not only to control the overall growth of the money supply, but also to direct funds to sectors targeted by the nation's industrial policy. This is handled through moral suasion—or window guidance, as it is known in Japan—and through direct controls. Since 1978, banks and other financial institutions have been required to submit their lending plans to the Bank of Japan, which may intervene if necessary to alter the volume or direction of credit.

The government also lends directly to nonfinancial corporations through a network of public financial institutions. These include the Japan Development Bank, which makes long-term loans to target industries; the Export-Import Bank; the Small Business Finance Corporation; and the Housing Loan Corporation. Governmental financial institutions account for about 28 percent of all financial-sector lending in Japan, compared to only 9 percent in the United States.[44] Thus, its role as a lender provides the Japanese government with an important lever to control the implementation of its industrial policy.

[42]Masayoshi Kanabayashi, "Japan's Latest Corporate Advantage," *Wall Street Journal,* September 16, 1982, 29.

[43]Management and Coordination Agency, Statistics Bureau, *Japan Statistical Yearbook 1984,* 394; and *Federal Reserve Bulletin* 70 (September 1984): A17, A26.

[44]Eisuke Sakakibara and Robert Feldman, "The Japanese Financial System in Comparative Perspective," *Journal of Comparative Economics* 7 (March 1983): 10.

The largest single source of funds for the governmental financial institutions is the postal savings system, which holds about 20 percent of total deposits in the nation. Individuals are able to open savings accounts at any of the 22,000 post offices around the country. In the past, interest on the first 3 million yen (about $18,000) deposited has been tax-free; it has been common practice (although illegal) to increase that tax exemption by opening multiple accounts. There are reportedly twice as many postal savings accounts in Japan as there are people.[45] Beginning in 1987, however, the interest on postal accounts became subject to a 20 percent tax.[46]

The Government

The role of the government in the Japanese economy is a subject of considerable disagreement. Pointing to conventional measures of governmental influence, such as taxation, expenditure, and nationalization (Tables A.15, A.17, A.18, A.19), conservative commentators maintain that "Japan teaches a lesson not about the value of economic planning, but about the vitality of the free market."[47] It is widely accepted that the low rate of taxation contributes to the high rate of saving, which finances the investment necessary for economic growth. The market system also fosters intense rivalry between Japanese firms, contributing to the efficiency of operations and the quality of goods.

On the other hand, many observers believe that the Japanese government, through its regulatory, advisory, and financial authority, has played a much more important role in the economy than the conventional measurements would imply. Their arguments are built around the conception of Japan, Inc.:

The Japanese government corresponds to corporate headquarters, responsible for planning and coordination, formulation of long-term policies and major investment decisions. The large corporations of Japan are akin to corporate divisions, with a good deal of operating autonomy within the overall policy framework laid down by corporate headquarters, free to compete with each other within broad limits, and charged with direct operating responsibility.[48]

The Japan, Inc. model is somewhat misleading; because it emphasizes the economic power of the government, but takes little notice of the political power of the business community. Furthermore, it should be noted that the corporate headquarters role is performed by at least three governmental agencies—the Economic Planning Agency (EPA), the Ministry of International Trade and Industry (MITI), and the Ministry of Finance—often in disagreement with one another. The EPA usually advocates stable growth and efficient re-

[45]David R. Henderson, "The Myth of MITI," *Fortune,* August 8, 1983, 4.

[46]*Wall Street Journal,* December 24, 1986, 14.

[47]Henderson, "The Myth of MITI," 4.

[48]James C. Abegglen, *Business Strategies for Japan* (Tokyo: Sophia University, 1970), 71.

Table 9.5   Japanese Economic Plans

Name of Plan	Original Plan Period	GNP Growth Target	Actual GNP Growth
Five-year Plan for Economic Self-Reliance	1956–1960	5.0	8.7
New Long-Term Economic Plan	1958–1962	6.5	9.9
National Income Doubling Plan	1961–1970	7.2	10.7
Mid-Term Economic Plan	1964–1968	8.1	10.6
Economic and Social Development Plan	1967–1971	8.2	9.9
New Economic and Social Development Plan	1970–1975	10.6	5.3
Economic and Social Basic Plan	1973–1977	9.4	3.8
1976–1980 Economic Plan	1976–1980	6.0	5.0
New Seven-Year Economic and Social Plan	1979–1985	5.7	4.5
Prospects and Guidelines for the 1980s	1983–1990	4.0	—

Source: Jon Woronoff, *The Japan Syndrome* (New Brunswick: Transaction Books, 1986), 122.

source allocation; MITI presses for rapid growth and technological innovation; and the Ministry of Finance attempts to maintain a balanced budget.

Economic Planning

The EPA, connected to the prime minister's office, performs a function quite similar to that of the General Planning Commissariat in France. It is the overseer of an indicative planning program that involves other government officials, business and labor leaders, and academics, all of whom are represented on the advisory Economic Council. The task of the EPA is to provide information, to improve communication between various segments of society, and to draw their individual proposals into a comprehensive and consistent plan. Adherence to the plan is voluntary, and the EPA, which has very little legal, administrative, or financial authority, must rely on the private sector and other government agencies for implementation.

As with French planning, the success or failure of Japanese planning is difficult to assess. Between 1956 and 1983, ten long-term plans were adopted (Table 9.5). While most of the plans were designed to run for 5 years or longer, their average length was only 3 years; the plans were scrapped as they lost touch with reality. In general, the first five plans, covering the era of miraculous growth, were insufficiently optimistic, while the four plans for 1970 to 1985 were overly optimistic. Nevertheless, defenders of indicative planning emphasize that "numbers have been less important to Japanese planners than trends," and that constant revision of the plans does not negate the "success of the system in directing the economy towards certain long-term goals for which particular forecasts have only been way stations."[49]

[49]William V. Rapp, "Japan: Its Industrial Policies and Corporate Behavior," *The Columbia Journal of World Business* (Spring 1977): 42.

Industrial Policy

Even among observers who believe that the EPA's comprehensive plans have had little impact on Japanese economic performance, many would ascribe an important role to the industrial policy of MITI. In collaboration with the Industrial Structure Council, MITI designates certain industries for priority development, based on their growth potential and their contribution to the growth of other sectors. These included the steel, automotive, shipbuilding, and petrochemical industries in the 1950s; consumer electronics in the 1960s; computer chips in the 1970s; and energy, computer, and other knowledge-intensive industries in the 1980s.

Governmental support of target industries has taken a number of forms. First, the Bank of Japan practices a selective policy of bank credit control—window guidance—and the Japan Development Bank and other public institutions account for more than one-quarter of all lending from the financial sector. Thus, MITI is able to channel governmental funds into targeted areas of investment, research, and export financing. In 1987, for example, MITI directed 117 billion yen ($816 million) to fund research in new energy sources, including electricity from solar cells, gasified coal, and sea water.[50]

Second, with cooperation from the Ministry of Finance, MITI is able to provide special tax concessions, such as accelerated depreciation, to target industries. Third, it has sponsored the formation of rationalization and recession cartels to promote efficient production and to support prices. Fourth, it has protected certain industries from import competition through various tariff and nontariff barriers and, until the 1960s, through a system of foreign exchange controls.

How much has industrial policy contributed to the Japanese miracle? Again, opinions are sharply divided. Proponents of the system find it difficult to believe that the postwar industrialization would have succeeded without governmental assistance:

Was it market forces alone that raised Japan's steelmaking capacity from the 6 to 7 million range of the war years to its current 150 million tons and made it the acknowledged leader in world steel production? Or was it market forces plus a package of measures that "socialized" a portion of the risk? It was the latter.[51]

Critics believe that Japan has succeeded despite industrial policy, not because of it. They note that some of Japan's most prosperous companies, including Sony and Honda, were picked as losers by MITI, while a number of sectors, including the bicycle and motorcycle industries, have blossomed without governmental aid.

Critics also insist that MITI is not as powerful as it seems. They point out that tax concessions are not terribly important in a country that has a light tax burden for everyone. Only a very small proportion of industrial investment is

---

[50]Stephen Yoder, "Japan Persists in Costly Energy Research," *Wall Street Journal,* June 2, 1987, 20.

[51]Eleanor M. Hadley, "The Secret of Japan's Success," *Challenge* (May–June 1983): 6.

financed with governmental loans; most of the government's investment funds are used for housing, railways, and highways.

Advocates of industrial policy admit that MITI-sponsored lending is small in relation to the entire economy, but they claim that it is important to the priority sectors. Furthermore, it could be argued that MITI supports its target industries in the same way that the Federal Deposit Insurance Corporation (FDIC) supports the banking system in the United States. The FDIC is able to maintain public confidence in insured bank accounts that are more than 50 times larger than its limited reserve fund because the FDIC represents the commitment of the U.S. government to support the banking industry. Likewise, in the 1970s, when the Japanese government committed $350 million to a research program for very large-scale integrated circuits, the companies in the project responded by spending 20 times more.[52] Today, Japan is the world's leading producer of 64K computer chips.

Pressure for Japan to reform or abandon its system of industrial policy has come principally from overseas, especially from the United States. In response to foreign complaints about unfair trading practices, the Japanese have been forced to dismantle a number of import barriers, cut subsidies, and amend the tax laws. In 1986, MITI announced that it would abandon a program initiated in 1958 to build an independent aircraft industry. Instead, it was announced that all government-funded projects to develop civilian aircraft would include foreign partners. The policy change was necessary, officials said, to provide more financing to the industry without alarming the West.[53]

Fiscal, Monetary, and Trade Policy

Monetary and fiscal policy both fall under the general oversight of the Ministry of Finance. Budgetary decisions must be approved by the cabinet and the Diet (parliament), and monetary policy is executed by the Bank of Japan, but the recommendations of the ministry usually are adopted with little opposition. Thus, the situation is quite different from that in the United States, where the Treasury Department is faced by a powerful Congress and an independent Federal Reserve.

The monetary policy of the Ministry of Finance and the Bank of Japan generally has been quite accommodative, allowing the growth in demand needed to sustain economic growth. The Japanese inflation rate was roughly equal, on average, to the American rate between 1971 and 1985 and was higher than the German, Swiss, and Dutch rates (Table A.5).

Although Japanese monetary policy generally has been accommodative, the government has occasionally stepped on the brakes to keep inflation from getting out of hand. Each of the five business recessions that occurred between

---

[52]Douglas Ramsey, et al. "Japan's High-Tech Challenge," *Newsweek,* August 9, 1982, 51.

[53]Stephen Yoder, "MITI Abandons Its Policy of Promoting Independent Japanese Aircraft Industry," *Asian Wall Street Journal,* February 10, 1986, 9.

1953 and 1973 was preceded by a period of monetary restraint. Thus, "postwar Japanese business cycles have been essentially policy generated."[54]

During the period of rapid economic growth—between 1955 and 1973—fiscal policy played a relatively unimportant role in Japan. During these years, particularly before the 1965 recession, the government was dedicated to the maintenance of a balanced budget. This was relatively easy to do because economic growth generated the tax revenues that were necessary to finance growth in expenditures and because military spending was kept at a very low level. If anything, the impact of fiscal policy on aggregate demand was probably negative during the high-growth era.[55]

The fiscal balance was upset by the oil price shock of 1974, slowing the rate of economic growth and the growth of tax revenue. The government, which recorded budget surpluses between 1970 and 1974, experienced rapidly mounting deficits between 1975 and 1978.[56] Reduction of the deficits began in 1979, but in 1982 the prime minister continued the warning that the government's finances were "on the brink of bankruptcy."[57] The total government debt, amounting to 12 percent of GDP in 1970, escalated to 69 percent in 1986, compared to 50 percent in the United States and 41 percent in West Germany (Table A.23).

Japanese fiscal policy presently is torn between two opposing forces. In the face of rising interest payments on the national debt and rising social security payments, the Ministry of Finance wishes to continue its course of fiscal tightening before the deficit becomes uncontrollable. The Ministry of International Trade and Industry favors a more expansionary fiscal and monetary policy for two basic reasons.

First, Japan has fallen under increasing pressure from the United States and other countries to stimulate its economic growth and import demand in order to reduce its balance of payments surplus. Failure to do so could contribute to protectionist sentiments in other countries and encourage the erection of barriers to Japanese exports. Second, rising unemployment is threatening the permanent commitment system with extinction, while fierce competition from Korea and other countries has reduced the dependability of foreign demand for Japanese goods. Thus, while the Ministry of Finance advocates belt-tightening, MITI calls for drastic measures to stimulate the economy.[58] In an apparent bow to MITI, the government announced a 6 trillion yen ($43 billion) package of spending measures and tax cuts in mid-1987.

---

[54]Gardner Ackley and Hiromitsu Ishi, "Fiscal, Monetary, and Related Policies," in *Asia's New Giant,* ed. Hugh Patrick and Henry Rosovsky (Washington, D.C.: The Brookings Institution, 1976), 184.

[55]Ibid., 213–216.

[56]International Monetary Fund, *World Economic Outlook* (Washington, D.C.: 1985), 221.

[57]Woronoff, *The Japan Syndrome,* 108.

[58]*Wall Street Journal,* March 12, 1987, 34.

Redistribution of Income

The period of rapid economic growth in Japan was accompanied by a very high investment rate, causing a rapid increase in the share of property income (profits, interest, and rent) in national income. Because property income tends to be distributed less evenly than wages, Japan also experienced a significant deterioration in income equality.[59] According to one recent study, by the late 1960s Japan had a more unequal distribution of income than any other major industrial capitalist country with the exception of France (Table A.25).[60] The Japanese government, however, spends less money on redistribution of income than any of its industrial peers (Table A.19).

Traditionally, the Japanese government has paid little attention to income redistribution because families, both biological and business, have been expected to care for their own. In addition to lifetime employment, many companies provide their employees with a number of welfare-like benefits, such as low-cost housing, subsidized meals, and free health care. Free of heavy responsibilities in the defense and social welfare categories, the government has been able to spend a great deal of its money on projects that contribute to economic growth.

In the past, Japan was able to maintain a low level of social security spending because it had a very young population. In 1970, less than 7 percent of the population was over 65, the lowest figure for any industrial country. This gap, however, is closing rapidly as the young people of the 1970s grow older. By the year 2000, more than 15 percent of the population will be older than 65 and Japan will have one of the oldest populations on earth. Thus, social security expenditures have risen rapidly and will continue to increase in the coming years.

The impact of the tax system on the distribution of income is very difficult to assess. On one hand, the individual income tax is steeply progressive, with a higher top rate (70 percent), a larger gap between the top and bottom rates, and a larger number of income brackets (15) than the systems in most other industrial countries. Furthermore, an unusually large proportion of tax receipts are levied on corporate profits, and a very small proportion is derived from regressive consumption taxes.[61] On the other hand, the distributive influence of the tax system is limited because the overall tax burden is relatively light. Judging by the difference between pre-tax and after-tax Gini

---

[59]Royal Commission on the Distribution of Income and Wealth, "The International Comparison of Income Distributions," in *Wealth, Income, and Inequality,* 2d ed., ed. A. B. Atkinson (Oxford: Oxford University Press, 1980), 95.

[60]Tadao Izhizaki, "Is Japan's Income Distribution Equal? An International Comparison," *Japanese Economic Studies* 14 (Winter 1985–1986): 31–55. Given the slippery nature of income comparisons, some analysts believe that the Japanese distribution is "one of the most equal in the world." For a defense of this view, and a broad discussion of the subject, see Andrea Boltho, *Japan: An Economic Survey 1953–1973* (Oxford: Oxford University Press, 1975), Chapter 8.

[61]The business community is lobbying for a major reform of this system, centered around a reduction of the corporate profits tax and a reduction of the progressivity of the income tax. See A. E. Cullison and Hiromitsu Ishi, "Moving Toward Tax Reform," *Sumitomo Quarterly* (Spring 1986): 4–8.

coefficients, the overall impact of the Japanese tax system is smaller than that in most other countries (Table A.25).

What Made Japan Grow?

Having surveyed the Japanese economic system, we return to that tantalizing question: Why did the Japanese economy grow so quickly during the decade of the 1960s? How did Japan, during the space of that decade, manage to overtake and bypass the levels of income per capita in Austria, Ireland, Italy, Spain, the United Kingdom, and the Soviet Union?[62] Can other countries repeat this performance by adopting the Japanese economic system?

Economic growth can be caused either by increasing the availability and employment of labor or capital inputs, or by improving factor productivity—growth in output per unit of factor inputs. During the 1960s, Japan did all three, simultaneously maintaining a higher growth rate for labor hours, the capital stock, and for factor productivity than any other major capitalist or socialist country (Table A.6). How was this accomplished?

According to careful measurements by Edward Denison and William Chung, the largest contribution was made by growth of the capital stock.[63] This high rate of capital accumulation was driven by a high rate of saving, which was, in turn, the result of several factors. These included the modesty of the social security system, the importance of bonus income, the tax exemption on accounts in the postal saving system, the low overall tax burden, and the tendency of consumer spending to lag behind the growth of income. Furthermore, the sharing of risk within *zaibatsu* and *keiretsu* families may have increased the willingness of the business community to engage in long-term capital investments.

Denison and Chung claim that the second largest cause of growth was the contribution of knowledge and technology to factor productivity. A major element here was the process of adopting technologies that were developed earlier in other countries. This, of course, is a dwindling source of growth; Japan has now caught up with—or surpassed—the rest of the world in many areas. The intellectualism of the Confucian heritage may have assisted the catching-up process, and the lifetime employment system may have encouraged employees to accept new technologies and employers to provide more training. In addition, the industrial policy of the government may have stimulated the development of new products and technologies.

Growth in the quantity, working hours, and educational quality of labor were collectively the third largest source of growth. Much of this was the result of fortuitous demographic trends that cannot be duplicated. Maintenance of low unemployment levels, however, may have resulted in part from

---

[62]According to estimates in Robert Summers and Alan Heston, "Improved International Comparisons of Real Product and Its Composition," *Review of Income and Wealth* 30 (June 1984): 207–262.

[63]Edward F. Denison and William K. Chung, *How Japan's Economy Grew So Fast* (Washington, D.C.: The Brookings Institution, 1976), 49.

the lifetime employment system and from the flexibility of the bonus income system. Undoubtedly, the rapid improvement in educational levels was encouraged by the perception that labor is Japan's only natural resource.

Two other elements that contributed to factor productivity were identified as important sources of growth. Economies of scale, made possible by expanding markets, were the fourth largest source. It surprises many people to learn that most of this growth was in the domestic, not the foreign, market. In 1984, exports accounted for only 15 percent of Japanese national income, compared to 25 percent in France and 31 percent in West Germany.

Finally, the improvement in the allocation of resources caused by movement of workers from agriculture and other low-productivity sectors into industry was the fifth largest source of growth. The proportion of the labor force engaged in primary goods production dropped from 33 percent in 1960 to 19 percent in 1970, and stood at 9 percent in 1984. Governmental subsidization of the farmers and protection from import competition have kept that figure from dropping even further.

The days of the Japanese miracle may be over. Many of the older sources of growth, such as catching up with technology and resource reallocation, are almot exhausted. In the face of international payments surpluses, Japanese consumers are being coaxed to save less money and buy more imports. International pressure has caused the government to drop many of the tools of industrial policy (such as exchange controls) that it once used. Growth in social security and governmental debt service costs have increased the tax burden, and the slower rate of economic growth has made it difficult for the corporations to maintain the lifetime employment system. Perhaps we should speculate less on the ability of other countries to adopt the Japanese economic system, and ask whether the Japanese will be able to keep the system themselves.

In closing, however, we should append a warning to those who underestimate the resilience of the Japanese. The following forecast was written in 1948 by a member of the American Occupation team:

In the light of an analysis of its resources, the Japan of the next three decades appears likely to have one of two aspects if its population continues to grow to 100 million or more. (1) It may have a standard of living equivalent to that of 1930–4 if foreign financial assistance is continued indefinitely. (2) It may be 'self-supporting', but with . . . a standard of living approaching the bare subsistence level.[64]

Summary

With few natural resources and devastated by World War II, Japan performed the ultimate economic miracle of the postwar era, but it still faces serious problems. Its homogeneous population is organized into a cooperative net-

---

[64]E. A. Ackerman, quoted in Boltho, *Japan: An Economic Survey,* 192.

work of interlocking families of individuals, companies, and conglomerates. However, cultural homogeneity may also impede technological creativity and encourage xenophobia and racism.

The business community is organized in a dual market structure—very large businesses and very small businesses with very few in the middle. Many of the big companies are members of *zaibatsu* and *keiretsu* conglomerates, which provide protected markets and financing for their members and exert considerable influence over governmental policies. The small companies are centered in distribution and subcontracting; they serve to reduce labor and inventory costs and to absorb the effects of business cycles for the larger firms.

The labor market, which is credited with much of Japan's success, is organized around a relatively docile network of company unions that participate in a semicentralized system of collective bargaining known as the Spring Labor Offensive. The lifetime employment system, which applies to about one-quarter of the work force, strengthens the family spirit of enterprises and may encourage technological innovation, but it reduces labor mobility and may impose a burden on employees who are not covered by the system. Pay is strongly influenced by seniority and about 20 percent is paid in bonuses. The latter may help to explain the high saving rate and the low unemployment rate in Japan. The saving rate is also supported by the tax and social security systems.

The government plays a limited role in the economy in direct taxation, expenditure, and nationalization. It plays an important role, however, in regulation, lending, and the formulation of indicative plans and industrial policies. Monetary policy generally has been accommodative, and fiscal surpluses turned to deficits in the 1970s. In recent years, macroeconomic policy has been split by the need for stimulus to reduce unemployment and excessive trade surpluses and the simultaneous need to control the public debt.

The rapid economic growth in the 1960s was caused first by the growth of the capital stock and then by the contributions of knowledge and technology, the growth of the size and quality of the labor force, economies of scale, and the shift of laborers from primary production to industry.

Discussion and Review Questions

1. What is the difference between the *zaibatsu* and *keiretsu* forms of industrial organization? What is the value of membership in one of these conglomerates?

2. How do the big companies allegedly benefit from the existence of small subcontractors in Japan?

3. How is the Shunto system in Japan similar to the centralized system of collective bargaining in Sweden? How do they differ?

4. What are the advantages and disadvantages of the permanent commitment system of employment? Would you be willing to enter such a commitment?

5.   What is a share economy? To what extent does Japan fit this theoretical model? Would you be willing to take a job under a share contract?

6.   Does the Japanese government play a strong role in the economy? What are its most important levers of influence?

7.   What are the most important factors that explain the rapid growth of the Japanese economy in the 1960s?

Suggested Readings

Denison, Edward F. and William K. Chung. *How Japan's Economy Grew So Fast.* Washington, D.C.: The Brookings Institution, 1976. *A comprehensive statistical picture of growth in the 1960s and comparisons with other countries.*

Johnson, Chalmers. *MITI and the Japanese Miracle.* Stanford: Stanford University Press, 1982. *An enthusiastic assessment of industrial policy.*

Morishima, Michio. *Why Has Japan 'Succeeded'?* Cambridge: Cambridge University Press, 1982. *Deals primarily with cultural factors in Japanese development.*

Patrick, Hugh and Henry Rosovsky, eds. *Asia's New Giant.* Washington, D.C.: The Brookings Institution, 1976. *A slightly dated but comprehensive collection of studies on trade and macroeconomic policy, the labor and finance markets, and other aspects of the Japanese system.*

Sethi, S. Prakash, Nobuaki Namiki, and Carl Swanson. *The False Promise of the Japanese Miracle.* Boston: Pitman, 1984. *Primarily concerned with the management system.*

Weitzman, Martin L. *The Share Economy: Conquering Stagflation.* Cambridge: Harvard University Press, 1984. *Attributes Japanese success to its system of bonus pay and provides a theoretical argument for this position.*

Woronoff, Jon. *The Japan Syndrome.* New Brunswick: Transaction Books, 1986. *Takes a critical view of permanent employment, quality circles, and the future of the Japanese economy.*

III
PART

SOCIALISM

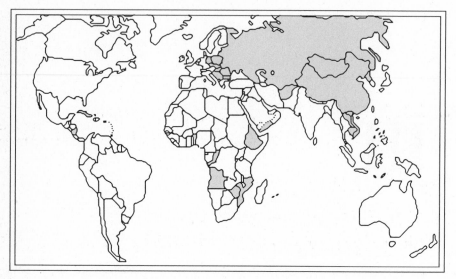

Countries Governed by Communist Parties and National Liberation Movements

10

HISTORY AND THEORIES OF SOCIALISM

The philosophers have only interpreted the world, in various ways; the point, however, is to change it.
—Karl Marx
  Theses on Feuerbach,
  1845

Under capitalism man exploits man, but under socialism exactly the opposite is true.
—A popular aphorism in
  the Soviet Union, origin
  unknown

In the first chapter we defined socialism as an economic and social system in which the greater part of the means of production—the nation's farms, factories, and mines—are owned socially. Today, about one-third of the world's population lives in the Soviet Union, China, the countries of Eastern Europe and others that fit this definition. Millions of people live in Third World "people's democracies" such as Angola and Zimbabwe, working toward social ownership. Political movements can be found all over the world that support socialist objectives.

In Chapter 3, we noted that citizens of the Western world tend to overestimate the antiquity of capitalism. Regarding socialism, the opposite bias is prevalent. Many Westerners believe that socialism began with the Russian Revolution, and many believe that Karl Marx was Russian. In actuality, socialism has a long and fascinating history.

There is also a tendency to underestimate the diversity of socialism. For example, when a socialist government encourages its factories to earn profits, the Western press invariably reports that the socialists are "adopting capitalist methods." The belief persists that there is something inherently capitalist about profits, money, and material incentives. While some socialists agree with this belief, many others insist that profits can be a useful measure of efficiency in any society—capitalist or socialist. The more important distinction, they would say, is whether the profits enrich the workers of the factory (socialism) or its owners (capitalism).

Since the eighteenth and nineteenth centuries, several competing socialist philosophies have struggled for the hearts and minds of those involved. One of the earliest disagreements concerned the proper range and level of social ownership. Should it be restricted to the means of production, or should it include consumer goods? Should social ownership be exercised at the level of the national government (that is, state socialism), or should it be limited to local cooperative and communal arrangements?

If the government is to be drawn into the operation or enforcement of socialism, how should this be accomplished? Will it be possible to develop socialist institutions through a gradual process of legislative reform, or will it be necessary to mount a forceful, sudden, and violent overthrow of the existing government and social system? If a revolution is necessary, how should it be initiated? Should the leaders try to build a broad-based political movement, or should they attack with a small, well-organized group of dedicated revolutionaries? And finally, if the state assumes ownership of the means of production, how should they be administered? Should factory managers be locally elected or centrally appointed? Should the activities of factories be coordinated by a central plan or a decentralized market?

These and other questions have occupied the socialist movement since its inception and are still being heatedly contested today. In this chapter we will briefly review the history and diversity of socialist theory and practice and take a closer look at the position of socialism in the world today.

Socialism in the Ancient World

In their study of primitive cultures, anthropologists have found evidence of both market exchange and socialist cooperation. Many of these cultures practiced a primitive form of communism, whereby the tribe owned productive goods and food was distributed by the chief.[1] Adam Smith, the father of classical economics, spoke of "that rude state of society which precedes both the accumulation of stock and the appropriation of land," when "the whole produce of labour belongs to the labourer."[2] Primitive communism was not the product of any ideal philosophical system; it was little more than a pragmatic response to the challenge of survival in the "rude state of society."

In ancient Greece, the birthplace of formal utopian philosophy, we find little consideration of socialism. In *Republic,* Plato advocated a system of social ownership and communal living arrangements, but only for members of the ruling class of philosophers and soldiers. The purpose was to prevent conflicts of interest, not to promote egalitarianism. In order to maintain work incentives, Plato favored individual ownership of property among members of the lower classes. First Democritus and then Aristotle defended the right of all social classes to own private property.

One of the earliest recorded collectivist experiments was performed by the early Christians in Jerusalem, for whom "all things were common property," and "there was not a needy person among them, for all who were owners of land or houses would sell them . . . and they would be distributed to each, as they had need."[3] This seems to have been a voluntary response to a situation of extreme need, not to a governmental or religious edict; the Christians outside of Jerusalem maintained ownership of their property.[4] Devoid of political or economic power, the early Christians directed their message to individual people and churches, not to the Roman government.

Modern Socialism before Marx

To trace the origins of socialism as a mass movement, we must leap forward to the late 1700s, when the political revolutions in America and France and the Industrial Revolution in England were laying fertile ground for a new social movement. The rebels in America and France supported private property rights; they also demonstrated the feasibility of revolutionary action and demanded political equality, the forerunner of economic equality. The Industrial Revolution generated, among other things, a Dickensian world of urban blight and child labor and a vast sum of new wealth to be redistributed.

---

[1]See, for example, Manning Nash, "The Organization of Economic Life," in *Tribal and Peasant Economics,* ed. George Dalton (Garden City, N.Y.: The Natural History Press, 1967), 3–4.

[2]Adam Smith, *An Inquiry into the Nature and Causes of the Wealth of Nations* (New York: P. F. Collier and Son, 1909, originally published in 1776), 50.

[3]Acts 4:32–35.

[4]Rom. 16:3–5; Col. 4:15; and Philem. 2.

Rousseau and Morelly

As early as 1755, the French philosopher Jean Jacques Rousseau (b.1712, d.1778) declared his belief in the superiority of the lowly savage over modern man. "How many crimes, wars, murders, sufferings, and horrors mankind would have been spared, if, when the first man enclosed a plot of land and said, 'This is mine,' someone would have torn down the fence and cried: 'Don't listen to this imposter; you are lost if you forget that the earth belongs to no one, and that the fruits are for all!' "[5] While Rousseau did not propose the abolition of private property, he inspired others to take that next step.

Also in 1755, a French philosopher named Morelly outlined several "sacred and fundamental laws that would tear out the roots of vice and of all the evils of society." His first proposal was that "nothing in society will belong to anyone, either as a personal possession or as capital goods, except the things for which the person has immediate use. . . ."[6] In Morelly's ideal society, production and distribution of goods, choice of occupations, location and arrangement of cities, rites of marriage, communal housing and training of children (including religious training), and many other activities would be regulated by governmental bodies. In order to "prevent all tyrannical domination," governmental leaders would be rotated and every head of a family would become a senator at the age of 50.

Babeuf and Saint-Simon

Morelly attracted little attention among his contemporaries, but both he and Rousseau influenced Francois Babeuf (b.1760, d.1797), a journalist who led the Society of the Pantheon. This group was organized in 1795 to denounce the decline of the French Revolution and to advance the cause of communist egalitarianism. According to Babeuf and his followers, the promise of political equality was empty and insufficient:

We are speaking of something more sublime and more equitable, the COMMON GOOD, *or the* COMMUNITY OF GOODS! *No more individual ownership of the land: the land belongs to no one. We are demanding, we desire, communal enjoyment of the fruits of the earth: the fruits belong to all.*[7]

Thus, Babeuf, like Morelly, favored communal control of producer *and* consumer goods and was dedicated to revolutionary tactics. Babeuf was executed in 1797 for plotting to overthrow the government, but his name became a rallying cry for later revolutionaries.

Also in France, Henri de Saint-Simon (b.1760, d.1825) developed a striking proposal for a national system of economic planning to organize public works and to make more efficient use of modern technology. Saint-Simon was not opposed to capitalist ownership; rather, he believed that people should be

[5]Jean Jacques Rousseau, "Discourse on the Origin of Inequality among Men," in *Socialist Thought: A Documentary History,* ed. Albert Fried and Ronald Sanders (Garden City, N.Y.: Doubleday and Company, 1964), 33.

[6]Morelly, "Code of Nature," in *Socialist Thought: A Documentary History,* 20.

[7]"Manifesto of the Equals," in *Socialist Thought: A Documentary History,* 53.

paid according to their work and had nothing but contempt for "idlers." According to the "one sole principle . . . given by God to men for the governing of their conduct," he said, "they must make it their goal in all of their efforts, in all of their activities, to ameliorate as promptly and as completely as possible the moral and physical existence of the most numerous class."[8]

According to the Saint-Simonian scheme, planning would be handled by a three-chamber industrial parliament. First, the Chamber of Invention, composed of engineers, poets, artists, architects, and musicians, would generate ideas for public works and prioritize them in a plan. Next, the Chamber of Examination, composed primarily of mathematicians and physical scientists, would evaluate the feasibility of the projects in the plan. Finally, the Chamber of Execution, composed of industrialists, would exercise veto power over the projects in the plan and develop a program to finance and implement them. Although his ideas were not adopted at the time, Saint-Simon is considered by many to be an inspirational force behind French indicative planning.

Cooperative and Communal Experiments

Early in the nineteenth century, interest in local cooperative and communal socialism reached a peak. In the year 1800, a prosperous Manchester businessman named Robert Owen (b.1771, d.1859) acquired the New Lanark factory in Scotland. Espousing ideas unusual at that time, Owen believed that environmental factors, rather than heredity or sinfulness, held back the progress of the lower classes. With the proper environment, "*any* habits and sentiments can be given to mankind," and "every individual may be trained to produce far more than he can consume."[9] Furthermore, he argued that an improvement in the educational and cultural level of the poor would benefit everyone, including the rich.

Based on this philosophy, Owen transformed New Lanark into a successful model community. He took young children out of the factories and established one of the first systems of universal education. He raised wages, shortened working hours, and provided good housing, sanitation, and nonprofit stores. To the amazement of his fellow industrialists, New Lanark continued to earn substantial profits after the reforms were introduced. Owen accepted a 5 percent return on invested capital and used any additional profits for the welfare of the workers.

After succeeding at New Lanark, Owen attempted to enlist the aid of the British government to establish a number of "villages of cooperation." When his proposals were spurned in England and on the Continent, he emigrated to the United States and established a cooperative society in New Harmony, Indiana, in 1826. Unfortunately, Owen was bilked by an associate and by 1828 the New Harmony experiment failed. Owen lost most of his fortune and re-

---

[8]Saint-Simon, "The New Christianity," in *Socialist Thought: A Documentary History,* 79.

[9]Robert Owen, "An Address to the Inhabitants of New Lanark," in *Socialist Thought: A Documentary History,* 173.

turned to England to spend the rest of his days working for the trade union movement.

Another important exponent of the cooperative movement was Charles Fourier (b.1772, d.1837), a businessman and writer in Lyons. Fourier, it should be noted in advance, was either eccentric or slightly insane. He believed, for instance, that the world will eventually reach a state of harmony, in which six new moons will replace the one in existence and all of the violent and repulsive beasts will be replaced by their opposites—lions by anti-lions, rats by anti-rats, bugs by anti-bugs, and so on. As you might expect, this part of his theory was never taken seriously.

Fourier was important to the cooperative movement because he developed a detailed proposal for a system of producer cooperatives. Each of his so-called **phalansteries** would include about 1,600 people, all of whom would live and work in one large building and its adjoining farmland. The shareholders who invested in the enterprise would receive one-third of its profits; the remaining profits would be divided between labor (five-twelfths) and management (one-quarter). In order to avoid the monotony of the factory system, participants would rotate job assignments every few hours and competitive games would be organized around the work process. Thus, Fourier foresaw the job enrichment movement in the Western world and the socialist competitions that are staged between factories in the Soviet Union.

Fourier was never able to raise the money to test his ideas in France, but more than 40 phalansteries were established in the United States. The most famous of these was Brook Farm, in Massachusetts, whose members included Nathaniel Hawthorne and Ralph Waldo Emerson. Brook Farm was reasonably successful until it burned to the ground in 1846. Almost all of the other American phalansteries disappeared by the mid-1850s.

Revolutionaries, Reformers, and Anarchists

With the exception of Babeuf, the early socialists had little to say concerning revolutionary strategy. Many of them believed that their proposals would be adopted voluntarily, with little need for governmental involvement. Before Marx, the most famous practitioner of revolutionary socialism was Auguste Blanqui (b.1805, d.1885). He advocated the expropriation of large estates, control over factories, free education, and a progressive income tax.

Blanqui did not believe that the workers would ever organize their own revolution or that socialist measures would be adopted in a democratic society, even if the poor were allowed to vote. The poor, he said, do not know the source of their miseries. Thus, he believed that a revolutionary coup must be initiated by a small, well-organized minority—a concept that was rejected by Marx and Engels, but later adopted by Lenin. Blanqui devoted himself to several insurrectionist causes and spent much of his adult life in jail.

Another Frenchman, Louis Blanc (b.1811, d.1882), believed that socialist reforms could be adopted by the democratic machinery of the existing government. To deal with the problem of unemployment, he proposed a system of state-owned workshops, whose policies would be determined by the workers. In February 1848, Blanc was given a position in the Provisional Government and attempted to implement his program of reform. His national workshops, like Franklin Roosevelt's WPA in the 1930s, were generally limited to public-works projects, such as planting trees along the boulevards. In June 1848, labor unrest and governmental budgetary problems mounted, and the workshops were closed. Thousands of workers and soldiers were killed in the riots that ensued, and Blanc fled to England.

The cessation of Blanc's reformism added fuel to the fire of a third group of socialists, the **anarchists.** Loosely organized around Pierre Joseph Proudhon (b.1809, d.1865), a Parisian, and Mikhail Bakunin (b.1814, d.1876), a violent Russian exile, the anarchists declared that all governmental power is corrupt—even if it is wielded by the workers. Thus, they rejected Blanqui's idea of a revolutionary takeover of the government and Blanc's faith in governmental reform. They anticipated many of the critics of modern Soviet-style socialism by warning that governmental ownership of the means of production could become the basis of a new form of oppression. Instead, they hoped to build all of society around a system of voluntary cooperatives and contracts. As Proudhon described it:

It is industrial organization that we will put in place of government. . . . In place of laws, we will put contracts. . . . In place of political power, we will put economic forces. . . . In place of standing armies, we will put industrial associations. In place of police, we will put identity of interests.[10]

John Stuart Mill

As we noted in Chapter, 3, John Stuart Mill (b.1806, d.1873) was the last prominent economist of the classical school. He was an advocate of the laissez faire principles of Adam Smith, but he lived to see the darker side of the Industrial Revolution and was profoundly influenced by the early socialists.

Putting together these strands of thought, Mill came to believe that capitalism would gradually and spontaneously evolve into socialist cooperation. "If mankind continues to improve," Mill said, production eventually will be dominated by "the association of the labourers themselves on terms of equality, collectively owning the capital with which they carry on their operations, and working under managers elected and removable by themselves."[11]

Mill looked forward to a system of democratic labor-managed cooperatives. He believed that socialism could and should be attained with a minimum of revolutionary fervor, governmental interference, expropriation of property, or central planning. He specifically rejected any scheme "which aims at taking possession of the whole land and capital of the country, and beginning at once to administer it on the public account." Aside from the injustice of that action,

---

[10]Pierre Joseph Proudhon, *General Idea of the Revolution in the Nineteenth Century,* in *French Utopias: An Anthology of Ideal Societies,* ed. F. E. Manuel and F. P. Manuel (New York: Free Press, 1966), 371.

[11]John Stuart Mill, *Principles of Political Economy,* ed. W. J. Ashley (New York: Augustus M. Kelley, 1965, originally published in 1848), 772–773.

"the very idea of conducting the whole industry of a country by direction from a single centre is so obviously chimerical that nobody ventures to propose any mode in which it should be done."[12] Nevertheless, Mill was an early supporter of governmental involvement in health, education, and welfare reform.

Because of his classical concern with economic efficiency, Mill rejected Fourier's idea to rotate work assignments. Likewise, he discounted the notion of many socialists that the competitive nature of the market system is morally degrading—"they forget that wherever competition is not, monopoly is; and that monopoly, in all its forms, is the taxation of the industrious for the support of indolence, if not of plunder."[13]

Mill was an early advocate of democratic market socialism and workers' self-management. He advanced the idea that socialism could be achieved through gradual reform rather than revolution. In the 1880s, democratic reform socialism became the central message of the Fabian Society, whose members included George Bernard Shaw, Sidney and Beatrice Webb, and Bertrand Russell; it is evident today in the writings of Michael Harrington, Alec Nove, John Kenneth Galbraith, and many others. Democratic socialism is the goal of many who reject the violence and authoritarianism of Marxist revolution and Soviet society, but believe that capitalist society is inherently unfair and unstable.

Marx and Engels

Karl Marx (b.1818, d.1883) and his associate Friedrich Engels (b.1820, d.1895) spent much of their time exposing the "true nature of capitalism" and the forces leading to its destruction; they spent little time preparing a blueprint for socialist society. Nevertheless, their ideas have been so influential that the words *socialism* and *Marxism* are often, in error, used interchangeably. Marx and Engels drew together many elements of earlier socialist philosophies and added many of their own. Their socialism was revolutionary and pragmatic in the short run, evolutionary and utopian in the long run. They defined a mainstream of socialism that drew many adherents on the Continent, at a time when reformism prevailed in England.

Marx and Engels declared that Owen, Fourier, Proudhon, and others had developed a system of **utopian socialism**—a label that is still used today. By declaration and implication, they dismissed the utopian program of voluntary cooperation as a quaint and naïve dream and replaced it with their own system of **scientific socialism.** Martin Buber, a twentieth-century advocate of voluntary cooperation, had this to say about Marx's method of "annihilation by labels":

The epithet "Utopian" . . . became the most potent missile in the fight of Marxism against non-Marxian socialism. . . . To be a "Utopian" in our

---

[12]Ibid., 988.
[13]Ibid., 792.

age means: to be out of step with modern economic development, and what modern economic development is we learn of course from Marxism. . . . But if socialism is to emerge from the blind-alley into which it has strayed, among other things the catchword "Utopian" must be cracked open and examined for its true content.[14]

In opposition to those who believed that socialism could be attained by peaceful means, and in opposition to the anarchists, who rejected the use of governmental authority, Marx answered that "someday the worker must seize political power . . . if he is not to lose heaven on earth, like the old Christians who neglected and despised politics," and "in most countries on the Continent the lever of our revolution must be force."[15] Furthermore, in opposition to those like Blanqui (and eventually Lenin), "who openly state that the workers are too uneducated to emancipate themselves," Marx countered that "the emancipation of the working class must be the work of the working class itself."[16]

Marx and Engels believed that after the revolution, socialism would proceed through several stages. During the first of these, the **dictatorship of the proletariat,** forceful measures would be necessary to protect the new socialist regime from lingering reactionary forces at home and abroad. "The class domination of workers over the resisting strata of the old world" must continue, Marx said, "until the economic foundations of the existence of classes are destroyed."[17]

Marx maintained that in the early stages of socialism, several of the defects of capitalist society would persist because socialism is "still stamped with the birth marks of the old society from whose womb it emerges."[18] In particular, some income inequality would have to continue in order to maintain work incentives and to make the new system politically acceptable.

Marx believed that several preconditions must be satisfied before communism, the final utopian stage of socialism, could be attained. First, society must reach a very high stage of economic development because the dialectical materialist theory of history maintains that development of the economic and social system is rooted in the development of the underlying forces of production. Second, an unselfish "new man" for whom "labour has become not only a means of life but life's prime want" must be created during the early stages of socialism.[19] And third, he apparently believed (as did Trotsky after him) that the socialist revolution must spread to all countries before communism could emerge. The working class in a single country could not put an end to class

---

[14]Martin Buber, *Paths in Utopia* (New York: Macmillan, 1950), 5–6.

[15]Karl Marx, "On the Possibility of Non-Violent Revolution," in *The Marx-Engels Reader,* 2d ed., ed. Robert C. Tucker (New York: W. W. Norton, 1978), 523. Interestingly, Marx believed that nonviolent revolutions could possibly occur in America and England because of the institutions, mores, and traditions in those countries.

[16]Karl Marx, "The Manifesto of the Three Zurichers," in *The Marx-Engels Reader,* 555.

[17]Karl Marx, "After the Revolution," in *The Marx-Engels Reader,* 547.

[18]Karl Marx, "Critique of the Gotha Program," in *The Marx-Engels Reader,* 529.

[19]Ibid., 531.

Table 10.1   Nineteenth-Century Socialists: A Typology

		Preferred Form of Social Ownership	
		State	Cooperative, Communal
Expected Method of Transition to Socialism	*Gradual Reform*	Blanc, Webbs	Fourier, Owen, Mill
	Revolution	Blanqui Marx (short run)	Proudhon, Bakunin, Marx (long run)

struggle because the bourgeois class of that country "is already linked up in a brotherhood . . . with the bourgeois of all other countries."[20]

Having fulfilled these conditions, it would be possible for the other features of communism to follow. The victory of the dictatorship of the proletariat and the gradual improvement of social consciousness would give rise to a classless society. With an abundance of goods and an unselfish, hard-working population, it would finally be possible to distribute consumer goods to each according to his needs.

Marx believed that many of the institutions of the old society would become obsolete when full communism is achieved. The use of money, for example, would pass away as abundance and unselfishness makes possible the distribution of goods according to need. The state, as we presently know it, would "wither away" because the cessation of domestic and international class conflict would reduce (possibly eliminate) the need for many of the legislative, law enforcement, and military functions of the government. Thus, Marx rejected the anarchist vision of a stateless society in the short run (during the dictatorship of the proletariat), but he embraced it in the utopian long run (Table 10.1).

Marx believed that the socialist economy would operate according to a plan that "distributes labour-power and means of production to the different branches of production," but he did not explain how the plan was to be formulated.[21] What agency would prepare the plan, especially after the state has "withered away"? How often should the plans be prepared? How would the central planners take account of the interdependence of the economy, and how would they control the implementation of the plans? Marx and Engels, who devoted most of their writing to the capitalist system, were silent on these and many other questions about socialism. According to one point of view, Marx and Engels believed that a blueprint of the socialist future was unnecessary, because "the planned, purposeful development of communist society would make everything clear and understandable. . . ."[22]

[20]Ibid., 533.

[21]Karl Marx, *Capital,* vol. 2 (Moscow: Progress Publishers, 1956, originally published in 1893), 362.

[22]Aron Katsenelinboigen, *Studies in Soviet Economic Planning* (White Plains, N.Y.: Sharpe, 1978), 29.

From 1848 to the Russian Revolution

After 1848, the year when Marx and Engels wrote their *Communist Mani-festo,* when Blanc attempted to establish his national workshops, and when workers' revolts were crushed in several countries, the socialist movement fell into disarray. The utopian experiments inspired by Owen, Fourier, and others continued through the 1840s, but most of them disappeared by the mid-1850s. The mood of the socialist movement in 1864 was reflected in Marx's speech to the founding convention of the Working Men's International Association (or the First International, as it is more commonly known):

After the Revolutions of 1848, all party organizations and party jour-nals of the working classes were . . . crushed by the iron hand of force . . . and the short-lived dreams of emancipation vanished before an epoch of industrial fever, moral morasme, and political reaction. . . .

At the same time, the experience of the period from 1848 to 1864 has proved beyond doubt that . . . co-operative labour, if kept within the narrow circle of the casual efforts of private workmen, will never be able to . . . free the masses. . . . To save the industrious masses, co-operative labour ought to be developed to national dimensions, and consequently, to be fostered by national means.[23]

While First International marked an important stage in the development of the trade union movement, it did very little to advance Marx's dream of a national socialist movement. Specifically, the International succeeded in coor-dinating the activities of trade unionists in several countries, preventing strike-breaking activities by workers in adjoining countries, and preventing the Brit-ish government from supporting the South in the American Civil War. It lost much of its influence, however, because of tactical disputes between the Marx-ist and Bakuninist wings of the association.

Rivalry within the First International was further intensified by the for-mation of the Paris Commune in 1871. In that year, the National Guard of Paris led a revolt against the national government; socialists of all stripes were elected to a majority of the seats on the new Commune Assembly. The Com-mune attempted to institute a number of social reforms, but it was crushed within a few weeks by the national government.

The Commune had little lasting impact on French history, but it was extolled by Marx, Engels, and Lenin as the first realistic attempt to establish a dictatorship of the proletariat.[24] This, in turn, intensified the debate in the First International between the Marxists, who believed in the necessity of a revo-lutionary dictatorship of the proletariat, and the reformers and anarchists, who rejected any proposal to take over the government. Marx had Bakunin and his supporters expelled from the International in 1872 and the organization col-lapsed over the next 4 years.

---

[23]Karl Marx, "Inaugural Address of the Working Men's International Association," in *The Marx-Engels Reader,* 516, 518.

[24]See Edward S. Mason, *The Paris Commune: An Episode in the History of the Socialist Move-ment* (New York: The Macmillan Co., 1930), Chapters 5, 6, and 7.

The Russian Revolution

The late 1800s witnessed the death of Marx (in 1883) and Engels (in 1895), the birth of an ineffectual Second International (in 1889), and the formation of social democratic or labor parties in Germany (1875), Austria-Hungary (1888), England (1893), and Russia (1897). From the very beginning, one of the prime movers among the Russian Social Democrats was a young lawyer named Vladimir I. Lenin (b.1870, d.1924). Lenin became a radical at the age of 16, when his older brother was executed for participating in a plot to assassinate Tsar Alexander III. He studied Marxian theory at home and abroad and in 1902 published a pamphlet, titled *What Is To Be Done?*, which echoed Blanqui in saying that the revolution must be initiated and led by an elite vanguard of professionals:

I assert: 1) that no movement can be durable without a stable organi-zation of leaders to maintain continuity; 2) that the more widely the masses are spontaneously drawn into the struggle and form the basis of the move-ment and participate in it, the more necessary it is to have such an organi-zation . . .; 3) that the organization must consist chiefly of persons engaged in revolutionary activities as a profession; 4) that in a country with an autocratic government, the more we restrict *the membership of this organi-zation to persons who are engaged in revolutionary activities as a profession . . .; and 5) the* wider *will be the circle of men and women of the working class . . . able to join the movement and perform active work in it.*[25]

When the Russian Social Democrats held their first congress in 1903, the followers of Lenin commanded a temporary majority and called themselves the **Bolsheviks** (from *bol'shinstvo,* majority). Their opponents, who rejected the idea of an authoritarian vanguard style of leadership, came to be known as the **Mensheviks** (minority). The names stuck, even when the Bolsheviks constituted a minority of the Social Democratic Party.

Initially, Lenin faced stiff resistance *within* the Bolshevik faction because he seemed to be violating the Marxian belief that the proletarian revolution would first occur in the most advanced capitalist countries. To this charge, Lenin answered that the Russian revolution could proceed "in a different way from that of the West-European countries," because the Russian proletariat had already demonstrated their revolutionary zeal and because the imperialist pol-icies of the advanced countries had shifted the focus of capitalist exploitation to Russia and other developing countries:

If a definite level of culture is required for the building of Socialism (although nobody can say just what that definite "level of culture" is, for it differs in every West-European country), why cannot we begin by first achieving the prerequisites for that definite level of culture in a revolution-ary way, and then, *with the aid of the workers' and peasants' government and the Soviet system, proceed to overtake the other nations?*[26]

[25]V. I. Lenin, *What Is To Be Done?* in *Essential Works of Lenin,* ed. Henry M. Christman (New York: Bantam Books, 1966), 147–148.

[26]V. I. Lenin, "Our Revolution," in *A Documentary History of Communism,* ed. Robert V. Daniels (New York: Random House, 1960), 229.

Lenin's arguments, supported by Leon Trotsky's (b.1879, d.1940) theory that a revolution in Russia would be supported by the encouragement of a "permanent revolution" in other countries, carried the day.

As we shall consider at length in the next chapter, the Bolsheviks took control of the government in November 1917 and the Soviet state was born. After experimenting with market socialism in the 1920s, the government eventually adopted a very centralized system of economic planning and administration. The individual enterprise manager in Irkutsk, Minsk, or Pinsk makes very few important decisions. Ideally, the central planners in Moscow tell him what his enterprise will produce, how much it will produce, where it will obtain raw materials, where the final products will be sold, what prices he will charge, and a host of other requirements. The manager and his employees are paid to carry out orders. Hence, the Soviet system is sometimes called a **command economy.**

The Efficiency of Socialism

After the Bolsheviks proved that it was possible to establish a socialist regime, a protracted debate began, which eventually included economists from several countries, concerning the possibility (or impossibility) of efficient management of a socialist economy. Adam Smith presented his view on this matter as early as 1776, when he said that "superintending the industry of private people, and . . . directing it towards the employments most suitable to the interests of society" is a task for which "no human wisdom or knowledge could ever be sufficient."[27]

The von Mises Critique

The debate began in earnest in 1920, when Austrian economist Ludwig von Mises (b.1881, d.1973) argued that efficient planning is impossible in a socialist state.[28] According to von Mises, market exchange of producer goods cannot occur in a socialist economy because producer goods are owned publicly. If producer goods are not exchanged, then it will be impossible to determine their market prices. If there are no market prices for producer goods, it will be impossible to perform the calculations that are necessary to make rational decisions.

If a steel mill is to be built, for example, where should it be located, and what technology should be employed? What energy source should be used, and what mix of raw materials? To answer these questions in a way that will minimize the social cost of building the steel mill, the cost of land, equipment,

[27]Smith, *The Wealth of Nations,* 466.

[28]Ludwig von Mises, "Economic Calculation in the Socialist Commonwealth," in *Socialist Economics,* ed. Alec Nove and D. M. Nuti (Baltimore: Penguin, 1972, first published in 1920), 75–91.

and raw materials must somehow be measured and added. Under socialism, von Mises argued, it may be possible to make vague estimates of cost, but no reliable yardstick will exist.

Lange's Theory of Market Socialism

The challenge presented by von Mises elicited a number of responses. In the Soviet Union, economists and officials maintained that centrally planned socialism could operate more efficiently than capitalism because the latter system is plagued by monopolistic distortions, business cycles, and unemployment. Some Soviet economists suggested that the problem of valuation, emphasized by von Mises, could be solved by using linear programming models and other mathematical techniques. Outside of the Soviet Union, however, few supporters of socialism defended the efficiency of Soviet-style central planning. Instead, they argued for a new form of socialism, based on decentralized market principles, that would surpass the allocative efficiency of the capitalist system.

Although John Stuart Mill proposed a system of **market socialism** as early as 1848, the first to answer von Mises with such a system was Fred M. Taylor, in his 1928 presidential address to the American Economic Association. His arguments were extended and amplified by Oskar Lange (a Polish economist), H. D. Dickinson (British), Abba Lerner (British-American), and Burnham Beckwith (American) between 1936 and 1949.[29] Their analyses were similar, but the version offered by Lange attracted the largest audience.

According to Lange, a decentralized socialist system could be devised that would operate in a way "quite analogous to that in a competitive market."[30] The pattern of production would be set by consumer sovereignty, and freedom of occupational choice would be maintained. The allocative efficiency of the economy would be greater than that of a capitalist economy, Lange believed, because it would be free of the distortions caused by monopolies and externalities.

According to Lange's scheme, the factory and industrial managers should be required to follow two rules. First, in order to minimize the average cost of production, they would be instructed to equalize the marginal products derived from the last unit of money spent on each of the factors of production. Second, in order to operate at the optimal level of production, they should expand factory and industrial output until the marginal cost of production is equal to the price of the final product. These are precisely the rules that are followed by a "perfectly competitive" producer in a capitalist economy.

The Central Planning Board (CPB) in Lange's model takes the place of the market. If a shortage or surplus of any commodity or productive resource

---

[29]For an annotated bibliography of these and other works on market socialism, see Burnham P. Beckwith, *Liberal Socialism,* 2d ed. (Jericho, N.Y.: Exposition Press, 1974), 445–455.

[30]Oskar Lange, "On the Economic Theory of Socialism," in *On the Economic System of Socialism,* ed. Benjamin E. Lippincott (Minneapolis: University of Minnesota Press, 1938), 82.

exists at the end of the accounting period, the CPB raises or reduces its price. Lange argued that this trial-and-error procedure would arrive at a set of equilibrium prices more rapidly than a competitive market because "the Central Planning Board has a much wider knowledge of what is going on in the whole economic system than any private entrepreneur can ever have. . . ."[31]

Lange claimed several additional advantages of market socialism over capitalism.[32] First, because the means of production are owned by the public, there are no property incomes; thus the distribution of income would be more even. Second, the managers of socialist factories would be willing to take fuller account of the social costs of production (including the cost of pollution, etc.) than the managers of profit-seeking capitalist enterprises.

Third, because the managers of socialist enterprises would be instructed to produce to the point where price equals marginal cost, production would not be restricted to an inefficient level, as it is in monopolistic capitalist firms.[33] Finally, a socialist economy would not be subject to the fluctuations of the business cycle because the planners would be able to keep a downturn in one sector of the economy from adversely affecting the others.

Lange's Critics

As one might expect, Lange's response to von Mises drew both praise and criticism.[34] His critics first allege that he underestimated the difficulty of the price-setting job of the CPB. There are literally millions of prices to set in a modern economy and these prices must be changed continuously to maintain equilibrium. In order to obtain the necessary information on shortages and surpluses, and in order to adjust all of the prices in a timely manner, the CPB would require a huge bureaucracy.

Even if Lange's planners and managers are able to match the performance of a market economy in static equilibrium, his critics say that the dynamic efficiency of the model is doubtful. In a world where decisions are based not only on present information, but also on uncertain expectations of future conditions, the two operating rules that Lange gives his managers may be insufficient to guide action. The prices set in a capitalist market are influenced by current conditions and by expectations; it is unlikely that the prices set by Lange's central planners would include all of that information.

Another objection concerns Lange's failure to describe the methods used to monitor performance of enterprise managers and how they would be mo-

[31]Ibid., 89.

[32]Ibid., 98–108.

[33]Recall that the profit-maximizing level of output for a monopolist is lower than the equilibrium level of output for a competitive industry.

[34]For critical evaluations of Lange's model, see Friedrich Hayek, "Socialist Calculation: The Competitive 'Solution'," *Economica* 7 (May 1940): 125–149; Abram Bergson, "Market Socialism Revisited," *Journal of Political Economy* 75 (October 1967): 655–673; and Peter Murrell, "Did the Theory of Market Socialism Answer the Challenge of Ludwig von Mises? A Reinterpretation of the Socialist Controversy," *History of Political Economy* 15 (1983): 92–105.

tivated to run their operations efficiently. Should profits be used as a measure of success? Should a share of profits be given to the manager? If this is done, some of the purported advantages of socialism may be lost. Profit-earning managers would have an incentive to take advantage of monopoly power and may ignore the social costs (for example, of pollution) in order to reduce their private costs. If profits are not used to measure the success of the enterprise and to reward its manager, what will take their place?

Other Market Socialist Models

In the 1950s and 1960s, Yugoslavia and a number of Eastern European countries began to experiment with market socialism. We will consider these experiments in the chapters that follow. In addition to their importance in the real world, the Eastern European systems have also inspired the creation of several new theoretical models of market socialism.

Ben Ward initiated a new round of theorizing in 1958 with his theory of labor-managed market socialism, based on an abstraction of the Yugoslav system.[35] In his model of the idealized nation of Illyria, the state owns the means of production but entrusts management to the workers in each enterprise. Commodities are exchanged in actual markets, where their prices are determined by supply and demand. Aside from taxes and rental fees paid to the government and funds retained for enterprise investment, any profits earned by the enterprise are divided among the workers.

Given these conditions, Ward assumes that the enterprise manager, who is elected by the workers, would attempt to maximize the income of the average worker in the enterprise. He thus hypothesizes very different behavior from that found in a capitalist enterprise where total profits, rather than profits-per-worker, are maximized. This model differs from the Lange model in that prices are set by the market rather than by central planners and the motivation system of the enterprise (retention of profits) is clearly defined. We will explore the implications of Ward's model, and other analytical theories it inspired, in Chapter 14 "Yugoslavia."

The Eastern European experience has also inspired several proposals for market socialist reform in advanced capitalist countries. Blueprint models of this kind include Alec Nove's **feasible socialism** and James Yunker's **pragmatic socialism,** both of which are predicated on the continuation of democratic institutions.[36] Unlike Lange, both Nove and Yunker would allow prices to be set by actual markets, rather than by central planners, although Nove would retain price controls in monopolistic industries. Yunker is not as concerned with monopoly power because he believes (with Arnold Harberger

---

[35]Benjamin Ward, "The Firm in Illyria: Market Syndicalism," *American Economic Review* 48 (September 1958): 566–589.

[36]Alec Nove, *The Economics of Feasible Socialism* (London: George Allen and Unwin, 1983); James A. Yunker, *Socialism in the Free Market* (New York: Nellen, 1979); and James A. Yunker, "A Market Socialist Critique of Capitalism's Dynamic Performance," *Journal of Economic Issues* 20 (March 1986): 63–86.

and others) that monopolies are not an important source of allocational inefficiency in the U.S. economy.

Whereas Lange would have enterprise managers follow a set of rules, Nove and Yunker would reward them for earning profits, although Nove is less enthusiastic about the profit motive than Yunker. Yunker believes that one of the most important advantages of market socialism is that it would inspire a *stronger* profit motive than presently exists under capitalism. This is true, he says, because a socialist system would remedy the problems caused by the separation of corporate ownership and control. Stronger adherence to the profit motive, in turn, would lead to reduction of costs, a higher level of x-efficiency, and a higher level of social welfare.

In Nove's system, smaller enterprises would be operated by Yugoslav-style self-management and cooperative principles and the largest enterprises would be run by state agencies. Yunker would leave the present system of management intact, but would nationalize all important businesses under a Bureau of Public Ownership (BPO). The BPO would allow enterprise executives to keep some of their profits as an incentive for efficient production and would use some of the profits to cover its own administrative costs. Most of the profits, however, would be paid to the public as a social dividend.

Both authors claim, of course, that a socialist system would yield a more equitable distribution of income and that socialism would significantly change the domestic political balance. This, in turn, would purportedly allow the government to pursue a more rational macroeconomic policy. It would also supposedly reduce the level of world tension caused by the opposition of capitalism and socialism. This could be the factor that tips the scales in the cause of peace, according to Yunker, but he says little about the potential conflict between democratic and totalitarian socialism.

The market socialism of Lange, Nove, Yunker, and others is open to criticism from both the left and the right. According to orthodox Marxists, the competitive rivalry and macroeconomic instability of the market system are inconsistent with socialist aspirations. According to libertarians, socialist restriction of property rights is the first step down Hayek's "road to serfdom." Even if the profit motive is maintained, and even if it motivates the production of high-quality goods at low cost, how will the manufacturers be motivated to increase the value of the capital entrusted to them without stake in its ownership?

This last point—the problem of establishing a property incentive in a socialist economy—has been addressed recently by Hungarian authors. For example, Barsony and Siklaky suggest that the right to manage public enterprises and the rental value of those enterprises should be established by a system of competitive bidding.[37] After paying rent, the socialist "entrepreneur" would keep a large share of the profits of the enterprise and would be able to

[37]J. Barsony and I. Siklaky, "Some Reflections on Socialist Entrepreneurship," *Acta Oeconomica* 34 (1985): 51–64. See also, L. Antal, "About the Property Incentive," *Acta Oeconomica* 34 (1985): 275–286.

deposit part of the rent in a bank account that could be used for innovation and other productive purposes. When the entrepreneur dies, the bank account would be inherited by society as a whole. Thus, the Barsony-Siklaky version of socialism comes precariously close to a capitalist system with a stiff inheritance tax.

The Growth of the Socialist World

Turning from theory to reality, we close this chapter by surveying the growth and scope of socialism in the modern world. In most cases, Marxist regimes have come to power during times of war and unrest. Revolutionary fires began to kindle in Russia during the populist movement of the 1870s. This spark became a flame during the Revolution of 1905, but it took the deprivation of World War I to break the power of the tsar in 1917. Two months before the October Revolution, Bukharin reported:

History is working for us. History is moving on the path which leads inevitably to the uprising of the proletariat and the triumph of socialism. . . . The continuing progress of the war is sharpening those tendencies which were observed at the very beginning of the war.[38]

In 1919, while the Bolsheviks were fighting the White Army in the Russian Civil War, China sent an army to Mongolia to impose authority over its feudal lords. The next year, a group of White Army forces under the command of the "mad" Baron von Sternberg entered Mongolia to support the feudal lords and to use the country as a staging ground to attack the Red Army and to restore the tsarist government. A group of Mongolian revolutionaries obtained assistance from the Red Army in a war of national liberation against Chinese and White Army forces; they managed to drive them all out of the country. The Mongolian People's Central Government was established in 1921 and was reorganized under a new constitution into the Mongolian People's Republic in 1924.

Until the latter years of World War II, the Soviet Union and Mongolia were the only strongholds of Marxist socialism in the world. Beginning in 1944, the Red Army installed communist governments in the countries of Eastern Europe and North Korea, liberating them from fascist and Japanese domination. Mock elections were held in Bulgaria, East Germany, Hungary, Poland, and Romania because the indigenous Marxist movements were rather weak in those countries.

The situation was somewhat different in Albania, Czechoslovakia, Yugoslavia, and Vietnam. Czechoslovakia had been friendly to the Soviet Union before the war; thus, it was allowed to hold a genuinely free election in 1946. The Communists won 38 percent of the vote and a rightful place on the

---

[38]Nikolai Bukharin, "Report on the War and the International Situation," in *A Documentary History of Communism,* 95–96.

coalition government. Within 2 years, all non-Communists were edged out of power.

Albania, Yugoslavia, and Vietnam drove out the Germans, Italians, and Japanese with little outside help. They all had relatively strong indigenous Marxist movements and none of them shared a common border with the Soviet Union. Furthermore, the Yugoslav and Vietnamese Communist leaders, Marshall Tito and Ho Chi Minh, were war heroes. Thus, Albania, Yugoslavia, and Vietnam were in a political and geographic position to act independently of Moscow.

All three countries were closely allied with the Soviet Union immediately after the war. The Vietnamese received substantial aid from the Russians and Chinese in their wars against the French, the Saigon government, and the United States. Conflicts between Tito and Stalin led to the 1948 expulsion of Yugoslavia from the Cominform, the international organization of the Soviet bloc. A few years later, Yugoslavia began to organize its unique system of labor-managed market socialism.

Under the leadership of Mao Zedong, the Chinese Communists came to power in 1949 by defeating the Kuomintang in a long civil war. The Chinese Communists received little help, and some hindrance, from the Soviet Union during the war, but afterwards the Soviet Union provided aid, equipment, and advisors to install Soviet-style socialism in China. However, the economic system designed for Soviet conditions did not work well in China.

The socialist world was shaken by Stalin's death in 1953 and by Khrushchev's denunciation at the 1956 Party Congress of Stalin's terror. The Albanian leaders were highly critical of Khrushchev and Albania dropped out of the Soviet bloc to continue its Stalinist policies. The Poles and the Hungarians were heartened by the de-Stalinization campaign; workers' demands for democracy, higher wages, privatization of agriculture, and Yugoslav-style worker self-management led to strikes and demonstrations in Poland and armed conflict in Hungary.

In China, Mao Zedong was troubled by Khrushchev's de-Stalinization campaign, by his policy of peaceful co-existence with the West, and by his shift toward consumer goods production at a time when China was attempting to establish an industrial base. Mao ignored his Soviet advisors in 1958 and initiated his ill-fated Great Leap Forward program of rural communes and small-scale industrial production. A war of words ensued between Moscow and Beijing, and Soviet advisors were withdrawn from China in 1960. The Communist Monolith, if it ever existed, was broken.

Nineteen sixty, the year of the Sino-Soviet dispute, was also the year Fidel Castro, the new leader of Cuba, began nationalizing foreign and domestic enterprises. In the next year, at the time of the U.S.-sponsored Bay of Pigs invasion, Castro declared his program of social reforms to be a full-fledged socialist revolution. Socialism thus gained an important new foothold in the Third World.

Despite a substantial influx of Soviet aid, Cuba has had little success in spreading the revolution to Latin America. Che Guevara, an Argentine with Cuban support, was slain in his 1968 effort to build a movement in Bolivia. In

Table 10.2   Definitions of the Socialist or Communist World

	1983 Population (millions)	Warsaw Pact	CMEA Members	Soviet Definition	Communist Affairs Yearbook
Africa					
Angola	8.2				*
Benin	3.8				*
Congo	1.8				*
Ethiopia	40.9				*
Mozambique	13.1				*
Zimbabwe	7.9				*
Asia and Middle East					
Afghanistan	17.2				*
China	1019.1			*	*
Kampuchea	6.1				*
Laos	3.7			*	*
Mongolia	1.8	*		*	*
North Korea	19.2			*	*
Vietnam	58.5		*	*	*
Yemen PDR	2.0				*
Europe and Soviet Union					
Albania	2.8			*	*
Bulgaria	8.9	*	*	*	*
Czechoslovakia	15.4	*	*	*	*
East Germany	16.7	*	*	*	*
Hungary	10.7	*	*	*	*
Poland	36.6	*	*	*	*
Romania	22.6	*	*	*	*
Soviet Union	272.5	*	*	*	*
Yugoslavia	22.8		**	*	*
Western Hemisphere					
Cuba	9.8		*	*	*
Nicaragua	3.0				*

**Associate member.

1970, the Chilean socialists and Communists won the presidential election for their candidate, Salvadore Allende, but they lost the congressional elections. Allende attempted to carry out a socialist program, but his congressional and military opponents, with covert aid from the United States, staged a military coup in 1973.

In 1979, toward the end of a long civil war, the Sandinista National Liberation Front toppled the ruthless Somoza dictatorship in Nicaragua. During the first year of their rule, the Sandinistas nationalized the locally-owned banks, insurance companies, and mining industry, and confiscated the holdings of the Somoza family. This was followed by the introduction of extensive land, educational, and social security reforms. In the 1984 elections, which were monitored by international organizations, 67 percent of those eligible voted and the Sandinistas drew 63 percent of the votes. The U.S. government declared the election a sham because the campaigns of opposition groups were limited. Thus, continuing U.S. support for the Contra opposition has slowed the Sandinista reforms.

National liberation movements have been more successful in Africa. As these countries have emerged from French and Portuguese colonial rule and as civil wars have been fought between native groups, Soviet aid and Cuban troops have supported the "progressive" factions. Marxist governments now rule in Angola, Benin, the Congo, Ethiopia, Mozambique, and Zimbabwe.

Measuring the scope of the socialist world today is a difficult task because no single definition of socialism has achieved general acceptance.[39] Academic and political studies of the socialist world are often confined to the Soviet Union and its six Eastern European allies in the Warsaw Pact (Table 10.2). Clearly, this is an overly restrictive definition of the socialist world.

A somewhat larger socialist grouping is the 11-member Council for Mutual Economic Assistance (CMEA), which promotes foreign trade and investment within the Soviet wing of the socialist world. This, too, is overly exclusive. According to the definition accepted by the Soviet government, the socialist world includes the 15 countries that are governed by recognized Communist parties—all of the CMEA members, plus Albania, China, Laos, and North Korea. The Marxist parties in other Third World countries are considered vanguard organizations that may develop into full-fledged Communist parties over time.

A broad definition of the socialist world is employed by the editors of the *Yearbook on International Communist Affairs,* published by the Hoover Institution at Stanford University. Their classification of countries is based on "rhetoric, the organizational model, participation in international communist meetings and fronts, and adherence to the USSR's foreign policy line."[40] According to their judgment, 25 countries were governed by Communist regimes in 1984. Interestingly, over half of these countries are members of the capitalist-dominated International Monetary Fund. If we include the other non-Marxist variants of socialism, however, even this listing is too restrictive. Various observers maintain that we should include Burma, Ghana, Guinea-Bissau, Iraq, Libya, Somalia, Syria, Tanzania, and several other countries.[41]

The socialist countries are geographically, culturally, and institutionally diverse. They include some of the poorest countries in the world (for example, Kampuchea and Ethiopia) and some that are relatively rich (East Germany and Czechoslovakia). Only time and experience will tell whether their ranks will grow or fade away.

---

[39]For a discussion of the definition problem, see Steven White, "What Is a Communist System?" *Studies in Comparative Communism* 16 (Winter 1983): 247–263; and Neil Harding, "What Does It Mean to Call a Regime Marxist?" in *Marxist Governments: A World Survey,* vol. 1 (London: Macmillan, 1981), 20–33.

[40]*Yearbook on International Communist Affairs 1985,* ed. Richard F. Staar (Stanford: Hoover Institution Press, 1985), i.

[41]For a discussion of alternative forms of socialism, see *Socialist Models of Development,* ed. Charles K. Wilber and Kenneth P. Jameson (Oxford: Pergamon Press, 1981).

Summary

In the primitive world, a form of communal ownership was sometimes practiced within the tribe and communal ownership was sometimes advocated or practiced in Greek and Biblical times. These, however, were usually voluntary responses to special circumstances. Revolutionary proposals for socialism as a mass movement began in the late 1700s, encouraged by the political revolutions in America and France and the Industrial Revolution in England. The French philosopher, Rousseau, criticized the system of capitalist ownership, and Morelly and Babeuf called for its abolition. Saint-Simon, in turn, devised a system of national economic planning.

In the nineteenth century, Robert Owen transformed the New Lanark factory into a successful model community and attempted to organize several other cooperative communities. A similar proposal for a communal society, including provisions to reduce the monotony of work, was developed by Charles Fourier; several of his communities were established in America. Auguste Blanqui argued that a socialist revolution would require the leadership of a small, well-organized minority, while Louis Blanc attempted to adopt socialism in France through a gradual process of reform. The anarchists, Proudhon and Bakunin, wished to replace the state altogether with a system of cooperatives. John Stuart Mill believed that society would eventually adopt a system of labor ownership and management and that it should do so without revolution or excessive governmental involvement.

Marx and Engels defined a mainstream of socialism that prescribed revolutionary tactics, state ownership, and a dictatorship of the proletariat in the short run, asserting that the state and monetary exchange would "wither away" in the long run. Their description of socialist society was not particularly detailed. Lenin followed Blanqui in saying that the revolution must be initiated and led by an elite vanguard of professionals; he provided a justification for beginning the revolution in Russia, a relatively poor country.

After the Bolshevik victory in the Russian Revolution, the feasibility of efficient socialist planning became a subject of extensive debate. Ludwig von Mises argued that efficient planning was impossible because the absence of a market to set prices for producer goods would make it impossible to calculate accurate costs and benefits. Oskar Lange, among others, argued that a system of market socialism could equal or exceed the efficiency of the capitalist system.

After systems of market socialism were actually adopted in Yugoslavia and Hungary, theoretical analysis of these systems was initiated by Ben Ward, and new proposals for the West were prepared by Nove, Yunker, and others.

From 1917 until the close of World War II, the Soviet Union and Mongolia were the only socialist countries in the world. Soon after the war, they were joined (in various ways) by China, North Korea, and the nations of Eastern Europe. A split developed in the socialist world in the 1960s, with China and Albania on one side and the Soviet bloc on the other. The socialist movement also traveled to the Western Hemisphere (centered in Cuba) during that decade, and national liberation movements began in Africa. The exact number of present-day socialist countries is a matter of some disagreement, but they include about one-third of the world's population.

Discussion and Review Questions

1.   What role did the French and American revolutions play in the early history of socialism?

2.   Describe and critically evaluate Saint-Simon's scheme for planning of public works.

3.   What was the philosophy that prompted Owen's experiments in social reform? Why was it revolutionary at the time?

4.   In what sense were Mill's socialist proposals consistent with the doctrines of Adam Smith and the classical school?

5.   According to Marx and Engels, how would the early stages of socialist society differ from the later stages?

6.   Explain the von Mises critique of the efficiency of socialism.

7.   How do the market socialist proposals of Lange, Nove, and Yunker differ from one another?

Suggested Readings

Buber, Martin. *Paths in Utopia.* New York: Macmillan, 1950. *A thoughtful polemic in favor of voluntary socialist cooperation by a noted theologian, with a particularly good discussion of Proudhon.*

Daniels, Robert V., ed. *A Documentary History of Communism.* New York: Random House, 1960. *Includes documents and classic works beginning with the Russian Revolution and extending through the movements in Vietnam and other countries in the 1950s.*

Fried, Albert, and Ronald Sanders, eds. *Socialist Thought: A Documentary History.* Garden City, N.Y.: Doubleday, 1964. *Selections from many of the prominent socialists from Morelly in the eighteenth century through Crosland in the twentieth century.*

Harrington, Michael. *Socialism.* New York: Saturday Review Press, 1972. *An engaging and accessible account of socialist history and philosophy.*

Lerner, Warren. *A History of Socialism and Communism in Modern Times.* Englewood Cliffs, N.J.: Prentice-Hall, 1982. *A clearly written textbook on the subject.*

Nove, Alec. *The Economics of Feasible Socialism.* London: George Allen and Unwin, 1983. *Nove's proposal is laid out in detail and defended in light of Eastern European experience.*

Nove, Alec, and D. M. Nuti, eds. *Socialist Economics.* Harmondsworth, Eng.: Penguin, 1972. *A book of readings, most from the twentieth century, including the von Mises and Lange contributions and other articles on socialist growth, planning, and reform.*

Tucker, Robert C., ed. *The Marx-Engels Reader.* 2d ed. New York: W. W. Norton, 1978. *Includes a good sampling of their work and several readings that are difficult to find elsewhere.*

Soviet Union

11

SOVIET UNION: HISTORY, POLITICS, and PLANNING

Fools win grace, wise men be wary, there he never spares the rod, god of everything contrary, that's him, that's your Russian god . . .

God of foreigners, whenever they set foot on Russian sod, god of Germans, now and ever, that's him, that's your Russian god.
—Prince P. A. Vyazemsky
  "The Russian God,"
  1828, translated by
  Alan Meyers

I cannot forecast to you the action of Russia. It is a riddle wrapped in a mystery inside an enigma; but perhaps there is a key. That key is Russian national interest.
—Winston Churchill, 1939

The Soviet Union is more a continent than a country. Reaching from the deserts of Uzbekistan to the Arctic Circle and from central Europe across 11 time zones to the Pacific Ocean, the Soviet Union sprawls over one-sixth of the world's land surface. China, Canada, and the United States, closest to it in size, are less than half as large; France, Germany, and the United Kingdom are *collectively* one-twentieth as large.

Within these boundaries, the Soviets hold one-fourth of the world's reserves of fossil fuels, almost half of its manganese, and a large share of its gold, silver, platinum, iron ore, cadmium, copper, and diamonds. They are the world's largest producer of oil, gas, iron, steel, cement, timber, mineral fertilizers, woolen fabrics, and tractors.

The Soviet population exceeds that of the United States by about 38 million and its people are as diverse as the land they inhabit. About half are Russians, a fifth are Ukrainian and Belorussian Slavs, and the remainder are drawn from more than a hundred European, Middle Eastern, and Asian nationalities. The Soviet religious community includes about 30 million members of the Russian Orthodox Church, a similar number of Moslems, 8 million members of other Eastern Orthodox and Catholic denominations, 3 million Protestants, more than a million Jews, and a significant number of Buddhists. Thus, roughly a quarter of the Soviet people openly profess some sort of religious belief; we can only guess the number of secret believers.

It is difficult to comprehend a country that is as culturally, geographically, institutionally, and historically complex as the Soviet Union. However, there is much that we know and many misconceptions to dispel. First, let us turn to the insights of history.

Economic History

Early History

During the tenth century, the first alliance of Russian city-states developed with its capital in Kiev, a major city on the trade route between Europe and the East. These Russians were a cosmopolitan people, with commercial and cultural links to most of the known world; a gradual shift began from agricultural production to urban crafts and services. Economically, culturally, and politically, Kievan Russia compared very favorably with the West.

This line of development was interrupted by a chain of events that isolated Russia from the Western world. Late in the tenth century, Kiev adopted Eastern Orthodoxy, whereas most of Europe adhered to Catholicism. Russian isolation deepened during the Fourth Crusade, when the Western powers opened a more direct trade route through Venice and the Italian city-states; it became complete after 1237, when the Mongol invasion of Russia initiated 200 years of foreign oppression. Kiev and several other cities were burned to the ground. The best craftsmen were deported to serve the Mongol rulers, forcing the remaining population back into agriculture. All ties to Western technology and philosophy were cut, and a tradition of subservience to autocratic rule was established. Russian economic development fell behind that of the West and never fully recovered.

Mongol rule also kindled a fear and suspicion of foreigners that has never disappeared from the Russian psyche. When independence was finally regained in 1452, the capital was moved to Moscow, a more remote outpost from Western Europe. Foreign travel and commerce were limited; the few outsiders permitted to live in the country were quarantined from the native population. In order to support a strong military, a strict set of feudal institutions was established under the control of the tsar. "In the sway he holds over his people," one sixteenth-century ambassador declared, the tsar "surpasses all of the monarchs of the whole world."[1]

Peter the Great

At the beginning of the eighteenth century, on the eve of the Industrial Revolution in England, Russian despotism was no match for Western technology. Peter the Great became convinced of this fact during his grand tour of Europe in 1697–1698. Drawing charges from pious Muscovites that he was the Antichrist, Tsar Peter initiated a crash program to introduce Western science, technology, art, and architecture in Russia. He hired foreign technicians, established an Academy of Sciences, built new state industries, and forbade his nobles to marry before they had some knowledge of mathematics. He forsook Moscow and moved his capital closer to the Western world, on the Gulf of Finland. At untold cost of resources and human lives he built St. Petersburg on swampland and patterned it after Venice and Versailles.

Similar to modern Soviet leaders, Peter was careful to avoid the adoption of Western political and economic philosophies while importing foreign technology. His Westernization program paradoxically led to stronger autocratic repression and a wider gulf between the aristocracy, who adopted Western ways, and the peasants, who did not.

His military adventures, his program of industrialization, and the building of St. Petersburg required that taxes be levied on everything imaginable: the wearing of beards, the keeping of bees, and the grinding of knives and axes to name a few.[2] Tax revenues increased five-fold during Peter's reign, requiring repressive measures to maintain domestic order and to support his system of forced labor.

Peter and his immediate successors accomplished most of his goals. Between the beginning of his reign and the end of the eighteenth century, new territory was added to the Russian Empire in the Baltic area, the Crimea, the northern Caucasus, the Ukraine, part of Central Asia, and Belorussia. Thus, Russia gained access to the Baltic and Black Sea trade routes, the farmlands of

[1]The ambassador of the Holy Roman Empire, quoted in Michael Kort, *The Soviet Colossus: A History of the USSR* (New York: Charles Scribner's Sons, 1985), 13.

[2]Peter I. Lyashchenko, *History of the National Economy of Russia* (New York: Macmillan, 1949), 269.

the Ukraine, and the iron and coal deposits of Krivoi Rog and the Donets Basin that would support the development of a steel industry in the next century. The number of factories increased from less than 200 in 1725 to about 2,500 at the end of the century.

Emancipation and Industrialization

The maintenance of autocratic and feudal institutions placed limits on Russian economic development. The immobility of the feudal labor force thwarted the growth of agricultural productivity. A repressive society may be able to buy, borrow, and steal technologies from abroad, but it provides a poor environment for the development of new ideas at home. Despite several significant achievements, the Russians have always lagged behind the West in technological progress.

The persistent backwardness of Russian society was dramatized by the Crimean War (1853–1856), when a disastrous defeat was handed to the army by a small but modern force of Europeans. Five years later, Alexander II signed the Emancipation Decree that nominally abolished serfdom in Russia. The decree was long and complex, and had positive and negative elements.

On the positive side, some 47 million serfs, making up about three-quarters of the population, were freed from the arbitrary rule of their masters. In contrast to the emancipated Poles and the victims of the European enclosure movement, the Russian serfs were not left landless. About half of the nation's agricultural land was assigned to them.

Unfortunately, the better land was kept by the gentry and the freed serfs were required to pay for their land through a system of redemption payments. The land was held by the peasants not individually, but as members of village communal organizations (the *mir* or *obshchina*). The commune was responsible for collection of taxes and redemption payments and for the fair apportionment of land to its members. The commune divided its land into small strips. Each family was assigned several strips to tend (sometimes as many as 40), some with higher fertility and some with lower. From time to time, the strips were rotated among the families.

The communal system of strip agriculture was somewhat equitable. (Marx suggested in 1882 that the Russian experience with "primeval common ownership" might make it possible to "pass directly to the higher form of communist common ownership.")[3] However, the system was grossly inefficient. The workers lost time traveling from one strip to another and the rotation of plots between families provided little incentive for improving the land. For these and other reasons, the level of productivity in Russian agriculture remained very low after emancipation, and chronic food shortages continued.

Despite low productivity, the peasants were forced to market a very large part of their output in order to pay taxes, redemption payments, and other

[3]Marx and Engels in their preface to the Russian edition of the *Communist Manifesto,* in *The Marx-Engels Reader,* ed. Robert Tucker, 2d ed. (New York: W. W. Norton, 1978), 472.

Table 11.1 Infant Mortality Rates in Europe, 1867–1911

	Annual Deaths of Infants Under One Year Old Per Thousand Live Births	
	1867–1869	1909–1911
Austria	248	202
Belgium	133	147
Denmark	135	102
England	155	115
Finland	252	114
France	180	128
Germany	304	175
Italy	225	151
Netherlands	204	115
Norway	120	67
Russia	272	252
Sweden	151	73

Source: B. R. Mitchell, ed., *European Historical Statistics, 1750–1975* (New York: Facts on File, 1980), 137–143.

monetary obligations. Thus, Russia became the world's largest grain exporter during the latter half of the nineteenth century. Grain exports made it possible to import more foreign equipment, and a wave of railroad construction began. Encompassing less than 700 miles of track before the emancipation, the Russian railroad network grew to more than 21,000 miles in 1894.

The railroads made it possible to link the coal of the Donets Basin with the iron ore of Krivoi Rog, and production of iron and steel tripled during the 1890s. Petroleum production also tripled during the decade and production of cotton cloth doubled.

Unfortunately, the industrialization program caused little improvement in the living standards of the common people. The benefits of economic growth were dissipated by rapid population growth and imperial taxation. Between the 1860s and the early-1900s, when infant mortality rates fell dramatically in most of Europe, the Russion rate barely declined (Table 11.1) and real wages barely increased.

In a vain attempt to control labor unrest, the tsarist government prohibited the formation of trade unions. This prohibition only contributed to the growth of underground revolutionary organizations. One of these organizations, Liberation of Labor, was founded by George Plekhanov in 1883. Plekhanov's group established close ties with socialist organizations in Western Europe, and laid the foundation for the Russian Social Democratic movement.

The Rise of Soviet Socialism
The Revolutions of 1905 and 1917

The Russian Social Democrats held their first congresses in 1903. Their program called for the overthrow of the tsarist monarchy and the eventual adoption of socialism. The faction that came to be known as the Mensheviks believed that Russia must pass through a bourgeois democratic period before it would be ready for socialism and that the party should be a broad-based mass organization. As we noted in the previous chapter, Lenin's followers, the Bolsheviks, believed that Russia was already ripe for socialism and that party membership should be restricted to an elite group of dedicated revolutionaries. While the Mensheviks won the vote on membership policy, the Bolsheviks gained control of the party's central committee and its newspaper, *Iskra* (The Spark).

The revolutionary movement gained momentum in January 1905 when the palace guard opened fire on thousands of workers assembled at the Winter Palace in St. Petersburg to protest the hardships caused by the war with Japan. Bloody Sunday, as it was called, precipitated a wave of demonstrations and strikes, culminating in a general strike in October. While few socialist goals were attained, the tsar was forced to grant several concessions, including the formation of a parliament (the Duma). The ensuing Stolypin reforms of 1906 to 1910 released the agricultural peasants from the communes and canceled their debts.

When World War I broke out across Europe in 1914, the situation in Russia went from bad to horrible. Two million Russians were killed in combat and governmental mismanagement and corruption compounded the economic problems at home. Food riots broke out in the capital in February 1917 and the tsar was forced to abdicate the throne. The Duma established a moderate provisional government, which was eventually headed by Alexander Kerensky of the Labor Party. The provisional government acted very slowly at a time when major reforms were needed and it gradually lost popular support. After several months of planning and a brief exchange of fire, the Bolsheviks (who split from the Mensheviks to form their own party in 1912) took control of the Winter Palace in November 1917.

War Communism (1918–1921)

After seizing power, the new Bolshevik leaders faced several immediate problems. First, they had to deliver on their promise to create a socialist society. To this end, on the very day of the overthrow they issued a decree that allowed the confiscation of all private and church land and livestock without compensation. Local committees were appointed to distribute the use of the land (but not its ownership) among the peasants in each area.

Second, the Bolshevik victory was won only in St. Petersburg; the consolidation of their rule in the rest of the empire required a long civil war against forces loyal to the tsarist regime. Their efforts to establish domestic control and reform were vastly complicated by Russian cooperation with the Allies in World War I.

After a heated debate, Lenin and his associates decided to cut their losses by negotiating a separate peace with the Germans. In exchange, they were required to recognize German control over several territories in Georgia, the Ukraine, Poland, and the Baltic states that were not yet under Bolshevik rule.

Thus, in the 1918 Treaty of Brest-Litovsk, the Bolsheviks signed away their rights to the trade routes, croplands, and iron and coal fields that were the backbone of the economy.

The truce with Germany precipitated an invasion of Allied soldiers, whose mission was to draw Russia back into the war, to recover munitions stored there, and to protect investments that had been nationalized by the Bolsheviks. The new leaders had traded German hostility for Allied intervention in 1918–1919 and were engaged in a civil war and a war with Poland until 1920.

The institutional response to these events was the formation of a military style of economic organization known as **War Communism.** The inefficiency of small-scale agriculture and the loss of the Ukraine contributed to severe food shortages; police and party activists were sent into the countryside to forcibly collect the agricultural "surpluses" of the peasants. These and other consumer goods were rationed to workers and their families by governmental agencies. Little use was made of money and private trade was outlawed. The leaders attempted to justify these measures in ideological terms, claiming that they represented a giant step toward the moneyless economy of full communism. In retrospect, they seem to have been little more than a pragmatic response to a desperate situation.

In industry, some 37,000 enterprises were nationalized, including all of those that employed more than ten workers and those with more than five workers where mechanical power was used. These were administered by a complex and confused bureaucracy of central and regional commissariats and councils, led by the Supreme Council of National Economy (*Vesenkha*). The ability of the government to coordinate the work of the nationalized industries was rendered all but impossible by the lack of centralized information. A committee of investigation set up in 1920 found that many of the central authorities not only "do not know what goods and in what amounts are kept in the warehouses under their control, but are actually ignorant even of the number of warehouses."[4]

A strict system of military discipline was exercised over much of the labor force. Labor armies were formed to rebuild the roads and railways (some 7,200 road and rail bridges had been destroyed by the hostilities) and to speed the recovery of coal mining, forestry, and oil extraction. The movement of workers was restricted and deserters were given severe penalties.

How did the system of War Communism perform? Agricultural and industrial production both plummeted during its operation. The uncompensated requisitioning of agricultural surpluses certainly reduced the farmers' work incentives and encouraged them to conceal their surpluses from the authorities. However, it is difficult to determine how much of the reduction in output was caused by poor work incentives and chaotic management practices and how much was caused by the disruption and devastation of war. According to

---

[4]Quoted in Maurice Dobb, *Soviet Economic Development Since 1917* (New York: International Publishers, 1948), 112.

Maurice Dobb, the Soviet authorities were forced by extreme circumstances to adopt their requisitioning and rationing system: "Without it there is small doubt that starvation in the towns in the winter of 1919–1920 would have been very much more extensive, and the army might well have collapsed."[5]

The New Economic Policy (1921–1928)

By the end of 1920, the Bolsheviks had won the civil war, consolidated their power, and regained most of the territory surrendered in the Brest-Litovsk Treaty. A series of workers' and soldiers' revolts made it painfully obvious that: (1) the government was not able to administer the entire economy; (2) forced requisitioning provoked anger from the peasants rather than productivity; and (3) the civilian labor force was no longer willing to work under military conditions.

The War Communism controls were no longer necessary or sustainable and in 1921 Lenin replaced them with his New Economic Policy (NEP). The NEP system was, in many ways, an experiment in market socialism. Lenin described it as a temporary step backward to capitalism, designed to get the economy back on its feet, so that it would become possible to take "two steps forward" toward full communism.

First, and perhaps most important, a progressive agricultural tax replaced the system of forced requisitioning and private trade was legalized. The farmers were able to keep or sell a larger part of any increase in their production and their incentive to work was restored. Governmental rationing of consumer goods was quickly replaced by private retail trade.

Second, the enterprises with 20 persons or less that had been nationalized under War Communism were leased to independent entrepreneurs. Many of the larger enterprises were allowed to operate as autonomous trusts and expected to operate at a profit. The only enterprises kept under direct governmental control were those in the commanding heights of industry—fuel, metallurgy, war industries, transportation, banking, and foreign trade. By controlling these industries, Lenin believed, it would be possible to set the course for the rest of the economy.

Third, the restrictions on labor mobility under War Communism were abolished and income equality gave way to market-determined wages. Labor legislation in 1922 entitled workers to an 8-hour day, a 2-week paid holiday, social insurance benefits, and collective bargaining rights. The return of the profit motive was accompanied by the return of unemployment, which climbed to 1.6 million in 1929.[6]

The performance of the NEP system, like the performance of War Communism, was obscured by exceptional conditions. A drought in 1920–1921 led to a famine in 1921–1922 that caused some 5,000,000 deaths—twice the number of Russian combat casualties in World War I. Even more deaths would

[5]Ibid., 103.

[6]Alec Nove, *An Economic History of the USSR* (London: Penguin, 1969), 115.

have occurred without $70 million of aid provided by the United States and smaller amounts given by other countries. After 1921, however, the NEP system supported a rapid recovery. The prewar levels of agricultural and industrial production were regained in 1925 and 1927, respectively.

The famine of 1921–1922 caused agricultural prices to rise at the beginning of the NEP period; they gradually declined as production recovered in 1922–1923. Industrial prices, on the other hand, were driven upward by monopolistic practices and by the slower recovery of industrial production. If drawn on a chart, the falling agricultural prices and rising industrial prices resembled a pair of scissors, giving rise to the so-called Scissors Crisis of 1923–1924. The Soviet leaders feared, irrationally it seems, that falling agricultural prices would eventually cause the peasants to reduce their marketing of food in the cities. They feared that in order to maintain their production incentives, it would be necessary to allow the farmers to accumulate more wealth. This policy seemed inconsistent with socialist ideals; thus, the entire NEP program came under attack.

The Industrialization Debate

The Scissors Crisis and Lenin's death in 1924 stimulated a heated debate over the proper strategy for Soviet industrialization. Impressed with the rapid recovery experienced after 1921, Bukharin and his "right-deviation" faction argued for continuation of the market-oriented policies of NEP. They admitted that the Soviet Union would remain an agrarian society for several years if market forces were allowed to operate: the country's comparative-cost advantage was currently in agriculture. They defended policies favoring agriculture, however, on both political and economic grounds.

First, the right believed that the legitimacy of the Soviet government was based on the so-called *smychka,* or alliance, between agricultural and industrial workers. Any serious effort to distort market forces to the advantage of industry would alienate the farmers. The *smychka* would be broken and the political basis of Soviet rule would disappear.

In economic terms, the right believed that investment expenditures directed toward modernization of the primitive agricultural sector would reap large returns and these would eventually generate the savings needed for industrial investment. Agricultural development in the short run would most effectively support industrial development in the long run, they argued.

In reply to the *smychka* argument, Trotsky and other members of the "left-deviation" wing of the Bolshevik Party warned that if NEP were continued, and if private agriculture and trade were allowed to grow and prosper, the capitalist system would return. They particularly disliked the slogan that Bukharin launched in 1925 to encourage the farmers: "Get rich." Furthermore, they warned that the Soviet Union, the only socialist country in the world, was surrounded by enemies and that a rapid expansion of heavy industry was necessary to support the military.

In economic terms, the left argued that a big push toward industrialization could be accomplished by exploitation—as they called it—of the private sector. Preobrazhensky, their leading theorist, estimated that between one-third and one-half of all profits in trade and industry in 1922 were accumulated by private traders and capitalists. These resources could be captured by the socialist sector, he suggested, by reviving the state trade monopoly that existed under War Communism, by levying high taxes on the peasants, and by controlling agricultural prices at low levels. If the peasants reacted by reducing their shipments of food to the cities, he suggested that they be forcibly assembled on collective farms where their actions could be controlled and where mass-production techniques could be used.

The industrialization debate was closely connected with two other important debates in the 1920s. The first concerned revolutionary strategy. Would the protection of socialism in the Soviet Union require a worldwide socialist revolution or would it be possible to build socialism in one country? Trotsky and the left adopted the former position, arguing that rapid development of heavy industry and military production was necessary to support the worldwide socialist revolution. Bukharin and the right believed that socialism must be strengthened in Russia before it could be carried to the outside world. They warned that coercive measures against the peasants would provoke a hostile reaction from Western countries (as evidenced by the aid received from the United States during the famine).

Industrialization strategy was also an important theme in the economic planning debate. On one side were the **geneticists,** who believed that any realistic long-term plan must be based on a careful analysis of present and past conditions and experiences—on the "genetic" heritage of the economy. The geneticists adopted the conservative (right) view that any shift from agricultural to industrial production should be gradual. On the other side were the **teleologists,** whose name comes from the Greek word for end. They believed that the purpose of economic planning was to accomplish a sharp break from tradition and market forces and that emphasis should be placed on goals rather than beginnings. The support of the workers for the socialist system should open a whole new realm of possibilities, they believed; thus their plans need not be constrained by conventional "genetic" criteria.

The Planning Era Begins

Stalin initially aligned himself with the right, but problems with grain procurement in 1927 turned him against the peasants and provoked the return of forced requisitioning. Bukharin began to speak of Stalin as a new Genghis Khan (recalling two centuries of Mongol domination) and of military-feudal exploitation of the peasantry. Stalin responded by declaring, early in 1929, that Bukharin was living in the past.

With the First Five-Year Plan, inaugurated in 1928, Stalin adopted a strategy that was unabashedly leftist and teleological. The plan was predicated on wildly optimistic assumptions and called for rapid rates of growth in all sectors of the economy (Table 11.2). The highest rates of growth were planned for producer goods, the next highest were those for industrial consumer goods, and the lowest priority was given to agriculture.

Table 11.2   The First Soviet Five-Year Plan

	Targets 1927–1928 to 1932–1933	Actual Growth, 1928–1933	
		Soviet Estimates	Western Estimates
Industrial production	136	113	49
Intermediate goods	181	95	98
Machinery	157	359	359
Consumer goods	84	63	1
Agriculture	55	− 19	

Percentage Increases

Sources: First column—Alec Nove, *An Economic History of the USSR* (London: Penguin, 1969), 145–146; second column—Roger Clarke, ed., *Soviet Economic Facts 1917–1970* (New York: John Wiley and Sons, 1972), 8–10, 68, and author's estimates; and third column—G. Warren Nutter, *Growth of Industrial Production in the Soviet Union* (Princeton, N.J.: Princeton University Press, 1962), 525–526.

Statistics on the fulfillment of the plan suggest an even more leftist orientation. A massive effort was devoted to expansion of machinery production and this portion of the plan was more than fulfilled. All of the other sectors of the economy fell short of their goals. According to Western estimates, production of industrial consumer goods increased by only 1 percent in 5 years. The official Soviet data reveal that agricultural production declined sharply.

What caused the drop in agricultural production? First, the plan devoted the lion's share of investment resources to industry, and pay incentives attracted millions of workers from agriculture into industry. Second, in his effort to maintain food deliveries to the cities, Stalin again borrowed from Preobrazhensky and, in 1929, launched a massive drive to collectivize agriculture. The land reform, he reasoned, had reduced the number of large, efficient farms and the size of the agricultural surplus marketed in the cities: "The way out lies, firstly, in the transition from the small, backward and scattered peasant farms to amalgamated, large-scale socialized farms, equipped with machinery, armed with scientific knowledge and capable of producing a maximum of grain for the market."[7]

Collectivization was violently resisted by the peasants, who wanted to keep their land, their livestock, and their independence. Rather than surrender them to the government, the peasants slaughtered millions of head of livestock and destroyed large numbers of buildings. The battle over collectivization, the consequent disruption of food production, and Stalin's use of forced labor in the Gulag caused at least 5 million deaths in the 1930s and some estimates run as high as 20 million.[8]

[7]From Stalin's 1928 address, "On the Grain Front," in *A Documentary History of Communism*, ed. Robert V. Daniels (New York: Random House, 1960), 303.

[8]Steven Rosefielde, "Excess Mortality in the Soviet Union: A Reconsideration of the Demographic Consequences of Forced Industrialization 1929–1949," *Soviet Studies* 35 (July 1983): 385–409.

Figure 11.1   The Soviet Communist Party and Government

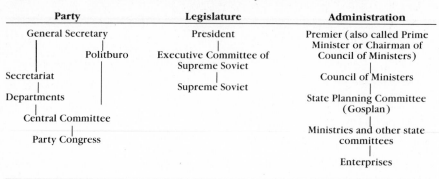

Party	Legislature	Administration
General Secretary	President	Premier (also called Prime Minister or Chairman of Council of Ministers)
Politburo	Executive Committee of Supreme Soviet	
Secretariat	Supreme Soviet	Council of Ministers
Departments		State Planning Committee (Gosplan)
Central Committee		Ministries and other state committees
Party Congress		Enterprises

Although it was accomplished at an enormous cost, the First Five-Year Plan and the collectivization of agriculture initiated a radical shift toward industrialization of the Soviet economy. Industrial production increased from 28 to 45 percent of net national product between 1928 and 1937, building the military-industrial base that repelled Hitler's invasion during World War II and contributing to the country's superpower status after the war. On the other hand, the low priority placed on agricultural production turned the world's largest exporter of grain into the world's largest importer. Stalin died in 1953, but his legacy is apparent today.

Political and Economic Institutions

In a country where the economy is run almost entirely by the government, the boundary between economics and politics is rather hazy. Before we begin our survey of the procedures and methods used in Soviet planning and management, it will be helpful to become acquainted with the major institutional actors. As we might expect, a society very different from our own has a very different form of political organization.

Soviet legal theory does not recognize the principle of separation of powers, but we can roughly divide the Soviet government into three interconnected branches: the Communist Party apparatus, the legislature, and the administrative apparatus (Figure 11.1). Of these, the most powerful is the Communist Party. A judiciary exists, but it is subordinate to the legislative branch and plays a relatively minor role in Soviet society. The Soviet Supreme Court, for example, has never claimed the right to review the acts of the legislature and the administration.

The Communist Party

The most powerful position in Soviet society, the office held by Stalin, Khrushchev, Brezhnev, Andropov, Chernenko, and Gorbachev, is the general secretary of the Communist Party (Figure 11.1). That the party leader has such an exalted position may seem strange to Americans, few of whom even know the names of the Democratic and Republican party chairmen. The Communist Party, however, enjoys a monopoly over Soviet politics. It has a large bureaucracy of its own and exercises authority over the other branches of government.

The Politburo is the board of directors of the Party, which means that it is the senior board of directors for all of Soviet society. It usually has about 12 voting members, including the general secretary, several of the other Party secretaries (who collectively compose the Secretariat), the leaders of the major regional Party organizations, and representatives from the other branches of government. The latter include the premier, the president, the minister of foreign affairs, and the head of the security police (the KGB). The Politburo holds weekly meetings and exercises control over all aspects of foreign and domestic policy.

The Secretariat also has about 12 members, all of whom are full-time Party leaders overseeing the work of the 21 central committee departments. The departments are the agencies through which the Party exercises control over the other branches of government. For example, the Agriculture and Food Industry Department oversees the work of the Ministry of Agriculture. The departments exercise their authority largely through their control of appointments to a list of some 200,000 key jobs—the so-called *nomenklatura.* The *nomenklatura* lists are never published, but Party approval is usually required to obtain a job as a factory manager, a foreign trade official, a director of a research institute, or any higher position in society.

The 307 (in 1987) voting members of the central committee of the Party are, with a few exceptions, the most powerful members of the national and regional Party and governmental agencies. The committee holds only two or three brief meetings per year, giving it hardly enough time to deal with complex decisions. Nonetheless, it is a very important organization. It elects the Politburo and the Secretariat and controls the Party's press organizations and journals. It also provides a forum for communication and debate among the national leaders. For example, central committee debates preceded the 1964 ouster of Khrushchev as general secretary and the 1968 invasion of Czechoslovakia.

The Party Congress, which is theoretically the supreme body of the Party, is convened once every 5 years. Each congress is an enormous media event. Thousands of delegates gather in the Kremlin to unanimously approve the new economic plan and to unanimously "elect" a new central committee. The congress provides an appropriate forum for the leaders to deliver their most important policy speeches and to set a tone for the following years.[9] Speeches are also given by local officials who wish to gain support for their pet investment projects.

[9]In the spirit of comparative analysis, I made a rough count of the words in General Secretary Gorbachev's speech to the 1986 party congress and President Reagan's 1987 State of the Union speech. Gorbachev's speech was about 10 times longer.

Below the national level, the Party maintains control through its network of regional, local, and enterprise organizations. These organizations enforce adherence to Party doctrine and ideology and attempt to instill a sense of social responsibility in workers and managers who are prone to follow their personal or departmental interests. In his speech to the 1986 Party Congress, Gorbachev attributed the poor performance of the economy in Uzbekistan to the leniency of local Party leaders:

In the republican Party organization discipline slackened, and persons for whom the sole principle was lack of principles, their own well-being, and careerist considerations were in favor. . . . All this could not but affect the state of affairs. The situation in the economy and the social sphere deteriorated markedly. Machinations, embezzlement, and bribery thrived, and socialist legality was grossly transgressed.[10]

The Legislature

The Supreme Soviet, the bicameral Soviet legislature, apparently plays a rather ornamental role in the government. Its 1,500 elected delegates, who generally hold other full-time jobs outside of the government, gather one or two times each year to approve the laws that have been prepared by others and to approve changes in the leadership of administrative agencies.

A more influential body is the Presidium of the Supreme Soviet. It has only 39 members, most of whom are full-time governmental officials, and holds meetings every other month. Between meetings of the full Supreme Soviet, the Presidium has all of the constitutional powers of the legislature. Thus, when the position of premier was passed from Khrushchev to Kosygin in 1964, and from Tikhonov to Ryzhkov in 1985, a meeting of the full Supreme Soviet was not required.

The chairman of the Presidium of the Supreme Soviet (presently Andrei Gromyko) is usually considered the head of state; he performs the traditional duties of signing legislation, receiving the credentials of diplomats, and the like. While the position is mostly ceremonial, like the vice presidency of the United States, its influence depends on the person who holds it. Brezhnev, Andropov, and Chernenko, for example, each served concurrently as general secretary of the Party and chairman of the Presidium.

The Administrative Branch

The premier (presently Nikolai Ryzhkov) is the head of the administrative branch. As a Politburo member, the premier is involved in all aspects of Soviet policy, the most important responsibility being management of the economy.

---

[10]Mikhail Gorbachev, *Political Report of the CPSU Central Committee to the 27th Party Congress* (Moscow: Novosti Press Agency, 1986), 101–102. For a fuller discussion of the economic role of the local Party organizations, see Gregory Grossman, "The Party as Manager and Entrepreneur," in *Entrepreneurship in Imperial Russia and the Soviet Union,* ed. Gregory Guroff and Fred Carstensen (Princeton, N.J.: Princeton University Press, 1983), 284–305.

It is the premier who presents the major report on the new five-year plan at the Party Congress.

Under the leadership of the premier, the Council of Ministers is composed of the 90 leaders of industrial ministries and state committees and the 15 chairmen of the councils of ministers of the union republics. Based on its authority to issue decrees, the Council has supplanted many of the legislative functions of the Supreme Soviet. The major economic reform that began in 1979, for example, was based on a decree (*postanovlenie*) jointly issued by the Central Committee and the Council of Ministers, with no involvement of the nominal legislature.

The most influential administrative agency below the Council of Ministers is the State Planning Committee, or Gosplan. Although many other agencies participate in the planning effort, it is the job of Gosplan to coordinate the process, to forge the proposals of other agencies into an internally consistent document, and to handle bottlenecks and conflicts that arise during the fulfillment of the plan.

Aside from Gosplan, several other agencies perform tasks that cut across all of the sectors of the economy. The State Price Committee is responsible for the control of all wholesale and retail prices in the country and sets many of the prices itself. The State Committee for Material and Technical Supply, or Gossnab, plays an important role in the planning of production and distribution; it operates a nationwide network of industrial supply warehouses and stores. The Ministry of Finance and the State Bank handle monetary and financial policy and administer a huge system of taxes and subsidies through the state budget. The Ministry of Foreign Trade prepares export and import plans and conducts almost all of the nation's international transactions through its worldwide network of trade organizations and representatives.

The actual production of broad categories of goods is administered by the 50-odd industrial ministries. There is, for example, a Ministry of Agriculture, a Ministry of Ferrous Metallurgy, and a Ministry of the Automobile Industry, each of which controls and evaluates the work of the farms and factories under its jurisdiction. The ministries prepare economic plans for their subordinate enterprises, administer the system of material incentives, and handle the hiring and firing of enterprise directors. According to Mikhail Gorbachev, the ministries have grown too powerful; he proposes that some of their authority be returned to higher and lower authorities—to the central planners and the subordinate enterprises.

At the bottom of the administrative hierarchy are the farms, factories, and other enterprises that actually produce goods and services. Each enterprise has a director appointed by the ministry with the advice and consent of the Party. It also has a Party committee and a trade union committee, each of which has its own leadership. The Soviet trade unions do not bargain for wage increases; they participate in the division of bonus payments between the workers, protect employee health and safety, provide legal aid to workers, and encourage labor discipline, training, and productivity.

An enterprise has little autonomy in the Soviet system. The ministry and the central planners tell it what to produce, what quantities to produce, how many workers to hire, what raw materials to use and where to buy them, what prices to charge for its products, and what to do with any profits that are earned. The performance of the enterprise and the income of its employees are based on its faithful performance of the instructions of superior authorities. An enterprise maintains a modicum of autonomy only because the central authorities do not have the desire, the ability, or the information necessary to monitor all of its actions. If Gorbachev is successful in reforming the system, enterprises will be allowed to make more of their own decisions in the future.

Central Planning

All of the organizations and institutions considered above are involved in one way or another in the formation and implementation of economic plans. General economic priorities are set by the Party and are incorporated into an operational economic plan by Gosplan and the other administrative agencies. The plan is given the force of law by the legislature and the ministries and enterprises, with the moral support of the Party, are responsible for its implementation.

The plans are prepared for overlapping time periods. The annual plan provides the greatest detail, including specific instructions for the individual enterprises. The five-year plan sets goals for the growth of national income and for broader commodity groups with only a few targets for individual enterprises. Even less detail is included in the perspective plans covering periods of 10–20 years.

In 1961, for example, Khrushchev issued a perspective plan designed to bring Soviet society to the threshold of full communism—that is, material abundance—by 1980. It was not fulfilled. Similarly, the program adopted by the 1986 Party Congress calls for a doubling of national income and industrial output by the year 2000. This would require a sharp acceleration of economic growth that is not likely to occur. Thus, the longer-term plans are often exercises in wishful thinking. The annual plans, however, are usually quite realistic and deserve emphasis here.

Planning of Production and Distribution

Several different plans are prepared every year in the Soviet Union. One covers the production and distribution of goods and services, another controls the allocation of capital investments, and others are prepared to regulate the financial and foreign trade systems. All of these plans must be coordinated, but the hub of the system is the production plan. All of the other plans are designed to support the production process and to keep the economy in financial balance.

The preparation of the production plan begins at the top of the hierarchy when the Politburo and other high-level political leaders formulate general priorities for the economy. Khrushchev, for example, set a high priority on the development of the chemicals industry, Brezhnev paid special attention to

Table 11.3   Material Balance Table for Product X in Year Y

Sources	Uses
Production	Productive uses
Imports	Exports
Beginning stocks	Ending stocks
	Personal consumption
Total	Total

agriculture (particularly after the American grain embargo of 1980), and Gorbachev has emphasized the development of computer technology and industrial robots.

Based on such general priorities and prospects, the economists at Gosplan prepare a set of **control figures**—a first draft of the plan for broad categories of commodities, designed to guide the planning activity of the ministries and enterprises. Based on these guidelines the ministries prepare a more detailed set of plan targets and pass them down to the individual enterprises. The ministries often inflate the initial targets knowing that the enterprises will bargain for lower, less demanding, goals.

The enterprises prepare an even more detailed set of plans based on the assignments of their ministries and on their knowledge of production capacity and the needs of their customers. They also engage in the bargaining process mentioned above. Because their income and career prospects depend on plan fulfillment, the enterprise directors will do everything in their power to assure the feasibility of their plans.

After this initial round of bargaining, usually in October or November, the ministries send their detailed plans back to Gosplan. The economists at Gosplan work out the consistency of the annual plan for the 4,000 most important product groups. The State Committee for Material and Technical Supply (Gossnab) handles about 15,000 items that are less important; the ministries prepare the final plans for some 40,000 to 50,000 items.[11]

In each case, the consistency of the plan is established through the so-called system of **material balances.** A material balance table (shown in Table 11.3) is a statement of the planned sources and uses of a product, each measured in physical terms. If this is, for example, a material balance for oil, the most important source is domestic production, and data for planned oil production and stocks are provided to Gosplan by the Ministry of the Petroleum Industry. Information on planned imports and exports of oil are furnished by the Ministry of Foreign Trade, based on trade agreements with other countries. The other industrial ministries provide estimates of their planned requirements for oil, and the Ministry of Trade estimates the level of consumer demand.

---

[11]N. F. Fedorenko, "Planning and Management: What Should They Be Like?" *Problems of Economic* 28 (December 1985): 45.

Based on these sources of information and many others, Gosplan compiles its 4,000 material balance tables. Ideally, the total sources of each product would match total uses. However, many of the tables tend to show deficits because the ministries and enterprises have a strong incentive to pad their requests for resources and to bargain for low output targets. In a market system, the shortages would lead to price increases, which would lead to a reduction of the shortages. In the Soviet system, with controlled prices and a weak profit motive, the shortages can be removed only through adjustment of the plans.

It is the difficult job of the central planners, therefore, to adjust the tables until they balance—at least on paper. Suppose, for a moment, that we are central planners and it is our job to remove a planned shortage of oil. First, on the sources side, we can tell the petroleum ministry that it will have to produce more oil. This can cause a number of problems. In order to produce more oil the industry is likely to need more drilling equipment. Thus, in our effort to reduce the shortage of oil we may create a new shortage of drilling equipment. Alternatively, we can tell the petroleum ministry to produce more oil and to do it without additional drilling equipment. We hope that we are not asking the industry to do the impossible, but from our office in Moscow we can only guess.

A similar problem arises when we reduce the productive uses of oil. Sending less oil to the chemicals industry, for example, may reduce the shortage of oil, but it is likely to create a shortage of chemicals. Alternatively, we can tell the chemicals industry to maintain its production with a smaller allocation of oil. Again, we may be asking the impossible, or we may be encouraging the production of low-quality goods.

We can increase our imports of oil or reduce our exports; either of these actions may cause a deficit in the international balance of payments and require additional exports of some other product. Finally, we can reduce the deliveries of oil to consumers. This is the strategy that has been used many times in the past, but it has its limits. In the extreme, attempting to solve too many of our problems at the expense of the consumers may cause political unrest. Short of this, insufficient provision of consumer goods will reduce the effectiveness of the material incentive system, which may lead again to shortages of other goods.

However we reduce our hypothetical shortage of oil, we run the danger of creating shortages of other products or of asking producers to do the impossible. Given the complex patterns of interdependence between the different sectors of the economy and the incomplete and imperfect information that is available to central planners, it is impossible to compile a fully consistent and feasible plan for a modern country with a population of 275 million people.

It is even less likely that the plan will be optimal in the sense of prescribing the best use of resources to maximize the satisfaction of the Party, the planners, or the public. While computers and mathematical methods, such as input-output economics, provide some help to the planner, they have serious limitations (see the Appendix to this chapter). In practice, the output targets for many products are simply derived from the **achieved level**—that is, the target for next year is equal to this year's production plus an arbitrary percentage mark-up.

After the sources and uses of each important commodity are drawn into balance on paper, Gosplan issues a new list of plan targets and raw material allotments to the ministries. These are disaggregated into targets and allotments for the individual enterprises. The final plan is approved by the Supreme Soviet; thus, noncompliance is an infraction of the law. The plan targets and product orders are not sent to the enterprises until April, so the enterprises must work through the first quarter of the year "practically in the blind."[12]

Implementation of the Output Plan

The Soviet plans are seldom implemented precisely as they are written for a number of reasons. First, it is virtually impossible for the planners to devise a program that is fully consistent and feasible. Economists working in Moscow simply do not have all of the information they need on production capacities, stocks of goods, technological relationships, consumer demand, future weather conditions, and future conditions on international markets. They would find it more than difficult to use all of this information if they had it.

Second, plan implementation is often interrupted by the uneven rhythm of Soviet production. Just as American college students tend to wait until the last moment to write term papers and study for tests, Soviet enterprises tend to wait until the last few days of the quarter and the year, when they must report on their plan fulfillment, to meet their production quotas. This process, known as **storming,** helps explain why some 70 percent of all construction jobs are routinely completed in the last quarter of the year.[13] It also helps to explain why industrial enterprises find it so difficult to obtain the right raw materials at the right time to meet their plan targets.

For these and other reasons, the plan is subject to constant revision and evasion. Throughout the year, troubled enterprises appeal to their ministries, and the ministries appeal to Gosplan, for reductions in their output targets and increases in their allocations of raw materials. Failing that, the enterprises send out their *tolkachy* (procurement agents), who operate on the fringe of legality to locate supplies of raw materials and to arrange unplanned transactions.[14]

The enterprises also deal with their supply problems through vertical integration, or self-supply. That is, they attempt to produce the necessary raw materials and subassemblies themselves, rather than depending on plan allocations and deliveries from other enterprises. Examples include a shoe plant

---

[12]Ibid., 47.

[13]A Soviet estimate, cited in Peter Rutland, *The Myth of the Plan* (La Salle, Ill.: Open Court, 1985), 128.

[14]For a discussion of the process of continuous plan revision and of the welfare effects of this process, see Raymond P. Powell, "Plan Execution and the Workability of Soviet Planning," *Journal of Comparative Economics* 1 (March 1977): 51–76.

that makes its own equipment and glue, an automobile plant that makes its own industrial robots, and a railroad car repair depot that built its own electric generating station. According to Soviet planning officials, only 3 to 4 percent of standard metalworking products are produced in specialized plants, compared to 70 percent in the United States.[15] This practice reduces the efficiency of the Soviet economy by encouraging small-scale production and discouraging specialization. It also reduces the controlling power of the central planners; each enterprise maintains its private hoard of raw materials.

Some of the problems in the plan are solved through black-market activities. The second economy, as it sometimes is called, provides everything from industrial raw materials to ballpoint pens and taxi rides. Although these activities reduce the authority of the central planners and give rise to graft and corruption, they also remedy some of the more glaring deficiencies of the planning system.

The continuous process of plan revision and other unplanned activities lead some analysts to describe the Soviet Union not as a centrally planned economy at all, but as a managed or administered economy.[16] Furthermore, the growing size and complexity of the economy, and the growing importance of several sectors that are difficult to predict and plan (for example, agriculture, consumer goods, and foreign trade), have made it even more difficult to take the initial plans seriously.

On the other hand, it should not be forgotten that the nation's system of managerial pay and bonuses is based on plan fulfillment. Much of the unplanned activity is directed toward the fulfillment of the plan itself. Economic planning has been likened to the building of Gothic cathedrals.[17] The architects had no mathematical structural theories or scaling methods, so their initial plans were imperfect. Corrections and adjustments were necessary during the construction phase, but the buildings were true to their architectural purpose, and they have lasted for 700 years.

Investment Planning

In a capitalist country, investment resources will flow to a particular sector of the economy if the rate of return in that sector, adjusted for risk, is higher than the market rate of interest. In other words, money will be borrowed to build widget factories if the widget industry is sufficiently profitable. Consumer and governmental demand influences profitability; profitability influences the pattern of investment; and the pattern of investment influences the pattern of production.

In the Soviet Union, the chain of causation is different. Political priorities (which are influenced by consumer demand) determine the structure of out-

[15]Vladimir Kontorovich and Vladimir Shlapentokh, "Soviet Industry Grows Its Own Potatoes," *Wall Street Journal*, January 11, 1985, 14.

[16]John Howard Wilhelm, "The Soviet Union Has an Administered, Not a Planned, Economy," *Soviet Studies* 37 (January 1985): 118–130.

[17]Powell, "Plan Execution," 74.

put; the structure of output determines the required structure of the capital stock; and profitability influences the operation of the financial system. Profitable enterprises are taxed heavily and unprofitable enterprises may be subsidized to pursue governmental priorities.

The political process used to allocate capital resources in the Soviet economy is similar to that used in the U.S. military. The U.S. Army, Navy, and Air Force compete for their shares of the new weapons systems, and states and municipalities compete for the location of military bases. In many cases, new installations are located in the home states of key members of Congress, regardless of economic or military justification. Similarly, Soviet industrial ministers, enterprise managers, and local officials vie for investment resources; their relative success is determined by their position in the government, their bargaining power, and a combination of other political and economic considerations.

After the general level of investment in a particular industry is determined through the political process and the output plan, economic criteria are used to make more specific investment decisions. Suppose, for example, that the chemicals ministry has been told to increase its production of sulphuric acid by a certain amount and has been allotted investment resources for that purpose. Further suppose that sulphuric acid can be produced by either of two processes, one of which is more capital intensive, the other more labor intensive. Which process should be used and what kind of factory should be built?

According to the official methodology issued by Gosplan, the ministry is supposed to build the factory that minimizes the cost of producing the planned quantity of sulphuric acid. The full cost of sulphuric acid production in each version of the factory would include wage and raw materials expenses and a charge for the use of the proposed capital investment. The percentage charge on capital in the calculations, which the Soviets call the **norm of relative effectiveness,** performs a function similar to a rate of interest in a capitalist economy. A high capital charge will encourage the use of capital-saving, labor-intensive techniques; a low charge will have the opposite effect. Unlike a market rate of interest, however, the capital charge is set by central planners and is differentiated according to industry.[18]

In recent years, the Soviet leaders have been particularly unhappy with their capital investment program. Prime Minister Ryzhkov reported to the 1986 Party Congress that "schedules for the construction of facilities have been flagrantly violated, their cost has gone up, and amounts of unfinished construction and stocks of uninstalled equipment have grown excessively. . . . The general falloff in discipline that took place in past years undoubtedly had an effect on the state of affairs in construction."[19] (Again, we note a similarity

---

[18]See David Dyker, *The Process of Investment in the Soviet Union* (Cambridge: Cambridge University Press, 1983); and Janice Giffen, "The Allocation of Investment in the Soviet Union: Criteria for the Efficiency of Investment," *Soviet Studies* 33 (October 1981): 593–609.

[19]"Ryzhkov's Report on the Five-Year Plan," *Current Digest of the Soviet Press,* April 23, 1986, 10.

to the cost over-runs and construction delays that plague the American military.) According to Ryzhkov, new facilities will no longer be built if older facilities can be renovated, and construction times must be cut in half.

Financial Planning

Soviet financial planning plays a subordinate role to output and investment planning, but it serves at least two important functions. First, because the financial plan is coordinated with the other plans, and because all major financial transactions are handled by the State Bank, the bank is able to monitor and enforce the fulfillment of the output and investment plans. This is what the Soviets call **control by the ruble.** Second, the plan is designed to ensure the financial balance of the household, business, governmental, and international sectors. This is necessary because interest rates, exchange rates, and other prices do not perform a spontaneous equilibrating role in a planned economy.

In the *household sector,* financial balance requires that the planned value of consumer goods provided to the population be roughly equal to planned disposable income, adjusted for desired saving. If an inflationary surplus of income over output—too many rubles chasing too few goods—is predicted, the central planners can increase retail prices, tax rates, and production of consumer goods, or they can reduce wage rates and social security benefits. Unfortunately, these remedies are either difficult (production increase) or politically sensitive (price increase or wage decrease). Traditionally, the planners have avoided the unpopular practice of raising retail prices, and this has contributed to financial imbalances and shortages of consumer goods.

In the *business sector,* financial balance requires that the state-owned enterprises receive sufficient incomes to cover their payroll and other costs of production. These enterprises are not fully responsible for their profits or losses because their output levels and prices are set by higher authorities. Accordingly, money-losing enterprises are kept afloat through subsidies from the government, and successful enterprises are required to surrender more than half of their profits to the government.

Financial balance in the *international sector* is reflected in the balance of payments. Sufficient funds must be generated from planned exports, arms sales, tourism, and international borrowing to finance the planned level of imports. Control of the international balance is complicated by two factors. First, international prices and exchange rates cannot be controlled by the central planners, they can only be forecast. Second, the Soviet Union conducts about half of its trade with Western countries in convertible currencies and the other half with socialist countries in bilateral barter arrangements. This means that several different balances of payments must be planned.

Finally, the financial balance of the *governmental sector* is planned through the state budget (Table 11.4). Business profits are the largest source of governmental revenue; subsidies and other payments to businesses are the largest category of expenditure. The budget is largely designed to mitigate the

Table 11.4   The Soviet State Budget, 1984 (Billions of Rubles)

Expenditures		Revenues	
National economy		Deductions from profits	115.6
(investment, subsidies, etc.)	211.7	Turnover tax	102.7
Social/cultural and science	119.7	Personal taxes	28.8
Defense	17.1	Social insurance contributions	24.5
Administration	2.9	Other	105.1
Other	19.8		
Total	371.2	Total	376.7

Source: Tsentral'noe Statisticheskoe upravlenie SSSR, *Narodnoe khoziaistvo SSSR v 1984 g.* (Moscow: Finansy i Statistika, 1985), 573.

financial imbalances that are caused in the business sector by the systems of price control and central planning.

The second-largest source of revenue, the turnover tax, is a differential sales tax. It arises from the differences between wholesale and retail prices. The income tax runs a distant third place as a source of revenue.

The figure included in the official budget for defense expenditure is clearly understated. The 1987 figure of 20.2 billion rubles converts to about $31 billion at the official exchange rate, compared to the $282 billion that the U.S. government budgeted for national defense in that same year. Since the Soviets claim they have reached military parity with the United States, the budget figure is patently absurd.[20]

The budget in Table 11.4 indicates a surplus of revenues over expenditures. This has been true of every Soviet budget published in peacetime. However, according to the controversial analysis of Igor Birman, these surpluses may be nothing more than the result of slippery accounting practices. Birman claims that the "other" unspecified sources of revenue claimed in the budget are much too large to be legitimate. He estimates that budget deficits were actually registered in 26 of the 29 years between 1950 and 1978 and that the deficits were financed through expansion of the money supply. Growth of the money supply, in turn, may have contributed to the shortages of consumer and producer goods.[21]

Summary

During its early history, Russia had strong ties with the Western world. The Catholic-Orthodox schism during the tenth century, the subsequent change of trade routes, and the Mongol invasion of 1237 cut these ties. The latter event

[20]For a fuller discussion of this point, see Raymond Hutchings, *The Soviet Budget* (Albany, N.Y.: The State University of New York Press, 1983), Chapter 9.

[21]Igor Birman, *Secret Incomes of the Soviet State Budget* (The Hague: Martinus Nijhoff, 1981), Chapter 10. See also, Igor Birman, "The Soviets Have Their Own Massive Deficit," *Wall Street Journal,* March 13, 1985, 34.

led to 200 years of foreign oppression and established autocratic and xenophobic traditions.

During the eighteenth century, Peter the Great initiated a period of closer contact with the West, imperial expansion, and industrial growth, while continuing the autocratic tradition. Although serfdom was finally abolished in 1861, several provisions of the emancipation decree restricted labor mobility and rural living standards. A railroad boom began in the 1870s and industrial production grew rapidly during the 1890s, but few of the benefits trickled down to the lower classes. Revolutionary activities gained momentum early in the 1900s. The privation of World War I led to riots that drove the tsar from the throne in February 1917, clearing the way for the Bolshevik revolution in November.

During the period of War Communism (1917–1921), the new leaders nationalized industry, confiscated agricultural surpluses, and used a military style of organization. This was followed by an experiment in market socialism known as the New Economic Policy (1921–1928). After an extended period of debate, the planning era began in 1928 with the publication of the ambitious First Five-Year Plan. Under this plan, heavy industry was given a higher priority than agriculture.

With centralized planning, the Soviets developed their current system of economic and political organization. National policy is established by the general secretary and the Communist Party hierarchy. The prime minister, the Council of Ministers, and the State Planning Committee coordinate the work of the ministries, which oversee the industrial enterprises. The roles of the parliament (Supreme Soviet) and the president are mostly ceremonial.

The economic plans are formulated for several time periods, with the annual plans being the most specific and operational. The production plans are formulated through a process of disaggregation and bargaining and are adjusted for rough consistency through the method of material balances. During its implementation, departures from the production plan are coordinated by administrative guidance, by the practice of self-supply within enterprises, and by black market transactions between enterprises. An investment plan is designed to provide the capital stock needed for the production plan. Financial plans are designed to balance the incomes and expenditures of the household, business, and governmental sectors, and to equilibrate the international balance of payments.

Discussion and Review Questions

1. Discuss the role of Peter the Great in Russian economic and political history. Why do you suppose that Maximillian Voloshin, a Russian poet, called Peter "the first Bolshevik"?

2. Discuss the Emancipation Decree of 1861, and explain its connection to the railroad boom of the 1870s.

3. Contrast the systems of War Communism and New Economic Policy. What purpose was each of these systems designed to serve?

4.   What were the positions taken during the industrialization debate of the 1920s? How were these positions supported?

5.   What functions are performed by the Communist Party in the Soviet system of government?

6.   Suppose that the material balance table for paper goods presently shows a deficit. What options are available to clear the deficit? What are the possible problems associated with each of these options?

7.   How does investment decision making differ in capitalist and planned socialist countries?

Suggested Readings

Dobb, Maurice. *Soviet Economic Development since 1917.* New York: International Publishers, 1948. *A vivid account of the confusion and terror of War Communism, the experimentation of the NEP period, and the early days of central planning.*

Erlich, Alexander. *The Soviet Industrialization Debate, 1924–1928.* Cambridge, Mass.: Harvard University Press, 1967. *A fascinating chronicle of the arguments, the changing positions and alliances, and the aftermath of one of the most important debates in world history.*

Gregory, Paul R. and Robert C. Stuart. *Soviet Economic Structure and Performance.* 3d ed. New York: Harper and Row, 1986. *A popular textbook on the Soviet economy, with an extended discussion of history and planning.*

Hough, Jerry F. and Merle Fainsod. *How the Soviet Union Is Governed.* Cambridge, Mass.: Harvard University Press, 1979. *A comprehensive and authoritative treatment of Soviet political institutions.*

Kort, Michael. *The Soviet Colossus: A History of the USSR.* New York: Charles Scribner's Sons, 1985. *Well written and accessible to a general audience.*

Nove, Alec. *An Economic History of the U.S.S.R.* London: Penguin, 1969. *An advanced treatment of Soviet economic history for further study.*

Nove, Alec. *The Soviet Economic System.* London: George Allen and Unwin, 1977. *Nove's analysis is somewhat advanced and should be preceded by simpler texts.*

Rutland, Peter. *The Myth of the Plan.* La Salle, Ill.: Open Court, 1985. *A critique of the planning system, harkening back to the von Mises–Lange debate.*

Voslensky, Michael. *Nomenklatura.* Garden City, N.Y.: Doubleday, 1984. *An explanation of the personnel system operated by the Party, and a biting account of the class structure it has created.*

INPUT-OUTPUT ECONOMICS

In our discussion of the material balance method, we saw that formulating a consistent plan is a difficult (some would say impossible) task. Adjustment of the production or use of one product logically requires that the production and use of many other products be adjusted as well, through a complex web of direct and indirect technological relationships. Steel is used to produce trucks and trucks are used to produce steel.

Faced by these complexities, the central planners are aided by a technique that earned its inventor, Wassily Leontief, the 1973 Nobel Prize in economics. Input-output analysis makes it possible, in principle, for a planner to formulate a set of mutually consistent gross output targets for each industry. A condensed input-output table for Soviet transactions in 1972 is presented in Table 11A.1. For the sake of pedagogical simplicity, we combined all the productive sectors of the economy into three large groups—industry, agriculture, and services. A more detailed table would be divided into hundreds of sectors.

Read horizontally, each line of the table shows how the gross output of a particular sector was distributed through the economy in 1972. For example, about half of the output of the industrial sector was used within industry itself for productive purposes. Part of the output of the steel industry, for example, was used by the automobile industry. Relatively small shares of industrial output were used by the agricultural and service sectors; less than half was used by consumers and other final demanders.

Looking down any of the first three columns in the table, the inputs that were delivered to a particular industry are shown. For example, in order to produce its 522 billion rubles of gross output, the Soviet industrial sector used 266 billion rubles of its own output, 62 billion rubles of agricultural goods, and 50 billion rubles of services.

Dividing the inputs in the first three columns by the gross outputs of the sectors that use them, we obtain a matrix of direct input coefficients, denoted by the letter A:

$$A = \begin{bmatrix} 266/522 & 18/115 & 10/60 \\ 62/522 & 24/115 & 0/60 \\ 50/522 & 6/115 & 1/60 \end{bmatrix} = \begin{bmatrix} .51 & .16 & .17 \\ .12 & .21 & 0 \\ .10 & .05 & .02 \end{bmatrix}$$

Matrix A is sometimes called a technology matrix because it contains useful information about the technical interrelationships between the different sectors of the economy. If it is multiplied by any vector of gross outputs, x, it will provide us with a vector of intermediate inputs that are needed to produce these gross outputs: Ax = intermediate demand. If, for example, we multiply matrix A by the actual gross outputs that were produced in 1972

Table 11A.1 Simplifed Input-Output Table for the Soviet Union, 1972 (Billions of Rubles in Purchasers' Prices)

From	To	Industry, Construction	Agriculture	Services, Other	Total Intermediate	Final Demand	Gross Output
Industry, construction		266	18	10	294	228	522
Agriculture		62	24	0	86	29	115
Services, other		50	6	1	57	3	60

Source: U.S. Bureau of the Census, Foreign Demographic Analysis Division, *Input-Output Structure of the Soviet Economy: 1972.* Foreign Economic Report No. 18 (Washington, D.C.: USGPO, 1983), 102.

(given in Table 11A.1), we obtain the vector of intermediate demands for 1972 (also given in the table):

$$\begin{bmatrix} .51 & .16 & .17 \\ .12 & .21 & 0 \\ .10 & .05 & .02 \end{bmatrix} \begin{bmatrix} 522 \\ 115 \\ 60 \end{bmatrix} = \begin{bmatrix} 294 \\ 86 \\ 57 \end{bmatrix}$$

If we use f to denote final demand, then:

$$x = Ax + f, \tag{1}$$

or gross output is equal to intermediate output plus final output. If we collect terms and solve Equation 1 for gross output, we obtain:

$$x = (I - A)^{-1}f, \tag{2}$$

where I is the identity matrix—a square matrix of the same order as A, but with ones along its principal diagonal (from upper-left to lower-right) and zeros elsewhere.

Equation 2 provides one of the principal conclusions of input-output analysis. If a political decision is made to provide a particular collection of goods (f) to consumers and other final demanders, we can multiply that vector by the matrix $(I - A)^{-1}$ to obtain the vector of gross outputs that will satisfy that final demand. In our example:

$$(I - A)^{-1} = \begin{bmatrix} 2.237 & .4776 & .3880 \\ .3998 & 1.338 & .0589 \\ .2456 & .1170 & 1.063 \end{bmatrix}$$

Hence, if we decided to supply final demanders with 100 billion rubles of industrial goods, agricultural goods, and services, we would need to set gross output targets of 310, 174, and 143 billion rubles, respectively.

Application and Limitations of Input-Output

In the 1960s, when electronic computers, input-output methods, and other mathematical techniques were in their infancy, it was widely believed that they would make it possible for the Soviet Union to compile fully consistent, and even optimal, economic plans. Subsequent events have caused many Soviet economists to lose this hope.

It is certainly true that computers have provided invaluable aid to the central planners, and the new generations of computers will be even more helpful. Input-output (I-O) and other methods have made it possible for the planners to explore alternative growth strategies for the economy and to compile highly aggregated versions of their plans. For several reasons, however, the application of mathematical techniques has not lived up to original expectations.

First, the I-O method has run into ideological and political opposition. It is not firmly grounded in the Marxist-Leninist theory of value, and its use is resisted by the ministries and other organizations that fear they will lose bargaining power under a computerized system of planning. Thus, according to an analyst at the Research Institute of Gosplan:

The true reasons for the insufficient use of input-output tables are to be found in the slow pace with which the organization and methodology of planning are being restructured. Planning practice has not yet completely overcome the outmoded approach that looks on the formation of a plan as a process of "meshing" the drafts submitted by the various agencies.[1]

Second, the I-O tables are not compiled often enough nor in sufficient detail to accurately guide the planning effort. Compilation of a large table is an expensive and complicated enterprise, much like taking a census. To date, Soviet tables have been constructed only for 1959, 1966, 1972, 1977, and, apparently, for 1982.[2] By the time a table becomes available for use, many of its technical relationships are already out of date. At most, they are disaggregated into hundreds of sectors; yet Gosplan alone must compile material balances for thousands of products.

Third, even if it were possible to compile much larger I-O tables, Soviet computers probably would not be able to perform the matrix inversions that are necessary for their effective use. Inversion of a table with 2,000 sectors would require billions of calculations, and Soviet computer technology is about 10 years behind that of the United States, with a special problem in the area of supercomputers.[3] According to Western economists who recently visited the Central Statistical Administration in Moscow, Soviet officials complained that they could not obtain one microcomputer equivalent to an IBM AT for each of their key offices or divisions.[4]

---

[1]F. Klotsvog, "The Utilization of Input-Output Tables in Planning Practice," *Current Digest of the Soviet Press,* May 7, 1980, 16.

[2]The 1959, 1966, and 1972 tables have been published (at least in part), but despite a policy of openness, the 1977 and 1982 tables have not yet been published.

[3]Assessment of the U.S. intelligence community, reported in U.S. Congress, Joint Economic Committee, *Allocation of Resources in the Soviet Union and China—1985* (Washington, D.C.: USGPO, 1986), 115. See also, S. E. Goodman and W. K. McHenry, "Computing in the USSR: Recent Progress and Policies," *Soviet Economy* 2 (1986): 327–353.

[4]Jan Vanous, "The Dark Side of 'Glasnost': Unbelievable National Income Statistics in the Gorbachev Era," *PlanEcon Report,* February 13, 1987, 13.

Fourth, if it were possible to compile and manipulate large, up-to-date input-output tables, the results of these calculations would still have limited application. An I-O table can reveal how many inputs were actually *used* during some previous year to produce a given level of output but not how many inputs were actually *needed.* Thus, the use of I-O tables can cause the inefficiencies of the past to be perpetuated in plans for the future.

In addition, a number of other technical problems stand in the way of input-output planning. The output plans usually are compiled in physical terms, while the I-O tables usually are aggregated in rubles. I-O analysis is based on an unusual assumption about the nature of the production function. Inputs, it is assumed, must be combined in fixed proportions to produce their output.

Finally, we should emphasize that I-O analysis may assist in the formulation of an internally consistent plan, but it does not generate an optimal plan—one that serves the objectives of consumers or political leaders at the lowest possible cost. For this purpose, we would have to go beyond I-O analysis to linear programming methods; the theoretical, statistical, and computational problems would become even larger.

For these and other reasons, I-O analysis is most useful during the early stages of the planning process—during the preparation of highly aggregated control figures. At this stage, I-O makes it possible to prepare several broad options for the plan, one of which is chosen by the political leadership. When the plan is disaggregated into thousands of product groups, no suitable substitute has been found for the traditional system of material balance tables. "Computopia," as Peter Wiles has called it, is still a distant dream.

Soviet Republics: Personal Income per Capita, 1978

☐ 700–999 rubles   1. Estonia   6. Ukraine
▨ 1,000–1,199 rubles   2. Latvia   7. Georgia
☐ 1,200–1,600 rubles   3. Lithuania   8. Armenia
                               4. Belorussia   9. Azerbaijan
                               5. Moldavia

Source: Gertrude E. Schroeder, "Regional Living Standards" in *Economics of Soviet Regions,* eds. I. S. Koropeckyj and Gertrude E. Schroeder (New York: Praeger, 1981), 120.

12
CHAPTER

SOVIET UNION: LABOR, INCENTIVES, AND PRICES

Don't we see that today the manager of an enterprise finds himself, to some extent, in a two-sided position? On the one hand, we demand of him independence, efficiency on the job, and socialist enterprise. On the other hand, we bind him hand and foot with countless instructions and unwarranted restrictions.
—Mikhail Gorbachev
Pravda, April 9, 1986

In the previous chapter we reviewed the history, organization, and mechanics of central planning in the Soviet Union. Next we discuss the factories and farms, and the people who work there. Although the plan is formulated in Moscow, it is executed in the surrounding industrial heartland, in the croplands of the Ukraine, the oilfields of Siberia, and the textile mills of central Asia. The performance of the Soviet economy hinges on its local systems of labor organization, industrial management, and work incentives. The incentive system is directly influenced by the system of price control. In this chapter, we will briefly review all of these topics.

Employment, Trade Unions, and Labor Mobility

Full Employment

One of the most remarkable features of the Soviet labor market is its very low level of unemployment. When the Soviet authorities are criticized for their abuses of human rights, they usually counter with their protection of the right to work and the abuse of this right in the West.

Soviet employers typically wish to hire more workers than they can find. This is true for several reasons. First, the political leaders and central planners have placed a high priority on rapid economic growth; much of this growth has been accomplished by the extensive use of labor. For example, about two-thirds of adult women have been drawn into the labor force; the Soviet Union is second only to Sweden (where almost 80 percent are employed) in its rate of female participation in the labor force.

Employment is also stabilized by public subsidies designed to keep unprofitable enterprises from failing. Protected by these subsidies, and determined to meet their output targets, industrial managers have little incentive to economize on the use of labor. A reserve of extra workers can be very useful when the time to file plan fulfillment reports nears. Furthermore, dismissing an employee can be very difficult to accomplish under Soviet law (see "The Firing of Nikolai Timofeevich," p. 273).

Unemployment is not, however, entirely absent in the Soviet Union, and the current round of economic reforms may cause it to increase. Workers who are moving from one job to another generate a small rate—about 1 to 3 percent—of frictional unemployment. Most of this movement is voluntary, but according to Tatyana Zaslavskaya, one of the architects of the reforms, in the future "the lazy worker and the inefficient manager will earn considerably less than they do now. If their company proves unnecessary or inefficient, it may be closed, and the employees may have to move to less desirable jobs in less pleasant parts of the country."[1] Likewise, another Soviet economist recently has suggested that fear of unemployment "is a very good medicine for laziness, drunkenness, and irresponsibility. . . . Many experts believe it would be

---

[1]Quoted in Paul Quinn-Judge, "Plenum in Moscow," *Christian Science Monitor,* June 26, 1987, 10.

THE FIRING OF NIKOLAI TIMOFEEVICH

Blair Ruble, an expert on Soviet labor law, tells the story of one Nikolai Timofeevich, a fictional composite of several litigants who have appeared before the supreme courts of the Soviet Union and the Russian Republic. Timofeevich, a war veteran, was a drunkard and was regularly late for work at a Leningrad machine shop. After a series of disciplinary actions, the factory manager moved him to a menial job in the supply office and reduced his pay. Nikolai maintained that the action was illegal because the factory trade union chairman was not consulted, and he asked the factory Disputes Committee to review the case. When this committee could not reach a unanimous decision, the matter went before the entire factory trade union committee, which ruled, 20 to 15, that the demotion was justified. Higher reviewing bodies at the city and district levels upheld the decision, but the process continued for about 9 months.

Nikolai Timofeevich continued to perform his duties so poorly that his co-workers in the supply office refused to work with him. Finally, the factory manager fired Nikolai and was given *ex post facto* approval for his action by the factory trade union chairman. Again, Nikolai appealed to higher authorities and this time he prevailed. With the help of a favorable ruling from the District People's Court, the city procurator (public prosecutor) forced the factory manager to reinstate Timofeevich at a level equal to his last position in the supply office, with full payment of back wages. The court's decision was based on the factory trade union committee's failure to approve Nikolai's dismissal *before* the actual order was issued. In order to prevent additional problems, the factory manager arranged with the trade union chairman to place Nikolai in charge of the factory trade union library.

How representative is the story of Nikolai Timofeevich? It is hard to say, but the available data suggest that Soviet courts find illegalities in dismissals and order employees to be reinstated in more than half of all cases.

Source: Blair A. Ruble, "Factory Unions and Workers' Rights," in *Industrial Labor in the USSR,* ed. Arcadius Kahan and Blair Ruble (New York: Pergamon Press, 1979), 60–63.

cheaper to pay temporary unemployment benefits for a few months than to keep masses of people in work who do nothing."[2]

In recent years, rapid population growth in Soviet central Asia has also caused a significant amount of rural unemployment. About 1 million people, most of whom are women, are unemployed in Uzbekistan alone, representing about 20 percent of the labor force in that republic.[3] Central Asia is also the home of thousands of vagrants, according to the current Soviet press. Most of these are alcoholics and drug addicts, but they also include a group of "old beatniks, hippies, Hare Krishnas, and various undefined individuals . . . who are characterized by utter passivity, infantilism, and a certain pseudophilosophicalness."[4]

On the national level, a more serious problem is "unemployment on the job," as Janos Kornai calls it, or underemployment.[5] In addition to the fact that employers hoard extra workers on their payrolls to insure fulfillment of output targets, the effort to maintain full employment has created millions of make-work jobs. Underemployment reduces the level of labor productivity, which reduces the average standard of living. In a country with no system of unemployment compensation, a make-work job is far better than no job at all.

Trade Unions

Labor unions in the Soviet Union and other socialist countries are quite different from their counterparts in capitalist countries. This fact was dramatized a few years ago by the abortive effort in Poland to create an independent union—Solidarity. According to the official view, there is no need for adversarial bargaining between labor and management in a socialist economy because all profits are used for the good of society at large. If the size of the total wage bill were a subject of negotiation, the authority of central planners to maintain a financial balance between consumer income and the production of consumer goods would be usurped. Thus, the unions are controlled by the Communist Party and are not allowed to stage strikes or other disruptive activities.[6] Their most important official function is to raise the ideological level of the workers and to prepare them for full communism. For this purpose, they provide lectures to the workers on Party policy and Marxism-Leninism, organ-

[2]Nikolai Shmelev, Institute of Economics of the World Socialist System, in *Novyi mir;* quoted in *Radio Liberty Research,* June 5, 1987, 7.

[3]According to the Deputy Director of the Uzbek Academy of Sciences Institute of Economics. See "Central Asia Faces Unemployment Problem," *Current Digest of the Soviet Press,* May 6, 1987, 4.

[4]The report of Aleksei Lebedev, a reporter for *Ogonyok* who lived among the vagrants. See "Profiling the Soviet Vagrant," *Current Digest of the Soviet Press,* May 6, 1987, 3.

[5]Janos Kornai, *The Economics of Shortage* (Amsterdam: North Holland, 1980), 255–256.

[6]Despite the inactivity of the unions, the illegality of strikes, and the tight control of the press, several reports of worker disturbances have leaked to the Western press since the 1960s. See Blair Ruble, "Soviet Trade Unions and Labor Relations after 'Solidarity'," in U.S. Congress, Joint Economic Committee, *Soviet Economy in the 1980s: Problems and Prospects,* Part 2 (Washington, D.C.: USGPO, 1982), 363–365.

ize socialist competitions to encourage productivity, and sometimes cooperate with factory managers in disciplinary actions against laggard employees.

Because the Soviet unions spend much of their time advocating the views of the Party, it is often alleged that they are not really unions at all. They do, however, represent the views of the workers in negotiations on several non-wage issues. For example, the local unions bargain with management on employee health and safety, administer the nation's social insurance fund, and protect workers from unfair and illegal demotions and dismissals (see "The Firing of Nikolai Timofeevich," p. 273). The unions give much more attention to labor advocacy now than they did during the Stalin era, and the role of a particular union chapter is affected by the history, location, and circumstances of that factory.

Labor Mobility

Within limits, Soviet workers are free to enter the occupation of their choice and to move between jobs. Like workers in other countries, they are guided by their interests, talents, family traditions, expected incomes and fringe benefits, geographical preferences, desire for prestige, and recruiting efforts of employers.[7] Soviet workers change jobs at roughly the same rate—about 20 percent per year—as their counterparts in the United States and Great Britain.

During the Stalin era, Soviet restrictions on labor mobility were quite severe. The rate of labor turnover was very high in the early 1930s and draconian methods were devised to solve the problem. Job changers were penalized with inferior housing and the loss of social insurance, and an internal passport system was established to monitor the movement of the population. In addition, millions of peasants who resisted collectivization, political prisoners, prisoners of war, resettled minorities, and others were sent to labor camps. Many of the camps were closed after 1956, and many other restrictions on mobility were abolished at that time. To this day, however, residence permits are required to live in the big, overcrowded cities.

Labor mobility is also limited by cultural factors and various forms of discrimination. For example, Party approval is necessary for thousands of high-level jobs on the *nomenklatura* lists. Church members (who are registered by the state) are not allowed to work as school teachers. Women play an active part in the Soviet work force, but their pay is between two-thirds and three-quarters of the average for males. Unemployed people of central Asia are unwilling to move to the European republics, where there is a labor shortage, because they are devoted to their homeland, language, religion, and cultural heritage.

The Incentive System

In Chapter 1, we spoke of three kinds of incentives: coercive, material, and moral. In the Soviet system, all three have been used extensively at one time

---

[7]Moscow television provides film footage and information about job openings in town and how to apply for them.

or another. Prison labor and other forms of coercion were used routinely during the Stalin era. Although human rights in the Soviet Union have improved drastically since that time, a 1983 study by the U.S. State Department alleged that the Soviets were still using a corp of 4 million political and religious dissidents and criminals to build pipelines, military facilities, and other projects.[8]

Maintenance of moral incentives is the special mission of the Communist Party apparatus and the labor unions. Laggards are criticized, socialist competitions for productivity improvement are organized, and the victory over fascism in World War II is memorialized, providing a constant reminder of the need for personal sacrifice and military-industrial readiness. The Party congresses are orchestrated to build enthusiasm for the five-year plans and to provide an occasion to expound socialist morality.

We, the Communists, are looked upon as a model in everything—in work and behavior. We have to live in such a way that the working person could say: "Yes, this is a true Communist." And the brighter and cleaner life is within the Party, the sooner we shall cope with the complex problems which are typical of the present time of change.[9]

Despite the continued use of coercion and moral incentives, the relative importance of *material incentives* has grown through the years. Coercion is a crude instrument in a modern economy where workers are free to move between jobs, and skills and creativity are more important than raw labor power. Moral sentiments are more difficult to arouse as the revolution and World War II fade farther into the past. Material incentives are now used to stimulate everything from technological development to childbirth (population policy), to encourage workers to relocate in Siberia, and to encourage soldiers to fight in Afghanistan:

"Soviet officers come here for the money," said Kolya, who was a private. "Instead of receiving their usual 250 rubles per month, in Afghanistan they earn 700 or 800 rubles. . . . And each year that a Soviet officer serves in Afghanistan is counted as three years."[10]

In most cases, Soviet workers receive two important forms of income. Their basic wage or salary is based on their industry, vocation, skills, location, and other factors and accounts for about 70 percent of the average worker's income. The other 30 percent is received in the form of salary bonuses, which are dependent on fulfillment of plan targets.

Wages and Salaries

Under the traditional Soviet system, the number of workers that an enterprise can employ in any given year and the average wage that the enterprise can

---

[8]Walter Mossberg, "Soviets Are Using Forced Labor to Build Pipelines, Other Projects, U.S. Study Says," *Wall Street Journal,* February 14, 1983, 7.

[9]Mikhail Gorbachev, *Political Report of the CPSU Central Committee to the 27th Party Congress* (Moscow: Novosti Press Agency, 1986), 99.

[10]Ludmilla Thorne, "Inside Afghanistan: War of Innocents," *Wall Street Journal,* September 21, 1983, 28.

Table 12.1   Average Monthly Wages and Salaries of Soviet Workers and Employees (Rubles)

	1940	1960	1970	1985
Industry				
Average	34	92	133	211
Professionals	70	135	178	233
Production Workers	32	90	131	212
Office Staff	36	74	112	165
Agriculture				
Average	23	54	101	183
Professionals	50	116	164	243
Production Workers	21	52	99	180
Office Staff	31	66	96	183
Transport	35	87	137	220
Communications	28	63	97	160
Construction	36	93	150	237
Trade and Catering	25	59	95	149
Health	26	58	95	147
Education	32	72	108	150
Art	39	64	95	145
Credit, Insurance	33	61	111	181
State Administration	39	86	123	166

Source: Tsentral'noe Statisticheskoe upravlenie SSSR, *Narodnoe khoziaistvo SSSR v 1985 g.* (Moscow: Finansy i Statistika, 1986), 397–398.

pay are both set by higher authorities in the ministries, the State Planning Committee, and the Ministry of Finance. Some enterprises are allowed to pay much higher wages than others. For example, during Stalin's industrialization drive workers were attracted from the farms to the cities by wages in industry that were far above those in agriculture. As shown in Table 12.1, the average rural wage was about 40 percent lower than the average industrial wage in 1960. Shortly thereafter, the Soviet Union became a net importer of food and agriculture was given a higher priority. By 1985 the wage levels of farmers were much closer to those of factory workers.

Enterprises are also able to pay higher wages in some geographic areas than in others. Like Americans who work for high wages in Alaska, Soviets can increase their pay by up to 50 percent in Siberia, 70 percent in some regions of the far north, and 100 percent in the islands of the Arctic ocean.[11]

Within each enterprise, managers and trade union representatives assign workers to occupations and skill levels according to standards that are set by the State Committee for Labor and Social Questions. Workers with higher skill ratings can receive higher wages according to a fixed schedule. For example,

[11]Janet G. Chapman, "Recent Trends in the Soviet Industrial Wage Structure," in *Industrial Labor in the USSR,* ed. Arcadius Kahan and Blair Ruble (New York: Pergamon Press, 1979), 160.

in 1975 workers in the machinery industry were paid the following multiples of the base wage for their factory:

Skill Level	Wage
1	1.00
2	1.09
3	1.20
4	1.33
5	1.50
6	1.71

During the Stalin era, large differentials were included in the wage schedules to encourage workers to upgrade their skills. During the years that followed, those differentials were reduced—minimum wage rates were increased more than the higher rates. By 1986, the pay of a bus driver was equal to that of a university professor.[12] One of the objectives of the current round of economic reforms is to strengthen material incentives by expanding these differentials again. Gorbachev also intends to give enterprise managers greater autonomy in setting wages. In a 1987 report to the Central Committee, he said that "no limit" should be set on the wage that can be paid to a worker: "There is only one criterion of justice: whether or not it is earned."[13]

Bonus Income

Reduced to its basics, the industrial bonus system is quite simple. If the physical plan targets (in tons, square meters, or other units) for the most important products are met, bonuses are added to the base salaries of the employees of the enterprise. Underfulfillment of the plan, even by a small margin, may mean that no bonus is paid at all; overfulfillment results in small increases in the bonus. According to a decree introduced in 1986, the bonuses of enterprise directors can amount to as much as 75 percent of their base pay.

An incentive system that rewards plan fulfillment is a necessary element of a centrally planned economy, but it presents several problems. First, it encourages enterprise managers to bargain for easier plan targets. To that end, they are likely to provide distorted information to the central planners concerning their production capacities and input needs. Enterprises are not likely to overfulfill their plan targets by a very large margin—even if they are able to do so—because a high level of production one year is likely to result in a difficult plan target the next year.

Second, the emphasis on plan fulfillment has contributed to production inefficiency. Industrial managers have a strong incentive to hoard labor, equipment, and raw materials to insure that their enterprise will be able to handle any plan target it is given. The enterprise may engage in small-scale production of the raw materials and components that it needs, rather than risk plan fulfillment on the supplies provided by other enterprises.

---

[12]N. Rimashevskaya, "Income Distribution and Justice," *Current Digest of the Soviet Press,* December 10, 1986, 6.

[13]*New York Times,* June 26, 1987, A8.

Third, even if the enterprise is able to abide by the letter of the plan, it is often necessary or convenient to ignore the spirit. The quality of output is routinely sacrificed to fulfill quantitative plan targets. Soviet automobile factories are reluctant to produce spare parts and accessories because they are rewarded more heavily for their most important products, finished cars. Soviet drivers lock their windshield wiper blades—a scarce item—in their glove compartments when they are not in use.

Between 1980 and 1982, Soviet factories produced goods worth about 17 billion rubles each year that were not ordered by trade organizations or other customers, while orders worth billions of rubles went unfilled.[14] Shoe factories often simplify their operations by producing all of their shoes in a few sizes. Thus, while there is no shortage of shoes, there is a shortage of usable shoes. A classic Soviet cartoon showed one enormous nail hanging in a large workshop. "The plan to produce 100 tons of nails is fulfilled," beamed the manager.

Fourth, the planning and incentive systems seem to discourage technological innovation. An enterprise that develops a new, more advanced product has traditionally received little reward for its work. The time and effort expended on innovation makes it difficult for the enterprise to meet its basic plan targets. The new product may also require raw materials that are difficult to acquire in the supply system. If an enterprise adopts a new technique that increases its production capacity, the plan targets assigned to the enterprise are increased accordingly, and the innovators are left where they started.[15]

Reform of the Incentive System

The characteristics of the Soviet material incentive system described above have proved to be remarkably persistent, despite several decades of revision and reform. Output planning seems to require that rewards be tied to the fulfillment of output targets, and narrow output targets discourage initiative, efficiency, and quality.

Some of the faults in the incentive system have been remedied. Beginning in the 1950s, special bonus schemes were established to encourage technological innovation and the production of higher quality goods. Traditionally, these supplementary bonuses have been too small to have any dramatic effect, but they have provided some compensation to enterprises that engage in innovative activity.

Success Indicators

Many of the incentive reforms have revolved around the so-called success indicator problem. Should enterprise plan fulfillment be measured in terms of

[14]V. I. Kletskii, "What Should Be Included in the Economic Mechanism of the Twelfth Five-Year Plan?" *Ekonomika i organizatsiia promyshlennogo proizvodstva,* No. 1 (1985): 27–42; translated in *Problems of Economics* 28 (January 1986): 73–88.

[15]For a full discussion of these issues, see Joseph S. Berliner, *The Innovation Decision in Soviet Industry* (Cambridge, Mass.: MIT Press, 1976).

physical output, the gross value of output, gross sales, value added, the share of high-quality goods in total output, profitability, labor productivity, adherence to contracts, or some combination of these? As we have seen, the logic of central planning requires that some attention be given to physical output, but all of these other measures have been used at one time or another.

Before 1965, the most common monetary success indicator was gross value of output (GVO). This is the simplest index of the total output of an enterprise, but its use causes two serious problems. First, because it is a measure of output rather than sales, it provides too little incentive to the enterprise to produce those goods demanded by consumers. Second, because it is a measure of gross output, it encourages enterprises to inflate the value of their product by including expensive components purchased from other enterprises.

The first of these problems was addressed in 1965, when gross sales began to replace GVO as the standard monetary measure of the output of the firm. A solution to the second problem was found in 1979, when **net normative value added (NNVA)** was chosen to replace gross sales. The NNVA of an enterprise is roughly equal to its gross output minus its purchases of intermediate inputs. The State Price Committee now has the difficult task of setting value added normatives for all manufactured goods, in addition to their traditional job of setting wholesale and retail prices.

Other reforms since 1979 have shifted more attention to quality, technological progress, and the assortment of goods in measuring the output of enterprises. Bonuses have been increased for enterprises whose products are certified to meet international standards, and, since 1983, enterprises that produce particularly shoddy goods have been liable for fines. Fulfillment of product-mix assignments has been encouraged by increasing the specificity of the physical output targets, and greater attention has been paid to the strict fulfillment of contract obligations.

In 1984 a major economic experiment was inaugurated in some 700 enterprises of five industrial ministries. In most cases, the number of success indicators used to calculate the size of bonus payments was reduced to three: (1) the volume of product sales, adjusted for adherence to the delivery dates, product mixes, and other provisions of sales contracts; (2) the proportion of products in the highest quality category in the overall volume of production; and (3) increase in profit. Before the experiment began, failure to adhere to 1 percent of the contracts in the enterprise delivery plan caused a 1 percent reduction in incentive payments. During the experiment, 1 percent underfulfillment of this plan caused a 3 percent reduction in incentive payments and fulfillment caused incentive payments to increase by as much as 15 percent.[16] The experiment was considered a success and this system of evaluation has been extended to other sectors of the economy.

Despite such changes, after 20 years of reform, Gorbachev reported that gross output targets still "play a major role in assessing the performance of

[16]Kletskii, "What Should Be Included," 76.

industries, regions, and enterprises." As a result, he said, "enterprise managers find themselves in an absurd position," and "costly materials often are used for the sake of increasing gross output."[17]

Calculation of Bonuses

Along with the success indicator problem, another subject of reform has been the formulas and procedures used to calculate bonus incomes. This has become an enormously complicated business and only the main outlines of the system are described here.

Since 1965 managerial bonuses have been paid out of the enterprise's material incentive fund, which is financed out of the profits of the enterprise. The amount of profit an enterprise is allowed to transfer to the incentive fund depends on the size of the wage fund of the enterprise (total wages approved by the central authorities) and on the degree of plan fulfillment. A higher level of plan fulfillment means that a larger percentage of the wage fund can be transferred out of profits into the incentive fund.

The system became more complex in 1971 when a new system of **counterplanning** was introduced to encourage producers to adopt more ambitious plans. Under this system, the enterprise first negotiates a set of directive plan targets with its ministry that are obligatory—no bonuses will be paid if these basic targets are not fulfilled. The enterprise is then encouraged to propose a more challenging counterplan, which, if fulfilled, will be rewarded with additional bonuses. As long as the directive plan is fulfilled, failure to meet the counterplan targets will not cause a complete loss of bonuses.

The counterplanning system has not been very successful. Since the directive plan must still be fulfilled before any bonuses are paid, enterprises continue their attempt to obtain easier directive plans. If an enterprise adopts and fulfills an ambitious counterplan one year, it will probably be given a more ambitious directive plan the next year, leading to a possible loss of bonuses. Thus, most enterprises are still unwilling to adopt counterplans (only 7 percent of all enterprises adopted them in 1981).[18]

The Shchekino Method

Soviet enterprises have very little incentive to economize on the use of labor because the success of the enterprise is measured in terms of output plan fulfillment rather than profitability. Enterprises usually try to maintain a reserve of excess workers to ensure the fulfillment of plan targets. Overstaffing is also encouraged by the dependence, in part, of managerial salaries on the size of their work force and by the political and legal obstacles involved in laying off Soviet workers.

[17]*Pravda,* June 17, 1986, 3.

[18]Philip Hanson, "Success Indicators Revisited: The July 1979 Soviet Decree on Planning and Management," *Soviet Studies* 35 (January 1983): 8.

Inefficient use of labor was not a serious problem in the 1950s, when the labor force and the capital stock were growing rapidly. In more recent years, however, as Soviet economic growth has decelerated, more attention has turned to the problem of overstaffing. One of the first efforts in this direction was an experiment at the Shchekino Chemical Combine, initiated in 1967.

According to the Shchekino Method, as it is called, if the factory reduces its work force, it is allowed to distribute the wages that have been saved to the remaining employees. During the years of the experiment (1967 to 1970) more than 1,000 workers out of an initial 7,500 were freed for other work, and the wage and productivity levels at Shchekino grew well ahead of the national average. Other problems developed at Shchekino in later years, as the potential for further improvements in labor productivity began to diminish, but the experiment was officially proclaimed to be a success.[19]

In his speech to the 1986 Party Congress, Gorbachev added his praise to the Shchekino Method and cited the experience of the Byelorussian railway, where the method freed 12,000 workers for jobs in other sectors.[20] However, talk of "freed" workers has raised a new fear that the labor shortage may turn into a labor surplus, or unemployment.

Implementation of Incentive Reforms

The problems that have plagued the Soviet reform programs over the last two decades can be divided into two categories: problems of design and implementation. Problems of design arise from the fact that most of the reforms involve decentralization of authority from the planners and ministries to the enterprises and the enterprises do not have the information they need to make rational decisions. In particular, reform of the system of price control may encourage enterprises to produce the wrong products in the wrong quantities.

Problems of implementation arise from the fact that the institutions that stand to lose the most from the reforms—central planners and industrial ministries— are largely responsible for carrying out the reforms. Asking the ministries to devise a program to transfer authority to the enterprises is something like asking the Department of Defense to negotiate a disarmament treaty. The reform programs of Khrushchev, Kosygin, and Brezhnev were undermined by ministerial footdragging; Gorbachev lamented that "the illusion of reconstruction is being created, and everything is proceeding well according to words, but no real changes have taken place."[21]

Opposition to the reforms from ministries and central planners takes several forms, mostly involving their effort to maintain control over the day-to-day activity of enterprises. Annual and 5-year plan targets and bonus formulas are revised frequently to take account of the level of production

[19]For a detailed appraisal, see Henry Norr, "Shchekino: Another Look," *Soviet Studies* 38 (April 1986): 141–169.

[20]Gorbachev, *Political Report,* 53.

[21]*Pravda,* June 17, 1986, 1.

achieved. A survey of 95 enterprises in the Novosibirsk area revealed that in an average year they received a total of 1,554 amendments to their annual production plans.[22] "Is it normal," Gorbachev asks, "when not only ministries and other agencies of branch management, but even the State Planning Commission and the Ministry of Finance take it upon themselves to resolve an immense number of trivial economic questions that, frankly, are none of their concern?"[23]

To curtail the dictatorial powers of the industrial ministries, Gorbachev plans to reduce their staffs of supervisory personnel and merge them into a few "superministries." The first of these, the State Agroindustrial Committee, was formed in 1985 through the merger of five ministries and one state committee. It led to the release of nearly half of the ministries' employees—about 3,200 bureaucrats lost their jobs.[24] Continuation of this trend may be the best indicator of Gorbachev's commitment to genuine reform.

The Price System

The role of prices in a centrally planned economy is quite different from that in a market economy. In the market system, prices react spontaneously and continuously to the forces of supply and demand, and production is guided by prices and profitability. Soviet prices, in contrast, are set and controlled by the State Price Committee, and production is guided by the annual plan. Setting millions of prices for a modern economy is an enormous task; thus they are not changed very often. Significant revisions of wholesale prices were undertaken in 1948, 1952, 1955, 1967, 1973, and 1982, and they were changed very little during the intervening years. According to a 1979 decree, the prices are to be revised at the beginning of each 5-year planning period.

Although prices do not play the same allocative role that they play in a market economy, they are still important for several reasons. They influence the managerial incentive system: plan targets for labor productivity, gross value of output, and profitability are set for many enterprises and are measured in monetary terms. For this reason, Gorbachev realizes that a more rational price system must be established before greater freedom can be given to the individual enterprises: "A radical reform of the price system is a most important part of the economic overhaul. Without it, a complete transition to the new mechanism is impossible."[25]

Prices are also among the variables used to regulate the financial balance of the economy. The incomes and outlays of consumers, enterprises, and the governmental budget are all influenced by prices; an imbalance in any of these sectors can cause shortages or surpluses of goods.

[22]Alec Nove, *The Soviet Economic System* (London: George Allen and Unwin, 1977), 104.

[23]*Pravda,* April 8, 1986, 1.

[24]Philip Hanson, "Superministries: The State of Play," *Radio Liberty Research,* April 21, 1986, 6.

[25]*New York Times,* June 26, 1987, A8.

Wholesale Prices

The rules and principles used to set wholesale prices, which Soviet enterprises receive for their products, and retail prices, which consumers pay, are quite different. In general, the wholesale price of a product is equal to the average unit cost of producing that item in the entire industry, plus a profit markup related to the capital intensity of the product. In recent years, enterprises have been allowed to keep about 40 percent of their profits to finance material incentive funds, internal investments, and the like. They have been required to pay about 60 percent to the governmental budget in taxes, rents (for the use of state-owned capital), and other payments.[26]

Basing wholesale prices on average industry costs is probably the simplest method available to the State Price Committee, but it has caused several problems. First, it means that many enterprises having higher costs than the industry average will automatically run losses and will have to be subsidized by the state budget. A large part of the state budget is used to redistribute income from profitable enterprises to unprofitable ones. This stands in contrast to the situation in a competitive market economy, where the price will normally rise to a level that will cover marginal costs for as many firms as are needed to meet the demand for a product.[27]

Second, while the use of average-cost prices may give enterprises an incentive to hold down their costs of production, it gives them little incentive to produce the goods that are demanded by other businesses and consumers. Thus, in recent years the regulations have been changed to allow enterprises to apply for higher wholesale prices for high-technology and high-quality products. For example, new products receiving the State Seal of Quality (intended to measure up to world standards), exported for convertible currency, certified as new inventions and discoveries, and replacing imported goods can be awarded an incentive price markup of up to 30 percent, depending on the cost savings they create for their purchasers. On the other hand, outdated and substandard products may be discounted at a rate of up to 30 percent.[28] Most significantly, a reform in the consumer goods industry stipulates that the wholesale prices of especially fashionable goods can be set in negotiations between the producers and the retail trade organizations.[29]

[26]Tsentral'noe Statisticheskoe upravlenie SSSR, *Narodnoe khoziaistvo SSSR v 1984 g.* (Moscow: Finansy i Statistika, 1985), 563.

[27]Some businesses are also subsidized in capitalist countries. In these cases, the subsidies are usually paid to maintain employment in industries that have experienced a reduction in the demand for their product (often caused by foreign competition).

[28]*Ekonomicheskaia gazeta,* 32 (1985): 12. For a more detailed description of these procedures, see the 1982 decree of the State Price Committee, "Prices for New Products: Procedure for Determining Wholesale Prices and Net Product Rates for New Machinery, Equipment, and Production and Technical-End Instruments," *Ekonomicheskaia gazeta,* 6 (February 1983): 11–14; translated in Joint Publications Research Service, *USSR Report: Economic Affairs,* March 16, 1983, 22–42. Also, see N. Glushkov, "Planned Pricing: Ways to Improve," *Kommunist* 3 (1985): 38–48; translated in *Problems of Economics* 28 (December 1985): 70–89.

[29]A decree of the Central Committee and the Council of Ministers, published in *Pravda,* May 6, 1986, 1–2; translated in *Current Digest of the Soviet Press,* June 11, 1986, 12, 22–23.

Finally, average-cost prices are poor guides for central planners who use them to make investment and foreign trade decisions. By their nature, these are usually marginal decisions: Will the cost of additional energy production outweigh the additional benefits? Will an increase in export production cost more or less than the domestic cost of import substitution? Such questions can be addressed most effectively with prices that are based on marginal, rather than average, costs and benefits, and several Soviet economists have called for a change of this kind.

Retail Prices

Several principles influence the determination of retail prices in the Soviet Union. Here again, most prices are not controlled by markets, but by the State Price Committee, and are changed very infrequently. The maintenance of stable retail prices traditionally has been claimed as one of the major strengths of the Soviet system. Second, in order to maintain some semblance of order and equilibrium in the consumer goods sector, the retail price of each product is originally set at level that roughly equates the quantity demanded with the quantity supplied (as controlled by the central planners). Third, an effort is made to redistribute purchasing power from the rich to the poor by holding down the prices of food, shelter, and other necessities and by padding the prices of luxuries.

Because price stability, supply-demand equilibrium, and distributive equity are competing objectives, none of them can be fully achieved. Concerning the distributive impact of retail prices, some indication of the Soviet record is given in Table 12.2. A Soviet industrial worker can earn enough income to pay his rent and ride the subway in less time than a worker in Paris, London, or Washington, D.C., because the prices of these necessities are very low in the Soviet Union. On the other hand, the relative prices of items such as televisions, cars, and other luxury items are very high.

The failure of retail prices to maintain an equilibrium between supply and demand gives rise to shortages, long lines, and black-market activities. These in turn give rise to corruption, dilution of work incentives, and other social problems. According to a survey of immigrants from the Soviet Union, Soviet women spend about 20 percent of their leisure time standing in lines.[30] Shortages and lines may also indicate the presence of pent-up inflationary pressure.

Inflation

Information concerning the inflationary process in the Soviet Union is limited and controversial. The Soviet authorities do not, for example, publish data on the growth of the money supply, an important determinant of inflationary

---

[30]Cullen Murphy, "Watching the Russians," *The Atlantic* (February 1983): 50.

Table 12.2   Work Time Required for an Industrial Worker to Buy Various Items in Moscow; Washington, D.C.; Paris; and London, 1986

	Moscow	Washington, D.C.	Paris	London
Hours of Work Time				
Monthly Rent	11	54	15	27
Color Television	669	30	106	75
Men's Suit	117	18	34	16
Months of Work Time				
Small Car	45	5	8	8
Minutes of Work Time				
Eggs (20)	100	10	34	20
Toilet Paper (1 roll)	22	2	6	5
Aspirin (1 bottle)	33	7	44	9
Cigarettes (1 pack)	15	7	12	25
Two-mile ride on:				
Taxi	33	25	20	32
Subway	3	7	5	9
One Pound of:				
Bread	8	3	9	5
Ground Beef	33	14	34	17
Sugar	24	3	5	4
Butter	89	18	29	17
Tomatoes	13	10	8	8
Apples	13	8	7	6
One Liter of:				
Milk	20	4	8	6
Beer	15	13	15	16
Vodka	1,216	156	194	156
Gasoline	17	2	7	6

Source: Keith Bush, "Retail Prices in Moscow and Four Western Cities in October, 1986," *Radio Liberty Research Bulletin*, supplement, January 21, 1987, 6–14.

pressure. Undoubtedly, the level of open inflation has been low by Western standards, due to the system of price control. The Soviet Union has experienced a certain amount of open inflation and perhaps a significant amount of hidden and repressed inflation.

Some of the possible sources of inflationary pressure in the Soviet Union are quite different from those in capitalist countries. First, the difficulty of maintaining balance in the economic plan, coupled with the goal of rapid economic growth, generates imbalances and shortages that put upward pressure on the prices of scarce goods.

Second, the managerial incentive system, which has traditionally rewarded the fulfillment of gross output or sales targets rather than profitability, encourages price increases. Under this system, a seller has much to gain from a price increase, while an industrial buyer, who is insensitive to costs, has little to lose. This problem has been acknowledged repeatedly in the Soviet press: "In the face of the customer's indifference toward the price, the producer, as is well known, overstates his planned expenditures . . . to receive large-scale bonuses."[31]

Third, inflationary pressure may be generated by a lack of control over enterprise wage funds. According to one Soviet economist, the authorities are compelled to increase retail prices primarily because the growth of money wages has traditionally been regulated by the planned growth in labor productivity. When productivity performance falls short of the plan, money wages grow more rapidly than output.[32] Thus, between 1975 and 1985, total wage payments increased at an average rate of 4.2 percent per year, while real production of consumer goods increased at a rate of only 2.3 percent.[33]

A fourth *possible* source of inflationary pressure is excessive expansion of the money supply. According to the controversial estimates of Igor Birman, the Soviet government ran budget deficits in 26 of the 29 years between 1950 and 1978 which were financed through monetary growth.

Interestingly, one of the most serious budgetary problems of the state is caused by the price system itself. Wholesale prices are based on costs of production, while retail prices are based on demand and equity considerations. In most cases, the retail prices are higher than the wholesale prices, and the difference between the two—the so-called turnover tax—is pocketed by the state. In the agricultural sector, however, the situation is quite different. Soviet agriculture is notoriously inefficient, requiring high cost-based wholesale prices, but the retail prices of food items are held down for ideological and political reasons. Consequently, retail prices of most agricultural goods are actually lower than the wholesale prices, requiring the payment of governmental subsidies. The subsidy for meat and milk products alone amounts to 40 billion rubles annually, or about 10 percent of all budgetary expenditures.[34]

Lastly, several deficiencies in the system of monetary control may contribute to inflationary pressure. According to an official of the Ministry of Finance, there is a lack of control over the lending activities of the various specialized banks and more loans are being made to industrial ministries rather than their constituent enterprises.[35] The ministries, he says, are more likely to be delinquent in repayment, and their repayment is more likely to be financed by the state budget.

---

[31]P. Bunich, "Wholesale Prices and the Mechanism of Providing Incentives for Collectives," *Ekonomicheskie nauki* 7 (1985), translated in Joint Publications Research Service, *USSR Report: Economic Affairs,* November 25, 1985, 42.

[32]Kletskii, "What Should Be Included," 78–79.

[33]*Narodnoe khoziaistvo SSSR v 1985 g.,* 39; and U.S. Central Intelligence Agency, *Handbook of Economic Statistics, 1986* (CPAS 86–10002, September 1986), 66.

[34]Interview with V. Yesipov in *Leningradskaia Pravda,* September 22, 1984, 2; translated in Joint Publications Research Service, *USSR Report: Economic Affairs,* January 3, 1985, 2. See also, Vladimir Treml, "Subsidies in Soviet Agriculture: Record and Prospects," in U.S. Congress, Joint Economic Committee, *Soviet Economy in the 1980s: Problems and Prospects,* Part 2 (Washington, D.C.: USGPO, 1982), 171–185.

[35]V. Zakharov, "Credit and Banks in the Economic Management System," *Voprosy ekonomiki* 3 (1982): 3–12; translated in *Problems of Economics* 26 (May 1983): 3–19.

Table 12.3   A Comparison of Official Retail Prices and Collective Farm Market Prices for Food, 1950–1985

	Collective Farm Market Prices as a Percentage of State Retail Prices	Food Price Index for:	
		State Retail Prices	Collective Farm Market Prices
1950	106	134	89
1965	141	100	88
1970	160	100	100
1975	183	101	116
1980	225	103	145
1985	236	112	165

Sources: Tsentral'noe Statisticheskoe upravlenie SSSR, *Narodnoe khoziaistvo SSSR* (Moscow: Finansy i Statistika, various years); the first and third columns were calculated by the author, using a method adapted from Barbara Severin, "USSR: The All-Union and Moscow Collective Farm Market Price Indexes," *The ACES Bulletin* 21 (Spring 1979): 33–34.

Aside from shortages and long lines, what are the evidences of inflationary pressure in the Soviet Union? A small amount of open inflation is reported by the Soviet authorities. In 1982, for example, the official index of retail prices increased by about 4 percent, caused in part by an 18 percent increase in the price of tobacco products. On the other hand, the Central Statistical Office reports that consumer prices fell 1.6 percent in 1985 and 3.8 percent in 1986.

The official index does not include the price increases that occur on the collective farm market, the only market where prices are legally set by the forces of supply and demand. Some indication of the relative levels and movement of official and free-market prices for food can be obtained from the data in Table 12.3.[36] According to these estimates, free-market prices have always been higher than official prices, and that margin has steadily increased. Food prices in the government-run stores increased at an annual rate of only 0.2 percent between 1970 and 1985, while the food inflation rate in the free market was about 3.4 percent.

The official price indexes also fail to capture a certain amount of **hidden inflation** that occurs when products are sold at prices that exceed their official levels (as they are on black markets) and when new or improved products are introduced at prices that exceed their improvement in quality. The State Price Committee is responsible for controlling this kind of inflation; in 1985 it confiscated more than 100 million rubles in profits received by enterprises engaged in illegal price-setting practices.[37] The committee has the impossible task of reviewing prices for more than 200,000 new products every year, and purchasers are happy to pay inflated prices to obtain scarce goods.

[36]The figures in Table 12.3, based on official Soviet statistics, may understate the difference between state retail and collective farm market prices. According to Western estimates, based on survey data, market prices exceeded official prices by a three-to-one margin in 1981–1983. See Vladimir Treml, "Purchases of Food from Private Sources in Soviet Urban Areas," *Berkeley-Duke Occasional Papers on the Second Economy in the USSR* 3 (1985): 23–27.

[37]*Pravda,* June 17, 1986, 3.

According to a CIA estimate of the Soviet GNP deflator, the rate of hidden inflation was about 2 percent per year between 1960 and 1980.[38] This is a moderate rate and does not include the price increases that occur on the black market.

Finally, there is the problem of **repressed inflation,** or inflationary pressure that is contained by price controls. The clearest evidence of this kind of inflation is the rapid growth of personal savings accounts. From 1975 to 1985, while money incomes grew at a rate of about 4 percent per year, the volume of personal savings accounts grew at an annual rate of 9 percent.[39] Many experts in the West and in the Soviet Union seem to agree that a large portion of this is the result of forced saving, as consumers are not able to spend their incomes on desired goods at current prices.[40]

The data seem to indicate that the Soviet inflation rate is very low by Western standards, even if repressed inflation is included. On the other hand, there is reason to believe that the Soviet public perceives a significantly higher level of price inflation, although the evidence is only anecdotal. For example, a reporter for *Literaturnaya Gazeta* who reports receiving hundreds of letters from readers concerned about rising prices, writes that "in recent times prices have risen out of proportion to wages . . . and not by kopecks, not even by just rubles."[41] During a visit to the Soviet Union, this author attempted to explain the inflationary psychology in the West to a young professional woman. "It is just the same here," she said, and explained how her efforts to purchase a color television were frustrated by the replacement of old sets with new "improved," higher-priced models. In the Soviet Union today, reality is still difficult to unveil and perceptions may be more important than reality.

Summary

The very low rate of unemployment in the Soviet Union is explained by the high priority accorded to economic growth, the managerial incentive system that stresses output targets, the prevention of bankruptcies through a large system of public subsidies, and a legal system that provides employment pro-

[38]U.S. Central Intelligence Agency, *Soviet Gross National Product in Current Prices, 1960–80* (SOV 83–10037, March 1983), 23.

[39]*Narodnoe khoziaistvo SSSR v 1985 g.,* 448. For further information on the inflationary implications of saving and lending data, and a discussion of the impact of inflation on planning and policy, see Gregory Grossman, "Inflationary, Political, and Social Implications of the Current Economic Slowdown," in *Economics and Politics in the USSR: Problems of Interdependence,* ed. Hans-Hermann Hohmann, Alec Nove, and Heinrich Vogel (Boulder, Colo.: Westview, 1986), 172–197.

[40]For a dissenting view, see Richard Portes and David Winter, "Disequilibrium Estimates for Consumption Goods Markets in Centrally Planned Economies," *Review of Economic Studies* 47 (1980): 137–159. See also, Jan Winiecki, "Portes Ante Portas: A Critique of the Revisionist Interpretation of Inflation Under Central Planning," *Comparative Economic Studies* 27 (Summer 1985): 25–51.

[41]Anatoli Rubinov, quoted in Mark D'Anastasio, "Soviet Media Admit Inflation's Existence," *Wall Street Journal,* May 22, 1987, 12.

tection to workers. A certain amount of frictional and rural unemployment exists and will probably increase under the Gorbachev reforms.

Trade unions are controlled rather heavily by the state and do not engage in adversarial wage bargaining or strikes. They do promote labor productivity, defend the rights of workers on certain issues, and handle the social insurance system. Although severe limits were imposed during the Stalin era, workers are generally free to enter the occupation of their choice and to move between jobs.

The material incentive system is based on wage and bonus payments. Workers receive a basic wage that is differentiated by industry, vocation, skills, location, and other factors. Bonuses are based on plan fulfillment; the methods used to calculate bonuses have been a subject of continuing revision and reform. One of these, the Shchekino Method, allows managers who reduce their work force to distribute the savings to their remaining employees.

Wholesale and retail prices are both heavily controlled. The former are designed to cover average costs of production, and the latter roughly equate the demand and planned supply of each product, with lower prices set for necessities. The system of price control seems to keep inflation at very low rates, but the situation is difficult to interpret because of gaps and uncertainties in the data and the possible presence of repressed and hidden inflation.

Discussion and Review Questions

1.   How has full employment been attained in the Soviet Union? How has it helped and hindered the operation of the economic system?

2.   What roles are played by Soviet trade unions? If you were a Soviet political official, what advantages and disadvantages would you see in the formation of an independent trade union, along the lines of Solidarity in Poland?

3.   Under the traditional Soviet system, who sets the average level of wages for each factory, and how are they differentiated between factories? How are individual wages set within the factory? How does this process resemble, and how does it differ from, that in a market economy?

4.   What is the purpose of the counterplanning system, and how does it work? What are its strengths and weaknesses?

5.   How are wholesale prices set? Why do you think this method was adopted? What problems does it cause?

6.   If we had access to full information on the Soviet economy, could we accurately measure the rate of repressed inflation? How would you measure or estimate it?

Suggested Readings

Abouchar, Alan, ed. *The Socialist Price Mechanism.* Durham, N.C.: Duke University Press, 1977. *Much, but not all, of this is rather advanced material.*

Berliner, Joseph S. *The Innovation Decision in Soviet Industry.* Cambridge, Mass.: MIT Press, 1976. *Provides a full, if slightly dated, description and discussion of prices and incentives and their impact on technological progress.*

Buck, Trevor and John Cole. *Modern Soviet Economic Performance.* Oxford: Basil Blackwell, 1987. *Includes a discussion of unemployment and overemployment based on Kornai's framework.*

Hanson, Philip. "Success Indicators Revisited: The July 1979 Soviet Decree on Planning and Management." *Soviet Studies* 35 (January 1983): 1–13. *Explains the historical progression from gross output to sales to net normative value added indicators.*

Kahan, Arcadius and Blair Ruble, eds. *Industrial Labor in the USSR.* New York: Pergamon Press, 1979. *Sixteen articles on the demography, organization, standard of living, and political positions of Soviet workers.*

Norr, Henry. "Shchekino: Another Look." *Soviet Studies* 38 (April 1986): 141–169. *An interesting description and analysis of an important experiment.*

Schroeder, Gertrude E. "Gorbachev: 'Radically' Implementing Brezhnev's Reforms." *Soviet Economy* 2 (December 1986): 289–301. *This, together with her earlier articles, provides a comprehensive history of the "treadmill" (as she calls it) of continuing incentive reforms beginning in 1965.*

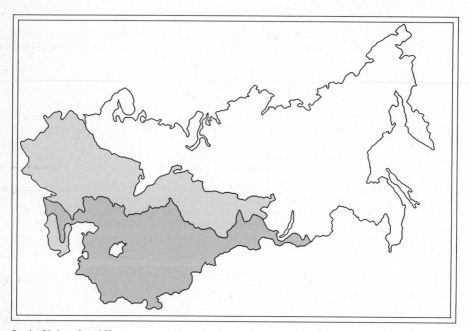

Soviet Union: Land Use
- ◱ Primary Agricultural Land
- ◪ Marginal Agricultural Land
- ☐ Non-Agricultural Land

13

CHAPTER

SOVIET UNION: PERFORMANCE AND PROSPECTS

In the coming twenty years the output of all the consumer goods industries is to increase approximately five-fold. . . . In the coming ten years all Soviet people will be able to acquire goods in adequate quantities, and in the subsequent ten years the consumer demand will be met in full. . . . At the close of the second decade every family will have a separate comfortable flat.
—Nikita Khrushchev
    Documents of the 22nd Congress of the CPSU, 1961

The long-term plans for the country's social and economic development envisage raising the people's wellbeing to a qualitatively new level. . . . All the efforts to perfect the distributive relations will have little effect . . . if we fail to saturate the market with diverse goods and services. . . . To provide every family with a separate flat or house by the year 2000 is, in itself, a tremendous but feasible undertaking.
—Mikhail Gorbachev
    Political Report to the 27th Party Congress, 1986

In this chapter we discuss the Soviet economy's past performance, its prospects for economic growth, and its current policies. We will begin with a discussion of the agricultural sector, surveying the factors that have dulled its performance, and look at the operation of the unplanned "second economy," assessing its positive and negative contributions. Next we will survey the causes of the deceleration in Soviet economic growth since the 1960s and consider the challenges facing the economic planners in the years ahead. Finally, we will examine and assess the policies adopted by Gorbachev and his associates.

Agriculture

With the possible exception of the military, no other sector of the Soviet economy is attracting as much attention as agriculture. Within the Soviet Union, the agricultural sector absorbs an enormous volume of resources and limits the growth of the rest of the economy. Grain prices in the rest of the world tend to rise and fall as Soviet production falls and rises.

Three basic kinds of agricultural institutions exist in the Soviet Union. First, the collective farm, or **kolkhoz,** is supposedly a cooperative organization, jointly owned and managed by its members, who jointly share in its profits. The members of a *kolkhoz* do not actually have any meaningful ownership rights. The chairman of the farm, elected by the members, is usually the single nominee recommended by the Party. A primary motive of the collectivization drive of the 1930s, which created the *kolkhozy,* was to extend state control over the independent farmers.

The state farm, or **sovkhoz,** is owned by the state; it has an organization similar to an industrial enterprise. Designed to take advantage of economies of scale, the state farms are enormous. The average *sovkhoz* has a harvested area of 12,000 acres, compared to about 2,500 acres of total area on the average U.S. corporate farm. The chairman of the *sovkhoz* is appointed by the government, and its employees are paid according to a wage and bonus system. According to Soviet dogma, the state farm is the highest form of socialist agriculture; thus the *sovkhozy* have been treated preferentially.

The third form of Soviet agricultural institution is the private plot. These are small holdings (about 1.5 acres per worker) allotted to families that work on the *kolkhozy* and *sovkhozy,* and smaller plots (usually .5 acres or less) that are cultivated by industrial workers in the towns and cities. The private plots are an unusual part of the Soviet economy because they are not subject to plan targets and their production can be freely consumed or sold at free-market prices.

The output and input shares of the three forms of agricultural organization are summarized in Table 13–1. Production of meat and milk are divided rather equally between the three sectors, grain is divided evenly between the state and collective farms, cotton and sugar beets are concentrated on the *kolkhozy,* eggs on the *sovkhozy,* and potatoes on the private plots.

Table 13.1   The Distribution of Agricultural Outputs and Inputs between Collective Farms, State Farms, and Private Plots, 1985

	Collective Farms	State Farms	Private Plots	Total
Gross Agricultural Output	34%	37%	29%	100%
Production of:				
Grain	51	48	1	100
Cotton	65	35	0	100
Sugar Beets	88	12	0	100
Potatoes	22	18	60	100
Meat	30	42	28	100
Milk	39	32	29	100
Eggs	6	66	28	100
Inputs:				
Labor Force	41	45	14	100
Sown Land	44	53	3	100
Tractors	41	46	13	100

Sources: Labor force data are from Stephen Rapawy, *Estimates and Projections of the Labor Force and Civilian Employment in the USSR,* Foreign Economic Report No. 10, U.S. Department of Commerce, 1976, 19; all other data are from Tsentral'noe Statisticheskoe Upravlenie SSSR, *Narodnoe khoziaistvo SSSR v 1985 g.* (Moscow: Finansy i Statistika, 1986).

A considerable amount of attention has been drawn to the fact that the private plots control only 3 percent of the land while accounting for 29 percent of all agricultural output. This is often taken, with some justification, as proof of the superiority of private agriculture over socialist agriculture. Other factors, however, should also be considered. The private plots are primarily used to produce high-priced, labor-intensive goods such as fruit, garden vegetables, spices, and meat, while the socialist sector provides the population with low-priced, land-and-capital intensive products such as grain. Also, private livestock are allowed to graze on socialist land, and the generous rewards for private activity often cause farmers to neglect their responsibilities on the *kolkhozy* and *sovkhozy.*

Agricultural Prices

A Soviet farm sells its products at several different prices. The farm is first required to deliver its planned quotas of agricultural goods to the governmental trade organizations at relatively low procurement prices. During the Stalin years, the compulsory quotas were very large and the procurement prices were far below costs of production. The *sovkhozy* were given subsidies to support the wages of their workers, but the *kolkhozy* were impoverished during those years. Since that time, procurement prices have been raised to cover costs of production. The procurement price of grain, for example, increased more than 12-fold between 1952 and 1965, and increased another 13 percent between 1965 and 1975.

After meeting their plan quotas, the *kolkhozy* are able to sell any additional output to the state at higher incentive prices (currently, 50 to 100 percent above procurement prices) or they can sell their additional goods directly to consumers on the collective farm market. There are about 8,000 collective farm market areas in the Soviet Union, half in the cities and half in rural areas. Prices on these markets are set by supply and demand.

The *sovkhozy* also are eligible to receive incentive prices for above-plan sales, but they were not allowed to sell these additional goods on the free market until a special decree was issued in 1986. The decree also states that the *kolkhozy* and *sovkhozy* can sell up to 30 percent of their *planned* output of some scarce fruits and vegetables on the collective farm market.[1]

While the government has paid higher procurement prices to farmers, it has sold food to consumers at stable prices. As noted in the previous chapter, the procurement prices of many products are now higher than the state retail prices. Buying high and selling low, the government loses about 60 billion rubles on its agricultural transactions each year, accounting for over 15 percent of the expenditures in the governmental budget.[2] Gorbachev and his advisers intend to reduce these subsidies and improve the operation of the agricultural sector through a radical reform of retail prices in the early 1990s. This plan, however, is meeting stiff political opposition.

Agricultural Performance

Within and without the Soviet Union, Soviet agricultural performance is considered a dismal failure. Before the revolution, from 1909 to 1913, Russia was the world's largest exporter of grain, accounting for 30 percent of the world total. The agricultural sector suffered during the Stalinist era of collectivization and industrialization, and did not respond well to the higher priority given to it by Khrushchev and Brezhnev. In the 1960s, the Soviet Union became a chronic importer of grain, and by the 1980s it was the world's largest importer, accounting for about 15 percent of the world total.

Data relating to the relative productivity of American and Soviet agriculture are presented in Table 13.2. Since 1960, Soviet agricultural output has been little more than three-quarters of the American level, despite the fact that the Soviets have consistently used at least 50 percent more land and eight times as many workers. In the earlier years, much of this productivity differential could be explained by the limited capital and chemical intensity of Soviet agriculture. Now, because of massive investments in the so-called agro-industrial complex, the Soviets have bypassed the United States in stock of grain combines and have nearly reached parity in their use of fertilizers and pesticides. As Gorbachev reported to the Central Committee in 1986, "we

[1]*Ekonomicheskaia gazeta,* No. 15, 1986, 2, 4–5.

[2]See the comments by Vladimir Treml in "Gorbachev's Economic Reform: A *Soviet Economy* Roundtable," *Soviet Economy* 3 (January–March 1987): 46–47.

Table 13.2   Agricultural Output and Inputs: The Soviet Union as a Percentage of the United States

	1960	1970	1980	1984
Output				
1. Total Farm Output	73	89	76	79
2. Grain Production	69	100	70	54
3. Meat Production	68	55	62	67
4. Milk Production	115	156	156	159
Inputs:				
5. Agricultural Labor Force	816	1050	912	867
6. Tractors	24	43	54	59
7. Grain Combines	48	79	111	128
8. Mineral Fertilizer per Acre of Land	29	55	72	94
9. Pesticide Production	11	35	43	72*
10. Acres Planted	155	174	151	153

*1983

Sources: Line 1—Douglas Diamond and W. Lee Davis, "Comparative Growth in Output and Productivity in U.S. and USSR Agriculture," in U.S. Congress, Joint Economic Committee, *Soviet Economy in a Time of Change,* vol. 2 (Washington, D.C.: USGPO, 1979), 45–48; updated by the author with data from CIA, U.S. Department of Agriculture, and Soviet sources. Lines 2, 3, 4, 5, 8: U.S. Central Intelligence Agency, *Handbook of Economic Statistics 1985* (CPAS 85–10001, September 1985). Lines 6, 7, 9, 10: Tsentral'noe Statisticheskoe upravlenie SSSR, *Narodnoe khoziaistvo SSSR v 1984 g.* (Moscow: Finansy i Statistika, 1985); U.S. Department of Agriculture, *Agricultural Statistics* (various years); and U.S. Bureau of the Census, *Statistical Abstract of the United States* (various years).

must recognize that the immense resources channeled into this sphere so far do not pay back as they should."[3]

What explains the continuing tendency of Soviet agriculture to lag behind? Several factors seem to be involved. First, cold climates cover much of the Soviet Union. Most of the sown area is comparable to the prairie provinces of Canada and to the northwestern United States, and very little can compare to the climate of the American corn belt. The annual distribution of precipitation is also unfavorable in the Soviet Union. In many of the major growing regions less than half of the annual precipitation occurs during the growing season. In much of North America, about three-quarters of all precipitation is received during this season.

However, in the words of a Soviet agricultural economist:

The main reasons for the instability of agriculture are not natural and climatic factors in themselves, but rather the technological and organizational-economic conditions of farming that have not been sufficiently flexible to make it possible to adapt continuously and efficiently to existing natural and climatic conditions.[4]

[3]*Pravda,* June 17, 1986, 3.

[4]V. Tikhonov, "The Soviet Food Program," *Problems of Economics* 26 (June 1983): 12.

In other words, central planning does not work well in the agricultural sector. Ideally, all of the important decisions in a centrally planned economy are made at the beginning of the year (or 5-year period) and are carried out during the remainder of the year. Agricultural decisions must be made and adjusted continuously to deal with the climate, insects, incidence of plant disease, consumer demand, and other factors. In most cases, a timely and informed opinion can be made only by the farmer on the scene, not by a central planner in Moscow.

Central planning was established in 1928, at the end of the industrialization debate, with the express purpose of transforming the Soviet Union from an agricultural country into a military and industrial power. Production of iron, steel, and other relatively simple industrial goods could be planned rather effectively because most of the important variables could be controlled by the planners. It was not until efforts were made to revive agriculture, to increase the level of foreign trade, and to improve the technological and qualitative level of production that the weaknesses of the Soviet system became clear. None of these activities have proved susceptible to central planning.

Along with these general environmental and systemic problems, Soviet agriculture suffers from a lack of infrastructure for transportation and storage of food. Although the land mass of the Soviet Union is more than twice as large as the United States, the Soviet road system is only one-fourth as large. More than one-quarter of the farms in the Russian Republic have no roads to connect them with the outside world, and those rural roads that exist are not paved. Storage facilities are too few and too distant from one another. The result is that about 20 percent of all the grain, fruit, and vegetables produced, and as much as 50 percent of the potato crop, rots in the field or is lost on the way to the grain elevator.[5]

Agricultural Policy and Reform

A number of measures have been taken since Stalin's death in 1953 to improve agricultural performance. Under Khrushchev, procurement prices were raised and the share of total investment directed to agriculture increased from 14 to about 17 percent. The Virgin Lands campaign brought about 90 million acres of marginal land under cultivation, the chemicalization drive expanded the production of mineral fertilizers, and the ill-conceived corn program expanded the acreage planted in corn approximately ten-fold. As a result, grain production grew rapidly between 1953 and 1963 but stagnated after 1963, contributing to Khrushchev's loss of political power.

Brezhnev and Kosygin, who took office in 1965, continued the drive to modernize agriculture. They further increased the share of agriculture in total investment from 17 percent (1966–1970) to 20 percent (1976–1980). Dur-

[5]Marshall Goldman, *USSR in Crisis: The Failure of an Economic System* (New York: W. W. Norton, 1983), 80–81.

ing the years 1970 to 1977, Soviet agricultural investment was more than six times the American level.[6]

Brezhnev's desire to achieve agricultural self-sufficiency was heightened by the American grain embargo of 1980. His so-called Food Program was initiated in 1982 and was embraced and extended by a series of agricultural decrees and plans issued by the Gorbachev government in 1986. Taken together, the Brezhnev and Gorbachev programs include the following provisions.

First, a high level of agricultural investment was maintained. One-third of all investment was allocated to the agro-industrial complex in the Eleventh (1981–1985) and Twelfth (1986–1990) Five-Year Plans. Although money has been allocated to build the much needed roads and storage facilities, little can be done to alleviate this problem in the near future. Special emphasis has been placed on investment in intensive technologies. That is, farms are given preferential access to inputs if they concentrate their efforts on the production of new high-yield crops on their most fertile land. Intensive techniques were used on 29 million hectares of grain farms in 1986 and are scheduled to encompass more than 50 million hectares in 1990.

Second, the administration of agriculture has undergone a series of revisions. At the local level, the 1982 program established a network of agro-industrial associations, each of which includes all state and collective farms in the district and all industrial enterprises and associations that serve agriculture. At the national level, a 1985 decree established the State Agro-Industrial Committee (*Gosagroprom*) by merging and liquidating five ministries (including the Ministry of Agriculture) and one state committee. Both of these moves were intended to reduce the size of the bureaucracy, eliminate petty rivalries between agencies, and unify the formation of agricultural policy.

Third, the Food Program has increased the availability of equipment, fertilizers, pesticides, and other resources to the private plots. In 1987, Gorbachev announced his intention to lease almost 800,000 unoccupied village houses with small plots of land to city dwellers who agree to farm them part-time. When this unused land has been allocated, he recommends further private leaseholds should be carved out of the huge state and collective farms.[7] The *sovkhozy* and *kolkhozy* should also be free to make more of their own decisions and to sell more of their output at free-market prices.

Fourth, state procurement prices were increased again in 1983 (generating about 16 billion rubles of new revenues for the agricultural sector) and the incentive markups for above-plan production were increased for some products in 1986. Finally, the Food Program and subsequent decrees extended financial support to ailing farms. About 10 billion rubles of indebtedness were

---

[6]Douglas Diamond and W. Lee Davis, "Comparative Growth in Output and Productivity in U.S. and USSR Agriculture," in U.S. Congress, Joint Economic Committee, *Soviet Economy in a Time of Change,* vol. 2 (Washington, D.C.: USGPO, 1979), 41.

[7]Bill Keller, "Gorbachev Urges Expansion of Family Farms," *New York Times,* July 1, 1987, A11.

written off by the 1982 act and the repayment periods were extended for another 11 billion rubles of debt.[8] According to a 1986 decree, farms that are unable to make their payments on State Bank loans due in 1986 to 1990 can reschedule their debts over a 10-year period starting in 1995 and are not required to pay interest on their debts in the interim.[9]

These programs have done little to reform the underlying institutional system in agriculture. The central planners still have too much authority to allow genuine local control. The farms are still too large (some have over 100,000 acres) to be run efficiently. Most prices remain unresponsive to market conditions. Gorbachev has said, "If we intend to truly succeed in agricultural industrial production we cannot hold to traditional paths."[10] The force of tradition, however, is very strong.

The Second Economy

Intertwined with the planned sector of the Soviet economy is a second economy of unplanned production and exchange. Much of this unplanned activity is legal; for example, the system of small-scale private-plot agriculture allows farmers to set their own production and price levels. Within strict limits, private activity among physicians, teachers, beauticians, photographers, and hunters is permitted, and the new Law on Individual Enterprise, which took effect in May 1987, legalized the private provision of repair and taxi services and a broader range of handicrafts.

On the other hand, the illegal part of the second economy is still very large. It flourishes, in part, because many activities that are legal in the West (or even in Eastern Europe) are still forbidden in the Soviet Union. The new Law on Individual Enterprise, for example, continues to disallow: (1) employment of workers outside of the immediate family; (2) production of certain prohibited items, such as fur hats, precious jewelry, weapons, and copying equipment; (3) operation of amusement rides or games; (4) giving instruction in subjects and courses that are not taught in the public schools and colleges; and (5) organization of entertainment activities. The law does not allow a worker to quit his regular job to engage in individual enterprise on a full-time basis, nor does it give the worker access to raw materials or supplies in the wholesale trade network. These must be obtained at the retail level where shortages abound.[11] Thus, it is now legal to run a private car repair service, but it is almost impossible to find the necessary spare parts.

For example, an apartment window broken in the dead of winter can be repaired by a governmental agency at little or no expense, but only after a wait of several weeks. If, instead, the tenant has a connection with a repairman who works for the governmental agency, it may be possible to have the job

[8]Tikhonov, "The Soviet Food Program," 17–18.
[9]*Ekonomicheskaia gazeta,* No. 15, 1986, 5.
[10]*Pravda,* June 17, 1986, 3.
[11]*Pravda,* November 21, 1986, 1, 3.

done after working hours. As Gorbachev mentioned in one of his speeches: "Try to get your apartment repaired. You will definitely have to find a moonlighter to do it for you, and he will steal the materials he needs from a construction site."[12]

Thus, the second economy includes many activities that are strictly legal, others that are legal but require theft and bribery for their success, and others that are strictly illegal. The Soviet newspapers have reported prosecution of cases in which entire factories produced goods for the plan during the day and for the black market at night. Some of the entrepreneurs who run these operations have amassed fortunes of hundreds of millions of rubles.[13]

A factory, run illegally at night, must obtain raw materials. These may be stolen from the state enterprise or purchased from other black-market outlets. A distribution network for the goods that are produced must be established, often involving bribes paid to local police, party, trade union, and government officials to avoid detection and prosecution. The ability of governmental officials to collect bribes, in turn, places an economic value on their positions.

On several occasions, the government has attempted to crack down on black-market activity and corruption. In 1972–1973, under the leadership of Georgian Internal Affairs Minister Shevardnadze, virtually the entire government of Soviet Georgia (including Party officials) was removed from office. For his efforts, Shevardnadze was promoted to foreign minister by Gorbachev.

A 1982 law imposed fines ranging from the equivalent of $420 (more than the average monthly wage) to $1,400 for economic crimes such as profiteering and stiffened the prison sentences for theft of public property. Judges were instructed to assign more convicts to forced labor brigades instead of sending them to prison. Between 1982 and 1985, according to the first secretary of the Kirghiz Communist Party, 1,100 members were expelled from the Party in that central Asian republic for corruption, abuse of office, or similar offenses.

Gorbachev spoke in 1986 of the need to "intensify the struggle against unearned income," stating "we should conduct an uncompromising fight against all parasitic elements, that is, against those who try to live off the money of others and of society."[14] This promises to be a long fight: central planning seems to generate shortages, shortages generate black markets, and black markets generate political corruption.

The second economy influence on Soviet economic performance seems to be a mixture of positive and negative effects. On the one hand, private activity fills many of the voids that are missed by central planning. Private-plot farmers and moonlighting workers contribute to the quantity, quality, and variety of goods and services that are available to the population. Industrial

[12]Quoted in Bruce Steinberg, "Reforming the Soviet Economy," *Fortune,* November 25, 1985, 96.

[13]For an amazing account of the underground business world, written by a former Moscow attorney, see Konstantin Simis, *USSR: The Corrupt Society* (New York: Simon and Schuster, 1982), Chapter 6.

[14]*Pravda,* March 17, 1986, 3.

expediters provide an invaluable service to factories needing raw materials to meet their plan targets.

On the negative side, the second economy tends to divert the efforts of workers from their official jobs. Agricultural workers, for example, seem to spend an inordinate amount of time on their tiny private plots. Industrial managers complain that workers are not interested in their full-time jobs because they can make more money working on the side. Worker morale is further reduced by the incidence of political graft and corruption, and the spontaneous second economy reduces governmental control over the centrally planned economy.

The second economy seems to have a significant impact on the level and distribution of household income. According to information gathered from 1,688 households of Soviet emigrants in Israel, the poorest decile obtained about 6 percent of their income from private sources while the richest decile obtained almost 39 percent of their income privately. The Gini index of income inequality (see Chapter 2) was 0.27 if private incomes were excluded, and 0.30 if they were included—a rise of 10 percent.[15] Not surprisingly, the possibility that Gorbachev's reforms will lead to more private activity and greater income inequality is a subject of heated controversy in the Soviet Union.

Performance and Prospects

We have already considered several aspects of Soviet economic performance. Unemployment and inflation are not entirely absent in the Soviet Union, but their rates are relatively low. Poverty exists, but its effects are ameliorated by the low prices charged for food, housing, health care, and other necessities. As an industrial producer, the Soviet Union climbed from the fifth largest in the world before the revolution to the second largest today. As a military superpower, the Soviet Union is second to none. Since the revolution, tremendous strides have been made in the areas of public health and education, scientific research and space flight, and popular promotion of athletics and culture.

On the negative side, we noted the poor performance of Soviet agriculture, but also that agriculture was given a low priority from 1928 to 1960 and that weather and soil conditions are unfavorable. Other economic and social problems include the limitation of political, economic, and cultural freedoms, the insufficient variety, quantity, and quality of consumer goods and housing, the high rate of alcoholism, the low level of work incentives, and the lag in computer technology (see "How I Bought a Computer," p. 303). Several of these successes and failures are related to the level or growth of national income.

In 1985, the national income of the Soviet Union was about two-thirds of the U.S. level according to Soviet estimates (which exclude service production in both countries), or about half the U.S. level according to American

---

[15]Gur Ofer, "The Distribution Effects of Private Incomes," *Radio Liberty Research,* June 19, 1987, 4–7.

HOW I BOUGHT A COMPUTER

We decided to buy a computer. After all . . . in the newspapers they write that soon computers will be in every family. Let one be in ours. . . .

The next day I, lucky person, decided to head to the Elektronika store and surprise my husband. . . . Here are electric clocks, radios, video cassettes, calculators, television sets. But I need a computer, and that I do not see. I go to the administrator's desk:

"I would like to buy a home computer."

"We sell them only to residents of Moscow."

"Yes, yes, I am from Moscow."

"Then leave a post card. Right now we are taking advance orders."

Well, I decided, if you're going to buy one, you should at least have a talk with someone knowledgeable, so I headed for the consultant . . .

"I read that besides computers with the Fokal language, there are also computers with Basic."

"You should read less," she advised me.

"Why?"

"Why? Because there aren't any and will not be any."

"And are game programs ever for sale?"

"They are not."

"And what kinds of programs show up for sale?"

"None at all . . ."

At home, my husband calmed me: "It's alright, there is still one more Elektronika store in Zelenograd. And they say that at Radiotekhnika there are sometimes other computers—the Mikrosha."

The next day I sat at the telephone. I called Zelenograd.

"What, a computer? No, we never have them."

I called Radiotekhnika.

"Mikrosha? What are you talking about? They still haven't been produced. We only had an exhibition . . . "

Finally, I decided to call the Ministry of the Electronics Industry.

"You need to get in touch with the Elektronika store."

"They only have post cards."

There were already short beeps [a disconnect signal] coming from the receiver.

Source: S. Beliaeva, "How I Bought a Computer," *Komsomol'skaia pravda,* January 11, 1987, 4.

estimates (which include services).[16] If we adjust for population, investment, and military expenditure, we find that Soviet per capita provision of consumer goods is only about one-third the U.S. level.[17] Many of the common conveniences of twentieth-century life—brooms with long handles, prepared breakfast cereals, liquid detergent, and toilet paper, to name just a few—are seldom available in Soviet stores.

In the early years, the Soviets admitted to a standard of living lower than that in the West, but they could claim that they were catching up. (A recurring theme in Khrushchev's speeches was the need to catch up to and overpass the United States.) Soviet GNP grew at an annual rate of about 6 percent during the 1950s, compared to the American rate of about 4 percent. Together with the spread of Soviet influence in China and Eastern Europe, the rapid growth of Soviet economic and military power contributed to the Red Scare and the McCarthy Era in the United States.

The Soviet growth rate decelerated to 5 percent in the 1960s, 3 percent in the 1970s, and about 2 percent in the first half of the 1980s.[18] Meanwhile, growth rates in the Western world fluctuated upward and downward, without following any clear trend. All together, the American and Soviet economies have been growing at approximately the same average rate in the most recent years. The Soviet standard of living is still far behind the American level and has no longer been catching up.

Part of the cause of the slowdown of Soviet economic growth is shown in Table 13.3. Growth in the labor force was fairly stable before 1980, the capital stock grew at a very rapid but declining rate, and the growth of land utilization dropped after 1960. If the growth rates of the factors of production are averaged together (using weights derived from a Cobb-Douglas production function), their combined growth was fairly stable through the 1950s and 1960s, decelerating in the 1970s and early 1980s. Taken together, this implies that the entire reduction in output growth between the 1950s and 1960s was caused by a deceleration of combined factor productivity, while the slowdown of output growth between the 1960s and the early 1980s can be blamed on slower input growth and negative productivity growth, equally.

The slow or negative growth of factor productivity, which explains most of the reduction in economic growth after 1950, seems to involve several problems. First, the capital stock grew so much more rapidly than the labor force or land utilization that diminishing returns to capital apparently slowed the growth of output. This is the conclusion of several econometric studies.[19]

---

[16]*Narodnoe khoziaistvo SSSR v 1985 g.*, 581.

[17]These are geometric means of ruble and dollar comparisons, drawn from U.S. Central Intelligence Agency, *Handbook of Economic Statistics 1986* (CPAS 86–10002, September 1986), 38.

[18]The Soviet growth rates for the last few years are obscured by inconsistencies in the Soviet data. See "1987 Panel on the Soviet Economic Outlook: Perceptions on a Confusing Set of Statistics," *Soviet Economy* 3 (January–March 1987): 3–24.

[19]See, for example, Robert Whitesell, "The Influence of Central Planning on the Economic Slowdown in the Soviet Union and Eastern Europe: A Comparative Production Function Analysis," *Economica* 52 (May 1985): 235–244, and the sources cited therein.

Table 13.3   Annual Average Growth Rates of Real GNP, Factor Inputs, and Factor Productivity, 1950–1985

	1951–1960	1961–1970	1971–1980	1981–1985
Real GNP	5.9%	4.9%	2.7%	2.0%
Factor Inputs:				
Labor Hours	1.3	1.8	1.5	0.7
Capital Stock	9.4	8.1	7.5	6.3
Land	2.7	0.1	0.0	− 0.1
Combined Factors	4.2	4.6	4.1	3.2
Combined Factor Productivity	1.7	0.3	− 1.4	− 1.2

Sources: 1950–1960— Rush Greenslade, "The Real Gross National Product of the USSR: 1950–1975," in U.S. Congress, Joint Economic Committee, *Soviet Economy in a New Perspective* (Washington, D.C.: USGPO, 1976), 279; 1961–1985: U.S. Central Intelligence Agency, *Handbook of Economic Statistics 1986* (CPAS 86–10002, September 1986), 70.

Second, the growth of factor productivity was undoubtedly fettered by the depletion of accessible natural resources. As deposits of oil, coal, iron ore, and other materials have dwindled in the European portion of the Soviet Union, it has been necessary to develop resources in Siberia and the Far East. This, in turn, requires the construction of new factories, roads, bridges, and living quarters, often under very unfavorable conditions. Thus, each unit of output requires a relatively large volume of capital investment.

Third, slower growth of technological progress apparently contributed to the slower growth of factor productivity. According to a recent study, the slowdown in technological improvement is indicated by a number of factors: slower introduction of new machinery into the economy, slower growth in the number and impact of technological innovations, and slower growth or decline in the importation of Western equipment.[20] Prime Minister Ryzhkov reported to the 1986 Party Congress that "the increase in the population's real income virtually stopped" in 1982, mainly because "the proper persistence was not shown in the utilization of the achievements of science and technical progress and in the restructuring of the economy and management in accordance with the demands of the times."[21]

Closely related to the slower growth of technological progress is the aging of the nation's capital stock and its detrimental effect on productivity growth. According to international statistical comparisons, the Soviets retire their old machinery and equipment less than half as quickly as the United States and other Western countries.[22] An aging capital stock is not only tech-

[20]Vladimir Kontorovich, "Technological Progress and Productivity Growth Slowdown in the Soviet Economy, 1951–1982," presented to the American Economic Association, Dallas, December 28–30, 1984, 54.

[21]*Pravda,* March 4, 1986, 2.

[22]Stanley H. Cohn, "Sources of Low Productivity in Soviet Capital Investment," in U.S. Congress, Joint Economic Committee, *Soviet Economy in the 1980s* (Washington, D.C.: USGPO, 1982), 181.

nologically backward, it also requires more repair. At times, 40 percent of the nation's stock of machine tools is reportedly used to repair old equipment, rather than to build new models.[23]

Finally, we may surmise that increasing strain on the system of central planning has contributed to the slowdown. As the economy has grown larger and more technologically advanced, as the size of the governmental bureaucracy has expanded, and as the Soviet Union has increased its involvement in international trade, the task of central planning has grown ever more complex. Moreover, as memories of the revolution and World War II fade, it becomes more difficult to draw on the ideological and nationalistic fervor of the population to inspire hard work and sacrifice.

In addition to the problems mentioned above, the planners face a number of new difficulties in the years ahead. First, for complex demographic reasons, the labor force has entered a prolonged phase of slow growth. After increasing by 24 million persons during the 1970s, the working-age population is expected to increase by only 5 million during the 1980s and by 8 million during the 1990s.[24] Compounding the problem, about 90 percent of this growth will occur in Soviet central Asia and Kazakhstan, where the workers have fewer skills, less education, and less productive capital than those in the European republics.

Soviet economic difficulties were also exacerbated by the disaster at the Chernobyl nuclear power station in April 1986—one month after a draft of a new 5-year plan was presented to the Party Congress. A summary of the final draft of the plan, approved by the Supreme Soviet 2 months after the accident, continued to call for an enormous increase in the share of nuclear plants in the generation of electrical power—from 11 percent of the total in 1985 to 21 percent in 1990.[25] This goal now seems rather far-fetched.

The Gorbachev Program

Against this backdrop of stagnation, the Gorbachev administration resolved in 1986 to double the level of national income (Soviet concept) by the year 2000. Considering that income grew by only 81 percent during the previous 15 years and that the labor force is expected to grow very slowly in the near future, fulfillment of this target will require an enormous improvement in labor productivity. Drawing on themes that were developed during the brief tenure of Yuri Andropov, resurrecting a number of ideas that were tried unsuccessfully by Leonid Brezhnev, borrowing several ideas from Eastern Europe and China, and adding a few concepts of their own, Gorbachev and his associates

[23]Herbert Levine, "Possible Causes of the Deterioration of Soviet Productivity Growth in the Period 1976–80," *Soviet Economy in the 1980s,* 159.

[24]Stephen Rapawy and Godfrey Baldwin, "Demographic Trends in the Soviet Union: 1950–2000," in *Soviet Economy in the 1980s,* 292.

[25]*Pravda,* June 19, 1986, 2.

have assembled a strategy for radical reform of the Soviet economic and political system.

Discipline

To stimulate labor productivity in the short run, Andropov and Gorbachev have attempted, with some apparent success, to impose stronger discipline over the work force. For example, soon after Andropov became general secretary, he sent the police into stores and shops to locate workers who were absent from their jobs and send them back to work. At higher levels, the campaign to clean up graft and corruption among Party and government officials was initiated.

Gorbachev opened his leadership with a campaign against alcoholism and drunkenness on the job. He cut the production of vodka, closed more than two-thirds of the country's liquor stores, forbade restaurants to serve drinks before 2 P.M., and increased the fine for drinking at work to 50 rubles (about one-fourth of the average monthly wage).

In order to strengthen discipline *within* enterprises, Gorbachev borrowed several ideas from the military. For example, most enterprises in industry and agriculture are now organized into work teams known as brigades (10 to 30 workers) and links (5 to 10 workers). The team concludes a collective contract with the enterprise, and bonuses are paid in a lump sum to the team based on their fulfillment of the contract. This system is apparently designed to combine moral incentives (peer pressure) with material incentives.[26]

The new system of product quality inspection is also based on the military experience. For years, the Soviet Ministry of Defense has stationed its own inspectors in defense plants to ensure adherence to their requirements. In the civilian economy, the factories were free to police themselves. According to a program inaugurated in 1987, the State Committee on Standards now has a team of its own inspectors in some 1,500 enterprises that produce the most important products. The inspectors are supposed to have broad powers to block the shipment of substandard goods and to work with the enterprise manager on improvements in product quality.[27]

In terms of financial discipline, Gorbachev intends to reduce governmental subsidies to business and close down unessential enterprises that fail to turn a profit. About 13 percent of the country's industrial enterprises currently operate at a loss; one of Gorbachev's advisors has estimated that plant closures, layoffs, and mergers will require the transfer of 15 to 20 million people to new jobs—many of them in the service sector.[28] The first bankruptcy of a state-owned enterprise was registered in 1987, when a Leningrad construction trust

[26]For more on this and other military precedents to the Gorbachev reforms, see George G. Weickhardt, "The Soviet Military-Industrial Complex and Economic Reform," *Soviet Economy* 2 (July–September 1986): 193–220.

[27]See Gertrude Schroeder, "Gorbachev: 'Radically' Implementing Brezhnev's Reforms," *Soviet Economy* 2 (October–December 1986): 294–295.

[28]Bill Keller, "Soviet Planning Big Labor Shift Out of Industry," *New York Times,* July 4, 1987, 2.

was closed for failure to meet delivery schedules, cost limits, and production standards. Its 2,000 employees, temporarily displaced, were offered new jobs without affecting their service records.[29]

Finally, imposition of discipline seems to be one of Gorbachev's prime motives in his campaigns for democratization and openness (*glasnost*). He believes that allowing workers to elect their factory managers from a field of candidates approved by the Communist Party will weed out corrupt and unqualified managers. Likewise, he has proposed multi-candidate elections for offices in local government, again under the control of the Party. Gorbachev has publicly reprimanded governmental and industrial officials who "continue to work in the old way," and he has encouraged the news media to humiliate those who do shoddy work:

When the subject of publicity comes up, calls are sometimes made for exercising greater caution when speaking about the shortcomings, omissions, and difficulties that are inevitable in any ongoing effort. . . . Those who have grown used to doing slipshod work, to practicing deception, indeed feel really awkward in the glare of publicity, when everything done . . . is in full public view.[30]

Incentives and Prices

In our review of the Soviet incentive system, we saw that the current leadership is attempting to reward enterprises for their adherence to the terms of delivery contracts, for improving the quality of their output, and for increasing their profits, rather than for simple fulfillment of gross output targets.

If Gorbachev successfully implements his reforms, enterprises that improve their performance will not be penalized with higher compulsory plan targets. Broader application of the Shchekino method will encourage enterprises to release their excess employees and pay higher wages to their most productive workers. As we noted earlier, Gorbachev told the Central Committee in 1987 that the only limit on income should be whether or not it is earned. In a recent survey of farm managers in the Altai region, almost two-thirds said that they needed additional workers. When asked how the situation would change if they were given greater control over pay and employment, almost half of the respondents said that part of their existing work force (15 to 20 percent average) would not be needed.[31]

With regard to the price system, Gorbachev says that greater attention should be paid to the consumer qualities of goods—including their style, workmanship, and technological sophistication—rather than their costs of production. He intends to increase simultaneously the flexibility of the price

[29]Mark D'Anastasio, "Soviets Declare the Bankruptcy of a State Firm," *Wall Street Journal,* March 27, 1987, 12.

[30]Mikhail Gorbachev, *Political Report of the CPSU Central Committee to the 27th Party Congress* (Moscow: Novosti Press Agency, 1986), 76.

[31]Tat'iana Zaslavskaia, "Social Justice and the Human Factor in Economic Development," *Problems of Economics* 30 (May 1987): 10.

system and the amount of price discipline exercised by the State Price Committee. On the side of flexibility, he has allowed some experimentation—principally in light industry—with contract prices negotiated between buyers and sellers. On the side of discipline, he intends to hold wholesale prices constant during the life of each 5-year plan.

At the retail level Gorbachev intends to increase the prices of meat, dairy products, and other foodstuffs in the early 1990s. One purpose of this action is to reduce the costly program of governmental subsidies; another purpose is regulate the consumer demand for those products. According to one of Gorbachev's advisors, Soviet citizens who travel to Yugoslavia (where most prices are not controlled) are astounded by the selection of food available in the stores. "Meat consumption per capita is lower [in Yugoslavia] than in the Soviet Union, but there is a sense of abundance. If I want, I can always come and buy it, as much as I want, without a line. It's not simple to create that feeling here, but if we succeed it will have a colossal psychological effect."[32]

Science and Technology

While Gorbachev's short-run policy is based on strengthening of discipline and incentives (the so-called human factor), his priority over the long run is radical acceleration of scientific and technological progress. He hopes to accomplish this, first of all, by increasing the rate of capital spending and by directing more of investments to machine building, electronics, and other technology-intensive sectors. Within each sector, Gorbachev advocates (as did Brezhnev) that a larger share of investment resources be used to modernize existing factories, rather than to build new ones.

Plans also call for increased spending on scientific education and research, rapid growth in the production of computers and industrial robots, organizational changes designed to bring scientific research closer to industry, and stronger incentives to produce and use new products and processes. Soviet legislation enacted in 1987 will make it possible for Soviet enterprises to have closer contact with Western firms through trade and joint venture arrangements. This, it is hoped, will increase the flow of foreign technology into the country and expose Soviet producers to some foreign competition.

Administrative Reform

Gorbachev realizes that most of his proposals are not new or original. Many of them were incorporated in the reforms initiated by Brezhnev and Kosygin in 1965 and 1979—reforms that never got off the ground. According to the analyses made by Gorbachev's advisors, the previous reforms were undermined by the bureaucracy of the industrial ministries.[33] Struggles for control

---

[32]Leonid Abalkin, director of the Institute of Economics of the Academy of Sciences, quoted in Keller, "Soviet Planning Big Labor Shift," 2.

[33]Tat'iana Zaslavskaia, "The Novosibirsk Report," *Survey* (Spring 1984): 91–95.

between the ministries made it difficult for the State Planning Committee to coordinate their activities; the ministries maintained jealous control over their subordinate enterprises, limiting their autonomy and initiative. In the words of Prime Minister Ryzhkov:

The apparatus of the ministries and departments, who are literally burying enterprises in mountains of paper, continues to be chained to obsolete administrative work methods. Instead of using economic forms of management, it thrives on the illusion that it is possible . . . to manage the entire range of work in enterprises from above.[34]

In order to reduce the rivalry between the ministries, and their capacity to interfere in the work of the enterprises, Gorbachev intends to reduce their staffs and merge them into a smaller number of **superministries.** The first superministry was created in agriculture through the merger of five branch ministries and one state committee, and almost half the former ministry employees lost their jobs. According to Central Committee staff members, the number of ministries in Moscow could shrink from around 80 to 20, and "those that remain will have a staff of 5,000 instead of 300,000."[35]

Limitations and Obstacles

Massive reductions in the ministerial bureaucracy, greater democratization and enterprise autonomy, bankruptcies and unemployment, unsubsidized consumer prices—if these and the other measures are fully implemented, they will truly constitute a radical reform of the Soviet system. Yet, the Gorbachev proposals are carefully limited and hedged. The enterprises will have greater control over their production and prices, but the systems of central planning and price control will be maintained. The incentive system will be rationalized, but it will continue to be based on plan fulfillment. Workers will lose their jobs, but the government will guarantee new ones. There will be greater scope for private activity, but only on a small scale. Multicandidate elections may be allowed at the local level, but all of the candidates will be approved by the Communist Party. Few departures from public ownership of the means of production will be allowed. For those who believe that Gorbachev is a market socialist or a closet capitalist, he made his feelings clear in a speech to his Eastern European allies:

Some of you look at the market as a lifesaver for your economies. But, comrades, you should not think about lifesavers but about the ship. And the ship is socialism.[36]

Despite concessions and limitations, Gorbachev's proposals have met stiff resistance. At the highest levels, they are opposed by officials and bureaucrats who fear the loss of their power and prestige. Thus, while Gorbachev has

[34]*Pravda,* June 19, 1986, 5.

[35]Quoted in Paul Quinn-Judge, "Plenum in Moscow," *Christian Science Monitor,* June 26, 1987, 10.

[36]Quoted in Seweryn Bialer and Joan Afferica, "The Genesis of Gorbachev's World," *Foreign Affairs* 64 (1986): 612.

enacted a number of general laws and decrees, much of the specific legislation needed to put these laws into practice has not yet gained Politburo approval. After a debate at the June 1987 meeting of the Central Committee, one of Gorbachev's advisors admitted that some of the speakers voiced harsh criticism of the experts who designed the reforms, but he declared that "total unanimity exists only in a cemetery."[37] Most pointedly, one Soviet daily newspaper attributed the following statement to the wife of a Communist Party official: "We are the elite, and you will not pull us down. You don't have the strength. We'll rip the flimsy sails of your restructuring. So dampen your enthusiasm."[38]

Gorbachev admits that his proposals are opposed at high levels, but he claims that the common people "are standing like a mountain behind restructuring."[39] Unfortunately, there is little logic or evidence to support this conclusion. Understandably, Soviet workers who have never had to deal with a significant threat of inflation or unemployment are apprehensive. A recent poll in the engineering and metal-working factories of Kazakhstan found that 40 percent of workers are opposed to any major change in the economic system.[40] According to the experience in Yugoslavia and Hungary, this opposition will grow stronger when bankruptcies, unemployment, inflation, and income inequality begin to rise. Will Gorbachev be willing and able to overcome opposition and press forward with his radical reforms? Many Western economists predict that the power of the status quo will be maintained, but Jerry Hough, a political scientist, reminds us of an important fact: "The one certain law of history is that the status quo is eventually certain to be transformed."[41]

Summary

Soviet agriculture is organized around collective farms (*kolkhozy*) that are owned and managed cooperatively, state farms (*sovkhozy*) that are run like factories, and small private plots. Procurement prices for the state and collective farms are set by the state; the private plots can sell all of their output at market prices. Retail prices of food are heavily subsidized. The poor performance of Soviet agriculture can be explained by climatic and geographic factors, the low investment priority that was placed on food production for many years, and the fact that agricultural production is difficult to plan and manage centrally. A higher priority has been accorded agriculture in recent years, and several reforms have been introduced, but the results are not clear.

---

[37]Abel Aganbegyan, quoted in *Dallas Morning News,* June 27, 1987, 9A.

[38]*Moskovskaya Pravda,* quoted in *Newsweek,* May 18, 1987, 48.

[39]*Pravda,* January 28, 1987, 2.

[40]Mark D'Anastasio, "Soviet Workers and Bureaucrats Resist Gorbachev Plan to Spur Factory Output," *Wall Street Journal,* June 2, 1987, 24.

[41]Jerry Hough, "The Gorbachev Reform: A Maximal Case," *Soviet Economy* 2 (October–December 1986): 303.

A second economy of unplanned production and exchange includes legal activity on private plots and in handicrafts and illegal production for the black market. While the second economy contributes in some ways to the performance of the planned sectors, it also seems to cause greater income inequality.

Although the Soviet level of real income is still far below that in the United States, the Soviet growth rate has decelerated to the point where it is no longer catching up. This deceleration may be caused by diminishing returns to investment, by a deceleration in technological progress, and by the growing complexity of planning a modern economy.

Gorbachev's system of economic reform calls for greater discipline and motivation of the labor force to accelerate production in the short run. Along these lines, important initiatives include the campaign against alcohol, the use of peer pressure in production brigades, a new system of quality inspection, the threat of bankruptcy and unemployment, public ridicule of laggard workers, greater enterprise autonomy in managing material incentives, and a new system of retail and wholesale prices. In the long run, growth will depend on better application of technology. A program of administrative reform is designed to weaken the resistance to other reforms and reduce ministerial meddling in the work of the enterprises. The reforms are opposed by officials who fear the loss of power and by many workers who fear the possibility of unemployment, inflation, and a range of other problems.

Discussion and Review Questions

1. What are several of the factors that explain the low level of productivity in Soviet agriculture? What has the government done in recent years to correct this problem? Do you believe that these measures will work?

2. How does the unplanned second economy support the performance of the planned economy? How does it interfere?

3. How has Soviet economic growth compared with American growth during the years since World War II? Discuss the factors that have influenced the trend in Soviet growth rates. How are demographic and geographic factors expected to influence the rate of growth in the future?

4. Describe the major initiatives that Gorbachev has proposed for economic and political reform. If the reforms are adopted, who will benefit in the short run and in the long run? Who will lose?

Suggested Readings

Bergson, Abram, and Herbert Levine, eds. *The Soviet Economy towards the Year 2000.* London: George Allen and Unwin, 1983. *A compendium of articles on the prospects for Soviet growth and development.*

Diamond, Douglas and W. Lee Davis. "Comparative Growth in Output and Productivity in U.S. and USSR Agriculture." In U.S. Congress, Joint Economic Committee. *Soviet Economy in a Time of Change,* vol. 2. Washington, D.C.: USGPO, 1979, 19–54. *Along with a statistical survey, this article contains a full discussion of the factors that explain the difference between Soviet and American agricultural performance.*

Goldman, Marshall. *USSR in Crisis: The Failure of an Economic System.* New York: W. W. Norton, 1983. *Somewhat polemical, a good description of the economic forces that are driving the process of reform.*

Gorbachev, Mikhail. *Political Report of the CPSU Central Committee to the 27th Party Congress.* Moscow: Novosti Press Agency, 1986. *In these speeches by Brezhnev and Gorbachev, change and continuity in Soviet political rhetoric can be recognized.*

Grossman, Gregory and Vladimir Treml, eds. *Berkeley-Duke Occasional Papers on the Second Economy in the USSR.* One of the richest sources of information on the unplanned portion of the Soviet economy; ten papers had been published by April 1987, including a general bibliography and studies of income, agriculture, alcohol production, poverty, and housing.

Levine, Herbert, et al. "Gorbachev's Economic Reform: A *Soviet Economy* Roundtable." *Soviet Economy* 3 (January–March 1987): 40–53. *The prospects for reform, discussed by 12 noted participants from academia, the think tanks, and the intelligence community.*

Levine, Herbert. "Possible Causes of the Deterioration of Soviet Productivity Growth in the Period 1976–80." In U.S. Congress, Joint Economic Committee. *Soviet Economy in the 1980s: Problems and Prospects,* Part 1. Washington, D.C.: USGPO, 1982, 153–168. *A clear, concise, and scholarly explanation of Soviet economic stagnation.*

Simis, Konstantin. *USSR: The Corrupt Society.* New York: Simon and Schuster, 1982. *An inside view of Soviet political corruption and its roots in the system of central planning.*

Zaslavskaia, Tat'iana. "The Novosibirsk Report." *Survey* (Spring 1984): 91–95. *One of the early analyses, by a controversial sociologist, that inspired and supported the Gorbachev program.*

Yugoslavia

14

YUGOSLAVIA: WORKER-MANAGED SOCIALISM

*Our road is socialism and
we shall build a socialist
state here. . . . The
methods are not fixed,
but the goal is. . . . It is
true democracy which
can be achieved only
through socialism.*
—Josip Broz Tito
    Interview with George
    Seldes, 1957

The countries in Eastern Europe have provided an invaluable laboratory for institutional experimentation. The results of these experiments have inspired economic reforms in the Soviet Union, China, and the Third World. All of the countries in this region had market systems before World War II and they all adopted the Soviet system of central planning after the war. However, several of these countries, particularly those dependent on agricultural production and foreign trade, found that the Soviet system was ill-suited for their needs. Thus, systems of market socialism were adopted in Yugoslavia and Hungary, major economic and political reforms were attempted (unsuccessfully) in Czechoslovakia and Poland, and cautious alterations of the Soviet system were undertaken in East Germany.

Eastern Europe has played an important and conspicuous role in world history. Between 359 and 323 B.C., Philip of Macedonia (now a part of Yugoslavia) and his son Alexander the Great carved out an empire that extended to Egypt and India. An assassination in the Yugoslav town of Sarajevo precipitated World War I, and World War II was initiated by the Nazi invasions of Czechoslovakia and Poland. In subsequent years, the delicate balance of East-West relations has been strained by the Berlin blockade (1948–1949), the Hungarian revolt (1956), the Soviet invasion of Czechoslovakia (1968), and the rise of Solidarity and martial law in Poland (beginning in 1980).

We will begin this chapter with a general survey of the Eastern European environment, noting some of the national similarities and differences in history, culture, and geography. We will take a more detailed look at Yugoslavia, the first country in the region to break from the Soviet model with its system of workers' self-management and market socialism. (Chapter 15 will cover the other countries of Eastern Europe, with special emphasis on the Hungarian reforms.)

The Eastern European Environment

Eastern Europe forms a land bridge between Western Europe, the Soviet Union, and Asia Minor. Thus, unlike the Japanese and Swedes who have spent much of their history in relative seclusion, the nations of Eastern Europe sustained invasions by the Romans, Huns, Byzantines, Ottoman Turks, Swedes, Habsburgs, Germans, and Russians. Having passed from empire to empire, they inherited a legacy of cultural and economic heterogeneity.

The cultural diversity of Eastern Europe is perhaps most evident in the languages of the region, which fall into several broad families. A variety of Slavonic languages are spoken in Bulgaria, Czechoslovakia, Poland, and Yugoslavia. Elsewhere, one can find representatives of the Romance (Romanian), Finno-Ugric (Hungarian), Albanian, and Germanic families. In Yugoslavia alone, four major languages are spoken and two different alphabets are employed.

In their religious traditions, Bulgaria and Romania are predominantly Eastern Orthodox; Czechoslovakia, East Germany, Hungary, and Poland are Roman Catholic. Yugoslavia is divided between Catholics in the west, Orthodox believers in the east, and Muslims in the south. Albania was traditionally a

Table 14.1   Basic Data for Eastern Europe

	1985 Population (million)	1985 GNP (billion U.S. dollars)	1985 GNP Per Capita (dollars)	1980 Agriculture Share of Labor Force	1984 Infant Mortality Rate (per 1,000)
Albania	3.0	6.4	2,133	56%	43
Bulgaria	9.0	57.8	6,422	18	17
Czechoslovakia	15.5	135.6	8,748	13	15
East Germany	16.7	174.4	10,443	11	11
Hungary	10.6	80.1	7,557	18	19
Poland	37.2	240.6	6,468	29	19
Romania	22.7	123.7	5,449	29	25
Yugoslavia	23.1	129.4	5,602	32	28

Sources: First three columns—U.S. Central Intelligence Agency, *Handbook of Economic Statistics 1986* (CPAS 86-10002, September 1986), 35, 55; figures for Albania are rough estimates. The last two columns are drawn from World Bank, *World Development Report 1986*, 233, 239.

Muslim country, but its intensely Stalinist regime forbids all public and private worship. In Poland, where 90 percent of the population adheres to Catholicism, the power of the Communist Party is tempered by the political activity of the Church. In Yugoslavia, where the country is divided by languages, religions, and regional animosities, the immobility of the labor force contributes to a high rate of unemployment.

The geographic landscape of Eastern Europe includes the fertile plains of Hungary, Poland, and Germany; the plateaus of Czechoslovakia; and the hills and mountains of Albania, Bulgaria, Romania, and Yugoslavia. Albania and Yugoslavia, geographically the two countries most isolated from the Soviet Union, have taken the most independent stance on political and economic issues. Traversing the Adriatic coast, Yugoslavia is particularly well-situated to benefit from the tourist trade.

The uneven record of economic development in the region is summarized in Table 14.1. The countries that were dominated for hundreds of years by the Ottoman Turks—Albania, Bulgaria, Romania, and Yugoslavia—are still relatively backward. Czechoslovakia, East Germany, and Hungary, countries that lie farthest to the west, have attained the highest levels of economic development. In terms of income per capita, Albania is roughly on a par with the nations of Central America and East Germany is in the same economic league as Great Britain.

Yugoslavia: A Brief Economic History

Yugoslavia has been described as one country with two alphabets, three major religions, four major languages (and ten others that are commonly spoken), five nations, six federal republics, seven neighbors, and eight national banks.[1] It did not exist as a single country until the end of World War I, when it was formed by the merger of two states freed from the Ottoman Empire in the 1880s (Serbia and Montenegro) and three territories of the defeated Austro-Hungarian Empire (Croatia, Slovenia, and Bosna-Hercegovina). Although a constitutional monarchy was proclaimed in 1921, regional animosities and economic decay kept the new nation in a state of chronic civil war until it was invaded by the Axis powers in 1941.

World War II had a devastating impact on Yugoslavia. Nearly 300,000 farms were destroyed, and the systems of transportation and communication were rendered inoperable. About 11 percent of the population lost their lives in the war and 3.3 million people were left without homes.[2] At the same time, the war helped to unite the feuding nationalities against their common enemy. The Yugoslavs are still very proud of the fact that they were the only inhabitants of Eastern Europe to expel the Nazis without foreign assistance.

The war also produced a national hero, Josip Broz, known affectionately by his code name, Marshall Tito (meaning "little bird"). Born in Croatia in 1892, Tito fought in the Austrian army during World War I. He was captured by the Tsarist Russians in 1915 and, as a result, lived in Russia during the revolution. When he returned to Yugoslavia in 1920, Tito became a founding member of the Yugoslav Communist Party (YCP). He was appointed general secretary of the YCP in 1937, and in 1941 he left Belgrade to lead the Partisans in their fight for national liberation.

Tito was seriously wounded in combat in 1943; this contributed to his reputation as a war hero. He established a new socialist government after the war and ruled until his death in 1980. Today, the Yugoslav leaders attempt to preserve the memory of Tito with national holidays, posters, speeches, books, and news reports, all designed to maintain some semblance of national unity.

1945–1950: Central Planning

Immediately after the war, Tito and his associates attempted to transplant the Soviet political and economic systems into Yugoslavia. Less than 3 months after the end of the war, a law was passed that broke up all farms larger than 87 acres (most of which were owned by churches and foreigners) and distributed the land to those who tilled it. In 1946 a new Soviet-style constitution was adopted and nationalization of industry began. The Yugoslav program of nationalization was accomplished rather easily because foreigners owned about half of the capital stock outside of agriculture and almost all of the mines.

Central planning began with the adoption of the First Five-Year Plan in 1947. In their early efforts, the Yugoslavs pushed detailed planning to its extreme. The 1949 program, for example, was broken into 13,000 groups of

[1]Branko Horvat, *The Yugoslav Economic System* (Armonk: M. E. Sharpe, 1976), 3.

[2]Martin Schrenk, Cyrus Ardalan, and Nadal A. El Tatawy, *Yugoslavia: Self-Management Socialism and the Challenge of Development* (Baltimore: The Johns Hopkins University Press, 1979), 12.

commodities and included quarterly, monthly, and ten-day plans. The paper it was printed on weighed some 3,300 pounds.[3] The First Five-Year Plan, calling for an extremely ambitious doubling of the prewar level of income, was carried out quite successfully during the first 18 months.

Joseph Stalin and the other Soviet leaders undoubtedly welcomed the establishment of another new, successful, centrally planned economy in Eastern Europe, but they were enraged by several of Tito's other activities. The Yugoslav leader wanted to accept Western economic aid to speed recovery from the war and establish an independent federation of Balkan nations. When he sent his troops into Albania during the Greek civil war, Tito did not bother to consult with the Soviets. An argument eventually erupted over the role of the Soviet army in the liberation of Yugoslavia from the Nazis. Furthermore, Tito did not believe that the Yugoslav farmers, who supported him in his struggle against the Nazis, should be forced to form collective farms.

For these and other reasons, a war of words developed between Stalin and Tito. In 1948, a meeting of the Comintern (the Soviet-bloc political grouping) expelled Yugoslavia from the organization, and in 1949 the Soviet Union and its allies attempted to topple the Tito government by imposing a trade embargo. The Yugoslavs attempted to regain Soviet favor—by continuing their practice of central planning and by accelerating the collectivization of agriculture—until the end of 1949.

1951–1965: Introduction of Labor Management

In 1950, the ill effects of the trade embargo were compounded by a severe drought and the Yugoslav leaders decided to abandon the Soviet economic model, turning to the outside world for help. During that year they accepted financial aid from the United States (about $2 billion between 1950 and 1961) and adopted the "Basic Law on the Management of State Industries by Work Collectives."[4] Under this law, each enterprise was given the right to handle its own affairs through an elected workers' council (analogous to the stockholders of a capitalist firm), an elected management board (analogous to the board of directors), and an appointed manager.

In the years that followed, the Yugoslavs rapidly increased their distance from the Soviet model. A 1951 law replaced the system of detailed central planning with a system that Egon Neuberger has called the **Visible Hand.** The enterprises were allowed to set their own production targets, while the planners in Belgrade reserved the right to control investment, foreign trade, and the basic proportions of the economy.

In 1952, compulsory deliveries of agricultural commodities were abolished and price controls were lifted from a wide range of goods. Forced

---

[3]Branko Horvat, "Yugoslav Economic Policy in the Post-War Period," *American Economic Review* 61 (June 1971): 88.

[4]An English translation of the Basic Law is available in Branko Horvat, Mihailo Markovic, and Rudi Supek, eds., *Self-Governing Socialism,* vol. 1 (White Plains, N.Y.: International Arts and Sciences Press, 1975), Chapter 35.

collectivization of agriculture was abandoned altogether in 1953. Thus, state and collective farms occupy only 16 percent of Yugoslav farm land today. The vast majority of the farms are run by private families and cooperatives.

Constitutional amendments in 1953 strengthened the system of self-management and provided for the gradual transfer of a great deal of power from the federal and republican governments to the local communes, committees, and workers' councils. Accordingly, the number of employees in the central administration was cut by almost 80 percent between 1948 and 1956.[5]

The 1965 Reforms: Market Socialism

The economy grew rapidly during the second half of the 1950s (about 7.6 percent per year), leading to an acceleration of inflation and a balance of payments crisis in 1964 (Table 14.2). In that same year, at the Eighth Party Congress, a debate was joined between a conservative faction, which called for the return of detailed central planning and price control, and a liberal faction, which supported a broader program of market reform. With support from Tito, the liberal faction was successful, and the conservative faction was removed from the Party leadership. An ambitious new program of market-socialist reforms was initiated in 1965, including the following:

- Additional authority was transferred from the federal government to the republics.
- The social investment funds, previously allocated on a political basis by the federal government, were transferred to the banks, which were instructed to lend them on a profit-and-loss basis.
- Price subsidies were reduced and controlled prices were adjusted upward to world market levels. About 56 percent of producer prices and 70 percent of retail prices were free of controls by the end of 1968.
- The domestic market was opened to more foreign competition, a cumbersome system of multiple exchange rates was replaced with a single rate, and the dinar (the Yugoslav currency) was devalued.
- Enterprises were given greater autonomy in distributing their profits between investment expenditures and personal incomes for their workers.
- Central planning of basic proportions gave way to a more aggregative and voluntary system of indicative planning.

Together with these systemic changes, the central bank also initiated a policy of monetary restraint, leading to higher unemployment rates between 1965 and 1969, and simultaneously slowed the rate of consumer price inflation from 34 percent to 7.5 percent. Since that time, Yugoslavia has experienced several rounds of stop-go cycles as the authorities have alternated between stimulative measures to reduce unemployment and contractionary policies to control inflation and the international balance of payments.

---

[5]Laza Djodjic, "Thirty-Five Years of Socialist Self-Management in Yugoslavia," *Socialist Thought and Practice* 25 (November 1985): 36–37.

Table 14.2   Yugoslav Business Cycle Statistics

	Consumer Price Inflation	Unemployment Rate	International Current Account Balance (million U.S. dollars)
1962	3.0%	6.7%	− 48
1963	2.9	6.4	− 80
1964	11.9	5.6	− 203
1965	34.0	6.1	70
1966	22.4	6.7	− 39
1967	7.3	7.0	− 75
1968	5.7	8.0	− 95
1969	7.5	8.2	− 63
1970	11.0	7.7	− 348
1971	15.3	6.7	− 357
1972	16.4	7.0	419
1973	19.4	8.1	485
1974	21.0	9.0	− 1183
1975	24.1	10.2	− 1003
1976	11.6	11.4	165
1977	15.4	11.9	− 1582
1978	14.2	12.0	− 1256
1979	20.3	11.9	− 3661
1980	30.1	11.9	− 2291
1981	41.0	11.9	− 946
1982	32.1	12.4	− 464
1983	40.4	12.8	274
1984	55.0	13.3	504
1985	71.5	13.8	833
1986 ·	88.1	13.9	na

Sources: Organization for Economic Cooperation and Development, *Economic Survey: Yugoslavia,* various years; and International Labor Organization, *Yearbook of Labor Statistics,* various years.

Although the 1965 reforms probably increased the flexibility and allocative efficiency of the economic system, they also had a number of negative effects. First, as control of investment financing was transferred from the central planners to the banks, the underdeveloped regions were no longer given preferential treatment and received a smaller share of the nation's investment. At the same time, high birth rates in the backward regions increased their share of the total population; the problem of regional income inequality worsened. The income of the average Slovenian, which was five times larger than the income of the average resident of Kosovo in 1964, was six times larger in 1975 (Table 14.3).

Second, the increase in foreign competition and the reduction of price subsidies caused financial problems for many of the smaller producers, forcing

Table 14.3   Regional Inequality in Yugoslavia

	GNP Per Capita (dollars)	Gross Material Product Per Capita (percent of national average)				Unemployment Rate	
		1955	1964	1975	1983	1971	1983
Slovenia	10,937	175	187	201	197	2.7%	1.3%
Croatia	6,940	122	119	124	125	4.0	5.2
Vojvodina	6,662	94	116	121	120	6.1	12.4
Serbia	5,496	91	95	92	99	7.9	15.8
Montenegro	4,275	77	72	70	77	6.0	14.7
Bosnia-							
Hercegovina	3,831	83	69	69	69	5.6	13.8
Macedonia	3,609	68	73	69	65	17.3	21.5
Kosovo	1,388	43	37	33	25	18.6	27.3
Yugoslavia	5,552	100	100	100	100	6.7	11.9

Sources: *Statisticki Godisnjak Jugoslavije* (Belgrade; various years); and Branislav Soskic, "Employment in Yugoslavia," *Socialist Thought and Practice* 25 (June 1985): 63. The first column is estimated by applying the percentages in the fifth column to an estimate of national GNP per capita derived from U.S. Central Intelligence Agency, *Handbook of Economic Statistics 1985*, 35, 55.

them to merge with larger and stronger enterprises. The merger movement, in turn, contributed to the monopoly power of the larger enterprises and allowed them to grow too large for effective labor management.

The 1970s: Crisis and Constitutional Change

In the 1970s, the problems of regional inequality and industrial concentration were compounded by rising international oil prices and the Yugoslav atmosphere grew more restive. The inflation rate increased each year between 1969 and 1975; unemployment climbed each year between 1972 and 1978. Criticism of the policies of the central government led to nationalist movements in several of the republics, strikes, demonstrations, and violent protests.[6] In response, a number of important constitutional amendments were introduced in the early 1970s and a new constitution was adopted in 1974.

To relieve tension between the eight regions, an unusual system of political institutions was created by the 1974 constitution. First, the regions were given equal representation in the collective leadership of the national League of Communists. Since Marshall Tito's death in 1980, the job of party president has rotated each year to a representative of a different region. The state, as opposed to the Party, is headed by a **collective presidency**, which includes one member from each of the eight regions, plus the current Party president.

[6]See Steven Burg, *Conflict and Cohesion in Socialist Yugoslavia* (Princeton, N.J.: Princeton University Press, 1983), Chapter 3.

The regional representatives on the presidency rotate each year in the job of president.

According to the Yugoslav press, the collective presidency reaches its decisions through "equality-based discussion, through the adjustment of differences," and through "unanimity . . . in the interest of the entire Yugoslav community," rather than through majority voting.[7] In the opinion of foreign observers, the instability caused by rotation of the leadership and the difficulty of reaching regional unanimity have crippled the mechanism of policy formation in Yugoslavia.[8]

Beginning with constitutional amendments passed in 1971, efforts were made to break the power of the larger enterprises and to strengthen the institutions of self-management and indicative planning. To give the workers a larger stake in management, the enterprises were divided into so-called **basic organizations of associated labor** (BOALs), each with its own workers' council. With regard to planning, it was decided that the enterprises and governmental agencies would continue to compile their own plans, but the plans would gain legal force by the negotiation of social compacts between governmental agencies and self-management agreements between enterprises and BOALs. Thus, the laissez faire system of indicative planning was replaced by a more binding system of **contractual planning.**

Introduced during a period of worldwide recession, the 1976–1980 Five-Year Plan had little chance to succeed. It called for 7 percent annual growth of gross material product and 14 percent annual growth of exports. Instead, the former grew by 5.6 percent per year, and the latter grew by only 6 percent per year—less than half of the planned rate. Even worse, the international balance of payments moved from a small surplus in 1976 to a record deficit in 1980.

From the 1980s to the 1990s: In Search of Stability

After 3 decades of reform, Yugoslavia entered the 1980s beset with problems. It had a high unemployment rate and the highest inflation rate in Europe. On a per capita basis, its international indebtedness was the largest in Eastern Europe, including Poland, and the international value of the dinar dropped by about 50 percent during 1980 to 1981. As regional conflicts continued, deadly riots in Kosovo province led to the long-term imprisonment of some 400 dissidents.[9]

To cope with the balance of payments crisis, in early 1982 the government appointed a Commission for Problems of Economic Stabilization, which issued a series of 17 documents in 1982 and 1983. Collectively, the documents constituted the Long-Term Program of Economic Stabilization, which was in-

[7]"New Presidency of Yugoslavia to Be Elected," *Yugoslav Life* 29 (February–March 1984): 2.

[8]Steven Burg, "Elite Conflict in Post-Tito Yugoslavia," *Soviet Studies* 38 (April 1986): 170.

[9]Frederick Kempe, "Rebel Province Troubles Yugoslavia," *Wall Street Journal,* June 10, 1983, 27.

tended to guide governmental policy and legislation to the end of the century. The following were among the many recommendations of the program:[10]

- Adherence to a stronger set of national priorities and basic proportions within the system of decentralized planning that had been introduced in 1976.
- Initial tightening of price controls, followed by tighter monetary policy, and eventually followed by removal of controls.
- Reduction of subsidies and eventual closure of unprofitable enterprises.
- Adoption of higher interest rates to encourage saving and to rationalize investment, and a requirement that enterprises must finance part of any new investment project out of retained earnings.
- Adoption of a unified and realistic exchange rate, and discontinuation of the central allocation of foreign exchange borrowing rights between the regions.
- Reduction in the overall tax burden, and a shift from indirect taxes, which are thought to be inflationary, to direct taxes on income.

The 1982 stabilization program was designed primarily to arrest the international debt crisis; it was successful. In 1983, Yugoslavia posted its first balance of payments surplus in 7 years; the surpluses continued in 1984 and 1985 (Table 14.2). After rising from $6.5 billion in 1975 to $20 billion in 1982, the Yugoslav external debt remained roughly stable in the 3 years that followed.

On the domestic front, the stabilization program was less helpful. The rates of unemployment and inflation both climbed in 1983 and 1984, and economic growth came to a halt. Thinking that it had the balance of payments under control, in 1985 the government turned to an expansionary fiscal and monetary policy and suspended regulations that would require the closure of unprofitable businesses.

Unfortunately, these measures did not reduce the rate of unemployment and caused an acceleration of inflation and a return of the international payments problem. In 1986 the government returned to austerity. A temporary ban was imposed on noneconomic investment in schools, hospitals, and other public buildings, and resources were directed to the export sectors. Price controls were tightened and the dinar was devalued by 14 percent. During the first half of 1986, 108 enterprises were forced into bankruptcy, causing a net loss of 2,200 jobs (compared with 61 bankruptcies in all of 1985).[11]

Early in 1987, faced with rapid inflation and a need to reschedule its foreign debts, the government decided to take stiffer measures. Wages were

---

[10]The following discussion of the Long-Term Program is based on John Burkett, "Stabilization Measures in Yugoslavia," in U.S. Congress, Joint Economic Committee, *East European Economies: Slow Growth in the 1980s,* vol. 3 (Washington, D.C.: USGPO, 1986), 561–574; Budimir Lazovic, "Long-Term Program of Economic Stabilization," *Yugoslav Survey* 24 (November 1983): 3–26; and Milan Jovanovic, "Changes in Yugoslavia's Economic System," *Review of International Affairs* 35 (March 5, 1984): 24–28.

[11]Organization for Economic Cooperation and Development, *OECD Economic Surveys 1986/ 1987: Yugoslavia* (Paris: 1987), 22–23, 29.

frozen at the end-of-1986 level (rolling back increases that many workers had already received) and consumer prices increased. This did not please the workers and more than 50,000 of them walked off their jobs in protest. (In one case, patients were left unattended for a day at one of the largest hospitals in Belgrade.) In response, the government was forced to restore many of the pay increases.[12]

Operation of the Yugoslav Economic System

Enterprise Management

The system of workers' self-management was introduced by the 1950 Basic Law on the Management of State Industries by Work Collectives. However, under this law the enterprises remained subject to the visible hand of state control over investment, foreign trade, and distribution of profits. The enterprises were given greater autonomy by the 1965 reforms and greater reliance was placed on the market mechanism. Decentralization was increased by a 1971 constitutional amendment that divided the enterprises into self-managed basic organizations of associated labor (BOALs). This system was reinforced and operationalized by the 1974 constitution and by the 1976 Law on Associated Labor.

According to Yugoslav law, an enterprise is now a community of independent BOALs. The enterprise is a legal entity, headed by a workers' council and a general manager, but it directs the work of the BOALs by their consent. A BOAL can be established for any department, factory, or other group of workers whose performance can be evaluated apart from the other workers in the enterprise.[13] For example, 20 BOALs were established in Beogradska Konfeksia, a clothing company with 5,600 workers. These ranged in size from an 80-member association of maintenance engineers to a 700-member association of retail workers; the BOALs in the production divisions ranged between 250 and 450 members.

Each BOAL includes administrators and workers at all levels of skill. Each has its own assets, its own workers' council, and its own delegate to the workers' council of the larger enterprise. Each BOAL is free to hire and fire its own workers, to set its own prices and production levels, and to negotiate contractual self-management agreements with other BOALs. Any BOAL is free to withdraw from the enterprise if this does not violate the terms of its contracts; it can join another enterprise or operate independently.

The possible advantages of the system of worker management are quite obvious. Ideally, the workers are made the masters of their own fate, and the

---

[12]"Striking at the System," *Maclean's*, April 13, 1987, 21; "Law on Wages Amended," *Yugoslav Life* (February–April 1987): 4.

[13]The following discussion is based on Schrenk, Ardalan, and El Tatawy, *Yugoslavia*, Chapters 3 and 4; and on Christopher Prout, *Market Socialism in Yugoslavia* (London: Oxford University Press, 1985), 65–67.

RAKOVICA: THE BATTLE OF THE BOALs

Until recently, the Rakovica Motor Works was a confederation of 10 basic organizations of associated labor (BOALs), operating in suburban Belgrade. One BOAL built engines, another chassis, another transmissions, another handled maintenance, and another operated a mountain resort for the workers.

Annual plans for Rakovica were prepared by the general manager and debated by the central workers' council. There they were amended and sent to the BOALs. Any one of the BOALs could veto the plan and initiate another round of bargaining. According to Dragutin Zujovic, an employee at Rakovica, "If a department wants to be stubborn, it goes on forever."

After a plan was finally approved, each BOAL had to negotiate a self-management agreement with all of the other BOALs. To conclude these agreements, about 18,000 labor-hours were devoted to meetings every year, and bureaucrats constituted about 45 percent of the work force.

The main subject of negotiations, of course, was distribution of the company's profits among its constituent BOALs. When workers at Rakovica called strikes (about twice a year, on average), their grievance seldom involved general pay increases. Instead, it usually concerned the way the factory's dwindling income was divided between the BOALs. "We will never exchange our system for another," says a former director of the central workers' council, "but we have found that in a number of cases it does not work."

To reduce the squabbling, Rakovica recently decided to return to the version of self-management that prevailed in the 1960s. The BOALs were dissolved and the whole factory is run by one workers' council and one general manager. The manager still is not able to fire his workers and they are able (collectively) to fire him, but much has changed. According to Strahinja Kostic, the general manager at Rakovica, a janitor could influence the organization of work under the BOAL bureaucracy, but now "managers make decisions."

Source: Adapted from Barry Newman, "Change of Heart: Yugoslavia's Workers Find Self-Management Doesn't Make Paradise," *The Wall Street Journal,* March 25, 1987, 1, 18. Reprinted by permission of *The Wall Street Journal,* © Dow Jones & Company, Inc. 1987. All Rights Reserved.

link between their labor and their income should be stronger than in either capitalism or planned socialism. Thus, there should be a lower level of alienation and a stronger system of incentives. These benefits must be balanced, however, against the time that is lost when thousands of workers are involved in council and committee meetings (see "Rakovica: The Battle of the BOALs," p. 326). Furthermore, theoretical analysis of the labor-managed enterprise suggests that it may behave inefficiently under certain assumptions (see Appendix 14A). A recent statistical study suggests that the level of labor productivity, adjusted for differences in educational levels and capital endowments, is higher in Yugoslavia than in other socialist countries, but lower than the level in the industrial capitalist world.[14]

From the consumers' perspective, self-management has an advantage over central planning because the former is driven by consumer demand, where the latter is controlled by planners' preferences. Thus, most observers would agree that Yugoslav consumer goods are superior in their style, variety, and quality to those in many of the more developed countries of Eastern Europe. For example, the Yugo was the first car from Eastern Europe to sell in significant numbers on the U.S. market.

The system of self-management may also provide a partial solution to the problem of environmental pollution. In capitalist and centrally planned economies, decisions to pollute the air and water in a locality often are made by stockholders and planners who live elsewhere. The decision to pollute Lake Michigan is made in New York, and Lake Baikal is sacrificed in Moscow. Under local control, a Yugoslav workers' council would presumably pay greater attention to the needs and desires of the community. If the profit that can be generated by polluting a lake is smaller than its perceived value for health and recreation, the lake will not be polluted.[15] In this sense, the system of self-management may allow a closer approximation to Milton Friedman's free-to-choose society, because it requires less governmental control of environmental quality.

It is difficult to say how much genuine labor management is conducted in Yugoslavia. In a 1980 survey of workers, 57 percent of the respondents agreed with the statement, "I don't have a feeling of being a self-manager in the work organization," and 62 percent said, "I don't have any influence on the members of the self-management bodies in the work organization."[16] Statements such as these do not reflect well on the depth of labor management, but, in comparison, voters in democratic societies are similarly uncertain of their influence on the political process. Yugoslav workers may question the power of their franchise, but they do not want to give it up.

---

[14]Abram Bergson, "Comparative Productivity: The USSR, Eastern Europe, and the West," *The American Economic Review* 77 (June 1987): 352–353.

[15]This, of course, is only a partial solution. For the sake of profit, an enterprise in one Yugoslav town may pollute a river with little consideration for other towns downstream.

[16]Vlado Arzensek, "Problems of Yugoslav Self-Management," in *International Yearbook of Organizational Democracy,* vol. 1, ed. Colin Crouch and Frank Heller (Chichester: John Wiley, 1983), 307.

Employment and Labor Relations

It is ironic that Yugoslavia, a labor-managed socialist economy, is plagued by more unemployment and labor unrest than many capitalist countries. About 13.9 percent of the labor force was unemployed in 1986, rising to more than 20 percent if it were to include those workers who have traveled to West Germany and other countries to find jobs.[17]

Yugoslav unemployment has several causes. First, for demographic reasons, the total labor force grows by about 100,000 per year and almost as many move out of agriculture every year. Many of these new entrants live in the most backward sections of the country where job opportunities are few. Because of linguistic and cultural barriers, workers are not willing to move from their native regions, causing a high rate of structural unemployment. Thus, in 1983 the unemployment rate was only 1.3 percent in Slovenia, but it was over 20 percent in Kosovo and Macedonia (Table 14.3).

Another possible cause of structural unemployment is the reluctance of some worker-managed enterprises to take on new workers. Successful enterprises are unwilling to absorb unemployed workers, it is said, because this will require them to divide their profits between a larger number of employees.

Finally, much of the unemployment in recent years has resulted from tight fiscal and monetary policies that are designed to reduce inflation and strengthen the balance of payments. The unemployment rate, which barely changed between 1962 and 1972 (the year before the first international oil crisis), has almost doubled since that time (Table 14.2).

It is interesting to note that worker management has not eliminated the need for labor unions. A Yugoslav social scientist gives the following explanation:

Irrespective of the fact that socialist self-management constitutes the gist of the political system, there are phenomena of bureaucratic or technocratic violations of the direct interests or needs of either individuals or groups. . . . It is in such instances that the Trade Union is brought under obligation to act directly. In case of a strike, the Trade Union is obliged to directly help in resolving the conflict. . . .[18]

Yugoslav law has never acknowledged the possibility that strikes would occur in a labor-managed economy. Thus, strikes are neither allowed nor forbidden. When they do occur, they usually take one of two forms. Strikes that are called within an enterprise usually involve disputes over the division of income between BOALs. These usually include only a few workers and end quickly—in one day or less. Concessions are usually made quickly by the enterprise management to avoid attention.[19] Broader strikes are sometimes

[17]In fairness, sample surveys indicate that high incomes abroad, not a lack of employment opportunities in Yugoslavia, is the major force motivating emigration. Prout, *Market Socialism in Yugoslavia,* 134–135.

[18]Rados Smiljkovic, "Role of Socio-Political Organizations," *Yugoslav Life* (November–January 1986–1987): 3.

[19]Prout, *Market Socialism in Yugoslavia,* 50–52.

called to protest governmental policies, for example, the 1987 strikes against a governmental wage freeze, which involved more than 50,000 workers.

The Financial System

The Yugoslav financial system has passed through several important stages. First, during 1945 to 1951, the traditional Soviet system was adopted. Prices were centrally controlled, causing some enterprises to earn large profits and others to sustain large losses. These differences were ironed out by a system of taxes and subsidies. Investment decisions were made by central planners, based on a mix of political and economic criteria, and financed out of governmental funds.

The introduction of worker management in 1951 led to some relaxation of price controls and provided the enterprises with a stronger profit motive. To encourage enterprises to economize on the use of capital, the government introduced a 6 percent annual interest charge in 1954. The government continued to provide generous subsidies to prevent bankruptcies and maintained budgetary control over investment.

Decentralization was introduced in 1963 in response to heated disputes between the rich and poor regions of the country caused by the centralized system of investment allocation. The Federal Investment Fund was abolished and its assets were distributed between the Investment Bank, the Bank for Foreign Trade, and the Agricultural Bank. In connection with the 1965 reforms, control of the banks was transferred from governmental authorities to the enterprises that use the banks' services. Enterprises could pool their funds to establish a new bank, and the enterprises, not the workers' council of the bank, would control its business and credit policy.

The 1965 reforms also gave the enterprises greater control over the distribution of their profits between retained earnings and personal income. With this freedom, the enterprises reduced their rate of saving by about 20 percent between 1965 and 1970. In a Yugoslav enterprise, the workers have little incentive to plow their profits back into investment because they do not have a true stake in the ownership of the factory. They share in the current profits of the enterprise, but they lose all rights to these profits when they leave or retire. Unlike a capitalist owner, who recaptures the value of saving and investment when he sells his stock, the Yugoslav worker leaves empty handed.[20]

Because of their reluctance to invest from retained earnings, Yugoslav workers generally prefer to finance investments with bank debt, to be repaid by future generations of workers in the enterprise. Their ability to obtain bank financing was enhanced by the 1965 reform, which placed the banks under enterprise control. Reliance on debt rather than equity may contribute to the

---

[20]This aspect of labor management has been emphasized in the work of Eirik Furubotn and Svetozar Pejovich, *The Economics of Property Rights* (Cambridge: Ballinger, 1974).

financial weakness of the enterprise and to the inflationary growth of the money supply.[21]

The 1965 reform was accompanied by a tight monetary and fiscal policy; this caused the inflation rate to slow from 34 percent in 1965 to 6 percent in 1968. Beginning in 1969, the rate began to rise again. It was decided that inflation was caused by rapid growth of the money supply, which, in turn, was caused by the factors outlined above. Under the new system of planning established in 1971, limits were again placed on the proportion of profits that enterprises could pay out as personal income.

According to legislation adopted in 1977 and 1985, Yugoslav business banks were divided into three categories: basic, associated, and internal banks. **Basic banks,** numbering 169 at the end of 1985, provide commercial and investment banking services to business and the general public. They are usually founded and owned by enterprises and governed by delegates of the founders, who vote in proportion to their investment shares. At most, 10 percent of the bank's lending can be directed to a single borrower.

The nine **associated banks** are founded and managed by two or more basic banks and provide check-clearing, foreign-exchange, and other services for their members. They cannot hold checking or savings accounts for the general public. Their role is somewhat similar to that of bank holding companies in the United States. **Internal banks** are established by groups of enterprises for their private use and to encourage the pooling of enterprise funds.[22]

In recent years, the ability of the central bank—the National Bank of Yugoslavia—to control inflation has been hindered by the extensive use of trade credits between enterprises. The central bank has slowed the growth of bank lending, but it has little control over the rate of business lending. Thus, the share of trade credits in enterprise liabilities increased from 37 to 46 percent between 1980 and 1985, while the share of bank credits dropped from 51 to 39 percent.[23] When these debts must be retired by payment with currency and bank deposits, the government falls under political pressure to inject new credit. These emergency measures are now so common that a number of Yugoslav economists believe that inflation is caused by uncontrolled, endogenous growth in the money supply.[24]

Prices

While Yugoslav inflation is caused in part by uncontrolled monetary growth, a number of other factors may also contribute to the problem. Under the system

---

[21]For a fuller discussion of these issues, see Saul Estrin and Michael Connock, "Ideas of Industrial Democracy in Eastern Europe: A Comment From the Yugoslav Perspective," *The ACES Bulletin* 25 (Spring 1983): 67–73.

[22]A detailed description and analysis of the financial system is provided in Organization for Economic Cooperation and Development, *OECD Economic Surveys 1986/1987: Yugoslavia,* 32–57.

[23]Ibid., 38.

[24]See Shirley Gedeon, "Monetary Disequilibrium and Bank Reform Proposals in Yugoslavia: Paternalism and the Economy," *Soviet Studies* 39 (April 1987): 281–291.

Table 14.4   Yugoslav Price Controls (Percentages of Producer Prices)

	January 1985	July 1986
Administered by the Federal Executive Council	16.9	7.4
Requiring approval of the Federal Bureau of Prices (FBP)	2.5	31.1
Requiring advance notice (30 days) to buyers and the FBP	48.0	—
Obligatory 120-day notice to the FBP	—	42.4
Freely changed without notification	35.1	37.6
Cost-linked automatic increases	—	6.8
Total	100.0	100.0

Source: Organization for Economic Cooperation and Development, *OECD Economic Surveys 1986/1987: Yugoslavia* (Paris: 1987), 69.

of labor management, workers may vote to grant themselves a pay increase and then attempt to pass the cost along to the consumers in higher prices. Their ability to increase prices may be strengthened by the high level of concentration on many markets. In addition, on a number of occasions Yugoslavia has been caught in a vicious circle of balance of payments deficits, which require devaluations of the dinar, which cause import costs to rise, which cause inflation, which cause another round of payments deficits.

For these and other reasons, the Yugoslav inflation rate remained in double digits during all of the years between 1970 and 1985. To deal with this problem, the government has maintained a complicated system of price control that is adjusted through time and varies from one commodity group to another. Since 1980, in keeping with the philosophy of self-management, a substantial part of the power to fix prices has been transferred from the federal level to so-called Communities for Prices, composed of producers and regional government officials. Recent trends in the system of price control are indicated in Table 14.4.

Self-Management and Economic Performance

Yugoslavia has maintained a very respectable rate of economic growth with its unusual economic system of self-management, despite its regional problems. Between 1965, the year of the market reform, and 1984, Yugoslav GNP per capita grew at an annual rate of 4.3 percent, compared to a rate of 3.3 percent for other upper-middle-income countries and 2.4 percent for other countries in Eastern Europe.[25] At the same time, Yugoslavia has maintained a better record of income equality than the majority of developing nations (Table A.24).

Other advantages of the Yugoslav system are more difficult to quantify. It is difficult to measure the psychological advantages, for example, that some

[25]The World Bank, *World Development Report 1986* (New York: Oxford University Press, 1986), 181; and U.S. Central Intelligence Agency, *Handbook of Economic Statistics 1985* (CPAS 85–10001, September 1985), 40.

workers gain from participation in management. Likewise, it is difficult to measure the impact of self-management on environmental quality and to place a value on the ability of the Yugoslav market system to meet the demands of consumers.

Finally, although it is difficult to separate cause from effect, the relatively liberal economic system in Yugoslavia is associated with a broader system of political and social freedom than one finds elsewhere in Eastern Europe. Yugoslavs have been allowed to travel freely outside of their country since 1963, and few limits are placed on religious and artistic expression. On the other hand, the press is still controlled by the government, and national elections usually offer one candidate for each office.

On the negative side of the ledger, Yugoslavia has chronic problems with its inflation, unemployment, and balance of payments. Another problem, expressed by the president of the Yugoslav Trade Union Confederation, is that worker management "is often slow, irrational, burdened by formalism and by the duplication of decisions concerning the same thing."[26] Labor unrest has increased in recent years, and the results of public opinion surveys cause us to question the true level of labor participation in management. Finally, the role of the individual entrepreneur is unclear in a system of collective management.

While Yugoslavia may not be the most successful country in the world, its independence and creativity is an inspiration to many.

Summary

Eastern Europe has played an important role in world history and in the history of economic systems. After centuries of invasions, the countries in the area exhibit a diversity of cultures, languages, religions, and levels of economic development. Yugoslavia, in particular, is internally divided by national and religious hostilities. World War II devastated Yugoslavia, but it also unified the country under Marshall Tito—a war hero.

Soviet-style central planning and management were conducted from 1945 to 1950, during which time agriculture was collectivized. Conflicts between Tito and Stalin led, however, to the expulsion of Yugoslavia from the Soviet bloc in 1948. Legislation in 1950–1951 created a system of workers' self-management and replaced detailed central planning with planning of basic proportions. Price controls were gradually released and forced collectivization of agriculture was abandoned.

Economic reforms in 1965 replaced the system of basic proportions planning with market relations and indicative planning. Control over investment resources was shifted from the governmental budget to the banks. In the 1970s, self-management was decentralized to the enterprise department level through creation of the BOALs and a new system of contractual planning was

[26]Laza Djodjic, "Thirty-Five Years," 40.

adopted. During the 1980s, a number of stabilization programs have been devised to handle balance of payments problems. These programs, which have caused rising unemployment, bankruptcies, and reductions in real income, have met stiff public opposition.

According to Yugoslav law, an enterprise is now a community of independent BOALs, each with its own assets and workers' council, coordinated by a central workers' council and a general director. If the BOALs are not cooperative, operation of the enterprise can be very slow and bureaucratic. Strikes, neither allowed nor forbidden by law, nonetheless occur.

Fixed investment is now financed through the banking system, and the banks are owned and operated by the productive enterprises. Yugoslavia usually has a high rate of inflation. Many economists believe that enterprise control over the banking system may be one of the causes, and worker control over wages may be another.

Along with chronic inflation, other problems in Yugoslavia include high rates of unemployment and foreign indebtedness, a limited role for individual entrepreneurs, and a limited amount of true self-management. On the other hand, Yugoslavia has out-performed other middle-income countries in terms of economic growth and income equality, and the system of self-management may have advantages in its control of environmental quality. The Yugoslav borders are open; thus those who dislike the system are free to leave.

Discussion and Review Questions

1.   How has the multinational character of the Yugoslav population affected the structure and performance of their economic system?

2.   Explain the differences between the three major forms of economic planning—directive, indicative, and contractual—that have been used in Yugoslavia.

3.   What is a BOAL? When and why were they created? What are their rights and responsibilities?

4.   What are some of the causes of Yugoslav unemployment? What governmental policies would you suggest to reduce it?

5.   Why is it widely believed that Yugoslav enterprises are unwilling to invest out of their retained earnings? Does this reluctance have any macroeconomic significance?

Suggested Readings

Burg, Steven. *Conflict and Cohesion in Socialist Yugoslavia.* Princeton, N.J.: Princeton University Press, 1983. *A scholarly discussion of Yugoslav regional affairs and their influence on the political and economic system.*

Horvat, Branko. *The Yugoslav Economic System.* Armonk, N.Y.: M. E. Sharpe, 1976. *An insider's account of the operation and performance of Yugoslav institutions and the academic debates that formed them.*

Horvat, Branko, Mihailo Markovic, and Rudi Supek, eds. *Self-Governing Socialism.* 2 vols. White Plains, N.Y.: International Arts and Sciences Press, 1975. *A compendium of articles and documents on the theoretical and practical roots of self-management.*

Prout, Christopher. *Market Socialism in Yugoslavia.* London: Oxford University Press, 1985. *A brief survey of the system with separate chapters on the markets for goods, labor, and capital.*

Schrenk, Martin, Cyrus Ardalan, and Nadal El Tatawy. *Yugoslavia: Self-Management Socialism and the Challenge of Development.* Baltimore: The Johns Hopkins University Press, 1979. *A wide-ranging World Bank report, this is one of the most comprehensive assessments of the Yugoslav system.*

Vanek, Jaroslav. *The Theory of Labor-Managed Market Economies.* Ithaca, N.Y.: Cornell University Press, 1970. *A good general introduction to the body of theoretical literature that is addressed in Appendix 14A.*

14A

APPENDIX

THE THEORY OF THE LABOR-MANAGED FIRM

A large body of theoretical analysis, now including hundreds of articles in the English language alone, was inspired by the introduction of workers' self-management in Yugoslavia after 1951. A brief look at this literature reveals something about the peculiarities of the Yugoslav firm and, equally interesting, about the role of assumptions in economic theory.

The seminal work in this field was Ben Ward's 1958 study of the idealized Illyrian firm (Illyria was the ancient name for part of Yugoslavia).[1] Unlike the capitalist firm, which theoretically attempts to maximize total profits, Ward assumes that the worker-managed firm will attempt to maximize profits per worker. Whereas the capitalist firm can hire additional employees at a market-fixed wage, the new employee in a worker-managed firm will receive a share of the company's profits.

Assume, for simplicity's sake, that a firm employs L workers as its only variable input, and it pays a fixed rent of R dinars per month to the government for the use of its factory. Also assume that the firm produces Q units of output according to the same kind of production function that is employed in the standard textbook theory of the capitalist firm, and it sells its output in a competitive market at a price of P dinars per unit. Income per worker (Y/L) is equal to total revenue (PQ) minus total cost (R), divided by employment (L):

$$Y/L = \frac{PQ - R}{L} = P\,(Q/L) - R/L$$

As rearranged, this equation states that income per worker is equal to the value of the average product of labor minus rental cost per worker. According to the standard production function, which states that the average product of labor (Q/L) first rises and then falls as more workers are hired, the value of the average product of labor will also rise and then fall. A graph of Q/L and P(Q/L) is presented in Figure 14A.1 for two different values of P. Notice that an increase in P shifts the P(Q/L) curve upward and changes its shape as its sides become steeper.

In Figure 14A.2, the graph of P(Q/L) is joined by a graph of R/L, the other half of the income formula. In the short run, with the amount of capital fixed, R/L slopes downward to the right as the fixed rental cost is spread over a larger number of workers (technically, it is represented by a rectangular hyperbola). Income per worker is represented by the vertical distance between the P(Q/L) and R/L curves.

[1]Benjamin Ward, "The Firm in Illyria: Market Syndicalism," *American Economic Review* 48 (September 1958): 566–589.

Figure 14A.1   The Average Product of Labor and the Value of the Average Product of Labor

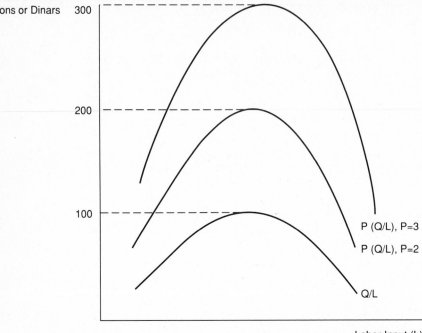

Tons or Dinars

300

200

100

P (Q/L), P=3

P (Q/L), P=2

Q/L

Labor Input (L)

How many workers should the firm hire to maximize income per worker? According to the graph, the firm can maximize sales revenue per worker—P(Q/L)—by hiring 30 employees. If additional workers are hired, it will reduce P(Q/L) but, up to a certain point, it will yield an even larger reduction in cost per worker—R/L. To maximize income per worker, hiring should continue until the last worker reduces P(Q/L) and R/L by the same amount. Graphically, this will occur at the level of employment where lines drawn tangent to the two curves (AA and BB) have identical slopes. Thus, the firm depicted in Figure 14A.2 will hire 40 workers.

Now, how will the firm react if the price of its product increases? As noted in Figure 14A.1, an increase in P will cause the P(Q/L) curve to shift upward and become steeper. In terms of Figure 14A.2, the slope of AA will become steeper than the slope of BB if 40 workers are employed. A reduction in employment will be necessary to flatten AA and to steepen BB until they are equal again and Y/L is at a new maximum. If the increase in P causes a reduction in employment, however, it will also cause a reduction in the output of the firm. The firm has a negatively sloped supply curve for its product.

The result just obtained is significant in several respects. First, if nothing else, it tells us that a seemingly small change in assumptions can cause a major change in the outcome of an economic theory. In this version of his theory,

Figure 14A.2   Maximization of Income Per Worker

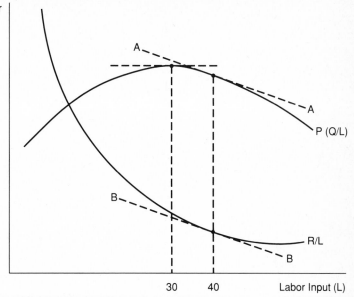

Ward retained all of the technology and market-structure assumptions of the theory of perfect competition, but replaced maximization of profits with maximization of profits-per-worker. This single alteration reversed the basic conclusion of the theory—the upward-sloping capitalist supply curve became a downward-sloping Illyrian supply curve.

More important, the theory suggests that markets in a Yugoslav-style economy could be unstable. If a particular product is in short supply, causing the price of the product to rise, this could cause a decline in production that would make the shortage even more severe. If the majority of markets were to work in this way, worker management would surely be an unworkable system.

Fortunately, the theoretical stability of the labor-managed market economy can be salvaged in any of several ways. First, even if the supply curves are negatively sloped, if they are steeper than the demand curves the markets will be stable. In this circumstance, a price above the equilibrium level will generate a surplus of the product in question, causing the price to fall back toward the equilibrium.[2]

Second, the labor-managed firm may have a positively sloped supply curve if labor is not its only variable input or if it produces more than one final product. Like a capitalist firm, the Illyrian firm will employ each non-labor

[2]Technically, this assumes a Walrasian price-adjustment mechanism rather than a Marshallian quantity-adjustment mechanism. For Marshallian stability, the demand curves must be steeper than the negatively sloped supply curves.

input up to the point where the value of its marginal product equals its price. Depending on the relative height and steepness of the marginal productivity curves of labor and other inputs, the supply curve may be positively or negatively sloped. In general, we can only say that the supply curve of the labor-managed firm will be less elastic than that of a comparable capitalist firm.[3]

Third, it has been shown that the current output of the labor-managed firm should depend not only on current prices, but also on future price expectations. If an increase in a price today causes us to expect that price to fall again in the future, then the supply elasticity of the firm will be greater than is usually supposed. On the other hand, if price expectations are elastic—a price rise causes us to expect more price rises—the possibility of a negative supply response is enhanced.[4]

Finally, several authors have disputed the validity of the entire body of Illyrian literature that is based on the static maximization of income per worker. In the opinion of Branko Horvat, a well-known Yugoslav economist, "It is a great merit of Ward's original article, which so bluntly stated the absurd neoclassical consequences, that it has forced us to undertake the reexamination of the theoretical foundations."[5] Horvat believes that the behavior of the Yugoslav firm can be described more accurately by the solution of a multiyear dynamic program, in which income per worker is maximized subject to a set of six constraints. These include upper and lower boundaries on wages and a requirement that a certain fraction of the firm's investments must be financed out of the firm's own funds. Horvat has not derived any solutions to his program, however, "since our knowledge about the behavior of worker-managers is still very imperfect."[6]

[3]Jaroslav Vanek, *The Theory of Labor-Managed Market Economies* (Ithaca, N.Y.: Cornell University Press, 1970), Chapter 3.

[4]David C. Wong, "A Two-Period Model of the Competitive Socialist Labor-Managed Firm," *Journal of Comparative Economics* 10 (September 1986): 313–324.

[5]Branko Horvat, "Farewell to the Illyrian Firm," *Economic Analysis and Workers' Management* 20 (1986): 29.

[6]Branko Horvat, "The Theory of the Worker-Managed Firm Revisited," *Journal of Comparative Economics* 10 (March 1986): 20–25.

Eastern Europe

15

HUNGARY AND EASTERN EUROPE: PLAN AND MARKET

It is essential that we should focus our thoughts on the stable resettlement of the affairs of East Europe and the Heartland. If we accept anything less than a complete solution of the Eastern question in its largest sense we shall merely have gained a respite, and our descendants will find themselves under the necessity of marshalling their power afresh for the siege of the Heartland.
—H. J. Mackinder
  Democratic Ideals and Reality, 1919

In this chapter, we continue our survey of Eastern European economies. With the exception of Albania, all of the countries in this chapter are members of the Warsaw Pact and the Council for Mutual Economic Assistance (CMEA)—a foreign trade and investment association based in Moscow. Thus, unlike Yugoslavia, which is the leader of the so-called nonaligned movement, the policies of these countries are constrained by Soviet economic and military power.

Our primary focus will be on Hungary; of the countries covered here, it has undertaken the most extensive economic reforms. More briefly, we will survey the East German reforms, the rise and fall of Solidarity in Poland, the "Prague Spring" in Czechoslovakia, and the economic systems of the Balkan Triangle—Albania, Bulgaria, and Romania.

Hungary: Administrative Market Socialism

Hungary did not provide a receptive environment for the Soviet version of socialism. Laszlo Nemeth, a noted Hungarian socialist, predicted in 1943 that Stalinism "would be barely distinguishable from slavery, since Hungary would be governed by alien outsiders."[1] Poor in natural resources, Hungary was the most trade-dependent country in the Soviet bloc, and central planning was (and is) too inflexible to respond effectively to the requirements of the international market.[2]

When relatively free elections were held in Hungary in 1945, the Hungarian Socialist Workers' Party (HSWP) could muster only 17 percent of the vote. This nonetheless gave them a role in the coalition government, including control of the Ministry of Interior. Using this as their power base, and backed by the occupying Red Army, they eliminated their opposition through imprisonment and exile. For example, Roman Catholic Archbishop Mindszenty was convicted of espionage in 1949 and sentenced to life imprisonment. Matyas Rakosi, the hard-line Stalinist head of the HSWP, candidly explained that they employed "salami tactics"—slicing off their enemies one by one. Nationalization of industry and collectivization of agriculture began in 1948, and in 1949 a new constitution proclaimed that the HSWP was the sole political actor in Hungary.

The First Five-Year Plan (1950–1954), formulated when Rakosi was concurrently premier and head of the HSWP, followed the Stalinist model of ambitious growth and emphasis on heavy industry. This strategy worked well enough for 2 years, but neglect of light industry and agriculture led to an actual decline in national income in 1952. In 1953, immediately after Stalin's death, Rakosi was summoned to Moscow and ordered to accept Imre Nagy as his premier. Nagy's agenda, the New Course, included a return to moderate

---

[1]Quoted in Adam Zwass, *Market, Plan, and State* (Armonk, N.Y.: M. E. Sharpe, 1987), 132.

[2]For comparisons of Eastern European dependence on foreign trade, see Eleftherios Botsas, "Patterns of Trade," in *Eastern Europe in the 1980s,* ed. Stephen Fisher-Galati (Boulder, Colo.: Westview Press, 1981), 90.

and balanced economic growth, a relaxation of forced collectivization, and freedom for political prisoners. The economy began to recover and the public gained a respite from Rakosi's terror.

In the Soviet Union, in February 1955, Khrushchev (the heavy industry–oriented Party leader) obtained a resignation from Malenkov (the consumer-oriented premier). It is no coincidence that shortly thereafter Rakosi (also a heavy industry–oriented Party leader) obtained a resignation from Nagy (a consumer-oriented premier). Rakosi attempted a return to his previous policies, but this time he led a divided party.

The 1956 Hungarian Revolt

In 1956, Hungary was again shaken by international events. In February, Khrushchev denounced Stalin's criminal deeds in his stunning "secret speech" to the Party Congress. This led to a violent strike against the Stalinist regime of Hilary Minc in Poland, and to its replacement in October with the more moderate leadership of Wladyslaw Gomulka.

Later in October 1956, a peaceful demonstration against Rakosi's Stalinist regime in Hungary drew a brutal response from security forces. The violence escalated and Soviet tanks joined the battle to restore order. The Soviets allowed Imre Nagy to regain leadership of the government and authorized him to initiate a series of moderate reforms. They got more than they intended. Nagy's government allowed freedom of the press, disbanded the security police, appealed to the United Nations to pressure Soviet troops out of Hungary, repudiated their association with the Warsaw Pact, and declared neutrality for Hungary. Yugoslav-style workers' councils were spontaneously established in many of the factories.

In November 1956, while the world's attention was distracted by the U.S. presidential election and the Suez crisis, Soviet tanks and troops crushed Hungary's attempt to defect from the Warsaw Pact. In connection with the hostilities, 2,900 Hungarians were killed, 13,000 were wounded, and 200,000 fled the country. At least 200 people were executed, including Nagy and his officials.

Agricultural Reforms

Janos Kadar, the new Soviet-installed leader, skillfully balanced Soviet demands for orthodoxy with Hungarian demands for independence. In 1957 he was required by the Soviets to resume the collectivization of agriculture. To satisfy domestic demands, he spread the program over 4 years and encouraged membership on cooperatives using incentives other than force.[3] New members were paid cash for the land they contributed to the cooperative, they were allowed to keep their livestock, and they were encouraged to maintain private

---

[3]See Michael Marrese, "Agricultural Performance and Policy in Hungary," *Journal of Comparative Economics* 7 (September 1983).

plots. Party appointment of farm leaders was replaced with a system of free elections. Compulsory delivery of agricultural goods was abolished, and the state increased the supply of equipment and chemicals to the farms.

Based on the success of the first round of agricultural reforms, another round began in 1965. Obligatory plan targets were abandoned and the farms were allowed to formulate their own plans for most products. State purchasing prices were raised to increase agricultural profits; the farms were allowed to use their profits for decentralized investment. Credit and tools were made available to individual farmers for use on their private plots.

The New Economic Mechanism

In industry, Kadar dissolved the workers' councils but also introduced a modest program of reforms in the late 1950s. He reduced the number of compulsory plan targets, amended the material incentive system to reward profitability and technological improvements, and introduced an interest charge on the use of fixed assets. These measures, however, had little lasting effect on economic performance. After a period of rapid growth in the late 1950s, the Hungarian economy began to decelerate in the early 1960s. In 1964, the Central Committee called for a full-scale discussion of the management of the economy. Based on the successes in agricultural reform, a 1966 decree called for major changes in the economic system.

Introduced in 1968, the so-called New Economic Mechanism (NEM) set Hungary on the road to market socialism. With the NEM, the Hungarians instituted a broader program of reform than the Soviet Union and its other Eastern European allies have accomplished in the 2 decades that have followed:

- Detailed central planning of output and delivery was replaced with a limited market mechanism and a system of macroeconomic indicative planning.
- In place of bonuses for plan fulfillment, the profit motive became the centerpiece of the material incentive system.
- Aside from raw materials and consumer staples, price controls were lifted from a wide range of products, and many other prices were allowed to fluctuate within limits.
- The state monopoly of foreign trade was weakened as a number of enterprises were given permission to trade on international markets without the intervention of the foreign trade ministry. To guide the decisions of the enterprises, the system of multiple exchange rates was replaced with a single, more realistic, rate.

Although these were revolutionary changes in the Eastern European context, several important features of the previous system were retained. First, in order to prevent the return of Soviet tanks, the reformers did not attempt to change the political system. They were careful to preserve a leading role for the HSWP and remained loyal to the Warsaw Pact. Hungary now had a system of market socialism, but unlike Yugoslavia, it did not adopt workers' self-management. The party/ministry hierarchy, not workers' councils, retained the authority to hire and fire enterprise managers. Furthermore, the government maintained direct control over half of all investment expenditures.

Second, in order to forestall domestic opposition, the reformers protected the population from many of the unpleasant consequences of the market system. Most important, they prevented an increase in unemployment by subsidizing enterprises that would have been driven into bankruptcy by market forces. Although the system of subsidies weakened the profit incentive, propped up a number of inefficient producers, and allowed the continued production of unwanted goods, it was deemed a political necessity.

The NEM proceeded smoothly for several years. The deceleration of economic growth was reversed, and the growth rate of total factor productivity doubled from 1962 to 1967, and again from 1967 to 1972.[4] During this time, Hungary began to experience several of the same problems that plagued Yugoslavia. In both countries, the reformers inherited a monopolistic market structure from the central planners, who found it easier to control and monitor a small number of large firms. Thus, in 1968 there were only 840 industrial enterprises in all of Hungary. Critics of the NEM questioned the efficiency of monopolistic market socialism and argued that it would promote income inequality. In fact, recent studies have shown that Hungarian wages grew more unequal from 1966 to 1974.[5]

The 1970s: Losing Ground

For these and other reasons, the NEM began to fail in 1972. A number of new controls were introduced in early 1973, followed shortly by the explosion of the international price of oil. In a vain attempt to protect the domestic economy from inflationary pressure, the government expanded its system of price subsidies. In 1974, for example, 70 percent of the increase in import prices was neutralized by payments from the state budget. In the words of Andras Hegedus, the former prime minister, "From the beginning of 1973 to the end of 1975 there was no more talk of reform in official circles. But it was also not criticized. It was simply forgotten that a reform had begun in 1968."[6]

Shielded from the international price increases, the Hungarian people had little incentive to reduce their demand for imports. The export-import balance moved from a small surplus in 1973 to a deficit of more than $1 billion in 1975. As the nation's reserves of foreign exchange began to dwindle, an expanded system of import quotas and other quantitative controls was introduced in 1976 to replace the disabled market mechanism. However, the exter-

---

[4]A study by Marton Tardos of the Hungarian Institute for Market Research, cited in Bela Balassa, "The Hungarian Economic Reform, 1968–1981," World Bank Staff Working Paper No. 506 (February 1982), 11.

[5]Henryk Flakierski, *Economic Reform and Income Distribution: A Case Study of Hungary and Poland* (Armonk, N.Y.: M. E. Sharpe, 1986), Chapter 2.

[6]Quoted in Adam Zwass, *The Economies of Eastern Europe in a Time of Change* (Armonk, N.Y.: M. E. Sharpe, 1984), 8.

nal situation continued to deteriorate. The Hungarian debt to the West increased from $3 billion in 1975 to $9 billion in 1980. In Eastern Europe, only Poland and Romania had a lower credit rating (and both of these countries were forced into insolvency in 1981).

The 1980s: The New Improved Mechanism[7]

In 1977, faced with the failure of central controls and restricted in their access to international borrowing, the Hungarian leaders began preparations for a new round of reforms that would reaffirm the principles of the New Economic Mechanism. Furthermore, the Solidarity movement in Poland prompted demands for a more effective system of employee participation in management. In contrast to the stable environment from 1968 to 1972 when the NEM was introduced, the reforms since 1979 have been superimposed on a backdrop of economic and political uncertainty.

Prices.   Measures were first taken to rationalize the subsidy-ridden price system. After increasing at an annual rate of only 4 percent during 1973 to 1978, retail prices were allowed to increase by an average rate of 7.8 percent during 1979 to 1986. Beginning in 1980 the competitive price system was introduced, which tied the domestic prices of goods accounting for about 70 percent of industrial output to world market levels, and allowed another 20 percent to be determined by domestic supply and demand. The purpose of the system is to set prices at the approximate levels that would prevail if all of the markets were competitive. As measures are taken to break up domestic monopolies, the number of prices that are set by domestic supply and demand is scheduled to increase.

Industrial Organization and Competition.   The Hungarian reformers say that the directors of the large industrial enterprises, who fear exposure to foreign and domestic competition, have been among the most formidable opponents of reform. Furthermore, the monopoly power of the large enterprises is a serious obstacle to further relaxation of price controls. Thus, in 1979 a special commission was formed to oversee the dissolution of large enterprises and trusts. By 1983 about 300 new enterprises had been broken off from the old giants, a rather significant number considering that there were only 702 state enterprises in all of Hungary when the process started in 1979.

Since 1982, the law has also allowed the establishment of several new kinds of small organizations. In the socialist sector, these include small enterprises and cooperatives established by ministries and local councils, independent subsidiaries established by state enterprises, and independent joint

---

[7]Much of the following discussion is based on Paul Marer, "Economic Reform in Hungary: From Central Planning to Regulated Market," in U.S. Congress, Joint Economic Committee, *East European Economies: Slow Growth in the 1980s* (Washington, D.C.: USGPO, 1986), 3: 247–271; and Ellen Comisso and Paul Marer, "The Economics and Politics of Reform in Hungary," *International Organization* 40 (Spring 1986): 421–454.

ventures established by two or more enterprises and/or cooperatives. By mid-1984, 567 small state enterprises and cooperatives were in operation, with a total payroll of 35,800 workers.[8]

Bridging the gap between the public and private sectors is the **enterprise contract work association (ECWA).** This is a partnership of 2 to 30 private individuals who enter a free contract with an enterprise to provide overtime labor—usually in the evenings and on weekends. The ECWA uses the equipment of the enterprise, so it does not require any capital investments; its workers usually earn about three times the standard rate of pay. For the enterprise, the ECWA is a convenient means of acquiring additional labor, and income paid to the association is not subject to a wage tax. In mid-1984, 13,572 ECWAs with 132,900 workers were in operation, most of them in industry and construction.

Organizationally similar to the ECWA, but more private in nature, is the **independent contract work association (ICWA).** Unlike the ECWAs, the ICWAs are not affiliated with a single enterprise. They own their own equipment, find their own work, and take entrepreneurial risks. In many cases, they are successors of underground operations. In mid-1984, 6,438 ICWAs existed, employing 32,000 people (about half of them full-time); they were rather evenly divided between industry, construction, and services. In one celebrated case, members of a mountain-climbing club formed an ICWA to wash the windows of high-rise buildings.

Enterprise Autonomy and Democracy.   To reduce the scope of bureaucratic meddling in enterprise affairs, three major industrial ministries were merged in 1980 into a single Ministry of Industry, with about half of the former personnel. The trend toward decentralization of foreign trade management was also accelerated at this time; increasing numbers of enterprises were given the right to deal directly on foreign markets without the intervention of the Ministry of Foreign Trade.

According to a law on enterprise democracy adopted in 1984, all state companies have been assigned to one of three groups with different forms of management. The first group, accounting for 58 of the 325 enterprises under the Ministry of Industry, includes the public utilities, defense industries, and other natural monopolies. Enterprises in this class have been kept under traditional administrative control, and their directors continue to be appointed by the ministries' municipal councils. Supervisory boards have been established in some of these enterprises to represent the interests of workers, consumers, and social organizations.

The medium-size and large competitive enterprises, which comprise the majority of Hungarian establishments, are now managed by an enterprise council that handles strategic decisions, and by a director who handles day-to-day operations. The councils can have up to 50 members, with equal representation from labor (elected by secret ballot for 5-year terms) and management

---

[8]"The Small Ventures Continue to Grow," *The Hungarian Economy* 14 (1985): 23.

(some of whom are elected and some of whom are appointed by the director). The director is appointed by the board, with the consent of the ministry, based on a competitive application process. Despite the important role played by the enterprise council in decisions relating to economic plans, investment, merger, and appointment of directors, this is still considered to be a modified "one-person" system of management.[9]

The smaller enterprises, generally those with fewer than 500 employees (accounting for about 25 percent of the firms switching to new forms of management), have been allowed to establish a Yugoslav-style system of labor self-management.[10] A general assembly of all enterprise employees has the authority to make strategic decisions and to elect a director without obtaining state approval.

Experience under the new systems of labor management is limited, and, like the Yugoslavs before them, the Hungarians are now trying to sort out the responsibilities of the actors:

What kind of difference can there be between the trade union, representing the interests of the workers, and the company council, representing the owners, which, in the final analysis, means also representing the workers' interests? Experiences indicate that the company council, the trade union, and the director all are trying to find their place in this triangle, and it will take a long time and numerous arguments to resolve the issue.[11]

As one collection of laws freed many of the enterprises from administrative control, another set established a more orderly system of legal checks and balances. A 1984 law, for example, prohibits enterprises from engaging in a wide range of unfair trade practices. The law forbids false advertising, abuse of trade secrets, charging of unfair prices, and actions that restrict competition.[12]

Banking and Finance.   The new round of reform reached the financial sector in 1983, when a small market for bonds issued by enterprises, cooperatives, financial institutions, and local governments was established. By mid-1986, 120 bond issues were made available to the public; these raised about $150 million of investment funds.[13] Ideological objections have prevented the creation of a market for equity share ownership, although some Hungarian economists favor such an action.

---

[9]"Changes in the Law on State Enterprises," *The Hungarian Economy* 13 (1984): 12.

[10]The Hungarian authorities have attempted to say that "this form of company does not mean a change-over to the Yugoslav style of self-management," because they "continue to be founded by the state, their assets are indivisible, there is no 'group ownership', and in case of their liquidation the assets of these companies remain in state ownership." By and large, however, these statements could be used to describe Yugoslav enterprises. See Tamas Sarkozy, "The Further Development of the State Sector in Hungary," *The Hungarian Economy* 14 (1985): 13.

[11]Judit Kozma, "In the Role of the Owner," *Nepszabadsag,* November 18, 1985, 3; translated in Joint Publications Research Service, *Eastern Europe Report,* February 4, 1986, 2.

[12]"Important New Legal Rules," *The Hungarian Economy* 13 (1984): 12–13.

[13]Michael Kaufman, "Hungarians Clip Coupons and Call It Communism," *New York Times,* July 8, 1986, A2.

In 1986 the authorities decided that the highly centralized banking system, which served a surveillance function under the old system of central planning, was not appropriate under the new conditions of enterprise autonomy. Accordingly, at the beginning of 1987 the National Bank of Hungary was transformed into a Western-style central bank, whose primary responsibilities are to control monetary growth and interest rates.

The commercial and investment banking offices were detached from the National Bank and dispersed between five big commercial banks and nine small venture capital operations. The commercial banks maintain company accounts, provide commercial and investment credits, perform securities transactions, participate in the founding of new ventures, and provide consulting services. They are expected to operate at a profit. Under the new competitive system, companies are free to choose between the competing banks (but they must do all of their business with a single bank), and the banks are free to accept and reject customers.[14]

Bankruptcy.   Despite their efforts to encourage competition and enterprise autonomy, in 1985 the Hungarian authorities provided 157 billion forints of budgetary subsidies to unprofitable enterprises, roughly one-quarter of national income.[15] The government decided that it could no longer provide such a large proportion of the nation's resources to inefficient enterprises. Thus, a new bankruptcy law became effective in September 1986. According to the law, a state enterprise that is delinquent in repaying its debts is required to engage in arbitration with its creditors before the Chamber of Commerce. If no agreement is reached, the possibility of a state-financed rehabilitation is considered. The state is to intervene only to prevent large-scale unemployment, violation of international obligations, or damage to national security. If the state does not choose to rescue the company, the law provides for an orderly process of reorganization or liquidation.[16]

The government has also established systems of job placement and financial support for workers who are displaced by the bankruptcies. The insolvent businesses are allowed to keep operating for as many as 9 months while their workers look for jobs. Unemployed workers are paid 75 percent of their average income during the first 3 months and 60 percent during the next 3 months.[17]

Taxation.   The most recent program of reform, still under consideration at the time of this writing, involves a major adjustment of the system of taxation. The proposed measures would reduce the taxes on enterprise profits and

[14]Tamas Bacskai, "Reform of the Banking System in Hungary," *The Hungarian Economy* 14 (1986): 5; *Economic Information,* No. 22 (HungaroPress, 1986), 3–5.

[15]Gyorgy Ney, "Official Interviewed on Workforce, Work Environment," in Joint Publications Research Service, *Eastern Europe Report,* October 28, 1986, 17.

[16]"New Regulations on Business Insolvency: Arbitration, Economic Reorganization, Liquidation," *The Hungarian Economy* 14 (1986): 12–13.

[17]Gyorgy Ney, "Official Interviewed on Workforce," 18–19.

introduce new personal income and value-added (sales) taxes. Not too surprisingly, the head of the Hungarian Chamber of Commerce believes that the reduction in business taxes would be "the most important reform step since the New Economic Mechanism was introduced in 1968."[18] On the other hand, the income and sales tax proposals are unpopular among the general population.

Evaluation of the Hungarian System

It is too soon to attempt a careful evaluation of the latest wave of Hungarian reform, because its implementation is far from complete. However, a number of successes and failures have begun to surface. First, supporters of the system can point to the fact that industrial labor productivity grew more rapidly in Hungary during 1976–1984 (4.6 percent per year) than in any of the other Eastern European countries.[19] Likewise, Hungary has consistently maintained the highest level of per capita agricultural production in Eastern Europe.[20] Just as important, Hungary managed to maintain its international solvency through the debt crisis of the early 1980s despite tremendous odds, while its neighbors in Poland and Romania failed.

The Hungarians are the first to admit that all is not well with the reforms. Release of the price controls led to an average inflation rate of about 6.5 percent from 1980 to 1986. Many workers joined the overtime contract work associations (ECWAs and ICWAs) simply to maintain their standards of living. In the words of one young entrepreneur, "As an electrician, today I work not 40 but 80 hours a week, but finally I can pay for an apartment for myself and my family. . . . It is true that the price for making a living has been the merciless exploitation of both my wife and myself, but at least we can make it."[21]

The situation is more desperate for those who are not able to engage in overtime work. The rising cost of living has driven 68 percent of retired industrial workers below the state-calculated poverty line.[22] According to Farenc Havasi, in his address to the 1985 Party Congress, "While the budgetary expenditure on welfare has continuously been growing, social tensions have not lessened, but, on the contrary, have grown sharper."[23] That conclusion is supported by the results of recent public opinion surveys (see "Polling the Proletariat," p. 351).

[18]Peter Lorincze, "Hungary Must Press On with Reforms," Wall Street Journal, July 3, 1987, 8.

[19]United Nations Economic Commission for Europe, Economic Survey of Europe in 1984–85, Part 2 (Geneva: 1986), 4.71.

[20]Gregor Lazarcik, "Comparative Growth of Agricultural Output, Inputs, and Productivity in Eastern Europe, 1965–82," in East European Economies: Slow Growth in the 1980s, 1: 419–420.

[21]Quoted in Ivan Volgyes, "Hungary: A Malaise Thinly Disguised," Current History 84 (November 1985): 366.

[22]Ferenc Koszeg, "Hungary Doesn't Deserve Model Communist Image," Wall Street Journal, June 18, 1986, 23.

[23]F. Havasi, "The Economic Situation of Hungary and the Tasks To Be Faced," Acta Oeconomica 34 (1985): 200.

POLLING THE PROLETARIAT

The Soviet and Eastern European leaders have attempted to manipulate public opinion, but until recently they seldom tried to measure it. Public opinion, they explained, was still captive to the old bourgeois ideology, and this is why the enlightened communists were supposed to play the leading role in society. More likely, they simply did not want to be graded on their performance.

In 1968, when the New Economic Mechanism was introduced in Hungary, a small polling organization was formed in the state radio and television organization to monitor the impact of the reforms. In 1985, this office was transformed into an independent Institute of Mass Communications; it now runs 40 big surveys each year, 50 flash polls, and a weekly canvass of television viewers. Poland established a similar organization in 1981. Tat'iana Zaslavskaya, one of the architects of the Soviet reforms, is a sociologist who draws heavily on public opinion research.

According to a 1985 Polish poll, economic reform was rated third in importance, behind social peace and hard work, among the factors that would lead that country out of its crisis. Lower ratings were given to international cooperation and governmental policies. Large majorities of those polled were in favor of workers' self-management, competition between enterprises, and discharging workers who are not needed by the plant. At the same time, three-quarters of the respondents were opposed to the release of price controls. Some 52 percent said that no effects could be seen from the most recent round of reforms, and another 16 percent answered that it was "hard to say."

In Hungary, two-thirds of college students agreed in 1986 that economic life in socialist countries was "characterized mostly by problems." A 1983 survey said that managers and executives have the highest level of social prestige, followed by intellectuals, other nonmanual laborers, and skilled workers. Nonagricultural self-employed workers were fifth in prestige, but first in income.

Beyond the realm of economics, 70 percent of Hungarians believe that the United States already has weapons in space and 60 percent are sure the Soviets do, too. Some 41 percent believe that the luckiest countries are those that have remained neutral and kept their distance from the arms race. Should Soviet troops be ordered out of Hungary? Should the Communist party be exposed to competition? These questions have not been asked—yet.

Sources: Barry Newman, "Budapest Embraces a Democratic Device: The Survey of Opinion," *Wall Street Journal,* January 8, 1987, 1, 12; Witold Morawski and Wieslawa Kozek, "Society on the Reform," in Joint Publications Research Service, *East European Economic and Industrial Affairs,* August 14, 1985, 112–116; and R. Kulcsar, "Results of the First Nationwide Prestige Survey in Hungary," *Acta Oeconomica* 36 (1986): 155–167.

Finally, in the opinion of several prominent Hungarian economists, the economic significance of the reform program has been overestimated. According to Marton Tardos, for example, in 1984 the scope of governmental control remained sufficiently large to say that Hungary had a system of modified central planning rather than a market socialist economy.[24]

Similarly, according to Janos Kornai, "I have the impression that the words about 'hard financial discipline' and 'hard credit conditions' have not been sufficiently coupled with deeds."[25] Without the discipline of a "hard budget constraint," Kornai argues that the market mechanism cannot control and coordinate the economy, creating continued demand for administrative guidance. "In our country. . . the intention is to simulate live competition with extremely complicated rules devised on a desk—with little success."[26]

Since Kornai wrote these words in 1983, considerable progress has been made toward the creation of a hard budget constraint for Hungarian companies and workers. In 1986–1987 the banks were transformed into competitive institutions and instructed to provide loans according to financial criteria, and new procedures were devised to liquidate unprofitable firms and to provide for unemployed workers.

Most important, the political leadership is determined to extend the reforms. Karoly Grosz, installed as prime minister in 1987, has a reputation as a tough young reformer in the Gorbachev mold. Grosz favors the closure of unprofitable enterprises, even in the face of unemployment, and larger income differentials to reward talent and effort.[27] These policies will meet stiff domestic opposition, but it is clear that Hungary will continue to point the way for other socialist countries.

East Germany: Life beyond the Wall

At the beginning of World War II, the area that is now the German Democratic Republic was the most economically developed region in Eastern Europe. The income of the average East German was roughly equal to that of the average West German and about 80 to 100 percent larger than that of the average Czechoslovak, the closest rival in Eastern Europe.[28]

[24]Marton Tardos, "How to Create Efficient Markets in Socialism," a paper presented to a conference at the Kennan Institute for Advanced Russian Studies, Woodrow Wilson International Center for Scholars, Washington, D.C. (October 18–19, 1984), 17.

[25]Janos Kornai, "Comments on the Present State and the Prospects of the Hungarian Economic Reform," *Journal of Comparative Economics* 7 (September 1983): 230.

[26]Ibid., 229.

[27]Eric Bourne, "Shuffle in Hungary Shows Intention to Reform Economy," *Christian Science Monitor,* June 29, 1987, 7, 9.

[28]For alternative estimates of Eastern European income levels in 1937–1938, see Zwass, *The Economies of Eastern Europe,* 45; and Ivan T. Berend and Gyorgi Ranki, *Economic Development in East-Central Europe in the 19th and 20th Centuries* (New York: Columbia University Press, 1974), 309. For prewar comparisons between East and West Germany, see Paul Gregory and Gert Leptin, "Similar Societies under Differing Economic Systems: The Case of the Two Germanies," *Soviet Studies* 29 (October 1977): 519–542.

All of this was changed by World War II. East Germany suffered less wartime destruction than West Germany, but it suffered far more from the confiscation of its assets at the end of the war. All together, about 41 percent of the East German capital stock was destroyed or dismantled, compared to about 33 percent in the West.[29] Division of the country forced the East Germans to redirect their foreign trade from the developed West to the backward East and caused many of the most talented East Germans—about 200,000 per year between 1945 and 1961—to flee to the West.

By 1950, East German income per capita was about 20 percent lower than the West German level and about 30 percent lower than the Czechoslovak level.[30] The burden of reparations led to a mass uprising in 1953 that required the intervention of Soviet tanks to restore law and order. The system hit its lowest ebb in 1961, when the Berlin Wall was built to stem the flow of emigration.

The 1960s: The Rise and Fall of the NES[31]

Based on their tradition of ingenuity and hard work, by 1963 the East Germans regained their position as the most well-to-do country in Eastern Europe. In that same year, it was decided that the Stalinist system of centralized planning was not appropriate for an advanced socialist society, and the New Economic System (NES) was introduced. At that time (before the NEM was introduced in Hungary), the NES was the most extensive program of economic reform attempted in the Soviet bloc, excluding Yugoslavia.

Unlike the Hungarian NEM, which was introduced 5 years later, the NES was not a program of market socialism. Instead, it was designed to decentralize the system of planning and to make greater use of financial criteria in the formulation of plans. The incentive system was changed to reward profitability, and an interest charge was introduced on the use of capital. Price controls were not released, but the controlled prices were rationalized, and they were revised more frequently. The State Bank of the GDR was transformed into a Western-style central bank and several new banks assumed its commercial operations.

Under the NES, the central authorities were supposed to concern themselves with long-term goals, while the enterprises and unions of state enterprises (VVBs) were supposed to formulate the short-term detailed plans. The traditional sequence—in which material balances were used to formulate central plans, and central plans guided the formulation of contracts between producers—was reversed. Instead, contracts were first negotiated between

---

[29]Zwass, *The Economies of Eastern Europe,* 25.

[30]Based on estimates in Robert Summers and Alan Heston, "Improved International Comparisons of Real Product and Its Composition: 1950–1980," *Review of Income and Wealth* 30 (June 1984): Appendix.

[31]For a full discussion of the New Economic System, see Gert Leptin and Manfred Melzer, *Economic Reform in East German Industry* (Oxford: Oxford University Press, 1978).

enterprises, based on profitability criteria, and these contracts were used by the VVBs and ministries to compile their material balances and plans. When potential shortages were uncovered in the material balances, the enterprises were told to renegotiate their contracts, and compensation was paid from a special fund to those who suffered damages.

Like many other limited reforms that have been introduced in the Soviet bloc, the NES did little to improve economic performance in the GDR. The profit motive encouraged cost efficiency, but neither the central planners nor the market system was given sufficient authority to coordinate the actions of producers or to ensure balanced growth of the producer and consumer goods sectors. The East Germans were neither the first nor the last to learn that price controls and the profit motive are incompatible.

In 1968, the Soviet intervention in Czechoslovakia cast a cloud over the program of reform, and 1970 was a year of bad weather, bottlenecks and shortages in the energy sector, and a workers' revolt in Poland. For these and other reasons, the German authorities decided to recentralize authority and launch a strategy of balanced economic growth. The number of centrally determined plan targets was increased, and stronger central control was exerted over prices, investment, and material supply. Interestingly, the return to central control was followed by a modest acceleration in economic growth in the early 1970s.[32]

The Kombinate *Reform*[33]

When much of the NES reform was abandoned in the early 1970s, the authorities turned their attention to improvements in the organizational structure of central planning. They decided that planning could be handled more effectively if the lines of communication between planners and producers were shorter. Thus, they decided to dissolve the VVBs created during the NES to mediate between the enterprises and the central authorities. This meant, however, that the planners would have to communicate with a very large number of individual enterprises. Thus, the enterprises were merged together into much larger units.

The first wave of merger, between 1970 and 1977, cut the number of enterprises in half, and a second wave, which began in 1977, created 226 huge vertically integrated *kombinate* organizations. Each *kombinate* is composed of a group of enterprises under the leadership of a general director. Where the VVBs had had only advisory powers, the general director of the *kombinate* has authority over all aspects of the production process. The *kombinate* is designed to take advantage of scale economies and to perform a wide range of

[32]This acceleration is evident in the official NMP data and in the CIA estimates of GNP, but the reliability of these data is questioned by Michael Keren. See "The Return of the Ancien Regime: The GDR in the 1970s," in U.S. Congress, Joint Economic Committee, *East European Economies Post Helsinki* (Washington, D.C.: USGPO, 1977), 732–740.

[33]See Manfred Melzer and Arthur Stahnke, "The GDR Faces the Economic Dilemmas of the 1980s," in *East European Economies: Slow Growth in the 1980s,* 3: 139–147.

functions, including planning, production, research and development, and, in some cases, foreign marketing.

The East German leaders credit their fidelity to central planning for their relatively high standard of living (compared to other East Europeans) and their relatively small burden of international indebtedness. A number of other environmental factors have also contributed to the German performance; not least of these is the special relationship between East and West Germany. Since it is not recognized as a foreign country, goods from East Germany are allowed into West Germany duty-free. West Germans send gifts to their friends and relatives in the East, travel to the East to make visits, and make payments to the East German government to obtain permissions for emigration. According to one estimate, these and other benefits are worth about $1.5 billion per year to the East Germans.[34] Add to this the value of Western technology that passes over the border (overtly and covertly) and the impact of Western television and radio programs on the East German population. Despite these exchanges, East is clearly East, and West is West.

Czechoslovakia: Two Decades after Prague Spring

Amid the diversity of Eastern Europe, Czechoslovakia and Poland hold several features in common. They are the two Slavic nations in the region that adopted Roman Catholicism. Forming a bridge between Germany and the Soviet Union, they were the first two countries to be invaded by Hitler. Aside from East Germany, they are the two largest military powers in Eastern Europe. Most important for present purposes, they are the two countries where attempts to reform the Stalinist system were crushed by tanks and guns. They provide a reminder to the other countries in the region that economic reform must not threaten the political monopoly of the Communist Party.

Czechoslovakia was the only country in the region to maintain a relatively democratic government before World War II; after the war Czechoslovak democracy survived somewhat longer—until 1948—than in any of the other nations of Eastern Europe. Significant movement toward reform of the Stalinist system began in 1963, concurrent with an actual decline in national income. A commission headed by Ota Sik, a leading Party economist, was formed to study the problem; it recommended a program of market-socialist reforms quite similar to those that were eventually adopted in Hungary. When implementation of the reforms moved slowly, Sik and others concluded that a reform of the political system would be necessary to remove the bureaucratic barriers. Thus, in 1967 they proposed reforms that would have gone far beyond the Yugoslav experiment in self-managed market socialism and would have established democratic political institutions.

Under pressure, Antonin Novotny resigned as Party Secretary in early 1968 and was replaced by Alexander Dubcek. During the so-called Prague

[34]Paul Marer, "Economic Policies and Systems in Eastern Europe and Yugoslavia: Commonalities and Differences," in *East European Economies: Slow Growth in the 1980s,* 3: 613.

Spring, Dubcek attempted to introduce the remaining reforms.[35] Workers' councils were established in the factories (illegally, but with governmental cooperation), and some of them held elections to replace the politically-appointed enterprise directors. Likewise, the workers took control of the trade unions from the Party, and governmental officials proclaimed the legitimacy of strikes. Wholesale prices were revised and price controls were released on some consumer goods. Enterprises were allowed to engage directly in foreign trade. Free speech and a free press were allowed, and Dubcek said that he was even ready to allow the revival of the Social Democratic Party.

The Soviets were willing to cope with the 1968 Hungarian reforms, which were confined to economics, but Dubcek's flirtation with political reform, workers' councils, and independent trade unions drew a very different response. On the evening of August 20, 1968, a few weeks before the Party Congress that would have formalized the new reforms, Czechoslovakia was invaded by a quarter of a million Warsaw Pact troops. Opposition groups were crushed, and the Dubcek government was replaced by the authoritarian regime of Gustav Husak. Since that time, no significant program of reforms has been attempted. Czechoslovakia has maintained a relatively high standard of living by Eastern European standards, but it has had one of the slowest rates of output and productivity growth in the region.

Poland: The Legacy of Solidarity

In Poland, the program of forced industrialization led to workers' riots in 1956 and 1970, but these upheavals did not lead to any significant programs of economic reform. After the 1970 riots, the Gierek government initiated an ambitious economic development program based on foreign technology and debt. When the imported technology did not generate enough exports to repay the debts, a problem exacerbated by the oil crisis of the 1970s, Poland faced a balance of payments crisis. Restriction of imports and expansion of exports required a reduction in the standard of living of the average Pole and precipitated a reduction in national income between 1979 and 1982 that has not been matched in the industrial West since the Great Depression.[36]

As part of its austerity program, the government increased meat prices in 1980, and this action touched off the Solidarity movement under the leadership of Lech Walesa. On August 14, 1980, the entire force of 17,000 workers stopped production at the Gdansk shipyard, and 4 days later Gierek announced his readiness to negotiate. In the Gdansk agreement the government agreed to condone the existence of the union and to grant workers the right to strike.

[35]For a description of the unfolding reform process, see Vaclav Holesovsky, "Planning and the Market in the Czechoslovak Reform," in *Plan and Market: Economic Reform in Eastern Europe,* ed. Morris Bornstein (New Haven, Conn.: Yale University Press, 1973), 313–345.

[36]David Kemme and Keith Crane, "The Polish Economic Collapse: Contributing Factors and Economic Costs," *Journal of Comparative Economics* 8 (March 1984): 27.

Wages were increased, political prisoners were freed, censorship almost disappeared, and the workweek was reduced from 6 to 5 days.

Unfortunately, two major problems remained. First, on the economic side, the burden of international debt did not disappear with the creation of Solidarity. The strikes and the shorter workweek caused a reduction in export production. On the political front, the concessions of the government emboldened some members of Solidarity to make more radical demands. Many of them called for the establishment of a Yugoslav-style system of workers' management, and a few suggested that elections should be held in which Solidarity would oppose the Communist Party. Responding to these economic conditions and political demands, the Jaruzelski government imposed martial law in late 1981, and the major Solidarity activists were imprisoned.

In mid-1981, General Jaruzelski decided to go ahead with a Hungarian-style system of economic reforms that had been prepared before the imposition of martial law. The reforms called for more enterprise autonomy, labor management, and price flexibility, and for a move from microeconomic to macroeconomic central planning.

The martial-law government was not very well-suited to enact a program of liberalizing reforms. Beginning in 1983, martial law was gradually lifted and the 1980 level of national income was finally regained in 1984. In recent years, Polish reform has been encouraged by the Gorbachev program in the Soviet Union. A 22–member reform commission is preparing proposals, and members of the commission favor the closure of inefficient firms and additional price increases. To these ends, a 3-week course was established in 1985 to train a cadre of specialists in the technicalities of bankruptcy law.[37]

To gain control over the country's $30 billion debt burden, many of the recent reforms are designed to boost export earnings. The zloty was devalued by about 20 percent in September 1986 and by a similar amount in February 1987. Exporters were granted ownership of the foreign exchange that they earn (previously it was confiscated by the state), and an Export Development Bank was established.[38] One of the most interesting proposals comes from a member of the reform commission who is willing to see the rebirth of independent labor unions: "Reform requires much harder conditions for all working people. You have to pay something for their help."[39]

Albania, Bulgaria, and Romania: The Balkan Triangle

Albania, Bulgaria, and Romania (together with Yugoslavia) constitute the Balkan rim of Eastern Europe. The Balkan nations share a mountainous terrain and, more importantly, a common heritage. From the fifteenth century until

---

[37]"Training Personnel to Run Firms in Receivership," in Joint Publications Research Service, *East European Economic and Industrial Affairs,* July 10, 1985, 68.

[38]*IMF Survey,* February 23, 1987, 59–61.

[39]Barry Newman, "Polish Leader Mulls Economic Overhaul," *Wall Street Journal,* April 10, 1987, 16.

the 1878 Council of Berlin, all of the nations in the area were vassals of the Turkish Empire. The significance of this era is explained by two Hungarian historians:

There were essential differences between the parts of Southeastern Europe occupied by the Turks and the other parts of East-Central Europe. The degree of feudal stagnation and backwardness in the two regions was so unequal as to be more than a quantitative difference. . . . Unlike other countries of Europe which had lost their independence, in these subjugated countries the conquerors not only settled down but also transformed the existing socio-economic system.[40]

Like Russia under the Mongols, the Balkan nations inherited a tradition of economic backwardness and political despotism that has never completely disappeared. Economic reforms in Bulgaria and Romania have been extremely conservative; Albania has rejected all reform of the Stalinist economic system. Per capita income in the four Balkan nations is about 30 percent lower than income in the other four nations of Eastern Europe (based on weighted averages of the figures given in Table 14.1), and Albania has the highest infant mortality rate in Europe.[41]

The human-rights record in the Balkans is poor, even if judged against the other countries in the Soviet bloc. The worst of the three is Albania, which has refused to sign any of the United Nations covenants on human rights. Albania forbids dissent, foreign travel, blue jeans, cosmetics, and chewing gum; it takes the world's strongest stance against religion—all public and private worship has been outlawed since 1967. The death penalty is imposed for more than 30 different crimes.

Romania reportedly has the most extensive system of security personnel in the world—one secret policeman for every 15 citizens.[42] Admission to a doctoral program has required Communist Party approval since 1975, and in 1983 the state required the registration of all typewriters and calculators. Bulgaria has a better human-rights record than the other two countries, but it has taken an unusually hard line against ethnic groups (Turks and Pomaks) that have resisted Bulgarianization.

While they hold much in common, the Balkan nations differ substantially in their economic and political relations with the Soviet Union and the Western world. At one extreme, Albania has poor relations with both the East and the West. All diplomatic relations with the Soviet Union, including participation in the Warsaw Pact, were broken during the 1960–1961 Sino-Soviet dispute, and economic relations with China were severed in 1978. Since 1985,

[40]Berend and Ranki, *Economic Development in East-Central Europe,* 4.

[41]Information on infant mortality is taken from World Bank, *World Development Report 1986* (New York: Oxford University Press, 1986), 232–233.

[42]See the testimony of a former deputy director of the Romanian foreign intelligence service, Ion Mihai Pacepa, in "Ceausescu: America's Most Favored Tyrant," *Wall Street Journal,* January 13, 1986, 24. For a more comprehensive picture of human-rights records, see the semiannual reports of the U.S. Department of State, Bureau of Public Affairs, *Implementation of Helsinki Final Act,* which are included in the department's Special Report series.

when the death of Enver Hoxha led to some moderation of policy under Ramiz Alia, long-term trade agreements have been signed with the other countries of Eastern Europe, and trade has resumed with China and several West European countries. However, Albania remains one of the most isolated countries in the world.

Romania is a member of the Warsaw Pact, but its leaders have been openly critical of Soviet policies on a number of occasions—including the invasion of Afghanistan. Romania also has been relatively independent in its foreign trade relations. In contrast to Bulgaria, which transacts about three-quarters of its trade with socialist countries, Romanian trade is almost evenly divided between the East and the West. Based on heavy importation of machinery and equipment, Romania posted the highest rate of economic growth in Eastern Europe during the 1970s, but it was driven into insolvency and austerity during the early 1980s.

Bulgaria faithfully supports the foreign policy of the Soviet Union and trades with it on preferential terms. In 1984, for example, the Soviet Union provided oil and other products at subsidized prices that saved about $200 for every man, woman, and child in Bulgaria.[43] This fact helps explain how Bulgaria has maintained the lightest burden of Western indebtedness in Eastern Europe.[44]

Summary

Stalinist central planning proved to be an inappropriate economic system for trade-dependent Hungary, and the Socialist Workers' Party seized control of the government with little popular support. Opposition to political repression and forced collectivization eventually led to the rise and fall of moderation under Nagy's New Course and then to the 1956 revolt. The latter was crushed by Soviet forces, and Janos Kadar was installed as the new national leader. Kadar resumed collectivization, but simultaneously introduced a program of agricultural reforms. Based on successes in agriculture, he carried moderate reform to industry, and in 1968 the country moved toward market socialism with the New Economic Mechanism (NEM).

The NEM replaced detailed central planning with indicative planning and a limited market mechanism. It based the incentive system on profits, lifted some price controls, and allowed some enterprises to engage directly in foreign trade. These measures led to both productivity growth and greater

---

[43]This is the largest subsidy, on a per capita basis, that the Soviets provided to any of the Eastern European countries. See Michael Marrese and Jan Vanous, "The Content and Controversy of Soviet Trade Relations with Eastern Europe, 1970–84," a paper presented to a conference at the Kennan Institute for Advanced Russian Studies, Woodrow Wilson International Center for Scholars, Washington, D.C. (October 18–19, 1984), 7a.

[44]For debt figures, see United Nations Economic Commission for Europe, "Recent Changes in Europe's Trade," *Economic Bulletin for Europe* 38 (December 1986): 602–603.

income inequality; when the international oil crisis of 1973 threatened an acceleration of inflation, the NEM floundered. Centralized price control was strengthened in the 1970s, causing repressed inflation and contributing to balance of payments problems. To deal with these problems, the principles of the NEM were reaffirmed in 1980. Since that time, price control has been eased, monopolistic firms have been broken into smaller units, other small firms have been established, the state bureaucracy has been trimmed, the banking system has been reformed, and bankruptcy laws have been adopted.

The Hungarian economy has recorded rapid productivity growth in industry and a high level of agricultural production per capita, while maintaining international solvency. Rapid inflation, though, has reduced living standards for a large segment of the population, and extension of the reform is opposed by many.

East Germany had the highest average income in Eastern Europe before World War II. It lost that position to Czechoslovakia after the war, but regained the lead in 1962. During that same year, planning was decentralized under the New Economic System (NES), a program leading to disproportional growth. In the 1970s, planning was recentralized, and the enterprises were merged into giant *kombinate* organizations designed to communicate more effectively with the planners.

In Czechoslovakia, an ambitious program of market-socialist reform was introduced in 1967, but it was broken by Soviet military power in 1968 when questions were raised about Warsaw Pact membership and the leading role of the Communist Party. In Poland, a policy of rapid import-led growth failed in the 1970s and left the nation with a huge Western debt. The government responded to the debt with an austerity program, leading to the formation of the Solidarity labor union. After initial successes, the demands of Solidarity were met by the imposition of martial law. The Jaruzelski government initiated a new program of reform in 1981, based on decentralization, export promotion, price increases, and closure of inefficient enterprises; these reforms have accelerated since martial law was lifted in 1983.

The countries on the Balkan rim of Eastern Europe—Albania, Bulgaria, and Romania—share a heritage of foreign domination, economic backwardness, and political despotism. They have relatively low income levels and poor human rights records, and they have accomplished few meaningful economic reforms. Bulgaria and Romania are both members of the Warsaw Pact, although about half of Romania's trade is with the West. Albania is not a member of the Pact and trades little with the East or the West.

Discussion and Review Questions

1. In 1968, when the Czechoslovak reforms drew the intervention of Soviet troops, why was Hungary able to introduce the New Economic Mechanism?

2. How did the Hungarian New Economic Mechanism resemble the Yugoslav system of market socialism? How did it differ?

3.   What caused the decline of the New Economic Mechanism in the 1970s? What caused its recovery in the 1980s?

4.   According to the Hungarian enterprise law of 1984, what are the three forms of state enterprises and how is each managed?

5.   What are the purposes of the *kombinate* organizations in East Germany, and how do they differ from the VVBs that they replaced?

6.   What were the events that led to the formation of Solidarity in Poland? What led to the imposition of martial law?

Suggested Readings

Bornstein, Morris, ed. *Plan and Market: Economic Reform in Eastern Europe.* New Haven, Conn.: Yale University Press, 1973. *A collective volume including theoretical analyses and country studies focused on the amazing events of the 1960s.*

Gomulka, Stanislaw. *Growth, Innovation, and Reform in Eastern Europe.* Madison, Wisc.: University of Wisconsin Press, 1986. *Includes a theoretical analysis of socialist innovation and several statistical studies on this subject.*

Hare, P. G., H. K. Radice, and N. Swain, eds. *Hungary: A Decade of Reform.* London: Allen and Unwin, 1981. *Several articles on industrial and agricultural reform in the 1960s and 1970s.*

Kornai, Janos. *Contradictions and Dilemmas.* Cambridge, Mass.: The MIT Press, 1986. *A critical analysis of the Hungarian reforms by one of the leading Hungarian economists.*

Nove, Alec, Hans-Hermann Hohmann, and Gertraud Seidenstecher, eds. *The East European Economies in the 1970s.* London: Butterworths, 1982. *Articles on each of the countries, describing developments during the first half of the 1970s.*

U.S. Congress, Joint Economic Committee, *East European Economic Assessment.* 2 vols. Washington, D.C.: USGPO, 1981. *The first volume is parallel to the Nove, et al. book; the second provides comparative regional assessments of policy and performance.*

U.S. Congress, Joint Economic Committee, *East European Economies: Slow Growth in the 1980s.* 3 vols. Washington, D.C.: USGPO, 1985–1986. *A compendium of articles on a wide range of Eastern European themes, covering the period through the early 1980s.*

Zwass, Adam. *The Economies of Eastern Europe in a Time of Change.* Armonk, N.Y.: M. E. Sharpe, 1984. *Useful surveys on each of the countries, covering the entire postwar era.*

China

16
CHAPTER

CHINA: THE CONTINUING REVOLUTION

History has shown that equalitarian thinking is a serious obstacle to implementing the principle of distribution according to work, and that if it is unchecked, the forces of production will inevitably be undermined. Naturally, a socialist society must guarantee its members a gradual improvement in material and cultural life and their common prosperity. But, common prosperity cannot and will never mean absolute equalitarianism. . . .
—Central Committee of the Chinese Communist Party, 1984

China is a land of ceaseless continuity and revolutionary change. In many ways, the life of the average rural family has changed little in the last millennium. With a national income of about $350 per capita (less than $250 in some provinces), the continuing struggle for survival occupies much of the population. On the other hand, the Chinese economic system has undergone a number of radical transformations in recent years. After thousands of years of dynastic rule and uneven economic development, the Communist Party took control of the country in 1949 under the leadership of Mao Zedong. They experimented with Soviet-style central planning in the 1950s, with several different versions of Maoist equalitarianism in the 1960s and 1970s, and with pragmatic market socialism in the 1980s. Chinese economic policy is as unpredictable as the weather.

History and Environment

Centuries of imperial conquest and unification made China a very large country. With over 1 billion people, China accounts for over a fifth of the world's population. Their territory, stretching from the Pacific coast and the eastern lowlands to the larger region of mountains and plateaus in the west, is exceeded only by the Soviet Union and Canada in overall size. Unfortunately, only 10 percent of the land is suitable for cultivation. With a large proportion of the Chinese labor force engaged in agriculture (about 70 percent), the average farm worker has less than 1 acre of land at his disposal, compared to about 2 acres for the average Indian and 100 acres for the average American farmer.

The Chinese Empire was the only giant of the ancient world to survive into the twentieth century. Despite several instances of barbarian conquest and internal strife, the Chinese nation remained intact long after the Egyptian, Persian, Greek, and Roman empires were dismembered. Let us briefly consider the economic significance of China's longevity.[1]

Sometime between 3000 and 2000 B.C., Chinese civilization began to take form in the lower Yellow River basin, several hundred miles from the Pacific coast. According to one interpretation of Chinese history, the arid climate of this region encouraged the formation of centralized institutions to coordinate flood control and agricultural irrigation.[2] At the beginning of recorded history, during the Shang dynasty (1766–1122 B.C.), this authority structure already included a network of feudal states.

The Chinese Empire was established during the Qin dynasty (221–207 B.C.) as the feudal states were merged into a system of prefectures and counties under central control. In order to protect his people from the military and

---

[1]For an interesting analysis of the endurance of the Chinese Empire, see Mark Elvin, *The Pattern of the Chinese Past* (Stanford, Calif.: Stanford University Press, 1973).

[2]Karl Wittfogel, "Imperial China—A 'Complex' Hydraulic (Oriental) Society," in *The Pattern of Chinese History,* ed. John Meskill (Lexington, Mass.: D. C. Heath and Co., 1965), 85–95.

cultural influence of the northern barbarians, the first emperor joined the local fortifications into the Great Wall. Behind the real and symbolic protection of the wall, a process of cultural unification began and spread to the south and west with the conquests of the Han dynasty (206 B.C.–A.D. 220). Today, the Hanren (Han people) constitute over 90 percent of the Chinese population, the remainder being Mongols, Koreans, and several other ethnic minorities.

Imperial China made remarkable strides in the development of science and technology. Iron replaced wood and bronze in the manufacture of Chinese weapons and tools long before it appeared in the western world. Gunpowder had been invented in China by the sixth century A.D., about 500 years before it was discovered by a British alchemist. Woodblock printing developed during the ninth century and movable type was invented during the eleventh century, about 400 years before Gutenburg's discovery. By the thirteenth century, Chinese mathematicians had discovered theorems in algebra and trigonometry that were not known in Europe for another 300 years, and a machine was introduced that could simultaneously spin 32 spindles of hemp thread. In sum, medieval China was "the most numerate as well as the most literate country in the world," and by the thirteenth century it "had what was probably the most sophisticated agriculture in the world."[3]

After the thirteenth century, for reasons that are not entirely clear, Chinese cultural and technological development lost its vitality. This was probably caused in part by the period of Mongol domination (1234–1368), which subjected the Chinese people to harsh taxation and slave-like servitude. However, the Mongol influence was not entirely negative. The Grand Canal, which was repaired and completed during this period, reduced transportation costs between the north and the south, and the economy was temporarily opened to foreign trade and technology. Marco Polo visited China, for example, between 1275 and 1292. When the Chinese expelled the Mongols, they entered a period of xenophobic separation from foreigners.

Beginning in the early days of the Manchu dynasty (1644–1911), China began to experience excessive population growth. Several possible causes have been suggested. The high level of agricultural productivity and the gradual abolition of feudal serfdom caused a huge increase in the number of people who could be fed. Manchu rule, following a period of prolonged struggle, gave the country about a century and a half of peace. Widespread epidemics, common during the sixteenth century, were noticeably absent after 1644, and advances in medical science slowly brought certain infectious diseases under control. By 1776, the burden of excess population had become evident:

China has long been one of the richest, that is, one of the most fertile, best cultivated, most industrious, and most populous countries in the world. It seems, however, to have been long stationary. . . . The poverty of the lower ranks of people in China far surpasses that of the most beggarly nations in Europe. In the neighborhood of Canton many hundred, it is commonly said, many thousand families . . . live constantly in little fishing boats upon the

---

[3]Elvin, *The Pattern of the Chinese Past,* 129, 181.

*rivers and canals. The subsistence which they find there is so scanty that they
are eager to fish up the nastiest garbage thrown overboard from any European ship.*[4]

Along with excessive population growth, another important economic
and social problem that emerged during the late imperial period was drug
addiction. Although opium had been used for medicinal purposes for centuries, its abuse became so widespread by 1729 that the emperor forbade its
sale. When this had little effect, importation of the drug was prohibited in
1800.

The ban, in turn, drew a hostile reaction from the British, who profited
from the opium trade between India (a British colony) and China. The British
were victorious in the Opium Wars of 1839–1842 and forced China to open
five additional treaty ports. Domestic cultivation of opium poppies expanded
along with imports; by 1923 they accounted for about two-thirds of the winter
planting in Yunnan province. This aggravated the food shortage, and in some
cities it was said that 90 percent of the men and 60 percent of the women
were opium addicts.[5]

Burdened by population pressure, foreign colonialism, political corruption, and social decay, the economy continued to stagnate. The dynastic system finally collapsed in 1911, and a republic was established by Sun Yat-sen.
The republic was weak, however, and the government in Beijing eventually
fell under the control of war lords.

Sun Yat-sen moved to the south in 1917 and established a rival government in Canton under the control of his Nationalist (Guomindang) Party.
Although he was opposed by many provincial officials, Sun was supported by
the working population. His "three fundamental principles" were nationalism,
democracy, and socialism, and he secured wage increases for the Canton
workers.

In 1923, Sun turned to the Soviet Union for help in his campaign against
the northern government. Moscow sent aid and advisors and persuaded Sun
to cooperate with the Chinese Communist Party, which had been organized
in Shanghai 2 years earlier. Sun died in 1925 and Chiang Kai-shek, the new
leader of the Guomindang, joined hands with the Communists in a northern
military expedition to unify the country. In 1927, with victory and national
unification in sight, Chiang launched a bloody purge against his Communist
allies.

The Communists who survived the purge established headquarters in
southern Jiangxi province; Mao Zedong became their leader. Guomindang
forces attacked in 1934 and forced them to retreat to the north. During the
famous Long March, covering a distance of some 6,000 miles, the Communists
fought their way through the southern and western provinces of China for

---

[4]Adam Smith, *An Inquiry into the Nature and Causes of the Wealth of Nations* (New York:
P. F. Collier and Son, 1909), 75–76.

[5]L. Carrington Goodrich, *A Short History of the Chinese People,* 3d ed. (New York: Harper and
Brothers, 1959), 223.

over a year. They eventually established their headquarters in Yanan, a desolate and remote outpost in northern Shaanxi province.

In 1937, Japan moved to occupy a large part of northern China and the Nationalist government fled to Chongqing in the south. Thus, the Communist government in Yanan became the command center for a growing number of anti-Japanese bases in the north. By 1945 the Party claimed over 1.2 million members and governed areas with a population of 95.5 million.[6] The Yanan period also had an important impact on Chairman Mao's philosophies of self-reliance and mass political participation and on his preference for moral over material incentives.

When World War II ended, the Communists and Nationalists no longer faced a common enemy and the civil war resumed. With their strength in the rural areas, the Communists were able to drive the Nationalists onto the island of Taiwan in 1949, establishing the People's Republic of China on the mainland.

Importing the Soviet Model, 1949–1957

Three months before the People's Republic was established, Mao Zedong dismissed those critics who said that he was "leaning to one side," and pledged his allegiance to the Soviet model of economic and social development:

We must overcome difficulties, we must learn what we do not know. *. . . We must not pretend to know when we do not know. . . . The Communist Party of the Soviet Union is our best teacher and we must learn from it.*[7]

A 20-year Treaty of Friendship, Alliance, and Mutual Assistance was signed between the Soviet Union and China in 1950, and the Soviets provided an extensive package of economic aid. Territories and military bases that were taken from the Japanese were returned to China, factories were built for low prices and financed at low interest rates, thousands of Soviet economists and technicians were sent to work in China, and tens of thousands of Chinese specialists were trained in the Soviet Union.

The initial challenge faced by the Communists was to speed the recovery from the disruption of the civil war and to begin a program of nationalization and land reform. During 1950 to 1952, about 45 percent of all farmland was confiscated from the former landlords and distributed to the poorer peasants. A system of local tribunals was established to implement the land reform and "to try and punish . . . the hated despotic elements who have committed heinous crimes, whom the masses of the people demand to be brought to justice, and all persons who resist or violate the provisions of the Land Reform Law."[8] At least 2 million landlords died in the process.

[6]James R. Townsend and Brantly Womack, *Politics in China,* 3d ed. (Boston: Little, Brown, 1986), 74.

[7]"On the People's Democratic Dictatorship," in *Mao Tse-tung and Lin Piao: Post Revolutionary Writings,* ed. K. Fan (Garden City, N.Y.: Anchor Books, 1972), 19.

[8]*The Land Reform Law of the People's Republic of China* (Peking: Foreign Languages Press, 1976), 13.

In industry, the Communists assumed ownership of about two-thirds of the nation's capital stock from the outgoing Nationalist government. Firms were also obtained from foreign "imperialists" who fled the country. Following the example of the Soviet New Economic Policy of the 1920s, the Chinese attempted to nationalize only the commanding heights of industry, including metallurgy, energy, chemicals, engineering, electrical machinery, and railroads. The remaining enterprises were left in private hands, with the understanding that they would gradually be socialized. Thus, the program of nationalization avoided the excesses that were experienced in the Soviet Union during War Communism, and it proceeded with little domestic opposition.

Soon after the revolution, the Communists also enacted an extensive program of social reforms. Their campaign to improve public health included stiff penalties for consumption or sale of opium. A new marriage law strengthened the legal status of women and protected them from "tyrannical husbands." Educational reforms were undertaken, but a shortage of teachers made it impossible to introduce compulsory schooling.

By 1952 the Chinese economy had regained its prerevolutionary peak level of production, and the First Five-Year Plan (1953–1957) was prepared (with the help of Soviet economists) to speed the process of industrialization. Reflecting the traditional Soviet emphasis on heavy industry, the plan called for 20 percent annual growth of gross industrial output and 5 percent annual growth of agricultural production. These targets were exceeded with the help of Soviet financial and technical aid; the 1949 level of GNP per capita had roughly doubled by 1957.

The Great Leap Forward, 1958–1960

Despite the steady growth of agricultural production during the First Five-Year Plan, the industrial labor force grew even more rapidly and urban food shortages appeared in 1956 and 1957. By early 1958, Chairman Mao began openly to question whether the Soviet development model was appropriate for the Chinese economy. He questioned whether nationwide central planning and the emphasis on industry over agriculture were appropriate in a poor, overpopulated country with a primitive communications system. Dogmatic adherence to the Soviet model fell out of favor:

In the period following the liberation of the whole country (from 1950 to 1957), dogmatism made its appearance both in economic and in cultural and educational work. . . . In economic work dogmatism primarily manifested itself in heavy industry, planning, banking, and statistics, especially in heavy industry and planning. Since we didn't understand these things and had absolutely no experience, all we could do in our ignorance was to import foreign methods. . . . In short, the Soviet Union was tops.[9]

---

[9]Chairman Mao quoted in Alexander Eckstein, *China's Economic Revolution* (Cambridge: Cambridge University Press, 1977), 55.

To declare his independence from the Soviet model, Mao introduced a leftist program that was inaccurately called the Great Leap Forward (GLF). The GLF was meant to serve several purposes. First, it replaced the Soviet pattern of unbalanced growth with a Chinese policy of "walking on two legs"—simultaneous development of industry and agriculture. Second, the GLF was designed to spread industrial development into the interior of the country, away from the traditional industrial centers on the Pacific coast.

Third, somewhat like the system of War Communism in the Soviet Union, the GLF was represented as a bold move toward the utopian communist state. Material incentives and technological expertise were sacrificed, respectively, at the altars of the new communist man and the wisdom of the worker. The centralized authority of the state was allowed to fade as more authority was shifted to the local communes. Monetary exchange was partially replaced by rationing.

The People's Communes

Probably the most important single component of the GLF was the reorganization of the rural sector into people's communes. Each of these was formed by combining several rural cooperatives and/or Soviet-style collective farms and placing them under a single administration with many of the powers of a local government. Thus, in addition to the farms, each commune typically would operate its own tax offices, schools, hospitals, power stations, irrigation systems, and recreational facilities. This integrated form of organization was retained with modifications until 1979, when the political and economic functions were again divided between townships, Party organizations, cooperatives, and households.

Each commune was hierarchically divided into 10 to 20 production brigades and 100 to 200 production teams, encompassing about 3,000 to 5,000 households. The production team was the basic unit of agricultural organization. Its leaders would decide which specific crops to grow and issue work assignments to the households. The brigade leaders coordinated the activity of the teams in areas such as equipment repair and construction and assisted the teams in obtaining fertilizer, insecticides, electricity, and other inputs.

In line with the radicalism of the GLF, the communes were formed very quickly, causing disruption of economic management and local governmental services. Furthermore, the administrators of the communes initially gave greater attention to ideology than to incentives. A large portion of income was distributed "to each according to his needs," and households were deprived of their private plots. Some communes drove the doctrine of social ownership to the extreme and collectivized all personal property down to cooking pots.

Small-Scale Industry

Industrial policy during the GLF emphasized the development of small-scale, labor-intensive industries in the rural areas. This strategy was designed to provide industrial inputs to agriculture, absorb underemployed and unemployed labor, and modernize some of the more isolated parts of the country. Thus, small plants were established by local governments all over the country to produce agricultural tools, fertilizers, pesticides, iron, steel, and a broad range of other goods. About 2 million so-called backyard blast furnaces were reportedly built in 1958 alone, and about 50 million people were said to be involved in their construction.

The GLF succeeded in spreading industrial production through a larger part of the country. The share of pig-iron production contributed by the northeastern region dropped from 48 to 18 percent between 1957 and 1960, while the share of the central region increased from 6 to 21 percent.[10] With the exception of Tibet, all of the provinces, autonomous regions, and central government municipalities were steel producers by 1959.

On the negative side, many of the small factories were extremely inefficient. Many found it difficult to obtain raw materials and the quality of their output was often very poor. They were often operated only a few hours a day by those unskilled agricultural workers with some time to spare. When industrial production fell in 1961, it became clear that money invested in larger enterprises would yield larger returns, and many of the smaller plants were closed.

The Legacy of the Great Leap

In most respects, the Great Leap Forward was a disaster. The chaotic formation of the communes, the destruction of material incentives, and bad weather caused grain production to plummet by 24 percent between 1958 and 1960. The Chinese government, which is now very critical of the "leftist" GLF, claims that the resulting famine caused millions of deaths. Equally important in the context of world history, the GLF started an argument over ideology between Beijing and Moscow that led to a rupture in their diplomatic relations in 1960. Soviet advisors were called home, technological and financial aid was withdrawn, and border conflicts erupted.

The collapse of agricultural production, the withdrawal of Soviet aid, and the introduction of inefficient production techniques (for example, the backyard steel mills) combined to reduce industrial production by roughly 40 percent in 1961. The GLF also had a devastating effect on education, science and technology, foreign trade, and population control. On the other hand, the formation of the communes made it possible to mobilize millions of workers each year to dig irrigation ditches and build dikes and dams for flood control.

Readjustment and Recovery, 1961–1965

As the Great Leap Forward faltered, Chairman Mao was criticized in the Chinese press. One account, for example, alleged that he suffered from amne-

---

[10]Willy Kraus, *Economic Development and Social Change in the People's Republic of China* (New York: Springer-Verlag, 1982), 146.

sia and was cut off from reality.[11] In 1959, Mao stepped down as president of the People's Republic (although he continued as Party chairman) and handed the position to Liu Shaoqi, the leader of the moderates. Liu rolled back many of the excesses of the GLF.

Whereas the Soviet model had assigned the highest priority to industrial production and the GLF was predicated on simultaneous rapid growth of industry and agriculture, the slogan of the early 1960s was "Agriculture First." The average commune was reduced in size from about 5,000 households in 1959 to 1,700 households in 1963. Individual incomes were linked to the performance of the production team, rather than the commune, and the private plots were restored. Thus, the individual laborer could perceive a closer connection between his work and his rewards.

In industry, investment was tilted toward the production of agricultural equipment and the inefficient small-scale factories were closed. The system of central planning was strengthened to deal with raw material shortages, and trade was increased with Japan and the West.

In terms of social policy, readjustment meant that the focus of the educational system shifted from politics and ideology to technical subjects. The moderates reduced the number of operating schools and universities to improve their quality. Birth control and family planning were encouraged under the slogan: "Two children are just right, three are too many, and four is an error."

In economic terms, these moderate policies were quite successful. After touching bottom in 1961, real GNP recovered to the pre-GLF level by 1964. Other problems began to appear, however, on a political and social plane. In the upper reaches of power, the bureaucracy expanded its size, power, and privilege. In the countryside, the free markets and private plots created a class of relatively wealthy farmers who could potentially threaten the authority of the Communist Party. Because of the shortage of qualified teachers, the educational system tended to promote elitism.

Beginning in 1962, Mao staged a political comeback with his socialist education campaign, which was designed to broaden the base of the educational system and to increase its ideological content. Mao consolidated his power by the beginning of 1965 and began to criticize those in power who were "taking the capitalist road." The stage was set for the Great Proletarian Cultural Revolution.

The Cultural Revolution, 1966–1976

The Cultural Revolution was primarily a political and ideological movement, but it had important economic consequences. Its underlying purpose was to get China back on the road toward full utopian communism. With this in mind,

---

[11]See M. Goldman, "The Unique 'Blooming and Contending' of 1961–62," *China Quarterly* 37 (1969): 54–83.

Mao and his followers had at least three objectives: (1) to overturn the existing power structure and to reverse the Soviet-style trend toward bureaucratism and state capitalism, (2) to cleanse "New China" of all traditional Chinese and Western cultural expressions that could encourage the resurgence of feudalism or capitalism, and (3) to raise the socialist consciousness of the masses.

In his effort to break the bureaucratic power structure, Mao carried his appeal to the masses. In place of the Communist Youth League and other orderly political organizations, Mao formed the Red Guard—a vast, loosely organized, revolutionary army of disaffected young people. With some of its members only 12 and 13 years old, the Red Guard conducted a series of tribunals and purges that were reminiscent of the Inquisition—but in this case the victims were "capitalist roaders" rather than Manichaean heretics. All counterrevolutionaries and rightists were subject to their condemnation, from shopkeepers and teachers to journalists and governmental leaders at local and national levels. Confessions of guilt were often obtained by torture.

All in all, the government now says that as many as 2.9 million people were persecuted during the Cultural Revolution and its aftermath; it caused about 34,000 deaths (in comparison, about 34,000 Americans died in the Korean War and 47,000 Americans died in Vietnam). Chief among the victims was Liu Shaoqi, the moderate leader who was president of the People's Republic, deputy Party chairman, and chairman of the National Defense Council. Liu was expelled from the Party and stripped of all of his governmental duties. He eventually died while under house arrest.

In 1967, Chinese politics degenerated into utter chaos. The relatively pluralistic Central Committee of the Party and its apparatus ceased to function and was replaced by a Central Cultural Revolution Group, dominated by radicals. Red Guard groups roamed the countryside performing their rites of rectification and feuding with rival Red Guard groups. Anyone in any office, shop, or commune who thought its leadership was corrupt or revisionist was encouraged to openly criticize it and engage in conflict. Industrial production fell for the first time since the latter days of the Great Leap Forward.

To restore some semblance of order, Mao finally instructed the People's Liberation Army to intervene. Once in control, the army placed **Revolutionary Committees** in charge of the factories and the local governments. Each committee included representatives from the army, the Red Guard, and the repentant veteran managers—the "three-way alliance." With the purge of the political leadership and the formation of the Revolutionary Committees, the old power structure had been thoroughly undermined.

The cultural component of the Cultural Revolution was pursued with similar zeal. Campaigns were waged against Confucianism, Western fashion, art, and music (including classical music), and traditional Chinese literature and performing arts. All of this had a devastating effect on foreign economic and political relations. Foreign ambassadors and crews on foreign ships were attacked, losing China its friends in both the East and the West. After growing by about 60 percent between 1962 and 1966, the dollar value of Chinese foreign trade fell by about 11 percent between 1966 and 1968.

The campaign against bourgeois culture was closely connected with the third phase of the Revolution—the effort to create a new proletarian society with its own philosophy, technology, music, and style of dress. Maoist philosophy was presented as a replacement for Confucianism and everyone was expected to study it. Intellectuals, bureaucrats, and capitalist roaders were required to work in the fields to get in touch with the masses. The masses, in turn, were admonished to learn from Tachai—a production brigade in the mountains that increased its agricultural yields against serious obstacles. "The Tachai spirit meant working for the revolution and not for 'filthy lucre,' seven-day work-weeks and twelve-hour working days, remuneration according to political reliability, doing without private plots and side occupations, . . . and especially self-reliance and delivery of large amounts of grain to the state."[12]

Despite all of this, the leaders of the Cultural Revolution did not order any basic institutional changes in the countryside, apart from the formation of the Revolutionary Committees. No national effort was made to abolish private-plot agriculture or to move the focus of rural organization from the production teams to the communes, although these actions were taken by some of the more zealous Revolutionary Committees. Accordingly, the disruption of agricultural production that attended the Great Leap Forward was not repeated during the Cultural Revolution. With the exception of a small weather-related downturn in 1968, advances in grain production were registered in all of the years between 1960 and 1971.

The end of the Cultural Revolution found Chairman Mao in his 70s and the country under military rule. The military elite was led by Defense Minister Lin Biao, who was officially designated as Mao's successor at the 1969 Party Congress. For reasons that are not entirely clear, Lin allegedly attempted to assassinate Mao in an aborted coup d'etat in 1971.[13] In their effort to escape from the country, Lin, his wife (who was also a Politburo member), and his lieutenants in the military hierarchy died in a mysterious plane crash in Inner Mongolia.

The chief political beneficiary of Lin's death was Premier Zhou Enlai, one of the few moderates to remain in power during the Cultural Revolution. Within a month of Lin's death, Zhou held talks with Henry Kissinger that led to President Nixon's historic visit to Beijing. Zhou strengthened his power base by rehabilitating many of the moderates who were purged during the 1960s. Chief among these was Deng Xiaoping, who as general secretary of the Central Committee had been denounced as the number-two person taking the capitalist road (Liu Shaoqi was number one). Zhou made Deng his vice-premier in 1973 and vice-chairman of the Party and chief of staff of the army in 1975.

---

[12]Kraus, *Economic Development and Social Change in the People's Republic of China,* 193.

[13]For documentation and analysis, see Michael Y. M. Kau, ed., *The Lin Piao Affair: Power Politics and Military Coup* (White Plains, N.Y.: International Arts and Sciences Press, 1975). For a fascinating fictionalized interpretation of the affair, see John Ehrlichman's novel, *The China Card* (New York: Simon and Schuster, 1986).

Under the leadership of Zhou and Deng, many of the policies of the Cultural Revolution were reversed. Material incentives, foreign contacts, and the bureaucratic machinery of the government were all strengthened. Knowledge of foreign languages was again encouraged, and English language courses were introduced in some primary schools. Greater attention was given to economic planning, which had fallen into disarray during the 1960s. After falling during the early years of the Cultural Revolution, national income increased during each year between 1969 and 1975. At the 1975 Party Congress, Zhou introduced his plan to achieve **Four Modernizations**—in agriculture, industry, defense, and technology—by the year 2000.

In 1976, both Mao Zedong and Zhou Enlai died. An intense battle for succession erupted between Deng Xiaoping, Zhou's hand-picked successor, and Jiang Qing, Mao's widow, a leader of the Cultural Revolution, and a member of the radical Gang of Four. The power struggle, punctuated by mass demonstrations and riots in Beijing's Tien An Men Square, caused a cessation of economic growth in 1976. The outcome stripped Deng Xiaoping of his titles once again, and the Party was left in the hands of a compromise candidate—a relative newcomer named Hua Guofeng. Late in 1976, 1 month after Mao's death, Hua had the Gang of Four arrested in an attempt to consolidate his power.

China after 1976: The Post-Mao Era

As a compromise leader, Hua vainly attempted to please both ends of the political spectrum. For the moderates and rightists, he arrested the Gang of Four and strengthened the system of material incentives. In 1977 he ordered the first general wage increase in 20 years and restored the payment of bonuses for plan fulfillment. Most important, he grudgingly allowed Deng Xiaoping to be rehabilitated for the second time in 2 years.

Despite his relative moderation, Hua stood to the left of Deng on several issues. First, he supported the so-called whatever faction—those who adopted the slogan: "We must resolutely support whatever decision Chairman Mao made and follow whatever directives Chairman Mao issued." Deng, on the other hand, said that Mao made serious mistakes during the Cultural Revolution. He agreed that Chairman Mao should be revered as the founder of the People's Republic, but he challenged the dogmatic application of Maoist ideology. "Practice should be the sole criterion for testing truth," and "It doesn't matter whether a cat is black or white if it can catch mice." These became his favorite slogans.

In agriculture, Hua continued to promote the old Maoist Tachai production brigade as an ideal organizational model. Deng and his followers supported stronger material incentives and the sovereignty of the individual production team. In 1980, after Deng had gained firm control, he disclosed that the Tachai brigade had falsified production figures and that its successes were the result of brutal suppression and large investments rather than self-reliance.

In industry, Hua announced a plan in early 1978 to build 120 large-scale projects by 1985—most of them in heavy industry, energy, and transport. An industrialization drive of this kind had not been attempted since the 1958 Great Leap Forward, and Hua adopted some of the Maoist rhetoric that was used during the GLF. The heavy-industry emphasis of the plan caused shortages of consumer goods and its expense caused the government to run a record deficit in 1979. Just as the 1958 leap forced Mao into temporary retirement, the 1978 leap had a devastating effect on Hua's political career.

By the end of 1978, the supporters of Deng Xiaoping constituted a plurality of the Politburo. Since that time, and particularly since 1980 when Hua was removed from leadership, the policies of the moderates have prevailed. Among the significant actions that have been taken or announced are:

- A shift from revolutionary to pragmatic ideology.
- Moderation of the planned rate of economic growth.
- An increase in the autonomy of farms and enterprises, and a shift from detailed central planning to broad indicative planning and macroeconomic control.
- Greater reliance on the market mechanism and greater flexibility of prices.
- A shift of investment priorities from heavy industry to agriculture and light industry.
- Greater emphasis on material rather than moral incentives.
- Greater allowance for small-scale private enterprise.
- Greater emphasis on control of population growth.
- A stronger educational system, including a doubling of the number of college graduates during 1986 to 1990, and the introduction of 9 years of compulsory education.
- Expansion of foreign trade and foreign educational, cultural, technological, and military cooperation.

The Ideology of Pragmatism

China has long been obsessed by its philosophies and ideologies. Public servants were expected to learn the sayings of Confucius before the revolution and the sayings of Mao afterwards. The results of Party meetings are often announced to the public through the adoption of new national slogans. The present leaders have not abandoned ideology, but they are modifying the Maoist teachings on revolution and class struggle with a new ideology of pragmatism and modernization.

In 1986, the Central Committee declared that the Party made a "serious miscalculation" after the revolution when it "continued to adhere to the policy of taking class struggle as the key link. . . . " Under present conditions, "the principle contradiction in Chinese society . . . is the one between the ever-growing material and cultural needs of the people and the country's backward production." Indeed, Marx's materialist conception of history, as interpreted by the Chinese, implies that modernization is a necessary condition for further

STUDENT UNREST—CHINESE STYLE

China has a long tradition of campus activism. One of the first salvos in the Cultural Revolution was fired in May 1966, when a group of philosophy lecturers erected a poster that denounced the president of Beijing University. The text of the poster was published a month later in *People's Daily* and encouraged additional criticism of national leaders. In July, Chairman Mao closed all of the schools and universities to unleash the revolutionary fervor of the students; in August he held a rally of 1 million young Red Guard members in Tienanmen Square.

On New Year's Day 1987, a crowd of 2,000 college students and teachers returned to Tienanmen Square to air a very different list of demands. Together with protesters in Hefei, Wuhan, Chongqing, Kunming, and Shenzhen, they called for free speech, freedom of the press, and freedom to form new political parties. In the words of one Beijing undergraduate, "A lot of things about Marxism are good, but I don't agree with everything. Marxism denies other truths. . . . Why is Japan so developed and we are so backward? Because Japan accepts more than one truth."

When the government mounted its campaign against bourgeois liberalization, it provoked a new group of dissidents. Three weeks after the demonstration in Tienanmen Square, an open letter was signed by 1,000 Chinese students studying in American universities and almost half of them allowed their names to be published. In part, the letter said the following:

We, the Chinese studying abroad . . . are extremely concerned about the recent changes in the political situation in China. . . . We fear the recurrence of the . . . Cultural Revolution in which ruthless struggle and merciless criticism were rampant. . . . The recent development . . . seriously violates the spirit of the constitutional rights such as freedom of speech. If this continues, the economic and political reforms of China will be ruined. . . . We sincerely hope that the party and the government will persist in reforms, oppose retrogression, preserve the principle of the rule of law, and avoid punishing people for voicing their opinions.

Sources: Willy Kraus, *Economic Development and Social Change in the People's Republic of China* (New York: Springer-Verlag, 1982), 172–174; *Wall Street Journal*, January 8, 1987, 18; and January 23, 1987, 14.

development of ideology: "Material progress lays the groundwork and furnishes practical experience for cultural and ideological progress."[14]

The leaders made it clear in 1987 that ideological relaxation has its limits. When college students held demonstrations in several cities calling for Western-style democracy, a campaign was launched against bourgeois liberalization (see "Student Unrest—Chinese Style," p. 376). In a major speech on the subject, Prime Minister Zhou Ziyang ruled out the possibility of major political reforms, but he also promised that there would be no return to the hysteria of the Cultural Revolution: "Disciplinary action will be taken against a very small number of Party members who have committed serious mistakes. . . . " Furthermore, he promised that the opposition to bourgeois liberalization will cause no change in the program of economic reform or in the policy of opening to the outside world.[15]

Plan and Market

When Deng Xiaoping and his associates consolidated their power, they quickly scaled back the leftist plan targets that were set by Hua Guofeng and strengthened the role of the market mechanism. Hua's goal of 10 percent annual growth in industrial production from 1978 to 1985 was reduced to 8 percent for 1981 to 1985, and then to 7.5 percent for 1986 to 1990. Slower industrial growth, it is hoped, will relieve chronic raw materials shortages and inflationary pressures, and will provide for higher living standards by reducing the bite of capital investment.

Also designed to raise living standards and material incentives, a higher priority has been given to investment in the production of consumer goods and services. As resources were shifted to housing, facilities for public health and culture, and urban public utilities, the share of heavy industry in total capital investment dropped from 50 to 40 percent between 1977 and 1985, and investment in productive capacity dropped from 83 to 63 percent of the total.[16]

The shift toward enterprise autonomy, decentralized planning, and greater reliance on the market mechanism is also designed to meet the needs of consumers and to strengthen work incentives. According to a 1984 decision of the Central Committee, "We must be realistic and admit that for a considerably long time to come, our national economic plans . . . can only be rough and elastic and that we can do no more than . . . exercise effective control over major issues while allowing flexibility in minor ones."[17] In a way quite

---

[14]"Resolution of the Central Committee of the Communist Party of China on the Guiding Principles for Building a Socialist Society with an Advanced Culture and Ideology," *Beijing Review,* October 6, 1986, supplement.

[15]Zhou Ziyang, "On the Two Basics of the Party Line," *Beijing Review,* February 9, 1987, 28.

[16]Zhang Zhongji, "End of Turmoil Brings Economic Growth," *Beijing Review,* September 29, 1986, 20–21.

[17]*China's Economic Structure Reform,* October 1984 Decision of the CPC Central Committee (Beijing: Foreign Languages Press, 1984), 14.

similar to Lenin's New Economic Policy of the 1920s, the Chinese leaders intend to control the production and allocation of grain, coal, steel, petroleum, and other strategically important products, while allowing local authorities and market forces to handle secondary goods. Thus, the number of industrial products controlled by the State Planning Commission's mandatory plan was cut from 120 in 1984 to 60 in 1986.[18]

The growth of market activity has been quite dramatic, particularly since the government lifted price controls from some 1,800 food items in 1985. Food prices increased by 14.4 percent in 1985 and 7.4 percent in 1986, and state subsidies on vegetables sold in the larger cities dropped from nearly 1.2 billion yuan in 1984 to 700 million yuan in 1986. As for industrial products, the prices of more than 1,000 small commodities have been decontrolled, and the remaining commodities with fixed prices account for only 40 percent of total sales volume.[19]

By 1986, China had 66,000 free markets and bazaars which handled about 20 percent of all retail sales of consumer goods. In Hebei province, the markets handled 81 percent of the sales of lamb, 57 percent of the beef, 68 percent of the eggs, and 66 percent of the vegetables. In addition, China had 11.7 million registered private enterprises—and many others that were unregistered—that included everything from home-based restaurants, medical and repair services to manufacturing, shipping, and taxi services with hundreds of employees.[20]

Out of total retail sales, the fraction handled by state outlets dropped from 90 percent in 1978 to 40 percent in 1986; the collective sector's share rose from 8 percent to 36 percent; and the private sector jumped from 2 percent to 24 percent.[21] How much further will the scope of market activity expand? According to Chen Yun, a veteran conservative on the Politburo who is opposed to Deng's pragmatism, central planning must remain "fundamental and predominant," and the role of the market system, though "indispensable," should remain "supplementary and secondary in nature."[22]

Agriculture

Similar in some respects to a program that was introduced during 1961 to 1965 by Liu Shaoqi, the first major economic reform of the post-Mao era was the establishment of the **household responsibility system** in agriculture.[23]

[18]Gao Shangquan, "Progress in Economic Reform (1979–1986)," *Beijing Review,* July 6, 1987, 21.

[19]Ibid.; and "Communique on the Statistics of 1986 Economic and Social Development," *Beijing Review,* March 2, 1987, 24.

[20]James Sterba, "Peking's Streets Teem with Merchants Again as State Loosens Reins," *Wall Street Journal,* June 16, 1986, 1.

[21]Shangquan, "Progress in Economic Reform," 20.

[22]Chen Yun, "Planning and the Market," *Beijing Review,* July 21, 1986, 14.

[23]The following discussion of the responsibility system draws heavily on Frederick W. Crook, "The Reform of the Commune System and the Rise of the Township-Collective-Household System," in U.S. Congress, Joint Economic Committee, *China's Economy Looks toward the Year 2000,* 1: 354–375.

Instead of working collectively under the direction of team leaders, participating households were given their own allocation of land to cultivate under their own initiative. Legally, the land was still owned by the state, but the household could obtain an exclusive right to use it for a 15–year period (longer for pastures and woodlands). Thus, the household was given an incentive to invest in the land and to develop its fertility.

In exchange for its allocation of land, the household agreed to provide fixed quotas of certain agricultural commodities to the state each year at fixed prices. Any output in excess of the agreed level could be consumed by the household, sold on the free market, or sold to the state at negotiated prices. In 1985, the state monopoly for distribution of agricultural goods was abolished and a contractual system of state purchasing replaced the mandatory fixed quotas. The contracted amounts generally are smaller than the previous quotas.[24] In effect, the responsibility system amounts to a sharecropping or family tenant farming arrangement in which the state (represented by the team or cooperative) plays the role of the landlord.

The responsibility system was introduced in stages beginning in 1979 and 98 percent of all farm families were involved in the program by 1984. At the same time, the government strengthened work incentives by increasing its procurement prices for farm products by more than 40 percent between 1977 and 1981.[25] Together with increased planting of high-yield hybrid rice, these measures had an enormous impact on productivity. After growing at an annual rate of only 3.3 percent during the previous decade, agricultural output advanced by 9 percent per year between 1977 and 1985.[26] For the first time in 25 years, China became a net exporter of grain in 1985.

Of course, these successes have imposed their costs. The increases in procurement prices, for example, were introduced without corresponding increases in state retail prices; the difference was filled by budgetary subsidies. By 1981, subsidies absorbed about one-quarter of all governmental budget revenues and amounted to about 30 percent of the wage bill of state workers and employees. They were much larger than the considerable subsidies in other centrally planned economies.[27] The subsidies have been reduced since 1985, but this has required large increases in retail prices.

Another problem is caused by the very success of the agricultural reforms. The responsibility system, the price subsidies, and the variations in the fertility of the land have made it possible for some farmers to become relatively wealthy, while others have remained miserably poor. As the reformers say, the collective is no longer "eating from the big rice bowl." In the Chinese context, wealthy farmers are those who are able to build houses and purchase some electrical appliances; the poor are those who live on the brink of starva-

---

[24]Duan Yingbi, "Opening Markets for Rural Products," *Beijing Review,* May 11, 1987, 14–17.

[25]Nicholas R. Lardy, "Prices, Markets, and the Chinese Peasant," in *Perspectives on Development in Mainland China,* ed. King-yuh Chang (Boulder, Colo.: Westview, 1985), 181.

[26]Zhongji, "End of Turmoil Brings Economic Growth," 18.

[27]Lardy, "Prices, Markets, and the Chinese Peasant," 183.

tion. The widening gulf of inequality has prompted criticism and violent attacks against the rich, some of whom have required police protection. Nonetheless, a 1986 resolution of the Central Committee says that "we shall encourage some of the people to become prosperous first, before the objective of common prosperity is achieved."[28] This is reminiscent of Bukharin's call for the Russian kulaks to get rich in the 1920s, leading to their victimization by Stalin in the 1930s.

Industrial Reform

Although the transformation of the agricultural sector has been dramatic, it should be noted that rural production teams were already relatively autonomous before Deng Xiaoping and his moderate faction gained control of the leadership. Thus, agricultural reform was far simpler to implement than industrial reform. In 1979, when the responsibility system was introduced in the rural sector, industrial reform was limited to experimentation in the Sichuan and Guangdong provinces. Five years passed before the Central Committee announced that "our successes in rural reform . . . provide highly favorable conditions for restructuring China's entire national economy, focusing on the urban economy."[29]

The industrial reforms are being implemented gradually and many are still on the drawing board. First, important changes have been made in the systems of enterprise ownership and management. By the end of 1986, a **factory director responsibility system** had been adopted by about 43 percent of the state-owned enterprises. Under this system, the factory manager signs a contract with state authorities to provide a certain output quota. The greater the amount by which the quota is exceeded, the more profits the manager and his workers are allowed to retain. About 8 percent of the small state-owned enterprises were placed under the control of collectives or leased to individuals. The industrial factories are subject to the broad administrative guidance of local authorities, but most of them are otherwise intended to be free of bureaucratic meddling of ministries, provinces, and autonomous regions.[30]

To strengthen the financial initiative and autonomy of the enterprises, an orderly system of profit taxation is replacing the arbitrary transfer of excess profits to the state budget. The proportion of profits retained by enterprises rose from 4 percent in 1978 to 25 percent in 1986; enterprises in some industries have been allowed to retain 90 percent of their profits to finance investments and incentive payments.[31]

The most radical reform experiments have been undertaken in the industrial city of Shenyang. The authorities there have allowed the formation of

---

[28]"On the Guiding Principles for Building a Socialist Society," *Beijing Review,* October 6, 1986, iv.

[29]*China's Economic Structure Reform,* 2.

[30]"Communique on the Statistics of 1986," 22.

[31]Shangquan, "Progress in Economic Reform," 20.

small securities markets, auctioned a few shops and factories, and plan to sell steel, which is usually subject to central allocation, in the marketplace. Perhaps most significantly, the Shenyang Explosion-Prevention Equipment Factory was forced to close its doors in 1986, making it the first factory to declare bankruptcy in the history of the People's Republic. Although the Shenyang factory employed only 72 staff members, its closure sent shock waves through the whole country. In the words of one Chinese worker:

I think the bankruptcy regulations link the fates of me and my enterprise. In the past, I did not do my best and had a lot of complaints. I thought I could always have a job, no matter how well or badly I did it. . . . Now it would be impossible for me to do that.[32]

Whether the Shenyang experiment will spread across the nation is far from clear, but a 1986 national survey of factory workers provided some interesting results. About 56 percent of the respondents believed that the old guarantee of a lifetime job should be abolished, 89 percent said that it is reasonable for enterprises to lay off workers who are not equal to their jobs, and almost 100 percent believed that enterprises should be closed if they suffer long-term losses, are unable to clear heavy debts, and cannot be saved through reorganization.[33]

Financial Reform

In a traditional centrally planned economy, capital investment is regulated by the plan and financed by budgetary appropriations and bank loans that are also controlled by the plan. Interest rates and rates of return have little impact on investment decisions; loan decisions do not hinge on the ability of the enterprise to repay debts. Slowly and gradually, all of this seems to be changing in China.

Although the central planners and politicians in Beijing still have veto power over all large capital investments, many investment projects are now formulated by local officials and enterprises. These investments may be financed from retained profits or bank loans and bankers are now instructed to base their loan decisions on the economic viability of the projects. "Now our first test," according to a People's Bank official, "is to make sure the borrower can repay."[34] Borrowers that fail to repay now risk bankruptcy.

Even more controversial in the socialist context, some enterprises have raised investment capital by selling ownership shares. Stock issues were introduced in 1980 by a furniture store in northeastern Heilongjiang province and a textile mill (the nation's largest) in Shanghai; they were originally offered only to workers in the respective enterprises and their ownership was not transferable. These limitations were lifted in 1984 when the state-run Foshan

---

[32]Quoted in Li Rongxia, "First Bankruptcy Shocks China," *Beijing Review,* September 8, 1986, 25.

[33]Xin Lin, "Popular Support for Reform," *Beijing Review,* January 26, 1987, 4.

[34]Frank Ching and Neil Ulman, "In China these Days, Bankers Lend Money and Expect It Back," *Wall Street Journal,* January 8, 1982, 1.

Trust and Investment Company tendered the People's Republic's first full-scale public offering.[35] In 1986, China's first stock exchange opened in Shanghai, involving securities issued by 1,480 enterprises. Similar exchanges have been opened subsequently in several other cities.

An interesting example of a share offering is provided by the Shanghai Yanzhong Industrial Company, an offshoot of an existing collective enterprise (state enterprises have been forbidden to issue shares since March 1987). The new enterprise was launched through a sale of 100,000 shares in 1985. Ninety percent of the shares were bought by 18,000 individuals and only 1.5 percent of these were employees of the company. Six percent of the shares went to the collective parent company and 4 percent were bought by a state shipyard. The shares sold for 50 yuan each, about half of an average monthly wage, and the largest individual shareholding was 800 shares. Purchasers receive a guaranteed interest of 7.2 percent per year and may receive an additional net dividend of up to 6 percent, depending on the company's performance. Owners of at least 100 shares—400 people in this case—are invited to the annual shareholders' meeting, where a board of directors is elected. The board elects a director who recommends a general manager. All of this is accomplished with little involvement of the national government, the local government, or the Party.[36]

Chinese critics of stock ownership say that it is leading their country on the slippery path to capitalism—a path that leads to speculative activity, income inequality, and exploitation. Defenders of the system invoke Marxian theory to say that a dose of capitalism may be appropriate in China—given the current stage of development of the forces of production. They also note that the proportion of total investment financed through the sale of securities is still quite small, is heavily regulated, has absorbed some of the excess savings of the population, and has created new jobs.

Population Growth and Employment

Chairman Mao and his leftist faction had little interest in controlling population growth. Mao once said, "It is a very good thing that China has a big population . . . as long as there are people, every kind of miracle can be performed."[37] Encouraged by this permissive policy, the Chinese population grew from about 542 million in 1949 to 937 million in 1976, the year of Mao's death—an annual growth rate of about 2 percent.

With the rise of the pragmatists, population growth has been regarded as a bane rather than a blessing. The surplus population exerts pressure on the

---

[35]Vigor Fung, "Chinese Snap Up Corporate Shares," *Wall Street Journal,* July 19, 1984, 35.

[36]Paul Bowles and Gordon White, "China Struggles with the Concept of Shares," *Wall Street Journal,* July 6, 1987, 15.

[37]Mao Zedong, "The Bankruptcy of the Idealist Conception of History," in *Mao Tse-tung and Lin Piao: Post Revolutionary Writings,* ed. K. Fan (Garden City, N.Y.: Doubleday, 1972), 70–71.

nation's natural resources, slows the growth in living standards, and generates unemployment, crime, and other social problems. The government reported a 1.9 percent overall unemployment rate in 1984; the urban unemployment rate was probably closer to 20 percent.[38]

A rigorous birth control campaign was first enacted in the cities in 1977 and efforts began in the villages in 1979. The authorities initially attempted to encourage two-child families—the guideline was set by Liu Shaoqi before the Cultural Revolution; since 1980 they have advocated one-child families. To meet these goals, a broad range of actions have been taken. In terms of positive incentives, bonuses are given to couples who pledge to have only one child, and they may also be publicly honored in their workplaces and neighborhoods. One-child families are given longer maternity allowances, larger pensions, and priority in housing, education, and medical care. On the other hand, families with additional children may be subject to fines and taxes that are designed to compensate for the extra burden imposed on society.

On the medical front, family planning services, contraceptives, abortions, and tubal ligations are provided free of charge. In 1983, 71 percent of the married women of childbearing age were reportedly using contraceptives, compared to 35 percent in India and less than 10 percent in the majority of low-income nations.[39] According to official pronouncements, participation in the family planning program is supposed to be voluntary, although it is encouraged by severe material and moral incentives. Unfortunately, in several provinces the program has been taken to extremes and scores of reports have documented the performance of compulsory abortions and sterilizations.[40] In some rural areas, tight population controls and the traditional desire to have male children have combined to cause an epidemic of female infanticide. Alarmingly, every year the number of registered male births exceeds the number of registered female births by several thousand. These practices have been condemned officially and some of the perpetrators have been prosecuted as criminals, but the underlying causes have not disappeared.

The population control measures have shown tangible results. The annual growth rate of the population slowed from 2 percent between 1949 and 1976 to about 1.3 percent between 1976 and 1985. In keeping with the one-child policy, the proportion of first births out of total births increased from 21 percent in 1970 to 47 percent in 1981; by 1982 this proportion exceeded 80 percent in some cities and provinces.[41]

The benefits that will flow from a slower rate of population growth are clear enough, but the Chinese will also have to cope with some troublesome

[38]Peng Xianchu, "Providing Jobs for China's Hundreds of Millions," *China Reconstructs* 35 (February 1986): 12; and Jurgen Domes, *The Government and Politics of the PRC: A Time of Transition* (Boulder, Colo.: Westview Press, 1985), 224.

[39]The World Bank, *World Development Report 1986* (New York: Oxford University Press, 1986), 230.

[40]For example, see Steven Mosher, *Broken Earth: The Rural Chinese* (New York: Free Press, 1983), 254f.

[41]The World Bank, *World Development Report 1984* (New York: Oxford University Press, 1984), 178.

side effects. The one-child policy means that the working-age population will grow by only 41 percent between 1980 and 2000, while the elderly population will double. Thus, it will become increasingly difficult to provide for pensioners. Equally interesting, the Chinese are beginning to ponder the social and political consequences of raising a generation of only children. Will these stereotypically spoiled, self-centered, and demanding children be willing to submit to the authority structure and common will of the socialist state, or will they be more comfortable in a world of capitalist individualism?[42]

Foreign Contacts

After the isolationism of the Cultural Revolution, one of the most dramatic and significant shifts in policy during the post-Mao era has been the acceptance of foreign economic, political, and cultural contact—the open door policy. Foreign trade and investment relations have grown rapidly, foreign language study has been reintroduced in the schools, thousands of students have been sent to study abroad, and foreign educators have been invited to teach in Chinese universities. The share of exports in national income increased from approximately 6 percent in 1976 to 11 percent in 1984. Furthermore, the government claims that between 1979 and 1986 it negotiated contracts for $18.1 billion of overseas investment, including 2,513 joint ventures (which are jointly owned by Chinese and foreign interests), 3,971 cooperative ventures in manufacturing and services (which are wholly owned by Chinese organizations), and 127 projects that are wholly owned by foreigners.[43] Although foreign estimates indicate that these official numbers may be inflated, the significance of the open door policy is beyond question.

The rapid growth of foreign contact has required several institutional changes in the Chinese system. Following the lead of Yugoslavia and Hungary, China broke the monopoly of the Ministry of Foreign Trade, giving some of its industrial enterprises the right to deal directly with foreigners. A number of joint venture laws have been passed to create a framework for foreign investment, and special tax breaks have been offered to foreign firms that invest in certain cities and special economic zones. China has gained membership in the World Bank, the International Monetary Fund, and other organizations that were formerly regarded as tools of capitalist exploitation.

China's Future

Will China continue on its path of pragmatism, consumerism, decentralization, population control, and international openness, or will it take still another turn to the left? This question nags a billion people in China and countless

---

[42]John Aird, "China Must Adapt to the Only Child," *Wall Street Journal,* July 15, 1985, 15.

[43]James Sterba, "Firms Doing Business in China Are Stymied by Costs and Hassles," *Wall Street Journal,* July 17, 1986, 1.

people elsewhere who recognize its political and economic importance. This is a question, it seems, on which reasonable people can differ.

To this author, it seems that the process of moderate reform is likely to continue. Chairman Mao, the spiritual leader of the left, has passed from the scene, and most of his followers have been purged from the leadership. Very few people seem to have fond memories of the Great Leap Forward and the Cultural Revolution, and living standards have improved markedly in recent years. Moreover, after the process of decentralization has been accomplished and individuals feel that they have greater control over their own lives, it may be difficult to turn back.

On the other hand, a number of eminent critics have questioned the depth and legitimacy of the recent Chinese reforms and assert that "one of the most widespread, costly, and obvious mistakes made in the past by American China specialists has been their assumption of a consensus or stable coalition existing among the top leadership group or the ability of a single person to dominate the top leadership group."[44] Deng Xiaoping may have purged his opposition, but Deng himself has been purged twice. The reforms have given rise to charges of income inequality, profiteering, corruption, inflation, and female infanticide. The leaders recognize the value of the open door policy, but they also fear the forces of "bourgeois liberalization" and "complete Westernization."

Perhaps it is best to simply say that all things are possible—from Maoism and Stalinism to Titoism and capitalism. China's growth and power may stagnate or it may, as one observer has suggested, close the century with the largest national income in the world.[45] For a great empire with a history that spans the millennia, all things are possible indeed.

Summary

China, a large country with a shortage of arable land, is the only giant of the ancient world to survive into the twentieth century. Flood control required the early development of centralized institutions. Surprising advances in technology were accomplished between the ninth and thirteenth centuries and then slowed, perhaps because of Mongol domination. Rapid population growth began in the 1600s, and the standard of living as assessed by Adam Smith became stationary. This fact, together with political corruption, opium addiction, and foreign imperialism, combined to cause the dynastic system to collapse. After 38 years of political instability, civil war, and two world wars, the Communists took control in 1949.

During 1949 to 1957, the Chinese Communists emulated the Soviet economic system and followed that development model. Chairman Mao even-

---

[44]Robert Dernberger, "Economic Policy and Performance," in *China's Economy Looks toward the Year 2000*, 41.

[45]Gianni Fodella, "China's Economy in the Next Twenty Years," *The World Today* 39 (November 1983): 463–464.

tually decided it was inappropriate for Chinese conditions and launched his Great Leap Forward (1958–1960). The GLF was intended to give greater priority to agriculture and small-scale industry and included campaigns to strengthen moral incentives and establish communes. These policies were implemented poorly and the economic results were disastrous.

During a period of recovery from the GLF (1961–1965), the systems of planning and material incentives were strengthened, and the economic, educational, and population policies turned to the right. Mao then staged a political comeback and launched the Cultural Revolution (1966–1976). This was a period of international isolationism, political and ideological fervor, and inquisitional purges. Its economic consequences were less harmful than those of the GLF, but they continued over a longer period.

When Mao died in 1976, Deng Xiaoping and his rightist moderate faction eventually won the power struggle and gradually introduced their program of reforms. These include a shift from revolutionary to pragmatic ideology, a more moderate rate of economic growth, autonomy and responsibility of farms and enterprises, a shift from detailed central planning to broad indicative planning and macroeconomic control, greater reliance on the market mechanism and material incentives, emphasis on control of population growth, and expansion of foreign trade and foreign educational, cultural, technological, and military cooperation.

Discussion and Review Questions

1. According to Adam Smith, China was transformed from "one of the richest" to one of the "most beggarly" countries in the world between the sixteenth and eighteenth centuries. What were some of the possible reasons?

2. What were the people's communes? When were they formed? How did they differ from Soviet collective farms? How did they change through time?

3. What is the household responsibility system? The managerial responsibility system?

4. Describe the changes that have occurred in the Chinese financial system in recent years. Are they consistent with socialist principles?

5. How do the opinions of the Chinese right and left differ on the subject of population control? What methods have been used by the government in recent years to deal with this problem?

Suggested Readings

Beijing Review. This is a Chinese weekly that is available in English in many university libraries.

Chang, King-yuh, ed. *Perspectives on Development in Mainland China.* Boulder, Colo.: Westview Press, 1985. *A collective volume with 22 articles on Chinese political, economic, military, and international affairs. Most of the authors are American or Taiwanese.*

U.S. Congress, Joint Economic Committee. *China's Economy Looks toward the Year 2000.* Washington, D.C.: USGPO, 1986. *Like all of the JEC volumes, this one provides a wealth of information, statistics, and analysis.*

Eckstein, Alexander. *China's Economic Revolution.* Cambridge: Cambridge University Press, 1977. *Written just before Deng Xiaoping ascended to power, this scholarly work gives a full description of the Chinese development model under Mao's leadership.*

Elvin, Mark. *The Pattern of the Chinese Past.* Stanford, Calif.: Stanford University Press, 1973. *An analysis of Chinese history that attempts to address the big questions: why did the empire stay together, what caused the technological revolution, and what caused it to decline?*

Fan, K., ed. *Mao Tse-tung and Lin Piao: Post Revolutionary Writings.* Garden City, N.Y.: Anchor Books, 1972. Even today, one of the Four Cardinal Principles of Chinese ideology is to "study Mao Zedong thought."

Kraus, Willy. *Economic Development and Social Change in the People's Republic of China.* New York: Springer-Verlag, 1982. *This book combines an analysis of the economy with a study of social policy—particularly health, education, and population policy.*

Mosher, Steven. *Broken Earth: The Rural Chinese.* New York: Free Press, 1983. *Written by an anthropologist, this is an unvarnished account of the extreme privation that still exists in the countryside.*

Muqiao, Xue. *China's Socialist Economy.* Beijing: Foreign Languages Press, 1981. *A general survey of the economy by one of the architects of the reforms.*

Riskin, Carl. *Political Economy of Chinese Development since 1949.* Oxford: Oxford University Press, 1985.

IV
PART

ECONOMIC DEVELOPMENT, TRADE, AND THE FUTURE

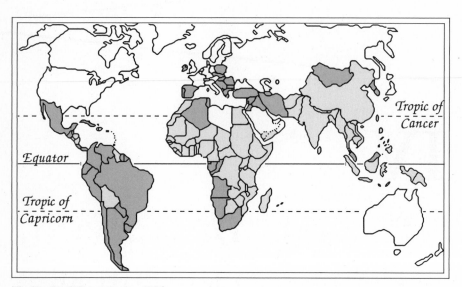

The World: GNP per Capita, 1984
- ☐ $100–$999
- ▨ $1,000–$4,999
- ☐ $5,000–$25,000

17
CHAPTER

THE DEVELOPING COUNTRIES

Most of the people in the world are poor, so if we knew the Economics of being poor we would know much of the Economics that really matters.
—Theodore W. Schultz
  Nobel Lecture
  Journal of Political Economy, August 1980

Two centuries after the Industrial Revolution, the World Bank reports that 1 billion people still live in absolute poverty—a condition of life "so characterized by malnutrition, illiteracy, and disease as to be beneath any reasonable definition of human decency."[1] These people and 2.5 billion others constitute that not-so-silent majority known as the Third World. They invade our consciousness when we hear of another famine in Africa or South Asia, another civil war in Latin America, another reversal of world commodity prices, or another report of the international debt crisis.

Who are the poor? Why do they remain poor? What can be done about it? Why hasn't it been done? These are important, difficult, and immortal questions; they extend far beyond the scope of comparative economic systems. For our present purposes, we will survey only a few of the relevant issues and hope that these will inspire additional study.

Obstacles to Development

Although social scientists do not agree on the causes of prolonged Third World poverty, there are a few premises that few would dispute. First, if a country wishes for sustained economic growth, it must somehow increase its stock of physical and/or human capital (factories, machinery, equipment, health, and education). If this is to be done without massive foreign aid, the country must begin by producing an output that exceeds the subsistence needs of the population. Furthermore, some group of people, whether they be private entrepreneurs, government leaders, or foreign colonialists, must mobilize that surplus toward productive ends (building factories, schools, roads, etc.) rather than allowing it to dissipate on extravagant consumption, military adventures, or civic monuments, or transferring it to other countries.

Speaking very generally, countries that remain poor are those that fail to generate a sufficient investable surplus or those that fail to invest it in productive activities. Within this framework, the various camps of economists differ on the causes of the low saving and investment rates. Traditional theories usually stress environmental and institutional barriers, and the "vicious circles of poverty." Radical economists believe that the surplus of the Third World is transferred to the industrial countries by an exploitive system of investment and trade.

Environment and Culture

In their search for the underlying causes of poverty and underdevelopment, some social scientists have argued that the Third World is accursed by geographic, environmental, and cultural conditions that are difficult to overcome. The average developing country, for example, has only half as much arable

---

[1]The World Bank, *World Development Report 1982* (New York: Oxford University Press, 1982), 78; and The World Bank, *Poverty and Human Development* (New York: Oxford University Press, 1980), v.

land per capita as the average industrial country (Table A.1). Accordingly, it is difficult to generate an investable surplus of output above the subsistence needs of the population.

Most of the developing world, and very little of the industrial world, is located in a band around the equator that stretches from the Tropic of Capricorn to the Tropic of Cancer. Most of this region receives heavy rain all year (within 1,000 miles of the equator) or heavy monsoon rains for half of the year and no rain for the rest of the year (1,000 to 1,500 miles from the equator), or has turned to desert. Except in high-altitude areas, temperatures range from hot to very hot, placing a strain on human bodies and automotive radiators.

Through much of the region that is not covered by jungle, desert, or volcanic or alluvial soil, excessive heat has burned away the organic matter of the soil and excessive rain has washed away its nutrients. The tropical climate and poor sanitation foster the reproduction of insects, parasites, and pests that attack people, plants, and animals; winter, the great exterminator, never comes.[2]

The cultural and religious impact on economic development is more difficult to explain. With the exception of Japan, all high-income industrial countries are predominantly Christian and all Protestant countries have high incomes. No Muslim country has advanced beyond the lower-middle income level without the help of petroleum exports.[3] According to cultural determinists, patterns such as these can be explained by religious and cultural attitudes toward freedom, conformity, equality, work, education, birth control, and wealth accumulation.

A cultural determinist would say, for example, that Latin America is relatively poor and North America is relatively rich because of differences between their Spanish and British colonial heritages. Spain was overpowered by the Moors (or Muslims) in the eighth century and, despite centuries of civil war, did not fully regain its independence until 1492, the year of Columbus's voyage. Thus, some would say that Spain inherited an authoritarian culture from the Moors and the long process of reconquest created an extremely orthodox and intolerant brand of Roman Catholicism. This intolerance led Spain to launch its Inquisition in 1480 and to expel all Jews from its territory in 1492. Spanish corruption, authoritarianism, inequality, and intolerance were allegedly transplanted in Latin America, where they have stood in the way of economic development.[4]

In Asia, rough cultural lines can be drawn between the Muslim countries of the Middle East and Pakistan, the Hindu countries of the south (India, Bangladesh, and Nepal), and the Confucian and Buddhist countries of the east.

---

[2]Andrew Karmarck, *The Tropics and Economic Development* (Baltimore: The Johns Hopkins University Press, 1976).

[3]Everett Hagen, *The Economics of Development,* 4th ed. (Homewood, Ill.: Irwin, 1986), 44.

[4]For an extended discussion of Latin American development by a cultural determinist, see Lawrence E. Harrison, *Development Is a State of Mind: The Latin American Case* (Lanham, Md.: University Press of America, 1985).

Some say that the Confucian work ethic has contributed to the successful growth of Japan and the East Asian Gang of Four—Hong Kong, Singapore, South Korea, and Taiwan. Conversely, certain aspects of Hinduism have allegedly retarded development in South Asia. The caste system, for example, places limits on labor mobility, income equality, and work incentives. The law of *karma*, which says that one's fate in this life is the reward or punishment for actions in a previous life, supposedly evokes a fatalistic acceptance of the status quo.

As many questions are left unanswered by geographic and cultural determinism as they are by any one-factor theory of development. Why were the ancient civilizations of Egypt, Mesopotamia, China, and the Mayas able to flourish under the curse of tropical geography? Why has it taken so long for the Confucian work ethic to take its place beside (or ahead of) the Protestant ethic? The links between geography, culture, and development are indisputable, but they are not well understood.

The Economic System

Quite often in the Third World, economic growth and development is fettered by the backwardness of economic institutions. The specific problems vary tremendously from one country to another, but a few are rather common.

Land Tenure.   Several different systems of land ownership are used in the Third World; few of them promote economic development. In much of Africa and Asia, particularly in nomadic areas, the land is held in common with no identifiable owner or controlled by a village, tribe, or extended family. In order to insure equity, the right to use the best land is rotated between families. Thus, an individual family has little incentive or opportunity to engage in long-term projects to irrigate and improve the land. If such efforts are undertaken, they usually require the cooperation of an entire community (see "Rural Self-Help: Harambee in Kenya," p. 395).

In most of the countries of Latin America, the land is held privately, but its distribution is very uneven. With the exception of countries that have implemented major land reforms (Mexico, Bolivia, Cuba, and Nicaragua), the *latifundia* (very large farms) usually constitute less than 5 percent of the farms while holding more than 50 percent of the land. The sharecroppers on the *latifundia* have little incentive to improve land that they do not own and the landlords have a poor record of investment. The small farms are usually so tiny that they barely provide a living for their owners.

Beginning in 1917, the Mexican government seized the large estates and distributed them to peasant communities—the *ejidos*. At first, the *ejidos* rotated the best land between families; later they recognized the need to provide stronger incentives for land improvement. Now, the land is assigned to a family for an indefinitely long period, and its use can be inherited (similar to the responsibility system in China).

In 1961, 2 years after the Cuban revolution, President Kennedy launched the Alliance for Progress, an ambitious program of aid and reform. The charter

RURAL SELF-HELP: HARAMBEE IN KENYA

In Kenya, comprehensive national planning was initiated in 1963 to promote industrial growth, while the task of rural development was entrusted to the time-honored tradition of local cooperation, or Harambee (Swahili for "let's all pull together"). In earlier times, the typical Harambee project involved a team of men or women who voluntarily joined to cultivate one another's fields. Nowadays, about half of the projects are organized to build schools; they are also devoted to the construction of health facilities, churches, cattle dips (tanks filled with water and chemicals to kill ticks), roads, bridges, and dams.

A Harambee may be initiated by anyone in the community. They have been launched by local politicians, clergy, business leaders, teachers, and farmers. They usually begin with a local meeting where a need is discussed and a committee is elected. The committee formulates a timetable of action that usually begins with a fundraising ceremony. The latter is attended by local and national governmental officials and by people from all of the surrounding communities who are attracted by the entertainment of drummers and dancers.

Ideally, contributions are made on a voluntary basis (although sometimes beneficiaries of the project are illegally forced to contribute) and may include cash, materials, or pledges of labor. Quite often, for example, a parent group will provide the labor to build and maintain a school. About 90 percent of the contributions are made by individuals; the remainder is made by governments, businesses, foundations, and others.

The practice of voluntary community self-help is not unique to Kenya. Churches, schools, houses, and barns are raised by similar cooperative arrangements in many countries. What is unique, perhaps, is the scope of the Harambee movement. More than 14,000 such projects were completed in Kenya from 1980 to 1984, accounting for over one-third of all capital development in the rural areas. The result? Kenyan agricultural production has grown at more than twice the average rate for other countries of sub-Saharan Africa. Primary school enrollment, which included only half of the nation's children in 1965, is now almost complete. Voluntarism is alive, well, and working in the villages of Kenya.

Sources: Peter M. Ngau, "Tensions in Empowerment: The Experience of the Harambee (Self-Help) Movement in Kenya," *Economic Development and Cultural Change* 35 (April 1987): 523–534; Barbara P. Thomas, "Development through Harambee: Who Wins and Who Loses?" *World Development* 15 (April 1987): 463–481.

of the alliance advocated "programs of comprehensive agrarian reform leading to the transformation of unjust structures and systems of land tenure and use, with a view to replacing *latifundia* and dwarf holdings by an equitable system of land tenure" so that "the land will become for the man who works it the basis of his economic stability, the foundation of his increasing welfare and the guarantee of his freedom and dignity." The vast majority of Latin American peasants are still waiting for the fulfillment of this promise.[5]

Market Structure.   In some countries, the market mechanism is operating at such a primitive level that it can do little to coordinate and guide the development of the economy. In the late 1970s, for example, it was estimated that about 25 percent of all economic activity in Africa took place outside of the monetized sector.[6] In countries with poor transportation and communication systems, the markets are disconnected from one another and from those in the outside world. Price controls, which cripple the operation of the market system, are used to control inflation in many Third World countries.

Recent research indicates that producers in the developing countries can react quite well to market signals. Niger, for example, is one of the poorest countries in the world; its farmers traditionally have relied on sales of groundnuts for their cash income. In the 1970s, the price of cowpeas increased more rapidly than the price of groundnuts, and things began to change. Production of cowpeas increased by more than 250 percent during the 1970s and sales of groundnuts nearly ceased. According to the World Bank staff economists, "All of this happened primarily in response to market signals, despite poor infrastructure, embryonic market information, and generally imperfect market conditions."[7]

Labor Markets.   A wide gulf usually exists between the modern sector of a developing economy, which typically involves capital-intensive industrial production in the cities, and the traditional sector of labor-intensive agricultural production and crafts. Thus, many countries have a **dual labor market** in which urban wages are two or three times larger than rural incomes. It is difficult to explain these differences in terms of skill or productivity; several other factors are apparently involved. The urban workers are more likely to be unionized, more likely to work for nationalized companies, and more likely to have the protection of a legal minimum wage. Thus, urban wages are heavily influenced by the ebb and flow of politics, while rural incomes are determined by local market conditions. The dual wage structure promotes income inequality and attracts large numbers of people into the cities, contributing to urban unemployment.

[5]See Mike Rose, "Agrarian Reform: Rhetoric and Reality," *Latin America and Caribbean Review 1986,* 7th ed. (Essex, Eng.: World of Information, 1985), 30–32.

[6]Anand G. Chandavarkar, "Monetization of Developing Countries," *International Monetary Fund Staff Papers* 24 (November 1977): 678–679.

[7]The World Bank, *World Development Report 1986* (New York: Oxford University Press, 1986), 69.

Financial Markets.   The limited quantity and quality of financial intermediation is a serious problem in many developing countries. The entire financial system is usually organized around a few banks, which are heavily regulated because they have excessive market power. Securities markets are rudimentary or nonexistent, making it difficult to raise money through stock or bond issues. Few people channel their savings through life insurance companies. Governmental taxation and control of interest rates reduces the incentive to save.

Vicious Circles of Poverty

If environmental, cultural, and institutional factors explain some of the initial causes of poverty, a number of vicious circles help to explain why the poor remain poor.

Saving and Investment.   It is difficult for a destitute country to generate the savings that are needed to finance investment. As shown in Table A.1, the investment rate of the 32 low-income countries is much lower than that of any other group of countries. Their low rate of investment, in turn, contributes to their low rate of economic growth.

Health and Education.   Similarly, it is difficult for a poor country to set aside the resources that are needed to provide health and education services to the population, and it is difficult for the children of the poor to take time off from work for their education. Thus, poverty begets disease and illiteracy, which cause the continuation of poverty.

Market Size.   Low income levels and primitive transportation systems restrict the market demand for any given commodity in a developing country. With limited demand, it is impossible to increase efficiency through mass production. A low level of efficiency leads to a continuation of poverty.

Political Instability.   Poverty also regenerates itself by provoking political instability, often in a senseless series of coups d'etat. Bolivia, for example, has had more than 150 governments since it declared independence in 1825; President Hernan Zuazo appointed 74 ministers and 6 cabinets during his first 2 years in office (1983–1984). Short terms of office, in turn, encourage rulers to undertake short-sighted economic policies, such as inflationary creation of money. In 1984 the Bolivian inflation rate was 1,281 percent, while the average for Latin America was 123 percent.[8] According to one comprehensive study, the initiation of economic growth in Latin American countries "usually

---

[8]To buy a television set in 1985, a Bolivian had to carry 68 pounds of 1,000-peso bills (the most common denomination) to the showroom. Tons of paper money are printed for Bolivia in West Germany and Britain and flown in twice a week to meet the demand. Purchases of money cost Bolivia more than $20 million in 1984, making it the country's third-largest import. See *Wall Street Journal,* February 7, 1985, 1.

Table 17.1   The Kuznets Hypothesis: Income and Inequality

	1983 GDP Per Capita Range (dollars)	Average Share of Poorest 40 Percent of Households in Total Income
9 Low-income countries	130–400	15.5
19 Middle-income countries	560–3,840	12.6
21 High-income countries	4,780–16,290	18.5

Source: World Bank, *World Development Report 1985,* 174–175, 228–229, and author's calculations.

dates from the emergence at long last of a stable government able to exercise effective control of the country for an extended period."[9]

Population Growth.   The percentage rate of population growth is about three times larger for the developing countries than it is for the industrial countries. It is even higher if only the low-income countries (Table A.1) are taken into consideration. The populations of poor countries tend to grow rapidly because of their rural lifestyles and their inability or unwillingness (for religious and other reasons) to practice birth control. The poorest countries also tend to have the highest **dependency ratios**—that is, the percentage of the population that is not of working age. In 1984 the dependency ratio was 45 percent in the low-income countries (excluding China), 44 percent in the middle-income developing countries, and only 33 percent in the industrial countries.[10] Until they pass through the demographic transition to lower birth rates, developing countries tend to have high rates of population growth and high dependency rates, both making it difficult to climb out of poverty.

Income Inequality.   Poor countries tend to experience greater income inequality than high-income countries, and efforts to promote economic development may cause inequality to grow worse before it improves. This pattern, known as Kuznets's Law, is illustrated by the data in Table 17.1. On average, income inequality is greatest in the middle-income countries, and lowest in high-income countries. By implication, as a country grows out of the low-income category, it may take a long time for the benefits of economic growth to trickle down to the lower classes of society. Economic growth accompanied by increasing income inequality may contribute to political instability, which may put an end to economic growth.[11]

[9]Lloyd G. Reynolds, "The Spread of Economic Growth to the Third World: 1850–1980," *Journal of Economic Literature* 21 (September 1983): 964.

[10]The World Bank, *World Development Report 1986,* 238.

[11]For a more optimistic assessment, which proposes that the Kuznets effect is too small to negate the welfare effects of economic growth, see Gustav Papanek and Oldrich Kyn, "The Effect on Income Distribution of Development, the Rate of Growth, and Economic Strategy," *Journal of Development Economics* 23 (September 1986): 55–65.

Imperialism and Dependency

Marxists and many others do not accept the environmental and vicious-circle explanations of Third World poverty. The industrial countries, they say, have employed a number of methods to extract the investable surpluses of the developing countries. The rich have grown richer by causing the poor to remain poor.

Most observers would agree that the developing countries were exploited during the colonial era. For example, the American Revolution was fought to end the burden of British colonial taxation. Spanish colonial rule in Latin America was more harsh and covered a longer period of time. One observer in the area that is now Peru described the payment of tribute to the Spaniards:

The Indians of Parinacocha have to carry their tribute over two hundred miles to Cuzco: wheat, maize, cloth, bars of silver, etc. Indian men are loaded with it, and so are the women, the pregnant ones with their heads on their swollen bellies. . . . [They] climb with their loads up slopes that a horse could not climb.[12]

Colonialism continued in India, the Middle East, and the Philippines until the end of World War II and in much of Africa and Indochina until the 1960s. The impact of colonial rule was not entirely negative, particularly under the British and the Japanese. The rulers generally built schools, ports, railways, electric power systems, and other utilities. Karl Marx gave the British credit for breaking the power of the village communities in India, which "had always been the solid foundation of Oriental despotism," and he attributed great importance to the building of railways: "Modern industry, resulting from the railway system, will dissolve the hereditary divisions of labor, upon which rest the Indian castes, those decisive impediments to Indian progress and Indian power."[13]

Now that overt colonialism is largely a thing of the past, Marxists and so-called **dependency theorists** believe that the industrial countries have continued their exploitation of the developing countries through their trade and investment. Multinational corporations (MNCs) are said to play an important role in this process; they engage in direct exploitation of Third World workers through their foreign operations. In Brazil, the country that has received the largest stock of foreign investment, foreign-controlled companies accounted for almost 45 percent of local sales of manufactured goods in 1977.[14]

Defenders of the MNCs say that they provide jobs, training, capital, technology, and tax revenues in the host countries. Brazil, it may be noted, has experienced the highest rate of economic growth in Latin America. A recent study by the World Bank concluded that "equity forms of investment can

---

[12]Quoted in Peter Worsley, *The Three Worlds: Culture and World Development* (Chicago: The University of Chicago Press, 1984), 8.

[13]Marx in the *New York Daily Tribune,* June 25, 1853, quoted in H. A. Reitsma and J. M. G. Kleinpenning, *The Third World in Perspective* (Assen, Neth.: Van Gorcum, 1985), 217.

[14]The World Bank, *World Development Report 1985,* 127.

clearly be beneficial to developing countries, and it is desirable that they be increased."[15]

Critics say that the MNCs extract excessive profits from the host countries and that they fund some of their operations out of local credit markets, crowding out domestic borrowers. Because of their foreign orientation, they introduce products and technologies that are inappropriate for the needs of the developing countries. They create low-skill jobs in the developing countries and shift the high-skill jobs elsewhere. Most important, they encourage governmental corruption and manipulate policies to the detriment of the local populations. Accordingly, many developing countries (and all of the Communist countries) have placed strict limits on foreign direct investment. In India, for example, foreign ownership is normally restricted to 40 percent of a company's equity, although a higher percentage may be allowed if the company is highly export oriented or provides a needed technology.

Marxists found it difficult to build a strong quantitative case for the link between foreign investment and Third World poverty. The profits that are taken out of the developing countries by the MNCs are relatively small as a proportion of national income, particularly for countries such as India. Thus, the dependency theorists have shifted attention from investment to international trade and specialization. In their view, the core (industrial) economies have manipulated the patterns of trade to their own advantage and to the detriment of the peripheral (developing) economies.

Dependency theory grew out of the writings of Raul Prebisch, an Argentine economist, who argued in the 1950s that the developing countries are victimized by their specialization in primary-goods production. The international terms of trade tend to deteriorate for the developing countries, he said, because growth in world income increases the demand for manufactured goods more rapidly than the demand for primary products. Prebisch attempted to support his theory with statistical evidence, but subsequent research has cast doubt over the declining-terms-of-trade hypothesis.[16]

More recently, the French economist Arghiri Emmanuel has argued that regardless of their historical trends, the export prices received by the Third World are simply too low. Thus, the developing countries are forced to surrender their primary goods in an **unequal exchange** for high-priced industrial goods. The prices of primary goods are low, he says, because they incorporate the low labor costs of the developing countries. Thus, poverty begets low prices and low prices beget poverty.[17]

According to traditional analysis, the unequal exchange hypothesis is just as invalid as the cheap-foreign-labor argument of protectionists in the indus-

---

[15]Ibid., 134.

[16]For a review of the evidence, see John Spraos, "The Statistical Debate on the Net Barter Terms of Trade between Primary Commodities and Manufactures," *Economic Journal* 90 (March 1980): 107–128.

[17]For a discussion of Emmanuel's theory and other radical perspectives on development, see Keith Griffin and John Gurley, "Radical Analyses of Imperialism, the Third World, and the Transition to Socialism: A Survey Article," *Journal of Economic Literature* 23 (September 1985): 1089–1143.

trial countries. International trade based on comparative advantage, according to theory, is mutually beneficial to the rich and the poor countries. However, the traditional theory says nothing about the equity with which the gains from trade are distributed between the rich and the poor.

Dependency theorists argue that the developing countries are crippled in many other ways by their peripheral role in the world capitalist system. They are jolted by broad swings in commodity prices during the boom-and-bust phases of the world business cycle, while the prices of manufactured goods remain relatively stable. The international arms race, which is allegedly manipulated by the arms merchants in the industrial countries, forces the developing countries to squander much of their investable surplus. More generally, dependent development means that "some countries can expand through self-impulsion while others . . . can only expand as a reflection of the dominant countries, which may have positive or negative effects on their immediate development."[18]

Development Strategies

Just as explanations of Third World poverty differ from country to country and economist to economist, proposals to alleviate poverty are similarly diverse. If one is persuaded by geographic or cultural determinism, or by vicious-circle theories, or by theories of imperialism and dependency, or by some combination of these, one may decide that the situation of Third World development is hopeless, or that it merely requires the removal of a few obstacles, or that it requires the adoption of a system of national planning, or that it requires the erection of a so-called new international economic order. A few of the more prominent strategies are surveyed below.

Smith, Ricardo, and Surplus Labor

Always the optimist, Adam Smith declared in 1755 (21 years before his *Wealth of Nations*) that "little else is requisite to carry a state to the highest degree of opulence, but peace, easy taxes, and a tolerable administration of justice; all the rest being brought about by the natural course of things." Economic development is the natural order of things, and little is needed to promote it, but excessive governmental activity can stop it. When they attempt to encourage economic growth, governments often disregard the basics: keeping the peace, ensuring justice and the sanctity of contracts, maintaining roads, bridges, and other public goods, and safeguarding the value of the currency.

David Ricardo, one of Smith's disciples, believed that British growth was threatened by restrictions on agricultural imports under the Corn Laws. The restrictions, he said, kept an artificially large labor force in the agricultural

---

[18]Theotonio Dos Santos, "The Structure of Dependence," *American Economic Review* 60 (May 1970): 289–290.

sector, working at very low marginal productivity. If the Corn Laws were repealed, market forces would move these excess workers into industry, where their productivity would be greater. The rise in productivity would create a surplus of output over the subsistence needs of the population, which would open the door for investment and economic growth.

In 1954, W. Arthur Lewis revived the idea that a surplus population of underemployed rural labor could be shifted into industry to increase productivity, generate savings, and fuel economic growth.[19] Lewis said that rapid population growth had created a rural **labor surplus** in the Third World—a surplus that could be mobilized:

The [developing countries] have within themselves all that is required for growth. They have surpluses of fuel and the principal minerals. They have enough land to feed themselves, if they cultivate it properly. They are capable of learning the skills of manufacturing, and of saving the capital required for modernization. Their development does not in the long run depend on the existence of the developed countries, and their potential for growth would be unaffected even if all the developed countries were to sink under the sea.[20]

Although Lewis believes that economic planning and governmental action may be needed to move the surplus agricultural workers into industry, his description of planning is reminiscent of Smith: "The economics of development is not very complicated; the secret of successful planning lies more in sensible politics and good public administration."[21]

Rosenstein-Rodan, Nurske, and Balanced Growth

As the world faced recovery from World War II, several economists agreed that industrialization could be launched by mobilizing the underemployed rural population, but few of them shared Lewis's view that development was "not very complicated." Writing as early as 1943, Paul Rosenstein-Rodan emphasized the obstacles to development and believed that industrialization would require a **big push:**

Launching a country into self-sustaining growth is a little like getting an airplane off the ground. There is a critical ground speed which must be passed before the craft can become airborne. . . . A big push seems to be required to jump over the economic obstacles to development. . . . An atmosphere of development may only arise with a minimum speed or size of investment.[22]

[19]W. A. Lewis, "Economic Development with Unlimited Supplies of Labor," *The Manchester School* (May 1954): 139–191.

[20]W. A. Lewis quoted in Gerald Meier, *Emerging from Poverty: The Economics that Really Matters* (New York: Oxford University Press, 1984), 207.

[21]Ibid., 208.

[22]Rosenstein-Rodan quoted in Meier, *Emerging from Poverty,* 138. Note the apparent influence of Rosenstein-Rodan on Rostow's conception of a "take-off into self-sustained growth," discussed below.

Supporting Rosenstein-Rodan's call for a big push, in 1953 Ragnar Nurske popularized the idea that economic progress is not a spontaneous or automatic affair because vicious circles of poverty, limited investment, malnutrition, and limited market size have stunted the growth of the Third World. Industrialization requires a comprehensive policy of **balanced growth,** accomplished by a wave of capital investments in a number of different industries. No single industry can go it alone, he says, because of the operation of Say's Law—the demand for one product is generated by the production of other goods.

Rostow, Hirschman, and Unbalanced Growth

Nurske's strategy of balanced growth was a counsel of despair in many of the poor countries: it implied that one must somehow support a wide range of industries or do nothing at all. Walt Rostow, also writing in 1953, struck a more responsive chord with Third World leaders when he said that development could be initiated by launching a few **leading sectors.**[23] Based on his reading of European and American history, Rostow concluded that societies pass through several distinct stages on their way to affluence.

According to Rostow's theory, societies emerge from the backward traditional stage as they fulfill the "preconditions for take-off." During the preconditions stage, attitudes toward economic and scientific progress begin to change, an entrepreneurial class is formed, and an infrastructure of transport and communications facilities is built. When the "old blocks and resistances to steady growth are finally overcome," the nation can begin its "take-off into self-sustained growth." The trends in social change, production, and scientific progress that were initiated during the preconditions stage will begin to accelerate, and the rate of investment will roughly double. A few leading sectors will grow most rapidly and will serve as a locomotive for the rest of the economy. The leading sector that launched the British Industrial Revolution, for example, was the cotton industry; the railroads led the way in the United States. After its take-off, our stereotypical society progresses to "technological maturity," then to "mass consumption," and finally to the "search for quality."

In the eyes of its critics, Rostow's theory is too neat, clean, and deterministic to serve as a description of the development path of all societies. The same criticism has been applied to the Marxian stage theory, which Rostow hoped to displace. The leaders of many developing countries have adopted Rostow's analysis as a how-to guide for growth; the take-off and leading sector concepts have entered the vernacular of economic development.

In his theory of **unbalanced growth,** Albert Hirschman gives guidance to those who must choose the leading sectors for a particular country. Most important, he says, special attention should be given to the growth of industries that have strong **linkages** to other industries. These may take several forms. Industries such as automotive manufacturing that create a strong de-

---

[23]Rostow's theory of leading sectors, which first appeared in a 1953 essay, was popularized in his book, *The Stages of Economic Growth* (London: Cambridge University Press, 1960).

mand for inputs from other industries are said to have strong **backward linkages.** Those that produce important inputs for other industries are said to
have **forward linkages.**

Import Substitution and Export Promotion

As Nurske emphasized, one of the dangers of an unbalanced growth strategy is
that the domestic market will not be able to provide sufficient demand for the
output of an isolated industry. One way to get around this problem is through
a policy of **import substitution.** If an industrial product is being imported,
then a domestic demand for that product obviously exists. All that must be
done is to develop an indigenous industry and protect it from foreign
competition.

Import substitution has been employed extensively in Latin America.
Dependency theorists are particularly supportive of this approach because it
shifts the developing countries to more progressive lines of production,
reduces their vulnerability to fluctuations in the world market, and should
alleviate their balance of payments problems. For example, American manufacturing was launched behind the protection of the Non-Importation Act of 1806
and President Jefferson's Embargo Act of 1807.

Critics of import substitution say that it distorts the allocation of resources by restricting foreign trade and the benefits of comparative advantage.
It requires that the government decide which sectors to protect from foreign
competition; these decisions invite governmental bribery and corruption. The
reduction in imports causes a reduction in the demand for foreign exchange,
which causes the exchange rate of the local currency to rise, which makes it
more difficult to sell the country's exports. Thus, the balance of payments may
not improve. Maintenance of high import barriers will often require an enormous system of controls to prevent smuggling. Infant industries that are created by the program will often fail to mature. Finally, the strategy is self-
limiting, in that it must stop when all of the nation's imports have been
replaced.

Encouraged by the successes of Brazil, Hong Kong, South Korea, Singapore, and Taiwan, many critics of import substitution have championed **export
promotion** as an alternative. Instead of levying heavy taxes on imports, the
government should choose a few industries in which the country has a potential comparative advantage and give subsidies, tax relief, import duty rebates,
and low-interest loans to prospective exporters and their customers.

Advocates of export promotion say that it keeps the country open to
foreign trade and competition, thus maintaining the benefits of international
specialization, and it imposes a healthy discipline on the governments and
businesses of the developing countries to maintain their competitiveness. In
particular, the government must resist inflationary policies and overvalued
exchange rates, while businesses must produce at cost and quality levels that
are competitive on the world market. Because no effort is made to restrict
anything, the strategy is accomplished through positive incentives rather than

a bureaucratic system of direct controls, creating less pressure for political corruption.[24]

Critics of export promotion say that it increases the dependence of the local economy on the international business climate. It may create an enclave of export-oriented companies with weak linkages to the rest of the economy. Even if one accepts the idea that an export orientation would be better for the economy in the long run, the adjustment from a tariff-ridden system of import substitution to a more market-oriented allocation of resources is likely to cause unemployment and income inequality in the short to medium term.

Development Planning and the Market

In order to pursue the kinds of growth strategies considered above—balanced or unbalanced growth, import substitution or export promotion—the leaders of the developing countries have prepared more than 300 economic plans since 1950. According to a recent World Bank study, these can be divided into three broad categories.[25] First, Soviet-inspired central planning has been employed in all of the Communist countries and weaker versions were attempted in India, Pakistan, and Turkey in the 1950s and 1960s, and in Bangladesh, Sri Lanka, and Ethiopia in the 1970s. In developing countries, these plans generally cover a 5-year period and include targets for all of the major sectors of the economy. However, a large part of economic activity in these countries continues to be controlled by markets and hand-to-mouth subsistence sectors; thus their plans are not as comprehensive as those in the Soviet Union. Adherence to the plans is controlled through nationalized companies and through licensing and production quotas.

Second, the eastern Asian countries of Japan, Korea, and Singapore developed their own style of indicative planning, based on their Confucian traditions and influenced by French planning. The plans are comprehensive in scope—they cover all major sectors—and they are prepared by cooperation between the public and private sectors. According to the World Bank study, the eastern Asian plans are "characterized not by technical sophistication or strict adherence to targets, but by consultations and flexibility."[26] Because of the export orientation of these countries, plan fulfillment is encouraged through positive incentives rather than direct controls.

In most of the other Third World countries, including those in Latin America, Africa, and Southeast Asia, planning has been encouraged by colonial powers and international aid agencies. After the war, for example, the socialist government in the United Kingdom required planning under its Colonial De-

[24]Anne O. Krueger, "Import Substitution versus Export Promotion," *Finance and Development* 22 (June 1985): 20–23.

[25]Ramgopal Agarwala, "Planning in Developing Countries," *Finance and Development* 22 (March 1985): 13–16.

[26]Ibid., 14.

velopment and Welfare Act of 1945. With little pressure for planning from the United States, Latin America was the last area to develop plans; Mexico in the 1950s and 1960s had no plans at all.

The developing countries use their plans to support applications for project loans and grants from agencies such as the World Bank and for rescheduling of debt with the International Monetary Fund and the major banks. Thus, the plans give special attention to projects and macroeconomic variables that interest the foreign audience. Targets for the private sector are usually indicative rather than coercive and are often exercises in wishful thinking.

Based on the success of the eastern Asian countries, the World Bank study provides a few suggestions for development planners. First, they recommend that, because the future is uncertain, more attention be given to flexibility than to strict adherence. Each plan should have a selective focus, rather than dealing with all of a nation's problems at once. Greater attention should be given to incentives rather than output and investment targets. For example, the operation of markets and prices was the major focus of Korea's Fifth Plan (1982–1986). Finally, the plan should be used to share information, promote cooperation and consultation, and build consensus between the private and public sectors.

Achievements and Challenges

As a group, the Third World nations have made tremendous progress since World War II, but they still have a long way to go. Their per capita income, for example, has almost tripled since 1950, but it is still only one-seventh of that in the industrial West (Table A.1). The lowest income levels are found in South Asia and sub-Saharan Africa; these two regions account for over half of the world's "absolute poor." Although the *proportion* of humankind living in absolute poverty has fallen during the past 2 decades, population growth has caused the *number* of absolute poor to increase.

Life expectancy in the developing countries increased from an average of 43 years in 1950 to 61 years in 1984, but it is still 15 years longer in the industrial West. Infant and child mortality rates have been cut in half, but about 20 percent of all children in countries such as Ethiopia, Malawi, Mali, Sierra Leone, and Guinea die before their fourth birthday. This is 20 times higher than the mortality rate in the industrial West. A quarter of the developing world's urban population and over half of its rural population do not have access to reasonably safe water. Only 50 percent of its urban and 14 percent of its rural dwellers are served by public sewers or other sanitation systems.[27]

Another indicator is the educational status of the developing countries. Although literacy rates have doubled, less than half of the adult population can

[27]Fredrik Deck, "Community Water Supply and Sanitation in Developing Countries, 1970–1990," *World Health Statistics* 39 (1986): 10–11.

Table 17.2   Actual Growth of GDP Per Capita and World Bank Forecasts, 1965–1995 (Annual Average Percentage Change)

	1965–1973	1973–1980	1980–1985	Forecast 1985–1995	
				High	Low
Industrial countries	3.7	2.1	1.7	3.8	2.0
Developing countries	4.0	3.2	1.3	3.9	2.0
Low-income countries	3.0	2.7	5.2	4.4	2.5
Africa	1.2	− 0.1	− 2.0	0.8	0.0
Asia	3.2	3.0	5.9	4.8	2.8
Middle-income oil exporters	4.5	3.1	− 1.1	2.3	0.9
Middle-income oil importers	4.5	3.2	− 0.1	4.1	1.9

Source: From *World Development Report,* 1986, p. 45. Copyright © 1986 by The International Bank for Reconstruction and Development/The World Bank. Reprinted by permission of Oxford University Press, Inc.

read or write in Africa or South Asia. In the low-income developing countries, which account for half of the world's population, less than one-third of all teenagers are enrolled in secondary education.[28]

Particularly discouraging is the fact that Third World economic growth has slowed dramatically since the oil crises of the 1970s (Table 17.2). During 1980 to 1985, the GDP per capita of the developing countries grew at less than half the rate that was experienced in 1965 to 1973 and income levels declined absolutely in Africa. To make matters worse, many of the countries have accumulated enormous debts that stand in the way of additional economic growth. Debt repayment absorbs more than one-third of the foreign exchange earnings of Brazil and Egypt, and about half of the earnings of Mexico and Chile.[29]

Despite all this, there is room for cautious optimism. The staff economists at the World Bank say that 1985 to 1995 is a decade of opportunity when growth rates can return to their pre-1973 levels if the right policies are pursued.[30] Most important, they say that the governments of the developing countries must increase their domestic savings to finance investment and debt repayment. In many countries, this will require smaller budget deficits and slower growth of the money supply. In others, saving can be encouraged by tax reform, particularly by reducing the taxation of interest income. In Bangladesh, Kenya, Nigeria, Peru, Thailand, Turkey, and Uruguay, financial reforms are needed to encourage saving. Governmental control of interest rates should be abolished and competition between financial institutions should be encour-

[28]The World Bank, *World Development Report 1986* (New York: Oxford University Press, 1986), 232–233, 236–237.

[29]Ibid., 212–213.

[30]Ibid., 40–60. The staff of the IMF has reached fairly similar conclusions. See International Monetary Fund, *World Economic Outlook* (Washington, D.C.: October, 1986), 18–20.

aged. Measures should be taken to strengthen the efficiency of investment expenditures and the flexibility of prices and exchange rates.

This is more easily said than done. Monetary and fiscal austerity is difficult to implement in any nation; it is particularly difficult in a poor country with a fragile political system. Successful adjustment in the developing world will require the support and cooperation of the industrial countries. If their macroeconomic situation can be put in order, and if the other political, cultural, and institutional barriers can be broken, then the Third World may indeed experience a decade of opportunity.

Summary

Very generally, countries that remain poor are those that fail to generate a sufficient investable surplus or those that fail to invest it in productive activities. In many countries, the effort to produce an investable surplus is complicated by such environmental factors as geography, soil, and climate, and the utilization of this surplus is influenced by religion and other aspects of culture. Institutional factors that stand in the way of economic development include inefficient and inequitable systems of land tenure, primitive market structures, dualism in labor markets, and limitations in the quantity and quality of financial intermediation. Poverty sustains itself through the operation of several vicious circles. While people with low incomes find it difficult to save, saving is needed to finance investment. Likewise, poverty places limits on educational opportunity, health, and market size, and it promotes rapid population growth, income inequality, and political instability.

Marxists and dependency theorists believe that the industrial countries, with their imperialist policies, shoulder much of the blame for Third World poverty. This form of exploitation was clear enough during the colonial era; they believe that it continues today through the operations of multinational corporations and through an unfair system of international prices.

Adam Smith and his followers believed that economic development is the natural order of things and that little is needed to promote it. In the 1950s, Arthur Lewis argued that independent development could be promoted by shifting rural surplus labor into industry. Rosenstein-Rodan agreed that this was possible, but added that it would require a big push to begin. Nurske proposed that such a push should be made simultaneously in several sectors, while Rostow argued for confining the initial push to leading sectors and Hirschman recommended that growth be encouraged in sectors with strong linkages. In many cases, particularly in Latin America, unbalanced growth has been linked with a policy of import substitution. In support of this, economists note that several Asian countries have undertaken successful programs of export promotion.

Economic plans in the Third World fall into three categories: Soviet-style central plans, Japanese-style indicative plans, and project plans that are required by aid agencies. According to the World Bank, development plans should be selective and flexible, and they should recognize the importance of incentives.

The Third World nations have made tremendous progress since World War II, but they have a long way to go. According to the World Bank, the growth rates of the 1960s can be restored if the right policies are pursued, including promotion of saving, the rationalization of investment, and flexibility of prices and exchange rates.

Discussion and Review Questions

1. Do you believe that cultural and religious traditions can have an important impact on economic development? Is it possible to study these influences in a scientific way?

2. How do traditional systems of land tenure influence economic development? What kinds of forces stand in the way of land reform?

3. What is a dual labor market? What are its causes and effects?

4. What kinds of vicious circles were discussed in the chapter? Can you think of others? What kinds of policies would be necessary to break them?

5. What is dependency theory? How does it explain the problems of the developing world? What policy recommendations are derived from the theory?

6. What are the relative advantages of import substitution and export promotion strategies of economic development?

7. Describe the different kinds of economic plans that are prepared in developing countries. What factors would influence a country's choice of a particular style of planning?

8. Describe the policies that are advocated by the staff of the World Bank to usher in a decade of opportunity. Do you agree with their suggestions and predictions?

Suggested Readings

Griffin, Keith and John Gurley. "Radical Analyses of Imperialism, the Third World, and the Transition to Socialism: A Survey Article." *Journal of Economic Literature* 23 (September 1985): 1089–1143. *A supportive assessment of dependency theory and other radical perspectives on development.*

Harrison, Lawrence E. *Development Is a State of Mind: The Latin American Case.* Lanham, Md.: University Press of America, 1985. *Presents an interesting example for cultural determinism.*

Karmarck, Andrew. *The Tropics and Economic Development.* Baltimore: The Johns Hopkins University Press, 1976. *Presents an interesting case for environmental determinism.*

Meier, Gerald. *Emerging from Poverty: The Economics that Really Matters.* New York: Oxford University Press, 1984. *An extended essay, written for a general audience, presenting a mainstream view of the history and performance of development economics.*

The World Bank, *World Development Report.* New York: Oxford University Press, annual. *Every year, the staff of the World Bank provides a wealth of authoritative statistical information, analysis, and policy guidance.*

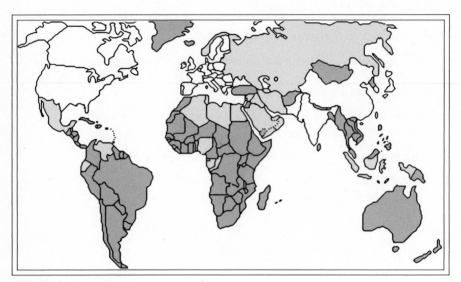

World Trade: Predominant Exports

☐ Fuel
▨ Other Primary Products
☐ Manufactured Goods

18

ECONOMIC SYSTEMS AND WORLD TRADE

It is commerce which is rapidly rendering war obsolete, by strengthening and multiplying the personal interests which are in natural opposition to it. And it may be said without exaggeration that the great extent and rapid increase of international trade, in being the principle guarantee of peace in the world, is the great permanent security for the uninterrupted progress of the ideas, the institutions, and the character of the human race.
—John Stuart Mill
  Principles of Political Economy, 1848

The real reason that the war we have just experienced took place was that Germany was afraid her commercial rivals were going to get the better of her, and the reason why some nations went into the war against Germany was that they thought Germany would get the commercial advantage of them.
—Woodrow Wilson
  Congressional Record, September 8, 1919

International trade can contribute to world poverty or prosperity, to cooperation or alienation, and to war or peace. It played an important part in the economic successes in Europe, America, and Japan; its disruption added depth to the Great Depression. Today, the world is knit together in an intricate web of commerce and even the large superpowers, which once considered themselves immune to the vagaries of the international market, can no longer ignore its risks and rewards.

Here we are interested in the impact of economic systems on world trade and payments. We will find that trade is handled quite differently among and between the industrial capitalist, socialist, and Third World countries. Each group has its own historical experience, ideologies, and attitudes, and each has its own system of institutions to promote, facilitate, and regulate trade.

Based on the data in Table A.26, we can make several observations about world trade: About 85 percent is conducted between countries with market economies. Half is conducted between industrial market countries, and half of this is conducted within Western Europe. North-south trade (trade between the industrial and developing market economies) accounts for more than one-quarter of the total. Trade among the Third World countries accounts for less than 10 percent.

Trade among Market Economies

In many respects, trade between market economies is simply an extension of trade within such countries. Import decisions, for example, generally are made by individual consumers, based on their comparisons of prices and other characteristics of domestic and foreign goods. Likewise, export decisions are made by individuals and businesses, based on the profits they can earn on the domestic and foreign markets. Within each country, the profit motive encourages each producer to specialize according to his comparative advantage—that is, he specializes in those goods and services that he can produce at a relatively low opportunity cost. Thus, without the guidance of any governmental agency, countries with rich deposits of coal and iron will tend to export steel and countries with fertile soil will tend to export food.

International trade also differs from domestic trade in several respects. First, each country has its own monetary system and sellers in each country desire payment in their domestic currency. Thus, if a Frenchman wishes to buy a Japanese car, he (or his dealer) must first exchange francs for yen, and then use the yen to buy the car. The price of the car in francs will be determined by the combination of the price in yen and the franc-yen exchange rate. The franc-yen exchange rate will be determined by the forces of supply and demand (as modified by governmental intervention) in the international exchange market.

Second, governmental treatment of international and domestic trade are quite different. Tariffs, quotas, and exchange controls impose a special burden on import transactions. Export subsidies make it profitable to sell certain

Table 18.1   Growth of World Output and Trade, 1968–1985

	Annual Average Percentage Rate at Constant Prices	
	Output	Trade
1963–1967	5.3	7.4*
1968–1972	4.9	8.8
1973–1977	3.7	6.8
1978–1981	2.9	3.6
1982–1985	2.6	3.0

*1963–1967 trade data do not include developing countries.

Sources: International Monetary Fund, *International Financial Statistics: Supplement on Output Statistics* (Washington, D.C.: 1984); and International Monetary Fund, *World Economic Outlook* (Washington, D.C.: 1986).

products overseas rather than on the domestic market. Governmental intervention in the foreign exchange market, designed to support or devalue the currency, can affect both exports and imports.

Third, a number of other barriers, including language, culture, distance, differences in quality and safety standards, and the complexity of international financial transactions tend to favor domestic trade. As Adam Smith observed in 1776, "every wholesale merchant naturally prefers the home trade to the foreign trade of consumption" because "he can know better the character and situation of the person whom he trusts, and if he should happen to be deceived, he knows better the laws of the country from which he must seek redress."[1]

By and large, the market system has coordinated the vast network of world production and trade remarkably well. The individual decisions of billions of consumers and producers have been held roughly in balance through the movements of international prices and exchange rates. Since World War II the volume of world trade has consistently grown more rapidly than world output of goods and services (Table 18.1).[2]

However, the operation of the international market is far from perfect. In 1986, for example, the global capacity to produce automobiles, petrochemicals, semiconductors, and steel was 15 to 30 percent larger than the world demand for these products.[3] Why has the market failed to maintain a closer balance between supply and demand? Part of the blame falls on governmental protectionist policies, which encourage the creation of excess industrial capacity, requiring even more protectionism. Another part of the blame falls on

[1]Adam Smith, *An Inquiry into the Nature and Causes of the Wealth of Nations* (New York: P. F. Collier, 1909), 349.

[2]Before World War II, with the exception of the period between 1840 and 1870, world industrial production generally grew more rapidly than world trade. For data on world trade and output reaching back to the year 1700, see Walt Rostow, *The World Economy: History and Prospect* (Austin, Tex.: University of Texas Press, 1978), 67.

[3]Bruce Stokes, "Coping With Glut," *National Journal,* November 1, 1986, 2608–2614.

Table 18.2   Average U.S. Tariff Rates, 1821–1984

Total Duties as a Percentage of Total Dutiable Imports

Year	Average Tariff	Year	Average Tariff
1821	45%	1920	16%
1830	62	1925	38
1835	40	1932	59
1850	27	1940	36
1861	19	1950	13
1865	48	1960	12
1893	50	1970	10
1900	49	1980	6
1910	42	1984	5

Sources: U.S. Department of Commerce, Bureau of the Census, *Historical Statistics of the United States* (Washington, D.C.: 1985); and U.S. Department of Commerce, Bureau of the Census, *Statistical Abstract of the United States 1986* (Washington, D.C.: 1986).

the competitive battle to increase market share and reduce unit costs by expanding the scale of production. Given the time and expense of creating modern production facilities, the stakes are very high in the international race for market share. Finally, part of the overcapacity problem is caused by the traditional inflexibility of industrial prices.

Western Trade Policy

International trade policy has always been one of the principal concerns of economists and politicians. For example, it was the argument over protection between the mercantilists, the physiocrats, and Adam Smith that gave birth to modern economics. Smith and his classical disciples (with help from the Anti–Corn Law League and the Irish potato famine) finally carried the day and England followed a policy of free trade from 1846 until the outbreak of World War I.

Outside England, the principle of free trade found stiffer resistance. Early in the nineteenth century, Alexander Hamilton in the United States and Friedrich List in Germany argued that free trade may be good for England, given its dominant position in the world economy, but inappropriate for countries that are nurturing infant industries. American protectionism was particularly strong after the War of 1812 (when an effort was made to maintain industries that had been established during the naval blockade), after the presidential campaign of 1828, and after the outbreak of the Civil War (when the political balance shifted in favor of industrial protectionists in the North) (Table 18.2). In France, Spain, Italy, and Russia, where the government traditionally played an active role in the economy, free trade was hardly considered.

The Great Depression of the 1930s precipitated a severe trade war. The first to act was the United States with the Smoot-Hawley tariff of 1930; within 2 years another 60 countries retaliated with large tariff increases. The result? By 1932, American trade fell to less than one-third of its 1929 level. The

Depression encouraged protectionism and protectionism added depth to the Depression.

The United States' Trade Agreements Act of 1934 called a truce. It shifted some tariff-setting authority from the legislature, which is particularly vulnerable to special interest groups, to the executive branch. In particular, it authorized the president to negotiate bilateral agreements with other countries to reduce tariffs by up to 50 percent in exchange for similar reductions. Furthermore, the 1934 act provided for Most-Favored-Nation (MFN) clauses in the agreements. If country X is given MFN status by the United States, then any tariff reduction that is granted to another country is also automatically granted to country X. By the outbreak of World War II, the United States had reached 21 agreements with other nations and the level of protection was substantially reduced (Table 18.2).

After World War II, the trading nations met in Havana and agreed to form the International Trade Organization (ITO); the agreement, however, was not ratified by the U.S. Senate and the ITO was never functional. Instead, the countries decided to establish an informal organization, known as the General Agreement on Trade and Tariffs (GATT), in which the United States could participate without congressional approval. Under the GATT umbrella, the trading nations have completed seven major rounds of multilateral tariff negotiations and reductions; an eighth round—the Uruguay Round—is under way.

During the Kennedy Round of GATT negotiations completed in 1967, the 90 participating nations agreed to average tariff reductions of about 35 percent. The Tokyo Round (1973–1979) provided for a similar reduction of tariffs and opened negotiations on the thorny problem of nontariff barriers to trade. On this last point, the participants agreed on codes of behavior to regulate unfair government procurement policies, production subsidies, customs valuation methods, import licensing procedures, and national quality and safety standards. The participants also agreed to establish a system of multilateral committees to settle disputes arising under the new codes.

The Tokyo Round was conducted during a decade of recession and the growth of world trade decelerated seriously after 1973 (Table 18.1). Although tariff rates have continued to fall, these reductions have been offset by new and creative forms of protectionism and unfair competition. For example, instead of placing tariffs and quotas on steel and automotive imports, the United States has persuaded Japan to exercise **voluntary export restraint** (see "Japan's Voluntary Export Restraint," p. 416). Until the OECD nations concluded an agreement in 1987 to phase out the practice, a number of countries promoted their exports by offering **tied aid**—a package of export financing and foreign-aid grants.[4] Subsidies to export industries were expanded through national industrial policies, while trade in services was limited by foreign exchange restrictions and national banking and security regulations.

[4]Art Pine, "OECD Nations Reach Accord on 'Tied Aid'," *Wall Street Journal,* March 16, 1987, 14.

JAPAN'S VOLUNTARY EXPORT RESTRAINT

In 1980, in the face of intense lobbying from the U.S. auto industry, the new Reagan administration persuaded the Japanese government to impose a system of voluntary export restraints (VERs). In the year ended March 1982, the Japanese limited their exports to the United States and Puerto Rico to 1.83 million units, down from 2.01 million in the previous year. This ceiling was kept unchanged in 1982–1983, but it was increased to 1.85 million in 1983–1984 when sales rebounded for American producers. Although the American government did not formally request an extension of the program beyond 1984, the Japanese limited their sales to 2.3 million cars in 1984–1985 to prevent a protectionist backlash in the U.S. Congress.

The VER program created an artificial shortage of Japanese cars on the American market; by 1984 this caused the average price of a new car to be about $1,600 higher than otherwise expected. Part of this increase was caused by actual price changes and part of it was caused by a change in the composition of imports. To maintain their dollar earnings, the Japanese replaced their sales of economy cars with larger models. Japanese restraint also allowed high-priced European manufacturers to maintain their market shares.

The rise in automobile prices (adjusted to exclude the effect of quality changes) cost American consumers an estimated $4 billion per year during 1981 to 1984. Of that increase, $1 to 3 billion represented a transfer to the U.S. auto industry; thus, the net annual cost of the VER program was the remaining $1 to 3 billion. The number of American jobs saved each year by the program is estimated at 10,000 to 19,000. The American consumer paid an annual net cost of $110,000 to $145,000 to maintain each of these jobs.

These statistical estimates are little more than educated guesses, but they seem to indicate that protectionism is an inefficient way to maintain employment. The vocational training programs of the U.S. government (such as the Job Corps) could have been almost twice as large during 1981 to 1984 if the net cost of the VERs had been directed to that purpose. Sweden has found that a system of training, placement, and relocation can help the labor force to meet the future, where protectionism vainly seeks to avoid it.

Sources: Charles Collyns and Steven Dunaway, "The Cost of Trade Restraints: The Case of Japanese Automobile Exports to the United States," *International Monetary Fund Staff Papers* 34 (March 1987): 150–175; and Robert C. Feenstra, "Automobile Prices and Protection: The U.S.–Japan Trade Restraint," in *The New Protectionist Threat to World Welfare,* ed. Dominick Salvatore (New York: North-Holland, 1987), 333–351.

The Uruguay Round of multilateral trade negotiations was launched in September 1986. Its goals are to: (1) continue the reduction of tariff and nontariff barriers; (2) guide, for the first time, trade in services, including banking, insurance, and telecommunications; (3) protect patents and other intellectual property rights, while ensuring that "procedures to enforce intellectual property rights do not themselves become barriers to legitimate trade"; and (4) "develop a multilateral framework of principles, rules, and disciplines dealing with international trade in counterfeit goods."[5]

Western Regional Trade Areas

Alongside the GATT framework for trade liberalization throughout the West, an important role is also played by several regional organizations, which are allowed by the GATT to depart from the most favored nation principle. The simplest of these, a **free-trade area or association** is a group of countries that agree to eliminate tariffs among themselves; each country maintains the right to set its own tariffs against nonmember nations. A higher level of integration is achieved by a **customs union,** which is a free-trade association in which all of the member countries establish a common set of tariffs against nonmembers. Higher still is a **common market**—a customs union with the additional removal of all barriers to factor movements between members. Finally, a group of countries may advance to an **economic union,** in which all of their economic policies—monetary, fiscal, antitrust, etc.—are integrated. All of these arrangements stimulate trade between members and discriminate against trade with nonmembers.

The European Common Market was formed in 1958 with six member nations; it has since expanded to include 12 countries.[6] In their effort to move toward economic union, the European Common Market nations have adopted similar systems of taxation (with emphasis on the value-added tax); they have coordinated their agricultural, industrial, transportation, and energy policies; and they have taken steps toward a monetary union. The European Common Market has its own parliament, which can levy taxes for its own purposes and fine member governments that violate its agreements.

Seven European countries that were not willing to adopt the uniform tariff schedule of the European Common Market formed a separate European Free Trade Association (EFTA) in 1959. Since that time, the EFTA has added two new members, while three of its founders have switched their affiliation to the European Common Market, leaving the EFTA with a current member-

[5]"GATT Ministers Agree to Launch New Round of Trade Talks," *IMF Survey,* September 30, 1986, 289, 299.

[6]The formal name of the European Common Market was originally the European Economic Community (EEC), shortened to European Community (EC) in 1976. The founding countries were West Germany, France, Italy, Belgium, the Netherlands, and Luxembourg. Later additions were Great Britain, Denmark, and Ireland in 1977; Greece in 1981; and Spain and Portugal in 1986.

ship of six countries.[7] The tariff reductions accomplished by the European Common Market and the EFTA help to explain the fact that about 25 percent of world trade is conducted within Western Europe (Table A.26).

The European experience has encouraged attempts by many other groups of countries to create free-trade areas and common markets. The United States formed a free-trade area with Israel in 1985 and has contemplated similar arrangements with Canada and Mexico. Integration efforts between developing countries have not been very successful. The West Indian Association and the union of Kenya, Tanzania, and Uganda have been dissolved. The Latin American Integration Association (LAIA), which includes Mexico and most of South America, and the Caribbean Community and Common Market (CARICOM) have made little progress toward trade liberalization. The Central American Common Market (CACM) had successfully removed almost all trade barriers within that region by 1967 and adopted a common system of external tariffs. The CACM, despite its small size, seems to have made a modest contribution to the standard of living within the region, but Central American cooperation began to crumble in 1969 when the soccer war broke out between Honduras and El Salvador. Since that time, the region has been plagued by insurgency, civil war, and international conflict.

North-South Trade Relations

Many statesmen and social scientists believe that the developing countries have been victimized by their status as exporters of primary products with low, unstable, and possibly declining relative prices (see Chapter 17). In order to address this concern, the first United Nations Conference on Trade and Development (UNCTAD) was held in 1964; it was subsequently converted into a permanent agency with a secretariat in Geneva. A 55-member Trade and Development Board meets twice each year and plenary meetings of all 165 member-countries are now held every third year. These meetings provide an important forum for the north-south dialogue; they led to the passage of the Declaration on the Establishment of a New International Economic Order by the U.N. General Assembly in 1974.

The proposals for a New International Economic Order have many specific provisions, but two have attracted special attention. First, in order to raise and/or stabilize the prices of primary products, UNCTAD called in 1976 for an integrated program of **international commodity agreements (ICAs).** These can employ one or both of the following methods of price stabilization: (1) a cartel arrangement can control production and supply of the commodity, or (2) a special fund can be established to purchase buffer stocks of the commodity when its international demand is weak; the fund can be replenished by selling the buffer stocks when demand is strong. Under the UNCTAD

---

[7]The founding members were Sweden, Norway, Switzerland, Austria, Great Britain, Denmark, and Portugal. Presently, the members are Sweden, Norway, Switzerland, Austria, Finland, and Iceland.

proposal, a common fund of about $6 billion would be contributed by the industrial countries to finance the management of buffer stocks for ten important commodities.

Some 40 ICAs covering 13 commodities have been concluded since 1931, but few of them have achieved any success. The strongest is the International Coffee Agreement, a coordinated system of export quotas that has operated with few interruptions since 1962. The International Tin Agreement, first concluded in 1956, was forced to discontinue its operations in 1985 when its financial resources were exhausted by a collapse of commodity prices. Of the ten ICAs envisioned by the 1976 UNCTAD proposal, agreements were actually concluded only for cocoa and rubber, and the cocoa agreement expired in 1986. In order to maintain its solvency, the International Rubber Agreement was forced in 1985 to reduce its minimum price.

The other important provision of the New International Economic Order is the **generalized system of preferences (GSP).** The developing countries claim that they are trapped in their role as primary commodity producers because the industrial countries place low tariffs on raw material imports and progressively higher tariffs on finished goods. Even when an industrial country reduces its tariffs on manufactures during GATT negotiations, the concessions usually apply to goods that are specifically requested by other industrial countries—sophisticated goods that the developing countries may not be able to manufacture.

Under a GSP the industrial countries reduce their tariff barriers on the specific kinds of manufactured goods that the developing countries are able to produce. The European Common Market enacted a GSP in 1972 that allows duty-free entry of manufactured goods from developing countries, but these are subject to quantitative restrictions. The United States GSP, which began in 1976, also allows duty-free importation (with quantity limits) of many manufactured goods, but footwear, glass products, steel, textiles, and several other politically sensitive items are excluded. Duty-free imports under the American GSP amounted to $13.3 billion in 1985. Between 1973 and 1985, the share of the developing countries in world exports of manufactures increased from 7 percent to 12.5 percent.

Trade Behavior of Centrally Planned Economies

In a traditional Soviet-style economy, where price controls and production targets stand in the way of the market mechanism, foreign-trade decisions are controlled and coordinated by the central authorities. Individual consumers and producers cannot be trusted to buy and sell the right goods overseas in the right quantities to fit the requirements of the plan, and they cannot be trusted, under the influence of inflexible prices and exchange rates, to maintain an acceptable balance of international payments.

In order to administer foreign trade in a centrally planned economy, a specialized Ministry of Foreign Trade (MFT) is usually established under the leadership of the State Planning Committee (SPC). The MFT, in turn, operates

Figure 18.1   The Soviet-Style Foreign Trade Planning Bureaucracy

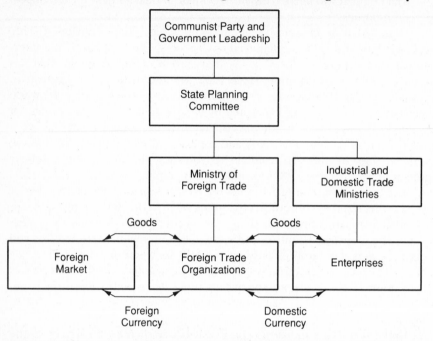

Foreign
Currency

Domestic
Currency

several Foreign Trade Organizations (FTOs), which handle the actual negotiation and conclusion of export and import transactions (Figure 18.1). In the Soviet Union, about 65 FTOs have been given the exclusive right to export and/or import a particular category of goods. For example, *Eksportkhleb* handles almost all Soviet exports and imports of grain products and *Soyuznefteeksport* handles almost all of the country's trade in petroleum products.

The profits and losses of the FTOs are largely determined by the differences between international market prices and controlled domestic prices. Consider, for example, the case of Soviet coal exports in 1972. *Soyuzpromeksport,* the relevant FTO, purchased coal from industrial enterprises at the controlled domestic price of 23 rubles per ton. It sold the coal abroad at the international price of $14 per ton, which translated into a price of 13 rubles per ton at the official exchange rate of $1.11 per ruble. Accordingly, because the foreign-trade ruble export price was lower than the domestic ruble purchase price, *Soyuzpromeksport* suffered a financial loss of about 10 rubles per ton on its 10 million tons of net exports of coal in 1972. The FTO engaged in these unprofitable exports because it was told to do so by the central planners. Subsidies from the governmental budget were required to spare *Soyuzpromeksport* and many other FTOs from bankruptcy, and profitable FTOs were taxed to balance the budget.

Because of the intervention of the Ministry of Foreign Trade and its FTOs, the industrial ministries and their enterprises have little direct contact with foreign customers and suppliers. They transact their business with the FTOs at roughly the same prices that would prevail in any other domestic transaction. The privileges of foreign contact and travel are reserved for the Party faithful who work for the FTOs, and the domestic economy supposedly is protected from foreign inflationary pressures.

The export and import plans are prepared in conjunction with the other sections of the annual and 5-year plans (see Chapter 11). After the Party and government leaders have established their general priorities for the economy, the State Planning Committee compiles an aggregative set of **control figures** for the production and utilization of several broad categories of goods. Based on these guidelines, and on their knowledge of existing trade agreements, international market conditions, and the specific resources and requirements of the domestic economy, each of the FTOs prepares a detailed plan for the export and/or import of its commodity group. The FTO plans are adjusted by other officials at the Ministry of Foreign Trade to assure an acceptable balance of payments and are assembled into a comprehensive (but preliminary) foreign-trade plan. The latter is sent to the State Planning Committee, which makes additional adjustments to the plan during the compilation and revision of its material balance tables. Finally, the entire plan is resubmitted to the political leaders for their approval.[8]

Weaknesses of Centrally Planned Foreign Trade

Of the many problems associated with the traditional Soviet-style system of foreign-trade administration, the most fundamental is this: Most of the important variables that must be considered in a foreign-trade plan—international prices, exchange rates, and international production and demand—cannot be controlled by the central planners of any single nation. Therefore, it is virtually impossible to construct a reliable foreign-trade plan for a 1-year period; a 5-year trade plan is little more than a forecast.

The socialist countries attempt to make trade more predictable by coordinating their plans and by signing long-term trade agreements among themselves and with the governments of capitalist countries. These agreements, however, are often made to be broken. For example, according to the Soviet-American Long-Term Grain Agreement for 1983–1988, the Soviet Union was obligated to purchase at least 4 million tons of wheat each year from the United States. Instead, the Soviets bought about 3 million tons in 1984–1985 and less than 200,000 tons in 1985–1986.

Even if the actions of foreigners were perfectly predictable, central planners still would find it difficult to take full advantage of the gains from international trade. Without a system of market prices, they have no dependable way to identify the particular products that their country should export and import. Remember, a country with a market economy will import a product if its

[8]For a detailed account of this procedure, see H. Stephen Gardner, *Soviet Foreign Trade: The Decision Process* (Boston: Kluwer-Nijhoff, 1983).

foreign price, converted into domestic currency at the market exchange rate, is lower than the domestic cost of that product. A planned economy, with inflexible, irrational, and tightly controlled prices and exchange rates, has little objective basis to compare domestic and foreign costs of production. As Ludwig von Mises observed in the 1920s, meaningful economic calculation is difficult to perform in a planned economy.[9]

Still another problem is presented by the system of material incentives in the Soviet-style planned economies. Because their factories are oriented toward the fulfillment of quantitative output targets, these countries generally produce low-quality manufactured goods and have never developed a tradition of providing service after the sale. Thus, they find it difficult to sell their manufactures on the highly competitive world market. This problem is exacerbated by the fact that domestic manufacturers have little knowledge of the international market because foreign contacts are usually handled by the Ministry of Foreign Trade.

The industrial enterprises generally avoid export production; the extra time that they must spend to prepare their goods for the foreign market may endanger the fulfillment of their overall output targets. Although they may be compensated for some of their additional costs of production, the payment that they receive for a sale to an FTO is roughly equal to the price they would receive on any other domestic transaction. As a Soviet foreign-trade official once put it, "Our manufacturers sometimes say that exporting is a form of punishment, while importing is a reward."

Foreign-Trade Management Reforms

For these and other reasons, most of the small, trade-dependent countries of Eastern Europe have discovered that Soviet-style central planning is inappropriate for their needs. Their need to make better use of the international market has prompted many of these countries to adopt economic reforms (see Chapter 14). This was perhaps the most important reason that Yugoslavia and Hungary established systems of market socialism.

In recent years, the Soviet Union has also undertaken foreign-trade management reform. Beginning in the 1960s, the Soviets established a modest system of supplementary material incentives for exporters and attempted to improve communication between the industrial ministries and the Ministry of Foreign Trade by establishing a number of export councils. Because these actions had little effect, a law was passed in 1978 that placed representatives from the industrial ministries on the boards of directors of the FTOs. Again, it was hoped that a closer working relationship between the producers and the

[9]A small number of very optimistic Soviet economists believe that mathematical programming methods can be used to identify an optimal structure of foreign trade in a planned economy. However, if these methods were used to make trade decisions in a continuous, dynamic, and flexible way for a detailed list of products, the data and computational requirements would be unthinkable. Very little progress has been made toward the construction of large-scale programming models. See Gardner, *Soviet Foreign Trade,* Chapter 6.

MFT would improve the Soviet export performance; however, the results were still discouraging. The share of machinery and equipment in Soviet exports fell from 22 percent in 1970 to 14 percent in 1985.

Most recently, in connection with the Gorbachev reforms, the Soviets have taken another step toward the dissolution of the state monopoly of foreign trade. Beginning in 1987, 21 industrial ministries and 70 manufacturing enterprises were given the right to handle their own foreign-trade transactions, without the intervention of the Ministry of Foreign Trade, and several of the existing FTOs are being placed under the direct control of industrial ministries. New export incentives have also been established, including a system whereby the exporting enterprises will have greater control over the foreign currency that is earned by their efforts. For the present, the Ministry of Foreign Trade will maintain control over trade in fuels, raw materials, and several categories of manufactured goods, accounting for about 90 percent of the value of Soviet exports.

Economic Relations between Socialist Countries

Before World War II, the Soviet leaders believed (with some justification) that their country was surrounded by capitalist enemies. For this reason, and because it is difficult to forecast and plan foreign trade, the Soviets followed a policy of autarky—independence from foreign trade. A few years later, Soviet troops occupied a number of new trade-dependent socialist states, and Stalin proclaimed the establishment of a socialist trading area:

The disintegration of the single, all-embracing world market must be regarded as the most important economic sequel of the Second World War. . . . The economic consequence of the existence of two opposite camps was that . . . we now have two parallel world markets also confronting one another.[10]

Determined to consolidate control of Eastern Europe, and facing a partial embargo from the West, Stalin required the "fraternal" countries to break most of their ties with the West. He vetoed the plans of Poland and Czechoslovakia to apply for Marshall Plan aid and countered by establishing a socialist Council for Mutual Economic Assistance (CMEA).[11] For several years the CMEA remained little more than a press release. It provided little assistance to Eastern Europe; the Soviet Union required its wartime enemies—East Germany, Romania, and Hungary—to pay exorbitant reparations. The East Germans, for example, were required to deliver commodities worth about $4 billion; they were also required to dismantle factories and equipment worth about $12

[10]Joseph Stalin, *Economic Problems of Socialism in the USSR* (New York: International Publishers, 1952), 26.

[11]The CMEA is also known as Comecon. Presently, its members include the Soviet Union, Bulgaria, Czechoslovakia, the German Democratic Republic, Hungary, Poland, Romania, Mongolia (since 1962), Cuba (since 1972), and Vietnam (since 1978). Yugoslavia, North Korea, Angola, Laos, and Ethiopia have observer status. Albania dropped out in 1962.

billion and move them to the Soviet Union. Before the war, the Eastern European nations purchased only 17 percent of their imports from one another and from the Soviet Union. By 1953, the figure was 72 percent.[12]

The CMEA became a more active organization after 1953, when Stalin died and Khrushchev rose to power, particularly after the Polish and Hungarian uprisings of 1956. Twelve standing commissions were established in 1956 to exchange technical information. A fledgling attempt was made to coordinate the national 5-year plans for 1956–1960. A detailed set of rules was formulated in 1958 for the negotiation of CMEA foreign-trade prices and plans were approved in that same year to build the 3,000-mile Druzhba (Friendship) Pipeline, which today carries most of the Soviet exports of oil to East Germany, Czechoslovakia, Hungary, and Poland. A set of CMEA articles was finally published in 1960 to codify the structure and governance of the organization.

As the Soviet strategy of economic development was adopted in all of the socialist countries, wasteful duplication of production facilities became an obvious problem. All of the countries built huge iron and steel complexes and started or increased production in all major lines of machinery, chemicals, and other products of heavy industry. A 1962 policy statement, the Basic Principles of the International Socialist Division of Labor, called for improvements in efficiency through greater specialization and integration of production.

In order to implement the Basic Principles, Khrushchev called for an amendment to the articles that would give the CMEA new powers of compulsory plan coordination for large investment projects. Romania, the most backward country in the organization (after Albania left in 1962) was afraid that a supranational planning body would force it to specialize in primary production and abandon its modern industries; thus it threatened to withdraw from the CMEA if the amendment was adopted. Khrushchev capitulated and the principle of voluntarism prevailed.

In 1964, all of the CMEA countries except for Romania and Mongolia formed Intermetall, a new organization that had limited supranational powers to coordinate research, investment, production, and trade in ferrous metals among its members. Since that time, other organizations of its kind have been formed for several other industries. Also in 1964, the International Bank for Economic Cooperation was established to handle payments between the socialist countries.

Despite efforts to strengthen the CMEA, the "world socialist market" exhibited disintegrating tendencies in the 1950s and 1960s. Freed from Stalin's grip, the CMEA share of Eastern European imports exhibited a downward trend from 72 percent in 1953 to 64 percent in 1970. Unrest in the region led to the Soviet invasion of Czechoslovakia in 1968 and the 1970 replacement of Gomulka by Gierek as the leader of Poland.

In an effort to get CMEA integration back on track, a new Comprehensive Program was adopted in 1971. The program established a Committee on Co-

[12]Franklyn Holzman, *International Trade under Communism* (New York: Basic Books, 1976), 70.

operation in Planning, headed by the chairmen of the national planning agencies, to strengthen the system of plan coordination and promote joint planning among interested parties. In addition, a new International Investment Bank was established in the same year to finance joint investment projects under the program. Joint investments are now included in the 5-year Coordinated Plan for Multilateral Integrational Measures (beginning with the plan for 1976 to 1980) and the 15- to 20-year Long-Term Target Programs. The largest of the joint projects, the Soyuz natural gas pipeline, was completed in 1978. The Mir (Peace) Electrical Power Grid came into service in 1979.

Although these actions stimulated CMEA trade, East-West trade grew even more rapidly in the 1970s and CMEA integration remained little more than a slogan. In 1978, the Soviets apparently repeated Khrushchev's attempt to bestow supranational powers on the CMEA. According to a story in the Yugoslav press, the Soviets attempted to repeal the interested parties doctrine, so that all CMEA countries could be required to participate in an investment project if the majority decided to participate. Again, Romania resisted the change and the Soviets relented.[13]

Finally, in the early 1980s, the CMEA countries were forced to strengthen their mutual ties by the course of international events: the Western recession, the rapid increase in CMEA indebtedness to the West (from $8 billion in 1971 to $87 billion in 1981), and the Western reactions to the Soviet invasion of Afghanistan and martial law in Poland. After decreasing for 3 decades, the CMEA share of Eastern European imports increased from 51 percent in 1981 to 66 percent in 1984.[14] According to an official of the CMEA Secretariat, eliminating unwarranted imports from the capitalist countries was one of the five top priorities pursued during the coordination of national plans for 1986 to 1990.[15]

Trade between centrally planned economies differs from trade between market economies in at least three important respects. First, as noted above, socialist trade is usually conducted in accordance with national plans and long-term agreements and is negotiated by officials from the ministries of foreign trade, with limited participation by producers and end-users. Second, trade between the socialist countries is usually conducted on a bilateral barter basis; money is used only as a unit of account (not as a medium of exchange) because socialist currencies are inconvertible. Third, because a true market does not exist in trade between planned economies, special arrangements must be employed to set foreign-trade prices.

---

[13]J. L. Kerr, "The 32nd Session of the Comecon Council," *Radio Free Europe Research,* Background Report No. 154, July 7, 1978, 8–10.

[14]Based on the 1982 and 1985 editions of the CMEA statistical yearbook, *Statisticheskii ezhegodnik stran-chlenov soveta ekonomicheskoi vzaimopomoshchi* (Moscow: Finansy i Statistika, annual).

[15]For further discussion of the CMEA drive for self-sufficiency, see H. Stephen Gardner, "Soviet Foreign Trade Decision-making in the 1980s," *Columbia Journal of World Business* 18 (Winter 1983): 17–19.

Table 18.3 Soviet Foreign Trade in 1985: Bilateralism with the East and Multilateralism with the West

	Soviet Exports*	Soviet Imports*	Trade Balance as Percent of Soviet Exports
All Socialist Countries	44,283	42,210	4.7%
Bulgaria	6,435	6,040	6.1
Czechoslovakia	6,813	6,587	3.3
East Germany	7,652	7,553	1.3
Hungary	4,560	4,850	− 6.4
Poland	6,517	5,525	15.2
Romania	1,949	2,277	16.8
Cuba	3,849	4,140	− 7.6
All Capitalist Countries	28,181	26,892	4.6
West Germany	3,992	3,094	22.5
Italy	2,468	1,325	46.3
Japan	928	2,287	− 146.4
United States	326	2,376	− 628.8
United Kingdom	1,218	684	43.8
Argentina	62	1,230	− 1,883.9
Canada	18	949	− 5,172.2

*Millions of rubles.

Source: Official Soviet statistics.

Inconvertibility and Bilateralism

In trade between Western countries, the U.S. dollar serves as an international medium of exchange. Thus, if a Western country runs a surplus in its balance of payments, that country will accumulate a stock of dollar reserves. At the end of 1985, for example, Japan held reserves of about $22 billion. Countries outside of the United States are willing to accept dollars in payment for their goods and hold large stocks of dollars because they know that other countries will also accept the dollars and that the dollars can easily be exchanged for goods in the U.S. economy. Thus, a Western country can run a trade surplus with one country and accumulate dollar reserves to finance a trade deficit with another country. There is no need for trade to be balanced between any single pair of countries.

In socialist trade, the situation is quite different. One must have both money and an allocation in the annual plan to buy large quantities of any particular product in a centrally planned economy. Thus, because it is relatively difficult to exchange Soviet-bloc currencies for goods, foreigners have little desire to accumulate these currencies, which are **inconvertible**—that is, they are not traded on international currency markets. Thus, none of the socialist currencies can serve as an international medium of exchange for the centrally planned economies.

Without the use of an international medium of exchange, the socialist countries are forced to conduct their mutual trade by a complex system of barter. Every year, teams of central planners and foreign-trade officials from each pair of socialist countries (Soviet Union-Poland, Poland-Romania, Soviet Union-Romania, etc.) must negotiate a trade agreement, which must strike an export-import balance between each pair of countries. The constraint of such bilateralism tends to reduce socialist trade below the level that could be attained with an effective medium of exchange.

The influence of bilateralism on Soviet trade is illustrated by the data in Table 18.3. Soviet trade with each of its major socialist partners is roughly balanced—seldom does an imbalance with a socialist country amount to more than 10 percent of Soviet exports to that country. In its trade with the West, the Soviet Union trades with dollars and other convertible currencies. Thus, it is able to accumulate large surpluses in its trade with Western Europe (principally through sales of oil and gas) and use these to finance large deficits (principally caused by grain and equipment imports) in its trade with North America, Japan, and Argentina. Socialist trade is bilaterally balanced, while trade with capitalist countries is multilaterally balanced.

Socialist Foreign-Trade Prices

When we say that socialist trade is bilaterally balanced, we mean that it is balanced in terms of value—not in terms of weight or bulk. But how do the socialist countries measure the value of their exports and imports? In other words, how do they set their foreign-trade prices?

Price policy has been a difficult and controversial issue in the CMEA since its inception. Although some socialist authors (primarily in Bulgaria and the Soviet Union) have argued that an independent price system should be established for CMEA trade—based on average domestic wholesale prices or production costs, or on the solution of a huge linear programming model— actual foreign-trade prices in the region have always been related in one way or another to prices on the capitalist world market. It is said (in jest) that if the worldwide socialist revolution ever comes, at least one capitalist country must be preserved to set foreign-trade prices.

Despite their ideological discomfort, the socialist countries base their foreign-trade prices on capitalist market prices for two basic reasons. First, capitalist prices are the objective standard against which all other price bases are judged. Any other price system generates identifiable "winners" and "losers," and a political tug of war. Second, if CMEA prices are too far out of line with world market prices, socialist countries that export products with relatively low CMEA prices will have a strong incentive to divert their trade to the West.

Generally speaking, during the years before 1966, CMEA prices were usually based on world market prices during the current year or one of the years in the recent past. For the 1966–1970 and 1971–1975 plan periods, the CMEA countries agreed to base their prices on average world market prices during the previous 5-year periods (for example, 1966–1970 CMEA prices were based on 1960–1964 world prices); they also agreed to hold their prices constant during the 5-year periods. The purpose of this arrangement was to protect the socialist countries from wide fluctuations in world prices, but it soon caused problems. In 1974, when the world price of oil quadrupled, the Soviet Union found itself selling oil to Eastern Europe at a relatively low fixed price. The Soviets demanded a change in pricing policy. Since 1975 the CMEA prices have changed every year, although they are still based on average world prices over the previous 5 years. According to one set of estimates, the Soviets implicitly subsidized the Eastern European economies in the amount of $7.7 billion per year between 1970 and 1984 by exporting their oil and other primary goods at prices below the world market and by paying relatively high prices for Eastern European manufactures.[16] However, the situation has apparently been reversed since 1985, when the world market price of oil fell below the slow-moving CMEA price.[17]

East-West Economic Relations

In 1985, exports from the industrial West to the Soviet Union and Eastern Europe amounted only to 2 percent of world exports, to 0.4 percent of the combined GNP of the West, and to 1.3 percent of the combined GNP of the East. Statistically, East-West trade is far less important than West-West, East-East, or north-south trade. However, the political and strategic importance of trade between potential adversaries is quite obvious. East-West trade is perceived by many to be a vehicle for world communication, understanding, and peace, while many others believe that it provides support to a collection of dictatorial regimes. Furthermore, the potential level of East-West trade may be far more significant than the existing level. According to one estimate, trade between the CMEA countries and Western Europe in 1970 was only 20 to 30 percent of the level predicted by the proximity, populations, and incomes of the two regions.[18]

Obstacles to East-West Trade

Several economic and political factors combine to explain the low level of East-West trade. First, foreign trade does not fit neatly into the system of central planning. Planners prefer to avoid that which is unpredictable. Socialist

[16]Michael Marrese and Jan Vanous, "The Content and Controversy of Soviet Foreign Trade Relations with Eastern Europe, 1970–84," a paper presented to the Conference on the Soviet Union and Eastern Europe in the World Economy, Kennan Institute for Advanced Russian Studies, Washington, D.C., October, 1984, Table 1. According to several authors, Marrese and Vanous may have exaggerated the size of the implicit subsidy. See, for example, Raimund Dietz, "Soviet Foregone Gains in Trade with the CMEA Six: A Reappraisal," *Comparative Economic Studies* 27 (Summer 1986): 69–94.

[17]Raimund Dietz, "Advantages and Disadvantages in Soviet Trade with Eastern Europe: The Pricing Dimension," in U.S. Congress, Joint Economic Committee, *East European Economies: Slow Growth in the 1980s* (Washington, D.C.: USGPO, 1986), 1:283.

[18]Edward A. Hewett, "A Gravity Model of CMEA Trade," in *Quantitative and Analytical Studies in East-West Economic Relations,* ed. Josef Brada (Bloomington, Ind.: International Development Research Center, Indiana University, 1976).

enterprises that are oriented toward the fulfillment of quantitative plan targets have a poor reputation for high-quality production and service after the sale. Furthermore, socialist producers have little direct knowledge of their foreign competition because of the intervention of the ministries of foreign trade. For these and other reasons, the Eastern nations find it difficult to sell their manufactured goods on the intensely competitive world market.

On the political front, the West has a long tradition of trade controls, restrictions, and sanctions directed against the East. The Coordinating Committee (COCOM), which now has representatives from 15 Western industrial nations, was established in 1947 to maintain an agreed list of strategic goods that cannot be exported to the Soviet bloc. Under the Export Control Act, first passed in 1949, the United States has maintained its own more extensive list of prohibited products.

In 1951, as the Cold War grew hot in Korea and during the period of Marshall Plan aid, the U.S. Congress passed the so-called Battle Act, which empowered the president to terminate all military and economic aid to any COCOM member that shipped products on the COCOM lists to the East. During that same year, the Trade Agreement Extension Act denied most-favored-nation (MFN) status to all of the Eastern countries except Yugoslavia. Thus, products imported from the socialist countries were subject to the prohibitive tariffs set during the trade warfare of the Great Depression in the Smoot-Hawley Tariff Act of 1930. More generally, during the McCarthy Era and its aftermath, any American who had business, personal, or cultural contact with the Communist monolith was open to suspicion.

After Stalin's dictatorship, the Korean War, and the Marshall Plan all came to an end in 1953, many of the barriers to East-West trade began to crumble. The new Soviet leadership allowed a little more freedom in the East and the United States could no longer use Marshall Plan aid to influence the West. In Europe, the proximity of the two blocs provided a strong impetus for renewal of traditional trade relations. Vienna, after all, is less than 200 miles from Budapest, and Nuremberg is less than 200 miles from Prague. In Germany, the desire for reunification of families, friendships, and the nation has never died.

Following the European lead, and encouraged by large sales of grain to the Soviet Union in 1963, President Johnson attempted to extend MFN status and Export-Import Bank credits to the Eastern countries, but he was defeated by Congress. It was President Nixon, with his strong credentials as an anti-Communist, who was able to pursue a policy of detente. He visited Moscow in 1972 to meet with General Secretary Brezhnev; later in that year a trade agreement was signed between the two countries calling for: (1) Soviet repayment of $722 million of its First World War Lend-Lease debt to the United States; (2) extension of MFN status to the Soviet Union; and (3) greater Soviet access to U.S. credit.

Again, however, implementation of the trade agreement ran into trouble in the U.S. Congress. Late in 1974, Congress passed an extension of the Export-Import Bank Bill which limited lending to the Soviets to $300 million over a 4-year period, and passed an amendment to the Trade Reform Act which made MFN treatment contingent on Soviet immigration policies. Disappointed by the credit restrictions (they hoped to borrow billions of dollars) and enraged by American efforts to intervene in their internal affairs, the Soviet leaders withdrew from the trade agreement early in 1975. Congressional efforts were made later in that year to rehabilitate the trade agreement, and similar attempts were made in 1979, but they were undermined by the Soviet involvements in Angola and Afghanistan.

The Soviet intervention in Afghanistan precipitated a broad program of sanctions from the Carter administration. New limits were placed on technology, grain, and phosphate (for fertilizers) exports. U.S. athletes were barred from participating in the Moscow Olympics; other commercial, scientific, and cultural exchanges were curtailed; Soviet fishing rights were restricted in U.S. waters; and Aeroflot's landing rights were cut from three to two flights per week. The partial grain embargo became a major issue in the 1980 presidential election and President Reagan fulfilled his campaign pledge to lift the embargo early in 1981. At the same time, he exercised tighter controls on technology exports and tried unsuccessfully to dissuade the other Western nations from participating in a huge project to build a gas export pipeline from Siberia to Western Europe.

In December 1981, one week after martial law was imposed in Poland, President Reagan declared that the Soviet Union bore a heavy and direct responsibility for the Polish action and announced a range of new sanctions. These included restriction of exports for the oil and gas industry, suspension of all Aeroflot service, and suspension of negotiations on maritime and long-term grain agreements. In June 1982, the United States attempted to prevent the European subsidiaries of U.S. firms from selling American-designed energy equipment to the Soviet Union, which placed a heavy strain on American relations with its European allies. Meanwhile, it was argued that American nonparticipation in the Siberian pipeline project was costing thousands of American jobs without appreciably slowing progress on the pipeline. Late in 1982, the effort to control sales of European subsidiaries was dropped and some sales of petroleum equipment originating in the United States were allowed.

Early in 1987, as the United States experienced huge trade deficits, the Reagan administration was forced to reassess its export control policy. A National Academy of Sciences study estimated that the controls cost $9.3 billion in lost sales and 188,000 in lost jobs annually.[19] The millions of products on the export control list could be cut dramatically, according to the Academy, without adding appreciably to the military might of the Soviet bloc. Early in 1987, the Reagan administration announced that it would lift the remaining foreign policy controls on exports of oil and gas equipment to the Soviet

---

[19]Jeff Copeland, "Easing the High-Tech Sales Ban," *Newsweek,* January 26, 1987, 38. These estimates may overestimate the impact of the controls, because they probably do not account for the adaptation of the market economy to controls. See H. Stephen Gardner, "Assessing the Cost to the U.S. Economy of Trade Sanctions against the USSR," in *The Politics of East-West Trade,* ed. Gordon Smith (Boulder, Colo.: Westview, 1984), 175–197.

Union; it also lifted the sanctions against Poland that were imposed 6 years earlier. Also in 1987, although IBM personal computers were still on the control list, the Commerce Department began to approve applications for their export to the East.

The Distribution of Gains from East-West Trade

Adam Smith and his followers in the classical school argued that international trade, because it is beneficial to all participants, should be unrestricted.[20] Even in countries that traditionally espouse liberal principles, the theoretical foundation of East-West trade is often borrowed from Friedrich List, the nineteenth-century German statesman and economist. List argued that trade with a potential adversary, even if it is mutually beneficial, may be undesirable if it bestows *more* economic benefits on the adversary than on the home country. If the gains from trade are distributed unevenly, they could tip the international balance of power.

For several reasons, it is widely believed that the gains from East-West trade flow disproportionately to the East. First, it is said that the Eastern nations can use their governmental foreign-trade monopolies to exercise market power and to whipsaw Western exporters against one another in their attempts to obtain large Eastern contracts. However, according to comparisons of the prices paid by Western and Eastern purchasers of American exports, there is no clear evidence that the Eastern countries have been able to drive a harder bargain.[21] In fact, the socialist countries find it difficult or impossible to make efficient use of the foreign market through central planning and the state monopoly of foreign trade.

Second, because the West is ahead of the East technologically, it is argued that trade allows the Eastern nations to modernize their industries, maintain their economic growth, and upgrade their military. This is undoubtedly part of the situation, but the importance of Western technology to the East should be kept in perspective. Through the decade of the 1970s, Western machinery imports into the Soviet Union amounted to only 2 to 4 percent of domestic machinery investment; less than half of these machinery imports were high-technology items.[22] Furthermore, several econometric studies of the contribution of Western equipment to Soviet economic growth have found that "no superiority can be claimed for Western capital employed in the Soviet Union over indigenous Soviet capital," although Western equipment is important for

---

[20]This overstates the case of classical liberalism, because even Adam Smith condoned protection of domestic industries that are necessary for national defense. "Defense," he said, "is of much more importance than opulence." See *The Wealth of Nations,* 361.

[21]Jacob S. Dreyer, "Countervailing Foreign Use of Monopoly Power," in *Challenges to a Liberal International Economic Order* (Washington, D.C.: American Enterprise Institute, 1979).

[22]John Martens, "Quantification of Western Exports of High-Technology Products to Communist Countries," in U.S. Congress, Joint Economic Committee, *East European Economies: Slow Growth in the 1980s* (Washington, D.C.: USGPO, 1986), 2:91–114.

its complementarity with domestic capital.[23] It should also be remembered that Western technology is (usually) sold for a price.

A third source of uneven gains from East-West trade may be the access of the East to subsidized credit. Of the $92 billion hard currency debt of the Soviet Union and Eastern Europe at the end of 1985, more than one-third was loaned or guaranteed by Western governments and official agencies. Government-backed credits are offered, almost by definition, at subsidized rates. Thus, Western governments sometimes engage in bidding wars with one another to create jobs in their export industries and the Eastern countries are the beneficiaries. The argument remains that the culprit here is not East-West trade, but the failure of Western governments to cooperate with one another.

International trade is not a panacea—a universal remedy for all of the ills of the world. Although it provides an important vehicle for international cooperation, many friendships have been strained or broken and many hot and cold wars have been fought over the field of trade. International commerce can contribute mightily to the world's standard of living as the advantages of specialization and technological progress are shared by its participants. At the same time, trade warfare in the 1930s added depth to the Great Depression, while the erratic behavior of international oil prices is one of the principal causes of economic instability today. In the end, trade is an expression of hope—the hope that cooperation will eventually triumph over chaos and conflict.

Summary

Trade between market economies, which accounts for 85 percent of the world total, is an extension of trade within such countries. However, it differs from domestic trade in that each nation has its own monetary system and because international trade is restricted by governmental policies, languages, customs, and many other factors. While Great Britain adopted a policy of free trade in the nineteenth century, other countries rejected the idea. The Depression of the 1930s encouraged protectionism, and trade restrictions caused further damage to the international economy.

Liberalization of trade began in the mid-1930s and continued after World War II with the General Agreement on Trade and Tariffs (GATT). Although the seven rounds of GATT negotiations have caused large reductions in tariffs and an eighth round is under way, obstacles remain in the removal of nontariff barriers and limits on services trade. Several groups of countries have attempted to promote trade by forming free-trade areas, customs unions, common markets, and economic unions. The U.N. Conference on Trade and

[23]Josef Brada and Dennis Hoffman, "The Productivity Differential between Soviet and Western Capital and the Benefits of Technology Import to the Soviet Economy," *Quarterly Review of Economics and Business* 25 (Spring 1985): 15–16.

Development (UNCTAD) was created in 1964 to promote trade between industrial and developing countries. It called in 1976 for an integrated program of international commodity agreements (ICAs). To date, however, the ICAs have not been very successful.

In a centrally planned economy, foreign trade is usually administered by specialized organizations that have an exclusive right to export and/or import a particular category of goods. This system allows central control of trade, but since trade is unpredictable, it does not fit well in a central plan. A centralized system usually provides poor information and incentives to exporters. Thus, the small, trade-dependent countries of Eastern Europe were the first to adopt economic reforms that allow producers to engage directly in foreign trade. The Soviet Union adopted a similar reform in 1987.

Trade between the socialist countries is promoted and coordinated by the Council for Mutual Economic Assistance (CMEA). The CMEA provides a forum to negotiate prices, trade agreements, international payments, and joint investment projects. Trade between centrally planned economies differs from trade between market economies in that it is based on long-term agreements, it is usually conducted on a bilateral barter basis, and it employs a special system of prices that are based on averages of world market prices.

East-West trade represents only 2 percent of world trade, but its political importance is far greater. The level of East-West trade is limited by the system of central planning and by Western trade, credit, and technology controls. Many people believe that the gains from East-West trade flow disproportionately to the East because of the power of the governmental trade monopoly. Others believe that the East is able to gain unfairly from its access to Western technology and subsidized credit. All of these gains are reduced, however, by the inefficiency of centrally planned foreign trade.

Discussion and Review Questions

1.   What are the differences between a free-trade area, a customs union, a common market, and an economic union? What are the advantages and disadvantages of participating in one of these arrangements?

2.   What is an international commodity agreement? What is its purpose? How does it work?

3.   What are the causes and consequences of inconvertibility and bilateralism in trade between socialist countries?

4.   How are prices determined in trade between socialist countries? What are the purposes, advantages, and disadvantages of this system?

5.   Do you favor a significant expansion of East-West trade? What kinds of goods should and should not be sold to the East? Under what political or military conditions, if any, should international contracts be broken?

Suggested Readings

Bornstein, Morris. *East-West Technology Transfer.* Paris: OECD, 1985. *Discusses the organizational mechanisms and methods of technology transfer from Western countries to the Soviet Union, and the impact of such transfers on the Soviet economy.*

Holzman, Franklyn. *International Trade under Communism.* New York: Basic Books, 1976. *Slightly dated, but still the best general introduction to the peculiarities of socialist foreign trade.*

Salvatore, Dominick, ed. *The New Protectionist Threat to World Welfare.* New York: North-Holland, 1987. *Includes 26 brief papers, ranging from broad theoretical treatments of protectionism to specific industry studies.*

Smith, Gordon, ed. *The Politics of East-West Trade.* Boulder, Colo.: Westview, 1984. *A collective work by economists, political scientists, business people, and government officials.*

International Monetary Fund. *World Economic Outlook.* Washington, D.C., annual. *Provides current data and analysis on the trade, payments, and macroeconomic performance of the industrial, developing, and socialist countries.*

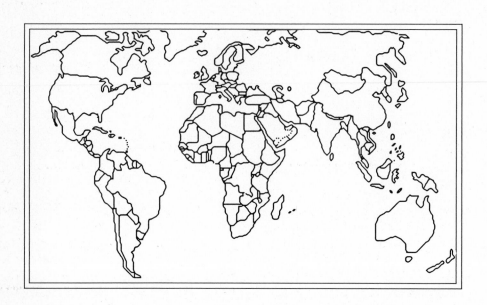

19
CHAPTER

The Future: Confrontation, Coexistence, or Convergence?

*Our little systems have
their day; They have their
day and cease to be;
They are but broken
lights of thee, And thou,
O Lord, art more than
they . . .*

*Behold, we know not
anything; I can but trust
that good shall fall At
last—far off—at last to all,
And every winter change
to spring . . .*
—Alfred Tennyson
  "In Memoriam," 1850

Now that we have surveyed the origins of capitalism and socialism, and the incredible diversity of capitalist and socialist societies in the world today, we can indulge in a bit of speculation. This indulgence is justified by our natural interest in the future and by our knowledge, as economists, that expectations of the future often control our actions in the present. Soviet behavior is influenced, no doubt, by their doctrine of the inevitable victory of socialism, and other countries are led by a variety of philosophies and expectations.

Our vision of the future is usually rooted in the experiences and ideas of the past. As John Maynard Keynes put it so forcefully, "Practical men, who believe themselves to be quite exempt from any intellectual influences, are usually the slaves of some defunct economist."[1] We should add that we are also slaves of defunct philosophers, political scientists, sociologists, and historians who have contributed to the conventional wisdom of our culture. If we hope to get in touch with our own fears, hopes, and expectations, we must continually review events and ideas that have passed before us.

A Brief History of the Economic Future

Adam Smith, the father of the classical school of economics, was a product of the Newtonian Age. Just as Isaac Newton formulated natural laws of gravity and motion to explain the behavior of planets in the solar system, Smith employed the laws of supply and demand to explain the operation of the economic system. To Smith, the market economic system was a permanent part of the natural world. He spoke of a system of natural liberty that was governed by a system of natural prices. Mercantilist restrictions could interrupt the natural progress of opulence, but they could not fundamentally change or replace the underlying laws of the system.

The Smithian view of the world and its future was quickly challenged. Hegel, the German philosopher, and Darwin, the British naturalist, introduced the dialectical and evolutionary modes of thought that questioned all static conceptions of life and social organization. The French and American revolutions demonstrated the feasibility of revolutionary action and led to demands for political, economic, and social equality. In 1848, John Stuart Mill published his *Principles of Political Economy,* which predicted the evolution of a system of labor-managed market socialism, and Marx and Engels published their *Communist Manifesto,* which explained the forces leading to an "inevitable" socialist revolution.

The possibility of a socialist revolution was finally demonstrated in 1917, when the Bolsheviks seized power in Russia. From the beginning, observers in the West found it difficult to believe that the system would last. In late May 1921, an English noble made the following entry in her diary: "Nansen was here to tea and gave me the reassuring news that our troubles with Russia are

---

[1]John Maynard Keynes, *The General Theory of Employment, Interest, and Money* (New York: Harcourt, Brace and World, 1935), 383.

over. Lenin is introducing a New Economic Policy which restores a free market and represents a return to capitalist exchange of goods in Russia."[2] Since that time, every Soviet program of reform has been greeted by many Westerners as a return to capitalism.

Origins of the Convergence Hypothesis

During the Great Depression, the old conceptions of capitalism and socialism seemed to lose their meaning. In the Soviet Union, Stalinist repression of the workers made a mockery of socialist ideals. In the United States, the New Deal policies seemed to modify the nature of the market system. A path-breaking study by Berle and Means revealed that many capitalist firms were no longer controlled by capitalists.[3] An elite corps of professional managers had taken charge, they said, because ownership of the large corporations was divided between thousands of powerless stockholders.

In 1941, James Burnham thought he saw a common thread in the evolutions of Russia, America, and Nazi Germany; he argued that all of the industrial countries were converging away from capitalism and socialism toward a middle ground that he called the **managerial society**. In this new society, he said, the means of production would be owned by the state so that the government would be able to eliminate the mass unemployment of the capitalist system, but no progress would be made toward a socialist classless society. The managerial and technocratic elite would "gain preference in the distribution of products, not directly, through property rights vested in them as individuals, but indirectly, through their control of the state. . . ."[4] Russia had already "advanced furthest along the managerial road," but all of the other industrial countries were on the way. Burnham's gloomy view of the future was shared by Friedrich Hayek in his 1944 book, *The Road to Serfdom.*[5]

In the year that Burnham's work appeared, a far more significant event captured the attention of the world and temporarily changed the Soviet image. The German invasion of Russia broke the bond of totalitarianism formed between Hitler and Stalin in 1939, and the Soviet Union joined in an alliance against Hitler with the Western democratic forces. In 1942, Wendell Willkie—the Republican candidate in the 1940 presidential race—spent ten days in the Soviet Union during a round-the-world ambassadorial trip for President Roosevelt. Upon his return, Willkie published his best-selling book, *One World,* which contained a plea for postwar cooperation between nations:

No, we do not need to fear Russia. We need to learn to work with her against our common enemy, Hitler. We need to learn to work with her in the

---

[2]The diary of Lady Kennet of the Deane, quoted in Bertram Wolfe, "A Historian Looks at the Convergence Theory," in *Sidney Hook and the Contemporary World,* ed. Paul Kurtz (New York: John Day, 1968), 55.

[3]A. A. Berle and Gardner C. Means, *The Modern Corporation and Private Property* (New York: Commerce Clearing House, 1932).

[4]James Burnham, *The Managerial Revolution* (New York: John Day, 1941), 72.

[5]Friedrich A. Hayek, *The Road to Serfdom* (Chicago: University of Chicago Press, 1944).

world after the war. For Russia is a dynamic country, a vital new society, a force that cannot be bypassed in any future world.[6]

Captured by that same wartime spirit of cooperation, a Russian-born Harvard sociologist, Pitirim Sorokin, argued that Russia and the United States "exhibit an essential similarity . . . in a number of important psychological, cultural, and social values."[7] Both countries, he noted, are continental in scope, are cultural and racial melting pots, and have similar family structures.

Because of their environmental similarities, Sorokin predicted a "mutual convergence" of the economic and social structures of the two countries, with growing political and religious freedom in Russia and stronger governmental control in the United States. This convergence, he believed, could provide a basis for international cooperation. He called on the American and Soviet leaders to create a framework for lasting peace by establishing a "real, efficient, and powerful international authority empowered with the right of decision in all international conflicts between all states."[8] One year later, his hopes were partially fulfilled when the United States, the Soviet Union, and 49 other countries signed the United Nations charter.

Convergence and Divergence since World War II

After the war, several circumstances seemed to support the contention of Burnham and Sorokin that capitalist and socialist countries were converging toward a middle ground. England and several other capitalist countries initiated large-scale nationalization of industry, and countries such as France and Japan established systems of indicative planning. In West Germany, the new system of codetermination placed labor representatives on corporate boards of directors. The Yugoslavs broke from the socialist mainstream in 1950 to establish their system of workers' self-management and gradually replaced central planning with market exchange.

In 1956, 3 years after Stalin's death, Nikita Khrushchev delivered two historic speeches to the Twentieth Party Congress. The first speech, delivered publicly, proclaimed that Lenin's doctrine of the inevitability of war between capitalist and socialist countries was rendered obsolete by the danger of nuclear extinction. He announced a policy of **peaceful coexistence**—a shift from military confrontation to economic and political competition. Furthermore, he attempted to draw Yugoslavia back into the fold by recognizing the legitimacy of different roads to socialism. In his second speech, delivered to a secret session of the Party Congress, Khrushchev denounced the despotism and personality cult of Stalin.

The Party Congress sent shock waves through the Communist world. The de-Stalinization campaign cleared the way for release of political prisoners and improvement of relations with the West. In the late 1950s and early 1960s,

---

[6]Wendell L. Willkie, *One World* (New York: Simon and Schuster, 1943), 87.

[7]Pitirim A. Sorokin, *Russia and the United States* (New York: E. P. Dutton, 1944), 26.

[8]Ibid., 239.

economic and political reforms were launched in Poland, Hungary, and Czechoslovakia. In 1962, an article in *Pravda* by Evsei Liberman initiated the discussion of economic reform in the Soviet Union.

In the West, the Kennedy-Johnson administration opened the 1960s with an emphasis on governmental activism and civil rights. In Great Britain, the Conservative government established the National Economic Development Council in 1962, influenced by the French record of rapid economic growth under indicative planning. Even in West Germany, a bastion of anti-Keynesianism, a Council of Economic Experts was established in 1963 to strengthen the nation's fiscal policy.

As the Eastern nations dabbled with markets and democracy, and the Western nations enlarged the roles of their governments, the convergence theory gained broad acceptance. Jan Tinbergen, who would eventually share the first Nobel prize in economics, published his "Theory of the Optimum Regime" in 1959, and in 1961 he argued that systemic changes "are in fact bringing the communist and free economies closer together," although he was quite aware that "there are very large differences still."[9] After scores of academic articles were written on the subject, the theory finally reached a popular audience in 1967, when John Kenneth Galbraith published *The New Industrial State.*

The theory also drew attention from the Soviet side in the 1960s. According to the official Marxian position, the capitalist countries were still destined to experience socialist revolutions, not gradual transitions to a mixed economy. The convergence theory, they said, was designed to "trick the toiling people, to lead them astray with pseudo-socialist slogans. . . ."[10] As Khrushchev told a group of diplomats who visited the Kremlin in 1956, socialism would not converge with capitalism, but it would eventually witness the submergence of capitalism: "Whether or not you like it, history is on our side. We will bury you."

A few voices in the Soviet Union drew inspiration and hope from the idea of convergence. Andrei Sakharov, the so-called father of the Soviet hydrogen bomb who later received the Nobel Peace Prize, proposed a plan in 1968 for economic and political convergence and disarmament.[11] Thirteen years later, while exiled in Gorky, Sakharov summarized his position as follows:

My ideal is an open, pluralistic society, with an unconditional observance of the fundamental civil and political rights of man, a society with a mixed economy which would make for scientifically regulated, comprehensive progress. I have voiced the assumption that such a society ought to come

[9]Jan Tinbergen, "The Theory of the Optimum Regime," in his *Selected Papers* (Amsterdam: 1959); and Jan Tinbergen, "Do Communist and Free Economies Show a Converging Pattern?" *Soviet Studies* 12 (April 1961): 333–341.

[10]L. F. Il'ichev, Soviet Party Secretary, quoted in Leon Goure, et al., *Convergence of Communism and Capitalism: The Soviet View* (Miami, Fla.: Center for Advanced International Studies, University of Miami, 1973), 41.

[11]Andrei Sakharov, *Progress, Coexistence, and Intellectual Freedom* (New York: W. W. Norton, 1968).

about as a result of a peaceful convergence of the socialist and capitalist systems. That is the main condition for saving the world from thermonuclear catastrophe.[12]

From the late 1960s until the late 1970s, the international trend seemingly turned from convergence to divergence. In 1968, although the Hungarians were able to introduce their New Economic Mechanism, Soviet troops ended a more significant revolution in Czechoslovakia. In the United States, 1968 was the year the Republicans regained the White House and liberalism lost two of its most important spokesmen—Martin Luther King and Robert Kennedy. In the Soviet Union, some of the 1965 economic reforms were rolled back in 1971. Each enterprise was required to meet a larger number of plan targets and new limits were placed on the handling of bonus funds. When international oil prices shot upward in 1973, even the Hungarians were forced to scale back their reforms.

A new era of reform began in the East in the late 1970s and this time the results were breathtaking. China adopted the agricultural responsibility system in 1978, 2 years after Mao's death, and Hungary turned its attention back to the New Economic Mechanism in 1979. Both of these countries expanded the scope of private activity, experimented with competitive local elections, loosened price controls, and threatened to close inefficient firms. The independent Solidarity union was established in Poland in 1980 and won a number of concessions from the Communist government. Under pressure from the Soviet Union, Poland imposed martial law in 1981, threatening an end to the entire era of reform.

The degenerative rule of Brezhnev finally ended with his death in 1982. A new program of reform began under the leadership of Andropov; it was continued, enlarged, and extended by Gorbachev. Indeed, Gorbachev has championed openness and restructuring throughout Eastern Europe. Polish martial law was lifted in 1983 and Poland is back on the road to reform. According to General Jaruzelski, the Polish leader, his policies are convergent with those in Moscow, and he is sure that Gorbachev will succeed in the Soviet Union: "It isn't a case of his objective desires. It is a historical principle at work here." The Soviet Union, he says, has been "simmering under a lid. The cover just had to fly off. The corset had to break."[13]

While the Eastern nations have moved dramatically toward the West, little convergence toward the East has been sponsored by leaders such as Reagan, Thatcher, and Helmut Kohl. In 1981, the Socialist government of Francois Mitterrand entered office in France with plans leaning to the left, but they were short-lived. Today, France has joined Great Britain and many other Western countries in their policy of privatization.

Nevertheless, the trend away from state ownership has been balanced, in part, by a trend toward employee ownership and producer cooperation. In

---

[12]Sakharov's open letter to the president of the Soviet Academy of Sciences, published in *Wall Street Journal,* February 5, 1981, 22.

[13]"Jaruzelski Seeks Major Economic Reform," *Wall Street Journal,* July 30, 1987, 16.

1983, when the Weirton Steel Mill in Pennsylvania closed, its 10,000 workers bought the business for $200 million to create the largest employee-owned firm in the world. The next year, when most steel firms lost money, Weirton boasted earnings of $48 million. Employees have taken over several other failing firms in the United States and about 6,000 firms operate Employee Stock Ownership Plans (ESOPs), including Sears, AT&T, Chrysler, Eastern, and MCI.[14]

Although producer cooperatives have a long tradition in Europe, governmental policies and economic conditions have caused their numbers to grow rapidly in recent years. Between 1970 and 1984, the number of British cooperatives increased from about 12 to about 900, and the number in France grew from 300 to 1,400. According to recent econometric evidence, the European firms with high levels of employee ownership and profit sharing have a significant productivity advantage over conventional firms.[15]

Arguments for Convergence

The authors who support the convergence hypothesis are drawn from many different intellectual traditions, but several common themes appear in their work. First, almost all of their theories are based on the idea, which dates at least to Aristotle, that a golden mean is better than an extreme. Thus, an optimum regime, as Tinbergen called it, must exist somewhere between the poles of traditional capitalism and socialism. According to most of the authors, this system would employ economic planning to coordinate long-term decisions, while the market system would regulate supply and demand in the short run. Monopolies, externalities, and other causes of market failure could be controlled through nationalization and/or regulation, but many of the authors would reserve an important place for private enterprise.

If a middle-of-the-road economic system is optimal, then how will all of the nations of the world eventually adopt it? One group of convergence theorists, the **perfectionists,** base their belief on little more than optimism. They share the hope of the French philosophers of the Enlightenment, who spoke of the perfectibility of man. Thus, John Stuart Mill, who was profoundly influenced by the French, predicted the gradual adoption of market socialism if mankind continues to improve. Likewise, Sakharov speaks of convergence as an ideal that can reduce the danger of nuclear war, but stops short of any firm prediction.

Another group, the **economic determinists,** implicitly accept the Marxian proposition that the economic and social system is captive to the development of resources and technology. In the writings of Burnham, Gal-

---

[14]William E. Halal, *The New Capitalism* (New York: John Wiley and Sons, 1986), 184–186.

[15]Saul Estrin, Derek Jones, and Jan Svejnar, "The Productivity Effects of Worker Participation: Producer Cooperatives in Western Economies," *Journal of Comparative Economics* 11 (1987): 40–61. For additional evidence on the effects of employee ownership, see Keith Bradley and Alan Gelb, *Worker Capitalism: The New Industrial Relations* (Cambridge, Mass.: The MIT Press, 1983), Chapter 4.

braith, and many others, the developed nations are driven toward convergence by the logic of industrial society:

> *Convergence begins with modern large-scale production, with heavy requirements of capital, sophisticated technology, and, as a prime consequence, elaborate organization. These require control of prices and, so far as possible, of what is bought at those prices. That is to say that planning must replace the market. In the Soviet-type economies, the control of prices is a function of the state. . . . With us, this management is accomplished less formally by the corporations. . . . But these, obviously, are differences in method rather than purpose.*[16]

Third, the **cultural determinists** believe that closer contact between the peoples of the world—fostered by trade, tourism, Olympic sports, artistic activities, the international news media, and other forms of communication—will strengthen international understanding, dismantle cultural and ideological barriers, and encourage all countries to adopt the best ideas from other cultures. Sorokin was one of the leading exponents of this view:

> *Without even diplomatic pressure the United States will strongly influence the Soviet regime in the direction of terminating its dictatorial violation of the elementary rights of Russian citizens. . . . On the other hand, Russia will continue to fructify the culture—particularly the fine arts—of the United States; and it may facilitate a decrease of the commercial hypocrisy, selfishness, and exploitation inherent, to a certain extent, in any private business on a large scale.*[17]

Arguments against Convergence

There are several reasons to doubt the existence of a single economic system that is optimal for all of the industrial nations. In Chapter 1, we discussed the fact that the economic performance of a country is influenced by its historical, cultural, natural, and international environment, by its economic system, and by its policies. The performance of the economy is judged in terms of national objectives and priorities. Hence, it follows that the optimal system for any single country would depend on its objectives and environment and on the skill of its policy-makers. Economic systems are not transplanted easily from one country to another. For example, the Soviet economic system, which was formulated in a large country with an autocratic political tradition, was wholly inappropriate for the small, trade-dependent countries of Eastern Europe.

Supposing an optimal economic system, or an optimal range of economic systems, could be identified, would it be found half-way between Soviet-style socialism and American-style capitalism, as the convergence theory suggests? If we examine the experiences of countries such as Yugoslavia and Hungary that have travelled in uncharted institutional regions, we see that a suitable compromise between central planning and the market system is hard to find.

[16]John Kenneth Galbraith, *The New Industrial State* (New York: Signet, 1967), 396–397.

[17]Sorokin, *Russia and the United States,* 210.

Suppose, for example, that Hungarian enterprises are given greater autonomy and told to follow a profit motive, while central planners are allowed to maintain their control of prices and credit. Under such circumstances, the country may find itself without any effective coordinating mechanism. The central planners do not have the authority needed to regulate the economy, because autonomy has been given to the enterprises, and the market cannot balance supply and demand, because prices are controlled by the central planners. A system at the middle of the spectrum may incorporate the worst of both worlds, rather than the best. Thus, Frederic Pryor, in his analysis of reforms in Eastern Europe, found that the mixed economies "tended to be unstable and move either toward more centralized or decentralized property patterns."[18]

Finally, if we were to accept the idea of an optimal system, and if we were to find it midway between the traditional models of capitalism and socialism, we may still doubt that all of mankind will adopt that system. Human institutions are resistant to change. Systemic reform almost always requires a shake-up of the existing power structure of society and power is seldom relinquished without a fight.

Economic reform is also a costly process. Suppose that the Soviet Union were to become a full-fledged market economy tomorrow. With production regulated by consumer demand rather than planners' preferences, the output of many products would need to increase substantially and others would need to decline or stop altogether. These adjustments would require retraining and relocating millions of workers and thousands of enterprises would be candidates for closure, reconstruction, or retooling. This would require time and many workers would probably suffer unemployment in the meanwhile. The reforms may improve the operation of the economy in the long run, but they risk a reduction of employment and output in the short run.

For this reason, public support for reform is fragile in many of the socialist countries.[19] If the market is allowed to operate, and unprofitable enterprises are forced to close their doors, many people fear that they will have to endure the capitalist problems—income inequality, unemployment, and inflation— without any assurance that they will be quickly relieved of the socialist problems—restricted freedom, shortages, and low-quality goods. Like tax reform in the West, the need for economic reform is widely acknowledged in the East, but it is difficult to gain broad support for any specific set of proposals.

The Future: A Plausible Scenario

If we take the foregoing arguments to an extreme, we may erroneously conclude that the future will be identical to the recent past. Mixtures of plan and

[18]Frederic Pryor, *Property and Industrial Organization in Communist and Capitalist Nations* (Bloomington, Ind.: Indiana University Press, 1973), 368.

[19]For evidence in the Soviet case that "the most significant brake on the pace of 'restructuring' is the lack of broad-based public support for change," see Elizabeth Teague, "Charges of Resistance to 'Restructuring' Intensify," *Radio Liberty Research,* RL 37/87 (January 26, 1987), 1–5.

Table 19.1   National Expectations

Percentages who responded to the question: "Do you think
for people like yourself that the world in ten years' time will
be a better place to live than it is now, a worse place, or just
about the same as it is today?"

	Better	Worse	Same	No Opinion
Uruguay	54%	23%	15%	9%
Greece	46	29	15	10
*Argentina**	44	27	12	8
United States	30	30	35	5
Brazil	27	48	17	8
Turkey	26	38	12	24
Switzerland	23	33	40	4
Philippines	21	29	42	8
Canada	19	35	41	4
Great Britain	18	45	31	6
Portugal	16	37	9	38
Belgium	15	31	37	17
Netherlands	15	26	53	6
Australia	14	41	38	7
*South Africa***	13	52	28	7
Japan	12	53	18	17
West Germany	4	31	46	19

*Buenos Aires only.
**Whites only.

Source: A 1985 poll administered to an average of over 1,000 citizens of each country, reported in *The Gallup Poll: Public Opinion 1985* (Wilmington, Del.: Scholarly Resources Inc., 1986), 78–80. Reprinted with permission.

market are unstable and reforms always meet political resistance, thus the East shall remain East, and the West shall remain West, and never the twain shall meet.

In all probability, some things will change and some things will stay the same for a very long period of time. All countries are faced by the challenge of rapid technological progress, by competition in a world economy that is increasingly integrated through trade and finance, and by the depletion of important natural resources. The old Soviet-style system of detailed central planning and price control does not seem sufficiently flexible to weather these storms. The Soviet planners and bureaucrats have been in operation for half a century and they will not pass quietly from the scene, but in the words of Keynes, "Soon or late, it is ideas, not vested interests, which are dangerous for good or evil."[20]

If detailed central planning does eventually give way to the market system, some of the levers of authoritarianism that operate in the East will inevitably be broken. On the other hand, considerable leeway will be left for

[20]Keynes, *The General Theory,* 384.

national and regional differences in economic, political, and social systems. Market failures and inequities will need correction; they will be handled through various combinations and forms of regulation, nationalization, employee ownership, codetermination, redistribution, indicative planning, fiscal and monetary policy, and other devices that have not yet been imagined. On this side of eternity, for as long as nations are divided by languages, cultures, objectives, traditions, and environmental differences, they will perceive their problems differently and they will devise their own solutions.

Opinion polls currently reveal little optimism in the world. In most countries where such polls have been taken, the people who believe the world will be a better place in the future are outnumbered by those who expect conditions to grow worse (Table 19.1). If we wish to outperform our expectations, we must learn to coexist and cooperate with other nations. We must learn to compete in a peaceful and constructive way. On these points, the leaders of the East and the West claim to agree. Our most difficult task for the coming years is to transform some of this rhetoric into reality.

Summary

To Adam Smith, the capitalist economic system was a permanent part of the natural world. Dialectical and evolutionary theories, including those of Karl Marx, challenged the conception of an economic universe governed by immutable economic laws. The Russian Revolution finally proved that capitalism could be replaced on a national scale.

The traditional views of capitalism and socialism were confounded in the 1930s by Stalinist repression in the Soviet Union and the separation of corporate ownership from control in the West. Hence, Burnham predicted that a managerial revolution would invade all of the industrial countries. The convergence hypothesis gained adherents during World War II, when the Soviet Union joined forces with the Western alliance against Hitler.

After the war, nationalization programs in Great Britain, indicative planning in France and Japan, codetermination in West Germany, and workers' self-management in Yugoslavia provided further evidence of convergence. Then, in the 1960s, the popularity of the theory peaked with the introduction of reforms in the East and social welfare programs in the West. Convergence seemed to give way to divergence beginning in the late 1960s, as the Czech reforms were crushed, the Soviet reforms were rolled back, and conservatism made new gains in the West. The Eastern reforms gained new life, in the late 1970s, with historic developments in China and Poland and throughout the region. Privatization was the prevailing trend in the West during the 1980s, but it was accompanied by a trend toward employee ownership.

Arguments in favor of the convergence hypothesis are usually based on the implicit or explicit assumption that an optimal regime exists somewhere between the poles of traditional capitalism and socialism. This system, according to the usual formulation, would employ a mix of long-term planning, short-term markets, and various patterns of ownership. The more deterministic models say that convergence is propelled by a technological or sociological imperative.

Opponents of the convergence hypothesis doubt the existence of a single optimal regime, due to the continuing differences of national objectives, cultures, and environments. If an optimal system did exist, it may not be found half-way between traditional capitalism and socialism; such a hybrid system may tie the hands of both the planners and the market. Furthermore, institutional change has its economic and political cost, possibly preventing the adoption of an optimal system. One plausible scenario is a trend toward wider use of a regulated market system, with broad differences in national management of market failures.

Discussion and Review Questions

1. How did the events of the 1930s and 1940s give rise to the convergence hypothesis?

2. What converging and diverging trends do you see today among Western countries, among Eastern countries, and between the East and the West?

3. Do you believe that technology is a force that encourages countries to adopt a common set of institutions, or does technology help countries to maintain their differences?

Suggested Readings

Burnham, James. *The Managerial Revolution.* New York: John Day, 1941. *One of the earliest, and gloomiest, predictions of convergence.*

Galbraith, John Kenneth. *The New Industrial State.* New York: Signet, 1967. *This book probably played the most important role in carrying the convergence hypothesis, based on technological determinism, to a popular audience.*

Goure, Leon, Foy D. Kohler, Richard Soll, and Annette Stiefbold. *Convergence of Communism and Capitalism: The Soviet View.* Miami, Fla.: Center for Advanced International Studies, University of Miami, 1973. *A documentary record of Soviet reactions, most of them denials.*

Halal, William E. *The New Capitalism.* New York: John Wiley and Sons, 1986. *This is primarily a treatise on the future of business management, but it is set in a broader cultural framework. It proposes the development of a democratic free enterprise economy, based on free markets, employee stock ownership, and broader participation of business and labor in government.*

Kerr, Clark. *The Future of Industrial Societies: Convergence or Continuing Diversity?* Cambridge, Mass.: Harvard University Press, 1983. *Provides a broad literature review, a typology of convergence and divergence theories, and a balanced set of conclusions.*

Sakharov, Andrei. *Progress, Coexistence, and Intellectual Freedom.* New York: W. W. Norton, 1968. *This is a plaintive cry for convergence, viewed as a precondition for world peace and cooperation.*

Sorokin, Pitirim A. *Russia and the United States.* New York: E. P. Dutton, 1944. *A sociological perspective, emphasizing the similarities between Russia and the United States.*

Zwass, Adam. *Market, Plan, and State: The Strengths and Weaknesses of the Two World Economic Systems.* Armonk, N.Y.: M. E. Sharpe, 1987. *Written by a former official of the Polish and CMEA banking systems, this book argues for the superior flexibility of the market system and surveys a broad array of topics related to comparative systems.*

APPENDIX OF
STATISTICAL TABLES

Table A.1   Basic Data on the World Economy

	Population		1982 Arable Land Per Capita (acres)
	1982 (millions)	1970–1981 Growth	
World	4,584	1.8%	0.8
Industrial Capitalist	723	0.7	1.2
Soviet Union/Eastern Europe	381	0.8	1.8
High-Income Oil Exporters	17	5.0	0.4
Developing Countries	3,463	2.1	0.6
Developing by Region:			
Sub-Saharan Africa	401	2.8	0.9
Middle East/North Africa	171	2.9	0.7
East Asia/Pacific	1,474	1.7	0.3
South Asia	945	2.2	0.6
Southern Europe	98	1.6	1.1
Western hemisphere	374	2.3	1.2
Developing by Income Group:			
21 Upper middle-income	489	2.2	—
39 Lower middle-income	670	2.6	0.8
32 Low income	541	2.6	—
China	1,008	1.5	0.2
India	717	2.1	0.6

*Gross domestic investment as a percentage of GDP.

Sources: World Bank, *World Development Report,* various years; World Bank, *World Tables,* 3d ed. (Baltimore: Johns Hopkins, 1983); Ruth Leger Sivard, *World Military and Social Expenditures 1985* (Washington: World Priorities, 1985); and U.S. Central Intelligence Agency, *Handbook of Economic Statistics 1985.* GNP per capita was roughly converted to a purchasing-power–parity basis using deviation indexes found in Irving Kravis, et. al., *World Product and Income* (Baltimore: Johns Hopkins, 1982), and other publications of the International Comparisons Project.

GNP Per Capita		1981 Investment Rate*	1982 Infant Mortality (per 1,000)	1981 Adult Literacy
Dollars (1982)	1960–1981 Growth			
3,492	3.1%	24%	66	69%
10,849	3.4	22	10	99
6,400	2.9	30	21	99
24,453	6.2	25	96	42
1,533	3.0	26	82	60
1,269	1.8	24	121	43
2,509	2.8	34	97	43
1,632	4.7	27	54	74
385	2.0	24	116	40
4,089	4.4	27	81	76
3,212	2.7	26	61	81
4,407	4.2	25	58	76
1,487	3.4	25	89	59
663	0.8	14	114	40
2,062	5.0	28	67	69
814	1.4	23	94	36

Table A.2 Alternative Measures of Living Standards, 1984*

	GDP Per Capita		Physical Quality of Life**	Food Calories Per Capita
	Market/Par Exchange Rate	Purchasing Power Parity		
Industrial Capitalist Countries				
Australia	76	80	100	85
Canada	86	91	100	95
France	63	83	101	97
Italy	42	56	99	97
Japan	69	81	101	73
Netherlands	62	69	101	96
Sweden	77	91	101	86
Switzerland	106	82	101	96
United Kingdom	56	63	99	89
United States	100	100	100	100
West Germany	72	85	100	96
Socialist Countries				
Bulgaria	28	44	95	101
China	2	18	82	72
Czechoslovakia	37	54	97	98
East Germany	46	63	98	103
Hungary	32	49	96	98
Poland	27	42	96	92
Romania	18	35	94	92
Soviet Union	30	48	93	93
Yugoslavia	25	40	90	99
Developing Countries				
Bangladesh	1	5	44	51
Brazil	11	23	76	70
Egypt	5	17	58	87
India	2	7	56	58
Mexico	13	31	84	81
Nigeria	5	10	48	56

*For each index, United States = 100.

**The Physical Quality of Life index is explained in Chapter 2.

Sources: Columns 1 and 3, and data to calculate column 4—World Bank, *World Development Report 1986* (New York: Oxford University Press, 1986), Tables 1, 27, 28; and Ruth Sivard, *World Military and Social Expenditures 1986* (Washington, D.C.: World Priorities, 1986), Table 3. For the Soviet Union and East Europe, columns 1 and 2 are based on the 1975 estimates in Paul Marer, *Dollar GNPs of the USSR and Eastern Europe* (Baltimore: Johns Hopkins, 1985), Table 3–15, and growth estimates in U.S. Central Intelligence Agency, *Handbook of Economic Statistics 1986*, Table 8. For other countries, column 2 is based on Robert Summers and Alan Heston, "Improved International Comparisons of Real Product and Its Composition, 1950–1980," *Review Of Income and Wealth* 30 (June 1984): 207–262; and growth estimates in International Monetary Fund, *International Financial Statistics*, Supplement on Economic Indicators, No. 10 (1985).

Table A.3   Gross Domestic Product, 1820–1985*

	France	West Germany	Japan	Sweden	United Kingdom	United States	Russia/ Soviet Union
1820	22.2	11.6	n.a.	n.a.	19.7	8.4	n.a.
1870	55.6	31.6	20.0	4.2	63.6	71.7	60.2
1913	112.5	103.8	56.9	13.7	142.5	414.6	172.7
1928	130.1	126.2	98.3	19.9	155.0	636.9	195.4
1933	131.6	112.5	102.6	21.1	155.8	476.8	223.2
1940	116.8	191.0	145.5	26.2	209.8	739.7	359.7
1950	162.6	167.1	110.7	38.3	229.2	1,147.7	436.9
1960	254.1	359.7	258.0	53.5	301.6	1,576.0	758.6
1970	436.7	569.5	741.8	83.7	397.8	2,320.6	1,246.5
1985	661.1	791.3	1,441.3	110.7	523.3	3,432.4	1,845.1

*Valued in billions of 1983 U.S. dollars at purchasing-power–parity exchange rates.

n.a.—not available.

Sources: For countries other than the Soviet Union and Sweden, 1950–1970 estimates are based on Irving Kravis, *World Product and Income* (Baltimore: Johns Hopkins, 1982), Table 8–3. The estimates for Sweden are taken from Robert Summers and Alan Heston, "Improved International Comparisons of Real Product and Its Composition," *Review of Income and Wealth* 30 (June 1984): 207–262. These are extrapolated forward using official indexes of real GDP, and extrapolated backward to 1820 using estimates in Angus Maddison, *Phases of Capitalist Development* (Oxford: Oxford University Press, 1982), Appendix A and B. All estimates are moved to a 1983 price base with the U.S. GNP deflator.

For Russia/Soviet Union, estimates for 1960–1983 are taken from U.S. Central Intelligence Agency, *Handbook of Economic Statistics 1986* (CPAS 86–10002, September 1986), Table 8. They are extrapolated backward with the CIA estimate for 1950 found in *USSR: Measures of Economic Growth and Development, 1950–80,* U.S. Congress, Joint Economic Committee (Washington, D.C.: USGPO, 1983), Table A-5, and to 1870 using the index found in Angus Maddison, *Economic Growth in Japan and the USSR* (New York: W. W. Norton, 1969), Appendix B. The U.S. GNP deflator was used to move the price base to 1983.

Table A.4   Gross Domestic Product Per Capita, 1820–1985*

	France	West Germany	Japan	Sweden	United Kingdom	United States	Russia/ Soviet Union
1820	886.6	466.7	n.a.	n.a.	950.7	877.1	n.a.
1870	1,447.1	804.9	582.0	1,007.1	2,031.0	1,797.7	728.4
1913	2,825.9	1,549.3	1,099.6	2,448.2	3,119.0	4,265.6	1,093.1
1928	3,166.4	1,960.3	1,574.5	3,265.6	3,398.0	5,285.1	1,289.7
1933	3,140.8	1,704.9	1,527.1	3,400.0	3,350.3	3,793.3	1,293.8
1940	2,847.8	2,736.5	1,993.7	4,087.5	4,352.9	5,599.4	1,843.7
1950	3,890.9	3,342.6	1,335.8	5,470.0	4,547.6	7,535.5	2,425.7
1960	5,559.7	6,492.4	2,765.7	7,128.0	5,734.0	8,721.4	3,539.9
1970	8,597.2	9,382.0	7,174.1	10,461.3	7,167.9	11,314.5	5,134.0
1985	12,020.0	12,972.1	11,941.2	13,337.3	9,278.4	14,385.6	6,615.6

*Valued in 1983 U.S. dollars at purchasing-power–parity exchange rates.

n.a.—not available.

Sources: See Table A.3.

Table A.5   Performance and Priorities: Economic Growth, Inflation, and Unemployment

	1971–1985 GNP Per Capita Growth	1971–1985 Annual Average Inflation	1980–1985 Annual Average Unemployment	Percent Polled Who Say Worst Problem Is:	
				Inflation	Unemployment
Industrial Capitalist Countries					
Australia	1.6%	9.7%	7.6%	41%	66%
Canada	2.2	7.8	9.9	—	—
France	2.2	9.7	8.3	21	47
Italy	1.9	13.9	9.2	—	—
Japan	3.5	6.9	2.4	25	n.a.
Netherlands	1.7	6.2	11.1	20	65
Sweden	1.6	9.2	2.8	26	18
Switzerland	1.0	4.8	0.6	14	9
United Kingdom	1.7	11.4	11.0	18	59
United States	1.6	7.0	8.0	53	11
West Germany	1.9	4.7	6.4	27	23
Socialist Countries					
Bulgaria	1.9	4.2	—	—	—
China	5.3	2.3	—	—	—
Czechoslovakia	1.8	2.1	—	—	—
East Germany	2.7	1.2	—	—	—
Hungary	1.8	6.0	—	—	—
Poland	1.7	14.5	—	—	—
Romania	3.4	4.6	—	—	—
Soviet Union	1.5	2.0	—	—	—
Yugoslavia	2.9	27.8	12.7	—	—
Developing Countries					
Brazil	3.5	76.2	—	—	—
India	1.2	8.5	—	—	—
Mexico	1.9	31.7	5.1**	—	—
Nigeria	0.1	17.1*	—	—	—
South Korea	5.9	13.4	4.3		

*1971–1984

**1980–1984

Sources: *OECD Economic Outlook,* No. 40 (December 1986), Tables R10, R12; Central Intelligence Agency, *Handbook of Economic Statistics 1986* (CPAS 86–10002, September 1986), Tables 13, 14, 26; International Monetary Fund, *International Financial Statistics,* Supplement on Economic Indicators, No. 10 (1985). Inflation data for socialist countries are based on CIA alternative estimates; unemployment rates for industrial capitalist countries are adjusted by OECD for consistency. Columns 4 and 5—Results of polls taken in 1980, reported in *The Gallup Poll: Public Opinion 1981* (Wilmington, Del.: Scholarly Resources, Inc., 1982): 9–11.

Table A.6   Average Annual Growth Rates of Real Product, Factor Inputs, and Total Factor Productivity, 1960–1973

	Real Product	Labor Input	Capital Input	Factor Productivity
Canada	5.1%	2.0%	4.9%	1.8%
France	5.9	0.4	6.3	3.0
Italy	4.8	0.2	5.4	2.6
Japan	10.9	2.7	11.5	4.5
Netherlands	5.6	0.3	6.6	2.6
United Kingdom	3.8	0.0	4.6	2.1
United States	4.1	2.2	4.0	1.1
*Soviet Union**	4.7	1.8	8.1	0.4
West Germany	5.0	− 0.7	7.0	3.0

*1961–1975

Sources: Laurits R. Christensen, Diane Cummings, and Dale Jorgenson, "Economic Growth, 1947–1973: An International Comparison," in *New Developments in Productivity Measurement and Analysis,* ed. John W. Kendrick and Beatrice N. Vacara (Chicago: University of Chicago Press, 1978), Table 11. For the Soviet Union, U.S. Central Intelligence Agency, *Handbook of Economic Statistics 1984* (CPAS 84–10002, September 1984), Table 44.

Table A.7   Structure of Output and Employment

	1984 Distribution of GDP			1980 Distribution of Employment		
	Agriculture	Industry	Services	Agriculture	Industry	Services
Industrial Capitalist Countries						
Canada	3	24	72	5	29	65
France	4	34	62	9	35	56
Italy	5	40	55	12	41	48
Japan	3	41	56	11	34	55
Netherlands	4	32	64	6	32	63
Sweden	3	31	66	6	33	62
United Kingdom	2	36	56	3	38	59
United States	2	32	66	4	31	66
West Germany	2	46	52	6	44	50
Socialist Countries						
Bulgaria	21	40	39	18	45	37
China	36	44	20	69	19	12
Czechoslovakia	16	39	45	13	49	37
East Germany	15	45	40	11	50	39
Hungary	20	42	38	18	44	38
Poland	15	52	33	29	39	33
Romania	28	40	32	29	44	27
Soviet Union	20	34	46	20	39	41
Yugoslavia	15	46	40	32	33	34
Developing Countries						
Bangladesh	48	12	39	80	8	12
Brazil	13	35	52	31	27	42
Egypt	20	33	48	46	20	34
Ethiopia	48	16	36	80	8	12
India	35	27	38	70	13	17
Mexico	9	40	52	37	29	34
Nigeria	27	30	43	68	12	20

Sources: World Bank, *World Development Report 1986* (New York: Oxford University Press, 1986), Tables 3 and 30. Distributions of output for East European countries were calculated on the basis of data found in Thad P. Alton, et al., "Economic Growth in Eastern Europe, 1970 and 1975–1984," Occasional Paper No. 85 of the Research Project on National Income in East Central Europe (New York: L. W. International Financial Research, 1985), Tables 1–6.

Table A.8   Selected Data on Financial Markets in Industrial Capitalist Countries

	Contribution of Finance, Insurance, Real Estate, and Business Services to GDP, 1981		Percentage Composition of Liabilities of Nonfinancial Corporations, 1984			
	U.S. Dollars (billions)	Percentage of GDP	Equity	Short-Term Debt	Long-Term Debt	Total
Canada	28.9	10.1%	57.7%	21.7%	20.6%	100%
France	95.5	17.7	30.1	52.4	17.5	100
Italy	61.4	18.5	—	—	—	—
Japan	176.8	15.4	17.3	59.6	23.1	100
Sweden	11.9	11.6	34.7	39.4	25.9	100
United Kingdom	63.2	13.4	45.4	46.2	8.4	100
United States	598.7	20.6	61.8	18.3	19.9	100
Germany	73.5	10.7	36.2	40.5	16.3	100

Sources: Organization for Economic Cooperation and Development, *National Accounts: 1964–1981* (Paris: 1983); and Organization for Economic Cooperation and Development, *Non-Financial Enterprises Financial Statements 1986* (Paris: 1986).

Table A.9   Average Industrial Concentration Ratios

	Scherer	Pryor	George/Ward
Belgium	—	1.46	—
Canada	71	1.52	—
France	66	.90	24
Italy	—	.97	20
Japan	—	1.05	—
Netherlands	—	1.17	—
Sweden	83	1.58	—
Switzerland	—	1.49	—
United Kingdom	60	1.04	32
United States	41	1.00	—
West Germany	56	.98	22
Yugoslavia	—	1.50	—

Sources: Column 1—Simple averages of three-firm concentration ratios for 12 identically defined industries in 1970. F. M. Scherer, et al., *The Economics of Multi-Plant Operation: An International Comparisons Study* (Cambridge, Mass.: Harvard University Press, 1975), 218–219, 426–428. Column 2—Ratio of simple average four-firm concentration ratio to average U.S. ratio. Most data are from early 1960s, and sample sizes range from 16 to 72 industries. Frederic L. Pryor, *Property and Industrial Organization in Communist and Capitalist Countries* (Bloomington, Ind.: Indiana University Press, 1973), 204. Column 3—Employment-weighted average of four-firm concentration ratios for 90 EEC census industries in 1963. Kenneth D. George and T. S. Ward, *The Structure of Industry in the EEC* (Cambridge: Cambridge University Press, 1975), 17.

Table A.10 Nationalities of Largest Industrial Corporations, 1985

	Number of Corporations among the Capitalist World's:		
	100 Largest by Sales	Second 100 by Sales	200 Largest by Sales
United States	48	38	86
Japan	12	16	28
West Germany	7	11	18
United Kingdom	5	8	13
France	5	6	11
Canada	3	3	6
South Korea	4	1	5
Netherlands	3	2	5
Italy	3	1	4
Other	10	14	24

Sources: "The International 500," *Fortune,* August 4, 1986, 180–185; and "The Largest U.S. Industrial Corporations," *Fortune,* April 28, 1986, 182–201.

Table A.11 Union Membership and Work Stoppages

	Union Members as Percent of Labor Force (early 1980s)	Average Annual Days Lost Per Thousand Employees		
		1955–1960	1961–1970	1971–1982
Canada	30	393	587	883
Denmark	75	159	193	257
France	20	184	185	198
Italy	37	406	1,260	1,193
Japan	22	254	137	99
Netherlands	26	49	14	37
Sweden	80	18	22	130
Switzerland	20	1	4	2
United Kingdom	44	203	192	524
United States	20	446	358	265
West Germany	35	43	16	45

Sources: Labor union membership estimates are taken from Central Intelligence Agency, *The World Factbook 1983* (CR 83–11300, 1983); and *Business Week,* November 26, 1984, 88. Work stoppage data are from U.S. Department of Labor, Bureau of Labor Statistics, *Handbook of Labor Statistics,* Bulletin 2217 (Washington, D.C.: USGPO, 1985), 448–449.

Table A.12   Unemployment Rates, 1920–1985

	1920	1933	1950	1960	1970	1980	1985
Industrial Capitalist Countries							
Australia	4.6%	17.4%	1.5%	2.5%	1.6%	6.0%	8.2%
Canada	—	19.3	3.6	6.8	5.6	7.4	10.4
France	—	—	2.3	1.8	2.4	6.3	10.1
Italy	—	5.9	6.9	3.9	5.3	7.5	10.5
Japan	—	—	1.9	1.7	1.1	2.0	2.6
Netherlands	1.7	9.7	2.8	1.2	1.0	6.0	13.0
Norway	—	9.7	1.2	2.3	1.6	1.7	2.5
Sweden	1.3	7.3	1.7	1.7	1.5	2.0	2.8
Switzerland	—	3.5	0.0	0.0	0.0	0.2	1.0
United Kingdom	1.9	13.9	2.5	2.2	3.0	6.4	13.0
United States	3.9	20.5	5.2	5.4	4.8	7.0	7.1
West Germany	1.7	14.8	8.2	1.0	0.8	3.0	8.6
Socialist Countries							
Yugoslavia	—	—	—	—	7.7	11.9	13.8
Developing Countries							
Chile	—	—	—	—	3.4	12.0	17.0
Hong Kong	—	—	—	—	—	3.8	3.2
Philippines	—	—	—	—	—	4.8	6.1
Puerto Rico	—	—	—	—	10.7	17.1	21.8
South Korea	—	—	—	—	4.5	5.2	4.0
Trinidad, Tobago	—	—	—	—	12.5	10.0	15.5

Sources: For industrial capitalist countries, 1920–1960 data are from Angus Maddison, *Phases of Capitalist Development* (Oxford: Oxford University Press, 1982), Table C-6; for 1970–1985, standardized rates found in *OECD Economic Outlook,* No. 40 (December 1986), Table R-12; for other countries, International Labour Office, *Yearbook of Labour Statistics 1980* (Geneva, 1980), Table 10; and United Nations, *Monthly Bulletin of Statistics* 41 (January 1987), Table 8.

Table A.13 Youth Unemployment

	Percent of Labor Force, Aged 15–24	
	1980	1984
Canada	13.2%	17.9%
France	15.0	26.1
Italy	25.2	34.1
Japan	3.6	4.9
Norway	5.4	7.6
Sweden	5.1	6.0
United Kingdom	14.1	21.8
United States	13.3	13.3
West Germany	3.9	10.1

Source: *OECD Economic Outlook,* No. 37 (June 1985), 29.

Table A.14   Hours of Work Per Week in Manufacturing

	1978	1981	1985
Industrial Capitalist Countries			
Australia	38.1	37.8	37.2
Canada	38.8	38.5	38.8
France	41.0	40.3	38.6
Japan	40.6	41.0	41.5
Netherlands	41.1	40.8	40.5
Norway	31.3	30.8	30.6
Sweden	37.8	37.5	37.9
United Kingdom	40.3	41.0	41.8
United States	40.4	39.8	40.5
West Germany	41.6	41.1	40.7
Socialist Countries			
Czechoslovakia	43.5	43.3	43.1
Soviet Union	40.4	40.7	40.3

Sources: International Labour Office, *Yearbook of Labour Statistics 1984* (Geneva, 1984), Table 12; United Nations Statistical Office, *Monthly Bulletin of Statistics* 41 (January 1987), Table 7; and U.S. Department of Labor, Bureau of Labor Statistics, *Handbook of Labor Statistics,* Bulletin 2217 (Washington, D.C.: USGPO, 1985), Table 131.

Table A.15   Role of Public Enterprises in Industrial Capitalist and Developing Countries (Late 1970s)

	Percentage Share of Publicly-owned Enterprises in:		
	GDP	Employment	Gross Fixed Investment
Industrial Capitalist Countries			
Australia	9.3	—	19.9
Austria	14.5	12.4	20.4
Canada	—	4.5	16.1
France	—	4.4	11.3
Italy	7.6	6.4	17.0
Japan	—	—	12.1
Netherlands	—	3.8	14.0
Sweden	—	8.0	17.1
United Kingdom	11.1	8.2	19.1
United States	—	1.6	4.9
West Germany	10.2	7.9	12.7
Developing Countries			
Argentina	4.7	—	19.5
Bolivia	12.1	—	40.9
Burma	—	—	50.1
Chile	14.3	—	17.0
Ethiopia	—	—	27.1
India	—	9.9	33.8
Kenya	—	—	17.7
Mexico	—	—	27.6
Pakistan	—	—	44.2
Philippines	—	—	9.8
Taiwan	13.5	—	33.9
Tanzania	—	12.3	25.6
Venezuela	21.3	—	29.3
Zambia	—	—	61.2

Sources: Data on employment and investment for the industrial countries are taken from "Big Government—How Big Is It?" *OECD Observer* (March 1983): 9. All other estimates are derived from the data for 1975–1980 in Robert Floyd, Clive Gray, and R. P. Short, *Public Enterprise in Mixed Economies: Some Macroeconomic Aspects* (Washington, D.C.: International Monetary Fund, 1984), Table 1.

Table A.16   Role of the Socialist Sector in the Socialist Countries

| | Percentage Share of the Socialist Sector in: | | | | | |
| | National Income | | Employment | | Capital Stock | |
	1960	1984	1960	1984	1960	1984
Bulgaria	—	—	100	100	99.6	99.9
Cuba	—	96.7	—	—	—	—
Czechoslovakia	98.5	99.3	99.8	99.9	97.9	99.3
East Germany	84.7	96.5	83.1	96.3	93.2	99.0
Hungary	91.0	95.9	98.3	98.9	91.9	99.1
Mongolia	99.9	100	100	100	99.9	100
Poland	62.1	79.8	95.5	93.1	—	78.4
Romania	83.3	95.5	100	100	86.7	99.5
Soviet Union	99.9	100	100	100	99.9	100
Vietnam	—	51.9	—	—	—	—
Yugoslavia	72.8	85.9	—	—	—	—

Source: *Statisticheskii ezhegodnik stran-chlenov Soveta Ekonomicheskoi Vzaimopomoshchi 1985* (Moscow: Finansy i Statistika, 1985), 51, 399.

Table A.17   Central Government Expenditures as a Percentage of GNP, 1983

	Total Expenditures	Health, Education, and Welfare Expenditures
Industrial Capitalist Countries		
Australia	26.7	12.0
Canada	25.6	12.2
France	44.8	31.5
Italy	52.8	28.7
Japan	18.6	—
Netherlands	59.4	37.8
Sweden	46.9	28.2
Switzerland	19.4	12.8
United Kingdom	41.4	19.7
United States	25.3	12.4
West Germany	31.1	21.7
Socialist Countries		
Bulgaria	54.8	18.7
Czechoslovakia	51.6	26.7
East Germany	63.6	19.7
Hungary	58.3	20.5
Poland	34.8	11.3
Romania	27.4	7.7
Soviet Union	50.1	16.1
Developing Countries		
Brazil	21.4	9.9
India	14.9	1.3
Iran	28.1	9.2
Kenya	26.6	7.5
Mexico	27.9	6.9
Sri Lanka	33.6	7.9
Zaire	27.5	5.5

Sources: For industrial capitalist and developing countries, World Bank, *World Development Report 1986* (New York: Oxford University Press, 1986) 222–223. For socialist countries, budgetary data in domestic currency were taken from United Nations, *Statistical Yearbook 1982* (New York, 1985), 265; GNP in domestic currency was estimated by adjusting 1983 NMP data, found in United Nations, *Monthly Bulletin of Statistics* (January 1987), special table E, with GNP/NMP ratios found in Paul Marer, *Dollar GNPs of the USSR and Eastern Europe* (Baltimore: Johns Hopkins, 1985), 18–19.

Table A.18 Government Current Expenditures on Goods and Services as a Proportion of GNP, 1870–1985

	1870	1913	1938	1954	1970	1985
Canada	4.6%	8.1%	10.9%	14.6%	19.2%	20.8%
Italy	8.1	9.7	15.7	12.1	13.8	19.5
Japan	6.8[a]	9.1	25.0	11.0	7.4	9.8
Norway	3.8	6.3	9.9	12.5	16.9	18.6
Sweden	4.7	5.6	10.4	15.0	21.4	27.4
United Kingdom	4.9	7.0	13.0	18.0	17.6	21.1
United States	3.7	4.2	10.1	17.3	19.2	18.3
West Germany	5.9[b]	8.7	23.1	14.0	15.8	19.9

[a]1879
[b]1871–1890

Sources: 1879–1938: Angus Maddison, *Economic Growth in Japan and the USSR* (New York: W. W. Norton, 1969), 13. 1954–1982: Organization for Economic Cooperation and Development, *National Accounts: 1953–82,* vol. 1 (Paris: 1984).

Table A.19 Transfer Payments to Households as a Percentage of GDP, 1953–1981

	1953	1960	1970	1981
France	12.4	12.9	17.2	24.7
Italy	8.3	12.1	12.7	17.7
Japan	2.9	5.0	4.8	11.2
Norway	6.5	9.3	12.3	14.6
Sweden	6.5	9.0	11.6	19.7
United Kingdom	6.2	6.9	9.3	14.0
United States	3.3	5.1	7.9	11.5
West Germany	11.8	12.4	13.4	18.0

Sources: 1953, 1960: Organization for Economic Cooperation and Development, *National Accounts: 1953–1969* (Paris: undated); 1970, 1981: Organization for Economic Cooperation and Development, *National Accounts: 1964–1981,* vol. 2 (Paris: 1983).

Table A.20   Defense Expenditures as a Percentage of GNP, 1965–1982

	1965	1970	1975	1982
Capitalist				
Australia	4.4	3.3	2.2	2.5
Belgium	3.1	2.9	3.0	3.4
Canada	3.0	2.4	1.9	2.2
France	5.2	4.2	3.8	4.2
Italy	3.3	2.5	2.5	2.6
Japan	1.0	0.8	0.9	1.0
Netherlands	4.0	3.4	3.2	3.3
Spain	2.7	3.1	2.7	2.1
Sweden	3.9	3.6	3.3	3.3
United Kingdom	5.9	4.7	4.9	5.1
United States	7.1	7.4	5.4	5.8
West Germany	4.3	3.3	3.6	3.4
Socialist				
Bulgaria	3–11	2–9	3–10	3–10
Czechoslovakia	4–6	3–5	3–5	4–5
East Germany	3–4	4–6	4–6	4–6
Hungary	3–6	3–6	2–5	2–5
Poland	3–6	4–6	3–5	4–7
Romania	2–8	2–7	2–6	1–5
Soviet Union	11–13	11–13	13–14	13–14

Note: The estimates for Eastern Europe are presented as a range, where the lower number is based on calculations in the domestic currencies, and the higher number is based on U.S. dollar valuations. This is an example of the index number problem, which is discussed in Chapter 2.

Sources: Capitalist countries: U.S. Central Intelligence Agency, *Handbook of Economic Statistics, 1985* (CPAS 85–10001, September 1985), Table 19. Eastern Europe: Thad P. Alton, et al., "East European Defense Expenditures, 1965–1982," in U.S. Congress, Joint Economic Committee, *East European Economies: Slow Growth in the 1980s,* vol. 1 (Washington, D.C.: USGPO, 1985), 476–479. Soviet Union: Estimates were presented in CIA testimony recorded in U.S Congress, Joint Economic Committee, *Soviet Military Economic Relations* (Washington, D.C.: USGPO, 1983), 131; and U.S. Congress, Joint Economic Committee, *Allocation of Resources in the Soviet Union and China—1984* (Washington, D.C.: USGPO, 1985), 8.

Table A.21   Composition of Central Government Current Revenue, 1983 (Percentages of Total Current Revenue)

	Taxes on:				
	Income, Profits	Goods and Services	International Trade	Social Security Contributions	Other
Industrial Capitalist Countries					
Australia	61.7	23.3	4.7	—	10.2
Canada	48.3	19.2	4.8	14.1	13.5
France	17.7	29.5	—	44.2	8.6
Italy	35.7	22.9	0.2	33.1	8.1
Netherlands	24.3	19.8	—	41.4	16.6
Sweden	14.5	29.0	0.6	34.1	21.8
Switzerland	14.2	19.4	8.3	49.3	8.8
United Kingdom	38.7	28.6	—	17.7	15.0
United States	49.9	5.4	1.3	31.3	12.0
West Germany	17.0	22.0	—	55.1	5.9
Socialist Countries					
Hungary	17.7	38.7	7.1	17.4	19.1
Soviet Union	37.5	28.8	—	6.4	27.3
Developing Countries					
Argentina	4.3	38.5	16.2	16.9	24.1
Brazil	15.1	25.3	4.1	24.6	31.0
Egypt	17.8	12.5	16.2	11.1	42.4
India	17.2	41.1	24.0	—	17.6
Mexico	22.0	63.2	6.9	11.0	—
Venezuela	56.1	6.0	18.0	3.8	16.2

Sources: World Bank, *World Development Report 1986* (New York: Oxford University Press, 1986), Table 23. For the Soviet Union, *Narodnoe khoziaistvo SSSR v 1984 g.* (Moscow: Finansy i Statistika, 1985), 574.

Table A.22   Marginal Income and Payroll Tax Rates on Earnings of Average Production Workers, 1976

	Excluding Payroll Taxes	Including Payroll Taxes
Austria	19	28
Belgium	27	37
Canada	30	30
Denmark	51	55
France	6	16
Italy	15	23
Japan	17	21
Netherlands	26	42
Norway	34	42
Sweden	63	63
United States	26	32
United Kingdom	35	41
West Germany	18	34

Source: Organization for Economic Cooperation and Development, *The Tax/Benefit Position of Selected Income Groups in OECD Member Countries* (Paris: 1978), 94, 96.

Table A.23   Governmental Deficits and Indebtedness

	Central Government Budget Balance as Percentage of GDP			General Government Debt as Percentage of GDP		
	1972	1983	1986*	1970	1980	1986*
Industrial Capitalist Countries						
Canada	—	−6.2	−5.3	53.7	45.9	73.0
France	0.7	−3.3	−3.1	29.4	29.1	38.7
Italy	−9.4	−16.4	−15.1	44.4	65.3	109.4
Japan	—	−5.7	−4.8	12.0	52.9	68.6
Sweden	−1.3	−10.1	—	—	—	—
United Kingdom	−2.7	−3.2	−2.7	86.2	55.5	55.3
United States	−1.7	−5.6	−4.8	46.2	40.1	50.4
West Germany	0.7	−2.0	−0.7	18.4	32.5	41.1
Socialist Countries						
Bulgaria	—	0.3	—	—	—	—
Czechoslovakia	—	0.0	—	—	—	—
East Germany	—	0.0	—	—	—	—
Hungary	—	−0.7	—	—	—	—
Poland	—	−0.3	—	—	—	—
Soviet Union	—	0.6	—	—	—	—
Yugoslavia	−0.4	—	—	—	—	—
Developing Countries						
Brazil	−0.4	−3.6	—	—	—	—
Egypt	—	−8.2	—	—	—	—
India	—	−7.0	—	—	—	—
Iran	−4.6	−6.1	—	—	—	—
Mexico	−3.0	−8.5	—	—	—	—
Nicaragua	−4.0	−26.8	—	—	—	—
Singapore	1.3	1.5	—	—	—	—

*Estimates

Sources: World Bank, *World Development Report 1986* (New York: Oxford University Press, 1986), Table 22; International Monetary Fund, *World Economic Outlook* (April 1986), Table A16; and Antonio Maria Costa, "The Need for New International Trade Negotiations," in *The New Protectionist Threat to World Welfare,* ed. Dominick Salvatore (New York: North Holland, 1987), Table 2. For the socialist countries, see the sources and methods described in Table A.17.

Table A.24   Measures of Income Inequality

	Reference Year	Percent of Total Household Income Received by:		Gini Ratio*
		Poorest 10%	Richest 10%	
Industrial Capitalist Countries				
Canada	1969	1.8	25.4	.34
Denmark	1976	2.9	22.4	.30
France	1975	1.8	30.5	.39
Sweden	1979	2.6	21.2	.30
United Kingdom	1979	2.8	23.8	.32
United States	1971	1.6	29.0	.39
West Germany	1974	2.9	28.8	.37
Socialist Countries				
Bulgaria-Romania	1970	4.5 (4.3)	18.1 (22.0)	.24 (.27)
East Germany	1972	4.9 (4.6)	23.0 (27.8)	.24 (.28)
Hungary	1977	2.7 (2.6)	20.6 (24.8)	.29 (.32)
Poland	1975	3.0 (2.8)	22.0 (26.7)	.29 (.33)
Soviet Union	1975	4.0 (3.7)	25.0 (30.4)	.30 (.34)
Yugoslavia	1973	2.6	25.2	.35
Developing Countries				
Argentina	1970	1.5	35.2	.44
Bangladesh	1973	2.7	27.4	.35
Brazil	1972	0.6	50.6	.61
Egypt	1974	2.1	33.2	.40
India	1975	2.5	33.6	.42
Iran	1973	1.4	41.7	.52
Mexico	1968	0.7	46.7	.56
Tanzania	1969	2.1	35.6	.42

*The Gini ratio is defined in Chapter 2.

Sources: Data for the industrial capitalist and developing countries are based on adjusted available income per household and are taken from Wouter van Ginnekin and Jong-goo Park, *Generating Internationally Comparable Income Distribution Statistics* (Geneva: International Labour Office, 1984), Tables 1 and A.1. Data for socialist countries are based on net household income; the figures in parentheses include a rough adjustment for nonmonetary income, such as access to special shops and the use of official cars. Data are taken from Christian Morrisson, "Income Distribution in East European and Western Countries," *Journal of Comparative Economics* 8 (June 1984): Table 2.

Table A.25 Income Inequality before and after Taxes in OECD Countries (Gini Coefficients)

	Dates	Before Taxes	After Taxes	Before Minus After
Australia	1966–1967	.313	.312	.001
Canada	1969	.382	.354	.028
France	1970	.416	.414	.002
Japan	1968	.408	.400	.008
Netherlands	1967	.385	.354	.031
Norway	1970	.354	.307	.047
Sweden	1973–1974	.346	.302	.044
United Kingdom	1973	.344	.318	.026
United States	1972	.404	.381	.023
West Germany	1973	.396	.383	.013

Sources: Malcolm Sawyer, "Income Distribution in OECD Countries," *OECD Economic Outlook: Occasional Studies* (July 1976): 16–17; and Tadao Izhizaki, "Is Japan's Income Distribution Equal? An International Comparison," *Japanese Economic Studies* 14 (Winter 1985–1986): 32, 36.

Table A.26   The Network of World Trade, 1985 (Billions of Dollars)

Exports from	Destination			
	Total World	North America	Western Europe	Other Industrial
Total world	1,933	392	735	156
North America	294	113	57	37
Western Europe	761	84	492	25
Other industrial*	220	78	36	17
OPEC	157	19	49	34
Other developing	300	93	61	35
Asian Socialist**	29	3	3	4
Soviet Union/Eastern Europe	172	2	37	2

*Japan, Australia, New Zealand, South Africa

**China, Mongolia

Source: United Nations, *Monthly Bulletin of Statistics* (June 1986).

Destination			
OPEC Countries	**Other Developing**	**Asian Socialist**	**Soviet Union Eastern Europe**
91	338	43	155
12	60	5	4
42	77	7	30
16	50	13	4
4	45	—	5
16	61	11	15
0	14	—	3
1	30	3	94

Table A.27　Selected Data on International Trade and Payments, 1984

	Export Share of GDP	Primary Products Share of Total Exports	Current Account Balance of Payments (million $)	External Public Debt (million $)
Industrial Capitalist Countries				
Australia	15%	77%	−8,302	—
Canada	29	45	1,974	—
France	25	36	−802	—
Italy	27	15	−2,902	—
Japan	15	3	35,148	—
Netherlands	63	50	4,879	—
Sweden	37	22	356	—
Switzerland	38	7	4,019	—
United Kingdom	29	35	1,417	—
United States	8	30	−1,780	—
West Germany	31	13	6,130	—
Socialist Countries				
Bulgaria	32	33	700	700
China	10	43	2,509	—
Czechoslovakia	19	20	700	2,100
East Germany	21	26	1,300	7,100
Hungary	40	42	290	7,380
Poland	18	35	−800	25,300
Romania	—	38	1,500	6,296
Soviet Union	7	69	6,600	14,200
Yugoslavia	31	24	656	8,690
Developing Countries				
Bangladesh	8	39	−521	5,154
Brazil	14	59	53	66,502
Egypt	28	92	−1,978	15,808
India	6	47	−2,429	22,403
Mexico	18	73	3,905	69,007
Nigeria	16	—	346	11,815

Sources: World Bank, *World Development Report 1986* (New York: Oxford University Press, 1986), Tables 3, 11, 14. For socialist countries, estimates of GDP are explained in notes to Table A.2. Information for column 2 is taken from *Statisticheskii ezhegodnik stran-chlenov Soveta Ekonomicheskoi Vzaimopomoshchi 1985* (Moscow: Finansy i Statistika, 1985), Table 181. Data on socialist payments and debt are taken from United Nations Economic Commission for Europe, *Economic Bulletin for Europe* 38 (December 1986): Tables 2.10 and 2.16.

Table A.28   Human Rights Ratings, 1985

| | Composite Score | Freedom of: | | | Freedom from: | | Womens' Rights |
		Political Parties	Press	Religion	Unlawful Detention	Capital Punishment	
Industrial Capitalist Countries							
Australia	94%	A	A	A	A	B	B
Canada	96	A	A	A	A	A	B
France	94	A	A	A	B	A	B
Italy	87	A	A	A	C	A	B
Japan	88	A	A	A	A	D	C
Netherlands	98	A	A	A	A	A	B
Sweden	98	A	A	A	A	A	B
Switzerland	95	A	A	A	A	A	B
United Kingdom	94	A	A	A	A	A	B
United States	90	A	A	A	A	D	B
West Germany	97	B	A	A	A	A	B
Socialist Countries							
Bulgaria	23	D	D	B	D	D	B
China	23	D	D	B	D	D	B
Czechoslovakia	36	D	D	C	D	D	B
East Germany	33	D	D	B	D	D	B
Hungary	55	D	C	B	B	D	B
Poland	41	D	D	A	D	D	B
Romania	20	D	D	B	D	D	B
Soviet Union	20	D	D	B	D	D	B
Yugoslavia	50	D	C	B	C	D	B
Developing Countries							
Bangladesh	43	C	B	A	D	D	D
Brazil	73	B	B	A	C	A	C
Egypt	59	B	B	B	B	D	C
Ethiopia	13	D	D	C	D	D	C
India	60	B	B	A	C	D	C
Mexico	62	D	B	A	D	A	B
Nigeria	54	D	B	B	D	D	C

Key: A—respect for rights or freedoms.
      B—some violations or infringements.
      C—substantial oppression, violations, or restrictions.
      D—continuous violations or total denial.

The composite score is based on assessments of respect for 40 human rights (6 of which are included here) that are embodied in United Nations covenants. Obviously, the objectivity and accuracy of any assessment of this kind is open to criticism. A socialist may object, for example, to the fact that the right to work is not included in the composite.

Source: Charles Humana, *The Economist World Human Rights Guide* (London: Hodder and Stoughton, 1986), passim. Reprinted with permission.

INDEX